SEXUALITY COUNSELING

SEXUALITY COUNSELING

LARRY D. BURLEW
DAVID CAPUZZI
EDITORS

Nova Science Publishers, Inc.
New York

Senior Editors: Susan Boriotti and Donna Dennis
Coordinating Editor: Tatiana Shohov
Office Manager: Annette Hellinger
Graphics: Wanda Serrano
Editorial Production: Jennifer Vogt, Matthew Kozlowski, Jonathan Rose and Maya Columbus
Circulation: Ave Maria Gonzalez, Indah Becker and Vladimir Klestov
Communications and Acquisitions: Serge P. Shohov

Library of Congress Cataloging-in-Publication Data

Sexuality Counseling / [edited by] Larry D. Burlew and David Capuzzi.
    p. cm.
  Includes bibliographical references and index.
  ISBN 1-59033-172-9
1. Sex counseling. I. Burlew, Larry D. II. Capuzzi, Dave.

HQ60.5.S49
361'.06--dc21

2002070978

Copyright © 2002 by Nova Science Publishers, Inc.
                    400 Oser Ave, Suite 1600
                    Hauppauge, New York 11788-3619
                    Tele. 631-231-7269 Fax 631-231-8175
                    e-mail: Novascience@earthlink.net
                    Web Site: http://www.novapublishers.com

Printed in the United States of America

CONTENTS

SECTION 1
SEXUALITY: A DEVELOPMENTAL PERSPECTIVE

Sexuality Counseling: Introduction, Definitions, Ethics, and Professional Issues

Larry D. Burlew
University of Bridgeport
David Capuzzi
Portland State University

Introduction

They sat close together, yet may as well been miles apart. The one too shy to make the first move, yet clearly felt a thump-thump somewhere deep within the body. The other coy, bolder, ready to make the first move, yet clearly aware how the body attracts.Both knew they wanted more than a kiss, [but that a kiss was better than the consequences of unmanageable lust]. So there they sat, staring gooey-eyed at each other.

What do you think is going on here? Who is involved? What reaction does this passage elicit from you? Would it surprise you to know that this passage (slightly edited) is from the movie, *The Lady and The Tramp*? Yet some people might have interpreted this as a "steamy" love/sex scene from a romance novel. In which case, was the man being coy or was the woman or was it two men or two women? Would your reaction be different if they had been dating for 6 months as compared to if they were out on a first date? How would you respond if they were two 12 year olds? 92 year olds? Two married people, but not married to each other? We suspect that seeing this scene in the movie causes an "ah, isn't that sweet" reaction from most people. However, seeing only the words and changing who the participants are and what their intentions are probably produces a host of different reactions from different people. These reactions are coming from a very personal side of our identity, our **sexuality**.

Many people may believe that sexuality only relates to **sexual acts** such as intercourse (Greenberg, Bruess, Mullen, & Sands, 1989) and, thus, may not relate the introductory passage to sexuality at all, unless they envisioned the sexual act that might occur. However, Crooks and Baur (1987) claimed, "Sexuality is governed more by psychosocial factors (motivation, emotional, attitudinal) and by social conditioning (process by which we learn our society's expectations and norms) than by the effects of biological factors such as hormones or instincts" (p. 3). Therefore, any reaction (i.e., emotions, attitudes) you experienced to this introductory paragraph concretely represents aspects of your own sexuality, which is, from our perspective, not easily or openly explored by Americans.

Human sexuality is a complex process involving the interaction of biological, psychological, sociological, cultural, and spiritual/ethical dimensions. Similarly, the development of one's sexuality is a complex process that is forever evolving and changing. **Mental health practitioners**, such as **counselors, psychologists** or **social workers**, can help individuals gain knowledge about healthy sexual functioning and about their own sexuality in general. They can also help with anxiety-producing issues that occur as people struggle with their developing sexuality. Learning more about sexuality, "results in improved sexual knowledge, helps clarify personal sexual attitudes and values, improves the decision-making process, and improves personal well-being (individuals suffer less anxiety and enjoy better interpersonal relationships)" (Greenberg, et al., 1989, p. 9).

The issues surrounding sexuality are varied and relate to factors such as the body, love, contraception, cultural heritage, communication, etc. Some of these issues are actual life events, such as pregnancy, that occur within the life of most individuals; others stem from reactions to or feelings about any life event or aspect of sexuality. For our purposes, the life events can be classified as either **normative** or **nonnormative life events** (Papalia, Olds, & Feldman, 1998). Papalia et al. claimed that a **normative "age-graded"** influence is when a life event "occurs in a similar way for most people and is highly similar for people in a particular age group" (p. 12). These type of events should be viewed as developmental in nature, typical or "normal" experiences for most people, even though people will experience them differently with different reactions, and they can be considered **developmental tasks**.

For example, a young boy having his first "**wet dream**" may be perplexed and worried about the experience, wondering if something is physically wrong with him, if nobody explained the event to him. While this is a normative age-graded life event that most young boys will experience during adolescence, it can still cause stress and anxiety and impact a young boy's thinking about his developing body and his sexual self. Using Erik Erikson's (1963) concept of development, such events might be considered conflicts or crises of a critical nature where "'critical' [is] a characteristic of turning points, of moments of decision between progress and regression, integration and retardation" (p. 271). Even though most young boys work through this event without the help of a counselor, for some young boys, counseling might help them more successfully "progress and integrate" the experience into their evolving sexuality.

On the other hand, Papalia et al. defined nonnormative influences or life events as "unusual events that have a major impact on individuals' lives and may cause stress because they are unexpected; either typical life events that happen at an atypical time of life or atypical events" (p. 13). Some of these unexpected, often traumatic or stressful nonnormative life events are also considered **developmental hazards** that can cause delays or barriers to one's continued healthy development. For example, a woman who experiences acquaintance rape, at any age, doesn't expect it and experiences a traumatic life event related to sexuality. This nonnormative life event is a life crisis that may cause her to re-evaluate her relationships with men, to alter her thinking about her sexuality, and to make her question a society that allows women to be so vulnerable. She may feel depressed, lose interest in sex, and feel insecure and stressed. While she may have been "progressing and integrating" aspects of her evolving sexual self fairly successfully, without intervention, this traumatic life event may cause a sense of "regression or retardation" in her continued sexual development. In such cases, counseling oftentimes helps the survivor work through the traumatic event "to reestablish a sense of personal competence and control and to regain a sense of continuity and meaning in life" (Kelly, 1995, p. 474).

The mental health practitioner (here on in referred to as counselor) can assume a critical role in helping clients achieve a healthy perspective about their sexuality. **Developmental counseling** can be offered, either through sex education/community workshops (e.g., safe sex workshops) or individual/group counseling, related to the more typical, normative, developmental life events that occur as one's sexuality is evolving and developing. This developmental counseling will help people work through the developmental crises of normative life events and lead them to more naturally and effectively integrating the experience into an evolving healthy sexual identity. Counselors can offer individual or group counseling for all nonnormative life events and traumatic developmental hazards that cause anxiety and stress around one's sexuality. Without intervention, these nonnormative life events related to one's sexual self oftentimes leave deep scars and feelings of shame or doubt regarding sexual functioning, attitudes and beliefs. Counseling should help the traumatized client to regain that sense of competence and control related to sexuality and to find meaning in a healthy sense of his/her sexual identity.

DEFINITIONS

This text is not about the study of human sexuality; rather it focuses on the counseling related to issues that arise around an individual's sexuality. Therefore, we do not intend to define every term related to human sexuality like intercourse, puberty, love, and STDs in this section. Some of the terms/concepts we exclude will be defined in other chapters of this text because they relate to a specific topic on sexuality. The definitions we do include below are only a way to introduce concepts we consider important to the study/practice of **sexuality counseling**. However, we did not require our contributing authors to follow these specific definitions in their own chapters. Therefore, you might find the terms/concepts that we included below defined slightly differently in another chapter of this text.

Sexuality and Sexuality Counseling

Sexuality is not a "thing," but rather a life-long process evolving and changing over time. Sexuality might generally be defined as any biological, psychological, sociological, cultural, or spiritual/ethical attribute that comprises one's perception of who he/she is as a sexual person. Additionally, issues related to sexuality may include any normative or nonnormative life event that impacts one's perceptions, feelings about, or actions related to sexuality and sexual behavior.

Sexuality counseling, then, deals with all issues related to attitudes about, characteristics of, or behaviors related to one's sexuality, including one's sexual identity. Additionally, sexuality counseling deals with issues around sexual problems, satisfactory sexual relations, or feelings related to sexual activity in general (Weinstein & Rosen, 1988). This text will not specifically deal with sexual dysfunctions considered more physical or biological in nature such as ejaculation problems, erection failure, priapism, preorgasmia, vaginismus, or dyspareunia, even though these dysfunctions may be symptoms presented in discussions around sexuality.

The role of one's culture cannot be ignored in discussing sexuality and the issues that often are presented as sexual issues in counseling usually have cultural implications. For example, culture sets boundaries on what is right and wrong in sexual behavior; appropriate traits for males and females; and even creates myths about various ethnic groups. Beverly Greene (1998) claimed, "What [one's sexual identity means] will be related to the meaning of sex and sexuality in the culture. It will be important to explore the range of sexuality that is sanctioned, whether or not or to what degree sexuality can be expressed or must be repressed, whether or not it can be expressed directly or indirectly, and so forth. It will also be important to explore the nature of repercussions for those who deviate from or conform to such norms" (p. 43).

Sex and Gender

These terms are oftentimes used interchangeably, even though distinctions can be made between them. Additionally, sex is often equated with **intercourse**, and when people talk about "having sex," they're referring to some physical behavior related to sexual activity usually leading to an **orgasm**. While we also use the term sex in this manner, we include it under the rubric of sexual behavior that is a more comprehensive and inclusive term for all types of sexual activity.

Sex and gender are actually inseparable in many ways. Sex is a genetic factor related to whether you are born male or female with appropriate male or female genitalia (Craig, 1999; Rice, 1992). So, if you are born with a penis, you are automatically labeled a boy and with a vagina a girl. Of course, this is not as easily determined with **intersexed** children who are technically born with both a penis and a vagina. The situation with intersexed children is an example of where gender concepts become important.

Gender refers to the cultural expectations of what it means to be a boy/girl, male/female and is developmental in nature and acquired (Craig, 1999). Therefore, children learn what society considers appropriate behavior, emotions, and reactions for girls and boys, thus developing what Sandra Bem (1983) referred to as a **gender schema**. The gender schema dictates how the little boy or little girl should behave, and he/she acts accordingly (or not). Ultimately, a **gender role** is adopted which Papalia, Olds, and Feldman (1999) defined as "behaviors, interests, attitudes, skills, and traits that culture considers appropriate for males or for females" (p. 358).

The concept of gender role defines what is considered **masculine**, **feminine** or **androgynous** in nature. Androgyny is a "mixing of male and female traits in one person; not sex-typed with respect to roles (although they are distinctly male or female [biologically]" (Rice, 1992, p. 220). If an individual becomes too rigid about exhibiting the appropriate gender role based on sex and feels anxious when not doing so, she/he might be **gender-role stereotyping** (Craig, 1999; Rice, 1992). Gender-role stereotyped individuals may hold others accountable to their standards also and may be intolerant of any variations from those standards. This attitude can cause problems if they act on their intolerance and discriminate against or violate the rights of individuals who do not meet their gender-role stereotypes.

Gender identity is another important concept, and we define it as the internalized sense of who we really are as a man or woman. This "sense" is an aspect of our self-concept and based partly on **gender-typing** which is the "socialization process by which [we], at an early age, learn behavior deemed by the culture as appropriate for a boy or a girl" (Papalia et al., 1999, p. 358). While we all experience gender-typing, our gender identity is based more on our inner feelings of what traits, attitudes, and interests of the gender roles we really identify with, even though we may not exhibit those beliefs/feelings publicly through our behavior.

Some people report knowing at a very early age, as young as 2-3 years old, that their sex did not match what they were feeling inside in terms of their gender identity; others report a similar feeling later in childhood or adolescence. These individuals fit the category of Gender Dysphoric Persons in the *DSM-IV* (American Psychiatric Association, 1994), even though we are not labeling this as a mental disorder. On the other hand, such individuals are certainly **transgendered** meaning that while they have the biological genitalia of a man or woman, their gender identity is that of the opposite sex to what their physical body is. Therefore, they may exhibit **cross-gender behaviors** in public like **cross-gender dressing** and **cross-gender talking** and, later in life, experience **sex reassignment surgery** (Rakic, Z., Starcevic, V., Maric, J., & Kelin, K., 1996).

Sexual Identity/Sexual Orientation

Some researchers (e.g., Cass, 1984) may use these terms interchangeably, and they may very well be. While we focus on sexual orientation in this section, we believe that sexual identity is the broader of the two categories. Sexual identity includes a comprehensive sense of who we are as sexual individuals, which includes our sexual orientation. This broader category of sexual identity includes attitudes, perceptions, beliefs, and images that create an internal sense of our sexuality, which ultimately directs our behavior. In some ways, this is our sexual self-concept and can motivate or inhibit sexual behavior/desires. It can be influenced by thoughts about the body like, "I must be a more virile man because I have a hairy chest," or ethical/religious beliefs like, "I'm a Southern Baptist and feel 'dirty' because I have sexual fantasies." Ultimately, a person's perception about his/her sexual identity is what is most important because perception is the filter to reality. So, if the man above believes his hairy chest makes him more virile, he will more likely act as he thinks a "virile man" should act assuming no other aspects of his sexual identity interfere.

Sexual orientation, on the other hand, is an aspect of one's sexual identity relating to a person's affectional/erotic attractions. Lesbians and gay men (homosexuals) are primarily attracted to members of the same sex, while heterosexuals are attracted to members of the opposite sex and bisexuals to both men and women (Greene, 1998). Asexuals, on the other hand, do not have strong affectional/erotic attractions to either sex.

As early as 1948, Kinsey developed a seven-point scale suggesting a continuum of sexual orientation as opposed to the thinking that one can only be exclusively homo- or heterosexual (Crooks & Baur, 1987). This looking for exclusivity of sexual orientation may stem from our tendency to only identify sexual orientation through sexual behavior/activities (i.e., with whom do we have sex). We refer to this as "sexualizing" sexual orientation. If relying on sexualizing, then the majority will dominate, thus heterosexuality becomes the normal and right orientation, and anything else is deviant. This type of thinking has labels like erotocentrism (i.e., your own sexual orientation is the right way) (Weinstein & Rosen, 1988) or heterosexism (i.e., having sex with members of the opposite sex is being normal) (Greene, 1998).

"Normalizing" any sexual orientation requires re-focusing our thinking that sexual orientation is determined only by sexual behavior. Rather, the focus becomes whom are you "attracted" to in which situation. For example, while an individual might be exclusively heterosexual in his/her sexual behavior, his/her very best friend might be a member of the same sex, thus a homosexual orientation. Similarly, a person might be bisexual, but not be able to become truly intimate with anybody, thus he/she might be asexual when it comes to true intimacy. And, another person might be exclusively homosexual in her/his sexual behavior, but have a heterosexual orientation and involve several people of the opposite sex when doing recreational activities like shopping or going to sports activities. Normalizing, rather than sexualizing, creates a stronger framework for avoiding heterosexist explosions like that which occurred in Wyoming to Matthew Shephard.

Sexual Behavior/Activities

Sexual behavior is another complex topic that needs to be explored from a broader perspective. Oftentimes, clients think of sexual behavior only as sex, or those specific acts leading to **ejaculation** or an **orgasm**. Therefore, when any problems occur that would impede that experience (e.g., **impotence**), then clients might conclude that their sexual life is over. Nothing could be further from the truth because sexual behavior includes a range of emotional, social, and physical behaviors.

For example, a man who is in an automobile accident leaving him a quadriplegic is not **"sexually dead"** as many people might think. He might be in a long-term relationship where he feels great love for his partner, has feelings of sexual excitement when near his partner, enjoys his partner caressing and kissing his lips, his eyes, and behind his ears, and feels fulfilled in providing **cunnilingus** or **fellatio** on his partner. On the other hand, the man's attitude about what constitutes sexual behavior may greatly affect his outlook and willingness to continue with a fulfilling, albeit changed sexual relationship.

Sexual behavior has many emotions attached to it. These emotions include such things as general interest, jealousy, sexual/emotional arousal, love, and intimacy. We have experienced clients who come into counseling reporting that they are **"love-starved"** because their long-term partners aren't paying enough attention to them or talking with them intimately at the end of the day. Some report that they miss the intense excitement that occurred during the early stages of the relationship. Others report a general malaise with their partners and wonder where the "love" feelings went. When their emotional issues are explored in more detail, they ultimately relate the physical sexual behaviors they are missing.

Physical sexual behaviors include anything of a physical nature on a continuum from an action that suggests a romantic/sexual interest in a person to actual vaginal/anal intercourse. A gay man **"cruising"** another man in a grocery store is a physical sexual behavior, just like a heterosexual woman winking at a man in a restaurant could be. **Sexual communication** is a form of sexual behavior and includes something as simple as saying, "I really like you and want to get to know you better." Or, it includes the idea that some people get sexually aroused when their partner "talks dirty" to them. We find it helpful to broaden clients' perspective on what physical sexual behavior is, particularly if they're feeling uncomfortable with or wanting more of "sexual behavior/intimacy." Holding hands, staring lovingly through candlelight, sharing sexual fantasies, masturbation, mutual masturbation, massages, kissing lightly or French kissing, and shared touching are all forms of physical sexual behavior included within the rubric of "**outercourse**" (Crooks & Baur, 1987). These behaviors don't necessarily require ejaculation or orgasm to perform yet can fulfil a "longing for sexual intimacy." **Oral-genital stimulation** (i.e., cunnilingus and fellatio) and **vaginal or anal intercourse** are more likely to lead to ejaculation or orgasm. Additionally, **sexual variety** can be an issue for some clients; this could include anything from trying different **coital positions** to wanting the use of **sex toys** during **foreplay** or alternative types of human interaction (e.g., **S & M, open marriages, menage á trois**).

The social aspects of sexual behavior are also varied but, for our purposes, include any interpersonal interaction revolving around sexuality and sexual issues. Watching "Sex in the City" with friends and comparing notes about the characters' **social/sexual experiences** is an example of the social aspects of sexual behavior. Additionally, the various forms of **social interactions** that people experience around sexuality like **dating, relationships, marriages, partnerships, and casual sexual contacts** are included in the social aspects as well.

The social aspects of sexual behavior are probably even more intensely controlled by culture. For example, most gay and lesbian couples do not hold hands or kiss in public, socially acceptable sexual behavior for heterosexual couples, because of the ostracism against public displays of homosexual behavior. However, psychologically, like other couples, they are experiencing the love and passion that might lead to the open expression of these intense emotions via handholding and/or kissing, but inhibit their behavior in the larger, public social environment. In private, with close social networks like friends and accepting family members, they may express their feelings for each other by kissing or holding hands openly.

Sexual Communication

Communication, whether verbal, nonverbal, or written, is often the most difficult aspect of sexuality for clients. Crooks and Baur (1987) wrote: "Why do so many people find it difficult to talk candidly with their companions about their sexual needs? There are many reasons: Some of the most important lie in our socialization; the language available to talk about sex; and the fears many people have about losing spontaneity or expressing too much of themselves" (p. 235). Communicating about sexuality should begin early in the life of a child with parents openly answering questions about "Where babies come from?" at the cognitive and language level of the child. Sex education in schools is helpful to provide children and adolescents with appropriate and accurate sexual knowledge so that they can make informed decisions related to sexuality and sexual behavior (Greenberg et al., 1989).

What we've found is that clients are often uncomfortable talking about sexual behavior and struggle using words like penis, vagina, and testicles. More importantly, they resist asking partners for sexual behavior that may be more pleasing for them which probably requires using more familiar jargon like sucking dick, eating pussy, or rimming. On the other hand, some clients use sexual terms freely like fucking, sucking, faggot, prick, and snatch. In these cases, the counselor must not react like parents, giving the impression that either sex can only be discussed with "clinical or proper terms" like intercourse and fellatio or it shouldn't be discussed at all.

And, every client is different; for example, an older female client may say that her husband of fifty years isn't intimate with her anymore and a young teenage girl may say that her boyfriend doesn't want to fuck her anymore, and both are talking about the same physical sexual behavior, intercourse. However, the underlying messages are probably different as well. The older client might be saying that she's concerned for her husband's health because they, until recently, had a fulfilling sexual life or that she's questioning whether or not she is still attractive to him. The teenage client might be saying that she thinks her boyfriend is "screwing around" on her or that she's fearful that he's breaking up with her.

Ultimately, as part of treatment around sexuality issues, clients often need help in developing sexual communication skills. It has become critical in education around safe sex, for example. Learning skills of talking about sex, listening and getting feedback, exploring sexual needs, making requests about sexual behavior, learning to be assertive, examining impasses related to sex, and thus demonstrating "mutual empathy – the underlying knowledge that each partner in a relationship cares for the other and knows that the care is reciprocated" (Crooks & Baur, p. 234). Even sexual perpetrators need training in more effective sexual communication to be less aggressive, understand prosocial, empathic behavior, and to communicate within socially acceptable boundaries to get their sexual needs met, rather than demonstrate sexually aggressive behavior that translates into control and violence.

PROFESSIONAL ISSUES IN SEXUALITY COUNSELING

Many counselors can use this text because they see clients struggling with sexuality issues, yet do not necessarily consider themselves a **sex counselor**, **sex therapist**, or a specialist in sexuality issues. Therefore, such counselors should be properly licensed and/or certified by state and/or national agencies to provide counseling/therapeutic services and belong to professional associations like the **American Counseling Association (ACA)** or the **American Psychological Association (APA)**. Their professional associations will provide **ethical guidelines** for the practice of counseling. **Standard of practice** should be followed with regard to **competency and training** (i.e., courses in human sexuality and sexuality counseling), **confidentiality**, type of relationship, **duty to warn**, freedom to choose, and other important categories related to ethics in the profession of counseling.

Additionally, if counselors find themselves more involved in sexuality counseling, then they might want to affiliate with professional organizations like the **American Association of Sex Educators, Counselors, and Therapists (AASECT)**. AASECT is a "not-for profit, interdisciplinary professional organization. In addition to sexuality educators, sex counselors and sex therapists, AASECT members include physicians, nurses, social workers, psychologists, allied health professionals, clergy members, lawyers, sociologists, marriage and family counselors and therapists, family planning specialists and researchers, as well as students in relevant professional disciplines. These individuals share an interest in promoting understanding of human sexuality and healthy sexual behavior" (AASECT, 2000, p. 1). You can contact AASECT as follows: P.O. Box 238, Mount Vernon, IA 52314-0238; fax, 319-

895-6203; or e-mail at AASECT@worldnet.att.net. ASSECT also has a publication titled "The Journal of Sex Education and Therapy" that is useful to keep current in the field.

AASECT 1993 Code of Ethics

AASECT's *1993 Code of Ethics* is an important document to guide professionals who specialize in sexuality counseling, particularly if one is a sex counselor or therapist. While we will not review the entire Code, it can easily be obtained from AASECT. However, we do want to provide an overview of the main categories in the Code. AASECT's Code begins with a statement about self regulation which is as follows.

> **Self Regulation:** Integrity, competence, confidentiality, responsibility, and other applicable standards are not always subject to finite definitions, descriptions, prescriptions, or proscriptions. Virtually every professional situation requires that the practitioner make judgments as to propriety. Through setting forth rules of ethical conduct for practice-related conditions, qualities, skills, and services, the Code of Ethics is intended to assist AASECT members with such judgments. Each member must exercise self regulation and satisfy governmental-regulatory and legal requirements. *(AASECT, 1993, p. 13)*

Self regulation is an important concept because it is placing responsibility for **ethical practice** in the hands of the professionals seeing clients with sexuality issues. AASECT requires its members to follow the Code of Ethics and that disciplinary action can be taken if they are not properly followed.

The Code of Ethics is divided into five categories called "Principles." Each principle is only briefly reviewed below.

Principle One: Competence and Integrity

Competence and **Integrity** refers to your own ability to provide sexuality counseling in terms of your training, as well as your basic integrity as a human being and practitioner. It requires members to: have appropriate training in sex education, counseling, therapy, and supervision; recognize your limits of competence; help the consumer identify your **credentials** and training; participate in **continuing education**; demonstrate integrity in all interactions with the public (e.g., not paying for referrals); and refer when you are **emotionally, physically, or otherwise impaired**.

Principle Two: Moral, Ethical, and Legal Standards

Moral, Ethical, and Legal Standards refers to your judgment as it relates to ethical practice in such situations as dual relationships and supervision. It requires members to: have some type of supervision, regardless of level of experience or training; avoid dual relationships; not violate any consumer's legal and civil rights; not discriminate; be honest in advertising your services; act in accordance with AASECT ethics; follow the ethical guidelines of other professional affiliations; and report ethical violations within thirty (30) days to the Chair of the AASECT Ethics Committee.

Principle Three: Welfare of the Consumer

The Code of Ethics begins this section with: "The AASECT member shall accept that the consumer is in a unique position of **vulnerability** in respect to services related to sex education, counseling, therapy, and supervision, and shall constantly be mindful of the responsibility for protection of the consumer's welfare, rights, and best interests and for the rigorous maintenance of the trust implicit in the educational, counseling, or therapeutic alliance" (p. 15). This principle requires members to: make sure consumers are clear about your abilities/training, nature of services, **limitations**, **personal values**, exceptions to confidentiality, and **financial** issues; keep all information from a consumer confidential; obtain legal determination for the **release of any information** about a consumer; divulge a consumer's information only under certain circumstances (e.g., consumer provides a **written and informed consent**; **clear and imminent danger** to the consumer or another); get written consent from any consumer to use his/her information in any **research or publication**; deal with **records** within the guidelines provided; address with **minors** the issue of limits of confidentiality; use **standard of practice** for **diagnosing**, **treatment planning**, **evaluation**; not engage in sexual behavior at any time because "the counseling or therapeutic relationship is deemed to continue in perpetuity" (p. 16); terminate when appropriate.

Principle Four: Welfare of Students, Trainees, and Others

This principle relates directly to dealing with and treating **students, trainees** and others in a professional and ethical manner. It is best described in the opening statement: "The ASSECT member shall respect the rights and dignity of students, trainees, and others (such as employees), maintain high standards of scholarship, and preserve academic freedom and responsibility" (p. 16).

Principle Five: Welfare of Research Subjects

This principle requires that individuals involved as **subjects** in research must be treated professionally and appropriately. It begins with the statement: "The ASSECT member shall conduct his/her investigations with respect for the dignity, rights, and welfare of the subjects. Research must be ethical and legal at its inception and not justified solely by its intended or achieved outcome" (p. 17). Seven guidelines are provided including concepts like informed consent, providing a clear purpose of the research, and a proposal for the research to be peer reviewed before beginning.

Professional Organizations Related to Sexuality Counseling

Other organizations exist that might help counselors in their work with clients dealing with sexuality issues. For example, the **Society for Human Sexuality** can be browsed at *http://www.sexuality.org/email.html*, and it has information on sexuality via books/resources, local events, erotica guide, video rentals, and matchmaking. They also provided the following numbers on their web site to help with answering questions related to sexuality: **San Francisco Sex Information** (415-989-SFSI); **Planned Parenthood** (1-800-230-PLAN); **Emergency Contraception Hotline** (1-888-NOT-2-LATE); **National STD Hotline** (1-800-227-8922); and **National AIDS Hotline** (1-800-342-2437).

Many organizations exist that help clients with special issues related to sexuality (e.g., for sexual abuse victims). Some of these organizations may be identified in various chapters throughout the text. However, we list a few additional organizations that represent examples where information on sexuality issues can be located.

- The **Foundation for the Scientific Study of Sexuality**: *http://www.ssc.wisc.edu/sss/fssgia.htm*
- Information Services, **The Kinsey Institute**: Email: *kinsey@indiana.edu*
- **American Association for Marriage and Family Therapy (AAMFT)**: Email: *WebMgr@aamft.org*
- **American Society for Reproductive Medicine**: Email: *asrm@asrm.org*
- **Association for the Treatment of Sexual Abusers**: Email: *atsa@atsa.com*
- **Harry Benjamin International Gender Dysphoria Association**: 1300 S. 2nd St., Ste. 180, Minneapolis, MN 55454. Ph: 612-625-1500
- **National Coalition to Support Sexuality Education**: SIECUS-DC, 1711 Connecticut Ave. NW, WDC 20009
- **North American Menopause Society**: Email: *info@menopause.org*
- **Sexuality Information and Education Council of the U.S. (SIECUS)**: Email: *siecus@siecus.org*
- **Society for the Scientific Study of Sexuality: Email**: *Society@worldnet.att.net*

Sex Counselor Certification

If a practitioner wants to specialize in sexuality counseling, then he/she might want to become a certified sex counselor. AASECT provides certification for sex educators, sex counselors, sex therapists, and supervisors. Additionally, the **American Board of Sexology** certifies practicing counselors holding a doctorate or a terminal degree in their field as **Diplomates**. Specialty certification is provided for sex therapists, **sexological educators** and **sexological research**. Information about the Diplomate can be found at *http://www.sexologist.org/home/certific.htm*.

As an example of the requirements to be certified, we review the sex counselor certification from AASECT. The information included below is only a summary of the requirements, and is directly from AASECT's "Certification Requirements" which can be obtained at *http://www.aasect.org/html/certify.htm*. Anybody interested in complete certification details should contact AASECT directly.

Academic and Sex Counseling Experience

A minimum of a Bachelor's degree is required in a **human service program** from an accredited university. With this degree, you must have at least four (4) years of professional experience involving 1,000 hours per year of practice. The higher the level of degree, the less years of experience required. You must also hold an appropriate certification or license as required by your state in one of the following: counseling, psychology, medicine, social work, nursing, or marriage and family therapy. If a state does not have such a requirement in your field, then you must be certified by a national board like the Certification by the **Academy of Certified Social Workers**, Clinical Membership in the **American Association of Pastoral Counselors**, or Certification by the **National Board of Certified Counselors**.

Human Sexuality Education

At least ninety (90) clock hours of general knowledge about human sexuality must be obtained through academic courses and training workshops. The core areas include: sexual and reproductive anatomy and physiology; a lifespan perspective on sexuality from a psychobiological framework; dynamics of interpersonal relationships; gender-related issues; sociocultural factors (ethnicity, religiosity, socioeconomic status) in sexual values and behavior; marital and family dynamics; medical factors that may influence sexuality including illness, disability, drugs, pregnancy, contraception and fertility, sexually transmitted diseases; sex research; sexual abuse and neglect; personal theories; substance and emotional addictions; and varieties of sexual orientation.

As part of the educational experience, ninety (90) clock hours of training in basic counseling skills and specific sex counseling strategies must occur. Forty-five (45) of these hours should be related to basic counseling skills and can be undergraduate or graduate courses and the other 45 hours must be directly related to sex counseling. The specific courses relate to topics like: personal counseling; assessment and diagnosis of **Psychosexual Disorders** according to the *DSM-IV*; relationships and sex and intimacy problems; medical interventions for psychosexual disorders; ethical issues; consultation practices; and evaluation of clinical outcomes.

Attitudes and Values Training Experiences

The certification requirements include the following statement about this category: "The applicant shall have participated in a minimum of twelve (12) hours of structural group experience consisting of a process-oriented exploration of the applicant's own feelings, attitudes, values, and beliefs regarding human sexuality and sexual behavior. Such training is not to be construed as personal psychotherapy or as an academic experience in which the primary emphasis is on cognitive information. It is strongly recommended that this experience occur early in the applicant's training" (AASECT, 1993).

Clinical, Field Work or Practicum Training Experience

In order to be certified, an applicant must have completed a minimum of two hundred (200) hours of supervised counseling involving different human sexuality issues and psychosexual disorders. Additionally, the applicant must have received a minimum of one hundred (100) hours of individual supervision with a qualified supervisor (e.g., AASECT Certified Sex Counselor).

In order to be certified through AASECT, an applicant must be a full, institutional, or life member in AASECT and remain a member. Appropriate documentation like official transcripts, copy of license, and letters of recommendation from approved supervisors must be provided. There is a fee for certification, and it is subject to renewal every three (3) years. Once certified, you will be listed in the National Register of AASECT as a Certified Sex Counselor.

SUMMARY

In their practices, counselors are more than ever before being confronted with sexuality issues like family planning, childhood sexual abuse, teenage sex, gay and lesbian sexuality, HIV/AIDS, the sexual and intimacy needs of people with disabilities, and sexual compulsivity. However, the study of sexuality in counseling programs at the master's level is often not included or perhaps theoretically reviewed in a lifespan human development course. Doctoral programs in counseling are more likely requiring a human sexuality or sexuality counseling course. What seems apparent is that counselors must have an intensive introduction to the dynamics of various types of client sexuality issues, along with suggested strategies and treatment recommendations to help clients with their personal well being related to sexuality and their overall sexual identity.

Our text is written specifically for mental health practitioners, like counselors, psychologists, psychiatric nurses, social workers, who work on a daily basis with client sexuality issues. Additionally, it can be used in graduate human sexuality courses if counseling strategies are an integral part of that course and it can specifically be used for sexuality counseling courses.

The text is divided into three sections: 1. Sexuality: A Normal Developmental Process; 2. Special Populations and Sexuality; and 3. Sexual Problems and Trauma. Section 1 is an introduction to the study of sexuality counseling. The goal is to examine normal or typical sexual development from a lifespan and cultural perspective, as well as to introduce some common concepts related to sexuality. Issues identified in this section might easily fall under the heading of developmental counseling around normative age-graded life events/influences.

The commonly occurring sexuality issues and needs of selected special populations are included in Section 2. Additionally, counseling strategies and treatment recommendations are provided for each special population. Topics include the sexuality issues and needs of couples, bisexuals, lesbians, gay men, transgendered individuals, older adults, HIV/AIDS patients, and addicts. In each chapter, you will find a general description of the population, cultural/gender implications, developmental/diagnostic factors (issues related to sexuality), and a case study with counseling and treatment strategies/recommendations.

Section 3 of this text includes sexuality issues that might be considered nonnormative life events and/or developmental hazards. Topics include the sexual concerns of sexual compulsives, adult survivors of childhood sexual abuse, rape victims, sexually harassed employees, women considering abortion, and clients with STDs. Each chapter is written like those of the previous section with a description of the population, cultural/gender implications, diagnostic factors, and a case study with counseling and treatment strategies/recommendations.

Each contributing author believes that sexual development is a critical aspect of one's self-concept, and something that should be discussed openly and freely with clients and the public in general when appropriate. More importantly, while it is important to understand the theoretical aspects of sexual development, it is even more important to share suggested counseling strategies and treatment recommendations that help all types of clients struggling with sexuality issues. This text will serve as a useful clinical tool to counselors already encountering clients with sexuality issues. For students, it provides an introduction to sexuality counseling throughout the lifespan and special populations of clients with specific needs related to sexual development.

REFERENCES

American Psychiatric Association. (1994). *Diagnostic and Statistical Manual of Mental Disorders-IV.* Washington, D.C.: Author.

AASECT. (1993). *1993 code of ethics [for the] American Association of Sex Educators, Counselors and Therapists.* Mount Vernon, IA: Author.

Bem, S. L. (1983). Gender schema theory and its implications for child development: Raising gender-aschematic children in a gender-schematic society. *Signs, 8,* 598-616.

Cass, V. C. (1984). Homosexual identity formation: A theoretical model. *Journal of Sex Research, 20,* 143-167.

Craig, G. J. (1999). *Human development* (8th ed.). Upper Saddle River, NJ: Prentice Hall.

Crooks, R., & Baur, K. (1987). *Our sexuality* (3rd ed.). Menlo Park, CA: The Benjamin/Cummings Publishing Company, Inc.

Erikson, E. H. (1963). *Childhood and society* (2nd ed.). New York: W.W. Norton & Company, Inc.

Greenberg, J. S., Bruess, C. E., Mullen, K. D., & Sands, D.W. (1989). *Sexuality: Insights and issues* (2nd ed.). Dubuque, IA: Wm. C. Brown Publishers.

Greene, B. (1998). Family, ethnic identity, and sexual orientation: African-American lesbians and gay men. In C.J. Patterson & A.R. D'Augelli (Eds.). *Lesbian, gay, and bisexual identities in families: Psychological perspectives* (pp. 40-52). NY: Oxford University Press.

Kelly, G. (1995). *Sexuality today: The human perspective* (5th ed.). Chicago, IL: Brown & Benchmark.

Papalia, D. E., Olds, S.W., & Feldman, R. D. (1999). *A child's world: Infancy through adolescence* (8th ed.). Boston, MA: WCB/McGraw-Hill.

Rakic, Z., Starcevic, V., Maric, J., & Kelin, K. (1996). The outcome of sex reassignment surgery in Belgrade: 32 patients of both sexes. *Archives of Sexual Behavior, 25*(5), 515-525.

Rice, F. P. (1992). *Human development: A life-span approach.* New York: Macmillan Publishing Company.

Weinstein, E., & Rosen, E. (1988). *Sexualtity counseling: Issues and Implications.* Pacific Grove, CA: Brooks/Cole Publishing Company.

Chapter 2

SEX AND GENDER IDENTITY ACROSS THE LIFE SPAN

Larry Phillips
University of Bridgeport

Sex and **gender** have a pervasive influence on the person, affecting and affected by all human dimensions: emotion, cognition, behavior, self-concept, family dynamics, interpersonal relations, religious belief, and culture. With such a pervasive effect sexuality is also implicated in mental health dysfunction (Gilbert & Scher, 1999). Obviously when clients present problems involving situations or symptoms that involve sexuality or gender, their development as a sexual being can be a critical area of investigation. This aspect of development, however, is often overlooked for other non-sexual situations and symptoms. In fact, it has been my experience from training counselors that there is reluctance on the part of many counselors to delve into this realm of life, as too private and personal. Consequently it is frequently overlooked or avoided. Although privacy should be respected, clients could be invited to present a full history including their sexual and gender development, milestones, and personal issues. In this chapter, it is my intention to provide information for the counselor to consider regarding a person's development as her/his sexuality unfolds and gender role is established. This can be an aid to building a historical perspective on the client as well as a way to ascertain how sexual-gender development impacts on many of clients' presenting situations and symptoms.

Additionally, counselors cannot be removed from their own developmental history and how it impacts on their counseling service. A practicum student I once supervised had a client on tape who repeatedly raised a sexual issue, while the counselor responded to other data and ignored the plea for consideration. Was the counselor just missing the repeated cues, or was he personally unable or unwilling to attend to them? A self-understanding of sexual-gender development can be growth producing for the counselor, as well as help her/him build understanding of important formative issues and dilemmas in the life of the client. In this chapter I explore the interrelated aspects of sexuality, gender, and society in human development as the life span is crossed.

I suppose it would be easy (but not nearly so interesting) if we could determine that males and females were only the product of physiology and all developed along the same identity timelines according to genetically coded script. The truth is far more complicated than just male and female. To start we do have the essential influence of chromosomes and hormones and the development of sexual characteristics as part of the reproductive function. Supplementing nature, however, is the profound influence of socialization, capable of altering or modifying physical sex and resulting in gender identity and social roles. Most follow the patterns and dictates of the culture according to sex. But for others there may be different scripts that do not conform to the most typical development. Besides male and female, we have **androgynous** variants, who have characteristics of both sexes, those with chromosomal and hormonal abnormalities, or **transgenders** whose sexual features and self-view do not match. Additionally there are differences in **sexual orientation**---the romantic and physical attraction to members of the other, same or both sexes.

SEX, GENDER, AND SEXUAL ORIENTATION

Two interrelated issues are important to address at the outset: first the distinction between sex and gender, and secondly the influence of biology (nature) and society (nurture) on the development of the person's sexuality. Social scientists have differentiated sex from gender (Diamond, 2000), referring to sex as the differential anatomy and the physiology of the reproductive system determined by genetics, while gender represents the socially constructed attributes that are bestowed on each sex by society. These social designations are based on the influence of historical, economic, social, political, and cultural factors (Fassinger, 2000; Lott & Maluso, 1993). Sex, based on physiological facts, may be the major precipitating influence but many other social conventions mold it and shape it into **gender identity**. It might be viewed as *what* we are (by looking) versus *who* we are (what we think about ourselves relative to what we see).

One can argue the precise differential importance of the biological and societal (nature versus nurture) influences on the development of the person. Genetics, physiology, and anatomy give us what is possible, but most researchers would agree that social and cultural influences determine what we make of it as it evolves over the life span (Ruble, 1988). Some move beyond the strictures of sexual physiology (Simon & Gagnon, 1998) and, in particular, some transgenders change it. In the computer world one might see the hard drive as analogous to the "equipment" of sexuality, while the input of operating system and software make it both functional and useful (or in the case of some social input toward sexuality just the opposite).

Gender, according to Gilbert and Scher (1999), is made up of four factors. They view it (1) as difference (anatomy), (2) as an organizer or structurer (norms, laws, policies and organizational structure), (3) as language and discourse (e.g. value-laden terms used in relation to gender), and (4) as an interactive process (how mental ideas and values regarding the other sex are acted out).

Money and Ehrhardt (1996) presented a further elaboration on gender identity as an aspect of gender role. View of self and self in relation to others of same and other sex comprises an identity formed by both internal-physiological and societal factors. Gender role comprises one's activity (including the erotic) and is the outward expression of one's gender identity. The gender identity is an internal, private experience of one's sex. One's anatomical biological sex and social gender identity or mental view may not be consistent as seen in the experience of the transgendered individual. They may first alter their role in order to match this gender identity, but may eventually alter their sex through medical intervention to achieve anatomical conformity with it.

This disparity can also be applied to sexual orientation. **Homosexuals**, although having conformity between their biological sex and their gender identity, respond affectionately and sexually to members of the same sex. They may be acting out a role (sexual response toward other sex), while internally having a different identity (sexual attraction to same sex). Although there are numerous theories and growing evidence from research, the origins of sexual orientation (homosexual, heterosexual or bisexual) remain a complex mystery (Rathus, Nevid, & Fichner-Rathus, 1997). Money and Ehrhardt (1996) view sexual orientation as an essential component of gender identity. Those of any sexual orientation do identify with their sexuality and gender. However, while most in society develop both a gender role and a sexual orientation that is consistent with the majority, others gravitate to the same sex partners for romantic and sexual relationships. Although homosexuality remains a major religious, social, and political issue in the United States, there has been a growth in acceptance from the elimination of homosexuality as a psychiatric disorder by the American Psychiatric Association (1994) to the institution of homosexual civil union by the state of Vermont.

GENDER IDENTITY ACROSS CULTURES

"Gender appears to be a socially constructed category because it differs across cultures in its content and form" (Beall, 1993, p.134). "Although gender is a social category in every culture, it does vary in what it means and how it is used in society" (Beall, 1993, p.133). When put into a cross-cultural perspective, differences in social role based on gender and sexual orientation become more pronounced and clearer. Of course the United States is a culturally rich and diverse country, but it is in comparison to cultures in more remote parts of the world that the differences are clearest. As humans we may be able to be divided into two groups based on hormones, glands, and organs, but what we ascribe to those two groups vary considerably. The only given across all cultures is the biological fact that women carry and give birth to the children.

Margaret Mead (as cited in Rathus et al., 1997) portrayed the difference in gender roles assigned and practiced by various cultures in New Guinea. The Mundugumor's men and women are equally aggressive and warlike. Although child bearing and rearing is delegated to the women, they resent the interruption from their warrior role. By contrast the men and women of the Arapesh are gentle, peaceful and both nurture children. The Tchambuli designate the gender-ascribed tasks of child caretaking to the males while the women are the designated fishers and the more aggressive of the sexes. In this culture men are self-adorning, while women have disdain for self-decoration. Also of New Guinea, the Sambians have rigid gender roles with separation of men and women, while the !Kung of Africa permit women autonomy and an active role in tribal affairs (Herdt, 1987; Rathus et al., 1997).

Best and Williams (1993) reported on their research regarding gender role differences across cultures. Some of their research is on sex role ideology, which they defined as "beliefs about the proper role relationships between women and men" (p. 222). They classify the ideologies as generally traditional (men are more important) versus modern (more egalitarian with dominance of one gender over the other rejected). They concluded that the ideology is more modern in countries that are more developed, urban, Christian, and of higher altitude.

In studies regarding sex stereotypes of college students in 25 countries, Best and Williams reported considerable agreement concerning the psychological characteristics attributed to men and with women, but they found that some countries had a higher degree of variance on certain characteristics than other countries. Those variances tended to be higher in the developed countries, the Protestant (vs. Catholic) countries, and the countries where the male work-related values were higher on individualism with less emphasis on money, power, assertiveness, and things (possessions). Perceived strength and activity differences between the stereotypes for men and women were greater in the less developed countries and tended to be greater where literacy was lower and the percentage of women attended higher education. They asserted that educational and economic progress may be accompanied with a reduced view of women as weaker and less active.

Best and Williams, attending to self-concept, concluded a decided difference between the sexes in psychological makeup across cultures. Both gender group's wishes to be more masculine was thought to reflect the stronger, more active stereotype noted above. The self-concept difference between men and women was greater in less developed countries and the differences were lower when women worked outside the home.

Turning their attention to children, Best and Williams found that by age five much of the sex-trait stereotype learning had taken place and by age eight the knowledge was well established. Across the twenty-four countries included in the study, significant difference was found regarding the knowledge of gender stereotypes. The children in Pakistan had the highest scores on both male and female stereotypes, whereas Germany was lowest on male stereotype and France was lowest on female stereotype. In Taiwan there was the greatest disparity with significantly higher scores on male stereotype than female. In Germany the reverse was true with much higher female stereotype than male. Although universal models of males and females (stereotypes) were found, they were modified to some degree by the influence of culture.

Although there are some extreme examples, most cultures do share some degree of similarity regarding the stereotypes of males and females. The fact that there is cultural diversity in gender role, however, attests to the fact that these identities and roles are not determined solely by biological sex. Although it is beyond the scope of this chapter, by contrasting cultures, one can also see huge differences in sexual behavior. Like gender identity, the way a human conducts physical contact and sexual expression varies considerably from culture to culture.

DEVELOPMENT

Roughly speaking our sexuality develops over three stages. During the pre-pubescent years, children discover their sex, encounter socialization and develop their gender role with little sexually related behavior. During **puberty** and adolescence, the body undergoes its most dramatic changes, and children begin to apply their gender identity and role, while beginning their sexual life. Beyond adolescence, young adults establish and solidify their lives in many ways including sexually. Typically a person turns to mating (partnering, coupling, marriage) for sexual gratification. Across the years, individuals continue to express their sexuality, act in accordance with their gender identity and sexual orientation, and eventually encounter physiological aging.

In this section, I investigate more closely these changes, physiologically, psychologically, and socially by first presenting theories and processes involved in the development of the individual, her/his sexuality and gender identification. I will then turn to an application by chronological stages across the life span.

Theories and Processes

Different theories offer perspectives on the developmental of the person, and her/his personality inclusive of gender role definition. Freud presented a theory that relied heavily on physiology and drive, primarily sexual. Erikson offered a contrasting view of development of the person from a more social perspective. **Behaviorists** focus on the processes of learning as the primary force that determines one's development while **cognitive psychology** offers a perspective based on mental processes as central to development.

In regard to any of these perspectives, one must consider the role of physiology, that is, the unfolding of one's biology. Likewise the role of culture from a historical perspective is an important factor. Frequently cited in the development of Freud's theory is the Victorian era's sexual suppression as a context for many of his principles. In culture both social mores and laws govern sexuality. We can view sex in society from a historical perspective and note the development of many of the attitudes and values regarding sexual practices and the people's response within their cultural context. For example, one way to track the development of attitudes and values regarding sexuality is through entertainment. Early in the twentieth century kissing was considered risqué on the movie screen, now nudity and sexual acts are broadcast and available to the masses on television.

Psychoanalytic and Neo-analytic Perspectives

Freud's theory is the only one that holds sexuality as central to the development of the personality. Although no longer generally accepted (Brannon, 1999; Fast, 1993) many believe that Freud made major contributions to an understanding of the mind and behavior. He based his thought on innate biologically based sex drives or *libido* (identified with the *id*) which come into conflict with society (morality, conscience labeled *superego*) and is then mediated by a force (**ego**) that negotiates between the satisfaction of the instinctual urges and social demands. The ego acts to protect the conscious awareness of sexual urges with a number of defense mechanisms. A key role is played by the unconscious mind where these urges may be held from personal recognition. These urges may, however, emerge in indirect ways in behavior.

Freud posed a theory of psychosexual development based on the focus of the libido on the **erogenous zones** (parts of the body that respond to sexual stimulation) with stages named for the zones: oral, anal, phallic, latency, and genital (Craig, 1999). Viewed by Fast (1993), Freud identified three major phases of early gender development. First, the phase before awareness, followed by the emerging awareness of gender difference and the occurrences related to this discovery, and ending with the phase where gender identities are consolidated (the Oedipal period in which the child comes to identify with the same sex parent). In this way he saw sexuality as primary in the development of the personality.

Erikson incorporated Freud's psychoanalytic thought but expanded it with emphasis toward social interaction, beginning with caregivers in early life. In this psychosocial view,

Erikson saw development over the lifetime in eight stages. The key concept of **ego identity** incorporates a person's view of self (self-concept, self-image). Although Erikson did not target sexuality within his theory specifically as Freud did, one can view each stage from the standpoint of how it speaks to the development of one's sexuality as well as that part of self-image, which might be considered gender identity (Craig 1999). I return to the stages when I shift to consideration of development over the life span.

Learning Theories

Learning theorists stress the learning processes as central to development by focusing on the shaping of behaviors through experience with environmental factors. Behaviorists assert that our sexual behavior is a result of the reinforcements received. If some aspect of sexual or gender related behavior is rewarded, it will become incorporated into the individual's behavioral repertoire; if it is punished in a given context it will be suppressed. Reinforcing agents (e.g. parents) will determine what the child incorporates or learns regarding the expression of sexuality and gender (Rathus et al., 1997).

Social-learning theorists also support the role of reinforcement but emphasize observation and imitation, as well as cognitive factors such as thoughts, plans, and anticipation. The social learning theory draws a distinction between learning a behavior, which is cognitive, from performing it, which is behavioral and based on the reward or punishment perceived (Brannon, 1999). In this regard children observe models in action, learn behaviors or roles and then based on expectations, make decisions concerning their own roles and behaviors (Rathus et al., 1997). Additionally, people anticipate consequences and formulate viewpoints (self and others) based on past observations (Miller, 1989). Social situations, therefore, provide for learning of gender related behaviors and an opportunity for performing and being reinforced for what is learned.

Cognitive Theories

Cognitive theorists stress the role and impact of thought or thought process on development. According to information-processing theory, the child first encodes information. Events or objects encountered in the environment are identified then transformed into internal mental representations (Bem, 1981, 1983; Siegler, 1986). These representations become organized and categorized into data groups of similar information called schema. A gender schema is a grouping of mental representations regarding the different physical qualities, behaviors and personality traits of the sexes as presented by the culture (Rathus, et al., 1997). With gender identification as a guide the child develops stereotypes regarding the roles and behaviors of males and females, self and others. The child acquires an understanding of gender based on sequential activities or **script**. These scripts incorporate behaviors with gender and contribute to gender stereotypes having the potential for both positive and negative consequences as the child relates to self and others in the world. Although they provide a model for developing one's masculinity or femininity, they also can be limiting in what the child deems gender appropriate behavior (Levy & Fivush, 1993; Nelson, 1981). With a **schema** regarding his/her own gender identity, the child assesses new information and either assimilates or accommodates it. Consequently this has implications for the child's behavior and expectations and is likely to contribute to his/her self-concept (self schema for gender related behaviors) (Brannon, 1999) and self-esteem or the assessment one makes of his/herself (Rathus et al., 1997).

Cognitive-developmental theory emphasizes processes (thinking, reasoning, problem solving) and how they contribute to the development of the person.

Before the age of 2 1/2 children are not able to consistently label gender. Piaget offers a theory of stages of cognitive development. In the second stage or the **preoperational stage,** he poses that gender differentiation becomes possible. The child develops abilities that make possible a transformation to **allocentrism** from **autocentrism** (Fast, 1993). Although children gain the ability to competently label gender, it isn't until between the ages of 4 and 7 that they achieve "**gender constancy**" or the belief that genders will remain the same throughout life (Kohlberg, 1966). Then, between 5 and 6, gender identify develops. At this point the child is able to correctly label gender with the knowledge that the gender will remain constant (Brannon, 1999). So, progressively, a child acquires gender identity (use of gender labels), gender **stability** (gender does not change over time) and gender constancy (gender does not change even if dress or behavior do) (Kohlberg, 1966; Slaby & Frey, 1975). According to Perry and Bussey (1979), once these stages are achieved a child's behavior will be gender appropriate. In this paradigm the developing child gains cognition of gender identity and then moves to gain consistency with it.

Sexual Orientation Development

A component of one's development of self-view or identity is the orientation or response set to members of same and other sex. Whereas most people develop affectionate and sexual response to the other sex, some develop response to same or both sexes. A small group of people develops a homosexual (gay or lesbian) orientation. Brannon (1999), reporting on studies ranging from Kinsey's in 1953 to one by Sell, Wells and Wypij in 1995, concluded that between 2.8% and 13 % of males and 1.4 and 7 % of females identify themselves as homosexual.

In Freudian view, the development of sexual orientation is based on the resolution of the **Oedipus or Electra complex.** This has to do with the role of the parents and the quality of the parental response to the child. Incorporated in this differential development is the challenge of the resolution of "**castration anxiety**" for the male and "**penis envy**" for the female. Through interview data research, Bieber concluded that mothers who dominate and smother, and fathers who are passive and distant determine homosexual orientation. Although there is considerable debate about this research methodology and the application of psychoanalytic theory, it appears that in the development of sexual orientation family characteristics may play a role (Rathus et al., 1997).

Instead of the resolution of unconscious conflicts, learning theorists maintain that sexual orientation may be the product of reinforced early sexual behaviors. This theory is, of course, based on sexual experience but Bell et al. (in Rathus et al., 1997) noted that most homosexuals are aware of sexual interest in their own gender before any behavior could be reinforced and many heterosexuals engage in same-sex behavior early in life.

Another aspect of development that may have a bearing on sexual orientation is gender identity and role conformity. Rathus et al. (1997), although recognizing the exaggerated stereotypes of lesbian masculine and gay effeminate behavior, noted a body of research that subscribes to the fact that homosexuals more than heterosexuals acknowledge behavior in childhood that is more stereotypical of the other gender. Gay males recalled more sensitivity and artistic interest than their peers did. They preferred playing with girls and feminine toys and activities and were more likely to crossdress during childhood, but were more likely to engage in sex play with other boys rather than girls (McConaghy, 1987; Rathus et al., 1997; Whitman, 1977). The opposite patterns have been noted for lesbian girls (Bailey & Zucker 1995).

Finally, much of the recent investigation involves the biological perspective that targets the role of heredity, the influence of hormones and the structure of the brain in the development of sexual orientation. A number of studies have been done and cited in Rathus et al. (1997) and McDermott (2000) that focus on twin studies. Since identical twins share the exact genetic makeup, one would expect identical development if behavior were based solely on genetics. To determine possible influences many studies contrasted these twins with fraternal twins who do not share the same identical genetic makeup. More than twice as many identical twins have the same sexual orientation as fraternal twins, but it is not 100%, which leaves some room for speculation concerning the role of social forces. Sex hormones (e.g., testosterone) were thought to be an influence on sexual orientation, but research has failed to make that connection (Friedman & Downey, 1994). Another consideration has been forwarded by the work of Simon LeVay (1991) who found significant differences in the structure of the brains of heterosexual and homosexual men.

The distinct possibility exists that there is not one pathway to sexual orientation. Factors may be purely biological or social or experiential or may interact in some significant ways in individualistic fashion. Some people in response to social pressure may hide inner identity (from self or society) and act out a contradictory role (Siegal & Lowe, 1995).

Sexual orientation is assumed by the majority in society, which necessitates struggle for many homosexuals as they come to grips with the identification of difference and the potentially hostile reactions of others. The obstacles encountered by homosexual youth include entrenched defenses against self-recognition, severe stigmatization and fragile and diffuse adolescent ego (Savin-Williams, 1995). In a review of the literature Savin-Williams (1995) noted the vast differences experienced by homosexuals. Some become aware of and/or acknowledge their difference early in life, others not until their twenties, but most come to the recognition during childhood and adolescence when their sexual feelings are awakened. Furthermore, the majority of homosexuals engage in some form of heterosexual activity, which may play some role in their identity formation (D'Augelli, 1991).

What does seem to be a significant factor is the range of human difference as noted Kinsey's research (in Rathus et al., 1997). Whereas some individuals are decidedly heterosexual or homosexual, others are somewhere on the continuum between the extremes (some level of bisexuality). The same might be said for gender identity. Some may be distinctly male or female in gender but others may fall somewhere along the continuum, thereby identifying more as **androgynous** in identity.

LIFESPAN PERSPECTIVE ON SEXUAL DEVELOPMENT

Prenatal

From conception to birth chromosomes determine hormonal activity, that as early as the ninth or tenth week of pregnancy account for the formation of the genitalia. Signs of sexual arousal are evident even in utero, but they are signs of reflex not sexual interest (Rathus et al., 1997).

Since we now can determine the sex of the child before birth, we can conclude that the response to the child's sex happens even before birth. In many instances we might be able to walk into a room designated for the soon-to-be-born and make a pretty good guess at the sex of the baby. So begins the process of the building of gender identity.

Infancy (Up to Age Two)

Boys physically differ from girls in a number of significant ways and although not a stage of purposeful sexual activity, this is the period where gender socialization begins. Freud focused on the discharge of sexual energy on the oral and anal preoccupations as central to development and Erikson noted the building of trust and autonomy as central factors in the child's evolution in this period. The child also becomes exposed to various conditioning stimuli that may begin to build a sexual and gender behavioral repertoire. As early as 18 months some children are able to recognize and attach words to gender but by 27 months half could not apply gender labels correctly (Fagot & Leinbach, 1989).

From birth boys differ from girls, in greater size (weight, length, heart, lungs, and muscle mass), faster metabolism, more gross motor output, but they are less responsive to voices (McDermott, 2000; Stockard & Johnson, 1992). These differences contribute to gender identity by prompting behavioral differences and differences in response by caregivers.

With much of the activity of the baby being focused on the mouth (feeding, experiencing of objects), Freud postulated the *oral stage* as the first of five stages of psychosexual development. In each stage he believed that behavior was sexual by focusing on the quest for pleasure and gratification. Subsequently, in the *anal stage* the child focuses on the excretory functions for pleasure. Frustrations (e.g. toilet training) in this or any stage may have repercussions later in adulthood. In each of the first two stages Freud saw no differences in the sexes. Feminist psychoanalyst Nancy Chodorow posed some differing views of these early times in development. She focused on the significance of the difference in the mother-child relationship for each sex. Whereby the girl learns to be feminine due to the caretaking closeness, boys must separate and reject femininity (Brannon, 1999).

With a view of development from a more social perspective, Erikson posed eight stages over the life span, each of which requires a resolution of an essential conflict. In the first, the child encounters the stage of *trust vs. mistrust* where the child is dependent on the environment and the caregiver. Resolution of the dilemma of this stage may have a bearing on the way the child views his/her future sexual relationships. In the following stage of *autonomy vs. shame and doubt* the child begins to move away from caregivers and gain independence. Autonomy is an asset, which can lead one to a healthier sexual potential (Craig, 1999).

The socialization process begins at birth and in behavioral terms the conditioning process of gender role has begun. Although the child is unaware of her/his sex in this first period of life, he/she is likely to encounter differential response. These responses are based on the beliefs regarding the different sexes (e.g. sexual stereotyping) from parents and others. This can take the form of things like toy or color choice (McDermott, 2000), different levels of discourse for girls and boys, and different play practices between adult and child (Jacklin, DiPietro & Maccoby, 1984). The child is exposed to assumptions and expectations about her/his particular sex and actions. This, in turn, will influence the way the child will view her/himself and the world

Beall (1993) conceptualized the process as parents (society) providing a set of lenses that the rest of the culture is using, and then teaching the child how to use the lenses to view the world. A newborn will soon see models with different characteristics doing different things and learn ways to be and things to do or not do consistent with observed sex. "Appropriate" behaviors will be reinforced and gender identity and roles will begin to develop.

Early Childhood (3-8 years)

Distinctions between boys and girls expand based on physiological and behavioral differences as well as social response. The child is growing cognitively enabling language to be a vehicle for socialization and enhanced gender schema. Between the ages of 3 and 6 most children develop gender knowledge that includes gender labeling, knowledge of gender stereotypes, gender preferences, and finally gender constancy (gender does not change, is both stable and consistent) and by the age of 7 or 8, they have a complete understanding of all the components of gender (Brannon, 1999). Freud considered this period the *phallic stage* where the genitals become the focus of sexual energy and the child identifies with the same sex. Erikson cited the stages of initiative and industry as the child takes more responsibility for self and builds necessary skills.

At this stage of growth boys and girls are physically similar. Girls have more fine motor dexterity and a longer attention span, while boys engage in more activity especially of a rougher sort. Children begin to gain a broader awareness of themselves including their sexuality. They are curious and may be exploratory of self and other's genitalia through play. Masturbation and exhibitionistic behavior are not uncommon (especially in boys) and members of both sexes begin to identify and rehearse gender roles in play. Boys develop an understanding of the penis and link it to adult male identity, while girls continue with a more asexual perspective without a link to adult female sexuality (McDermott, 2000).

Money & Ehrhardt (1996) asserted that by the age of three, the core sex-role and gender identities are established. According to Spence (1985), sex and gender are so important in our culture that gender identity becomes the key component in self-concept. Kohlberg (as cited in Rathus et al., 1997) notes the progression in this stage toward a complete understanding of gender. With this understanding of gender, children develop gender schema differentiating the sexes and, except in unusual cases, identify with their anatomical sex.

From the cognitive developmental perspective of Piaget (as cited in Craig, 1999), a child moves through the preoperational stage and into the *concrete operational stage*. Language becomes a tool the child uses to build schema concerning gender roles and a tool parents use in the shaping of socialization toward cultural, and societal assumptions and expectations.

Socialization differences are noted at this time. Boys are weaned from contact and nurturing at an earlier age than girls are. There is more acceptance of gender role deviation for girls than for boys and more tolerance for sexual behavior and nudity for boys. Parents begin to qualify body parts with modifiers like "nice, bad or dirty" and sexuality becomes associated with something private and secret.

In these formative years, great learning takes place. Behaviors consistent with the dictates of parents and society are overtly or covertly rewarded, while undesirable behavior is punished. Additionally, traumatic events in this period and beyond can have profound effects on personality and may contribute to a life of dysfunctional behavior related to relationships and sexuality.

In Freudian terms, this is the *phallic stage* where the erogenous zone of focus is the genitals. It is here that the child must resolve the Oedipal or Electra complex, regarding the attraction to the other sex and competition with same sex. With a growing awareness of sexuality, girls experience *penis envy* while boys develop *castration anxiety*. Eventually this stage is resolved in identification with the same sex parent and the child enters a stage of *latency*, where sexuality becomes dormant until puberty.

In the Eriksonian paradigm this is the stage where the child is conceived of as reaching out into the world beyond themselves to new things and people. It is in this **initiative stage** that the child gains a broader conception of his/her sexuality, the sexuality of others, and gender specific behavioral expectations, which surface in play activity. Through school and other venues, the child then enters the stage of **industry** (ages 6-12) where important skills and competencies lead to a positive self-view. Failure in these stages leads to *guilt*, if overly criticized or punished and *inferiority* if one does not develop the needed abilities and self–view. Having a positive view of one's self, sexuality, and gender at these stages helps one navigate the difficult straits of puberty and interpersonal sexuality to follow (Craig, 1999).

Money and Ehrhardt (1996) asserted that when gender identity is established in late infancy and early childhood, sexual orientation is also established. According to Coleman (1985) and Siegal and Lowe (1995) this begins a difficult journey for homosexuals who are feeling different and alienated which inclines the child to low self-esteem, depression, and protective defenses. These writers caution that the development of homosexual orientation does not necessarily follow a time frame. Instead it is a process of stages that may be sequential or overlap. The initial stage has been labeled "turning points" by Siegal and Lowe and incorporates "pre-emergence," "self-acknowledgement," and "self-identification."

Late Childhood (9 to 12 years)

In this period of physical growth, the child's cognitive abilities expand along with social skills and morality. A greater awareness of sexuality, gender and relationships are also achieved.

During this period both sexes encounter a growth spurt, girls first. Physical and motor development progresses rapidly. Gender differences are noted in scholastic performance. Girls excel in verbal skills and boys in quantitative skills (Maccoby & Jacklin, 1974). A dramatic course is charted in cognitive and social skills that becomes essential in relationships. Children develop a more realistic and less self-centered but critical view of themselves. There is an expansion of gender roles including stereotyping, and social cognition (awareness and understanding of others) as behavioral determinants. They begin to make social inference regarding interpretations of the behavior of others, begin to respect the obligations of social responsibility, and develop an understanding of the customs and convention, known as social regulations (Craig, 1999). All these aspects of development contribute to a growing sense of self in relation to others and emergent sexuality.

In this period there is an increase in sexual involvement and a greater awareness of others as a source of sexual stimulation. About a quarter of children at this age engage in same-gender sexual play, and a third of girls and two-thirds of boys engage in focused masturbation. Through pursuit of sexual knowledge, intercourse is understood and children begin to fantasize and engage in the sharing of sexual jokes. Children may develop sexual attractions ("crushes") and engage in group dating, but socially segregate by gender. At this age they also become more private and modest as their self/sexual awareness increases, and girls became aware of their vulnerability and physical safety (McDermott, 2000).

D'Augelli and Patterson (1995) asserted an initial awareness of difference by homosexuals accompanied with confusion and alienation. But it is at this stage of life that this difference is noted in sexual terms. In reviewing the work of Boxer, Herdt and others in 1988 and 1989, it is apparent that roughly between the ages of 9.6 and 11.9 both gay and lesbian youth have their first homosexual attraction and fantasy.

Morality is another aspect of both social and cognitive development. Piaget and Kohlberg (as cited in Craig, 1999) detailed a progression of moral development. Children will learn the rightness and wrongness of behavior including sexual. Gilligan (1982) posed the perspective that boys and girls develop different kinds of moral reasoning. Boys, she believes, develops morality around the concept of justice, while girls focus more on caring and human relationships. This differential morality begins to enter the behavioral arena as boys and girls mingle and form relationships. Morality and religious views will become significant elements in sexual practice, as well as feelings regarding the sexual behavior that is chosen.

Adolescence (12 to 18 years)

From puberty through adolescence the most dramatic changes in development take place. Children begin to relate to others in a sexual way as their adult reproductive capability comes of age. Freud targeted this period as the *genital stage* or the re-awakening of sexuality after a dormant latency period and Erikson focused on ego *identity* as the child is provided with a new body and physical capabilities to integrate into a concept of self. Enhanced capabilities in the cognitive realm also enable more abstract and thoughtful responses to the many dilemmas of adolescence.

Certainly the most dramatic period in sexual development is puberty or the maturation of the reproductive system. Puberty typically begins for girls about two years earlier than boys. Differential hormonal activity in both sexes triggers the development of secondary sex characteristics (e.g. pubic hair) first, followed by the primary sex characteristics that are directly involved in reproduction. **Menarche** (first menstruation) and ovulation (which may lag by as much as two years) in girls typically occurs around the age of 12 or 13 (Etaugh & Rathus, 1995). For boys semen production begins, and boys typically experience a first ejaculation at about the age of 13 or 14.

From a cognitive development perspective, teens who enter the *formal operational stage* are provided with capacities of thought necessary to meet the multitude of dilemmas of adolescence. Abstract thought and the ability to speculate about possibilities and plans are the hallmarks of this stage and represent cognitive skills that can help teens make decisions regarding behavior in a sexual context (Green, 1990). In this stage of life with all of its emphasis on social comparison and self-assessment, these skills or the absence of them may be crucial in determining skills in the choices of behaviors. Some of these choices are crucial and have long lasting effects such as engaging in sexual activity, the use of contraception, dealing with pregnancy or sexually transmitted disease, or "**coming out**" for gay and lesbian youth. Unfortunately, not all people are capable of this level of cognitive ability resulting in behavior with insufficient thought, speculation, or planning (Craig, 1999; Piaget, 1972).

Erikson referred to this stage as *ego identity vs. ego diffusion* which is a time for consolidation of the different roles of the teen (child, sibling, friend, student, etc.) with the consolidation of different values and expectations of adolescence into a coherent identify. Adolescents merge from the reliance on parents to the social realm of peer influence with its increased independence and experimentation. As a challenge of maturity, they integrate their emergent sexuality (Freud's *genital stage*) and its reproductive realities with their gender roles and self-view. Furthermore, acceptance or rejection by peers becomes a critical factor in identity formation (Craig, 1999).

This is a time of increased social interaction, and dating provides the teen with learning opportunities in the social realm. Dating serves the functions of recreation, socialization, companionship and status. In regard to emerging psychosexual and physical development, it also more specifically serves the function of intimacy (establishing close meaningful relationships), mate selection (experience in ascertaining compatible qualities) and sex (experimentation with sexual satisfaction) (Roscoe & Brooks, 1987).

Masturbation is still the primary sexual activity for most adolescents, but a significant number of adolescents also experience guilt in relation to it. Coles and Stokes (1985) estimated that 97% of teenagers had experienced petting (and kissing) by the age of 15, and Rathus et al. (1997) noted that 41-53% of boys and 33-42% of girls reported engaging in oral sex. A steady increase in sexual intercourse among teenagers has occurred over the years due to both a more permissive attitude toward sexuality in the culture, as well as an erosion of the double standard dictating that sexual activity is acceptable for males but not for females. In 1953, Kinsey and Charles reported that fewer than 20% of 19 year-old women had experienced intercourse, which compares to 78% for metropolitan girls in a 1988 study (Zeman, 1990). Brooks-Gunn and Furstenberg (1989) noted that among European-American girls the incidence of intercourse had risen from 7% in 1938 to 44% in the 1980's. In the 1990's more than 50% of teenagers engage in intercourse and the percentage difference for males and females has changed over time resulting in nearly equal percentages now for both engaging in sex as well as first intercourse (Brannon, 1999). There are many reasons for teens to engage in sexual relations with a partner besides the pursuit of sexual stimulation. Other reasons include affection, a sign of maturity, reward for relationship loyalty, parental punishment, social pressure, or partner pressure (Coles & Stokes 1985; Michael, Gagnon, Laumann, & Kolata, 1994; Miller, McCoy, Olson, & Wallace, 1986). Roscoe, Kennedy, & Pope (1987) reported that young males associated intimacy with sex, whereas females associated intimacy with openness.

The relationship between parents and teens is an important determiner of sexual activity. Teens who engage in premarital intercourse are more likely to come from divorced or separated parents or parents who are permissive (Coles & Stokes, 1985; Hogan & Kitagawa 1985; Miller et al., 1986). Furthermore, teens more likely to engage in coitus believe they cannot talk to their parents (Rathus et al., 1997).

Teenage pregnancy is a major social issue in America. About 10% or one in five sexually active girls, nearly one million total, become pregnant each year (Kantrowitz, 1990). Ninety percent of these pregnancies are unplanned (Alan Guttmacher Institute, 1991) and 40% end in abortion. In 1960 15% remained unmarried as compared to 67% today, and the rate is 92%

for African-American mothers (National Research Council, 1993). Although no difference esxists in adolescent intercourse rates between teens in America and those in Canada, France, Great Britain, Sweden and the Netherlands, the American teenage pregnancy rate is two to five times higher. Reasons for the higher rate could be that Americans have less access to the services that provide contraceptives, choose ineffective contraceptive methods (or use them inconsistently), and have less availability of educational programs (Baker, Thalberg, & Morrison, 1988; Hess, Markson, & Stein 1993; Jones et al., 1985; Polit-O'Hara & Kahn, 1985; Rathus et al., 1997; Wallace & Vienonen, 1989).

These changing sexual mores are difficult enough for heterosexual youth, but a significant challenge for homosexual youth. Denied the societal sanction enjoyed by heterosexuals, the homosexual adolescent can experience feelings of isolation, despair and self-destruction (Savin-Williams, 1995). D'Augelli and Patterson (1995) quoted the works of Boxer, Herdt and others from 1988 and 1989 identifying that for homosexuals the age of first sexual activity is between 13.1 and 15.2 years old. This is also an age of first heterosexual activity, adding to the confusion for gay and lesbian youth. An interesting note is that homosexual activity precedes heterosexual activity for boys, but the reverse is true for girls. All of this uncertainty and pressure is certainly evidenced by the major mental health problems of teenagers, depression and suicide. Although one of the major causes of death for teenagers in general, suicide is especially high for gay youth. Herdt (as cited in Siegel & Lowe, 1995) reported that between twenty and thirty percent of gay youth have made suicide attempts.

In this age range with its great social expectations, homosexual youth are challenged by the stigma of their difference accompanied by peer ostracism and an absence of support. D'Augelli and Patterson (1995) cited the challenges of finding mates, the consequences of same sex dating (e.g. harassment) and the lack of public celebration or even recognition of these relationships. Siegal and Lowe (1995) contrast the gay man, who "runs cruel psychic gauntlets every day of his life" to the average straight man, who "can stumble through the psychic passages from boyhood to adolescence" (p. 30). While heterosexual youth explore and experiment with their emergent sexuality, at this stage homosexual youth may be repressed and delayed thereby being deprived of adolescence. Although they may hold their identity in private for many years to come or act out an inconsistent (heterosexual) role with their peers, it is a time for the potential of disclosure of sexual orientation ("coming out). This may be the first acknowledgement of sexual feelings and the facing of the next developmental task of telling others in part to gain acceptance (Siegal & Lowe, 1995; Weinberg & Williams, 1974). Gonsiorek (1985) described the stages of development of "exploration" and "first relationship" as this initial movement into the interpersonal arena. The opposite or attempting to "pass" as heterosexual, including dating, can ward off assault of various kinds. However, the passing can result in internal turmoil, retreat from intimacy and low self-esteem (Savin-Williams, 1995). The area of intimacy is specifically addressed by Remafedi (1990) asserting that sexual activity may substitute for and represent an escape from more meaningful or intimate expressions like kissing. The psychological repercussions of the denial of social sanction for homosexuality might result in isolation, despair and self-destruction (D'Augelli & Patterson, 1995). In spite of all the aforementioned difficulties it must be noted that most of these youth cope with the challenges and develop a healthy, happy and productive life (D'Augelli & Patterson, 1995; Savin-Williams, 1995).

Young Adult (19-40 years)

After passing through adolescence the person is ready to assume full adult sexuality and is likely to engage in serious romantic and sexual relationships with others. Mature thought processes enhance and expand these capabilities.

Having achieved sexual maturity and at the peak of physical development, young adults decrease dependence on the family of origin while increasing involvement with their peer social strata. In addition to establishing oneself in the occupational life the significant task of this time of life is relational, which may eventually lead to cohabitation or marriage and the possibility of starting a family. Erikson (as cited in Craig, 1999) refers to this stage as *intimacy*, which is the ability to share self with others or the opening to and the engagement with others. Although it includes sexuality it is not limited to it. However, over these years many will find a mate and settle into long-term relationships that include sexuality and the prospect of creating a family. Levinson (1978, 1986), in reference to men, noted that in this stage the young man gains awareness of the way he relates to the other sex and a deeper understanding of himself. In sexual intimacy he will define his strength and vulnerability.

Sarrel and Sarrel (1979) in reference to the beginning of this stage (college years) list nine processes of "sexual unfolding." The processes are: "evolving sense of body," moving beyond sexual inhibitions and associated feelings present in childhood, "loosening of libidinal ties to parents and siblings," gaining awareness of what provides erotic pleasure, overcoming sexual orientation confusion, "an increasingly satisfying and rich sexual life," recognition of the place and importance of sex in life, responsibility about oneself and one's partner, and finally the possibility of a "fusion of sex and love" (p. 19). Each of these processes plays a transitional role into adulthood.

Cognitive development also contributes to the intimacy equation, enabling richer relationship through enhanced thought process. Schaie (as cited in Craig, 1999) calls this the *achieving period* stressing the application of intellectual, problem solving and decision-making skills. Riegel (1975) proposed similar a stage of development, incorporating the power of adult cognition, called *dialectical thinking* which refers to the young adult's ability to ponder and sift through information, attempting to bring together opposing ideas and perceptions. Labouvie-Vief (1984) emphasized commitment and responsibility in cognitive development. This more mature cognitive ability to which they refer is put into service in the understanding of relationships and one's response to and from others, thereby allowing for deeper and more mature choices and selections in life.

The need for intimacy leads people to various lifestyles in relation to sexuality with others. Life as a single is the most common lifestyle of people in their early 20's (Barringer, 1992a, 1992b) and represents one in four of those 18 or older (Steinhauer, 1995). Cohabitation (unmarried adults of different gender living together) has grown with the greatest increase since 1980 for those over the age of 35 (Bumpass, 1995). This only reflects the heterosexual population; it must also be added that monogamous relationships with same-sex couples occur for almost 40% of gay men and 60% of lesbian women (Dunlap, 1994; Laumann, Gagnon, Michael & Michaels, 1994). Marriage remains the most common lifestyle in this age bracket, with about 65% of adult men and 60% of adult women living with a spouse (U.S. Bureau of the Census, 1990). Eventually a third of couples who cohabit marry (Demaris & Lesley, 1984) and over 90% of Americans will marry at some time in life (Craig, 1999).

Love plays a central role in the life of a young adult. Sternberg (1986) presented a triangular theory of love that addresses three interactional components. He cites the interacting components as *intimacy* (close feelings in love relationships), *passion* (physical attraction and sexual behavior) and *decision/commitment* (realization of love and becoming committed to another). When two of three of these are coupled without the other it results in *romantic love* (intimacy and passion), *companionate love* (intimacy and commitment), or *fatuous love* (passion and commitment); when all three are present it is *consummate love*. This model addresses the relational necessities of love, while also separating the related but distinct roles and how they may or may not co-exist.

Patterns of sexual activity have changed over time in America. Western societies have been among the most restrictive in sexuality, even within marriage, but the sexual revolution of the late 1960's has resulted in greater sexual freedom and activity (Hunt, 1974). In the late 1980's there was a shift back to more restricted sexual activity, in part due to the threat of sexually transmitted diseases (first the permanency of Herpes, then the fatality of AIDS), which will remain a concern for the foreseeable future. Recent research (Laumann et al., 1994; Oliver & Hyde, 1993) suggests that differences continue to exist between men and women. Females are less accepting of oral sex and casual sex, have more guilt and fear associated with sexual behavior, are less likely to masturbate or experience orgasm, and have a higher average age for first sexual intercourse.

Today married couples experience greater sexual satisfaction engaging in coitus that has greater duration, with more frequency and variety (Rathus èt al., 1997). The vast majority (90% of men, 70% of women) acknowledges reaching orgasm usually or always (Laumann et al., 1994). Compared to younger and older counterparts, women in their 40's have a greater likelihood of consistently reaching orgasm which is connected to closer relationships. Therefore, Rathus et al. (1997) concluded that there is a link between the satisfaction of emotional needs to sexual satisfaction for marital couples.

Whether dissatisfied, curious, seeking closeness or needing a boost to self-esteem 21% of married men and 12% of married women acknowledged engaging in extramarital sexual affairs (Rathus et al., 1997). Other sexual alternatives, although practiced by relatively few, are swinging (exchanging partners), open marriage (affairs sanctioned as part of marriage) and group marriage (several couples involved in a joint marriage).

Sexuality among gay men and lesbians is less based on age and stage than heterosexual development is because of the identity confusion, the prevailing societal attitudes, and the need to maintain secrecy to avoid ostracism or violence. Siegal and Lowe (1995) posed three aspects to "coming out" starting with identification as a homosexual, accepting it, and then "celebrating" it. This serves not only as self-definition and internal integration, but also a bid for the acknowledgement and acceptance of others.

Middle Adult (41-65 years)

At this stage of life most people are in relationships or marriage and many have families. Erikson (as cited in Craig, 1999) noted a shift in this period when the focus moves more from self onto others, referred to as ***generativity***. In this stage adult attention turns to others, perhaps as parents or grandparents or to society in a more general way. Peck (in Rathus et al., 1997.) offers an elaboration on the later years of life beyond that of Erikson. He cites a shift from physical to mental activity, forcing redefinition of relationships, stressing the social and companionship aspects over the sexual. A manifestation of this can also be seen in regard to sexual behavior. Weg (1989) sees a broadening of sexuality to include sensuality. Sex life takes on more interpersonal dimension to include more caring, affection and intimacy as well as genital contact. She views sexuality defined as behavior resulting in orgasm (quality and quantity) as too limited. Although sexual behavior continues, toward the end of this period physical changes take place and some abilities begin to decline.

Both men and women face obstacles in this period imposed by the stereotypes and expectations of a youth-oriented culture. These obstacles are a challenge to self-image, self-acceptance and a belief in one's competence. For females sexuality is equated with attractiveness and procreation, while men are held to a standard of virility. Although there are emerging physical limitations, the psychological impact on the midlife adult is greater (Weg, 1989).

In the middle years of adult life, physical decline occurs in the sensory and motor skills, and the internal working of the body (Birren, Woods & Williams, 1980). Many of these changes, characterized as "slowing down" have sexual implications. Masters and Johnson (1966) reported that those over 50 needed more time to be aroused and had a decrease in physical spasms at orgasm.

The most dramatic change is menopause or a "shutting down" for women in their late 40's. There is a change in hormonal activity (estrogen) which results in cessation of ovulation, and the ending of childbearing capability. Although there are both physical (e.g., decline in lubrication, increased time needed to achieve orgasm), and psychological (e.g. depression over the loss of feminine reproductivity) implications to this major life change most women do not view the experience as negative (Goodman, 1980; Neugarten, 1967; Neugarten, Wood, Kraines, & Loomis, 1968) and experience limited impact on sexual responsiveness. In fact, contrary to midlife myths, menopause may promote the opposite--heightened libido or sexual capacity characterized by increased sexual interest, initiative and pleasure (Weg, 1989).

At about the same age men too undergo similar but more gradual changes while retaining reproductive ability (Rucbsatt & Hull, 1975). Changes may be exhibited as diminished libido, less forceful ejaculation, longer refractory period, or occasional impotence. The impact on overall sexuality is not physiologically extensive but can result in increase sexual anxiety that results in sexual dissatisfaction. Unsatisfying experiences may threaten the ego and self-esteem inciting fear and a chain reaction that results in withdrawal from sexual activity or fleeing to new partners. More likely difficulties emerge as much based on other aspects of relationships like intimacy than on the elements of physical decline (Weg, 1989)

During midlife other factors begin to emerge in the lives of some that have an effect on overall functioning that spill over into sexuality. During the earlier years of midlife, career and family pressures may account for some decline in frequency of sexual activity. With progressing age, the advent of disease, illness, surgery and the effects of medication may also take a toll on sexual behavior (Weg, 1989).

D'Augelli and Patterson (1995) concluded that insufficient research has been directed toward mid-life homosexuality. For gay men generally the same issues and development prevail as they do for the heterosexual male. The challenges of mid-life are different for lesbians. Most are not confronted with life punctuated by children leaving home and the possibility of re-entry into the workforce (D'Augelli & Patterson, 1995). Cole and Rothblum

(1991) also noted that menopause is not as disruptive for lesbians as it is for heterosexual women in part due to less emphasis on the physiological intrusion of menopause on sexual performance for both partners.

Older Adult (Retirement and Beyond)

The last stage of life can span four decades, and the level of sexual satisfaction that remains can be based on health and the retention of functions and skills. Kaplan (1990) noted "because sex is among the last pleasure-giving biological processes to deteriorate, it is potentially an enduring source of gratification" (p. 204). Purifoy, Grodsky, and Giambra (1992) reported, however, that sexual drive and activity decline with age, while negative attitudes about sex increase. People at this stage may continue to engage in sexual activity but the type of activity or the frequency may change (Myers & Schwiebert, 1996; Schneider & Kropf, 1992). As people get on in years, mature sexuality may be redefined, stressing more hugging, touching and the like which may or may not lead to sexual acts (Weg, 1989).

Despite the potential for decline, Starr and Weiner (1981) reported that 95% of older people reported liking sex, and that 75% said orgasm was necessary for sexual fulfillment. Sexual relations were reported by half of the 60 to 91 year olds and half of those reported once a week or more. In the same study, masturbation was reported by 46%. In a study of healthy adults spanning ages 80 to 102, Bretschneider & McCoy, (1988) reported that 30% of the women and 62% of the men continued to engage in intercourse.

Many older adults maintain an ability to respond sexually but with considerable changes related to aging. After menopause women change little. Some deteriorating factors brought on by steroid starvation and hormonal imbalance relate to sexual functioning resulting in reduction in muscle tension, vaginal lubrication, vaginal wall elasticity, size of the ovaries and uterus, and muscle spasm intensity at orgasm (Bee, 1987; Masters & Johnson, 1966; Schneider & Kropf, 1992).

Testosterone decline results in changes for men including diminished sperm production, testes shrinkage, and reduction in seminal fluid. For men more time and stimulation are needed to achieve erection and orgasm and the refractory period is longer. Additionally erections are less firm and orgasmic contractions less intense. By the age of sixty, men may experience impotence (Bee, 1987; Rathus et al., 1997).

Although social expectations as well as physical decline may limit the elderly, most are able to continue with sexual activity late in life. Psychological barriers and the absence of partners are more responsible for decline in activity than are physical limitations (Schneider & Kropf, 1992).

Certainly society's views of age and sexuality have an impact on everyone at this stage of life. For the aged homosexuals who were born and raised before views of homosexuality began to change, the experience of old age may be tinged not only with the heavy impact of the youth culture, intensified in the gay society, but the more ingrained attitudes present during much of their developing life (D'Augelli & Patterson, 1995). If the challenges of younger years were not enough for homosexuals at the end of life restrictions from visiting partners in hospitals, helping to make decisions for ill or dying partners, and financial concerns of old age and death of a partner add further impositions (Poor, 1982). On the other hand, Friend (1991) also sees the strife associated with coming to grips with the stressors of homosexual orientation as promoting a different sense of psychological strength.

SUMMARY

Although sexuality is biologically determined and the same for all humans, gender identity and the roles for each sex are socially determined. Many theorists pose valuable understandings for the way a person's sexuality develops and gender identity is determined. Freud posed a model of development based on the placement of sexual energy in the erogenous zones. Erickson stressed the social aspects of development, which clearly affect one's identity and relationship to others, sexually and otherwise. Behaviorists stress the role of reinforcement as well as observation and imitation in sexual and gender role development. The cognitive theorists view development through the mental processes that will affect how one views oneself, his/her sexuality and gender.

In the years prior to puberty, children discovers their sexuality and learns their gender roles. Puberty represents the sexual maturation, resulting in a movement toward others in a sexual way. Having navigated the turbulent waters of adolescence the mature person settles into a life that includes sexuality and relationships. Through the years the person's sexual functioning matures, peaks, and finally ebbs in the later years.

REFERENCES

Alan Guttmacher Institute. (1991). *Facts in brief.* New York: Author.

American Psychiatric Association. (1994). *Diagnostic and Statistical Manual IV.* Washington, DC: Author.

Bailey, J.M., & Zucker, K.J. (1995). Childhood sex-typed behavior and sexual orientation: A conceptual analysis and quantitative review. *Developmental Psychology, 31,* 43-55.

Baker, S., Thalberg, S., & Morrison, D. (1988). Parents' behavioral norms as predictors of adolescent sexual activity and contraceptive use. *Adolescence, 23,* 278-281.

Barringer, F. (1992a, July 17). Rate of marriage continues decline. *The New York Times,* p. A20.

Barringer, F. (1992b, July 19). More Americans are saying, "I don't." *The New York Times,* p. E2.

Beall, A. E. (1993). A social Constructionist view of gender. In A.E. Beall & R.J. Sternberg (Eds.), *The psychology of gender.* New York: Guilford.

Bee, H. (1987). *The journey of adulthood.* New York: Macmillan.

Bem, S.L. (1981). Gender schema theory: A cognitive account of sex typing. *Psychological Review, 88,* 354-364.

Bem, S.L. (1983). Gender schema theory and its implications for child development: Raising gender-aschematic children in a gender schematic society. *Signs 8,* 598-616.

Best, D., & Williams, J.E. (1993). A cross cultural viewpoint. In A.E. Beall & R.J. Sternberg, (Eds.) *The psychology of gender.* New York: Guilford.

Birren, J.E., Woods, A.M., & Williams, M.V. (1980). Behavioral slowing with age: Causes, organization, and consequences. In L.W. Poon (Ed.), *Aging in the 1980's*. Washington D.C.: American Psychological Association.

Brannon, L. (1999). *Gender psychological perspectives*. Needem Heights MA: Allyn and Bacon.

Bretschneider, J., & McCoy N. (1988). Sexual interest and behavior in healthy 80 to 102 year olds. *Archives of Sexual Behavior, 17,* 109.

Brooks-Gunn, J., & Furstenberg, F., Jr. (1989). Adolesent sexual behavior. *American Psychologist, 44,* 249-257

Bumpass, L. (1995). Cited in Steinhauer, J. (1995, July 6). No marriage, no apologies. *The New York Times,* pp. C1, C7.

Coleman, E. (1985). Developmental Stages of the coming out process. In J.A. Gonsiorek (Ed)., *Guide to psychotherapy with gay and lesbian clients*. New York: Harrington Park Press.

Cole, E., & Rothblum, E. (1991). Lesbian sex after menopause: As good or better than ever. In B. Sang, J. Warshow, & A. Smith (Eds.), *Lesbians at midlife: The creative transition* (pp. 184-193). San Francisco: Spinsters.

Coles, R., & Stokes, G. (1985). *Sex and the American teenager*. New York: Harper and Row.

Craig, G. J. (1999). *Human development*. Upper Saddle River NJ: Prentice Hall.

D'Augelli, A.R. (1991). Gay men in college: Identity processes and adaptations. *Journal of College Student Development, 32,* 140-146.

D'Augelli, A., & Patterson, C.(1995). *Lesbian, gay and bisexual identities over the lifespan,* New York: Oxford.

Demaris, A., & Leslie, G. (1984). Cohabitation with a future spouse: Its influence upon marital satisfaction and communication. *Journal of Marriage and the Family, 46,* 77-84.

Diamond, M. (2000). Sex and Gender: Same or different. *Feminism & Psychology, 10*(1): 46-54.

Dunlap, D.W. (1994, October 18). Gay survey raises a new question. *New York Times,* p. B8.

Etaugh, C., & Rathus, S.A. (1995). *The world of children*. Forth Worth, TX: Harcourt Brace College Publishers.

Fagot B. I, & Leinbach, M. D. (1989). The young child's gender schema: Environmental input, internal organization. *Child Development, 60,* 663-672.

Fassinger, R. E. (2000). Gender and sexuality in human development: implications for prevention and advocacy in counseling Psychology. In S.D. Brown & R.W. Lent (Eds.), *Handbook of counseling psychology* (3rd ed.) (pp. 346-378). New York: Wiley.

Fast I., (1993). Aspects of early gender development: A psychodynamic perspective. In A.E. Beall & Sternberg (Eds.), *The psychology of gender*. New York: Guildford.

Friedman, R.C., & Downey, J. I. (1994). Homosexuality. *New England Journal of Medicine, 331,* 923-930.

Friend, R. A. (1991). Older lesbian and gay people: A theory of successful aging. In J.A. Lee (Ed.), *Gay midlife and maturity* (pp. 99-118). New York: Haworth Press.

Gilbert, L.A., & Scher, M. (1999). Gender and sex in counseling and psychotherapy: Current knowledge and directions for research and social action. In S.D. Brown & R.W. Lent (Eds.), *Handbook of counseling psychology* (2nd ed.) (pp 383-418). New York: Wiley.

Gilligan, C. (1982). *In a different voice: Psychological theory and women's development.* Cambridge, MA: Harvard University Press.

Gonsiorek, J. C. (Ed) (1985). *A Guide to Psychotherapy with gay and lesbian clients* New York: Harrington Park Press.

Goodman, M. (1980). Toward a biology of menopause. *Signs, 5,* 739-753.

Green, A.L. (1990). Great expectations: Constructions of the life course during adolescence. *Journal of Youth and Adolescence, 19,* 289-303.

Herdt, G.H. (1987). *The Sambia: Ritual and gender in New Guinea.* New York: Holt, Rinehart & Winston.

Hess, B.B., Markson, E.W., & Stein, P. (1993). *Sociology* (4th ed.). New York:Macmillan.

Hogan D., & Kitagawa E. (1985). The impact of social status, family structure and neighborhood on the fortility of black adolescents. *American Journal of Sociology, 90,* 825-55

Hunt, M. (1974). *Sexual behavior in the 1970's.* New York: Dell.

Jacklin, C.N., DiPietro, J., & Maccoby, E. (1984). Sex typing behavior and sex-typing pressure in child—parent interaction. *Archives of Sexual Behavior, 13,* 413-425.

Jones, E.F., Forrest J. Goldman, N. Henshaw, S. Lincoln, R., Rosoff, J.I., Westoff, C. F., & Wulf, D. (1985). Teenage pregnancy in developed countries: Determinants and policy implications. *Family Planning Perspectives, 17,* 53-62.

Kantrowitz, B. (1990, Summer/Fall Special Issue). High school homeroom. *Newsweek,* 50-54.

Kaplan, H. S. (1990). Sex, intimacy and the aging process. *Journal of the American Academy of Psychoanalysis, 18,* 185-205.

Kinsey, A. C., & Charles, A. (1953). *Sexual behavior in the human female.* Philadelphia, PA: W.B. Saunders.

Kohlberg, L. (1966). A cognitive—developmental analysis of children's sex-role concepts and attitudes. In E. E. Macocoby (Ed.), *The development of sex differences* (pp. 52-173). Stanford, CA: Stanford University Press.

Labouvie-Vief, G. (1984). In M.L. Commons, F.A. Richards, & C. Armon (Eds.) *Beyond formal operations: Late adolescence and adult cognitive development.* New York: Praeger.

Laumann, E.O., Gagnon, J.H., Michael, R.T., & Michaels, S. (1994). *The social organization of sexuality: Sexual practices in the United States.* Chicago: The University of Chicago Press.

LeVay, S. (1991). A difference in hypothalamic structure between heterosexual and homosexual men. *Science, 253,* 1034-1037.

Levinson, D. J. (1978). *The seasons of a man's life.* New York: Knopf.

Levinson, D. (1986.) A conception of adult development. *American Psychologist, 41,* 3-13.

Levy, G. D, & Fivush, R. (1993). Scripts and gender: A new approach for examining gender role development. *Developmental Review, 13,* 126-146.

Lott, B., & Maluso, D. (1993). The social learning of gender. In A. Beall & R. Sternberg (Eds.), *The Psychology of Gender.* (1993), New York: Guilford.

Maccoby, E.E., & Jacklin, C.N. (1974). *The psychology of sex differences.* Stanford: Stanford University Press.

McConaghy, N. (1987). Heterosexuality/homosexuality: Dichotomy or continuum? *Archives of Sexual Behavior, 16,* 411-424.

McDermott, L. J. (2000). *Human sexuality* (4th ed.) Needam Heights, MA: Pearson Custom Publishing.

Masters, W., & Johnson, V. (1966) *Human sexual response.* Boston: Little Brown.

Michael, R.T., Gagnon, J.H., Laumann, E.Ol, & Kolata, G. (1994). *Sex in America: A definitive survey.* Boston: Little, Brown.

Miller, B.C., McCoy, J.K., Olson, T.D., & Wallace, C.M. (1986). Parental discipline and control attempts in relation to adolescent sexual attitudes and behavior. *Journal of Marriage and the Family, 48,* 503-512.

Miller, P. (1989). *Theories of developmental psychology* (2nd ed.). New York: Freeman.

Money, J., & Ehrhardt, A. (1996). *Man & woman, boy & girl.* Northvale, NJ: Jason Aronson.

Myers, J.E., & Schwiebert, V.L. (1996) *Competencies for gerontological counseling.* Alexandria, VA: ACA

National Research Council. (1993). *Losing generations: Adolscents in high risk settings.* Washington, D.C.: National Academy Press.

Nelson, K. (1981). Social cognition in a script framework. In J. H. Flavell & L. Ross (Eds.), *Social cognitive development: Frontiers and possible futures* (pp. 97-118). Cambridge, England: Cambridge University Press.

Neugarten, B. (1967). The awarness of middle age. In B. Neugarten (Ed.), *Middle age and aging.* Chicago: University of Chicago Press.

Neugarten, B., Wood, V., Kraines, R., & Loomis, B. (1968). Women's attitudes toward menopause. In B.L. Neugarten (Ed.), *Middle age and aging.* Chicago: University of Chicago Press.

Oliver, M. B., & Hyde, J. S. (1993). Gender differences in sexuality: A meta analysis. *Psychological Bulletin, 114,* 29-51.

Perry D.G., & Bussey, K. (1979). The social learning theory of sex differences: Imitation is alive and well. *Journal of Personality and Social Psychology, 37,* 1699-1712

Piaget, J. (1972).Intellectual evolution from adolescence to adulthood. *Human Development, 15,* 1-12.

Polit-O'Hara, D., & Kahn, J. (1985). Communication and adolescent contraceptive practices in adolescent couples. *Adolescence, 20,* 33-43.

Poor, M. (1982). The older lesbian. In M. Cruikshank (Ed.), *Lesbian studies* (pp. 165-173). Old Westbury, NY: Feminist Press.

Purifoy, F.E., Grodsky, A., & Giambra, L.M. (1992). The relationship of sexual daydreaming to sexual activity, sexual drive, and sexual attitudes for women across the life-span. *Archives of Sexual Behavior, 21,* 369-375.

Rathus, S. A., Nevid, J. S., & Fichner-Rathus, L. F. (1997). *Human sexuality in a world of diversity.* (3rd ed.). Boston: Allyn and Bacon.

Remafedi, G. (1990). Fundamental issues in the care of homosexual youth. *Adolescent Medicine, 74,* 1169-1179.

Riegal, K. F. (1975). Adult life crisis: A dialectical interpretation. In N. Datan & L.H. Ginsberg (Eds.), *Life-span developmental psychology: Normative life crisis.* New York: Academic Press.

Riegel, K. (1984). In M.L.Commons, F.A. Richards, & C. Armon (Eds.), *Beyond formal operations: Late adolescence and adult cognitive development.* New York: Praeger.

Roscoe, B.D., & Brooks, R.H., II. (1987). Early, middle and late adolescents; views on dating and factors influencing partner selection. *Adolescence, 12,* 59-68.

Roscoe, B., Kennedy, D., & Pope, T. (1987). Adolescents' views of intimacy: Distinguishing intimate from nonintimate relationships. *Adolescence, 22,* 511-516.

Ruebsaat, H.J., & Hull, R. (1975). *The male climacteric.* New York: Hawthorn Books.

Ruble, D.N. (1988). Sex-role development. In M.H. Bornstein & M.E. Lamb (Eds.) *Developmental psychology: An advanced textbook* (2nd ed.) (pp. 411-460).Hillsdale, NJ: Erlbaum.

Sarrel, L., & Sarrel P. (1979) *Sexual unfolding.* Boston: Little Brown.

Savin-Williams, R.C. (1995). Lesbian, gay male, and bisexual adolescents. In A. D'Augelli & C. Patterson (Eds.), Lesbian, gay and bisexual identities over the lifespan. New York: Oxford.

Schneider, R., & Kropf, N. (1992) *Gerontological social work. Knowledge, service settings, and special populations.* Chicago: Nelson-Hall

Siegal, S. & Lowe E. Jr., (1995) *Uncharted lives,* New York: Penguin Books

Siegler, R.S. (1986) *Children's thinking.* Englewood Cliffs, NJ: Prentice Hall.

Simon & Gagnon (1998). Psychosexual development. *Society, 35, 60-67*

Slaby, R.G., & Frey, K.S. (1975). Development of gender constancy and selective attention to same-sex models. *Child Development, 46,* 849-856

Spence, J. T. (1985). Gender identity and its implications for concepts of masculinity and femininity. In T.B. Sonderegger (Ed.), *Nebraska symposium on motivation: Psychology of gender* (pp. 59-95). Lincoln, NB: University of Nebraska Press.

Starr, B.D., & Weiner, M.B. (1981). *The Starr-Weiner report on sex and sexuality in the mature years.* New York: Stein & Day.

Steinhauer, J. (1995, July 6). No marriage, no apologies. *The New York Times,* pp. C1, C7.

Sternberg, R.J. (1986). A triangular theory of love. *Psychological Review, 93,* 119-135.

Stockard J., & Johnson, M. (1992). *Sex and gender in society.* Englewood Cliffs, N.J: Prentice Hall.

U.S. Bureau of the Census (1990). Marital status and living arrangements: March 1990. *Current Population Reports,* Series P-20, No. 450. Washington D.C.: U.S. Government Printing Office.

Wallace, H.M., & Vienonen, M. (1989). Teenage pregnancy in Sweden and Finland. *Journal of Adolescent Health Care, 10,* 231-236.

Weg, R.B. (1989). Sensuality/sexuality of the middle years. In S. Hunter & M. Sundel (Eds.), *Midlife myths: Issues, findings and practice implications* (pp. 31-47*).* Newbury Park, CA: Sage.

Weinberg , M.S., & Williams, C.S. (1974). *Male homosexuals: Their problems and adaptations.* New York: Oxford Press.

Whitman, F. L. (1977). Childhood indicators of male homosexuality. *Archives of Sexual Behavior, 6,* 89-96.

Zeman, N. (1990, Summer/Fall). The new rules of courtship (special edition). *Newsweek, 24-27.*

Chapter 3

CROSS-CULTURAL PERSPECTIVES ON LOVE AND SEX

Arpana Inman
Lehigh University
Daya Singh Sandhu
University of Louisville

The **Hopi** forbid sexual activity in a cornfield, believing that such behavior offend the spirits. On the other hand, the **Navajo** and the **Mandon** believed the opposite to be true (Gregersen, 1983). In **Greek Orthodox** houses, having sex in the presence of religious symbols such as holy pictures and crosses is seen as sacrilegious; while the **Roman Catholic** see the crucifix over the bed as a form of blessing (Gregersen, 1983). Among **Haitians,** there is no stigma attached to **cohabitation** and family structures outside of marriage. Additionally, in some other **Caribbean** cultures (e.g., **Martinique**), births outside marriage are the norm (Gregersen, 1983). The Mayan culture allows men and women to find a mate without the involvement of family/community (Bertrand, Ward, & Pauc, 1992), while for **South Asians** finding a mate has typically involved familial and community decisions (Kumari, 1988).

Such instances suggest that people from divergent cultures reinforce different behaviors and provide distinct, yet acceptable ways for their expression of love and sex. **Culture** pervades everybody's lives and implicitly or explicitly imparts norms, rules, customs, and ideals that serve as guides or maps shaping one's expectations and perception of reality. Thus, one's roles, behaviors, values, and personal experiences are typically interpreted and sanctioned through the culture in which one operates (Opler, 1956). Culture influences which behaviors are considered deviant and which are consistent with one's society and socially approved (Comas-Diaz & Griffith, 1988).

The focus of this chapter is on examining these socially approved and distinct cultural **perspectives on love and sex**. While there are universals within a culture, when examining cultures from the outside, care should be taken to not take things out of context, to stereotype, or to devalue aspects of a culture that may appear strange. Furthermore, it is important to note that no **ethnocultural** group is unidimensional and that there are wide variations in **sexual attitudes and behavior** based in ethnicity, socioeconomic status, religions, politics, regions, education, early life experiences, and acculturation.

In order to provide a conceptually inclusive account of the **cross-cultural perspectives** on love and sex, the chapter begins with an historical perspectives based within the Western and Eastern dichotomy. This is followed by an examination of the concept of intimacy, identifying different types of love and different forms of sexual relations within the context of intimacy. The chapter also looks at the role of culture in relation to **sexual markers**, **sexual permissiveness**, **gender differences in mate selection** and cultural views on **long-term relationships**.

HISTORICAL PERSPECTIVES

Historically, both the Western and Eastern literature have abounded in stories of lovers caught up in the throes of passion and violence (e.g., Romeo & Juliet), and in tales where tormented lovers are caught between romantic love and familial duty (e.g., Laila-Majnu). In addition, the openness of sexual attitudes has been demonstrated widely in legends, history, philosophy, religion, arts, and literature within cultures. For example, wall carvings in ancient temples and manuals such as the **Kama Sutra** explain sexual activity in great detail. Erotic paintings, prints, illustrations (i.e., Shunga-illustrated manuals) were considered normal subjects for **Japanese** artists and this artwork reached a peak in the late 18th century (Hirayama & Hirayama, 1986; Lister, 1986). Interestingly, this liberal attitude with regard to sexual conduct and sexual attitudes has been prevalent in the Eastern cultures (e.g., **India**, **China**, **Japan**) long before the liberalization in the West (Carson & Sperry, 1999; Hirayama & Hirayama, 1986). Yet, ironically, there has been a great shift, in fact a reversal in these attitudes in recent years (Hatfield & Rapson, 1996). Different political, economic, social, and religious influences have put forth different social mores and expectations about love and sex. Attitudes have become more restrictive or liberal based on these influences. For example, through religious conversion, modernization and acculturation, some of these Eastern groups (e.g., Japanese, Filipino) have taken on moral attitudes and positions advocated by the European/Catholic cultures (Hirayama & Hirayama, 1986; Yap, 1986).

Despite there being great variations in **ethnic groups**, ethnocultural or cross-cultural differences in traditions, customs, values, and norms continue to be examined within a Western and Eastern dichotomy. Specifically, the focus has been on the West being seen as individualistic and the East as collective in their orientations to self or others (Hofstede, 1983; Markus & Kitayama, 1991; Triandis, 1994). Within this framework, these societies have been seen as differing in their physical (e.g., urban vs. rural, modern vs. traditional), social (e.g., independent vs. interdependent), and economic (e.g., developed vs. developing; industrial vs. agricultural; affluent, vs. poor) environments, respectively. These physical, social, economic factors are seen to significantly influence cultural traditions and conceptualizations about love and sex within their cultures (Hatfield & Rapson, 1996).

The West has emphasized and placed high value on passionate love in **romantic relationships**, **love marriages**, **egalitarian relationships**, **sexual freedom** for men and women, and sexual permissiveness prior to marriage (Gardiner, Mutter, & Kosmitzki, 1998; Hatfield & Rapson, 1993). This emphasis is seen as coming from a belief in the individuality, independence, separateness and uniqueness of a person. Furthermore, increasing industrialization, as well as the women's movement, is likely to have contributed significantly to these values. On the other hand, most Eastern or non-Western cultures emphasize a fundamental interconnectedness of human beings, a collective orientation, with the self not only defined in relation to family, friends, and the community, but the behaviors that one engages in are seen to be a reflection on one's family and community (Inman, Ladany, Constantine, & Morano, 2001; Triandis, 1989). This self-construal has been identified as defining one's view of oneself within the context of intimacy. Thus, within the Eastern cultures, there is a greater emphasis on **compassionate love**, focus on **hierarchical relations** with different sexual expectations for males and females, marriages are typically arranged with the assistance of family/community, and there is an emphasis on chastity prior to marriage (Buss, 1994b; Dasgupta & Dasgupta, 1996; Chu, 1985; Gardiner, Mutter, & Kosmitzi, 1998; Saran, 1985). Many of these values have also been influenced by these cultures being predominantly **patriarchal**, **agrarian**, and based in **traditional value** systems. Thus, the social, physical, and economic influences identified above seem to dictate the dichotomy between the West and the East. However, as one continues through the chapter, it becomes evident that these seems to be a trend towards a shift in attitudes due to a greater interchange of culture as a function of **migration**, **acculturation**, as well as changing **sociopolitical climates** within several regions in the West and East. Having examined the historical perspective on love and sex, it becomes necessary to examine some definitions and forms of love and sexual relationships across cultures and explore it within the context of intimacy.

INTIMACY

Intimacy according to Hatfield (1984) refers to " a process by which people attempt to get close to another; to explore similarities and differences in the ways they think, feel and behave" (p. 208). Cultural characterizations regarding emotional expression and intimacy vary widely across cultures. For example, those from the **Mediterranean** cultures or the **Eastern European** cultures appear to be comfortable expressing their emotions boisterously when compared to those from **Canada**, **England** or **Australia**. People from the **Far East** (e.g., Japan, Korea) or **Asia** are more likely to value restraint and discretion in emotional expression. **African Americans**, on the other hand, value expressiveness and openness while **New Englanders** (e.g., White Americans/Europeans) may treasure restraint and tact (Barnlund, 1989; Thiederman, 1991; Won-Doornink, 1985). These variations further extend to the manner in which intimacy is conceptualized and practiced.

America places a high value on intimacy in couple relationships, with romance, trust, open communication, and friendship as core features of intimacy (Hatfield, & Rapson, 1996). On the other hand, while intimacy is also valued in the Korean culture, the term intimacy does not exist within the Korean language, and romance is not an aspect of intimacy within several other Asian cultures such as Japan and India; (Berg, Sperry, & Carlson, 1999; Kumar, 1991; Roland, 1988). Intimacy within some Asian cultures may be thought of as symbolizing cooperation, harmony, friendship and a closeness that is accomodating rather than romantic (Berg, Sperry, & Carlson, 1999). For example, in Dion & Dion's (1993) study comparing Asian and European men and women, they found that Asians tend to view love relationships in terms of **friendship** when compared to their European counterparts. Ting-Toomey (1991) examined the extent to which **Americans**, French, and Japanese students would disclose very intimate things about themselves. She found that the Japanese students were least intimate, while the American students were most intimate. The French students were intermediate in their intimacy. Among the **Polynesian** inhabitants of **Mangaia**, personal affection is less of a requisite for sexual intimacy while the reversal is true of the western culture (Marshall, 1993). Thus, it appears that there are variations with the Western cultures being more open in their intimacy.

Love and Intimacy. Within the context of intimacy, love has been identified as taking many forms within relationships. **Passionate love** refers to an intense emotion and longing for union. Compassionate love refers to true or marital love, a love with less intensity but encompassing a deep attachment, affection and tenderness for the other person. It involves intimacy and commitment. **Romantic love** involves passion and intimacy, while **consummate love** is the ultimate form of love and involves passion, intimacy and commitment (Hatfield & Rapson, 1996).

Literature suggests that passionate love and romance are important components of intimacy within the American culture while compassionate love is more salient within the Eastern cultures (Hatfield & Rapson, 1996). For example, in America, intimacy and love are sought out in passionate affairs, and in the Chinese, Japanese, and Indian cultures, intimacy is sought amongst family and kin rather than in marital relationships (Chu, 1985; Kumar, 1991; Roland, 1988). Roland (1988) and Kumar (1991) discussed that in Japanese and Indian marriages respectively, husbands and wives have typically not been each other's best friends. Friendship and intimacy is typically sought among extended family and friends. Chu (1985) found that for most North Americans and Europeans, love and compatability between the couple had been a priority in relationships, while in China, compatibility of the families of the partners had been of greater importance. The concept of romantic love is idenitified as fitting better with the American perspective rather than the Chinese cultural orientation because within the Chinese culture, one is expected to consider not just one's own personal feelings but is obligated to others in the family (Hsu, 1985). While this may be true within the two contexts (i.e., East and the West), recent research (Aron & Rodriguez, as cited in Hatfield & Rapson, 1996; Doherty, Hatfield, Thompson, & Choo 1993; Sprecher, Aron, Hatfield Cortese, Potapova, & Levitskaya, 1994) conducted with **Mexican Americans**, **Chinese Americans**, **Anglo Americans**, **Russians**, **Japanese**, **Japanese Americans**, and **Pacific Islanders** provides evidence that men and women in all these cultures are just as romantic as Americans, are suceptable to falling in love, and experience passionate and companionate love similarly. Also, increasingly, men and women thoughout the world (e. g. Mexican-Americans, Chinese, Indians) are starting to look for similar characteristics in love relationships, for example, open communication, trust, shared values, happiness and intimacy in relationships (Castaneda, 1993; Xu & Whyte, 1990; Yelsma & Althappilly, 1988).

Sexual Unions and Intimacy. In addition to the different types of love, anthropologists and evolutionary psychologists have identified different types of **sexual** (i.e., marital) **unions** existing in cultures around the world. These include, **monogamy**, which involves men and women engaging in a relationship with one single person at a time; **polygamy**, in which men and women have more than one sexual mate or partner at a given time; **polygyny**, in which men have more than one wife or sexual partner at a time; **polyandry**, where women can have more than one husband or sexual partner at a time; and **polygynandry**, where both men and women can have as many sexual or marital partners as they may desire (Hatfield & Rapson, 1996).

Literature indicates that the most favored form of marriage is polygyny. **Mormons** engaged in polygyny to increase the family size due to the agricultural nature of the community. Although the U.S. Congress enforced a need to abandon this practice, there are still an estimated 50,000 people living in polygynous housholds (Johnson, 1991). Murdock (1967) found that 721 participants in his sample were polygynous, 137 were monogamous, and only 4 were polyandrous. More recently, Fisher (1989) found some similar statistics. She noted that about 84% of the societies permitted polygyny (e.g., **Nigeria, Zambia**) 16% prescribed monogamy (e.g., **Germany, Spain**), and 0.5% allowed polyandry (e.g., **Western Africa**). Interestingly, despite these statistics, it was found that men within polygynous societies rarely exercised this option and a large percentage of these societies prefer and practice monogamy.

Finally, in recent years, researchers have noted the growing phenomena of "cohabitation" (i.e., consensual union that does not involve marriage) as another form of an intimate relationship. The concept of cohabitation has long exited in the **Grecian** society where marriages were typically reserved for the wealthy (Duff & Truitt, 1991). However, with the spread of **Christianity**, the relationship between opposite sexes in the form of marriage became a universal **social sanction** and cohabitation came to be seen as sinful (Nicole & Baldwin, 1995).

Through the years, cultures have varied in their acceptance of this form of relationship for different reasons. For example, premarital or consensual cohabitation has been an acceptable form of family organization in Nigeria (Soyinka, 1979), as well as in some communities in the Caribbean (Smith, 1962). **Consensual unions** have appeared to serve the function of trial marriages among rural **Latin Americans** (e.g., **Columbia**, Mexico, **Peru**, and **Costa Rica**; Goldman & Pebley, 1981). Similarly, in **Canada**, cohabitation has been seen as a substitute for marriage rather than a prelude to marriage among Francophone students (e.g., women; Hobart & Grigel, 1992), and those favoring marriage seemed to be in strong support of cohabitation (Hobart, 1993). Cohabitation has long existed among certain cultural groups such as **Guam**'s predominantly Roman Catholic, Asian/Pacific population and **Haitians**, due to the lack of negative meanings or **stigma** attached to it (Gregersen, 1983; Pinhey & Perez, 2000). Family structures outside marriage have traditionally been accepted within these cultural groups.

Cohabitation, however, has been an increasing form of "**alternative lifestyle**" since the 1970s in the United States (Cherlin, 1991), with 25% of Americans practicing this form of lifestyle sometime during their adult lives (Larson, 1991). Several researchers have noted cohabitation in **Sweden** and **Norway** to be a **norm** before marriage and existing as a social institution alongside marriage (Duvander, 1999; Leven & Trost, 1999). The passing of the **Registered Partnership Act** in Norway in 1993 that acknowledged **gay and lesbian relationships** as having similar legal rights as heterosexual couples seemed to have contributed to legitimizing cohabitation among heterosexual couples in Norway as well (Halvorsen, 1998).

The increase in this type of lifestyle has been noted in several cultures. Societal changes that include changing roles of women, late marriages, increased acceptance of premarital intimacy, prolonged educational processes, financial constraints and increasing costs appear to be some of the contributing factors for people cohabiting in the United States (Sirica, 1993). Other factors such as **modernization** and changing views on marriage and sexuality (e.g., increase in **extramarital relations**, childcare problems, divorce, domestic violence) have created openness to cohabitation in certain urban areas in China (Huang, 1998). Structural and ideological changes and legal reforms in Australia have led to cohabitation being seen as a temporary or preparatory step to marriage rather than an alternative to matrimony (Sarantakos, 1994; Khoo, 1987). Thus, societal conditions rather than culture/**ethnicity** appear to be important factors in legitimizing alternative lifestyles and sexual practices (Davis, 1998).

Research on **racial and ethnic differences in cohabitation** shows that although cohabitation increases rates of premarital pregnancy for most women, the effect appears to be greater among Puerto Ricans than non-Hispanic Whites and African Americans. Also, cohabitation appears to force White women who get pregnant prior to marriage, towards marriage more quickly, while having no effect on Blacks and a strong negative effect among Puerto Ricans (Manning & Landale, 1996). Similar research (Oropesa, 1996) shows that Puerto Ricans are most approving of cohabitation when compared to Mexican Americans and non-Latino Americans. Mexican Americans have reportedly been more inclined towards cohabitation due to marriage being evaluated more positively than being single within this culture.

Research comparing married and cohabiting couples has shown cohabiting couples having lower levels of commitment, happiness, and relationship quality (Brown & Booth, 1996; Nock, 1995), but the relationship quality of both married and cohabiting couples that intended to marry seemed to be affected similarly by the presence of potential sources of stresses (e.g., children, past unions; Brown & Booth). Other related research (Cunningham & Antill, 1994) has shown that married couples with cohabiting experience, and cohabiting couples seem to have higher scores on feminism, wider sexual experiences, less stereotyped sex role expectation, when compared to married couples without cohabiting experiences. Shelton and John (1993) found marital status impacting household expectations for married women when compared to cohabiting women. Specifically, married women spent significantly more time on housework, whereas cohabiting women were similar to single, noncohabiting women.

Gender differences in cohabitation have shown that for women, willingness to cohabitate appeared to be related to being older, having lower levels of religiosity, less traditional views of marriage and sex roles, and more liberal attitudes towards sexual behavior. On the other hand, men's willingness to cohabitate seemed to be related to lower levels of religiosity and more tolerant views of rape (Huffman, Chang, Rausch, & Schaffer, 1994).

Finally, research comparing **opposite sex** and **same sex** couples with regard to cohabitation revealed that both types of couples shared similar issues, problems, and conflicts in cohabitation (Sarantokos, 1996). Similarly, Kurdek (1998) found that the strength of the relationship quality (i.e., intimacy, autonomy, equality, constructive problem-solving, and barriers to leaving) and its impact on relationship outcome (i.e., relationship satisfaction and dissolution of relationship over 5 years) for married couples and cohabiting gay and lesbian couples appeared similar. Furthermore, it has been found that social support from friends and family is positively related to relationship quality in gay couples (Smith & Brown, 1997). Thus, although intimacy exists within all cultures, not only does its expression vary across cultures, but the nature of intimate relationships is experienced differently as well. Furthermore, it appears that with the changing socio-political-economic conditions in the world, cultures seem to be converging in their attitudes on some aspects related to sexual practices and intimacy.

MARKERS OF SEXUAL MATURATION

Typically, there are clear universal **biological markers** of **sexual maturity** across cultures. For girls, it is the development of breasts and and onset of menarche; and growth of facial hair and change of voice in boys. However, each society also has its unique signals that communicate to the community when women and men have transitioned from adolescence to adulthood (Gardiner, Mutter, & Kosmitzki, 1998).

This transition from adolescence to adulthood typically involves instruction into the **cultural norms, mores,** and **values** regarding sex and sexuality (Weisfeld, 1997). It is often celebrated with elaborate **initiation ceremonies,** such as changing of clothing, use of tattoos, **circumcision/genital mutilation,** as well as change of hairstyle (Gardiner, Mutter, & Kosmitzki, 1998; Weisfeld, 1997). For example, in **Eastern Africa,** 10-12 year old boys within the **Kaguru tribe** are stripped of all their clothing, ritually circumcised and taught **sexual practices** of adulthood by the male members of this community (Beidelman, 1971). In other countries (e.g., Africa, Middle-East), **female circumcision** is a widely held practice (e.g., Armstrong, 1991).

Readiness for a sexual relationship also appears to vary from culture to culture. For example, the Mayan culture considers young women and men sexually mature and ready for a relationship when they begin experiencing **sexual desire** (Bernard, Ward, & Pauc, 1992). On the other hand, **South Asians** (e.g., **Hindus**) consider a woman to be sexually mature with the onset of menstruation (Kumari, 1988). In societies such as the **Masai** of **Kenya** or the **Hopi Indians** of North America, girls are allowed to become **sexually active** around thirteen or fourteen years of age (Ruan, 1991). Thus, despite there being **universal markers,** each culture has its prescribed, socially acceptable behaviors that signal the readiness for sexual activity among its men and women.

CULTURE AND SEXUAL PERMISSIVENESS

Behaviors are embedded in the social structure and culture of a society. Cultures create social systems that influence and shape people's sense of self, their beliefs, and values so as to meet the expectations of their roles with their respective societies (Eagly & Wood, 1999). Based on the different social structures, cultures not only have different sources for providing **sexual information,** but also emphasize different cultural attitudes. This section examines these sources of sexual information, as well as cross-cultural attitudes towards **sexual permissiveness** as it relates to sexual attitudes/knowledge/behaviors, premarital sex and dating relations, and extramarital sexual relations.

Source of Sexual Information. Talking about sexual matters is largely a taboo in several cultures (e.g., North and South America, Asia, the **Middle East**), while more easily discussed in other cultures (e.g., European). Thus, the manner by which information is gathered varies across cultures. While there are universal sources of sexual information, such as friends, school, books/magazines and parents, sexual information, sexual meanings and practices are all embedded in cultural processes (Lackey & Moberg, 1998). For example, in the past, women in China were prepared for marriage by older women telling the bride of her marital duties while massaging her breasts and vaginal area (Lister, 1986). In Japan, marriage gifts such as illustrated sex manuals have been a common method of imparting this information (Gregersen, 1983). In **Mexico** and **Puerto** Rico, communication or education about sexuality has often been nonverbal and indirect through innuendos and phrases with double meanings for both genders (Burgos & Diaz-Perez, 1986; Pavich, 1986).

In recent literature, studies indicate that Anglo-American females and individuals from rural areas have received more information from their parents when compared to Anglo-American males, **Hispanics**, **Native Americans**, and students from Urban areas. Males were more likely to get information from movies than females (Davis & Harris, 1982). In other cultures (e.g., China), boys learn about sexual matters from **prostitutes** or **unmarried women** (Ruan, 1991). Bertrand, Ward, & Pauc (1992), however, found that adolescents from the Mayan culture in **Guatemala** received little education about sex. Girls learn about **menstruation** after experiencing **menarche**. Boys, on the other hand, learn about sexual issues informally, from movies, television and school. However, culturally sanctioned information about marriage is typically received through a **traditional religious ceremony** (Bertrand et al., 1992). Lackey & Moberg (1998) found that the American popular culture, especially music, played a significant role in the information process by glamorizing and mystifying sex. Thus, cultural processes dictate the extent of information and the manner by which individuals learn about sexual issues.

Sexual Attitudes, Knowledge and Behaviors. Studies (Davis & Harris, 1982; Meston, Trapneck, & Gorzalka, 1998) conducted on differences in sexual knowledge and attitudes revealed that Asians were not only more restricted in their expression of sexuality, but also held more **conservative attitudes** and demonstrated significantly lesser **sexual knowledge** than the Europeans. It was also found that Anglo-Americans were more knowledgeable about sexual issues, followed by Hispanics and Native Americans. McLaughlin, Chen, Greenberger & Biermeier (1997) examined ethnic differences in sexual behaviors and found that **Caucasian** Americans reported more **sexual partners** by late adolescence to young adulthood as compared to Asian Americans.

Other studies examining racial differences in sexual behaviors found that **Blacks** view sexuality as natural and positive and often initiate heterosexual relations early in life (Wilson, 1986). Within the **Latino** cultures, for example, the Puerto Ricans, socialize women to reinforce dependency, virginity, and submission in relationships (Burgos & Diaz-Perez, 1986). In keeping with the above literature, studies have shown that Asians and Latinos have been more conservative than Blacks, White Americans have been less restrained than Asians, but more restrained than Blacks in their sexual behaviors and attitudes (Baldwin, Whiteley, & Baldwin, 1992; LaBeff & Dodder, 1982; Moore & Erickson, 1985; Rushton & Bogaert, 1987). In comparing men and women from universities in the U.S., Canada, England, Norway, and Germany, Luckey and Nass (1972) found that English students engaged in sexual activity at an earlier age and had more sexual activity, followed by the Norwegians and the Germans respectively. The North Americans, on the other hand, were the least experienced and most conservative of the four groups. Furthermore, in comparison to the British, Japanese students were found to be less permissible and less advanced in their sexual attitudes (Iwawaki & Eysenck, 1978).

Premarital Sex and Dating Relationships. There are large variations with regard to acceptance of premarital sexual activity and dating within different cultures. In examining the literature, it appears that attitudes towards these two behaviors are closely connected and hence will be discussed together.

Chastity until marriage is a norm across several cultures based in the traditional Catholic and Islamic values. Buss (1988) found that in India, China, Iran, Indonesia, Israel, and Taiwan, chastity was seen as "indispensable" in a partner; In contrast, men and women from Finland, France, Norway, the Netherlands, Sweden, and West Germany saw chastity as relatively unimportant. Other studies have shown that young people from Asia, the Middle East, Mexico, and South America strongly disapprove of premarital sexual activity. However, people of similar age groups in the U.S., France, Belgium, and the Scandinavians countries were seen to be relatively permissive in their attitudes (Christensen, 1973; Hanassab & Tidwell, 1996; Kontula & Haavio-Manila, 1995; LaBeff & Dodder, 1982).

In addition to sexual permissiveness, studies have shown variations in the value attached to premarital sexual activity based on the intent and extent of the relationship. In their study on students from the U.S., Japan, and Russia, Sprecher and Hatfield (1995) reported that students from all three cultures tended to disapprove of casual sex. However, Americans were more approving of premarital sex in serious dating relationships, when couples were pre-engaged, and when they were formally engaged. Americans seemed to see love and commitment as a criteria and prerequisite for premarital sex. The Russians and the Japanese on the other hand saw marriage as the essential factor. However, the Russians seemed to be more approving of sex on a first date than others.

Studies have further examined the role of **acculturation in sexual permissiveness**. Raschke (1976) compared American students in the midwest, Chinese students in the U.S. and Chinese students in Hong Kong about their **premarital sexual permissiveness**. They found the Chinese students in Hong Kong were less permissive about premarital sex. However, Chinese students in America seemed to adopt American standards of premarital sexual attitudes and behaviors. Vaidyanathan & Naidoo's (1990/1991) study exploring differences between first and second generation South Asian parents and children's (Indo-Pakistani) attitudes towards premarital sexual relationships revealed that participants from both generations felt that premarital sex was unacceptable, unless the couple was emotionally involved (30% second generation) or was engaged to be married (22.7% first generation). Huang & Uba (1992) found that over 60% of the Chinese students in the U.S. approved of premarital sexual relations when the partner was in love or engaged, with sexual permissiveness being related to level of acculturation. Similarly, Hanassab & Tidwell (1996) found that there was a positive relationship between Iranian women's permissive attitudes towards sex and premarital sex and the length of time they were in the U.S..

Similar differences are seen with regard to dating. Within the Asian cultural context, dating is less acceptable when compared to European/American cultures. For example, dating relationships are rare among Koreans and seen as inconsistent with the South Asian culture because of the belief in arranged marriages (Almeida, 1996; Berg, Sperry, & Carlson, 1999). Cultures that strongly emphasize chastity prior to marriage appear to be less supportive of dating. This may be a function of cultures perceiving premarital sex as implicit in dating relationships (Inman, Ladany, Constantine, & Morano, 2001).

However, similar to the literature on premarital sexual activity, research suggests that levels of acculturation influence attitudes towards dating. For example, Vaidyanathan and Naidoo's (1990/1991) study exploring differences between first and second generation South Asian parents and children's (Indo-Pakistani) attitudes towards dating practices showed that, compared to 80% of second generation South Asians, only 20% of the first generation South Asians believed in encouraging dating. Revilla's (1989) study assessing the relationship between acculturation levels and dating preferences among Philipino-Americans suggested that dating preferences appeared to be related to ethnic loyalty rather than cultural awareness. Thus, extent of ethnic identification may appear to be a significant factor impacting one's attitudes towards dating and premarital relations.

Extramarital Sex: Attitudes and Behaviors. There is a vast difference among ethnic and cultural groups in their reasons for engaging in extramarital relations, their attitudes towards extramarital sex, and their openness to engage in these behaviors. Glass and Wright (1992) found that low self-esteem, need for attention, need for love/understanding, emotional or sexual frustration, and curiosity were some of the reasons for infidelity. Studies on differences among genders in the United States have shown men to separate love and sex, and women to combine them. Glass and Wright noted that men have been tempted to have sex purely for sexual pleasure, while women would openly do so for love/emotionally intimate relationships. Similar studies done in England, Scotland, and Wales showed traditional men were likely to engage in casual sex, brief encounters, and one night stands, while traditional woman were more likely to do so for love (Lawson, 1988). Similar themes seem to appear for men and women in gay and lesbian relationships as well. For example, intimacy patterns appear to be more sexually focused in gay relationships while more emotionally focused in lesbian relatioinships (Patterson, Williams, Grauf-Grounds, & Chamow, 1998).

Literature on cultural differences in attitudes toward extramarital sexual relationships showed that cultures, like the **Toda** of India, a polyandrous society, who do not have a word like adultery in their language, allowed extramarital relations in special circumstances (Ford & Beach, 1951). In some societies, where a double standard exists, only husbands are permitted to have extramarital relations. In several tribal societies, both men and women are forbidden to engage in such behaviors (Hatfield & Rapson, 1996). Yet, in other cultures, men and women have been punished for their extramarital affairs. These punishments have ranged from mild (e.g., small fines, warnings) to severe forms of punishment (e.g., beaten, imprisoned, mutilated or killed) (Frayser, 1985). Typically within some non-Western cultures, extramarital affairs have been seen as an unforgivable sin with rituals such as clitoral mutilation being practiced to discourage women's sexual desires (Rosenthal, 1993; Upreti & Upreti, 1991).

Studies in North America show that most people disapprove of extramarital sex under any circumstances. However, there are some variations between genders on their tolerance levels for extramarital affairs. In a national survey on American attitudes, it was found that 86% of men and women thought marital infidelity was always or almost always wrong; however, men were typically more tolerant of extramarital affairs than women (Davis & Smith, 1991; Oliver & Hyde, 1993). Some other gender differences noted men to engage in affairs earlier in their marriages. They were also seen to engage in affairs more often than women, have more sexual partners, and feel less guilty than women about engaging in these affairs (Glass & Wright, 1992; Lawson, 1988; Spanier & Margolis, 1983). Similar differences have been found in studies conducted in Australia (Thompson, 1984), England, and the Netherlands (Buunk, 1980).

Typically, European countries appear to be more tolerant and sexually permissive in their attitudes when compared to North Americans and Asians. Asians seem to be the most restricted in their attitudes towards extramarital sex. A study (Christensen, 1973) done on college students from nine different countries showed that students from Denmark, Sweden, and Belgium were generally tolerant of extramarital sex. Students from Taiwan were more conservative with 71% indicating that infidelity was wrong. Buunk's (1980) study examining the differences between U.S. and Dutch couples on their attitudes towards extramarital affairs, showed that extramarital relations were identified as more acceptable within the Dutch culture. Dutch men and women had more permissive and positive attitudes towards infidelity than the U.S. couples. Maykovich's (1976) study comparing American and Japanese females found that Americans were more liberal in their attitudes towards extramarital sexual relations. Thus, in examining the literature on sexual premissiveness, variations in different cultures appear to be related to factors such as ethnicity, gender, and acculturation. Europeans seem to be the most liberal followed by Black Americans, White Americans, Latinos, and Asians.

GENDER & CULTURAL DIFFERENCES
IN THE DESIRES FOR A ROMANTIC PARTNER

There appears to be much variation across gender and culture with regard to characteristics individuals consider important in a partner. Buss's (1994a) study examining gender differences in *mate selection* revealed that women valued ambitions, financial prospects, a good earning capacity, social status, and industriousness more than men. Men, on the other hand, appeared to value women who were younger than them. Zambian and Nigerian men who were allowed to have multiple wives preferred women who were 7-8 years younger then them when compared to men from Germany, Spain, and France who were monogamous. These men preferred wives who were only slightly younger than them. Men in most cultures (e.g., Africa, South America, Madrid, London, Paris) placed a high premium on physical appearance in seeking mates. In another study, Buss (1994b) examined mate preferences within thirty seven cultures. Findings revealed that both men and women across cultures looked for mates who were understanding, kind, intelligent, healthy and had an exciting personality. However, in examining the value attached to chastity or lack of previous sexual experiences, he found that both men and the women from Netherlands, Sweden, & Norway viewed it as unimportant, while their Chinese, Indian, **Taiwanese** and **Iranian** counterparts viewed chastity as indispensable. Those from Columbia, **Estonia**, Japan, **Poland**, Nigeria, **South Africa** and **Zambia** thought it to be moderately desirable. Furthermore, chastity was found to be desirable more by men than women. Other aspects valued involved "good housekeeping." Findings revealed that good housekeeping was valued more highly in China and Estonia than in Western Europe and North America. "Neatness" was valued highly in Iran and Nigeria and less valued in **Great Britain**, Australia, and **Ireland**. "Religious" was valued highly in Iran, moderately valued in India, and the least valued in North America and Western Europe. Hatfield & Sprecher (1995) compared students from the U.S., **Russia**, and Japan with regard to mens and women's preference in marital partners. They found that men cared more about physical attractiveness, while women cared more about status and personality attributes. In general, women were more particular about their expectation than men. Also, results revealed that men and women in the U.S. and Russia expected more from their relationships than their Japanese counterparts. Men and women across cultures appear to be similar to their counterparts with regard to expectations of the opposite sex. However, culture and religion appear to influence the extent of liberalism expressed in these expectations.

CULTURAL VIEWS OF LONG-TERM RELATIONSHIPS

Motivation for long-term relationships or marriages is influenced by cultural values, norms and beliefs, such as procreation, the provision of a stable environment for children, or for spiritual growth. For example, Hindus consider marriage to be sacred and that a man without a wife is spiritually incomplete (Kumari, 1988). The Chinese propose the interaction of the yin (i.e., passive, female) with the yang (i.e., positive, male) to be a necessary spiritual component of all events, including the relationship between men and women. Marriage within the Asian cultures is viewed as a blending or alliance of two families rather than two individuals (Dion & Dion, 1993). In keeping with this, **arranged marriages** have been the typical practice in cultures with a **collective orientation** or cultures within the East (Gardiner, Mutter, & Kosmitzki, 1998), and love marriages have been the choice in the Western cultures (Hatfield & Rapson, 1996). However, cultures such as India, Japan, China, Thailand and Africa are undergoing a change due to modernization. For example, although arranged marriages still play a signficant role in India, Middle East/Muslim countries, people are engaging in a mixture of traditional and modern practices of marriage (Fukada, 1991; Gardiner & Gardiner, 1991; Hudgins & Williams-Snyder, 1995). Literature shows that parents, brides, and grooms consult with each other and all have some say in choosing mates (Hatfield & Rapson, 1996), with arrangements varying in each culture based on their ethnicity, class, religious underpinnings, regional differences and familial values (Bumroongsook, as cited in Hatfield & Rapson, 1996).

In light of these changes, reseachers debate whether love or aranged marriages are better. Sprecher & Chandak (1992) surveyed Indian women and men living in India, England, and the United States on their thoughts about the advantages of arranged and love marriages. Some pros for arranged marriages included family support, stability of marriage, compatibility, easier adjustment, ease of meeting partner, happiness of parents and family. Disadvantages identified included limited choice, family and in-law problems, treatment related to dowry, and not knowing each other well. Advantages of love marriages included love and romanticism, freedom of choice, dating and sexual freedom, getting to know each other, while disadvantages included anguish related to sex, pregnancy and immoral behavior, disapproval from parents and society, waste of time and money, bad reputation, and short-lived relationships, to name a few.

Blood (1967) questioned Japanese men and women about **marital satisfaction** in relation to love and arranged marriages. He found that men were equally happy in either forms of marriage. However, women who were married longer and had been in arranged marriages were unhappier than women in love marriages. In a study by Yelsma & Althappilly (1988), Indian couples in arranged marriages rated greater marital satisfaction than American or

Indian couples engaged in love marriages. Xu & Whyte (1990) studied Chinese women and found that women were the happiest when allowed to choose their own partner, with more arranged than love marriages ending in divorce. Regardless of these mixed results, there is a greater move towards men and women choosing their own partners and marrying for love.

Long-term relationships have also been discussed in terms of **sexual orientation**. Sexuality experts (Kinsey and others, as cited in Suggs & Miracle, 1993) identified human sexuality as existing along a continuum with **homosexuality** and **heterosexuality** falling at the extreme ends of this continuum. In keeping with this, there is an assumption that these extremes, along with the gradations of behaviors between them are natural and normal (Suggs & Miracle). However, despite human sexuality being discussed on a continuum, long-term relations are typically discussed within the context of a heterosexual and homosexual relationship. Such a dichotomy typically prevents one from fully appreciating the variety of sexual behaviors across cultures. Furthermore, while heterosexuality and homosexuality are at the extreme opposite ends of the continuum, cultures differ greatly in terms of their attitudes towards homosexuality. Heterosexuality appears to be seen as normal and natural and homosexulity as deviant (Suggs & Miracle, 1993).

Interestingly, while heterosexual relations are fostered and encouraged by most societies, Bolton (1994) found male homosexual relations to be common in 41-64% of the societies that he studied. Research in some cultures/societies (e.g., the Siwans of Africa, the Azande, Dahomey) indicates homosexuality to be a common and encouraged feature for both men and women (Blackwood, 1986; Ford & Beach, 1951). Sexual behavior of the Berdache among North American Indians shows that homosexual activity was stressed and encouraged (Callender & Kochems, 1983). According to Herdt (1993), the Sambia of New Guinea perceive homosexual contacts as a normative practive in terms of the intiation into adulthood, with heterosexual contacts discouraged. However, in adulthood, heterosexual relations are defined as the norm. Moroccans, while less homophobic than Americans or Europeans, appear to have similar mixed attitudes towards homosexuality (Davis & Davis, 1994). In **Zawiya**, young boys, as well as older boys, engage in homosexual acts without the label of homosexuality attached to it. However, homosexual acts among adult men may be seen as shameful. In China, only monogamous sexual relations within a heterosexual context are morally acceptable and homosexuality is typically unacceptable (Ruan, 1991). While there are great variations currently within modern India, in ancient times, homosexuality has resulted in mutilation, death or loosing one's caste (Kumari, 1988). However, there does appear to be some evidence that attitudes towards homosexuality are becoming more liberal.

In recent years, research indicates that greater percentages of men and women in the United States, France, Hong Kong, and China have engaged in homosexual relations (Family Planning Association of Hong Kong, 1987; Hatfield, & Rapson, 1996; Laumann, Gagnon, Michael, & Michaels, 1994; Ruan & Bullough, 1992). While homosexuality may still be on the fringes of society, both in the West and more slowly in the East, there is a greater tolerance with legal concessions being made towards individuals with this sexual orientation (Aries, 1985).

IMPLICATIONS FOR COUNSELING

Sexuality is an integral and intrinsic part of every human being. Even though sex is a biologically sustaining process, meanings attached to sexuality and sexual behaviors are most definitely experienced within a cultural context. Sexuality is culturally informed and based on cultural beliefs, mores, and customs. Typically, what one society might condone or see as natural, the other may condemn or see as unnatural. **Sexual meanings** are thus reflected in the cultural milieu of a society (Suggs & Miracle, 1993). This has important implications in terms of counseling.

The first recommendation in counseling clients and understanding their sexual behaviors is to contextualize their behaviors and explore it through an **emic** perspective, noting that certain behaviors are specific to the client's culture. Counselors should not conceptualize client issues through their own cultural lens and perspectives. Working within a cultural context may require understanding the meaning of intimacy and how it is experienced within cultural and gender role socialization within a specific culture. For example, it may be helpful to explore how aspects related to sexuality and intimacy are communicated in the client's culture and family; how affection is expressed within the cultural context; and to what extent intimacy is sexually and/or emotionally displayed.

Counselors may want to become aware of the taboos and stigmas associated with verbalizing sexual issues in some cultures (e.g., Asian, Middle-Eastern). Counselors may need to gently explore the extent to which discussion of sexual issues is typically accepted or repressed in a particular client's culture, and the extent to which these issues are expressed within the client's family directly or indirectly, as well as the potential consequences for nonconformity to the cultural/familial norms (Greene, 1998). Nonverbalization of sexual issues should not be seen as resistance, but should be addressed with sensitivity and respect for the client and his/her cultural norms. Furthermore, because within group differences are greater than between group differences, counselors should refrain from stereotyping client behaviors and concerns. While becoming familiar with different cultures becomes important, counselors need to listen to the subjective experience of clients.

Although the review of sexual history in this chapter has been examined within an East-West dichotomy, constantly changing influences have shown a shift occurring worldwide in terms of how intimate relationships are being examined and experienced. Thus, a second recommendation is for counselors to approach client concerns related to sexuality by examining such aspects as acculturation, modernization, religious conversions, feminist movements, and other social conditions that have been instrumental in this shift.

For example, it would be helpful for counselors to have some knowledge of the differences in the acculturation levels based on generational status of clients in the United States (Inman, Constantine, & Ladany, 1999). Assessing the level of acculturation involves understanding the extent to which a client identifies with and has retained aspects of his/her own culture (e.g., attitudes towards religion, gender role socialization, etc.) and taken on aspects of the dominant culture. This assessment needs to be done at the behavioral, attitudinal and cultural levels (Ibrahim et al., 1997). For recent immigrants (first generation) the influence of modernization and changing economic-political conditions in the country of origin should also be explored. Feminist movements may also be experienced and conceptualized in varying degrees in other cultures; understanding the impact of the feminist movements on sexuality and gender roles may be significant. In light of this, integrating the biological, historical, economic, political, social, cultural, and gender perspectives in assessment and conceptualization of client issues becomes relevant and indispensable. Thus, counselors are encouraged to use a multicultural and multisystemic perspective in their clinical work with culturally different clients.

Our goal in this chapter was to provide you with an overview of the current literature on cross-cultural perspectives related to sexual behaviors and some recommendations for counseling within a cultural framework. Although limited in our scope and focus, our intent was to stimulate discussion on the role of culture in shaping one's behaviors and elucidate how multiple influences may interact within a culture, creating shifts in one's attitudes and behaviors in general and in love and sexual practices in particular.

REFERENCES

Aires, P. (1985) Thoughts on the history of homosexuality. In A. N. Suggs & A. W. Miracle (Eds.) (1993). *Culture and human sexuality: A reader* (pp. 356-366). Pacific Grove: CA: Brooks/Cole Publishing.

Almeida, R. (1996). Hindu, Christian, and Muslim families. In M. McGoldrick, J. Giordano, & J. K. Pearce (Eds.), *Ethnicity and family therapy* (pp. 395-423). New York: The Guilford Press.

Armstrong, S. (1991, February 2). Female circumcision: Fighting a cruel tradition. *New Scientist, 129*, 42-47.

Baldwin, J. D., Whiteley, S., & Baldwin, J. I. (1992). The effects of ethnic gorup on sexual activities related to contraception and STDs. *Journal of Sex Research, 29*, 189-205.

Barnlund, D. (1989). *Commuicative styles of Japanese and Americans: Images and realities.* Belmont, CA: Wadsworth.

Berg, I. K., Sperry, L. (Eds.), & Carlson, J (1999) Intimacy and culture: A solution-focused perspective - An interview with I. K. Berg, L. Sperry, & J. Carlson. In J. Carlson & L. Sperry, *The intimate couple* (pp. 41-54). Philadelphia, PA: Bruner/Mazel.

Beidelman. T. O. (1971). *The Kagura: A matrilineal people of East Africa.* New York: Hold, Rinehard & Winston.

Bertrand, J. T., Ward, V., & Pauc, F. (1992). Sexual practices among the Quiche-speaking Mayan populations of Guatemala. *International Quarterly of Community Health Education, 12,* 265-282.

Blackwood, E. (1986). Breaking the mirror: The construction of lesbianism and the anthropological discourse on homosexuality. *The many faces of homosexuality: Anthropological approaches to homosexual behavior* (pp. 1-17). New York: Harington park Press.

Blood, R. O., Jr. (1967). *Love match and arranged marriage.* New York: Free Press.

Bolton, R. (1994). Sex, science, and social responsibility: Cross cultural research and same-sex eroticism and sexual intolerance. *Cross-cultural Research, 28,* 134-190.

Brown, S.L., & Booth, A. (1996). Cohabitation versus marriage: A comparison of relatioinship quality. *Journal of Marriage and the Family, 58,* 668-678.

Burgos, N. M. & Diaz-Perez, Y. I. (1986). An exploration of human sexuality in the Puerto Rican culture. *Journal of Social Work and Human Sexuality*, 4, 135-150.

Buss, D. M. (1988). The evolution of human intrasexual competition: Tactics of mate attraction. *Journal of Personality and Social Psychology*, *54*, 616-628.

Buss, D. M. (1994a). *The evolution of desire: Strategies of human mating.* New York: Basic Books.

Buss, D. M. (1994b). Mate preferences in 37 cultures. In W. J. Lonner & R. Malpass (Eds.), *Psychology and culture* (pp. 197-201). Boston: Allyn & Bacon.

Buunk, B. P. (1980). Extramarital sex in the Netherlands: Motivations in social and marital context. *Alternative Lifestyles, 3,* 11-39.

Callender C. & Kochems, L. M. (1983). The North American Berdache. In A. N. Suggs & A. W. Miracle (Eds.) (1993). *Culture and human sexuality: A reader* (pp. 367-397). Pacific Grove: CA: Brooks/Cole Publishing.

Carson, J. & Sperry, L. (1999). *The intimate couple.* Philadelphia, PA: Brunner/Manzel

Castaneda, D. M. (1993). The meaning of romantic love among Mexican-Americans. *Journal of Social behavior and Personality, 8,* 257-272.

Cherlin, A. (1991). Recent changes in American fertility, marriage, and divorce. *The Annuals of American Academy of Political and Social Science, 510,* 145-156.

Christensen, H. T. (1973). Attitudes towards marital infidelity: A nine-cultural sampling of university student opinion. *Journal of Comparative Family Studies, 4,* 197-214.

Chu, G. C. (1985). The changing concept of self in comtemporary China. In A. J. Marsella, G. DeVos, & F. L. K. Hus (Eds.), *Culture and self: Asian and Western perspectives* (pp. 252-277). London, England: Tavistock.

Comas-Diaz, L., & Griffith, E. E. H. (1988). *Clinical guidelines in cross-cultural mental health.* New York: John Wiley & Sons.

Cunningham, J.D., & Antill, J.K. (1994). Cohabitation and marriage: Retrospective and predictive comparisons. *Journal of Social and Personal Relationships, 11,* 77-93.

Dasgupta, S.D., & Dasgupta, S. (1996). Private face, private space: Asian Indian women and sexuality. In N.B. Maglin, & D. Perry (Eds.), *Bad girls, good girls: Women, sex, and power in the nineties* (pp. 226-243). New Brunswick, NJ: Rutgers University Press.

Davis, R.A. (1998). The norm of legitimacy in the Black family. *Western Journal of Black Studies, 22,* 145-152.

Davis, D. A., & Davis, S. S. (1994). Sexual values in a Moroccan town. In W. J. Lonner & R. Malpass (Eds.), *Psychology and Culture* (pp. 225-230). Boston, MA: Allyn & Bacon.

Davis, J. A., & Smith, T. W. (1991). *General social surveys, 1972-1991.* Chicago: National Opinion Research Center: University of Chicago.

Davis, S. M., & Harris, M. B. (1982). Sexual knowedlge, sexual interests, and sources of sexual information of rural and urban adolescents from three cultures. *Adolescence, 17,* 471-492.

Dion, K. L., & Dion, K. K. (1993). Gender and ethnocultural comparisons in styles of love. *Psychology of Women Quarterly, 17,* 463-473.

Doherty, R. W., Hatfield, E., Thompson, K., & Choo, P. (1993). Cultural and ethnic influences on love and attachment. *Personal Relationships, 1,* 391-398.

Duff, J., & Truitt, G.S. (1991). The transition from cohabitation to marriage: A longitudinal study of the propensity to marry in Sweden in the early 1990s. *Journal of Family Issues, 20,* 698-717.

Eagly, A. H., & Wood, W. (1999). The origins of sex differences in human behavior: Evolved disposition versus social roles. *American Psychologist, 54,* 408-423.

Family Planning Association of Hong Kong. (1987). *Adolescent sexuality study 1986.* Hong Kong: Family Planning Association.

Fisher, H. E. (1989). Evolution of human serial pair-bonding. *American Journal of Physical Anthropology, 78,* 331-354.

Ford, C. S., & Beach, F. A. (1951). *Patterns of sexual behavior.* New York: Harper & Row.

Frayser, S. G. (1985). *Varieties of sexual experience: An anthropological perspective on human sexuality.* New Haven, CT: HRAF Press.

Fukada, N. (1991). Women in Japan. In L. L. Adler (Ed.), *Women in cross-cultural perspective* (pp. 205-219). Westport, CT: Praeger.

Gardiner, H. W., & Gardiner, O. S. (1991). Women in Thailand. In L. L. Adler (Ed.), *Women in cross-cultural perspective.* (pp. 174-187). Westport, CT: Praeger.

Gardiner, H. W., Mutter, J. D., & Kosmitzki, C. (1998). *Lives across cultures: Cross-cultural human development.* Boston: Allyn & Bacon.

Glass, S. P., & Wright, T. L. (1992). Justification for extramarital relationships: The association between attitudes, behaviors, and gender. *Journal of Sex Research, 29,* 361-387.

Goldman, N., & Pebley, A.R. (1981). Legalization of consensual unions in Latin America. *Social Biology, 28,* 49-61.

Greene, B. (1998). Family, ethnic identity, and sexual orientation: African-American lesbians and gay men. In C.J. Patterson, & A.R. D'Augelli (Eds.), *Lesbian, gay, and bisexual identities in families: Psychological perspectives* (pp 40-52). NY: Oxford University Press.

Gregersen, E. (1983). *Sexual practices: The story of human sexuality.* New York: Franklin Watts.

Halvorsen, R. (1998). The ambiguity of lesbian and gay marriages: Change and continuity in the symbolic order. *Journal of Homosexuality, 35,* 207-231.

Hanassab, S., & Tidwell, R. (1996). Sex-roles and sexual attitudes of young Iranian women: Implications for cross-cultural counseling. *Social Behavior and Personality, 24,* 185-194.

Hatfield, E. (1984). The dangers of intimacy. In V. Derlaga (Ed.), *Communication, intimacy, and close relationships* (pp. 207-220). New York: Academic Press.

Hatfield, E., & Rapson, R. L. (1995). Historical and cross-cultural perspectives on passionate love and sexual desire. *Annual Review of Sex Research, 4,* 67-97.

Hatfield, E., & Rapson, R. L. (1996). *Love and Sex: Cross-cultural perspectives.* Boston: Allyn & Bacon.

Hatfield, E. & Sprecher, S. (1995). Men's and women's preferences in marital partners in the United States, Russia, and Japan. *Journal of Cross-Cultural Psychology, 26,* 728-750.

Herdt, G. H. (1993). Semen transactions in Sambia Culture. In A. N. Suggs & A. W. Miracle (Eds.), *Culture and human sexuality: A reader* (pp. 298-327). Pacific Grove: CA: Brooks/Cole Publishing

Hirayama, H., & Hirayama, K. K. (1986). The sexuality of Japanese Americans. *Journal of Social Work and Human Sexuality, 4,* 81-98.

Hobart, C. (1993). Interest in marriage among Canadian students at the end of the eighties. *Journal of Comparative Family Studies, 24,* 45-61.

Hobart, C., & Grigel, F. (1992). Cohabitation among Canadian students at the end of the eighties. *Journal of Comparative Family Studies, 23,* 311-337.

Hofstede, G. (1983). National culture revisited. *Behavior Science research, 18,* 285-305.

Hsu, F. L. K. (1985). The self in cross-cultural perspectives. In A. J. Marsella, G. DeVos, & F. L. K. Hus (Eds.), *Culture and self: Asian and Western perspectives* (pp. 24-55). London, England: Tavistock.

Huang, H. (1998). The impact of social change on family and marriage in China. In U.P. Gielen, & A.L. Comunian (Eds.), *The family and family therapy in international perspective* (pp. 168-185). Brooklyn, NY: Edizioni, Lint, & Trieste.

Huang, K., & Uba, L. (1992). Premarital sexual behavior among Chinese college students in the United States. *Archives of Sexual Behavior, 21,* 227-240.

Hudgins, J. E. & Williams-Snyder, V. (1995). *African wedding guide.* Netscape: New Perspectives Technologies Company. (http://www.melanet.com/wedding/wed.html).

Huffman, T., Chang, K. Rausch, P., & Schaffer, N. (1994). Gender differences and factors related to the disposition towards cohabitation. *Family Therapy, 21,* 171-184.

Ibrahim, F.A., Ohnishi, H., & Sandhu, D.S. (1997). Asian American identity development: A culture specific model for South Asian Americans. *Journal of Multicultural Counseling and Development, 25,* 34-50.

Inman, A.G., Constantine, M.G., & Ladany, N. (1999). Cultural value conflict: An examination of Asian Indian women's bicultural experience. In D.S. Sandhu (Ed.), *Asian and Pacific Islander Americans: Issues and concerns for counseling and psychotherapy* (pp. 31-41). Commack. NY: Nova Science Publishers.

Inman, A.G., Ladany, N., Constantine, M.G., & Morano, C.K. (2001). Development and preliminary validation of the cultural values conflicts scale for South Asian women. *Journal of Counseling Psychology, 48,* 17-27.

Iwasaki, S. & Eysenck, H. J. (1978). Sexual attitudes among British and Japanese students. *Journal of Psychology, 98,* 289-298.

Johnson, D. (1991, April 9). Polygamists emerge from secrecy, seeking not just peace but respect. *New York Times.*

Khoo, S. (1987). Living together as married: A profile of de facto couples in Australia. *Journal of Marriage and the Family, 49,* 185-191.

Kontula, O. & Haavio-Mannila, E. (1995). *Sexual pleasures: Enhancement of sex life in Finland, 1991-1992.* Brookfield, VA: Dartmouth.

Kumar, U. (1991). Life stages in the development of the Hindu woman in India. In L. L. Adler (Ed.), *Women in corss-cultural perspectives* (pp. 142-158). New York: Praeger.

Kumari, R. (1988). *Female sexuality in Hinduism.* Delhi: Joint Women's Programme by ISPCK.

Kurdek. L.A. (1998). The deterioration of relationship quality for gay and lesbian cohabiting couples: A five-year prospective longitudinal study. *Personal Relationships, 3,* 417-442.

LaBeff, E. E., & Dodder, R. A. (1982). Attitudes towards sexual permissiveness in Mexico and the United States. *The Journal of Social Psychology, 116,* 285-286.

Lackey, J. F., & Moberg, D. P. (1998). Understanding the onset of intercourse among urban American adolescents: A cultural process framework. *Human Organization, 57,* 491-501.

Larson, J. (1991). Cohabitation is a premarital step. *American Demographics, 13,* 20-22.

Laumann, E. O., Gagnon, J. H., Michael, R. T., & Michaels, S. (1994). *The social organization of sexuality: Sexual practices in the United States.* Chicago, IL: University of Chicago Press.

Lawson, A. (1988). *Adultery: An analysis of love and betrayal.* New York: Basic Books.

Levin, I., & Trost, J. (1999). Living apart together. *Community Work and Family, 2,* 279-294.

Lister, L. (1986). A conceptual framework for exploring ethnoculture and human sexuality. *Journal of Social Work and Human Sexuality, 4,* 1-27.

Luckey, E. B., & Nass, G. D. (1972). Comparison of sexual attitudes in an international sample of college students. *Medical Aspects of Human Sexuality, 6,* 66-107.

Manning, W.D., & Landale, N.S. (1996). Racial and ethnic differences in the role of cohabitation in premarital childbearing. *Journal of Marriage and the Family, 58,* 63-77.

Markus, H. R., & Kitayama, S. (1991). Culture and the self: Implications for cognition, emotion and motivation. *Psychological Review, 98,* 224-253.

Marshal, D. S. (1993). Sexual aspects of the life cycle. In A. N. Suggs & A. W. Miracle (Eds.), *Culture and human sexuality: A reader* (pp. 91-102). Pacific Grove: CA: Brooks/Cole Publishing Company.

Maykorvich, M. K. (1976). Attitudes versus behavior in extramarital relations. *Journal of Marriage and the Family, 38,* 693-699.

McLaughlin, C. S., Chen, C., Greenberger, E., & Biermeier, C. (1997). Family, peer, and individual correlates of sexual experience among Caucasian and Asian American late adolescents. *Journal of Research on Adolescence, 7,* 33-53.

Meston, C. M., Trapnell, P. D., & Gorzalka, B. B. (1998). Ethnic, gender, and length-of-residency influences on sexual knowledge and attitudes. *Journal of Sex Research, 35,* 176-188.

Moore, D. S. & Erickson, P. I. (1985). Age, gender, and ethnic differences in sexual and contraceptive knowledge, attitudes, and behaviors. *Family and Community Health, 8,* 38-51.

Murdock, G. P. (1967). *Ethnographic atlas.* Pittsburgh, PA: Pittsburgh University Press.

Nicole, F.M., & Baldwin, C. (1995). Cohabitation as a developmental stage: Implicatioins for mental health counseling. *Journal of Mental Health Counseling, 17,* 386-396.

Nock, S.L. (1995). A comparison of marriages and cohabiting relationships. *Journal of Family Issues, 16,* 53-76.

Oliver, M. B., & Hyde, J. S. (1993). Gender differences in sexuality: A meta-analysis. *Psychological Bulletin, 114,* 29-51.

Opler, M. (1956). *Culture and mental health: Cross-cultural studies.* New York: Macmillan.

Oropesa, R.S. (1996). Normative beliefs about marriage and cohabitation: A comparison of non-Latino Whites, Mexican Americans, and Puerto Ricans. *Journal of Marriage and the Family, 58,* 49-62.

Patterson, J., Williams, L., Grauf-Grounds, C., & Chamow, L. (1998). *Essential skills in family therapy: From the first interview to termination.* New York: Guilford Press.

Pavich, E. G. (1986). A Chicana perspective on Mexican culture and sexuality. *Journal of Social Work and Human Sexuality, 4,* 47-65.

Piney, T.K., & Perez, M.P. (2000). Recounting the wages of self-appraised sinfulness: A research note on divorce, cohabitation, and guilt. *Deviant Behavior, 21,* 1-13.

Raschke, V. (1976). Premarital sexual permissiveness of college students in Hong Kong. *Journal of Comparative Family Studies, 7,* 65-74.

Revilla, L.A. (1989). Dating and marriage preference among Philipino-Americans. *Journal of the Asian American Psychological Association, 13,* 72-79.

Roland, A. (1988). *In search of self in India and Japan.* Princeton, NJ: Princeton University Press.

Rosenthal, A. M. (1993, July 27). The torture continues. *The New York Times, A13.*

Ruan, F. F. (1991). *Sex in China: Studies in sexology in Chinese culture.* New York: Plenum.

Ruan, F. F., & Bollough, V.L. (1992). Lesbianism in China. *Archives of Sexual Behavior, 21,* 217-226.

Rushton, J. P. & Bogaert, A. F. (1987). Race differences in sexual behaviors: Testing an evolutionary hypothesis. *Journal of Research in Personality, 21,* 529-551.

Saran, P. (1985). *The Asian Indian experience in the United States.* New Delhi, India: Vikas.

Sarantokos, S. (1994). Unmarried cohabitation: Options, limits and possibilities. *Australian Journal of Marriage and Family, 15,* 148-160.

Sarantokos, S. (1996). Same-sex couples: Problems and prospects. *Journal of Family Studies, 2,* 147-163.

Shelton, B.A., & John, D. (1993). Does marital status make a difference? Homework among married and cohabiting men and women. *Journal of Family Issues, 14,* 410-420.

Sirica, J. (1993, December 13). Women are remaining childless in almost record numbers. *Atlanta Journal,* C8.

Smith, M.G. (1962). *West Indian family structure.* Seattle, WA: Washington Press.

Smith, R.B., & Brown, R.A. (1997). The impact of social support on gay male couples. *Journal of Homosexuality, 33,* 39-61.

Soyinka, F. (1979). Sexual behavior among university students in Nigeria. *Archives of Sexual Behavior, 8,* 15-26.

Spanier, G. B., & Margolis, R. L. (1983). Marital separation and extramarital sexual behavior. *The Journal of Sex Research, 19,* 23-48.

Sprecher, S., & Chandak, R. (1992). Attitudes about arranged marriages and dating among men and women from India. *Free Inquiry in Creative Sociology, 20,* 1-11.

Sprecher, S., Aron, A., Hatfield, E., Cortese, A., Potapova, E., & Levitskaya, A. (1994). Love: American style, Russian style, and Japanese style. *Personal Relationships, 1,* 349-369.

Sprecher, S., & Hatfield E. (1995). Premarital sexal standards among U.S. college students and a comparison with those of Russian and Japanese students. *Archives of Sexual Behavior, 25,* 261-288.

Sprecher, S. & Hatfield, E. (1996). Premarital sexual standards among U.S. college students: Comparison with Russian and Japanese students. *Archives of Sexual Behaviors, 25,* 261-288.

Sprecher, S., & McKinney, K. (1993). *Sexuality.* Newbury Park, CA: Sage.

Suggs, A. N., & Miracle, A. W. (1993). *Culture and human sexuality: A reader.* Pacific Grove: CA: Brooks/Cole Publishing Company.

Thiederman, S. (1991). *Bridging cultural barriers for corporate success.* New York: Lexington Books.

Thompson, A. P. (1984). Emotional and sexual components of extramarital relations. *Journal of Marriage and the Family, 46,* 35-42.

Ting-Toomey, S. (1991). Intimacy expressions in three cultures: France, Japan & the United States. *International Journal of Intercultural Relations, 15,* 29-46.

Triandis, H. C. (1989). The self and social behavior in differing cultural contexts. *Psychological Review, 96,* 506-520.

Triandis, II. C. (1994). *Culture and social behavior.* New York: McGraw-Hill.

Upreti, H. C., & Upreti, N. (1991). *The myth of sati: Some dimensions of widow burning.* Bombay: Himalaya Publishing House.

Vaidyanathan & Naidoo (1990/1991). Asian Indians in Western countries: Cultural identity and the arranged marriage. In N. Bleichrodt & P. J. D. Drenth (Eds.), *Contemporary issues in cross-cultural psychology: Selected papers from a regional conference of the international association of cross-cultural psychology* (pp. 37-49). Berwyn, PA: Swets & Zeitlinger.

Weisfeld, G. (1997). Puberty rites as clues to the nature of human adolescence. *Cross-Cultural Research, 31,* 27-54.

Wilson, P. M. (1986). Black culture and sexuality. *Journal of Social Work and Human Sexuality, 4,* 29-46.

Won-Doornik, M. (1985). Self-disclosure and reciprocity in conversation: A cross-national study. *Social Psychology Quarterly, 48,* 97-107.

Xu, X., & Whyte, M. K. (1990). Love matches and arranged marriages: A Chinese replication. *Journal of Marriage and the Family, 52,* 709-722.

Yap, J. G. (1986). Philippine ethnoculture and human sexuality. *Journal of Social Work and Human Sexuality, 4,* 121-134.

Yelsma, P. & Althappilly, K. (1988). Marital satisfaction and communication practices: Comparisons among India and American couples. *Journal of Comparative Family Studies, 19,* 37-54.

Chapter 4

SEXUALITY EDUCATION AND THE PUBLIC SCHOOLS

Jan R. Bartlett
Iowa State University
Tarrell A. Portman
The University of Iowa

Today a controversy rages in our schools regarding **sexuality education** in the United States. The debate and controversy regarding educating our youth on the topic of sex are not new, and there have always been extreme views regarding the topic of sex in the U.S. The issues that drive sexuality education are multifaceted and tied to sweeping societal concerns. Therefore, to ask a school district to resolve teen pregnancy, to prevent students from becoming sexually active, or to prevent the contraction of HIV/AIDS or other STDs is not possible. It must be acknowledged that many schools exert tremendous efforts toward preventing the above behaviors from becoming a reality for our students, often amidst controversy and opposing opinions. This is accomplished by providing information to students so that they can make informed personal decisions. Today's students engage in sexual activity at a younger age than in past decades and their decision to become sexually active is not based on their knowledge of sex. Sweden began compulsory sexuality education for students starting at age 8 in 1956. Swedish preadolescents have sexual knowledge far superior to that of most North American children of the same age, and research demonstrates that Swedish students are not promiscuous and that their teen pregnancy rate is substantially lower than United States teens (King, 1999).

To narrow sexual activity for teens to a simplistic phrase like, "just say no" ignores the complexity and the scope of sex in our schools and in our society. Various aspects of sexuality education are often divided and presented in a random fashion, rather than through a comprehensive K-12 curriculum. In many schools the school counselor functions in no formal role for the district regarding sexuality education. Therefore, the professional best trained to assist students, parents, administrators, and teachers during discussions of possibly embarrassing or uncomfortable sexuality topics is not included or invited into the conversation. Those counselors who involve themselves in sexuality education do so because they recognize the potential of their vital role. School counselors have the knowledge, skills, compassion, and established relationships that could profoundly and positively impact sexuality education in our schools.

BACKGROUND

Historical Perspective

In the 1880s the "**Free Lovers**" encouraged the joys of unabandoned fornication, but at the same time **John Harvey Kellogg**, the cereal tycoon, strongly cautioned against the risks and the menace of **masturbation** (Priluck, 1997). A few years later, the **National Purity Association** in 1895 published a pamphlet that warned girls about the dangers of male lust (Priluck, 1997). The polarization of opinions and powerful emotions that frequently accompany this topic among parents, counselors, teachers, and students is still prevalent. Often groups of people with differing moral or political ideologies find sexuality education a fruitful battleground. This is happening, when for the first time in history, educators are in a position to provide factual information regarding human sexuality to students (King, 1999). Since 1992, over 700 attacks have been launched against sexuality education, with parents, school board members, and faculty struggling to determine at what age what information is appropriate ("Fact Sheet," 2000).

Historically, the shifting saga of **sex education** in this country began formally in 1892 with a resolution passed by the **National Education Association (NEA)**, which declared the backing of sex education as a necessary part of the education curriculum (Priluck, 1997). The NEA strengthened their endorsement of sex education in **public schools** in 1912 (Czuczka, 2000; King, 1999) and encouraged the inclusion of courses such as "**sex hygiene**," which was a delicate way of addressing and then discussing **venereal diseases** (Priluck, 1997). This information may not appear earth shaking by today's standards, but it must be placed in the context of the laws of the time and the drama that evolved from the degree of enthusiasm and commitment on both sides of the issue.

In 1873 the **Comstock Law** was passed, which made it a felony to mail any materials considered obscene or lewd, which included information intended for the purpose of preventing conception or resulting in an abortion (Czuczka, 2000; King, 1999; Priluck, 1997). The law was named after Anthony Comstock, a moral crusader who became a special agent of the U.S. Post Office (King, 1999) and later formed the Society for the Suppression of Vice (D'Emilio & Freedman, 1988). In 1915, Comstock entered the architect studio of **William Sanger** with an arrest warrant because Sanger had provided the pamphlet, *Family Limitation,* written by his wife, **Margaret Sanger**, to a spy for the society (D'Emilio & Freedman, 1988). In order to evade prosecution for writing articles on contraception, Margaret Sanger had escaped the previous year to Europe, but with her husband's arrest she returned. The subsequent trials of both the Sangers created unexpected demonstrations by women demanding an open discussion on contraception (D'Emilio & Freedman, 1988).

By 1922, 40 percent of public schools conducted instruction on social hygiene and sexuality education (Priluck, 1997). A journal from this decade measured the emerging sexual freedom in terms of fabric yardage required for a woman's dress, for in 1913 it required 19.5 yards and in 1928 only 7 were required (Czuczka, 2000). The culture at this time was greatly influenced by the increased mobility of Henry Ford's affordable automobiles, the arrival of movies and film stars, and an overall atmosphere of affluence and increased leisure time (Czuczka, 2000). With the crash of the stock market and the following economic depression during the 1930s, a more conservative environment prevailed in the country, as the "advances of sexual liberalism came to a halt" (Czuczka, 2000, p. 16).

One text that emerged in 1930 was written by a Catholic theologian, *Sex Education and Training in Chastity*. He advised boys regarding wet dreams to "try to think of something else, forget about the emission, say a Hail Mary, and turn over and go to sleep" (Priluck, 1997, p. 11). Along this same line, in 1938 the **American Association of School Administrators** supported the new approach, which stipulated that sex should be within the bounds of love (Priluck, 1997). The AASA instructed that lessons in social hygiene center on homemaking and character building, and that masturbation, **necking**, and **petting** were to be discouraged (Priluck, 1997).

In the 1940s several important events occurred. As the U.S. entered the war, 12 million men went into the armed services and for the first time a policy of education and prevention developed around venereal disease (Czuczka, 2000). Antibiotics, a cure for some venereal diseases, were discovered during this decade. At this time the **U.S. Public Health Service** began to advocate for school-based education on sexuality and was supported by many other organizations. The emerging literature highlighted expression and pleasure, which was a break from the previous emphasis on reproduction and control (Czuczka, 2000).

Sexuality education received a powerful advocate in the mid-fifties with the joint publication of five pamphlets for elementary, secondary students, and adults by the **American Medical Association (AMA)** and the NEA (Priluck, 1997): *Parents' Privilege, A Story about You, Finding Yourself, Learning About Love, and Facts Aren't Enough* (Czuczka, 2000). These pamphlets were broadly utilized across the U.S.

In the sixties, scientific research on sexuality pushed the discussion into new areas and created social movement. A truly revolutionary event occurred in the early 1960s that would forever impact female sexuality; at this time the **Food and Drug Administration (FDA)** released a female contraceptive, "**the pill**," which became available to women across the nation (Czuczka, 2000; D'Emilio & Freedman, 1988; Priluck, 1997). One influential group formed at this time was the **Sex Information and Education Council of the United States (SIECUS)**, which sought to "affirm sexuality as a natural and healthy part of life" and to advocate around the sharing of information regarding sexuality (Czuczka, 2000, p 17). Critics labeled founders of the organization pornographers and communists (Priluck, 1997). The **U.S. Office of Education** encouraged programs for the training of teachers, sex education, and family-life (Czuczka, 2000). Many conservative groups, such as the **John Birch Society, Christian Crusade**, and **Mothers Organized for Moral Stability**, opposed sexuality education and their effect was far-reaching. By 1970, many states had eliminated or limited sexuality education in schools (Czuzcka, 2000).

Two major events served as a catalyst for twenty states to restrict sexuality education in schools by 1975 (Priluck, 1997). First, in 1973 the **U.S. Supreme Court** legalized abortions and then, in 1974, the **American Psychiatric Association (APA)** removed from its diagnostic manual and list of mental illness homosexuality (Czuzcka, 2000; D'Emilio & Freedman, 1988). The controversy over abortion, the right to choose and the expression of different sexual orientations are still explosive topics today. The women's movement, which took women's issues into classrooms across the country, led women to question sexual relationships traditionally confined exclusively to the institution of marriage. At the same time, gay men and lesbians became increasingly vocal in ascertaining their sexual selves in private and in public. The growing sense of freedom and openness sexually that many young people explored in the 1960s and 1970s transformed into an increasing sense of fear for young people in the next decade, as escalating numbers of deaths were attributed to a mysterious new disease that emerged in the 1980s. Much of the open and free expression of love became something else, because people became scared and terrified for loved ones and friends who began to die.

The word for the 1980s related to sexuality education was clearly AIDS. The first cases were diagnosed in the early part of the decade. The headline for *The New York Times* stated, "Rare Cancer Seen in 41 Homosexuals" and other publications referred to it as the "gay plague" (Czuzcka, 2000). The disease was clearly linked to IV drug use, Haitians, and gay men; therefore, many people assumed that the disease was not relevant to them. The attitude of many changed as research findings emerged and the threat of AIDS was re-evaluated. By 1986, the U.S. Surgeon General C. Everett Koop strongly stated, "There is now no doubt that we need sex education in schools and that it must include information on heterosexual and homosexual relationships" (Czuzcka, 2000, p. 18). At this same time in 1985, the television networks refused to run public service announcements on the topic of teen pregnancy (Priluck, 1997). Religious and political extremists used the threat of AIDS to further their agendas against homosexuality and for sexual abstinence education in the schools (Czuzcka, 2000).

In the 1990s, the reality set in that AIDS was not just a gay disease. New York City led the nation in 1995 with the number of reported cases of AIDS among adolescents and young adults (Priluck, 1997). In 1996, all 50 states either required or recommended public schools to provide sexuality and HIV/AIDS education, yet only 5% of high school students received comprehensive sexuality education (Priluck, 1997). Legislation in 1996 restricted the content and effectiveness of school-based sexuality education throughout much of the nation and shifted its support intensely toward abstinence education (Czuzcka, 2000). A lawsuit filed by Planned Parenthood in 1992 was settled in 1996, which stemmed from charges leveled at a Florida school district for providing erroneous and deficient information regarding sex (Priluck, 1997).

Overview

Nationwide in those public school districts that have policies requiring sexuality education, 86 percent stipulate that **abstinence** be endorsed as the preferred option for teenagers or as the only alternative beyond the institution of **marriage** (Alan Guttmacher Institute, 2000). This information is derived from the institute's survey of the nation's superintendents. The study also showed that in one-third of those schools with sex education polices, **contraception** was either discussed in the context of its ineffectiveness in averting unplanned pregnancy or sexually transmitted diseases or was prohibited all together as a topic for discussion (Alan Guttmacher Institute, 2000). These numbers may be attributed to the 1996 reform of welfare, which allocated "$50 million annually for chastity programs and required that states match three dollars for every four federal dollars if they wanted a share of it" (Klein, 2000, p. 9).

With a majority of public school districts sponsoring abstinence based sexuality education, very few are providing education on protection for students who decide to become sexually active. Leitman, Kramer, & Taylor (1993) examined the availability of condoms in the public schools, and the results determined that only 8% of middle school and secondary students were in schools where districts had approved condom distribution programs. Most of those school districts were on either the east or west coasts of the country and in the nation's largest school districts. Those school districts favoring contraceptive disbursement to students, can refer to a recent report stressing the reduction in teen pregnancies during the 1990s being directly related to contraceptive use ("Teenage Contraceptive," 1999).

Another emotionally charged issue is the discussion of **sexual orientation** in the schools. There are school districts and some school counselors who are becoming strong **advocates** against the oppression, discrimination, harassment, and threats students cope with because of their sexual orientation, and they try to educate faculty, staff, students and communities (Bauman & Sachs-Kapp, 1998; Moss, 1997; Rodriguez, 1998). School districts are now also dealing with sexual harassment through both policies and litigation." Sexual harassment has long been present in schools, but is now actively being addressed. The voices concerning sexuality education are loud and the messages mixed.

Related Definitions

Our examination of concepts and terms begins with **sexuality education**. This particular definition is from the **Sexuality Information and Education Council of the United States, Inc. (SIECUS)**. In the past, the term sex education was frequently used, now the preferred term appears to be sexuality education. The latter term is more encompassing, rather than sex education, which might imply simply information or education regarding sex. For the purpose of this chapter, we are applying this term in application to the school setting.

SIECUS, 1992– What is sexuality education? Sexuality education is a lifelong process of acquiring information and forming attitudes, beliefs, and values about identity, relationships, and intimacy. It encompasses sexual development, reproductive health, interpersonal relationships, affection, intimacy, body image, and gender roles. Sexuality education addresses the biological, sociocultural, psychological, and spiritual dimensions of sexuality from (1) the cognitive domain, (2) the affective domain, and (3) the behavioral domain, including the skills to communicate effectively and make responsible decisions. *(National Guidelines Task Force, 1996)*

Therefore, sexuality education relates to curriculum designed to address the categories above within the classroom in school districts or not, as the district choose.

Another term that appears frequently today is **abstinence based sex education**. This type of educational approach provides some information about sex, but not comprehensively. In some cases, the words "until marriage" have been added to the curriculum. The curriculum's platform for students is tied to these terms: "avoiding sexual intercourse as well as any genital contact or genital stimulation" (Medical Institute for Sexual Health, 1996, p. 7). Research actually demonstrates minimal connection between the sexual activity of students and the provision of information regarding sex. Telling students about sex has not encouraged the participation in sexual activity. On the other hand, not informing students about sex does not prevent sexual activity either.

A **comprehensive sexuality education** program is aimed toward providing complete and accurate information to students regarding sexuality. In addition to information, this model also strives to assist young people concerning interpersonal skills and the understanding of their own values, attitudes, and beliefs about sexuality. The use of contraception, as well as abstinence, is discussed in this type of program. More information concerning this type of program is presented in the section of the chapter on models.

GENERAL OVERVIEW OF CULTURAL PERSPECTIVES RELATED TO SEX EDUCATION

American public school systems are but a microcosm of the American multicultural, multilingual society. The diversity represented in public schools is representative of the greater population. Issues of prejudice, discrimination, and racism surrounding diversity of age, gender, ethnicity, disability, religion, sexual orientation, socioeconomic status, and citizenship status are not uncommon in elementary, middle, or secondary schools. These cultural perspectives cannot be ignored when considering curriculum incorporating sexuality education.

In considering cultural perspectives related to sexuality education, it is necessary to provide some insight into the current statistical evidence found regarding these various diverse factors. The two areas often considered related to the topic of sexuality education are STD/HIV infection and teenage pregnancy.

STD/HIV/AIDS

According to data collected by the U.S. Center for Disease Control, during the 1996-1997 years, African Americans had a higher number of reported cases of Chlamydia than did White, non-Hispanic individuals in the same two year period (STD Surveillance, 1997). Elementary and Middle School children ages 10 – 14 had a total number of reported cases of 9,338, which decreased slightly to 9,168 in 1997. Secondary School children had the largest number of reported cases during this time period of 151,120 cases in 1996, which increased to 158,554 in 1997. (STD Surveillance, 1997).

Acquired Immunodeficiency Syndrome (AIDS) cases were also reported according to age, gender, and race in a longitudinal table looking at 1985 data through 1998 data. African Americans males, age 13 years and older had the highest number reported cases at 145.3 cases per 100,000 population. The next highest group was American Indian/Alaskan Native males with 67.2 cases reported per 100,000 individuals. Females were reported as having fewer cases of AIDS but still African American females age 13 years and older had 54.1 cases reported per 100,000 individuals.

Results also indicated a difference by ethnicity in children (all children under age 13) during this 14-year period. White, non-Hispanic children had 18.5 % of the cases reported, and African American, non-Hispanic had 60.9 % of the cases reported. Percentage of cases reported for other groups are noted as 19.4 % for Hispanic children and for American

Indian/Alaskan Native 0.3%, and for Asian or Pacific Islander 0.6%. Cases reported for children less than 1 year of age were 39.7 %. Children ages 1-12 years made up 60.3 % of these reported cases (Centers for Disease Control and Prevention, 1998). These data indicate the need for sexuality education in our public schools. Children in the United States are suffering from sexually transmitted diseases.

Teen Pregnancy

The United States has the highest rates of teen pregnancy and births in the western industrialized world. Teen pregnancy costs the United States at least $7 billion annually. (National Campaign to Prevent Teen Pregnancy, 1997). Each year approximately one million girls in America conceive a child and an overwhelming majority (78%) of these teenage pregnancies are unplanned. Teenagers are rushed into premature adulthood by having the responsibility for their own offspring with more than half a million teenagers having a child (Haffner, 1995a; Henshaw, 1998). This number appears to be declining.

A comparison of data from 1991 to 1998 provides insight into declining birth rates. An overall decline of 18 percent for those aged 15 to 19 was noted, whereas, there was a 24-percent rise in the teenage birth rate from 1986 to 1991. The birth rate for African American teens aged 15 to 19 fell 26 percent from 1991 to 1998. Latino/a teen birth rates declined 13 percent between 1994 and 1998. The rates of both Latino/as and African Americans, however, remain higher than for other groups. Latino/a teens now have the highest teenage birth rates.

However, the teenage birth rate for 1998 is still higher than it was in the mid-1980s (Ventura, Mathews, & Curtin, 1999). American children are still disadvantaged by socioeconomic status and ethnicity, which puts them in groups at risk for early unintended pregnancy (Guttmacher Institute, 1994).

Religiosity and Sexuality Education

Major cultural diversity issues exist in the current literature surrounding sexuality education in public schools. The primary diversity factors that stand out are the conflicts between people's worldviews related to religious beliefs. In fact, three factors have been determined to be instrumental in determining people's attitudes toward sexuality education in public schools. These factors are religiosity, age and level of education (Ray, 1988).

Conflicts surrounding individual community members or the worldview of parents could be considered as ideological conflicts. These ideological conflicts over sexuality education in public schools typically are presented by opposing groups; one group favoring abstinence-only curriculum and the other group in favor of comprehensive sexuality curriculums (Nelson, 1997). Comprehensive sexuality education curriculum embraces the value of information sharing, decision-making and tolerance (Moore, Miller, Glei & Morrison, 1995). These two opposing groups are just a reflection of the greater American society as indicated in the next passage by Nelson (1997):

The conflicts over sex education are inextricably connected to larger contemporary cultural conflicts between the "Left" and "Right." Indeed, the debated sex education curricula themselves are merely symbols in a much larger struggle over which – and whose—definitions of sexuality, family, adolescence and national identity the public schools will teach .

This reflection of the greater society is also displayed in analyzing state statutes regarding sexuality education. Greer (1988) examined state statutes regarding sexuality education. Religiosity was found to be a determining factor for the state's decision-makers, which suggests that sexuality education is often viewed as religious education. This short excerpt provides information related to how school districts must determine implementation of sexuality education in their schools.

> The review of case law and state statutes reveals that sex education is permissible under several criteria, which are consistent with the United States Constitution and individual state constitutions. These criteria include: (1) student participation which is subject to parental approval must be voluntary; (2) parents can review instructional materials in advance; (3) decisions to implement the programs are delegated by state statutes or state boards of education to the local school boards; (4) course content is objective and relative to the course being taught; and (5) course content is neutral in the religious sphere having a secular health education purpose. *(Greer, 1988, p. 3)*

Sexuality education is a lifelong process of acquiring information and forming attitudes, beliefs, and values about identity, relationships, and intimacy. It encompasses sexual development, reproductive health, interpersonal relationships, affection, intimacy, body image, and gender roles. Sexuality education addresses the biological, sociocultural, psychological, and spiritual dimensions of sexuality from the cognitive domain (information); the affective domain (feelings, values, and attitudes); and the behavioral domain (communication and decision-making skills) (SIECUS, 1999). Although this definition appears to consider the worldviews of each of the opposing groups, there still remain many areas of conflict.

One of the areas of conflict between these groups is in teaching about sexual orientation. In her book, *Bridges of Respect: Creating Support for Gay and Lesbian Youth*, Katherine Whitlock states the experiences every school counselor is familiar with at both the elementary and secondary levels:

> In schools across the country, even very young children learn the codes, passed on in jokes and whispers: "Don't wear certain colors to school on a particular day, or you're queer." Lessons are learned each time a child discovers that one of the surest ways to deliver an insult is to accuse another of being a lezzy, a faggot, a sissy. Children may not always know what these words mean, but they know the pejorative power of this language. Lessons are learned each time adults speak and act as if everyone in the world in heterosexual, or should be. Adult acquiescence in homophobia places lesbian and gay youth at great emotional and sometimes physical risk. *(1988, p. 2)*.

It is important to teach actively about sexual orientation in elementary, middle/junior high and secondary schools. This is an issue often ignored or hotly debated among politically and religiously antagonistic groups. School Counselors serve all students and thus are advocates for all students. Ries (1998) conveys this message strongly to educators:

All students, regardless of their sexual orientation, learn mythology and hatred in school. All are hurt by it. Teachers can educate actively, replacing mythology with knowledge and hatred with respect, or they can educate passively as they have in the past. Those are the only alternatives. Either way, they communicate important messages. *(p. 5)*

Many gay, lesbian, and bisexual students tackle the developmental stage of adolescence with a supplemental burden, because of their sexual orientation. Identity development and the exploration of intimate relationships can be more complex for these students and their situation may be further complicated when the need for peer acceptance and the fear of persecution from others is added to their circumstances. In Fort Collins, Colorado, an alternative high school adopted the goal of promoting the tolerance of diversity. To achieve tolerance of others, they organized and facilitated school wide workshops on a variety of topics (Bauman & Sachs-Kapp, 1998). The trained student leaders selected the topics and organized the workshops, which included gender equity, racism, religious discrimination and sexual orientation. By far the most controversial and effective workshop dealt with the issue of sexual orientation. The students decided that there was a need for discussion on the topic after the observation of interactions around the school. The school counselors spent 20 hours training the students over a 3 week period (Bauman & Sachs-Kapps, 1998). The general theme employed throughout the workshops was that hate hurts.

In another school district in Maryland, school officials added the two words sexual orientation to the anti-harassment policy, which unleashed a storm and divided parents into two opposing groups (Moss, 1997). The initial opposition eventually subsided until a student produced a public affairs program that discussed same-sex marriage (Moss, 1997). The debate in this district began in 1995 when a student survey revealed that 53% of the high school students perceived that gay and lesbian students suffered more discrimination than any other group in school (Moss, 1997). The issue or topic of sexual orientation is no longer hidden to the extent that it once was, although many students may not feel safe expressing who they are sexually. The media and the bravery of certain individuals have allowed the discussion to begin earnestly in many of our schools because of broader exposure of the topic. As in most instances where sexual issues are addressed regarding young people, voices and emotions run strong on both sides of the issue.

One large school district in New Jersey boldly tackled the issue of diversity in spite of heightened anxiety and threats. More than 700 employees attended the training, which centered around an open discussion on a broad spectrum of issues including sexual orientation, disabilities, race, and gender. This open forum for conversation fostered genuine soul searching, rather than the expression of anger or resentment (Rodriguez, 1998). In an article entitled "There is No Hierarchy of Oppression," Lorde (as cited in Gordon, 1983) stated that both homophobia and heterosexism must be addressed, because as long as any segment of the population is subjected to ridicule, stereotyping, violence or name-calling we are all oppressed.

Gender Considerations

Curriculums for sexuality education increasingly focus on and attempt to provide educational answers to serious and multifaceted social issues (Whatley, as cited in Klein, 2000). One of these issues is sex equity. Sex equity should be addressed throughout the course of a sexuality education program, therefore the curriculum should not reinforce sexual behaviors with a double standard, nor should the curriculum reinforce restrictive sex-role stereotypes (Whatley, as cited in Klein, 2000). These statements present quite a challenge, as often the issue of female sex drive and the notion of female desire are evaded by both educators and the curriculum. The whole issue of hormones as a determining factor for sex drive and, at times an excuse for males, is an issue still debated by biologists. What is often missing from this discussion is that females also have levels of hormones that trigger desire, which students act upon. Conducting a conversation with students that communicates research findings and allows a healthy and open discussion on the issue is important. Many sexual myths exist around male hormones and male behaviors; these myths may contribute to occurrences of both date rape and dating violence.

Another prominent issue that surfaces around **gender** is **sexual harassment**, which is clearly most frequently experienced by female students. The women's movement virtually invented the phrase "sexual harassment" to explain the unwanted and repeated advances that women workers endured for generations (D'Emilio & Freedman, 1988). This issue was addressed in the work setting by the **Civil Rights Act of 1962**, when women started suing and winning lawsuits. Many corporations began to hire feminists to train employees around sexual harassment issues (D'Emilio & Freedman, 1988). Sexual harassment is now an issue in our schools. A statement was issued from the U.S. Department of Education's Office for Civil Rights in 1992 regarding sexual harassment in schools. The publication stated, "sexual harassment is a real and increasingly visible problem, one that can threaten a student's emotional well-being, impair academic progress, and even inhibit the attainment of career goals" (Roscoe & Strouse, 1994, p. 515). For some time sexual harassment has been examined in the workplace or the college setting, but now both professionals and the courts have recognized the occurrence of sexual harassment at considerably younger ages, in middle school and high school.

Two studies, one by the American Association of University Women (AAUW) and the other in *Seventeen Magazine* by the Wellesley Center for Research on Women and NOW's Legal Defense and Education fund, found that 75% of the students they surveyed reported being sexually harassed in school (Kopels & Dupper, 1999; Linn, 1999). In the AAUW study, entitled *Hostile Hallways*, because of sexual harassment 33% of the girls reported not wanting to attend school, 32% reported a reluctance to talk out in class, and 28% reported that it was difficult to pay attention in school (Kopels & Dupper, 1999). Additional information revealed that 64% of the girls were embarrassed, 52% reported self-conscious feelings, and 43% stated that they felt less confident of themselves because of the sexual harassment experience (Kopels & Dupper, 1999).

These percentages are powerful indicators of the prevalence of sexual harassment in today's schools. For too long this type of behavior has been viewed as a natural developmental pathway for males with rising hormone levels and not seen as especially harmful to the girls subjected to the abuse. Perhaps to only a small degree that was truer in the past decades than today, but today it seems that the behaviors have changed as well. The saturation of the media with sexuality may have impacted students' attitudes and values regarding what behaviors they deem acceptable. In the studies cited in the previous paragraph, boys were also subjected to sexual harassment, although not with the same frequency that girls were harassed. On the other hand, current research demonstrates that girls also sexually harassed students. Eighty-three percent of the girls and 60% of the boys reported sexual harassment experiences, and 53% of both sexes had been both the victim and the perpetrator (Bracey, 1997).

Difficulty surrounds the issue of defining what behaviors are considered appropriate and which are not. Often definitions of sexual harassment deal with the existence of a power differential between the individuals or may even be tied to legal terms linked with sexual assault. A sexuality program would be advisable to include school policy, and conduct role playing scenarios and discussions on this topic. The school counselor could easily function in a key role around these activities. Recommendations for this type of program might include defining sexual harassment for the students and providing specific examples that occur in students' lives. Also, it would be important to discuss with the students both the possible effects for victims and the consequences of sexual harassment for perpetrators (Roscoe & Strouse, 1994).

DEVELOPMENTAL FACTORS & SEXUALITY EDUCATION

Rudimentary information on health issues is important for youth. Reproductive health is just basic necessary health education. The opportunity for students to participate in sexuality education programs may be the only exposure young people have to accurate information about reproductive health. What better place to learn skills for improving knowledge, skills, and awareness than in a safe monitored environment (Barnett, 1997).

The National Commission on Adolescent Sexual Health has taken a stand by recognizing that adolescent sexuality is a highly charged emotional issue for many adults. The commission encourages policymakers to acknowledge that sexuality is an essential part of adolescence development. Policymakers must also realize that a large percentage of adolescents engage in sexual behaviors as part of their overall development (Haffner, 1995b). The Commission developed a consensus statement in an attempt to bridge the gulf between the opposing groups. More than 50 national organizations endorsed this consensus statement which states that adolescents should be encouraged to delay sexual activity until they are ready physically, cognitively, and emotionally for mature sexual relationships and the ensuing consequences (Haffner, 1995b).

Systemic Educational Cultures

Public schools are state institutions, which receive funding from both state governments and the federal government. Schools fall under the constitutional mandates of state governments and, therefore, are not required to seek or receive federal funding. Often however, federal funding proposals do influence the decisions of state governments, which in turn influence public schools. This is the case with the implementation of sexuality education in the schools.

At this time there are no federal laws or policies mandating sexuality or HIV education. In 1996 a very influential piece of federal legislation was signed into law by President Clinton entitled the Temporary Assistance to Needy Families Act (EL>104-193). This law created a new entitlement of funding program for "abstinence education" in Section 510, Title V of the Social Security Act. The provision reads:

Title V of the Social Security Act (the Maternal and Child Health Program) is amended by adding at the end the following section:

Section 510 (b)

(1) The purpose of an allotment under subsection (a) is to enable the State to provide abstinence education, and at the option of the state, where appropriate, mentoring, counseling, and adult supervision to promote abstinence from sexual activity, with a focus on those groups which are most likely to bear children out-of-wedlock.

(2) For the purposes of this section, the term "abstinence education" means an educational or motivational program which:

(A) has as its exclusive purpose, teaching the social , psychological, and health gains to be realized by abstaining from sexual activity;

(B) teaches abstinence from sexual activity outside marriage as the expected standard for all school age children;

(C) teaches that abstinence from sexual activity is the only certain way to avoid out-of-wedlock pregnancy, sexually transmitted diseases, and other associated health problems;

(D) teaches that a mutually faithful monogamous relationship in the context of marriage is the expected standard of human sexual activity;

(E) teaches that sexual activity outside of the context of marriage is likely to have harmful psychological and physical effects;

(F) teaches that bearing children out of wedlock is likely to have harmful consequences for the child, the child's parents, and society.

(G) Teaches young people how to reject sexual advances and how alcohol and drug use increase vulnerability to sexual advances; and

(H) Teaches the importance of attaining self-sufficiency before engaging in sexual activity.

After the passage of this abstinence education provision, Florida, Georgia, Indiana, Mississippi, Missouri, Nebraska, North Carolina, and Ohio adopted language similar to the federal definition of abstinence education into their state laws and/or education codes. This Federal Act is an example of how the federal government influences the affairs of American public schools.

States requiring schools to provide sexuality education include: AL, DE, DC, GA, HI, IL, IA, KS, KY, MD, MN, NV, NJ, NC, RI, SC, TN, UT, VT, WV. Of these states, 10 (DE, GA, HI, NJ, NC, RI, SC, TN, VT, WV.) require that abstinence-plus curriculum (inclusion of information about contraception) be taught in sexuality education. Four states (AL, IL, KY, UT) require an abstinence-only curriculum.

Some states do not require schools to teach sexuality education but have content requirements for schools that choose to include sexuality education in their curriculum. Thirty-one states do not require schools to teach sexuality education (AK, AZ, AR, CA, CO, CT, FL, ID, IN, LA, ME, MA, MI, MS, MO, MT, NE, NH, NM, NY, ND, OH, OK, OR, PA, SD, TX, VA, WA, WI, WY). California, Oregon and Virginia have abstinence-plus contraception content requirements for schools. Arizona, Colorado, Michigan, and Oklahoma require inclusion of information about abstinence in sexuality education. Arkansas, Florida, Indiana, Louisiana, Mississippi, and Texas specify the teaching of abstinence only until marriage. Thirty-four states and the District of Columbia require schools to provide STD and/or HIV/AIDS education. Sixteen states (AK, AZ, AR, CO, ID, LA, ME, MA, MS, MT, NE, ND, SD, TX VA, WY) do not require schools to provide STD and/or HIV/AIDS education.

Another major impact of this law on public schools was the large funding incentive, which encouraged the embracing of the federal government definition of sexuality education. The Sexuality Information and Education Council of the United States (SIECUS, 1998) reported:

> Congress allocated $50 million in federal funds for the program each year for federal fiscal years 1998-2002. By the end of the program's five guaranteed years, Americans will have spent nearly half a billion dollars on the abstinence-only-until-marriage education entitlement program. During the first year of the program, 48 states accepted the federal funds and provided support for 698 abstinence-only-until-marriage grants for education agencies, community-based organizations, and statewide programs

Other federal governmental agencies are involved in examining sexuality education in the public schools. The Division of Adolescent and School Health of the U.S. Centers for Disease Control and Prevention (CDC) explored sexuality curriculums taught in schools across the country. Results from 35 state surveys and 13 local surveys completed by school principals and health education coordinators were gathered. The School Health Education Profiles (SHEP) findings illustrate how many states require specific sexuality topics to be included in health education courses. Ninety-five percent of the states require information about HIV prevention. Ninety-four percent require information about STD prevention and 85% require information about pregnancy prevention. Among those schools that required HIV education, 99 percent taught about HIV infection and transmission, 97 percent taught about condom efficacy, and 48 percent taught how to use condoms correctly. In addition, 96 percent of the states' required health education courses taught skills to help students resist social pressures, 97 percent taught decision-making skills, and 90 percent taught communication skills (Morbidity and Mortality Weekly Report, 1998).

Most public schools allow parents to excuse their children from sexuality education programs (Reis, 1999). Each state either legislates the right of parents to either remove their children from sexuality education classes or defers that decision to the local school districts. This is illustrated by the following passage:

> In Washington State, each school district must conduct at least one presentation for parents on all sexuality education curricula that it intends to use. Parents must also be told that they can inspect all materials. Parents who attend a presentation may excuse their children from the instruction by submitting a written request. *(NARAL, 1995, p. 132)*

National Guidelines for Sexuality Education

SIECUS, the Sex Information and Education Council of the United States, is a private, nonprofit education organization established in 1964 to advocate for comprehensive sexuality education (SIECUS, 1996). This council originally published guidelines for sexuality education in 1991. In 1996, the national guidelines for sexuality education were updated. The intent of the guidelines is not to provide a curriculum kit but to help local communities create, develop, and evaluate their own selection of sexuality education curricula. Since the publication of the Guidelines, they have become the most widely recognized and implemented framework for comprehensive sexuality education in the United States. Local communities use these guidelines to plan new programs, evaluate existing programs, train teachers, educate parents, conduct research, develop peer programs, and write new materials. These materials can be used in communities to discuss sexuality education in the local schools.

Six key concepts that should be included in a comprehensive sex education program are provided in the guidelines. The six key concepts that should be considered are information about:

- Human development, which includes reproductive anatomy and physiology
- Relationships, which include relationships with families and friends, as well as relationships in dating and marriage
- Personal skills, which include values, decision-making, communication, and negotiation
- Sexual behavior, which includes abstinence as well as sexuality throughout the life cycle
- Sexual health, including contraception, STD and HIV prevention, abortion and sexual abuse
- Society and culture, which includes gender roles, sexuality and religion. *(Barnett, 1997)*

These six key concepts from the National Guidelines provide a foundation for sexuality education. The National Guidelines Task Force (1996) said it best, "There is no ideal curriculum that will meet the needs of every community in the United States. However, like other subject materials for school-based programs, there are key concepts and topics that should be presented to all children in a developmentally appropriate manner." School counselors need to constantly be aware of the responsibility they have to serve all students in a positive and appropriate manner.

MODELS FOR SEXUALITY EDUCATION

As mentioned earlier in the chapter, there are two basic models of sexuality education: the abstinence-only model and the comprehensive sexuality education model. Often a hybrid model is presented called the abstinence-plus model. The abstinence-plus model is a blend of the other two models. The problem with such a model is that it leaves too much room for ambiguity. The two basic models and some examples will be presented in the next sections.

Abstinence-Only Models

The Medical Institute for Sexual Health (MISH) defines abstinence as "avoiding sexual intercourse as well as any genital contact or genital stimulation" (Medical Institute for Sexual Health, 1996, p. 7). However, some abstinence-only models define it as avoiding any behaviors beyond hand holding and light kissing (Kantor, 1992).

Proponents of abstinence-only sexuality education promote abstinence as the only strategy for preventing teenage pregnancy and sexually transmitted diseases that is 100% effective (Haffner, 1995b). These groups also provide methods to evaluate sexuality education programs to ensure the content is abstinence-only. The fact sheet, *In Focus-Sex Education—What Works?* (Family Research Council, 1995) frames the values of some abstinence-only followers. The following statements from the Family Research Council provide a clearer understanding of these underlying philosophies.

> The growing interest in abstinence curriculum has caused many contraception programs to frame themselves as "abstinence-based," "abstinence-plus," or "comprehensive" because they mention abstinence as one of several options. Such programs, however, communicate a mixed message to students, which thereby tremendously weakens the abstinence message. Some common characteristics of these "comprehensive" and "abstinence-plus" programs are that they (1) assume that teenagers are inevitably sexually active, (2) emphasize contraception and abortion, and (3) include affective decision-making (presenting abstinence as one of many options from which to choose). Thus, parents and school boards should choose a curriculum that avoids these danger points, and instead upholds abstinence as the way to handle teen sex issues. *(p. 16)*

Abstinence-only proponents suggest abstinence education should be directive, emphasizing values and attitudes, and students should be taught to be in control and say "no" to sexual activity (Haffner, 1995b). Parents should monitor the content of sexuality education closely. Parents are encouraged to be particularly interested in information or pictures that may be too explicit for their children (Haffner, 1995b). While not all abstinence-only programs are this extreme, the common factor is that contraception and sexual orientation are not included in the curriculum. This may create controversy with comprehensive sexuality programs or any add-on programs that include instruction on contraception.

Many abstinence-only sexuality education curriculums exist and have been implemented but little empirical evidence exists, which would support the use of programs. There is, however, one abstinence education program that has been empirically examined. This program is entitled "Sex Can Wait" (Young & Young, 1994). The Sex Can Wait program provides curriculum modules for high school (Gephart, Hart, & Young, 1994a), middle school (Gephart, Hart, & Young, 1994b), and upper elementary (Young & Young, 1994). There is also a companion activity book (Young & Young, 1996). The program is implemented over a five-week period with 23 lessons at the upper elementary, and 24 lessons at the middle and high school levels (Denny, Young, & Spear, 1999). Several studies of the Sex Can Wait program (formerly titled Living Smart) have been conducted with positive results (Denny, Goldfarb, Donnelly, Duncan, Young, Eadie, & Castiglia, 1999; Young, & Spear, 1999; Young, Core-Gephart, & Marx, 1992;). School counselors need to be aware of abstinence-only sexuality programs if they are employed in a state where abstinence-only programming is mandated. Choosing programs that have been empirically tested can provide an appropriate educational foundation.

Comprehensive Models

The controversy continues as we explore comprehensive sexuality education. The proponents of comprehensive sexuality education are quick to negate the long-term effects of abstinence-only programs (Barnett, 1997). In fact, SIECUS (1992) has a statement on school-based sexuality education that proclaims the most effective sexuality education programs are comprehensive and skill-based. Support for the inclusion of abstinence in comprehensive programs does exist. SIECUS supports programs such as Postponing Sexual Involvement. This abstinence based program presents abstinence information within a broader, more comprehensive sexuality education program (Haffner, 1995b). The basic premise of SIECUS is the advice for young people to abstain, but if they choose not to abstain, they should act responsibly (Haffner, 1997).

Comprehensive models generally use the National Guidelines in developing sexuality education programs, which includes STD/HIV and contraception education. From this model, two messages are basically conveyed to young people. The first is that it is better to abstain from sexual activity until they are physically, emotionally, and cognitively ready for a mature sexual relationship. However, the second message states that these models include skills and knowledge on the appropriate use of contraceptives and condoms.

The goals of comprehensive sexuality programs are fourfold: 1) to provide accurate information about human sexuality; 2) to provide an opportunity for young people to develop and understand their values, attitudes, and beliefs about sexuality; 3) to help young people develop relationships and interpersonal skills; and 4) to help young people exercise responsibility regarding sexual relationships, including addressing abstinence, pressures to become prematurely involved in sexual intercourse, and the use of contraception and other sexual health measures. (National Guidelines Task Force, 1996, p.3-5).

Haffner (1995b) provided information based on the philosophical foundation of comprehensive sexuality proponents. Comprehensive sexuality education is, on the other hand, an effective strategy for giving young people the skills to delay their involvement in sexual behaviors. Several reviews of published evaluations of sexuality education, HIV prevention, and teenage pregnancy prevention programs have consistently found that:

- Sexuality education does not encourage teens to start having sexual intercourse or to increase their frequency of sexual intercourse *(Frost & Forrest, 1995;Grunseit & Kippax, 1993; Kirby, Korpi, Barth, & Cagampang, 1995).*
- Programs must take place before the young people begin experimenting with sexual behaviors if they are to result in a delay of sexual intercourse *(Kirby, et al., 1995).*
- Teenagers who start having intercourse following a sexuality education program are more likely to use contraceptives than those who have not participated *(Grunseit & Kippax, 1993).*
- HIV programs that use cognitive and behavioral skills training with adolescents demonstrate "consistently positive" results *(Frost & Forrest, 1995).*

Comprehensive sexuality education programs do provide an avenue for the presentation of a genuine, honest view of human sexual development across the life span, thus, normalizing sexuality as a necessary part of life.

Considerations for School-based Sexuality Education

Greer (1988) provided some recommendations on the inclusion of sexuality education. First, make sex education available to all students. Second, appoint an advisory board comprised of educators, parents, students, the health professions, and the clergy from the community. Third, and finally, personal questions regarding sexual activity or beliefs should be discouraged.

There are some characteristics, shared by most effective sexuality education programs.

- A clear focus on reducing one or more sexual behaviors that lead to unintended pregnancy or HIV/STD infection
- Materials that provide behavioral goals, teaching methods, and materials appropriate to the age, sexual experience, and culture of the students
- Theoretical approaches that have a demonstrated effectiveness in influencing other health-related risky behaviors
- Teaching methods designed to involve the participants and allow them to personalize information
- Basic, accurate information about the risks of unprotected intercourse and methods of avoiding unprotected intercourse
- Activities that address social pressures on sexual behaviors
- Opportunities to model and practice communication, negotiation, and refusal skills
- Teachers or peers who are trained and who believe in the program they are implementing. *(Kirby, 1997, pp. 27-31)*

IMPLICATIONS FOR SCHOOL COUNSELORS

The primary goal of sexuality education is the promotion of sexual health. School counselors often are only involved peripherally in school-based sexuality education. This is a result of considering sexuality education within the realm of the health education content areas. However, if sexuality education seeks to assist adolescents in gaining a positive view of sexuality by providing them with information, decision-making skills and peer refusal skills, school counselors must be actively involved in sexuality education development and implementation.

School counselors are responsible for the provision of services to students when they become pregnant or enter into sexual activity prematurely. These situations can affect the academic, career and personal/social decision making of students. Antecedents of early first intercourse include lower school performance, lower reading and writing skills, lack of parental support, depression, and other problem behaviors, such as substance use (including alcohol and nicotine), and school delinquency (Moore et al., 1995). School counselors are trained to address these antecedents. Information provided through sexuality education may help students to delay engaging in sexual activity before a young person is ready or may educate them on having sexual protection against STD/HIV.

Sexuality education can also open wounds that some children may have from past or ongoing sexual exploitation. The school counselor must be aware of the curriculum content in supporting students who have been sexually abused. Consultation with the student and with the health educator may be necessary to alleviate possible harmful situations. This may also mean the school counselor would need to be an advocate for students who are sexual minorities.

Counseling offices should maintain resources for students and their parents related to sexuality. These resources may be from community groups or from medical facilities. It is important that a school counselor knows the norms and policies of the state, community and school district in which they are employed. This knowledge may allow the opportunity to serve the needs of students and parents on both sides of the sexuality education continuum.

SUMMARY

From the resolution passed in 1892 by the NEA, deeming it essential that school curriculum address sex education in the schools, to the conflict today over how much information to share with students, the constant that remains is that students become pregnant, contract STDs, and others become sexually involved long before they are emotionally ready. The difference is that more students make these choices today than in 1892; our society is saturated with sexual messages and images for students to absorb. Whether they are dealing with relationships, breakups, pregnancy, abuse, violence, sexual orientation, teasing, sexual harassing, or discussing developmental issues, school counselors are involved everyday with students and issues related to sexuality and all the nuances associated with the word. The grade level of the students may vary the depth of the topic, but many discussions may relate in some way to sex. Sometimes students go to their counselor, because they feel it is a safe place to openly express themselves; in other settings, the student may feel the tendency to be more guarded in revealing both their words and feelings. Yet, as stated, school counselors are only peripherally engaged in the educational piece. Most discussions around sexual education occur in the science or health class or possibly with the nurse, but the exchanges tend to be centered on the facts with little to no attention to processing the information with students. Curriculum is geared toward the educator not the counselor.

One lone piece of literature emerged in our search entitled, "The Guidance Counselor as Sex Educator" by Gary F. Kelly. In this small booklet, Kelly (1976) discussed the changing role of the school counselor from the 1950s to the 1970s and stated the ways in which school counselors provide more than academic and vocational services to students. He also discussed school counseling in terms of assisting students in becoming fully functioning individuals who can adjust in a healthy manner to conditions in their lives. He shared how the new theories of the time were shaping and transforming counseling; these new and exciting ideas were existential and humanistic and included the names of Maslow, Rogers, Jourard, and Glasser. Kelly (1976) wrote,

> Probably at no other time in history has American society generated more confusion with regard to sexual identity than exists today. We live in a time in which traditional boundaries between male and female are becoming blurred...the changes appear to result from the breaking through of some of the superficial and even dishonest standards of

maleness and femaleness, which for many years have been accepted as valid. As people search for a more meaningful understanding of all human nature, we are discovering that men and women have much more in common than was ever realized before. *(p. 5-6)*

Reading this last passage reminds us that these transitions are still occurring in our society 24 years later and that school counselors are still defining their role. The linking of school counselors in some role or capacity with sexuality education, even as a team member, in our schools seems to have gotten lost somewhere and all but disappeared. Kelly (1976) presented a strong case for the value of what he terms "group guidance and counseling" in conjunction with a sex education program. He viewed the skills of the school counselor as unique and extremely helpful to any program, because of the counselor's ability to assist students in the group format in expressing their feelings.

School counselors might explore the possibilities of linkages with other school professionals on the topic of sexuality education. School counselor should be involved in the coordination of school-wide sexuality programming and/or classroom experiences. This can be done by having the school counselor sit on advisory committees or through consultation with the sexuality education teacher, school nurse, or other health professionals in the school district and the community. School counselors facilitating sexuality education in classrooms or in small groups is a topic rich with possibilities for research and inquiry, as little to none currently exists.

REFERENCES

Alan Guttmacher Institute (2000, February). School sex education focusing on abstinence. *Nation's Health, 14.*

Barnett, B. (1997). Education protects health, delays sex. *Network, 17*(3), 14.

Bauman, S., & Sachs-Kapps, P. (1998). A school takes a stand: Promotion of sexual orientation workshops by counselors. *Professional School Counseling, 1*(3), 42-45.

Bracey, G. W. (1997). The culture of sexual harassment. *Phi Delta Kappan, 78*(9), 725-727.

Centers for Disease Control and Prevention, National Center for HIV, STD, and TB Prevention, Division of HIV/AIDS Prevention, 1998 special data run.

Czuczka, D. (2000). The twentieth century: An American sexual history. *SIECUS Report, 28*(2), 15-18.

D'Emilio, J., & Freedman, E. B. (1988). *Intimate matters: A history of sexuality in America.* New York: Harper & Row Publishers.

Denny, G., Young, M., & Spear, C. E. (1999). An evaluation of the Sex Can Wait abstinence education series. *American Journal of Health Behavior, 23,* 134-143.

Fact Sheet on Opponents of comprehensive Sexuality Education. (2000, January). *SIECUS Report, 28* (2), 19.

Family Research Council (1995). *In focus-sex education-What works?* [Accession No. 01018384]. Washington, DC: Author.

Firestone, W. A. (1994). The content and context of sexuality education: An exploratory study in one state. *Family Planning Journal, 26,* 127-131.

Frost, J. J., & Forrest, J. D. (1995). Understanding the impact of effective teenage pregnancy prevention programs. *Family Planning Perspective, 27*(5) 188-196.

Gephart, P., Hart, S., & Young, M. (1994a). *Sex Can Wait: An abstinence-based sexuality curriculum for high school classrooms.* Santa Cruz, CA: ETR Associates.

Gephart, P., Hart, S., & Young, M. (1994b). *Sex Can Wait: An abstinence-based sexuality curriculum for middle school classrooms.* Santa Cruz, CA: ETR Associates.

Goldfarb, E., Donnelly, J., Duncan, D., Young, M., Eadie, C., & Castiglia, D. (1999). Evaluation of an abstinence-based curriculum for early adolescents: First year changes in sex attitudes, knowledge and behavior. *North American Journal of Psychology,(1),* 243-254.

Gordon, L. (1983). Homophobia and education. *Bulletin* [NY Council on Interracial Books for Children], *14* (3,4).

Greer, C. F. (1988). Implications of the first amendment of sex education in the public school system in the United States. Doctoral Dissertation, Pepperdine University, 1988). *Dissertation Abstracts International, 49-09A,* 133 pages.

Grunseit, A., & Kippax, S. (1993). *Effects of sex education on young people's sexual behavior.* Geneva: World Health Organization.

Guttmacher Institute (1994). *Sex and America's teenagers.* New York: The Alan Guttmacher Institute.

Haffner, D. (Ed.). (1995a). *Facing facts: Sexual health* for America's adolescents. National Commission on Adolescent Health, Sexuality information and Education Council of the United States (SIECUS).

Haffner, D. W. (1995b). What's wrong with abstinence-only sexuality education programs? *SIECUS Report, 25*(4), p 9-13.

Henshaw, S.K. (1998). Unintended Pregnancy in the United States. *Family Planning Perspectives, 30*(1), 24-29, 46.

Kantor, L. (1992). Scared Chaste: Fear-based education curricula. *SIECUS Report, 21*(2) 1-15.

Kelly, G. F. (1976). *The guidance counselor as sex educator.* New York: Human Sciences Press.

King, B. M. (1999). *Human sexuality.* Upper Saddle, NJ: Prentice Hall.

Kirby, D. (1997). No easy answers. Washington: National Campaign to Prevent Teen Pregnancy.

Kirby, D., Korpi, M. Barth, R.E., & Cagampang, H.H. (1997). Impact of the postponing sexual involvement curriculum among youth in California. *Family Planning Perspective, 29*(3), 100-108.

Klein, M. (2000). Coming attractions: Sexual expression in the next decade. *SIECUS Report, 28*(2), 9-14.

Kopels, S., & Dupper, D. R. (1999). School-based peer sexual harassment. *Child Welfare, 78,* 435-460.

Leitman, R., Kramer, E., & Taylor, H. (1993). A survey of condom programs. In S. E. Samuels & M. D. Smith, (Eds.), *Condoms in the schools* (pp. 1-23). Menlo Park, CA: The Henry J. Kaiser Family Foundation.

Linn, E. (1999). The role of school mental health professionals in resolving school-related sexual harassment complaints. *Social Work in Education, 2,* 263-268.

Medical Institute for Sexual Health (1996). *National Guidelines for Sexuality and Character Education.* Austin, Texas: Author.

Moore, K.A., Miller, B.C., Glei, D., & Morrison, D.R. (1995). *Adolescent sex, contraception, and childbearing;* A review of recent research. Washington, DC: Child Trends, Inc.

Morbidity and Mortality Weekly Report. (1998, September 11). Characteristics of health education among secondary schools – school health education profiles. Author, *47* (SS-4),.1-31.

Moss, J. J. (1997). Classroom warfare. *Advocate, 728,* 33-34.

NARAL (1995). *Sexuality Education in America: A state-by-state review.* Washington D.C.: NARAL, the NAP, AL Foundation.

National Campaign to Prevent Teen Pregnancy. (1997). *Whatever happened to childhood? The problem of teen pregnancy in the United States.* Washington, DC: Author.

National Guidelines Task Force (1996). *Guidelines for Comprehensive Sexuality Education, 2nd Edition, Kindergarten—12th Grade.* New York: Sexuality Information and Education Counsel of the United States.

National Institutes of Health, Consensus Development Conference Statement, Feb. 11-13, 1997.

Nelson, K. L. (1997). "It's all about an ideology"; An analysis of grass roots conflicts over sex education in the public schools. Doctoral Dissertation, Temple University, 1997. *Dissertatioin Abstracts International, 48-03A,* 282.

Priluck, J. (1997). A century of controversy. *Village Voice, 52,* (3), 10-11.

Ray, B. B. (1988). Religiosity and attitude toward sex education in public schools: A comparative study. Doctoral Dissertation, Mississippi State University, 1998. *Dissertatioin Abstracts International, 49-12A,* 143.

Reis, B. (1998) A Guide to Teaching Actively about Sexual Orientation. *SIECUS Report, 26*(4), 1998, p. 5-6 [Accession No.: 01024075].

Rodriguez , D. (1998). Diversity training brings staff closer. *Education Digest, 64*(1), 28-31.

Roscoe, B., & Strouse, J. S. (1994). Sexual harassment: Early adolescents' self reports of experiences and acceptance. *Adolescence, 29,* 515-523.

Sexuality Information and Education Council of the United States (SIECUS). (1998). Between the Lines: States' Implementation of the Federal Government's Section 510 (B) Abstinence Education Program in Fiscal Year 1998. New York: Author, pp7-8.

SIECUS (1996). Sexuality Education and the Schools: Issues and Answers. [SIECUS Fact Sheet Comprehensive Sexuality Education].

SIECUS Report (1999). Issues and answers fact sheet on sexuality education. *SIECUS Report, 27*(6), 29+ [Accession no.: 01038471].

STD Surveillance (1997). Website: Table 3A Chlamydia – Reported cases by age, gender, and race/ethnicity in the United States, 1996-1997.

Teenage contraceptive use credited with decline in pregnancies: A synopsis of an Alan Guttmacker Institute report. (1999, August/September). *SIECUS Report, 27*(7), 28.

The Henry J. Kaiser Family Foundation (1996). What they say teens today need to know, and who they listen to. (California: The Henry J. Kaiser Family Foundation, 1996) chart 8.

Ventura, S.J., Mathews, T.J., & Curtin, S.C. (1999). Declines in teenage birthrates, 1991-98: Update of national and state trends. *National Vital Statistics Reports, 47*(26).

Young, M., Core-Gebhart, P., & Marx, D. (1992). Abstinence-oriented sexuality education; initial field test results of the Living Smart curriculum. *Family Life Educator, 10*, 4-8.

Young, M., & Young, T., (1994). *Sex can wait: An abstinence-based sexuality curriculum for upper elementary classrooms.* Santa Cruz, CA: ETR Associates.

Young, M., & Young, T., (1996). *Pick and Choose: Abstinence Activities.* Santa Cruz, CA: ETR Associates.

Whatley, M. H. (1992). Goals for sex-equitable sexuality education. In S. S. Klein (Ed.), *Sex equity and sexuality in education* (pp. 83-95). Albany, NY: State University of New York Press.

Whitlock, K. (1988). *Bridges of respect: creating support for lesbian and gay youth.* Philadelphia, PA: American Friends Service Committee.

RESOURCES

Resource*: http://www.teenpregnancy.org/conflic1.htm*
Resource: *http://www.siecus.org/school/sex_ed/guidelines.guide0000.html*

SECTION 2
SPECIAL POPULATIONS AND SEXUALITY COUNSELING

INTRODUCTION

From a **developmental** perspective, dealing with one's **sexuality** is a **normal**, typical experience for all people that evolves over the **lifespan**. However, like other aspects of **human development**, at different stages of life and for various aspects of sexuality, this experience can be **stressful**, feel like a **crisis**, and involve **conflict**. Nobody can predict an individual's reaction to his/her evolving **sexual identity**. For example, at midlife, one individual may report becoming **celibate** because he/she gained weight and feels awkward about being sexually intimate. On the other hand, another person may report that expecting weight gain at midlife was "freeing" from obsessive worry about weight control that allowed him/her to be more sexual. Yet, each of these individuals may experience stress and/or conflict about the weight change and the choices made around it.

The midlife weight gain, a **normative age-graded** life event, is a typical event that most people can expect to experience. The psychological response to the changed **body image** and the effect on one's sexuality varies from individual to individual. However, changes in sexual identity and **sexual behavior** occur throughout the lifespan for many different reasons. Most people experience many of these changes, like the effect of weight gain on sexuality. Some of these changes, on the other hand, are specific to certain populations or stages of life, yet are normative life events for those particular groups of people. **Normalizing** all types of sexual development and addressing them openly in societal, group, and individual formats helps people deal with their evolving sexuality in a healthy manner so that they can retain a "sense of personal competence and control and [have] a sense of continuity and meaning in life" (Kelly, 1995, p. 474).

Normalizing **sexual development** is important for counselors working with clients dealing with sexuality issues. Sometimes this is an **educational** process helping clients realize that many people have the same sexual concerns and issues that they are presenting. Counselors must also be able to distinguish more normal or typical sexual developmental issues from **sexual disorders** or from **sexual trauma**. A counselor's own **values** can be the greatest **barrier** to making such distinctions. Clients presenting with sexuality issues can easily be labeled **pathological** if the counselor's own values rigidly adhere to a **religious**, **heterosexual** perspective on acceptable sexual behavior and sexuality.

Other barriers to normalizing sexual development in counseling are is a counselor's own discomfort with discussions about sexual behavior and sexuality and a lack of knowledge about **sexuality counseling** with different populations. If a counselor has not worked on his/her own sexuality issues, then discomfort can occur during a client's discussion about sex. A client who, is also feeling uncomfortable easily identifies a counselor's discomfort. Then, the client may perceive that he/she is experiencing some type of pathology related to sexuality, rather than experiencing a normative, sexual, developmental event. Therefore, counselors seeing clients with sexuality issues are recommended to seek counseling themselves if discomfort about sexual topics persists.

The chapters in Section 2 are included to provide counselors with more knowledge about some of the **special populations** or issues related to sexuality counseling. We consider these populations as part of the spectrum or continuum of normal sexual development. While some professionals may disagree with our choice of populations, they are purposely included because they can easily be **marginalized** in the study of sexuality.

The eight chapters included in Section 2 involve special populations struggling with normative or typical life events that most of the individuals within the populations experience to some degree. A unique commonality to most of these populations is the **stigma** attached to their sexuality. For example, Chapters 6 (**bisexuals**), 7 (**lesbians**), 8 (**gay men**), and 9 (**transgender**) deal with what some people refer to as **alternative lifestyles** because their sexuality deviates from the perspective that only sex within a **heterosexual** marriage is normal. These individuals struggle with the same sexuality issues that heterosexuals struggle with like dating, feeling good about their bodies, how to communicate sexual needs, etc. Additionally, they learn to cope with societal **oppression**, stigma, **pathology** labels, **hate crimes**, and general **heterosexism** that creates for them unique, but normative, life events not experienced by the dominant **sexual culture**. Our approach is that these are not alternative lifestyles, but rather different variations of sexuality on a continuum of sexual identities.

Chapters 11 (**HIV/AIDS**) and 12 (**Addiction**) involve special populations that include individuals from all variations of sexual identity. However, the stigma these populations deal with is attached to their **disease**, AIDS and addiction (if one believes in the disease model of addiction). While addiction might be considered a life-long event, **recovered addicts** must struggle with new issues surrounding their sexuality, particularly related to **relationship** and **intimacy** needs. AIDS individuals, on the other hand, become diagnosed with the disease typically in young adulthood, even though AIDS is a disease that strikes in all stages of life. Therefore, they have special needs related to rebuilding a sense of their sexuality as a person with AIDS and learning new skills, like disclosing the AIDS diagnosis despite the stigma attached to the disease.

Similarly, **older adults** (Chapter 10) deal with the stigma and **myths** of aging (i.e., old people should not be interested in sex). However, sexual development is a lifelong process that continues until a person's **death**. Older adults have special needs related to such factors as physical changes (e.g., **medication** causing **erection** difficulties); social changes (e.g., death of a lifelong spouse/partner); psychological considerations (e.g., **internalized ageism**); and **spiritual/religious** considerations (e.g., appropriateness of sexual relations with another after death of partner). Whether or not older individuals openly address their sexual development is an individual choice, but institutions (e.g., nursing homes) and families refusing to acknowledge the sexual needs of older adults is a reflection of societal ageism.

Finally, Section 2 begins with "Negotiating **Couple** Sexuality" (Chapter 5). This chapter is included because individuals evolve from a sense of their own individual sexuality, to (for most people) a level of intimacy related to being part of a "couple." How to share oneself at all levels of intimacy with another person is different from being single, dating, relating to another person for a short period of time, breaking up, and then dating again. Partnership involves a sense of **mutual empathy** or "the underlying knowledge that each partner in a relationship cares for thc other and knows that the care is reciprocated" (Crooks & Baur, 1987, p. 234). As individuals enter into a committed partnership, special needs emerge for the couple.

REFERENCES

Crooks, R., & Baur, K. (1987). *Our sexuality* (3rd ed.). Menlo Park, CA: The Benjamin/Cummings Publishing Company, Inc.

Kelly, G. (1995). *Sexuality today: The human perspective* (5th ed.). Chicago, IL: Brown & Benchmark.

Chapter 5

NEGOTIATING COUPLE SEXUALITY

Thomas W. Blume
Oakland University

Counseling for clients with sexual concerns has been dominated by theories of individual functioning. Even when a partner has been included in the counseling process, prevailing intervention models have explained the problem at the level of the individual(s) and have conceptualized change as *individual* learning, *individual* resolution of intrapsychic issues, and *individual* cognitive change (Rosen & Leiblum, 1995). This chapter derives instead from a theoretical tradition in which human behavior is seen as multiply determined but as especially influenced by the social context (Sarbin, 1986) and negotiated meanings in relationships (Gergen & Gergen, 1983; Mead, 1934). The counseling approaches summarized in this chapter focus on direct and indirect negotiations that can enable couples to enjoy and enrich their sexuality as they manage the intensity of their verbal, emotional, and physical interdependence over time.

BACKGROUND

This chapter has been influenced by **postmodernism**, a developing perspective that questions the assumptions of the rationality and scientific certainty that have been part of most mental health theories since Freud. Postmodern authors (e.g., Foucault, 1990) have argued that conventional assumptions about sexuality, mental health, and other aspects of human life represent incomplete world views in which certain kinds of experience are **privileged** as other kinds of experience are denied. Postmodern analyses of gender (e.g. , Hare-Mustin, 1998) have called attention to culturally embedded assumptions about power and desire that are acted out in relationships. The perspective of this chapter could be considered, then, "profeminist" in its recognition that both men and women are constrained by traditional gender assumptions.

The **Identity Renegotiation** perspective draws on several closely linked traditions including **social constructionism** (Gergen, 1994), **narrative** studies (Currie, 1998; Gergen & Gergen, 1983; Sarbin, 1986) and **symbolic interactionism** (Mead, 1934). These theoretical traditions agree that individual actions cannot be interpreted without an understanding of the social environments, contexts, and **discourses** that give them meaning. Such a view seems especially relevant for sexuality, which is an inherently social experience. In fact, sex has been defined and explained in many different ways across time and within different social groups (Foucault, 1990). Sexuality has variously been given a place of great power in some social groups and almost denied in others. Some societies have honored the priests and priestesses of sex cults, attributing magical powers to sexual organs and acts (Maxwell, 1996). In more ascetic societies the reproductive function has been emphasized, and pleasure has been considered an unfortunate and "animalistic" feature of a biological process.

Socially located ideas, or discourses, about sexuality have frequently included assumptions about similarity and differentness based on biological sex. These ideas are generally referred to by the term **gender**, to differentiate them from descriptions of physical structure and function (Baber & Allen, 1992; Knudson-Martin & Mahoney, 1999). Individuals, couples, and families incorporate aspects of this gender discourse into narratives through which they make sense of their experience and coordinate their actions (Gergen & Gergen, 1983; Hare-Mustin, 1998).

The final intellectual tradition underlying this work is a **conflict** perspective (Sprey, 1969), a view of human interaction that emphasizes the positive value of conflict as a force that promotes change when needed. Rather than presuming that conflict can be avoided, conflict researchers (Blume, 1987; Selman & Demorest, 1984) have studied ways in which people **negotiate** differences to better meet their expectations. Sager (1976) and others have demonstrated that couple relationships can be strengthened by defining areas of disagreement and negotiating new relationship "contracts."

Postmodern and feminist traditions have called attention to the dangers inherent in an illusion of universal truths and objective observers. It is important, therefore, that I acknowledge my experience as a heterosexual, divorced and remarried white male and father of sons. My understandings of other experiences are limited, although they continue to develop through my couple and other family relationships; relationships with colleagues and especially students, many of whom have written eloquently of their lives and their relationships; professional and self-help writings; and the families, couples, and individuals who open their lives to me in counseling. My couple counseling experience has been limited to heterosexual couples; however, the theories and the approaches presented below have been chosen for their gender awareness and apparent compatability with issues of same-sex couples.

The Relational Self

Gergen and Gergen (1983) have challenged psychological views of people as individuals, as self-contained units of action and experience. They and others (e.g., Sarbin, 1986) have noted that the individualistic perspective, rather than being limited to industrialized societies, has been glorified and celebrated for thousands of years in some cultures. This social convention, according to Gergen (1994), has contributed to many individual and social problems. Stress, isolation, and meaninglessness derive in part from the impossibility of any individual's resolving conflicting discourses, creating a self, and defending that self against all challenges.

Such an emphasis on the individual is not, however, universal; alternative views, including many cultural and religious traditions in addition to intellectual traditions such as social constructionism, place more emphasis on the person as a part of a family or other group (Gergen, 1994). The **self** is seen by Gergen and Gergen (1983) not as an entity but as a social product--a negotiated story of selfhood that incorporates memories, ideas, feelings, and even actions that extend beyond any individual. A sense of identity, that is, a sense that a person has behavioral continuity and autonomy, is essentially a **narrative co-construction** that comes into being through the sharing of expectations, experiences, and interpretations (Gergen & Gergen, 1983; Kerby, 1991; Mead, 1934).

A Contextual View of Couple Sexuality

Sexuality includes more than just sexual behavior; the sexual experience also includes positive and negative expectations, physical sensations, feelings, and understandings of self and other. All of these elements of sexuality are influenced by the relationship context, and at the same time the relationship is a context that shapes itself as expectations, meanings, and behavior are negotiated.

Because sexual experiences, fantasies, and intentions take place in the context of multiple overlapping historical and cultural discourses, sexual gestures such as a touch, a kiss, or a look often have different meanings for the people involved. By the time a person has a first interpersonal sexual experience --whether before puberty or after the age of 30--he or she has internalized community discourses that shape positive and negative reactions to sex. As an example, for one person underwear will be identified with elimination and will be embarrassing or nauseating. For another, underwear will be associated with hidden body parts that symbolize fun, defiance of authority, delightful physical sensations and passion. Many couples will find themselves, even after 20 or 30 years of individual and combined sexual experience, struggling with complex mixtures of such antithetical responses.

The couple's relationship as a whole will typically be found to have several levels of interaction with their current expression of their sexuality. Their sexual history, for example, may include previous challenging periods or it may have provided little experience with problem solving. Positive early sexual experiences have been known to give couples an unrealistic view of sex in committed relationships. On the other hand a couple may have shared sexual experiences that begin badly and, years later, remain troubling and unresolved for one or both partners.

Sexuality is, of course, only a part of either a couple's relationship history or their current interaction. The variety of couple experiences is difficult to describe. At one extreme are partners who were promised to each other in childhood, who may come together as strangers trying to create a successful physical and emotional relationship. At the opposite extreme are partners who have chosen each other with a belief that happy relationships must be based on love, attraction, and/or desire. Some couples struggle for moments of privacy, while others live a nearly symbiotic existence. Special couple experiences related to economic status, health, employment, and family responsibilities also contribute to unique relationship environments in which people's sexual behavior may have different meanings.

Sexual Narratives

Narrative clinicians (Knudson-Martin & Mahoney, 1999; Spence, 1986) and narrative scholars (Gergen & Gergen 1983; Kerby, 1991) have described the human tendency to organize experiences into a story that achieves **narrative coherence** by pulling together characters, scenes, and plot to make the world seem less random and more predictable. As characters in our own narratives, we discover our identities in the stories we tell and the stories others tell about us.

A nearly universal element in these narrative identities is an evaluative component (Gergen, 1994). Identity narratives do not merely report on a person's actions, they interpret those actions in terms of some kind of ideal image. Part of the appeal of a committed relationship is the hope that a committed partner will *know* the narratives--both the good and the bad--and confirm that one is lovable. When a relationship becomes sexual, it gains special power because a sexual partner knows secret--possibly upsetting--details. A supportive narrative of the self confirmed by a sexual partner is somehow more complete and has more validity than a supportive narrative confirmed by others.

When a sexual relationship is positive, the **sexual narrative** is a positive one: "I am a gentle but powerful, fascinating, god-like being. Just the sight of my body brings joy to my loved one, and he/she has never been this happy." Such a positive sexual narrative invites further (reasonable) risk taking and self disclosure, which in turn becomes more positive if the partner's love triumphs over potential problems such as scars, body odors; and asymmetrical organs . But when sex "goes bad," the story has equal power to feel disabling: "I am disgusting, incompetent, and worthless. I may look like a normal person, but no one can stand to get close to me. There's no use trying to be sexual." A negative sexual narrative can survive in the thoughts and memories of one person, unchallenged by opposing viewpoints, if sexual experiences are not discussed. A partner's misunderstood gesture or involuntary twitch can live on for years as a symbolic comment, not only on the individual's behavior, but on his or her self worth.

When the socially constructed sexual responses of two people are taken into consideration, it is not surprising that many couples' narratives incorporate a mixture of positive and negative sexual encounters. Ruth and Larry, for example, had enacted a rather traditional gender-related sexual pattern; Larry had been the pursuer, Ruth had been more passive. A turning point came when, in discussing their responses to a movie, they found that they felt quite differently about the idea of combining food and sex. When Ruth suggested that Larry lick chocolate syrup off her abdomen, Larry was repelled by the idea of ingesting a combination of chocolate and sweat. Ruth chose not to press what appeared to be a sensitive topic, and they resumed their routine of predictable but successful sex. The narrative now included some new elements, however. Ruth was now the "kinky" partner, as well as the "dissatisfied" partner; Larry had now become identified with "safe sex," sexual conservatism, and avoidance of risk. Future events and conversations would determine whether they would find this new narrative an acceptable one or they would make further changes.

Successful couple relationships, viewed from a narrative perspective, are those in which any negative sexual experiences are somehow incorporated into a shared set of narratives in which the positives outweigh the negatives. Increasing the positive sexual "charge" in relationships and reducing negative sexual encounters are both ways of achieving this overall positive tone, and therefore couples benefit from direct assistance with interpersonal issues such as sexual pacing, sensitivity, and appropriate technique. Sexual interactions, in fact, offer tremendous potential for changing the relationship narrative, especially as partners become more sensitive to each others' symbolic worlds. But in the end it is assumed that couples have the power, through their shared narratives, to acknowledge, integrate, and transcend sexual problems--their sexual relationship does not have to be solely dependent on "good sex."

Negotiation and Collaborative Problem Solving

Postmodern authors have expressed distrust of apparently conflict-free agreements which, on closer examination, result from accepting a dominant discourse that denies any other reality (Hare-Mustin, 1998). A full experience of couple sexuality requires ways of reconciling different expectations, physical sensations, feelings, and understandings of self and other (Love & Robinson, 1994).

Research based on a developmental model (Blume, 1987; Selman & Demorest, 1984), has demonstrated that people use a variety of "higher-level" and "lower-level" **interpersonal negotiation strategies** in their discussions and behavior in relationships. Lower-level strategies include passive control strategies--refusing to ask for anything, giving in at every opportunity--as well as active control strategies such as giving orders and making threats. Lower-level strategies are learned early in life, but they continue to be used in adult relationships (Blume, 1987). Especially relevant in sexual relationships is the strategy of reward and punishment--or promise of reward and threat of punishment. Sex, with its many levels of experience and meaning, has potential to be an especially powerful tool in negative patterns of coercion and struggles for dominance.

Higher-level negotiations, according to Selman and Demorest, are characterized by mutual exploration of goals and the recognition that a relationship may be more important than the goals being pursued by any of the individuals involved. Sexual interaction, in which mutual satisfaction and genuine expression of feelings are valued (Love & Robinson, 1994), clearly seems to call for higher-level negotiation strategies. At the same time, with sexual topics carrying multiple meanings that include identity, self-worth, and shame, many couples seem unable to comfortably discuss their sexual experiences and understandings (Snyder, 2000).

Higher-level negotiation patterns can be learned; the principles of effective conflict management have been articulated in a large body of literature (e.g., Edelman & Crain, 1994; Fisher & Ury, 1981). **Cooperative problem solving** processes seem to reduce coercive interactions and promote open exchanges about goals, perceptions, feelings, and behavior (Deutsch, 1973). Cooperative problem solving depends on an openness to other experiences than one's own. In this way the traditions of conflict management and narrative co-construction are quite similar. When applied to the sexual relationship, however, the conflict literature also offers guidelines for helping a couple counselor to identify and to creatively resolve the differences that arise as the partners attempt to reconcile the conflicting, many-layered cultural discourses of gender and gendered sexuality.

CULTURAL/GENDER DISCOURSES

Humans are biologically equipped to be sexual, and most people can experience sexual arousal through a variety of forms of stimulation, some of which are reproductively useful to the species. The fantasies, experiences, or activities that arouse an individual are only partially influenced by biology. Judith Butler (1993) described the "**regulatory norms**" that shape the sexual development of individuals through reiteration of normative messages, resulting in some degree of "materialization" in each person's body of sexuality that fits regulatory ideals. Cultural discourses that define emotional, cognitive, behavioral and physical similarities and differences among males and females, in combination with other cultural messages regarding sexual desire and behavior, shape the ways in which partners see themselves as sexual beings. Every couple faces the challenge of integrating different discourses and may be seen, over time, as defining their own culture as their sexual narrative constructs their social conventions regarding gender and sexuality.

During the past 200 years, our culture has experienced intense societal re-examination concerning gender and sexuality (Bailey, 1999; Foucault, 1990); no contemporary couple can be unaffected by these larger cultural trends. Medical science has contributed to recent changes, as oral contraceptives are generally credited with changing women's sexuality during the childbearing years (Bailey, 1999). Patriarchy, the tradition of male privilege and dominance, has been challenged by the increasing economic independence of women and the increase in social services; far more women have means to escape coercion and violence from their male partners. Many women have opportunities to achieve recognition outside the home, reducing their emotional dependence as well. Men, at the same time, are increasingly choosing to explore less aggressive and less achievement-oriented life choices, and they have support for exploring counternormative desires for intimacy and dependency (Meth, 1990).

Gender is, of course, only one of the cultural elements influencing sexuality and sexual problems. Among the wide variety of cultural traditions regarding sex, including religious traditions, many may be viewed as either anti-sexual or, at best, confused about sexuality (Foucault, 1990). Since Freud's challenges to the sexual repression of his time and place, it appears that the confusion has not lessened but has become more obvious and possibly more intense. The "sexual revolution" of the 1960s and 1970s promoted freedom of sexual expression, but it also led to new epidemics of sexually transmitted diseases and community backlash against sexuality (Bailey, 1999).

Some discourses about sexuality, including that of Freud, portray sexuality as a dangerous force that threatens society. Other sexual discourses in recent centuries have focused on gender issues: Do men and women have similar feelings? Are their early sexual experiences significantly different? Do they respond the same ways when they are sexually aroused? Do they have the same goals for sex? As the complexity of gender has become more visible, these questions have become more elaborate: Do all men and all women fit into mutually exclusive categories with consistently different experiences? Does knowledge of a person's biological sex predict anything about his or her sexuality? According to Butler (1993) and others, gender is a matter not of substance but of **performance**. Every couple is in the process of enacting gender and has opportunities to alter that performance, depending on successful negotiations between the partners and the various discourses of gender. The following examples demonstrate the implications of three typical gender discourses for the developing sexual relationships of couples.

*Gender Discourse: **Male Lust***. A powerful and seemingly universal gender narrative portrays the human male as "only interested in one thing." The story is an easy one to tell; the male body, with its obvious erections, clearly seems to communicate sexual interest. And even though high school students of both sexes tell stories of boys with noticeable erections in class or other school activities, boys and men are encouraged to interpret an erection as sexual interest and as having the goal of sexual activity. Human males in many cultures seem to give a priority to sexual interests and activities; prostitution and pornography, for example, both seem to be supported primarily by men (Maxwell, 1996). Furthermore, men's identity narratives often express even non-sexual ideas using sexual metaphors: Male ego strength is defined as "potency" and a seemingly powerless male is described as "castrated."

Depending on how it is expressed, this discourse of the lusty male either glorifies and celebrates the sex-obsessed male or ridicules him as helpless in the thrall of his hormones. The idea of a male "sex drive," though problematic, may be useful for relationships in sexually repressive cultures, ensuring that someone is taking primary responsibility for reproductive activity (e.g. Rainwater, 1960). The American film "Carnal Knowledge" (1971) portrayed this view of young men; they have a tough job, making sure that sex does not die out. Their methods may be suspect, but the goal is one on which they and the larger society agree. The male in such a tradition has the responsibility not only to initiate sex but also to be an expert on things sexual. He is expected to accumulate sexual experience so that he can do the important job of socializing his female partner. Many comedians have built their routines around this version of the lust theme, and some of their strongest laughter comes from women who can remember how their "good girl" identities were protected by blaming sexual activity on their sex-obsessed partners.

For many men and women, however, this theme has created more pain than joy. When Masters and Johnson (1970) began their work many of their women patients reported experiencing no sexual desire, a pattern the authors attributed to cultural influences. The assignment of desire to men is half of a discourse that also denies its existence in women; women's only option within this discourse are, on one hand, to be sexual and be masculine and, on the other hand, to deny their sexuality and be feminine. There are still many women who suppress any sexual feelings, and many others who acknowledge sexual feelings but who (with their partners) have difficulty accepting their deviant behavior.

For many men the expectation of unflagging sexual interest--regardless of moods, physical illness, distractions, and relationship problems--leaves them feeling inadequate at their primary responsibility. Men's partners, assuming that expressions of desire represent not caring but biological urges, may dismiss genuine feelings. And, some men continue to coerce women into sexual activity because they do not believe women's expressions of disinterest, discomfort, or rejection.

*Gender Discourse: **Physical Beauty/Attraction***. Just as prevalent, and distributed widely, is a discourse suggesting that men's desire is inextricably linked to visual stimulation from women whose bodies are young and match some ideal of physical beauty. This story, too, finds ready support in observations of human behavior; girls and young women whose appearance fits cultural ideals seem to attract more attention than more mature and less "beautiful" women.

Just as with the theme of male lust, this discourse has been experienced both positively and negatively. The clear priority placed on youth and looks has given some women a sense of empowerment, and knowing the rules has allowed them to focus their energy on the primary criteria for sexual success. The popularity of magazines such as *Seventeen* and *Cosmopolitan,* suggests that a large number of girls and women try to "win" at this highly valued game, and soap operas demonstrate the rewards of good looks.

Despite the comfort that this theme may have provided some people, the generally negative impact of this discourse is clear. Some women, driven by images of thinness, starve themselves; others risk their health in cosmetic surgery; and still others, attempting to avoid sexual attention, become dangerously obese. Girls whose intellect, athletic ability, and leadership skills might have propelled them to scholarships and successful careers abandon their strengths and devote themselves to becoming attractive. And men, in a contradiction of the male lust discourse, find that their sexuality is linked not only to beauty but to competition. Those who succeed in dating or marrying the most beautiful women are often consumed by jealousy, seeing every other man as threatening their sexual performance.

*Gender Discourse: **Dominance and Exploitation***. Recent history has seen a generalized rejection of social relationships that are characterized by power and dominance. Notable achievements have included the widespread elimination of slavery and some of the more extreme forms of economic exploitation. Women's movements have gained their public support from the ideal of economic liberation, as well as the ideal of gender equality (Burggraf, 1997).

The prevailing discourse of gender has been one of male dominance over decision making; male control of privileges and scarce resources; and male assignment of unpleasant and unprofitable jobs to women. Some authors (e.g., Adler, 1927) have explained this pattern in terms of physical and economic advantage; not only have women tended to be smaller than their male partners, they have until recently been denied access to jobs, military service, and sports in which men train their bodies and their aggressive responses. However, other authors have suggested the possibility that male efforts to dominate women have arisen not so much from the ease of such domination but rather from men's fears of the sexual and reproductive power of women. Boys grow up with clear messages about sexual dependency; the slang term "pussy-whipped" communicates both derision for a male who lets himself be dominated by a woman and a belief that women's sexual dominance is difficult to resist.

In a context of diminishing male privilege and increased opportunities for women, a new form of gender problem has become common. Faced with the need to create a couple narrative without the help of prescriptive relationship discourses, heterosexual couples and same-sex couples alike are challenged to create their own relationship goals and behavior patterns. If sex is not about male satisfaction and female cooperation, then the partners need cooperative problem-solving abilities to work through the process of co-narrating the story of their sexuality. Likewise, nonsexual aspects of a relationship may require mutual exploration and accommodation to achieve a smooth couple narrative.

If these negotiations take place within a discourse of male dominance, either a male or a female partner may suffer. Men in both heterosexual and same-sex relationships can find their identity narratives tied to behavior patterns that exploit others and deny their own feelings of helplessness or caring (Meth, 1990). Men in therapy report that their feelings of helplessness and caring become more prominent in midlife, but their partners, in such cases, may have little access to those feelings and may fear abandoning the established relationship narrative. On the other hand, women, especially in heterosexual relationships, can feel that their personal power and leadership gifts must be denied if they are to be loved; many women, too, have experienced a midlife discovery of "lost" parts of themselves.

In a successful case, such midlife discoveries have proved liberating for a couple, and they have found in their 40s or 50s a new level of comfort with their mixed dominant and submissive sides. When assertiveness, nurturance, aesthetic sensibility, and patience have been disengaged from gender, couples are free to explore their own differences, design their relationship goals, and negotiate their distribution of tasks based on who they see themselves to be.

THE COUPLES'S DEVELOPING SEXUAL NARRATIVE

At every point in a couple relationship at least one sexual narrative is being told, and often there are multiple sexual narratives in conflict. These narratives incorporate multiple discourses, but the characters in the narratives--the couple--bring the discourses to life in such narrative themes as loss of desire, mismatches in desire, sexual exploitation, and sexual dysfunction. These narratives change to incorporate new experiences, as well as to resolve internal discrepancies. They are different in every telling, as the audience co-narrates the story, and they change to incorporate new discourses.

Identity Narratives

The developmental counseling tradition (e.g., Ivey & Goncalves, 1988) incorporates the basic idea that human life is characterized by changes in self awareness and a sense of self. From a narrative perspective, this development is not strictly an internal cognitive process but rather the telling and retelling of a story over which the individual has only partial control (Gergen, 1994). A similar process seems to operate at the level of couples and families, where identity narratives also take shape and change over time (Gergen & Gergen, 1983; White & Epston, 1990).

Identity narratives communicate/construct meaning at many levels. At one level, they are behavioral descriptions, purporting to capture events as they might have been observed by a disinterested party. At another level, as these event descriptions are blended together, they fit into patterns that attempt to explain and interpret the events. Yet another level seeks to predict future behavior based on the past. Narratives accomplish this meaning making through such elements as plot, perspective, and metaphor. They often follow familiar plots such as victim-persecutor, exiled heir to the throne, or good-hearted simpleton. Skillful narrators can shift perspectives, creating the illusion of understanding by telling the story from one character's point of view. And the metaphorical nature of language permits a story to incorporate complex meanings into a few words.

Identity narratives incorporate contributions from many people, such as the family of origin, friends, co-workers, a religious community, or a recreational group. But in the lives of a typical American couple each partner has extraordinary input into the other's identity narrative. The validity of the partner's narrative voice is hard to discount when he or she has special access to extended observations, including times when it seems as if the "true self" might be more likely to emerge. During a sexual interaction (or the subtle negotiations leading up to a sexual interaction) people may express desires, thoughts, and responses that they would not feel comfortable revealing in public. At the same time, the emotional power of body contact gives special intensity to the partner's verbal and gestural responses.

Individuals and groups seem to construct mental images or identity narratives that represent both their "ideal" and "actual" identities (Gergen, 1994). An identity ideal, often unachievable, represents strivings and provides guidance in decision making. The actual identity, what is often referred to in the individual development literature as a self -concept, includes an awareness of characteristics that may not seem as ideal. The mentally or socially healthy, from this perspective, are the persons and groups who integrate their preferred and less-preferred aspects into a homogenous, somewhat predictable actual identity that is relatively congruent with the ideal identity (Kerby, 1991; White & Epston, 1990). Events and behaviors that do not fit the internal story represent challenges to this sense of continuity. Simple challenges can be handled by changing the story a little bit, while more severe challenges often result in symptomatic behavior and may need therapeutic intervention (White & Epston, 1990).

Of special interest at the couple level, however, is the *coordination* of identity narratives. Narratives and behavior must somehow fit together, and there are many possible mismatches. Early relationship struggles over identity can be intense, as can the negotiation throughout a relationship when partners use maladaptive strategies instead of pursuing a genuine mutual accommodation. Many couples, for example, find their "morning person" and "night person" identities in conflict. If sex is limited to the bedroom, their sexual interaction may be quite limited by not being in bed and awake at the same time. The discourse of domination makes it hard for either partner to "become a different person" by giving up long-standing behavior patterns. Furthermore, one or both partners may attempt to persuade the other one to make the majority of the changes.

Narrative Stability and Change

An Identity Renegotiation perspective normalizes the aspect of the relationship narrative that describes how much each partner is being encouraged to change or to remain the same. In some couples' narratives the theme is avoiding change, while others describe moving toward identity ideals. Following Sager (1976), I have described the expectation of change as a contractual issue; the committed relationship may be based on an assumption that there will be no changes, or it may be based on the assumption that certain changes will occur (Blume, 1996). In the case of sexuality, an individual who is struggling against desire can choose between two opposite strategies: choose a partner who will help to support desire by challenging that denial, or maintain the distance from desire by choosing someone who seems to know how to control sexual behavior.

Identity stability and/or change in a relationship can be negotiated successfully. Many people succeed in forming and maintaining couple relationships that accommodate changes in who each partner has been, wants to be, needs to be under certain circumstances, and has the resources to become. An occasional couple is able to begin dating at 16, keep their relationship together in some form during college and /or early career exploration, and remain intimately connected into old age as their relationship accommodates to the demands of (optional) parenthood and grandparenthood, illness, losses of loved ones, retirement, and death. Their sexual identity narratives, over a 70-year span, would change to incorporate discoveries about fluctuating levels of sexual characteristics such as desire, physical responsiveness, energy, patience, fantasy, and assertiveness.

But the majority of couples seem to struggle with such identity negotiations, and it is during those struggles that they are most likely to seek help with sexual problems. Their identities, after all, are intensely linked with their sexual narratives and behavior. Counseling from this perspective attempts to respect the centrality of sexual issues in larger identity concerns, as well as the impact of relationship changes on the quality of sexual interaction.

COUNSELING AND TREATMENT STRATEGIES

Because of the uniqueness of every couple, counseling begins with assessment of the various narratives that embody and shape the couple's relationship. The gathering of these stories is complicated by the fact that clients are often unaccustomed to talking about their sexual experiences. Therefore, I structure the early part of the conversation by providing the couple with a questionnaire (Blume, 1998) designed to elicit discussion of sexual conflict. The goal at this stage of counseling is not so much one of determining facts as one of gaining access to the sexual narratives that shape their interaction.

I envision the early stage of couple sexual counseling as what Fritz Perls (1965) referred to as a "safe emergency," a situation in which people can experience something they have feared and find out that it is not as uncomfortable as their fantasies would have suggested. I attempt to create an experience in which both partners feel safe. I explicitly discuss the discomfort the couple may feel, having their lives on display; I acknowledge the risk that I might take one partner's side against the other; admitting how hard it is to understand other people's lives; And I gently confront topics that seem to create discomfort. The centrality of identity issues, especially those related to gender, often leads to avoidance. I find that a less "clinical" style helps couples to more quickly open up about their doubts and fears.

I also take the opportunity in the first few counseling sessions to learn about the larger relationship context with a focus on the contract for change. Mutual trust and feelings of support seem to increase as the couple's story begins to incorporate positive problem-solving experiences and they reduce their use of coercive/passive strategies.

The most mature negotiation strategies involve openly sharing feelings and beliefs, hopes and fears, and honest observations of self and other (Edelman & Crain, 1994; Selman & Demorest, 1984). Such negotiations seek a resolution in which both partners are validated and the relationship is strengthened. Neither individual is wedded to a particular solution; instead, there is an honest exploration of the basis for the conflict and an openness to all possible resolutions. Even after a joint decision is made, there is continuing review of the process and the decision in hopes of improving future conflict management.

I have found that couples perform at their best in negotiations that are structured to encourage these positive patterns. First, I help them to identify issues in a non-blaming way, temporarily setting aside any assumptions about how they should be resolved. "We aren't in agreement about how frequently we'd like to be sexual with each other" is quite different, at this phase of negotiation, from "He wants sex all the time and I want him to let me alone." Fisher and Ury (1981) referred to this as part of "**interest-based**" rather than "**position-based**" negotiation; people tend to open with the positions they intend to take, and that impedes discussion.

Then I encourage partners to identify the shared values and principles that would be demonstrated by a good decision; equality of sexual enjoyment might be one, as might conformity to religious teachings. A good list may include ten or more items. People often need help doing this, as they are typically focusing not on shared values but on differences.

Once this supportive framework is established, things tend to go more smoothly. Each identified issue must be, to a great extent, processed separately, and yet many people are more sensitive to the overlaps among issues and they require a more circular than linear process. For each issue the couple needs to identify every possible alternative for resolving the impasse. The brainstorming model works well at this phase; no idea can be rejected on its face, even the most preposterous suggestion gets written down and evaluated later. I have found two strategies to be extremely helpful. The first involves taking a break--from five minutes to two weeks--from problem-solving discussions, giving the partners time to "find" alternatives they couldn't think of at the time. The second, even more powerful, involves asking each person to remember alternatives the other has proposed and has apparently forgotten. In the context of value-free brainstorming, people seem willing to do this, and it helps to create a positive climate of cooperation.

Once all the options have been identified, the bargaining phase involves the basic techniques that apply to tricycles, cookies, and the last glass of milk: dividing and distributing the rewards (masturbating you to orgasm leaves me worn out, but I'd be happy to masturbate you for up to ten minutes and then we could switch to intercourse) and taking turns (I agreed to your toe-sucking last night; you have to agree to my wearing costumes tonight).

No negotiated agreement is complete without documentation, an implementation plan, and a followup evaluation. The documentation is necessary to compensate for memory problems (But, I'm sure you said that you would start being responsible for birth control). A plan helps to build trust. And every agreement is best evaluated after implementation to see whether or not it accomplishes its goals.

When sexual identity issues are negotiated in such a way, sexual self discovery and sharing are life-long processes. Rather than being fearful of judgment, partners can feel that they are honoring each other when they identify problem areas that could grow into negative narratives. They also can feel assured that any change in appearance, desire, response, or ability will be treated with respect.

Approaches to Identity Narratives. The pioneers of narrative counseling (e.g., White & Epston, 1990) were strongly influenced by the analysis of literary texts. That is, these approaches tended to view narratives as discrete entities that could be gathered or collected, exhibiting some degree of closure (Sheehan, 1999). More recent approaches take a more tentative approach, hearing multiple narratives coexisting in every jointly-narrated story. The counselor seems to have three basic options for being helpful; modify the narrative, totally replace the narrative with a new one, or deconstruct the narrative-- develop a critical awareness of its assumptions so that it loses its power to control behavior.

The first option, modifying problematic narratives, is typified by the narrative strategy of **externalizing** (White & Epston, 1990). This type of intervention is based on the idea that clients who see themselves as responsible for creating their own problems feel inadequate or doomed to failure. They frequently fight over which family member will be blamed, rather than unite in solving the problem. Following this idea, in the early stage of treatment I encourage a couple to attribute their problems to their situation, to their past experiences, and to the surrounding society's discourse about sexuality. Such attributions may help people to avoid the "real" issues, but in this case external attributions are part of a temporary strategy that seems to reduce clients' anxiety as they talk about identity-threatening experiences.

An elaborate version of externalizing has been documented by White and Epston (1990); clients are encouraged to identify and name the problem as an entity external to themselves and their relationships. Orgasms, for example, might be described as having been "stolen" by Performance Anxiety. Performance Anxiety would then be built up as a character in the narrative, a character that is powerful but not invincible. United in opposition to the common enemy, the couple would find ways to keep Performance Anxiety from disrupting their efforts to be close to each other.

White and Epston (1990) were also among the first to describe another structural narrative intervention, replacing a problematic narrative. They wrote:

> ...we make the general assumption that persons experience problems, for which they frequently seek therapy, when the narratives in which they are "storying" their experience, and/or in which they are having their experience "storied" by others, do not sufficiently represent their lived experience, and that, in these circumstances, there will be significant aspects of their lived experience that contradict these dominant narratives. *(1990, p. 14)*

Problematic narratives are replaced through reviewing narratives and listening for **unique outcomes** that cannot be explained by the dominant story. Bob, for example, described his wife, Ellen, as "like a light switch--once something turns her off, she's turned off." Externalizing would have been a possibility in this situation, as Ellen agreed that she was "turned off" by Bob's giving in to Obsessive Neatness and he might have agreed that it was a common enemy. But such an approach would not have challenged his denial of her sexuality. I chose instead to invite Ellen to identify times when her sexual feelings didn't work the way Bob described. At first she didn't recall any incidents; the next week she came in with an example from the past. From that point on, they were an investigative team, looking for evidence that Ellen could recover her sexual interest even after Bob had upset her. Within a few weeks they had a new story, one in which Ellen had a long-term investment in sex, and was able to work with Bob to locate her sexual interest even when events seemed to have destroyed it.

A third narrative option is referred to by Zimmerman and Dickerson (1993) as "separating the couple from the problem-supporting discourse." In this approach, a couple's problematic narrative is identified and externalized--located outside them, in the family/cultural/community context (discourse). Similarly, several contemporary authors (e.g., Hare-Mustin, 1998; Sheehan, 1999) have described postmodern or poststructuralist narrative approaches. These approaches view narratives as open-ended works in progress rather than concrete, finished products. Attempting to capture the quality of a constantly-changing entity, I focus on problematic narrative "themes" or "streams" that exert varying degrees of influence on couple and family interactions.

As the partners learn to recognize the times when they are being affected by this discourse, therefore, learn to be on guard against its influence, they also learn to **deconstruct** the discourse—to understand the ways in which every discourse operates to serve the interests of some privileged group. David, a roofing contractor, and Andrea, a teacher, had formed their relationship around a stereotypical set of gender expectations. Andrea, who had been in a verbally and physically abusive relationship at the time she met David, viewed her options as choosing between one dominant male and another. David behaved more respectfully toward her than her husband did, and only later did she realize—after she was pregnant with his child—that his apparent respect could have represented competition with her husband. Once David had won the competition, he seemed to resent Andrea's refusal to be an obedient wife whose only sexual agenda was pleasing him. Both Andrea and David responded positively to a focus on the discourse of male dominance, a discourse that was hurting both of them. David began to identify the source of his rules for behavior, and started to appreciate the problems built into his assumptions about men and women. Despite living and working around men who expressed views of their wives as property, he gradually modified his individual and couple identity narratives to ones that supported Andrea's equality as a person.

A final approach addresses the question of narrative continuity (Spence, 1986). This approach emphasizes the challenges of achieving narrative integrity, incorporating various parts of one's experience into a recognizable self. If this "narrative smoothing" is hard for one person, it is even harder for two people to work together to achieve a couple identity that incorporates the valued parts of each. Kerby (1991) suggested that "unity" for an individual can only be achieved by either limiting the discrepant parts, leading to a life obsessed with routine, or telling the story in a way that makes the parts fit together. For a couple, this consolidation of narratives seems the only reasonable option. Reconciling the multiple discrepancies in two sexual stories is a challenge, but one that couples can meet with help.

CASE STUDY

Nancy's brother Jerry, a former client, called me to ask if I provided premarital counseling. Reassured that I did, he encouraged Nancy and Rodney to come see me. I opened the first session asking for their impressions of what was happening. They explained that they were engaged, with a wedding planned in FOUR months. But in the six months since the engagement had been announced, their sexual relationship had become increasingly problematic. Rodney "never" expressed a desire for sex, and, according to Nancy, when she made sexual advances he seemed to look for excuses to avoid intercourse. Several recent attempts at intercourse had been frustrated when Rodney "lost" his erection, ending in mutual blaming and self-protective withdrawal. As they talked, Rodney seemed inclined to be optimistic, attributing the sexual problems to work pressures and family interference, but Nancy said that she was almost ready to call off the engagement.

They agreed that sex had not been a problem when they first started dating. At that time Nancy, a 32-year-old divorced law student, had been living in an apartment shared with another student. Rodney, 28, who worked in the computer center at a local community college, had been sharing an apartment with a former college roommate. Neither had felt especially successful in previous relationships, but they reported a feeling of ease and comfort when they began to be sexual with each other. Both of them came from religious backgrounds that disapproved of sex outside marriage.

In the beginning, they agreed that their opportunities for private time had been limited. Possibly for that reason, they both had worked hard to arrange an occasional night together, and they found on those nights a passion that, they agreed, surprised them both. But, they also described many things that had changed in the intervening year. Nancy had completed her degree, and she was beginning to feel a new financial comfort. On the other hand, her work hours, which had once been rather flexible, had become much more limited. From being the partner who could always fit couple time into her schedule, she was now described as "hard to connect with" except late in the evenings and on weekends. And, Rodney was also under increased stress. He and a friend were starting a consulting business while he continued in his previous position. In preparation for marriage, Nancy had moved out of her apartment and moved in with Rodney, even though his roommate had not yet moved out.

Assessing the Contract for Change

The Identity Renegotiation approach suggests a simultaneous focus on both the couple's narratives and their interactions. In this case, the early sessions included explorations of the contract for change; the history of attempts to negotiate changes in self and other; and their current assessments of the most important changes they needed to negotiate. For Nancy, it seemed that their contract had initially called for her becoming less emotional and more independent. She had called him frequently and had complained of his long hours in the computer center, as well as his time with his roommate. Rodney, too, had been attempting to be less emotionally expressive, with the explanation that he had "led her to expect too much" in the early weeks. The couple had been successful in reducing Nancy's dependent behavior and Rodney's expressiveness. This change, however, meant that neither of them was making the gestures to reach out emotionally.

Rodney's career plans were also part of the contract for change. His relatively unambitious life style had been adequate before he became involved with a law student. At this time both of them expressed a belief that his lower status, combined with the age difference, would create tensions. His business plan, therefore, was essentially a condition of the marriage.

During the first few weeks we reviewed the change contract and explored possible modifications. Following the plan for cooperative problem solving, the first stage involved identifying the problems in nonjudgmental terms without proposing solutions. Two previously addressed issues were identified: a) They had difficulty coordinating their varying feelings about intimacy and autonomy, and b) They were afraid that their unconventional relationship would not survive unless they made it more "normal" in terms of job status and money. Coming to me had added a newer area of concern: c) They were experiencing difficulty being sexual together. As our conversations progressed, I heard a final issue in their couple narratives: d) Conflicts between their previously separate family and friendship groups were frequent, and they were worried that the conflicts would escalate.

Before attempting changes to resolve any issue, all of the possible alternatives needed to be explored; Nancy and Rodney were sent home more than once with instructions to reflect on any options that might have been overlooked. Their previously adopted plans were still options, but newer alternatives sounded attractive. As we carried on these direct, seemingly straightforward fact-finding conversations, it was possible to detect the level of the identity threats in their narratives By the fourth session, we were able to shift more directly to exploring the ways in which the discourses of gender, identity, and sexuality had limited their willingness and ability to enact and tell an honest, complete couple story.

Assessing Discourses and Narratives

I experienced a relatively low level of conflict in the first few sessions, something I find typical in couples who are facing threats to their narrative identities. Both Rodney and Nancy were vulnerable, depending on how their problems were viewed. According to the Physical Beauty/Attraction discourse, Nancy might be held responsible for Rodney's sexual performance problems, but her physical attractiveness also might be blamed for their unacceptable premarital behavior. The Male Lust discourse, on the other hand, would absolve Nancy of blame but then would label Rodney as "less than a real man." Both of them could be held responsible under the Dominance and Exploitation narrative. Nancy was guilty of being older, better educated, and too opinionated. At the same time, Rodney was vulnerable to both accusations of accepting a subordinate role and accusations of being the sex-obsessed male, taking advantage of Nancy. Neither of them wanted to create the pain that would have resulted from exposing these toxic story lines.

Therefore, as we explored the relationship contract, I encouraged the retelling of their individual and joint sexual narratives in a safe, nonjudgmental environment. The existence, in their narratives, of significant life changes provided opportunities for me to help them negotiate non-threatening, externalizing alternative narratives (White & Epston, 1990). These alternative narratives-- success, job/family conflicts, competition among friends and families, stress--also offered opportunities for each of them to identify with positive themes of flexibility, commitment to change, and courage. Their relationship narrative had to find ways of dealing with a number of dangerous gender and sexuality discourses, of which the following are only a sample.

Dominance and Exploitation. Dominance issues came up relatively early. As Nancy related others' advice and observations about her upcoming marriage, she reported that several of her advisers--friends and family--had worried that she was not appropriately submissive and that the practice of law would make her more "pushy." Further conversations about this theme produced other narrative inputs; for example, Rodney's friends were observing that Nancy did not afford him the privileges and freedoms that were due him as a man. Both partners recalled the pejorative terms used to describe a man who "let a woman lead him around by the nose" or was "whipped."

Rodney admitted that his sexual feelings were intimately tied up with the theme of domination. As he understood heterosexual relationships, a man who was dominated by a woman was not really a man; he would eventually be found out as sexually inadequate. But the domination was insidious; if Rodney felt sexual desire for Nancy, as a result she gained power over him, and he lost his masculinity. In a way, then, Rodney's last-minute withdrawal of sexual interest was a solution to this problem, a way to regain his self respect and his sexual potency. Nancy's attempts to initiate sex, though they were well intended, had the effect of increasing the intensity of Rodney's conflicts. He felt most comfortable being in charge sexually, but he distrusted his ability to follow through if he initiated sex.

Caring. Another gender-related theme, the idea of caring, presented a paradox. Both Rodney and Nancy knew that the woman was supposed to be the caretaker, and once again their friends and family had commented on the occasions when they violated the norms. Their attempts to reestablish traditional gender roles included a gradual elimination of Rodney's caring gestures toward Nancy. He stopped bringing her flowers and making her breakfast, and she was just as happy that he was becoming "normal." Unfortunately, caretaking was a major part of Rodney's sexuality. If no one was making gestures that--in Rodney's romantic love narrative--constituted foreplay, then sex was forced and lacked intensity.

Passion. As he described sex, it became obvious that Rodney believed in passion; according to his romantic love narrative, people who were in love were swept away by their sexual feelings (and their resulting behavior, though sinful, could be forgiven). Nancy's descriptions of sex were more those of a pragmatist who viewed sexual passion as a barrier to a true relationship. She recalled that she had found the intensity of their early sexual encounters to be troubling. Rather than excitement, what she wanted from sex was reassurance and comfort. A man who was excited by sex might go elsewhere looking for it, and therefore she wasn't going to encourage him to think of sex as thrilling.

Sexual Response. Rodney didn't like talking about his sexual "failure," and as a result he and Nancy had not discussed many of the possible reasons for his sexual reluctance and uneven performance. Like many couples, they had little information about the physiology of sex, and the information they had indicated that sex was automatically good if two people loved each other. Neither of them realized that men and women alike could respond to the emotional climate of lovemaking, or that a man might sometimes need direct physical stimulation to create a firm erection just as a woman might sometimes need direct physical stimulation to become fully aroused. Their discomfort with sexual topics had prevented them from making efforts to enhance their sexual interactions.

Male Lust. One of Rodney's greatest fears was that he would be sexually inadequate, and the fear seemed understandable when he described his image of "normal" men's performance. As he related his sexual anxiety narrative, it became clear that his inconsistent erections seemed to confirm a thought that dated back to high school. Friends had told him that he didn't seem "man enough" for his girl friend at the time, and had teased him about eventually needing them to help him keep her satisfied. He had, in fact, delayed his first intercourse until his junior year in college, and he had kept his slow sexual development a secret.

Nancy recalled that she had considered men's sexual obsession to be a biological fact, and remembered having made joking comments to Rodney about men being inexhaustible. She hadn't recognized her participation in creating expectations that he would fear he couldn't fulfill.

Obligation. As our conversations focused on the engagement itself, it became clear that since they had begun living together both Rodney and Nancy were starting to feel the obligation to be sexual with each other. Once sex had been voluntary and spontaneous and now it was becoming a duty. Nancy, who viewed sex on a more mundane level, did not see that this sense of duty interfered with her sexuality. Instead, she enjoyed the sense that she could experience desire, and that Rodney would be there when she came to bed. But this was one of the crucial overlaps among themes; she assumed that her desire would be matched by his, because she assumed that men were naturally obsessed with sex. When he failed to respond, she assumed that it was because he no longer found her attractive.

Physical Beauty/Attraction. In a society where advertising messages and media stories provide daily reminders that only the young and beautiful can be sexy, Nancy was insecure, and she was not comfortable expressing her insecurity. The age difference between her and Rodney was rarely discussed and, when discussions occurred, they focused on status rather than physical appearance. Our discussions brought out negative expectations on both sides, as they recognized their participation in a discourse that describes men as improving with age and women losing their attractiveness after the age of 25. Until we began examining other explanations for Rodney's sexual behavior, verbal reassurances from Rodney couldn't contradict Nancy's physical evidence that he, like everyone else, pitied her as her youthful beauty disappeared. Rodney, not understanding the power of the discourse underlying her doubts, needed help both articulating his feelings of attraction and explaining how he could find her mature looks preferable to the conventionally attractive younger women she envied.

Renegotiating the Sexual Narrative

At their stage of relationship development, it was not surprising that Nancy and Rodney's sexual narrative was full of gaps and inconsistencies. Even after 10 weeks of discussions the story was a work in progress, with further changes expected. Changes were negotiated in all three realms: expectations, experiences, and interpretations. Common to all the renegotiations was the critical examination and rejection of the many discourses that had defined their experiences before they came to counseling. Quoting again from White and Epston (1990):

> The externalization of the problem helps persons identify and separate from unitary knowledges and "truth" discourses that are subjugating them. In mapping the influence of the problem in the person's life and relationships, these unitary knowledges can be exposed by encouraging persons to identify beliefs about themselves, others, and their relationships that are reinforced and confirmed by the continued presence of the problem. *(p. 30)*

The four issues, as defined above, became the externalized problems. The problems were not Rodney and Nancy, but rather patterns that developed in their interaction. These patterns were addressed in a cooperative problem-solving mode, as follows:

1. *Difficulty coordinating their varying feelings about intimacy and autonomy.* This issue became much more comfortable to negotiate when the power of gender assumptions was weakened. They had been lying to themselves about their feelings and their behavior. They considered options that would have made coordination easier by reducing the variation and intensity of feelings. Those options were rejected in favor of new expectations and communication patterns. During the time we worked together, their new narrative began to develop as they showed that each one could feel, at different times, lonely, tense and unavailable, open and sensual, vulnerable and needy, or angry and rejecting. Their consistent choice to explore their feelings and find ways of working with those feelings provided them with a strong base of emotional connection, despite some intense disagreements.

2. *Fear that their unconventional relationship would not survive unless they made it more "normal" in terms of job status and money.* This fear became, in a way, the challenge that gave their relationship its meaning. The fear had nearly overwhelmed them, and they were determined to prove it mistaken. Having rejected solutions that involved adapting to match the conventional relationship story, they chose solutions that focused on their encounters with messengers who would keep reminding them of their deviance. They committed themselves to reporting any such encounters and sharing the process of either finding the flaws in the message or else taking the message as a challenge to locate and work on areas of possible vulnerability.

3. *Difficulty being sexual together.* This, the presenting problem, was difficult to negotiate before the negative effects of gender and sex discourses began to disappear from the couple narrative. By the end of our time together, new expectations were negotiated, including permission for either person to feel a wide range of sexual arousal and interest and permission for the partner to have different feelings at any given time. The assumption of knowing and understanding the other's sexual responses was replaced by an assumption of mutual discovery and partial mystery. Every sexual encounter, according to the new narrative, was a chance to learn something about self, partner, or the ways in which they fit together. New experiences as well were negotiated; both Nancy and Rodney were somewhat inexperienced, and they found a few sex guides that they began using to ensure that they would continue to discover new things about their sexuality. And they radically renegotiated their interpretations of the first year of their relationship. The new narrative described their sexual health and well being before finding each other; the courageous, if misguided, sacrifices each made because of a belief that it would be necessary to become someone different; and the deep love, commitment, and flexibility that was shown in their having survived the period when their sexuality was no longer a source of positive feelings and physical closeness.

4. *Conflicts between their previously separate family and friendship groups.* This issue is one that faces many couples in their early years. In Rodney and Nancy's case, the extent of the conflict had been denied as each of them protected the other from hearing about critical and discouraging comments. A new expectation was negotiated, with both partners accepting the possibility that some of their loved ones would neither share their excitement about the coming marriage nor relish the eventual meeting with the "other side of the family." With this more accepting view of their critics, Nancy and Rodney began to plan ways to support people's limited investment in their marriage, and they reworked several parts of the wedding plan. Most importantly, they decided to work with Rodney's mother, who had been threatening to stay away from the wedding. This was more easily accomplished because they also renegotiated the meaning of Mom's behavior.

SUMMARY

This chapter has presented a multidimensional approach to working with couple sexuality, based on assumptions that sexual behavior can only be understood in context. The context emphasized in this approach is one of social constructions and narratives that make meaning out of experience and give a sense of identity to a couple. Change in couple sexual relationships is explained as a negotiation process that focuses on changing three aspects of the sexual narrative: expectations, experiences, and interpretations.

The work presented here represents a further refinement of an Identity Renegotiation perspective that has been developing over a 15-year period, most recently attempting to clarify the location of relationship problems in "problem-saturated narratives" (White & Epston, 1990). The rich literature on narrative approaches suggests a variety of ways in which counselors can work with couples' own narratives and the discourses of gender and sexuality that surround them.

REFERENCES

Adler, A. (1927). *Understanding human nature.* Garden City, NY: Garden City Publishing Co.

Baber, K. M., & Allen, K. R. (1992). *Women and families: Feminist reconstructions.* New York: Guilford.

Bailey, B. (1999). *Sex in the heartland.* Cambridge, MA: Harvard.

Blume, T. W. (1987). *Cognitive and behavioral aspects of marital conflict: A test of a constructivist model.* Ann Arbor, MI: Dissertation Abstracts International.

Blume, T. W. (1996). Negotiating identity in couple relationships. Paper presented at the 26th Theory Construction and Research Methodology Workshop, National Council on Family Relations, Kansas City, MO. Published in *Papers for discussion, 26th theory construction and research methodology workshop,* pp. 69-74.

Blume, T.W. (1998). Couple intimacy and sexuality questionnaire. In L.L. Hecker & S. Deacon (Eds.), *The therapist's notebook: Homework, handouts, & activities* (pp. 197-200). New York: Haworth Press.

Burggraf, S. P. (1997) *The feminine economy and economic man: Reviving the role of the family in the postindustrial age.* Englewood Cliffs, NJ: Prentice-Hall.

Butler, J. (1993). *Bodies that matter: On the discursive limits of sex.* New York: Routledge.

Currie, M. (1998). *Postmodern narrative theory.* New York: St. Martin's Press.

Deutsch, M. (1973). *The resolution of conflict: Constructive and destructive processes.* New Haven: Yale.

Edelman, J., & Crain, M. B. (1994). *The Tao of negotiation: How you can prevent, resolve, and transcend conflict in work and everyday life.* New York: Harperbusiness.

Fisher, R., & Ury, W. (1981). *Getting to yes: Negotiating agreement without giving in.* New York: Penguin.

Foucault, M. (1990). *The history of sexuality. Volume I: An introduction.* New York: Vintage Books.

Gergen, K. J. (1994). *Realities and relationships: Soundings in social construction.* Cambridge, MA: Harvard University Press.

Gergen, K. J., & Gergen, M. M. (1983). Narratives of the self. In T. R. Sarbin & K. E. Scheibe (Eds.), *Studies in social identity* (pp. 254-275). N. Y.: Praeger.

Hare-Mustin, R. T. (1998). Challenging traditional discourses in psychotherapy: Creating space for alternatives. *Journal of Feminist Family Therapy, 10*(3), 39-56.

Ivey, A. E., & Goncalves, O. F. (1988). Developmental therapy: Integrating developmental processes into the clinical practice. *Journal of Counseling and Development, 66,* 406-413.

Kerby, A. P. (1991). *Narrative and the self.* New York: Indiana University Press.

Knudson-Martin, C., & Mahoney, A. R. (1999). Beyond different worlds: A "postgender" approach to relational development. *Family Process, 38,* 325-340.

Love, P., & Robinson, J. (1994). *Hot monogamy: Essential steps to more passionate, intimate lovemaking.* New York: Dutton.

Masters, W. H., & Johnson, V. E. (1970). *Human sexual inadequacy*. Boston: Little, Brown.

Maxwell, K. E. (1996). *A sexual odyssey: From forbidden fruit to cybersex*. New York: Plenum Press.

Mead, G. H. (1934). *Mind, self, and society from the standpoint of a social behaviorist*. Chicago: University of Chicago Press.

Mcth, R. L. (1990). Men and sexuality. In R. L. Meth & R. S. Pasick (Eds.), *Men in therapy: The challenge of change* (pp. 209-223). New York: Guilford.

Nichols, M. (Director) (1971). Carnal knowledge. Available from New Line Home Video.

Perls, F. (1965). *Three approaches to psychotherapy, Part 2*. Available from Psychological and Educational Films.

Rainwater, L. (1960). *And the poor get children: Sex, contraception, and family planning in the working class*. Chicago, IL: Quadrangle Books.

Rosen, R. C., & Leiblum, S. R. (1995). The changing focus of sex therapy (pp. 3-17). In R. C. Rosen & S. R. Leiblum (Eds.), *Case studies in sex therapy*. New York: Guilford.

Sager, C. J. (1976). *Marriage contracts and couple therapy: Hidden forces in intimate relationships*. New York: Brunner/Mazel.

Sarbin, T. R. (Ed.) (1986). *Narrative psychology: The storied nature of human conduct*. New York: Praeger.

Selman, R. L., & Demorest, A. P. (1984). Observing troubled children's interpersonal negotiation strategies: Implications of and for a developmental model. *Child Development, 55,* 288-304.

Sheehan, J. (1999). Liberating narrational styles in systemic practice. *Journal of Systemic Therapies, 18(3),* 51-68.

Snyder, M. (2000). The loss and recovery of erotic intimacy in primary relationships: Narrative therapy and relationship enhancement therapy. *The Family Journal: Counseling and Therapy for Couples and Families, 8,* 37-46.

Spence, D. P. (1986). Narrative smoothing and clinical wisdom. In T. R. Sarbin (Ed.), *Narrative psychology: The storied nature of human conduct* (pp.211-232). New York: Praeger.

Sprey, J. (1969). The family as a system in conflict. *Journal of Marriage and the Family, 31,* 699-706.

White, M., & Epston, D. (1990). *Narrative means to therapeutic ends*. New York: W. W. Norton.

Zimmerman, J. L., & Dickerson, V. C. (1993). Separating couples from restraining patterns and the relationship discourse that supports them. *Journal of Marital and Family Therapy, 19,* 403-413.

Chapter 6

COUNSELING THE BISEXUAL CLIENT

Thomas Arbaugh Jr.

University of Southern Mississippi - Gulf Coast

This chapter discusses counseling issues surrounding **bisexuality**. Various approaches are presented for the counselor who works with the individual self-identifying as bisexual. It is the author's intent to bring about a deeper understanding of potential issues for the counselor working with the bisexual client through presenting and exploring the information found in the literature. This presentation and these suggestions are not definitive answers for every bisexual person any more than counseling holds the only answer for every client. It is essential for the counselor to maintain a process of self-awareness while exploring with the bisexual client the unique issues that are a part of the counseling process.

Ongoing **self-awareness** on the part of the counselor is crucial for **diversity** sensitive counseling. What are the personal values and beliefs that the counselor has around bisexuality? The counselor may hold to a belief that there is no such thing as bisexuality and that bisexual behavior is part of the transition process from a heterosexual culture to the self identification of being lesbian or gay. Another counselor may believe that bisexuality is a discrete category without overlapping heterosexuality or homosexuality (King, 1997). What is known is that too much focus on categories or labels can interfere with effective counseling (Stokes & Miller, 1998; Zeeland, 1995). While some counselors and clients may want to avoid labels and categories of sexual behavior, it may be important for others to embrace a concept of sexuality so that they can more completely develop their identity. Ault (1996) concluded that ". . . larger **feminist** discourses on choice and sexual self-determination have motivated some feminist women to reclaim the bisexual category" (p. 452). Counselors may want to establish the level of importance of identity labels and to know what they think about definitions of bisexuality. Even the acknowledgment of the legitimacy of same sex relationships may be a difficult point for some counselors (Schwartzberg & Rosenberg, 1998).

The counselor's biases are often communicated in subtle ways, words, and mannerisms (Fontaine, 1998; Reynolds & Koski, 1995). While there continues to be a fluctuation of cultural nuances and a flow of sexual behaviors, counselors need to perpetuate self awareness for the client and the counselor. This is accomplished through a safe atmosphere in counseling, providing freedom to explore delicate issues and a knowledge of bisexuality, including the relationship of bisexual love to lesbian and gay love relationships.

BACKGROUND TO UNDERSTANDING BISEXUALITY

Through experience as a practitioner with bisexual, lesbian, and gay individuals, I have formatted a procedure to help a client in the formation of an identification process. As the client explores sexual experiences and sexuality, she or he often exhibits confusion around the issues of how the sexual activity relates to emotional and **spiritual** feelings. By segmenting the areas of sexual activity into personal, emotional completion, and spiritual fulfillment, a client can examine feelings, desires, and satisfactions with a new clarity. One bisexual client stated that although he was sexually satisfied by erotic activity with either males or females, he found that emotionally he felt more complete intimacy with a male partner. He also expressed that spiritually he found much greater growth and attainment with male sexual/emotional partners. On the other hand, some research (e.g., Stokes & Miller, 1998) that indicates men may have sexual experiences with other men merely because either the sexual opportunity is easier to obtain, or because of the enjoyment of sexual diversity. However, the opportunistic same gender sexual activity of some heterosexual men does not necessarily mean they identify, or should be identified as bisexual.

Once rapport is established with a client, sexual behaviors can more easily be discussed and tabulated. More difficult is the exploration of the emotions involved in sexual activity, and the role of spirituality in sexual activity. While **spirituality** in counseling is a challenging area to define (Chandler, Holden, & Kolander, 1992), it is relevant for counselors to include the element of spirituality in counseling sessions with a client (Miller, 1999; Shannon & Woods, 1998; Stanard, Sandhu, & Painter, 2000). By so doing, spirituality becomes an avenue in the healing process (Westgate, 1996). The terms "spiritual" and "higher power" can be defined and agreed upon and understood more completely as counseling progresses. Counsellors do not have to set aside the element of spirituality because it is unclear or because the counselor, and/or the client is not comfortable with religion. Penn (1997) wrote, ". . . it is practically impossible to imagine a gay man who has not been exposed to religion-based arguments against homosexuality" (p. 478). This could also be said about lesbian women and bisexual people who have had both gay and heterosexual experiences. In the Judeo-Christian tradition, same gender activity remains famous for being "unspeakable"and "unmentionable" (Sedgwick, 1985, p. 94). The perceived incompatibility of the spiritual, emotional, and fulfillment elements of sex with the issues of sin and evil often has to be addressed. Thus, bisexual clients are more able to incorporate both previous religious learning and a new spiritual fulfillment in sexual activity. Integration of spirituality and sexuality is a major component in the many facets of **wellness** and psychological well-being (Arbaugh, 1994; McNeill, 1995; Monteiro & Fuqua, 1995; Witmer & Sweeney, 1992). Moore (1998) presented the combination of sexuality and spirituality as ". . . discovering the depths and heights of sex, its inherent and unsentimental sacredness, the spirit and soul within the mechanics, techniques, and paraphernalia" (p. 109).

McWilliams (1993) clarified that any shift in consciousness can be perceived as a religious experience depending upon the belief system of the client. Therefore, it is important that the client have the flexibility to define and differentiate between a religious experience and personal spirituality. The counselor must continue to be sensitive to the individual's concepts of religion and higher power. "Because of the historical separation between many psychological theorists and religion, counselors may need to voice their openness to discuss religious issues with clients" (Favier, O'Brien, & Ingersoll, 2000, p. 158). Therefore, counselors are able to help clients discern personal forms of spirituality. The concept of spirituality is integral towards understanding one's self and becoming a whole person who is comfortable with his/her sexuality. The embracing of spirituality through sexuality is vital for becoming an authentic self (McNeill, 1995). Exploring sexuality through the lens of spiritual, emotional, and physical evolvement can be a helpful beginning in the process of understanding bisexuality.

Defining Bisexuality through Acceptance

It is often difficult to define bisexuality. The range of sexual behaviors is such that many people have experienced both encounters with a same gender partner and an encounter with someone of the opposite sex. Even when people identify themselves as being heterosexual, many have experienced a same gender sexual encounter of some sort during the experimental years of sexual development (Cantarella, 1992; Schwartzberg & Rosenberg, 1998; Udis-Kessler, 1992). These experiences may vary in degree from an experimental flirting and touching to any number of intimate sexual activities. All too often, a person is considered non-gay until proven gay (Savin-Williams & Rodriguez, 1993). This burden of proof falls even harder on the bisexual person because there is often little clarification of bisexuality or support for bisexual behaviors from either the gay community or the non-gay majority culture (Gibian, 1992; McKirnan & Stokes, 1995; Shuster, 1992).

A number of factors lead women and men to define their sexual identity and to self-identify as either heterosexual or bisexual. The true bisexual person is one who is emotionally, sexually and intimately willing to function with someone else of either gender. As a concept, the definition of bisexual activity and bisexuality is left to the person who is describing herself or himself. The counselor is most effective as a listener who starts the helping process by understanding how the client defines bisexuality and is supportive in the process of exploration into that definition (Stokes & Miller, 1998).

> Sexuality has to do with life and joy. How we express it is individual and ought to be . . .
> In counseling we must be prepared to assist clients with achieving a deeper and more humane understanding of how and when to express their sexual selves. (*Gilbert & Scher, 1999, p. 99-100*)

An older man may have experimented early in life and then put same gender sexual activity aside in order to live in what he considered a normal life (Berger, 1996). When first starting, or restarting sexual activity with another man, he often will identify as being bisexual. The concept of bisexuality as a transition from a heterosexual identity to a gay identity is supported in much of the literature and in experiential research (McKirnan & Stokes, 1995; Rhoads, 1997; Shannon & Woods; 1998; Stokes & Miller, 1998; Smiley, 1997; Wolf, 1992). The bisexual label may appear to be well justified when the man is functioning consistently in sexual relationships with his female spouse. Nevertheless, the counselor must work with the client to determine if the client chooses to identify as bisexual. It often becomes important for the client to adopt a label in order to solidify the element of sexual identity. King (1997) supported the conjecture that sexual orientation can be multidimensional and does not need to fall into strict boundaries of gay, non-gay, or bisexualism.

Some older men might not have acted upon the desire to have a same gender sexual experience because they want to be faithful to their wives. One man swore to himself he was not going to have sexual relations outside his marriage despite acknowledging various opportunities for same sex experiences. He held to this value for nearly 40 years of marriage. It was only when he reported that he "fell in love with his soul mate" that he was willing to set aside his long-held value and allow his friendship to take the next step of intimacy by becoming sexual. This individual never identified as being gay or bisexual for many years because he was not having any same sex activity. When he realized he was truly in love with another man, he also realized he was gay. While he continued to function sexually with his wife, he identified himself as solely gay and not bisexual. He felt complete with his male companion and acknowledged emotional, sexual and spiritual fulfillment not experienced with his female spouse.

In research of the qualitative evaluation of the **older gay man**, Berger (1996) concluded that, "Being openly gay can be personally liberating, but it is not adaptive in every situation" (p.11). When a person is perceived as being heterosexual and in an open heterosexual relationship, it is often important to hide same sex orientation. At best this can be a difficult and time consuming and, at worst, can put the bisexual person in physical, marital and even legal danger (Gutierrez, 1992; McKirnan & Stokes, 1995; Savin-Williams, 1994; Sedgwick, 1985). Kaufman and Raphael (1996) addressed the way any special attachment to one's own sex can make a person suspect of having bisexual activity. It can also bring shame to that person. The authors wrote, "The girl who feels drawn to other girls and the boy who feels drawn to other boys have now been taught to hide, to deny, to pretend, because their survival depends on it" (p. 126). Gilbert and Scher (1999) pointed out the devastating repercussions that may occur when people talk about their sexual identity. The cost of being discreet to everyone can bring out feelings of isolation and compartmentalization (Ault, 1996; Gibian, 1992; Gilbert & Scher,1999; Gutierrez, 1992, Sears, 1991).

DEVELOPMENTAL FACTORS

A contrast to the older gay man is the young woman who finds it "ludicrous" to not tell her extended family about her bisexuality. Mastoon (1997) described a 16 year old girl who agreed to keep her sexuality a secret from her family so that her mother did not have to face the negative response from extended family members. She was active in her high school gay/straight alliance group and found meaning in her high school career by her activism. While this open attitude is positive and shows maturity in this young adult, Blumenfeld (1995) points out that often times the younger a person is when she identifies her sexuality to others, the greater the problems she has to face.

Teenagers who have some element of a support system say they are more free to identify themselves as openly gay or lesbian without taking the journey through bisexual semantics (Blumenfeld, 1995; Mastoon, 1997; McFarland, 1998). Sometimes this is merely part of the journey to identification as gay and then having pride in sexuality (Wolf, 1992). A support system is a key element in a teenager's ability to respond to the desires that were required to be hidden by the present generation of older adults who felt they could not publicly acknowledge same gender sexuality (Fontaine, 1998; Isensee, 1991; Kaufman & Raphael, 1996; Savin-Williams & Rodriguez, 1993; Sears, 1991).

Sullivan (1996) postulated that humans can break through a crack in the culture of an oppressive social structure to express one's sexuality as one wishes. "That autonomy may be born out of pain, or misery, out of the very forces that seek to extinguish it; but its resilience suggests the existence of a human individual separate and independent from the culture in which he operates" (Sullivan, p. 73). As counseling and psychotherapy enable the client, young or old, to develop and exercise freedom of sexuality, the person can and will often draw on the power of the previous generation who express independence from cultural restraints by freely expressing sexual/affectional identification. This provides the incentive for a bisexual person to decide at what age, to whom, and to what extent one expresses sexuality. In addition, the person who is feeling internal power with external support can have the freedom to experience sexuality in the most personally fulfilling manner (Gilbert & Scher, 1999; Isay, 1989; Kaufman & Raphael, 1996; Murphy, 1992).

An important issue in counseling the bisexual client is providing educational material which will help expand the world-view of the client (Mastoon, 1997; Smiley, 1997). As a client goes through the process of development and learning, understanding the many alternatives in sexual desire can be a key factor in how well she or he is able to understand and accept herself or himself. Dissemination of educational material to a client is more difficult when that client is a school student or if the client resides in a rural town that does not acknowledge sexual diversity among its residents. The difficulty in discussing and providing information to a school student is exacerbated in parts of the United States where a school counselor can be dismissed for giving a student information on alternative sexual orientation. Some communities view the counselor as promoting homosexuality by even discussing alternative sexuality with a student. Discussing a forbidden topic may not necessarily be the reason given for the counselor's dismissal, yet there are still many communities which would quickly awaken in protest if the school counselor were known to give out information about bisexuality. School counselors can reference sexuality without being an advocate for the acting out of sexual desires. Because the gay or bisexual teen is curious about sexuality does not mean there needs to be sexual activity.

A counselor cannot be without an opinion regarding child or teenage sexual activity (Gilbert & Scher, 1999). It is effective to the counseling process when the counselor does not express immediate alarm at sexual activity, unless that activity is blatantly harmful. In harmful situations when the counselor must contact protective authorities, it is beneficial to the child to not express alarm and dismay at the sexual activity that has been described (Kaufman & Raphael, 1996). To do so is to retraumatize the child. It is essential that counselors and parents not further distress the child by quickly judging and reacting negatively when the child has behaved positively by reporting the sexual behavior.

School counselors can meet the challenge of maintaining an open environment for all students and still fulfill their jobs. A student may be hesitant to take the risk of bringing up alternative sexual activities to a school counselor. The student might need some sign that sex is a topic that can be discussed (Reynolds & Koski, 1995). There are strategies for demonstrating a safe environment for students without being identified as a counselor who promotes alternative sexuality. One possible suggestion is to have a book or two somewhere in the counselor's office with the words lesbian, gay, or bisexual (Marinoble, 1998). A print size that is easy to read is also a good idea. Keep these books among other books. When the counselor suspects alternative sexuality is an issue of importance, these books can be left on the counselor's desk when the teen is known to be coming to the counseling office. The books provide the adolescent a lead to open up the conversation. Counselors are misguided to think a teen will bring up the topic of bisexuality. Counselors realize that all schools are not ready to have open discussions about sexuality (Savin-Williams, 1994). Even in a strict school environment influenced by a conservative religious constituency, I have experienced freedom to answer all questions asked by students. Reynolds and Koski (1995) stressed that the school counselor needs not only to be tolerant of sexual diversity, but also be supporting, accepting and affirming. These authors concluded that "Sexual orientation should be presented not as a 'problem' but as another part of normal development" (p. 90). Although not an easy task, the importance of a supportive and open counseling environment is becoming more obvious in the culture of North American schools (Kaufman & Raphael, 1996; McWilliams, 1993; Rhoads, 1997).

Adolescents experiencing sexual attraction toward the same gender are beginning to see some portrayal of same sex attraction in television and movies. The sexual identity of music stars such as Elton John and Melissa Ethridge are known to many adolescents. Even though these mediums allow gay, lesbian and bisexual individuals to be more openly discussed (Savin-Williams & Rodriguez, 1993), the counselor is reminded that the attraction to someone of the same gender for an adolescent adds additional stress to an already tumultuous time in human development (Black & Underwood, 1998; Cooley,1998). In their writing emphasizing an understanding of the developmental process of gay men, Schwartzberg and Rosenberg (1998) posited the young adult gay male ". . . lacks the experiential learning that many heterosexuals gained during adolescence, and must address these tasks at a chronological age that does not match his developmental age" (p. 268).

Blumenfeld (1995) emphasized the advantages of organizational alliances for gay teens and non-gay teens. There are social and education support systems in place for heterosexual youth, while most bisexual youth must keep quiet about at least part of their sexual activity. "Enormous peer pressure to conform, coupled with the social stigma surrounding homosexuality and bisexuality and lack of support systems, causes many young people to turn inward" (Blumenfeld, p. 216). The need for counseling to reach out to lesbian, gay, and bisexual youth is underscored by reports which state that suicide is the leading cause of death among adolescents (Savin-Williams, 1994, p. 266). A method to reach young bisexual people is to provide a place where there is open dialogue about alternative sexual activity.

COUNSELING IMPLICATIONS AND STRATEGIES

As counselors seek to continually define bisexuality by understanding individual clients and the worlds of those clients, they must generate an awareness of cultural issues that relate to all counseling relationships. These **cross-cultural** issues apply to the bisexual client, the heterosexual client and the homosexual client. Some matters are going to be solely specific to the men and women who come to define themselves as bisexual. Maintaining an openness to the definition of bisexuality is the first step in assisting a client to explore issues around sexuality and to explore other areas presented as problems. The environment is critical to the feelings of emotional safety for the client and critical to the development of a trusting relationship between counselor and client (Young, 1998). The counselor has to maintain an awareness that some issue may cause confusion in defining one's sexuality. Yet these same issues may only be a minor theme in the counseling process. Not all clients lacking a clear definition of sexual identity are struggling with labels to put on sexual attractions or behaviors. Counselors cannot assume that because an immediate discussion or presentation of an alternative orientation occurs that the orientation or sexuality is the problem. More bisexual, lesbian, and gay clients are immediately disclosing their sexual orientation to their therapists. They choose to "get it out in the open" and avoid a misunderstanding that leaves the counselor guessing about their sexual orientation. Even among many counselors trained in **multiculturalism,** the assumption is often made that everyone is heterosexual (Atkinson & Hackett, 1998; King, 1997; Morrow, 1998). Because many men may have been sexual and/or involved with both men and women at some point in their lives (Isensee, 1990), a level of comfort may need to be established with labels by both the client and the counselor, or they may decide to seek comfort with not working from a defined sexual orientation. Establishing a comfort level is critical, whether the client be male or female, bisexual, gay, or non-gay (Gibian, 1992; Stokes & Miller, 1998).

When a client does identify as bisexual, one of the first challenges that the client faces is finding a place to fit within the social structure. As the dominate sexual culture, heterosexuals have people who "try to fix them up," have dating services in most communities, and even have personal ads on public access television. Some larger communities have personal ads in the local lesbian and gay newspapers (Penn, 1997). Yet in an informal review of Atlanta, New Orleans, and Dallas gay orientated newspapers, the section devoted to bisexual relationships was limited or nonexistent. This is one example of the invisibility of the bisexual person among the lesbian and gay community. Living in a majority culture of heterosexuals, many bisexual people prefer to allow others to think they are heterosexual to avoid confusion or explanations and dangerous repercussions (Savin-Williams, 1994). In a discussion of the tenuousness of bisexual self-identification, McKirnan and Stokes (1995) stressed that African American men are very careful to avoid identifying as gay or bisexual, even when actively participating in same gender sexual behavior. Instead of focusing on categories or labels, it is more beneficial to focus on the various aspects of the dual attractions and to explore what meaning those attractions have for the client (Stokes & Miller, 1998).

While many counselors have a cursory knowledge of the gay and lesbian community in their area of the country, such a community seldom exists for a bisexual client who can then search out, invest energy with, and learn from an organized group. In these situations, it is difficult to build a bisexual support system. The exceptions are bisexual organizations found in the following cities: Seattle, Los Angles, New York, Washington D.C., Philadelphia, Santa Cruz, Chicago, Toronto, Amsterdam and London (Weise, 1992). Even with a growing list of bisexual organizations, many bisexual clients rely on the counselor to help them come to terms with self-identification and with the realization that they are truly bisexual (Savin-Williams & Rodriguez, 1993). Further, the bisexual client may struggle with believing this is a phase one goes through, and not a progression toward homosexuality, since the attraction was only to one single person. The attraction, a client may believe, cannot be generalized to others of the same gender. Some clients struggling with their own gay identity choose a bisexual identity because it is less distasteful than to think of themselves as being "totally" gay (Isay, 1989). This may also be a symptom of internalized homophobia (Penn, 1997). These notions of bisexuality versus homosexuality that have been accepted from the majority culture will likely come out as they tell their stories (Semmler & Williams, 2000). Therefore, a first step in counseling a bisexual client may be to help the client learn about bisexuality. The counselor is then supportive in finding ways for the client to self-identify, if that is important to the client.

An issue in counseling with the bisexual client is the issue of monogamy. For the heterosexual couple, monogamy is an assumed part of the connubial agreement. Conversely, much debate exists in the gay male research literature as to the inherent value of monogamy (Carl, 1990; Isay, 1989; Isensee, 1990; Marcus, 1992; Penn, 1997; Weise, 1992). The topic takes on yet another angle for the bisexual individual who prefers to have both a husband and a wife.

Case Study

Alex, a client, would often state he did not want a divorce from his wife who was his best friend. He wanted to take a third partner in the marriage who would fulfill his spiritual, emotional, and physical desires for men. His sexual encounters with men usually resulted from contacts made at the gym. These men he would openly name and talk about as if they were merely other friends. He was convinced his wife never suspected these friends were his sexual outlets. Alex and his wife had many openly gay friends and were outspoken advocates for the rights of bisexual, lesbian, and gay people. Alex presented in counseling primarily with wonderment about the feelings of sexual attraction toward men. Alex had sought out a gay therapist, indicating the hope that a gay therapist would be more understanding of his being married and also being attracted to men. He stated that his sexual experience with men was very limited.

Alex was entrenched in his family heritage. He stated that all the men in his family were very masculine, and it was masculinity he found attractive in men. Likewise, it was femininity which he found attractive in women. Alex's emphasis on masculinity may have been a part of the process toward acceptance of his same sex attraction. Such emphasis is often called internalized homophobia (Schwartzberg & Rosenberg, 1998). Alex stated it would be like death for his family to know of his bisexuality. In his family he would be thought of as being a sissy if anyone knew he was having sex with men. Much of the counseling process with Alex was education on sexual activity, labeling feelings and behaviors. The counseling element important to him was having someone with whom he could discuss and decipher all the various confusing feelings and thoughts endemic to one who is newly exploring the world of same gender sexual activity. An ongoing issue with Alex and, with many married male clients who have same sex affairs, is that of being unfaithful to their spouse. These men are faced with a conundrum. They desire to have fluid sexual relationships that include sex with men. At the same time, they also have feelings of being disloyal to their wives with whom they would prefer to remain monogamous. Semantics surfaced in a similar incident with another client. The male client reassured his wife, when she told him of her suspicions of his having an affair, that he had never had sex with another women the entire many years of their marriage. At that point, she never even considered asking about his having a sexual liaison with a man.

Gibian (1992) wrote about feelings of disloyalty when she feared falling in love with a man after being so long embraced by her lesbian community. It was more than a matter of being unfaithful to one partner. She feared once again being presumed to be heterosexual when being seen with a man, yet her desire for monogamy with this boyfriend kept her from acting on a same gender sexual desire. Being monogamous brings security to the relationship whether in the gay or non-gay community. Monogamy also closes down potential feelings of sexual fulfillment that accompanies multiple relationships. In essence, monogamy means choosing one gender for a primary partner and accepting the distinctions which are connected to that people group. Lesbian feminists have much to offer women who are not lesbian. One example is the support and understanding the lesbian community can offer to women who have experienced abuse from men, or even women who merely want to promote and support a woman loving culture. While Gibian chose to maintain a long-term relationship with a man, she recognized that this single relationship did not meet all her sexual longings and feelings. "Learning to legitimate desire without necessarily acting upon it is a challenge any long-term monogamous relationship faces. To maintain a bisexual self-concept in a monogamous relationship, the challenge is imperative" (Gibian, 1992, p. 13).

An issue connected to monogamy within any relationship is that of sexually transmitted diseases (STDs), the most prominent of which is still the spread of HIV infection. In Alex's experimentation with men, he began to indulge in more and more sexual activities. At that point much of counseling centered around safer sex practices since there was the increased likelihood of his infecting his wife with HIV. The realization that he could contract HIV was a strong turning point for Alex. Many of his sexual behaviors changed. He was much more circumspect in regard to his choice of sexual partners and his sexual activities with them. He proceeded to be tested for HIV antibodies. This testing lead to great levels of anxiety and trepidation until the test results proved negative.

If Alex's wife truly had no idea that he was sexually active outside their relationship, she would not think to use protective measures for HIV or any other STD. There are ethical issues in circumstances such as this. The counselor has a duty to warn a potential victim if a client cannot or will not change behaviors which endanger the partner (Cooley, 1998; Kain, 1996). The counselor is responsible to help the client understand, a) the danger inherent in such behaviors, b) the ease with which infections are carried back to the partner, and c) the responsibility that is vital in any open relationship (Marcus, 1992). The counselor can work with the client around safer sexual practices. If that does not change the behavior, the counselor explains the procedure to be taken for protecting the unknowing potential victim. This is the last precautionary step in the attempt to change behaviors before breaking confidentiality (Herlihy & Corey, 1996).

Zeeland (1995) studied the use of drugs, and particularly alcohol, with many men who experiment in bisexual behavior. These men used alcohol and other drugs to help break down their own mental inhibitions for to engaging in same sex activity. The use of drugs (alcohol being the most common) increases the threat of contracting STDs since drug use often impairs the judgment of the user. Such men are more likely to try sexual activities which make them at a higher risk for contracting an STD. This enforces the tenet that the counselor must maintain open communication about the nature of the sexual activity. By so doing, the counselor can discuss the possible use of alcohol or other drugs coupled with sexual activity, and include dialogue about safer sex practices. Kain (1996) offered the strategy of focusing on helping clients develop skills in the area of safer sex activities. This strategy can be quite effective when working with adolescents who may have great anxiety about sexual orientation and who continually face peer influence on what behaviors are an acceptable part of sex.

CULTURAL CONSIDERATIONS

The bisexual person does not merely face issues of dealing with a label or not fitting into the **majority culture** group of people. Lesbian and gay people can be thought of as bicultural. Most grow up in heterosexual families and learn about heterosexuality as part of the developmental process (Schwartzberg & Rosenberg, 1998). "The societal oppression of lesbians and bisexual women attempts to coerce all women to participate in heterosexuality without question" (Shuster, 1992, p.149). In working with a minority client living in the majority culture, research indicates that counseling interventions can be developed more effectively after the level of stress related to racism has been explored with the client (Utsey, Ponterotto, Reynolds, & Cancelli, 2000).

The bisexual individual's ability to fluidly move from a heterosexual culture to an identification with gay people helps them reject negative messages from the heterosexual culture. These negative messages are often internalized, but will surface in life stories (Semmler & Williams, 2000). Numerous researchers (e.g., Ault, 1996; Isay, 1989; Kaufman & Raphael, 1996; Murphy, 1992; Sedgwick, 1985; Stokes & Miller, 1998) have identified an important component in wellness and **wholeness** for a bisexual person, which is dealing with the internalized negative feelings adopted from the barrage of negative messages against same sex activity by the dominant culture. In their work on the use of narrative therapy in multicultural counseling, Semmler and Williams (2000) discuss the power inherent in the dominant cultural systems. They distinguish how negative internal messages can shape a person's life and, subsequently, the personal power and growth one can gain as self-freedom from "cultural constraints on self-definition" begins to develop (Semmler & Williams, p. 53).

While the majority culture attempts to keep lesbian and gay activity quiet and hidden (Savin-Williams & Rodriguez, 1993; Sears, 1991; Zeeland, 1995), the bisexual individual can be invisible even among the lesbian and gay subculture (Schwartzberg & Rosenberg, 1998). Therefore, counselors working with bisexual clients have the responsibility to consider the bisexual person's background and social and work environments. Understanding ethnic and racial backgrounds is a powerful asset in helping a client who must consider family, friends, and community, when dealing with the unique issues connected to a bisexual identity (Gilbert & Scher, 1999). Because most counselors, it can be assumed, come from a heterosexual home environment, it can also be assumed they are unintentionally socialized into the ways of the dominate culture. Therefore, a counselor's lack of understanding of bisexuality, separate from heterosexuality or lesbians and gays, may cause the counselor to unwittingly discriminate against a bisexual person (Diller, 1999).

Shannon and Woods (1998) indicated that men in an ethnic subculture likely differ from men in the white culture in experience, attitudes and beliefs about same sex activity. An **African American male** engaging in sex with both men and women may not be comfortable with self-identifying as gay (Stokes & Miller, 1998), yet he is more likely than a European American man to label himself as bisexual (Monteiro & Fuqua, 1995). McKirnan and Stokes (1995) reported that black men have more female sexual partners than their white counterparts and are less likely to disclose bisexual activity to others. They concluded that the clandestine activity, coupled with having no connection with the gay community and its support group information on prevention measures, leads to a greater risk of HIV infection and transmission for African American men. When other oppressive forces, that is, lack of economic opportunity and racial discrimination, are combined with negative attitudes toward sexual activity, the African American bisexual man may not disclose yet another dimension of himself which would separate him from a supportive environment.

For the bisexual woman, an additional oppressive force might be a knowledge that her sexual activity would be a violation of societal expectations. If this woman is also a part of a patriarchal culture, she is likely to feel additionally oppressed (Browning, Reynolds, & Dworkin, 1998). A woman in this circumstance may have to choose between social interaction with the lesbian community or social interaction within her racial community. In the former, she may or may not be totally accepted and, in the latter, she may have to keep silent about same gender sexuality. This isolation lends to difficulty in finding potential sexual partners. It further leads to feelings of a lack of social support, and often loss of self-esteem (Browning et al., 1998; Gilbert & Scher, 1999). In his research, Sears (1991) wrote of receiving reports that African Americans are often more concerned with issues associated with race then with the gender of the sexual partner. He also pointed out that there are differing degrees of animosity toward same gender sexual activity amongst **African American communities** in his studies. These differences were based on the emphasis of religion in the family, the community mores and African history. Some participants reported that homophobia was rampant in African American life. He concluded, "Lesbians and gay men of color in this study often chose exile from either their homosexual feelings or their black communities" (p. 69). Utsey et al. (2000) found, ". . . gender differences existed regarding the types of coping strategies used by African Americans in their encounters with racial discrimination" (p. 78).

Chung and Katayama (1998) reported that the intensity of heterosexism and homophobia is stronger in Asian cultures than in the overarching culture of the United States of America. Any same sex activity is in conflict with traditional gender roles like family propagation for men and family caregiving for women. Since the family system is central to most **Asian** cultures (Atkinson & Hackett, 1998), the aberration of these roles brings at a minimum censorship for the bisexual, lesbian, or gay person. These data point to the counselor's need for understanding the bisexual Asian as an unique individual, who may not fit into the gay and lesbian community and who may not fit into the Asian American community. "A positive Asian-American lesbian or gay identity cannot be achieved without effectively dealing with one's double minority status" (Chung & Katayama, 1998, p. 23). This challenge for a positive identity is exacerbated until the counselor explores and determines if the Asian individual is comfortable with a bisexual identification. If the double minority status predominates counseling, the goal of counseling may then become the integration of ethnic and sexual identities with other identities important to the bisexual client.

For the **Latina or Latino** bisexual client, counseling may have to help clarify the three cultural communities which are an important part of emotional, social, and resource support (Morales, 1992). These cultures are as follows:

- The lesbian and gay community. This community provides freedom of sexual expression for the Latina or Latino client.

- The family history culture. This tradition-steeped culture provides a sense of security and responsibility for the client.
- The employment and education community. This community is the larger culture dominated by white heterosexuals. The support in this larger community depends upon the degree to which the Latin or Hispanic person has acculturated toward the mainstream. Underlying this acceptance in the community may be socioeconomic status, place of birth, language preferences, and the number of generations who have lived in the present country.

These factors are true across many diverse ethnicities and are an excellent preamble for the counselor's understanding more about a person's ethnic identity (Axelson, 1999; Morales, 1992). "Social class in particular is an important factor that influences Latina women's ability to redefine aspects of their gender role" (Gilbert & Scher, 1999, p. 21). A professional man or woman from a Latin background may find more opportunities for cultural separation and thus a greater availability for bisexual activities. Latina women who do not have financial freedom are reported to have more traditional attitudes about a woman's responsibility to her husband and her family (Gilbert & Scher, 1999).

The fact that **Native American** culture puts great emphasis on harmony (Baruth & Manning, 1999) is important when dealing with the bisexual Native American client. Just as religious conservative clients, regardless of the particular religion, are commonly taught that their sexuality is against a god, the Native American client may be concerned that bisexuality is against the **harmony of nature**. The extension of this concern is that the client does not know how she or he can fit into the traditional culture and still maintain alternative sexual outlets. Effective counseling with Native American clients involves quickly building trust and demonstrating appreciation for the acculturation level of the client (Garrett & Pichette, 2000). "By contrast, bicultural Native Americans are identified as having fewer personal, social, and academic difficulties because of their ability to effectively use a greater range in modes of social behavior and cultural communication that are appropriate in a variety of context and situations" (Garrett & Pichette, 2000, p. 7). Diller (1999) cited that full counselor awareness when working with a Native American client will probably mean the counselor is working with someone who either knows nothing about the culture of their ethnic group or who is bicultural.

Being both bicultural and being bisexual is still not an easy combination for the Native American client. Learning how the client's sexual identity fits or does not fit into a particular Native American culture is the first step. The counselor's responsibility is to both learn about the native culture and build an immediate groundwork of trust. If these crucial elements are not realized , the chances of a second counseling session are doubtful (Baruth & Manning, 2000). The counselor must explore with the Native American client how specific sexuality is perceived by elders and other people of importance in the tribal community. In doing this, it is essential for the counselor to support the client's need for privacy about sexual issues. A balance can be established between identifying supportive people in the client's life and recognizing situations which might exacerbate negative feelings. The responsible non-Native counselor will institute connections and resources in the Native American community (Diller, 1999). A second strategy in counseling is to present multicultural issues surrounding alternative sexuality. The Native American client is thus assured that bisexuality is not just pertinent to white culture and, therefore, is not perceived as antithetical to the Native American culture.

The counselor working with Native American youth has a higher degree of responsibility in working with clients in the area of sexuality. The suicide rate among gay and lesbian youth is three times that of their peers (McFarland, 1998). Other statistics show Native Americans having the highest suicide rate among a variety of North American people groups (Garrett & Pichette, 2000). The counselor working with Native American youth has reason for concern. A positive characteristic of Native American people is their demonstrated ability to cope with conditions of injustice. Affirmative counseling can build upon the individual's coping skills and upon the values of the culture and community. This approach gives the counselor an opening to address the issues presented in the counseling experience (Baruth & Manning, 1999; Diller, 1999).

Four cultural groups have been referenced above, although these presentations of each group has been cursory. The underlying principle of the presentation has been to illustrate how each group can bring into the counseling setting distinctive cultural characteristics regarding issues related to bisexuality. The intent is to bring consciousness and recognition that various racial and ethnic groups have special circumstances connected to being a bisexual person who is not part of the dominate culture.

SUMMARY

Effective counseling with the bisexual client is:

- Intentionally affirming.
- Sensitive to cultural, ethnic, and socioeconomic diversity.
- Open to learning client definitions of sexuality.
- Providing a societally safe environment where a client can openly explore all aspects of self and sexuality.

Awareness of gender issues connected to social and sexual expectations leads a client to understand sex-role constraints, expectations, and internalized cultural messages. The counselor is a critical component in the helping relationship for a bisexual person. The responsibilities and challenges which face the counselor have been presented to help counselors understand gender differences, variations on definitions around sexual identity, and the relationship of these elements to the individual's culture and to significant clinical details.

A counselor's values around sexual monogamy can also have repercussions without an ongoing awareness of the issue. Does the counselor hold different values for those who have the legal sanction of marriage versus lesbian and gay couples who are only beginning to obtain these legal rights? While working with the bisexual client, the counselor should utilize supervision or peer consultation to explore her or his own history regarding monogamy or open relationships. The counselor should examine personal views on marital privileges for same sex relationships. Additionally, religious opposition to homosexuality or the counselor's personal political views should be examined.

A primary consideration for counselors who may have bisexual clients is the degree of comfort in dealing with human sexuality. Counselor issues regarding a failed marriage, sexual abuse, impotence, or sexual desire, among others, can bring out elements of judgment when working with a client who is presenting on related topics. The counselor need not have worked through each factor in his or her own life to be helpful for a client. The counselor must maintain an awareness that her or his experiences could be an agent in what focus the counseling sessions are taking. It is the focus on the individuality of the bisexual client, coupled with the self awareness of the counselor, that is paramount to a counselor's work as a helper.

REFERENCES

Arbaugh, T, Jr. (1994). *Dancing with the dark side: A qualitative study of the life reports of men who have experienced sexual abuse.* Unpublished doctoral dissertation, Ohio University.

Axelson, J. A. (1999). *Counseling and development in a multicultural society* (3rd ed.). Pacific Grove, CA: Brooks/Cole.

Atkinson, D. R., & Hackett, G. (Eds.). (1998). *Counseling diverse populations* (2nd ed.). Boston: McGraw-Hill.

Ault, A. (1996). Ambiguous identity in an unambiguous sex/gender structure: A case of bisexual women. *Sociological Quarterly, 37,* 449-464.

Baruth, L. G., & Manning, L. (1999). *Multicultural counseling and psychotherapy: A lifespan perspective* (2nd ed.). Columbus, OH: Merrill.

Berger, R. (1996). *Gay and gray: The older homosexual man* (2nd ed.). New York: Haworth Press.

Black, J., & Underwood, J. (1998). Young, female, and gay: Lesbian students and the school environment. *Professional School Counseling, 1,* 15-20.

Blumenfeld, W. J. (1995). Gay/straight alliances: Transforming pain to pride. In G. Unks (Ed.), *The gay teen: Educational practice and theory for lesbian, gay and bisexual adolescents* (pp. 211-224). London: Routledge.

Browning, C., Reynolds, A. L., & Dworkin, S. H. (1998). Affirmative psychotherapy for lesbian women. In D. R. Atkinson & G. Hackett (Eds.), *Counseling diverse populations* (2nd ed.) (pp. 317-334). Boston: McGraw-Hill.

Cantarella, E. (1992). *Bisexuality in the ancient world.* London: Yale University Press.

Carl, D. (1990). *Counseling same-sex couples.* New York: W. W. Norton.

Chandler, C. K., Holden, J. M., & Kolander, C. A. (1992). Counseling for spiritual wellness: Theory and Practice. *Journal of Counseling and Development, 71,* 168-175.

Chung, Y. B., & Katayama, M. (1998). Ethnic and sexual identity development of Asian-American lesbian and gay adolescents. *Professional School Counseling, 1,* 21-25.

Cooley, J. J. (1998). Gay and lesbian adolescents: Presenting problems and the counselor's role. *Professional School Counseling, 1,* 30-34.

Diller, J. V. (1999). *Cultural diversity: A primer for the human services.* Belmont, CA: Wadsworth.

Faiver, C. M., O'Brien, E. M., & Ingersoll, R. E. (2000). Religion, guilt, and mental health. *Journal of Counseling and Development, 78,* 155-161.

Fontaine, J. H. (1998). Evidencing a need: School counselors' experiences with gay and lesbian students. *Professional School Counseling, 1,* 8-14.

Garrett, M. T., & Pichette, E. F. (2000). Red as an apple: Native American acculturation and counseling with or without reservation. *Journal of Counseling and Development, 78,* 3-13.

Gibian, R. (1992). Refusing certainty: Toward a bisexuality of wholeness. In E. R. Wise (Ed.), *Closer to home: Bisexuality and feminism* (pp. 3-25). Toronto: Seal Press.

Gilbert, L. A., & Scher, M. (1999). *Gender and sex in counseling and psychotherapy.* Needham Heights, MA: Allyn & Bacon.

Gutierrez, F. J. (1992). Eros, the aging years: Counseling older gay men. In S. H. Dworkin, & F. J. Gutierrez (Eds.), *Counseling gay men and lesbians: Journey to the end of the rainbow* (pp. 49-60). Alexandria, VA: American Counseling Association.

Herlihy, B., & Corey, G. (Eds.). (1996). *ACA ethical standards casebook* (5th ed.). Alexandria, VA: American Counseling Association.

Isay, R. A. (1989). *Being homosexual: Gay men and their development.* New York: Avon Books.

Isensee, R. (1990). *Love between men: Enhancing intimacy and keeping your relationship alive.* Los Angles: Alyson.

Isensee, R. (1991). *Growing up gay in a dysfunctional family: A guide for gay men reclaiming their lives.* New York: Simon & Schuster.

Kain, C. D. (1996). *Positive HIV affirmative counseling.* Alexandria, VA: American Counseling Association.

Kaufman, G., & Raphael, L. (1996). *Coming out of shame: Transforming gay and lesbian lives.* New York: Doubleday.

King, B. R. (1997). Challenging the traditional paradigm: Bisexuality as a catalyst [Review of the book Bisexuality: The psychology and politics of an invisible minority]. *Journal of Sex Research, 34,* 421-423.

Marcus, E. (1992). *The male couple's guide: Finding a man, making a home, building a life* (Rev. ed.). New York: HarperCollins.

Marinoble, R. M. (1998). Homosexuality: A blind spot in the school mirror. *Professional School Counseling, 1,* 4-7.

Mastoon, A. (1997). *The shared heart: Portraits and stories celebrating lesbian, gay, and bisexual young people.* New York: William Morrow and Company.

McFarland, W. P. (1998). Gay, lesbian, and bisexual student suicide. *Professional School Counseling, 1,* 26-29.

McKirnan, D. J., & Stokes, J. P. (1995). Bisexually active men: Social characteristics and sexual behavior. *Journal of Sex Research, 32,* 65-77.

McNeill, J. J. (1995). *Freedom, glorious freedom: The spiritual journey to the fullness of life for gays, lesbians and everybody else.* Boston: Beacon.

McWilliams, P. (1993). *Ain't nobody's business if you do: The absurdity of consensual crimes in a free society.* Los Angeles: Prelude Press.

Miller, G. (1999). The development of the spiritual focus in counseling and counselor education. *Journal of Counseling and Development, 77,* 498-501.

Monteiro, K. P., & Fuqua, V. (1995). African-American gay youth; One form of manhood. In G. Unks (Ed.), *The gay teen: Educational practice and theory for lesbian, gay and bisexual adolescents* (pp. 159-187). London: Routledge.

Moore, T. (1998). *The soul of sex: Cultivating life as an act of love.* New York: Harper/Collins.

Morales, E. S. (1992). Counseling Latino gays and Latina lesbians. In S. H. Dworkin, & F. J. Gutierrez (Eds.), *Counseling gay men and lesbians: Journey to the end of the rainbow* (pp. 125-139). Alexandria,VA: American Counseling Association.

Morrow, S. L. (1998). Toward a new paradigm in psychology training and education. *Counseling Psychologist, 20,* 797-809.

Murphy, B. C. (1992). Counseling lesbian couples: Sexism, heterosexism, and homophobia. In S. H. Dworkin, & F. J. Gutierrez (Eds.), *Counseling gay men and lesbians: Journey to the end of the rainbow* (pp. 63-79). Alexandria,VA: American Counseling Association.

Penn, R. E. (1997). *The gay men's wellness guide: The national lesbian and gay health association's complete book of physical, emotional, and mental health and well-being for every gay male.* New York: Henry Holt & Company.

Reynolds, A. L., & Koski, M. J. (1995). Lesbian, gay, and bisexual teens and the school counselor: Building alliances. In G. Unks (Ed.), *The gay teen: Educational practice and theory for lesbian, gay and bisexual adolescents* (pp. 85-93). London: Routledge.

Rhoads, R. A. (1997). A subcultural study of gay and bisexual college males. *Journal of Higher Education, 68,* 460-482.

Savin-Williams, R. C. (1994). Verbal and physical abuse as stressors in the lives of lesbian, gay male, and bisexual youths: Associations with school problems, running away, substance abuse, prostitution, and suicide. *Journal of Consulting and Clinical Psychology, 62,* 261-269.

Savin-Williams, R. C., & Rodriguez, R. G. (1993). A developmental, clinical perspective on lesbian, gay male, and bisexual youths. In T. P. Gullotta, G. R. Adams, & R. Montemayor (Eds.), *Adolescent Sexuality* (pp. 77-101). Newbury Park: Sage.

Schwartzberg, S., & Rosenberg, L. G. (1998). Being gay and being male: Psychotherapy with gay and bisexual men. In W. S. Pollack, & R. F. Levant (Eds.), *New psychotherapy for men* (pp. 259-281). New York: John Wiley & Sons.

Sears, J. T. (1991). *Growing up gay in the south: Race, gender, and journeys of the spirit.* New York: Harrington Park Press.

Sedgwick, E. K. (1985). *Between men: English literature and homosexual desire.* New York: Columbia University Press.

Semmler, P. L., & Williams, C. B. (2000). Narrative therapy: A storied context for multicultural counseling. *Journal of Multicultural Counseling and Development, 28,* 51-62.

Shannon, J. W., & Woods, J. W. (1998). Affirmative psychotherapy for gay men. In D. R. Atkinson & G. Hackett (Eds.), *Counseling diverse populations* (2nd ed.) (pp. 335-352). Boston: McGraw-Hill.

Shuster, R. (1992). Bisexuality and the quest for principled loving. In E. R. Wise (Ed.), *Closer to home: Bisexuality and feminism* (pp. 147-154). Toronto: Seal Press.

Smiley, E. (1997). Counseling bisexual clients. *Journal of Mental Health Counseling, 19,* 373-382.

Stanard, R. B., Sandhu, D. S., & Painter, L. C. (2000). Assessment of spirituality in counseling. *Journal of Counseling and Development, 78,* 204-210.

Stokes, J. P., & Miller, R. L. (1998). Toward an understanding of behaviorally bisexual men: The influence of context and culture. *Canadian Journal of Human Sexuality, 7,* (2) 101-114.

Sullivan, A. (1996). *Virtually normal: An argument about homosexuality.* New York: Vintage.

Udis-Kessler, A. (1992). Notes on the Kinsey scale and other measures of sexuality. In E. R. Weise (Ed.), *Closer to home: Bisexuality and feminism* (pp. 311-318). Toronto: Seal Press.

Utsey, S. O., Ponterotto, J. G., Reynolds, A. L., & Cancelli, A. A. (2000). Racial discrimination, coping, life satisfaction, and self-esteem among African Americans. *Journal of Counseling and Development, 78,* 72-80.

Weise, E. R. (Ed.). (1992). *Closer to home: bisexuality and feminism.* Toronto: Seal Press.

Westgate, C. (1996). Spiritual wellness and depression. *Journal of Counseling and Development, 75,* 26-35.

Witmer, J. M., & Sweeney, T. J. (1992). A holistic model for wellness and prevention over the life span. *Journal of Counseling and Development, 17,* 140-148.

Wolf, T. J. (1992). Bisexuality: A counseling perspective. In S. H. Dworkin, & F. J. Gutierrez (Eds.), *Counseling gay men and lesbians. Journey to the end of the rainbow* (pp. 175-187). Alexandria, VA: American Counseling Association.

Young, M. E. (1998). *Learning the art of helping: Building blocks and techniques.* Columbus, OH: Merrill.

Zeeland, S. (1995). *Sailors and sexual identity: Crossing the line between "straight" and "gay" in the U.S. Navy.* New York: Haworth.

Chapter 7

LESBIAN SEXUALITY

Colleen R. Logan
University of Houston-Victoria

BACKGROUND

Like it or not, even in the age of political correctness, the idea of women having relationships or being sexual with each other is likely to evoke an uncomfortable maybe even titillating, visceral response from a significant number of people. And let's face it, mental health practitioners aren't immune to this response. In a recent survey, Nystrom (1997) found that of gay men and women who sought psychotherapy 45.6% indicated that they experienced situations where therapists refused to acknowledge or ignored their sexual orientation, attempted reparative therapy, or made derogatory statements regarding their sexual orientation. Why is there such a knee-jerk negative response to gays and lesbians and more importantly and germane to this chapter is how can mental health practitioners overcome this almost inevitable discomfort and work effectively with lesbian clients who are struggling with issues related to sexuality and intimacy?

Basically, the discomfort many people feel stems from the overwhelming effects of societal **homoprejudice** (Logan, 1996). All of us, including counselors, are taught from an early age that lesbians are immoral and disgusting and any sex they might have is not only perverted but also completely inferior to "normal" heterosexual coupling. To overcome this onslaught of negativity requires constant self-monitoring and analysis along with a steadfast commitment to refute the constant barrage of cultural stereotypes and negativity toward lesbians. This enormous task is particularly critical for mental health practitioners who are likely to encounter lesbians seeking not only effective counseling services, but also practitioners who are affirming and accepting of non-heterosexual sexuality. To begin the process of understanding this often maligned and often ignored population, it's important to define the term "lesbian" and then explore what constitutes lesbian sexuality.

What Is a Lesbian?

Who are lesbians? What images come to mind when you hear the word lesbian or picture yourself counseling a lesbian? Stereotypical cultural images of lesbians range from mysterious witches to emasculating bullies and masculine mommas to dykes on bikes and lesbian chic. Be prepared and willing to separate the folklore from the reality because lesbians represent all of these and none of these images. Lesbians are chefs, business executives, professors, separatists, earth mothers, electricians, women of color, old, young, and disabled. Lesbians play sports, wear make-up and skirts, have long hair and short hair, cut the lawn and lead Fortune 500 companies. They typically aren't men-haters and didn't become lesbian because they couldn't get a man. As a couple, one doesn't necessarily "play" the husband to the other's role as the "wife" and they don't all secretly want to become men. These stereotypical notions of masculinity and femininity sometimes referred to as "butch" and "femme" respectively, primarily reflect lesbian choices to expand restrictive gender boundaries as opposed to assigned roles in a relationship.

Many of the stereotypical images of lesbians are deeply entrenched in sexism, stemming from the erroneous notion that the mere existence of lesbianism is an act of resistance against men. Suffice it to say, lesbians are a diverse group of women-who-love-women, in need of affirmative and effective counseling services.

For the purposes of this chapter, lesbian is defined as a woman who self-identifies as a lesbian and is sexually, emotionally and spiritually attracted to other women. In fact, the term lesbian may also be used to describe women who have sexual fantasies or erotic feelings toward women or who are asexual or who are even intermittently involved sexually with men (Morris & Rothblum, 1999). However, the issues related to the sometimes incongruous relationship between sexual identity and sexual behavior are beyond the scope of this chapter and, therefore, the discussion and treatment recommendations that follow are primarily focused on women who self-identify as lesbian and who, indeed, have sex with other women.

What Constitutes Lesbian Sexuality?

What is lesbian sexuality and what makes it unique from any other form of sexuality and sexual expression? Loulan (1984) described lesbian sex as "anything two lesbians do together." Lesbian sexuality itself is unlimited and may include masturbation, tribadism or sexually rubbing together, oral sex, toys, vibrators and sado-maschochistic activities (Caster, 1993). According to Newman (1999), contrary to popular folklore lesbians love sex, all types of sex. Lesbians have sex with long-time partners, new lovers, groups of friends and sometimes they masturbate all by themselves. On occasion, lesbians will have long languorous sessions of heart-melting, soulful sex and other times lesbians have loud, sweaty sex that wakes the neighbors (Newman,1999). Women have been having sex with other women throughout history and across every society and culture. So, the question remains, is lesbian sex any different from any other type of sex or intimacy?

In a review of the available literature, Schreurs (1993) found that in general, lesbians meet the cultural stereotypes for all women, regardless of sexual orientation, in that they are indeed more interested in romance and relationships. In fact, lesbians are more similar to heterosexual women than gay men in terms of their preferences for emotional intimacy and monogamy. In general, lesbians reported that they were satisfied with their sex lives just as gay and heterosexual couples say they are. Furthermore, lesbians have a higher rate of orgasm than their heterosexual counterparts and the most common sexual behaviors with a partner include mutual masturbation, manual-genital and oral-genital stimulation. And just like heterosexual couples, lack of communication, conflicts about sex, and an unequal power balance lead to dissatisfaction with the relationship. On the surface, at least, it appears that lesbians are fairly similar to heterosexual women in terms of relationship preference and satisfaction.

The pervasive and popular perception of lesbian sex is that it is rather passionless and virtually non-existent in long-term relationships. Jokes and stereotypes often refer to the dreaded "lesbian bed death" referring to the loss of sexuality or lack of sex in long-term relationships between women. These jokes propagate the myth that lesbians don't have sex and lesbian relationships are destined to becoming desexualized, dispassionate, and that partnered lesbians should prepare themselves for becoming best friends with their lovers, no longer sexual and intimate with each other. Another myth regarding lesbian sex is that lesbians don't have hot, satisfying sex or "real" sex because they don't have a man. Yet as noted before, studies indicate that lesbians self-report that sex is intensely satisfying and usually orgasmic (Schreurs, 1993). Clearly, the jokes and stereotypes belie the reality of lesbian sexuality and eroticism. In so many ways, lesbian sex is no different from heterosexual sex or gay male sex. There are, however, a number of unique culturally mandated challenges that are associated with the expression of sexuality and intimacy between women, primarily the combined effects of sexism, heterosexism and homoprejudice.

Clearly, the combined effects of these cultural prohibitions can have a lethal effect on lesbian libido. Homoprejudice refers to the pervasive cultural negativity, stereotyping and oppression of lesbians and lesbian relationships. The impact of societal homoprejudice must not be underestimated. From a young age, lesbian youth are bombarded by cultural messages that they are sick, immoral and disgusting. According to Coleman (1990), the negative bias against sexual minorities is often more intense than that directed toward any other minority group. For example, according to the results of the first national survey of sexual minority youth, conducted by the Gay, Lesbian and Straight Educators Network (1999), 69% reported having experienced some type of verbal, physical and sexual harassment/assault while on school property. Ninety percent reported that they have been harassed verbally by negative remarks or derogatory name-calling such as dyke, sissy or queer. Most reported hearing these comments from other students while 30% heard them from faculty or other staff members. More than a third reported that no one ever intervened in these situations and if someone did intervene, it was usually another student and rarely a faculty or staff member. To put this in context, GLSEN estimates that sexual minority youth hear anti-gay epithets at least twenty-five times a day or every fourteen minutes. Over 50% of the respondents said they experienced some type of verbal abuse on a daily basis, however, less than 2/3 of the respondents felt comfortable reporting the incidents to a staff member.

Previous studies revealed that sexual minority youth are frequently the targets of physical threats and violence, such as objects thrown at them, being chased or spat on (Pilkington & D'Augelli,1995). Annually, one in every six sexual minority youth will be beaten up so badly that they will have to see a doctor (Bart, 1998; "Safe Schools," 1996). Other studies indicate that dual or triple sexual minorities are at an even greater risk for violence and abuse both at home and in the community (Hunter, 1992; Savin-Williams, 1994). Given these frightening statistics, it is no wonder lesbians are afraid to be who they are and engage in loving and sexual relationships with other women.

Heterosexism refers to the belief that heterosexuality is preferred and/or superior to homosexuality, and sexism refers to the systematic subordination of women to men, based on the belief that men are far superior to women (McClintock, 1996). From an early age, both lesbian and heterosexual women are taught that they are not supposed to be interested in sex or sexuality and above all else, they are not supposed to initiate sex because that is a man's role (Roth, 1985). Clearly, this prohibition against initiating sex can be a double-whammy for lesbians. For lesbians these messages against female sexuality are exacerbated by homoprejudice in that women aren't supposed to be sexually involved with other women. Therefore, therapeutic interventions should be focused on exploring the effects of internalized homoprejudice and other negative messages regarding female sexuality, as well as specific skills and techniques to enhance intimacy and sexuality (Ossana, 2000).

The essential purpose of this chapter is to provide an overview of the issues associated with counseling lesbians, such as adopting a positive lesbian identity and learning how to form and maintain healthy relationships as well as to offer techniques and strategies to help clients celebrate and fully integrate sex and intimacy into their lives. Counselors are first and foremost challenged to explore their own views and issues regarding sex and intimacy. Second, counselors are challenged to explore their own homoprejudice and biases against lesbians and lesbian sexuality. Finally, counselors are challenged to empower and affirm lesbian clients both as women and as lesbians, recognizing the multiple effects of homoprejudice, heterosexism and sexism while collaborating with clients to navigate and attain healthy sexuality.

CULTURAL CONSIDERATIONS

There are two popular yet divergent views about lesbian sex. One view maintains that it is highly satisfying, usually orgasmic, emotionally fulfilling and gratifying. The other view is that lesbians have low sexual desire, and female couples are destined to experience the dreaded "lesbian bed death" or decreased sexual desire. To some extent, the phenomenon of decreased desire does appear to be true for many lesbian couples. For example, in a survey of both heterosexual and homosexual couples, Blumstein and Schwartz (1983) found that only about one-third of lesbians in relationships of two years or longer had sex once a week or more and almost half of those sampled had sex once a month or even less frequently. Indeed, subsequent studies indicate that lesbians may indeed have sex less frequently than heterosexual couples or gay male couples, however, they appear to spend much more time in each sexual encounter (Ossana, 2000). Seemingly, lesbians in couple relationships are having far less sex than heterosexual or gay couples. One must question, however, how "sex" is defined, because sexual encounters for women are defined by activities other than penetration or both partners reaching orgasm. For example, lesbians seem to spend more time cuddling, passionate kissing and holding each other and consider this time spent together as a sexual encounter (Ossana, 2000).

Moreover, this notion of lesbian bed death or lack of sexual desire may actually be mitigated by society in that deep emotional bonds with other women are socially sanctioned as long as they are non-sexual (Berzon, 1990). Lesbian couples are doubly constrained in that women are taught to repress sexual desire, and sexual relationships between women are forbidden. Lesbian bed death or lack of sexual intimacy between women may simply be the result of culturally programmed sexual repression or inhibited desire and reluctance to initiate sex due to a fear of appearing sexually aggressive or immoral.

Furthermore, lack of sexual desire between women is likely to be the result of the mixed messages that lesbians are given about sexuality in our culture. Brown (2000) identified the media as a significant culprit in the desexualizing of lesbians. Soft-porn movies show scenes of women sexually pleasuring other women until a man enters the scene and provides the "ultimate" pleasure by having sexual intercourse with one or both of them. These images imply that genuine sexual pleasure between women is impossible without a man. Even if the women are using dildos for penetration, they are almost "joyfully" put aside when the "real thing" or a male penis comes on the scene, painfully illustrating the widely held myth of sexual inadequacy and inferiority of sex between women (Brown, 2000). According to Brown (2000), even our language is heterosexist in that sex between women is often referred to as fondling and caressing, while the term "sex" is almost always a euphemism for "the real thing" or heterosexual sex. Other images of lesbians in the media portray them as dangerous, over-sexual, man hating and needing to be tamed by a man such as the Sharon Stone character in *Basic Instinct or* the Catherine Deneuve character in *The Hunger* (Brown, 2000*)*. Still other images portray lesbians as asexual, egalitarian and painfully polite with neither partner initiating or having more sexual power than the other and any kind of penetration is strictly avoided as it is seen as suspicious, male-like, and negative. Needless to say when any or all of these cultural messages are taken together and internalized, they can manifest in shame, anxiety, guilt or the avoidance or repression of sexual desire. (Browning, Reynolds and Dworkin, 1991).

Lesbian women of color are further challenged by the complexities of managing triple minority memberships, a phenomenon Greene (1994) referred to as "triple jeaopardy." Lesbians of color must try to manage the dominant culture's racism, sexism and homoprejudice, as well as negativity from their own cultural group, a group that has traditionally provided validation and safety in a racist world. With few exceptions, most ethnic groups devalue or completely disregard lesbians and lesbian sexuality, leaving lesbians of color feeling more vulnerable and perhaps, even more reluctant to be visible and out to family and friends (Greene, 1994). Homosexuality is often seen as a White disease that is chosen or "caught," therefore, lesbians of color are looked on with shame because they are being disloyal to their ethnic backgrounds. Furthermore, rather than disrupt these important family and community alliances, many lesbians of color may choose to accept an informal "don't ask, don't tell" that allows families and communities to continue to embrace lesbian members without having to name or face the issue directly. Unfortunately, efforts to gain support and validation from the lesbian community are often met with prejudice and discrimination. Lesbians of color are often caught between the two communities, never truly feeling part of either group as each requires a diminishing of a critical aspect of identity. Feeling marginalized and alone can lead to an increased sense of vulnerability and self-hate leaving lesbians of color at high risk for mental stress and maladaptive coping skills.

Another cultural consideration is the impact of homoprejudice. Adopting a positive lesbian sexual identity in the face of society's onslaught of negativity and oppression is daunting and likely to have a profound effect on one's ability to be sexual and intimate with other woman. Society teaches all of us that lesbians and lesbian sexuality is immoral, disgusting and perverted, which can have a devastating effect on clients who are trying to come to terms with a non-heterosexual orientation. Common reactions to this cultural squelching of one's identity may include **hyper-heterosexuality,** engaging in a frenzy of heterosexual relationships in an effort to somehow disprove one's lesbianism, or allowing oneself to be involved with another woman, yet completely avoiding sex and intimacy in order to somehow legitimize the relationship.

Given societal oppression, issues of comfort with sexual orientation, level of visibility or degree of "outness" are important to consider when working with lesbian clients. Seemingly minor issues which heterosexual couples take for granted, such as the inability to be intimate in public or the lack of legal sanctioning of lesbian relationships, can have a profound effect on intimacy and sexual expression. For example, public displays of affection between lesbian partners are generally looked upon with disdain, and couples are either forced into unnatural contact-free public situations or resort to furtive hand-holding and signs of affection when seemingly no one is looking. This cultural mandate to hide one's affection for your same-sex partner surely and insidiously seeps into the bedroom, as it is difficult to switch back and forth between silence and shame and untethered sexual celebration.

In recent years, there has been a shift in the lesbian community toward a more open, sexual scene more akin to the gay men's culture (Ersterberg, 1996). Women-made pornography, magazines, go-go clubs and other more frank expressions of sexuality have challenged the previously held myths about the nature of lesbian sexuality. Younger lesbians appear to be much more comfortable with themselves sexually, more open with public displays of affection and other types of intimacy. Clearly, this new openness is a reflection of society's gradual and tentative shift in terms of more tolerant attitudes and perceptions of homosexuality as evidenced by the revolutionary decision by the state of Vermont in affording civil rights to same-sex couples.

DEVELOPMENTAL/DIAGNOSTIC FACTORS

Discomfort with Lesbian Identity

In a homoprejudiced society, adopting a positive lesbian self-identity in the face of assumed heterosexuality can be extremely challenging. There is some evidence, however, that this life-long task may be relatively easier for some women than for others. For example, many women believe they were born lesbian and they will always be lesbian. To these women, being lesbian is a fixed and unchanging characteristic. Other lesbians remember having difficulty shifting from an assumed heterosexual identity to a more authentic lesbian identity. At some point, they were aware of consciously considering the possibility to become involved with women, perhaps because of involvement with the women's movement or friendships with other lesbians. Being sexual with a woman felt right in a way that being with a man never did. All of a sudden it made sense why relationships with men never worked or were always unfulfilling, yet identifying as a lesbian still felt awkward and uncomfortable primarily due to the effects of internalized homoprejudice.

The process of adopting a positive lesbian identity is a relatively new concept because lesbians have traditionally been subsumed under the rubric of gays or gay men and not seen as a unique entity. Existing gay identity development models have been criticized for being stage sequential and linear in progression and based primarily on the retrospective accounts of white, middle-aged, gay males, failing to recognize the more fluid and relationship-oriented aspects of lesbian identity development. According to McCarn and Fassinger (1996) these models also fail to recognize the effects of dual and triple minority statuses such as African-American, female and lesbian and multiple oppressive environments. In response, the authors proposed a dual lesbian identity developmental model which tracks individual or personal identity development and relationship identity development or how one relates to the reference group. This new model of lesbian identity development was derived from existing models of gay and lesbian identity development and information gleaned from the gender, sociopolitical and diversity literature. Borrowed from the feminist literature are the notions of sexual repression and the tendency of women to develop and come out in the context of a relationship. Women face a struggle when trying to incorporate their sexual identity that men traditionally do not (i.e., women are taught that sexual desire is dangerous and inappropriate and furthermore, the object of their sexual desire, a woman, is inferior). Moreover, women tend to come out later in life in the context of a relationship as opposed to an independent process of articulating and acting on sexual desire or feelings.

According to McCarn and Fassinger (1996) in Stage I or the **Awareness Stage**, individually she becomes aware of her feelings of differentness; " I feel pulled toward women in ways I don't understand, " and on a group level, the individual first begins to recognize there are sexual orientations other than just heterosexual and may begin thinking, " I had no idea there were lesbian/gay people out there." In Stage II or the **Exploration Stage**, individually, she may experience strong feelings toward other women, which may or may not be erotic, given the social sanctioning of close friendships between women and start realizing that, "The way I feel makes me want to be sexual with other women." On a group level, the individual begins to actively pursue information about lesbians, however, is likely not to see herself as a lesbian and may even think that, " Getting to know gays and lesbians is scary and exciting." In Stage Three there is a **Deepening Commitment** to one's sexual desire for women, and she begins to develop sexual clarity and commitment to fulfillment as a sexual being. She begins to combine her sexual identity with who she is actually sexual with and begins the process of grieving the loss of heterosexuality by thinking, "I clearly feel more intimate sexually and emotionally with women than with men." On a group level in Stage three, she begins to deepen her commitment to the lesbian culture. She begins to actively reject heterosexual norms and parameters and places a higher level on lesbians as a group. She may even experience anger and frustration with societal oppression and homoprejudice and angrily acknowledge that, " Sometimes I have been mistreated because of my lesbianism." The fourth and final stage is the **Internalization or Integration Stage**. In this stage, she has internalized and accepted her identity as a lesbian by feeling that, "I am deeply fulfilled in my relationships with women." In terms of her relationship with lesbians as a group, she feels secure, fulfilled and able to maintain her lesbian identity across contexts and believes that, "I feel comfortable with my lesbianism no matter where or who I am with."

This model is useful for Counselors as they help facilitate the identity development process for lesbian women. Clearly, lesbians can be in different phases, on both an individual and a group level simultaneously. Moreover, different stages will effect sexuality and intimacy in different ways. For example, in Stage I, she may be in a relationship with another woman, yet denying of her erotic feelings toward women or she may be in Stage II, and vacillate between her feelings toward women and the cultural mandate to be heterosexual.

Discomfort with one's lesbian identity may manifest in rigid love-making patterns, such as only being the aggressor rather than the receiver of sexual intimacy or even fear of being touched and discomfort with certain sexual acts such as oral sex or penetration. Clearly, the process of adopting a positive lesbian identity in a homoprejudiced society where heterosexuality is the norm is difficult and often overwhelming.

Counselors must be cognizant that some women who are trying to cope with the prospect of accepting their lesbianism and moving through the various stages of the coming out process may exhibit sexual dissatisfaction or dysfunction, hypersexuality, emotional upheaval, depression, stress, anger and even rage. It is important to normalize the sexual identity process and help the client move through the various stages, validating her feelings and experiences.

Fusion

Relationships between women tend to be emotionally intense and tightly entwined. In fact, as noted before, this type of intense "friendship" is sanctioned by society whereas sexual relationships between women are prohibited. This type of close relationship is often described as fused, a term that has traditionally been used to signify an unhealthy relationship, one that it is overburdened with emotion and lacking clear boundaries (Nichols & Schwartz, 1998). Fusion reflects a state of merging together, an intense emotional connection that causes the individual to lose sense of her separate self. Moving away from pejorative descriptions, Ossana (2000) defined fusion as a relationship in which the boundaries between female partners are blurred and a premium is placed on emotional intimacy and togetherness. In fact, emotional intimacy and togetherness between two women can be a source of strength because it fosters deep trust and a sense of safety and allows the couple to meet the challenge of ongoing homoprejudice and oppression. Fusion or merger is a problem only when it's too high or too low (Slater, 1995).

Too much fusion occurs when the individual begins to lose a sense of her separate self, and partners become merged to the point where they begin to limit contact with the outside world. It is at this point that sexual intimacy and physical connection feels much too threatening because all other aspects of life are merged. Infrequent sexual contact may actually be a strategy for obtaining a boundary or a sense of separateness when there's too much emotional intimacy and togetherness (Hall, 1984). Overinvolvement, and overemphasis on harmony and relational equality may inhibit direct expression of the individual's wants or needs. When overly fused, even seemingly small differences between partners can feel extremely threatening. Differences may feel like a threat to the emotional cocoon of the relationship and, therefore, should be avoided at all costs. Differences may occur in terms of identity development, level of outness, different sexual expectations and needs. It is helpful to validate differences and put them in perspective, that is differences are just that, differences.

Sexual Abuse

The high incidence of sexual trauma and incest against women can also serve as an obstruction to sex and intimacy. According to a survey conducted by Loulan (1987) 38% of lesbians have experienced sexual abuse by a family member or stranger before the age of 18.

And, although this high percentage is similar to the rates of sexual abuse in heterosexual women, there is a high probability in lesbian couples that not just one partner but both partners have experienced sexual abuse (Brown, 1995). Needless to say, the impact can have a devastating effect on intimacy and sexuality. For example, each partner may be at different stages of recovery or have different needs. One or both may experience flashbacks of the abuse during sex or avoid sex altogether which may anger, or frustrate or even trigger a flashback for her partner (Browning et al., 1991). Counselors must be prepared to address the myriad effects of sexual abuse and assist, both partners as they begin to negotiate the life-long process of recovery.

Substance Abuse

Research (e.g., Bux, 1996) indicates that lesbians tend to drink more than their heterosexual counterparts. Reasons for this phenomenon may include the effects of homoprejudice and the tendency of the overall gay community to socialize in bars or club settings. Many lesbians may find themselves abusing drugs and alcohol as way to numb the feelings of guilt and shame associated with having a different sexual orientation.

In the process of recovery, lesbians may be uniquely challenged by the following issues (Browning et., al., 1991):

1. Many lesbians in recovery struggle with the decision of whether or not to come out to potentially hostile and prejudiced staff in a chemical dependency treatment program. On the other hand, remaining hidden and closeted fuels shame and guilt and inhibits the recovery process. Be aware that there are a number of treatment facilities available nation-wide specifically designed to meet the needs of recovering sexual minorities.
2. Another consideration is the extent to which her partner or social support network will be involved in her recovery process. Given that lesbians are more likely to operate in a relational context, partner and peer support may be critical to her success.
3. Many lesbians in recovery find it difficult to accept the traditional male-dominated AA models and, therefore, never connect with an important source of support. Counselors can help lesbian clients in recovery locate meetings which are specifically for women or even meetings that are specifically designed for the overall gay community.

Domestic Violence

Traditionally, there has been a sense of reluctance to even admit that domestic violence between lesbians occurs. It somehow goes against how we perceive women and how we perceive lesbian relationships as happy, healthy, and violence-free (Coleman, 1996). Surprisingly, it appears that the prevalence and severity of domestic violence between women is comparable to those of heterosexual relationships. However, it is rarely talked about or even reported and, therefore, it is still not taken very seriously by the mental health system. Domestic violence between women is characterized by the need to dominate and control and likely develops from an overall sense of powerlessness fueled by homoprejudice, sexism, social isolation, and low self-esteem. Just like heterosexual relationships, abuse between women can take the form of verbal abuse, sexual coercion and physical violence (Peplau,Veniegas & Campbell, 1996).

When seeking help, lesbians may encounter at least four significant challenges (Browning, et al., 1991). The first, and perhaps the most formidable, challenge is the culturally pervasive denial that domestic violence occurs between women. Second, the victim may have trouble identifying battering as abuse because she may have reacted violently in self-defense and, therefore, she may inaccurately perceive violence as mutual aggression. A third challenge is the resistance to report incidents of domestic violence due to a perceived lack of sensitivity and understanding by service providers. The fourth and final reason is the resistance of women's shelters to deal with domestic violence between women openly and sensitively.

COUNSELING AND TREATMENT STRATEGIES

Explore Effects of Homoprejudice

First and foremost, counselors are challenged to explore and address their own internalized homoprejudice. Counselors need to conduct an active and ongoing exploration and excavation of culturally ingrained and inaccurate stereotypes and biases toward lesbians. In addition, counselors need to explore their own internalized attitudes and beliefs about lesbian sexuality and intimacy. To enhance this process the following books may be useful to both counselors and clients:

Lesbian Sex by JoAnn Loulan
Lesbian Passion; Loving Ourselves and Each Other by JoAnn Loulan
The Lesbian Sex Book by Wendy Castor
The Whole Lesbian Sex Book by Felice Newman
Sapphistry: The Book of Lesbian Sexuality by Pat Califia

Normalize Lesbian Sexuality

The onus is on the counselor to normalize lesbianism and lesbian sexuality. To empower lesbian clients be prepared to provide accurate information and address the myths associated with female sexuality. To augment this process, counselors are encouraged to gain an understanding and appreciation for the feminist movement. Have a list of feminist books and other materials available in your waiting room and on your bookshelves. Be aware of resources in the community such as women's support groups and networks. Become familiar and comfortable with lesbian sexuality and its expression. In addition, be familiar and ready to address the multiple effects of sexual abuse and trauma.

Facilitate the Coming Out Process

It is important that mental health practitioners understand and appreciate how difficult it is to adopt a positive lesbian self-identity. Denying one's sexual orientation and same-sex attractions can have a devastating effect on one's sexuality. Some clients will have trouble self-identifying as lesbian, while others will have trouble labeling themselves as gay or even non-heterosexual. Remember, adopting a lesbian identity is a difficult and often complex process; avoid prematurely imposing labels and allow the client to self-identify and label herself. At the same time, provide accurate and affirmative information regarding homosexual, bisexual and heterosexual sexual orientations.

As noted earlier in the chapter, the McCarn and Fassinger (1996) lesbian identity development model is a useful tool that can help counselors and their lesbian clients understand the different stages of the coming out process. Introduce the model and have the client identify her stage both on an individual level and in reference to the overall gay and lesbian community. Encourage the client to explore her evolution specifically addressing when she first became aware of her feelings of attraction toward other women, identify and explore her current feelings and then, have her visualize where she would like to see herself in the next five to ten years. This model is also helpful when working with lesbian couples who are at different stages of the identity development process. Have each partner identify what stage she feels she is at and facilitate an open and honest dialogue about the challenges associated with being at different stages and different levels of comfort.

The **Klein Sexual Orientation Grid** (Klein, Sepekoff & Wolf, 1985) is a useful tool to help clients explore the different aspects of sexual identity and sexual behavior because it looks at the elements of sexual identity and attraction across seven factors including: 1. Sexual attraction. 2. Sexual behavior. 3. Sexual fantasies. 4. Emotional preference. 5. Social preference 6. Life-style, and 7. Self-identification or the way one self-identifies. In addition, the following set of questions may help guide the client's journey as she begins to discover her sexual identity:

Which gender(s) is prominent in her sexual fantasies? To which gender(s) does she find herself sexually attracted? With which gender does the client find herself falling in love? What are her emotional preferences? Which gender has the client had sexual experiences and what has been the quality of those experiences? And probably the most important question, how does the client self-identify? (Golden, 1994).

In addition, it may be helpful to have clients rate themselves and respond to the questions across time (i.e., according to how she felt or perceived herself in the past five years, currently and her vision of the future).

Empathically Address Fusion

When working with fused couples, it is important to teach lesbian clients that intimacy and autonomy can co-exist. In an empathic manner, teach clients that differences are just that, differences and not necessarily a threat to the relationship. Address differences in desire. Emphasize communication and understanding, as well as willingness to be flexible. Avoid pre-judging close lesbian relationships as unhealthy. Teach clients how to maintain autonomy while building togetherness. At the same time, be prepared to address the question of monogamy vs. non-monogamy. Avoid being trapped by the stereotype that women who love women are always monogamous—not true. The decision to be non-monogamous requires open communication and clear guidelines, such as sex with other partners is allowed as long as it's discussed or kept secret, not with mutual friends, only as a threesome or not at home or in the couple's bedroom, etc. (Clunis & Green, 2000).

Help clients build a vocabulary for sex and intimacy. Teach the partners how to give and receive sensual and sexual pleasure, and learn how to say what feels good and what doesn't.

Explore the effects of internalized homoprejudice. Examine the effects of sexism and heterosexism. Write down negative sexual messages and refute them with positive, counter statements. Encourage your clients to talk openly and honestly with each other; sexual intimacy is another way to communicate so if talking shuts down, so will sex.

Help your clients avoid getting stuck in roles where someone is *always* the initiator and the other is always passive---take turns initiating. Explore feelings and attitudes toward being the "sexual aggressor" –address negative self-talk and societal prohibitions. Have partners talk about their sexual fantasies and act them out. Encourage your clients to avoid saying "no" for unimportant reasons. If they don't have time or energy for a long, languorous session, teach them how to compromise or meet their lovers halfway or discover ways to satisfy a partner when one isn't as interested as the other. Teach clients to avoid using sex to punish or hurt their partners. If they're hurt or angry, risk talking about it and working it out. Teach your clients to have fun in the bedroom. Have them read erotica, masturbate or watch sexy movies. Encourage them to vary the places they have sex, like in the kitchen or the back seat of a car. Experiment with costumes, sex toys or a vibrator (Clunis & Green, 2000; Tessina, 2000).

Teach Lesbian Clients Dating Skills

Societal sanctioning of female same-sex friendships and relationships may push some clients to mate before they have had time to date and get to know potential partners. Encourage clients to attend community events where they are likely to meet other single women. Volunteering is another way to meet other women, as are sports or other group activities.

Be Culturally Sensitive

Seek to understand the effects of racism and sexism. Be willing to explore your myths and biases regarding lesbian women of color. What are your images? Stereotypes? Be sensitive to the realities of multiple oppressions. Be cognizant of the stressors lesbians of color face when grappling with the decision to "come out" to family and friends. Ethnic communities and the family unit, in particular, have traditionally provided a safe haven in a racist world. Coming out as a lesbian could threaten these important ties, leaving the client feeling alone and isolated from the community. And unfortunately, there is no guarantee that the overall lesbian community will accept and embrace lesbians of color (Greene, 1994). Be aware of your own cultural baggage. White therapists need to be cognizant of the effects of privilege and the potential to feel guilty for having membership in the dominant culture. Explore how these dynamics might have a detrimental effect on the counseling relationship.

As a counselor of color, avoid collusion or assuming that your clients of color share your feelings and attitudes as this assumption may be inaccurate and harmful to the therapeutic relationship.

Counseling Lesbians in Recovery

Be aware of lesbian-friendly AA programs and treatment facilities. Remember that substance abuse can be a symptom of internalized homoprejudice. Be willing to explore why the client is abusing alcohol or drugs and avoid prematurely labeling clients as chemically dependent.

Domestic Violence Does Occur

Recognize that domestic violence does occur in lesbian relationships. Be prepared to offer appropriate and affirming resources. Make sure you keep an up-to-date list of lesbian-friendly shelters and other sources of support. Avoid potential pitfalls such as minimizing battering or blaming the victim. Domestic violence between women does occur and counselors must be prepared to take immediate and empathic action.

Address Sexual Abuse

Counselors must be prepared to address the myriad effects of sexual abuse and assist, perhaps both partners as they begin to negotiate the life-long process of recovery. Lesbian clients may believe their lesbian identity results from prior sexual abuse and will require accurate information about the prevalence of abuse among heterosexual women, affirming that sexual orientation is an attraction to women not a rejection of men (Browning et al., 1991).

The high incidence of sexual trauma and incest against women can also serve as a double whammy against a lesbian couple (Browning et al., 1991). Counselors must be prepared to address the myriad effects of sexual abuse and assist, perhaps both partners as they begin to negotiate the life long process of recovery. Issues to address may include the fear and shame associated with disclosure, personal safety and trust. Incest survivors often have trouble feeling emotionally safe with their partners and, as a result, may vacillate between feeling and wanting closeness and trying to place distance between them. The recovery process requires patience and understanding, as well as clear personal boundaries. For example, while working on abuse issues, the client may not want to be sexual with her partner. This can be hurtful and confusing to her partner and will require open communication and willingness to negotiate other ways to be intimate, such as romantic dinners, non-sexual massages or love notes (Clunis & Green, 2000). It is important to remind both partners that this process is about healing the past and not reflective of feelings toward each other or commitment to the current relationship.

CASE STUDY

Denise was a thirty-three year-old professional woman who had been to therapist after therapist but never felt completely comfortable with anyone. She attributed these feelings of discomfort to her own fear and lack of trust, as she had never been willing to reveal to her therapists that she was a lesbian. She was so afraid of being judged or hated because she had relationships with other women that she never shared this aspect of her life with her counselors and, therefore, counseling had been limited and unproductive. Moreover, several counselors had made disparaging remarks about gays and lesbians and that only confirmed Denise's fears about coming out in a counseling relationship.

Denise had grown up on a farm in the Midwest as the only girl out of five children. The kids were forced to work on the farm as soon as they were old enough and life revolved around school and work, work and school. Both of Denise's parents were alcoholics. Once the chores were done for the day, both parents started drinking until they fell into bed and passed out. Most nights were filled with loud arguments and slamming doors, and the kids learned to stay out of the way—especially Denise. It was her job to try and keep the peace, keep everyone happy, be a good girl and not make any trouble. She was being such a good girl, making sure not to upset anyone, and trying not to make anyone mad, that she never told anyone that her uncle was sexually abusing her on a regular basis. Denise had been working on dealing with the effects of the abuse for several years now. She had begun to accept that the abuse was not her fault, but was still struggling to find her voice and learning how to draw healthy boundaries.

Over and over in her life there were situations where Denise would just not assert herself. This was true in business, in relationships and with her family. For example, it took her years to come out to her family as a lesbian, even though she had known since she was a little girl. Unfortunately, they didn't handle her revelation about her sexual orientation very well. To this day, they firmly believed that the abuse had made her queer and that if she just found the right man she would give up this crazy, man-hating, lesbian phase. "And you know," Denise would say, "I really have tried to please them and make myself straight for them—I dated man after man after man, and nothing ever worked. I am a lesbian and that's that and believe me, my uncle didn't make me that way, in fact, I believe I was born this way." Denise was so tired of always trying to please everyone. She didn't know how to say no and she didn't know how to deal with her emotions, especially her anger. For example, her current relationship has been fraught with conflict. In fact, all they ever did was argue—well, actually, her partner would get angry and start yelling and Denise would just try to calm her down. Three years ago her partner had an affair and the relationship has been on the brink of ending ever since.

The tenuous situation with her partner had been absolutely devastating for Denise. Her partner was the love of her life, and Denise wasn't going to give up without a fight. She knew there had been problems in the relationship but never in a million years would she have thought her partner would have an affair. Although in retrospect, one of their biggest areas of conflict had been the bedroom. Over the years, they had just stopped having sex. They never talked about it, it just happened. Denise described herself as very sexual, and she didn't understand why they weren't having sex anymore. " I mean, you should have seen us at the beginning of the relationship, we barely came up for air and water and, then, over the years, it happened—the dreaded lesbian bed death." Denise laughed when she said this, although her eyes welled up with tears and she started to sob. " I don't want to lose her, what can I do?" Denise stated that she and her partner wanted to come to couples counseling, but she also knew she had lots of work to do on her own. Intuitively, she realized that she was smothering her partner but she was just so afraid of losing her.

Kelly, Denise's partner, felt overwhelmed by Denise. She felt that they had become one and she had lost herself somewhere along the way. "People don't even refer to us as individuals anymore, we're just one long name—KellyandDenise—I feel like I'm suffocating." Kelly shared that she wanted more alone time and time away from Denise to spend with her own friends. As for sex, Kelly said she always felt pressured by Denise, it felt like Denise was always asking for sex at the wrong time. She never just let it "naturally unfold." Requests for time apart felt very threatening to Denise and, in fact, Kelly's desire to spend time away felt like she was being punished, like she was being abandoned. In addition, Kelly liked to be vaginally penetrated but was afraid to admit it to Denise because she didn't want to be disloyal or hurtful, afraid that her partner would think she wanted a man or that penetration would bring up the ghosts of Denise's history with sexual abuse.

Counseling and Treatment Strategies

When the counselor first started working with Denise, she spent time exploring validating her sexual orientation and addressing all the myths and stereotypes about lesbians, particularly the one about incest turning girls into man-hating lesbians. She was also concerned that Denise might not trust her because she was heterosexual, given her prior experiences with less than understanding and non-empathic therapists. One day, Denise pointed to the picture on her desk and asked if that was her husband and her kids and her counselor answered yes. The counselor asked if that would be a problem for Denise, and she answered, "No," because for the first time she felt comfortable with who she was and she appreciated that the counselor was supportive and affirming of her sexual orientation.

The counselor worked hard with Denise to help her establish boundaries and learn how to assert herself with others. Part of this work required cognitive re-framing and refuting of internal negative messages. For example, saying no was okay, it didn't mean she was a bad person and asking for what she needed was not selfish or indifferent to others. She also worked with Denise to help her learn how to appropriately express her anger. Based on her parent's behavior, Denise had such a skewed view of anger, all she knew was drunken rage. The counselor spent a great deal of time working with Denise to help her to first identify feelings of anger and then express those feelings in appropriate ways.

In addition, to help Denise as she recovered from the effects of sexual abuse, the counselor encouraged her to attend a female incest survivors support group. She also provided her with a list of books designed to help her develop a sense of self and a self in relation to others.

Couples sessions with Denise and Kelly quickly illuminated some of the reasons for the lack of sexual intimacy. Fortunately, the therapist was comfortable with her own sexuality and not at all uncomfortable when lesbian clients talked about sex or sex practices during counseling sessions. First, the therapist normalized Kelly's desire to be penetrated, regardless of her sexual orientation and then helped facilitate the discussion with Denise regarding her feelings and desires. Her therapist also referred the couple to a feminist-owned sex-toy store and encouraged them to explore the possibilities of incorporating non-representational dildos into their lovemaking. In addition, the therapist encouraged Denise to share her concerns and fears about penetration, teaching both partners to respect each other's desires and openly communicate during lovemaking. The therapist validated and normalized Kelly's desires while honoring Denise's fears and discomfort with the idea of penetration,

In addition, the counselor helped Kelly and Denise begin to balance the need for autonomy and the need for togetherness. The counselor had encountered this difficulty before with her lesbian clients. Partners would become so enmeshed with each other that the individual felt lost and trapped. In fact, she remembered a former supervisor telling her that this was actually an inherent flaw in lesbian relationships, women would engulf each other and eventually have to break up in order to reestablish their own identity. She disagreed. This emotional connection and deep involvement with each other was actually a strength. In too large a dose, yes, it could be overwhelming. However, in moderation a closely knit relationship was a rich source of strength in an oppressive society that negated and discriminated against same-sex couples. In many cases, the bedroom would be the arena in which the struggle for autonomy would be acted out. To address this issue, the therapist would typically draw a Venn diagram, that is, two circles that overlap to varying degrees in order to illustrate the two separate individuals and their overlap as a couple. In addition, the therapist consistently affirmed Kelly and Denise as a couple and validated their commitment to the relationship at the same time. She encouraged each to have alone time and time when they weren't with each other. She also helped them work through the issues of sexual intimacy. One step was for Denise to stop pursuing Kelly and trust that Kelly would initiate sex. The therapist also helped them to communicate better about sex, to ask for what they wanted, to experiment and have fun.

SUMMARY

The purpose of this chapter was to provide a broad overview of the issues related to lesbians and lesbian sexuality, as well to provide suggestions and strategies for intervention. First and foremost, clinicians must not underestimate the combined impact of homoprejudice, heterosexism and sexism when working with lesbian clients. To be effective, therapists need to explore their own internalized homoprejudice and biases toward lesbians and lesbian sexuality. Given how misunderstood and often underserved this population can be, counselors are encouraged to remain current with the available literature, to serve as social activists and advocates for their lesbian clients and above all, to provide affirmative counseling to lesbian clients.

This said, unfortunately, there is a significant dearth in the literature regarding lesbian sexuality and sexual practices. For additional information and literature, one is well advised to access resources in the feminist community and the gay and lesbian community. In terms of future research, empirical studies need to be conducted on what exactly constitutes lesbian sex rather than simply relying on heterosexual and gay male paradigms as parameters for sexual encounters between women. In addition, the combined effects of sexism, heterosexism and homoprejudice must be examined in terms of their effects on lesbian sexual and intimacy practices. And, finally, process and outcome studies need to be performed in order to understand the both the short and long-term effects of affirmative individual, couple and group therapies on lesbian sexuality and intimacy.

REFERENCES

Bart, M. (1998, September). Creating a safer school for gay students. *Counseling Today*, p.26-39.

Berzon, B. (1990). *Permanent partners: Building gay and lesbian relationships that last.* New York: Plume.

Blumstein, P., & Schwartz, P. (1983). *American couples: Money,work and sex.*New York: Morrow.

Brown, L. S. (1995). Therapy with same-sex couples: An introduction. In N.S. Jacobson, & A.S Gurman (Eds.), *Clinical handbook of couples therapy* (pp.274-291). New York: Guilford Press.

Brown, L. S. (2000). Dangerousness, impotence, silence, and invisibility: Heterosexism in the construction of women's sexuality. In C.B. Travis, & J.W. White (Eds.), *Sexuality, society, and feminism* (pp. 273-297). Washington, D.C.: American Psychological Association Press.

Browning, C., Reynolds, A. L., & Dworkin, S. H. (1991). Affirmative psychotherapy for lesbian women. *The Counseling Psychologist, 19*(2), 177-196.

Bux, D.A. (1996). The epidemiology of problem drinking in gay men and lesbians: A critical review. *Clinical Psychology Review,16*(4), 277-298.

Caster, W. (1993). *The lesbian sex book.* Los Angeles: Alyson Publications.

Coleman, D. (1990, July 10). Homophobia: Scientists find clues to its roots. *The New York Times*, pp. C1, C11.

Coleman, V. E. (1996). Lesbian battering:The relationship between personality and the perpetration of violence. In L. K. Hamberger, & C. Renzetti (Eds.), *Domestic partner abuse* (pp. 77-102). New York, NY: Springer Publishing Company.

Clunis, D. M., & Green, G. D. (2000). *Lesbian couples: A guide to creating healthy relationships.* Seattle, WA: Seal Press.

Esterberg, K. G. (1996). Gay cultures, gay communities: The social organization of lesbians, gay men, and bisexuals. In R.C. Williams, & K.M. Cohen (Eds.), *The lives of lesbians, gays and bisexuals: Children to adults* (pp.377-393). Fort Worth: Harcourt Brace.

Gay, Lesbian, Straight Educators Network (1999). *First-of-its-kind school climate surveys lesbian, gay, bisexual, transgender students, showing pervasive harassment at school* Retrieved October 10, 1999 from http://www.glsen.org/pages/ sections/library/news/9909-241 article.

Greene, B. (1994). Lesbian women of color: Triple jeopardy. In L. Comas-Diaz, & B. Greene (Eds.), *Women of color: Integrating ethnic and gender identities in psychotherapy.* New York: Guilford Press.

Golden, C. (1994). Our politics and choices: The feminist movement and sexual orientation. In B. Greene, & G. M. Herek (Eds.), *Lesbian and gay psychology: Theory, research and clinical applications* (pp. 54-70). Thousand Oaks, CA: Sage.

Hall, M. (1984). Lesbians, limerence, and long-term relationships. In J. Loulan (Ed.), *Lesbian sex* (pp. 141-150.) New York: Spinsters.

Hunter, J. (1992). Violence against lesbian and gay male youths. In G.M. Herek, & K.T. Berill (Eds.), *Hate crimes: Confronting violence against lesbians and gay men* (pp. 297-316). Newbury Park, CA: Sage.

Klein, F., Sepekoff, B., &Wolf, T.J. (1985). Sexual orientation: A multi-variable dynamic process. *Journal of Homosexuality, 11*(1-2), 35-39.

Logan, C. (1996). Homophobia? No, homoprejudice. *Journal of Homosexuality, 31*(3), 31-53.

Loulan, J. (1984). *Lesbian sex.* San Francisco: Spinsters Ink.

Loulan, J. (1987). *Lesbian passion: Loving ourselves and each other.* San Francisco: Spinster press

McCarn, S. R., & Fassinger, R. E. (1996). Revisioning sexual minority identity formation: A new model of lesbian identity and its implications for counseling and research. *The Counseling Psychologist, 24*(3), 508-534.

McClintock, M. (1996). Lesbian baiting hurts all women. *In women's voices in experiential education* (EDRS Publication No. ED412 049, pp. 241-250). Washington, DC: U.S. Department of Education.

Morris, J. F., & Rothblum, E. D. (1999). Who fills out a "lesbian" questionnaire? The interrelationship of sexual orientation, years "out," disclosure of sexual oreintation, sexual experience with women, and participation in the lesbian community. *Psychology of Women Quarterly, 23,* 537-557.

Newman, F. (1999). *The whole lesbian sex book: A passionate guide for all of us.* San Francisco: Cleis Press, Inc.

Nichols, M. P., & Schwartz, R. C. (1998). *Family therapy: Concepts and methods.* Needham Heights, MA: Allyn and Bacon.

Nystrom, N. (1997). Oppression by mental health providers: A report by gay men and lesbians about their treatment (Doctoral dissertation, University of Washington, 1997). *Dissertation Abstracts International, 58,* p. 2394.

Ossana, S. M. (2000). Relationship and couples counseling. In R. M. Perez, K. A. Debord, & K. J. Bieschke (Eds*.), Handbook of counseling and therapy with lesbians, gays, and bisexuals* (pp.275-302). Washington, D.C.: American Psychological Association Press.

Peplau, L. A., Veniegas, R. C., & Campbell, S. M. (1996). Gay and lesbian relationships. In R. C. Williams, & K. M. Cohen (Eds.), *The lives of lesbians, gays and bisexuals: Children to adults* (pp.351-270). Fort Worth: Harcourt Brace.

Pilkington, N., & D'Augelli, A. R. (1995). Victimization of lesbian, gay and bisexual youth in community settings. *Journal of Community Psychology, 23,* 33-56.

Roth, S. (1985). Psychotherapy with lesbian couples: Individual issues, female socialization, and the social context. *Journal of Marital and Family Therapy, 11*(3), 273-286.

Safe Schools Coalition of Washington. (1996). *Safe schools anti-violence documentation: Third annual report.* Seattle,WA: Author

Savin-Williams, R. C. (1994). Verbal and physical abuse as stressors in the lives of lesbian, gay male and bisexual youths: Associations with school problems, running away, substance abuse, prostitution and suicide. *Journal of Consulting and Clinical Psychology, 62,* 261-269.

Schreurs, K. M. G. (1993). Sexuality in lesbian couples: The importance of gender. *Annual Review of Sex Research, 4,* 49-66.

Slater, S. (1995). *The lesbian family life cycle.* New York: Free Press.

Tessina, T. B. (2000, January). Fanning the flames. *Girlfriends, 6*(7), p. 29.

Chapter 8

Counseling Gay Men toward an Integrated Sexuality

Mark Pope
University of Missouri - St. Louis
Bob Barret
University of North Carolina

Background

Sexual behavior for all males in our society is an important issue and is subject to societal messages. "Male sexuality in our cultural view is shaped by the scripts boys are offered almost from birth, by the cultural lessons they learn throughout the life course, among them the belief in a sometimes overpowering male sex drive and the belief that men have immutable sexual needs that are manifested over and above individual attempts at repression" (Blumstein & Schwartz, 1990, p. 310). One does not have to look far to see the overt sexual messages that infuse every aspect of our culture. Desirable male images appear in all media as strong, aggressive, sexually skillful, athletic, and, above all, confident. Both heterosexual and homosexual men have to deal with these images, and undoubtedly both must struggle with their inability to embody all of those idealized masculine traits (Pollack, 1998). Depictions of masculinity are particularly visible within the gay male culture and include such hyper-masculine images like massive bodybuilders, men dressed in leather, men who have abundant sex, and even its opposite, men dressed in drag. Because most gay men must overcome the negative stereotype that they are effeminate and not "real" men, such strong male images can be particularly oppressive.

In this chapter we examine some of the complexities in understanding sexual orientation, the various terms that are common in this area, and, from a developmental perspective, gay male sexuality for adolescent, adult, and older gay males. We also address the implications for counseling, as well as present a case study with our analysis of this case.

COMPLEXITIES IN UNDERSTANDING SEXUAL ORIENTATION

The topic of sexual orientation is complex, evocative, and confusing. No one really knows yet how sexual orientation is determined. And, because conservative religious and political groups tend to view homosexuality as a moral issue, and others see it as a civil rights issue, it cannot be separated from either context: being gay has both political and religious implications. Finally, given the lack of definitive answers from scientific research, confusion and uncertainty tend to underlie the often intense discussions about the sexual behavior and mental health needs of gay men (Barret & Logan, 2001; Barret & Robinson, 2000).

The lack of strong scientific evidence about the etiology of homosexuality allows those on either side of the "nature vs. nurture" discussion to claim that their view is the "right" one. Research in human sexuality is complex and riddled with many challenges (Barret & Robinson, 2000). Most studies draw their findings from self-reports as opposed to objective observations or measurements, sample sizes are often small and not representative of the populations being studied, and many research participants volunteer for studies because they want to prove a particular point. It is only recently that genetic studies have appeared in research on homosexuality. LeVay (1991, 1999) reviewed the growing scientific data on the causes of sexual orientation. He found a few medical studies that clearly show a relationship between genetics/hormones and sexual orientation, and he surmised from this evidence that sexual orientation is determined rather than chosen. These studies point to differences in sizes of particular parts of the brain, ear lobes, and even thumbs when comparing gay subjects with those who identify as nongay.

On the other side is the "nurture" argument which is advanced by practitioners who believe that homosexuality is caused by environmental factors. The view that homosexuality is inherently pathological has its roots in the psychoanalytic community (Beiber, 1965; Socarides, 1968, 1973). Using studies drawn from their own patients who have sought treatment for homosexuality, those in this camp promote the notion that homosexuality emerges after birth in particular family structures. Their neo-Freudian analysis goes something like this: gay males were "feminized men" since they grew up in households that had strong, dominant mothers and weak, ineffective fathers. If they had grown up in families that had a "normal" constellation of strong, dominant fathers and weak, ineffective mothers, then the children would be heterosexually-oriented. Freedman (1971), Lewes (1988), and Isay (1989), respected members of the psychoanalytic community, have refuted this approach by showing that both gay men and non-gay men come from families that meet both descriptions.

Social attitudes toward homosexuality have also undergone many changes. From the acceptance and integration of same-sex persons into the native American tribes of North America (Roscoe, 1994), to the acceptance of same-sex unions by the Christian church in the middle ages (Boswell, 1995), to the persecution of homosexually-oriented persons under the Victorians (Rowse, 1977), to the enlightened approaches of pre-Nazi Germany (Hirschfeld, 1935), pre-Stalinist Russia (Thorstad, 1974), and imperial China (Ruan, 1991), and finally to the removal of homosexuality from the psychiatric manual of mental disorders (Bayer, 1981), history has seen an ebb and flow in the social acceptance of same-sex orientations.

Another issue that makes research on homosexuality complex is the rapidly changing nature of the gay experience. Studies conducted prior to 1990, reflect the gay male experience in a culture that no longer exists. Today gay men appear in virtually every aspect of daily life.

They are more out to their families and co-workers, visible in their neighborhoods, assertive in demanding equal rights, and have moved beyond the fear and shame that used to keep most of them invisible. This change is seen in all aspects of the media, gay-positive-statements from national and local political candidates and in the debates within virtually all Christian denominations about the role of gay men and lesbians within the church (Barret & Logan, 2001).

A similar public debate is occuring about the ability to change sexual orientation. Nicolosi (1991) described an approach called "reparative therapy" (RT). RT's claim is that sexual orientation (always from gay to straight, rather than the opposite) can be changed, which parallels another "treatment," "conversion therapy," hailed by conservative Christian groups as proof that prayer and meditation can "drive the sin out" and bring the "sick" homosexual back to health. As to queries regarding whether sexual orientation is open to change, Money (1990) stated:

> The concept of voluntary choice is as much in error (as applied to sexual orientation) as in its application to handedness or to native language. You do not choose your native language as a preference, even though you are born without it. You assimilate it into a brain pre-natally made ready to receive a native language from those who constitute your primate troop and who speak that language to you and listen to you when you speak it. Once assimilated through the ears into the brain, a native language becomes securely locked in -- as securely as if it has been phylogenetically preordained to be locked in pre-natally by a process of genetic pre-determinism or by the determinism of fetal hormonal or other brain chemistries. So also with sexual status or orientation, which, whatever its genesis, also may become assimilated and locked into the brain as mono sexually homosexual or heterosexual or as bisexually a mixture of both. *(pp. 43-44)*

Further, according to Coleman (1982),

> It is unethical and morally questionable to offer a 'cure' to homosexuals who request a change in their sexual orientation. While there have been reports that changes in behavior have occurred for individuals seeking treatment, it is questionable whether it is beneficial to change their behavior to something that is incongruent with their sexual orientation. *(p.87)*

Both RT and CT have received abundant attention and both have been soundly condemned by the American Counseling Association, the American Psychiatric Association, the American Psychological Association, the National Association of Social Workers, the National Association of School Psychologists, the American School Health Association, the American Federation of Teachers, the National Education Association, and the American Academy of Pediatrics. Mental health workers are warned that research indicates both of these "treatments" are more likely to be harmful than helpful. Many believe it is unethical for mental health professionals to practice CT or RT (Barret,1999; Just the Facts Coalition, 2000).

This debate (i.e., nature/nurture) is not explored in detail in this chapter. Rather, we make the assumption that the causes of sexual orientation are not known definitively, but that sexual orientation is not mutable. Likewise, we believe that the negative stereotype of gay men as effeminate, less functional, and inherently unhealthy individuals does not represent gay men in general.

DEFINITIONS

Prior to 1869, same sex attraction was a concept without terminology. "Homosexuality" was coined by K. M. Benkert, writing under the pseudonym "Kertbeny," in 1869 (Bullough, 1976). Others had proposed "homophilic" (falling in love with same sex) or "homogenic" (attracted to same sex). Supported by Havelock Ellis (1942) and Magnus Hirschfeld (1948), homosexuality became the correct and recognizable term.

Many homosexual men, uncomfortable with homosexual because it emphasizes the sexual nature of their identity, use the term "gay" to describe themselves. Money (1990) says that "falling in love" is the definitive criteron of sexual orientation. Any person can participate in a sexual act; however, a man falling in love with another man and wanting to spend the rest of their lives together is the definition of "gay." More recently, Thompson (1997, 1994) and others have promoted the understanding that being gay goes beyond erotic attraction to identifying with a particular culture that includes same sex love and relationships but also includes a literature, social expectations, and history. In brief, being gay is much more than simply having sexual attraction to persons of the same sex.

There is a tendency to subsume many aspects of gay sexual experience under one term, sexual orientation. Actually, in order to understand gay male sexuality one must examine sexual behavior, sexual identity, sexual orientation, and gender role (Barret, 1998). "Sexual orientation (heterosexual/bisexual/homosexual), the expression of gender role (masculine/feminine), and gender identity (an individual's self-identification as either male or female) are conceptually distinct phenomena" (Sanders, Reinisch, & McWhirter, 1990, p. xx). Sexual orientation is usually discovered as one begins to experience erotic attraction (Barret & Logan, 2001).

Sexual identity is a name that we give to ourselves. Most men identify as straight and have sex exclusively with females. Some men prefer sex with women but also have sex with men without seeing the latter behavior as indicative of their sexual identity. Some men label themselves as bisexual. Some men internally identify as gay but externally identify as straight. And, some men want everyone to know them as gay. Gender, unlike sexual identity, is defined by physiology. If you have a penis, you are male.

Sexual behavior is what people do. Sex is a mechanical process involving the stimulation of various parts of the anatomy. It is clearly possible for men and women to experience sexual satisfaction from both same and opposite sex partners, as well as by masturbation and the use of "sex toys." The range of human sexual behavior includes more common practices, as well as sadism, masochism, and other even more controversial practices.

Finally, it is important to underline that sexual orientation is not *determined* by sexual identity or even sexual behavior (Barret, 1998). Sexual orientation is a discovery that one makes about self. Generally this discovery comes about through the awareness of strong erotic attraction to a person of the same sex. It may be repressed, denied, hidden, selectively embraced, or pronounced to all. As noted above, it is not something that one chooses, an implication of the term sexual "preference." Sexual orientation appears to be a given. The challenge for both gay and straight people is to understand and express their sexual orientation in ways that build confidence, healthy relationships, and a sense of well-being.

CULTURAL CONSIDERATIONS

Gay males in American society, contrary to popular belief, come in many different sizes, colors, and economic classes. Gay male culture includes special groups which cross racial, ethnic, and other culture boundaries, such as Black and White Men Together (gay African American males), Men of All Colors Together, Pacific Friends (gay Asian males in USA), Trikone (gay South Asian males), Long Yang Clubs (gay Asian males around the world), Gay Asian Pacific Alliance, Lavendar Godzilla (gay Asian males in San Francisco), Gay & Lesbian Latinos Unidos (gay Latinos in Los Angeles), Rainbow Deaf Society (gay deaf men), Girth and Mirth Clubs (large gay men), and many others.

There are special considerations in counseling gay men that follow from variations in ethnicity, race, and other culture. For example, Pope and Chung (2000) discussed the cultural considerations in conducting psychotherapy with gay and lesbian Asian Americans.

> Gay and lesbian Asian and Pacific Islander Americans (APIAs) are by their nature a cultural hybrid -- the dominant Asian/Pacific Islander culture mixed with the dominant American culture stirred with the gay and lesbian cultures within both -- and this mixture produces a new and challenging task for those who would provide counseling and psychotherapy services for this group. To appreciate lesbian and gay APIAs, it is important to understand their cultural roots, the acculturation process of immigrants in a new land, and their social status as a variant from the modal sexual orientation (p. 233) Pope and Chung (2000) recommended that counselors look at the role of family, religion/philosophy, acculturation, and identity development in the lives of their gay Asian and Pacific Islander clients, as these four issues are what bind together all Asian cultures.

The primary cultural consideration in doing sexuality counseling with gay men from non-dominant cultures is to identify the stages associated with that individual's cultural identity development. Cultural identity development refers to all of the many cultures of which a person may be composed, including racial, ethnic, gender, socioeconomic status, geographic as well as sexual orientation. These data are crucial in designing an effective treatment plan. For example, if a gay man who is seeing you for relationship issues is at the identity confusion stage (Cass's [1979] stage 1, where previously accepted heterosexual identity is just beginning to be questioned) and you, as a helping professional, are treating him as if he is at the identity acceptance stage (Cass's stage 4, gay or lesbian identity is accepted, and selective disclosure to other is begun), you may recommend certain behavioral options which your client would strongly resist, such as wrongly assuming that the identified partner is male. A gay male client at the first stage is just beginning to explore a same-sex sexual orientation. More often than not, the major relationship issues at stage 1 are with opposite-sex partners.

DEVELOPMENTAL/DIAGNOSTIC ISSUES

Sexuality for gay men is a complicated area filled with issues their mother and father never discussed with them when they were growing up. In this section, the issues which will be discussed include: the cultural identity development process for gay men; how coming out to self is a developmental task important to conquer during adolescence; on disclosing sexual orientation to others; on conducting an "environmental homophobia assessment;" on passing as a straight man; on oppression and discrimination; on STDs and AIDS and their effects on the community; on homoprejudice and internalized homoprejudice; and legal issues.

"Coming Out": The Cultural Identity Development Process for Gays

"Coming out" has been defined by Altman (1971) as

> the whole process whereby a person comes to identify himself/herself as homosexual, and recognizes his/her position as part of a stigmatized and semi-hidden minority. . . . The development of a homosexual identity is a long process that usually begins during adolescence, though sometimes considerably later. Because of the fears and ignorance that surround our views of sex, children discover sexual feelings and behavior incompletely, and often accompanied by great pangs of guilt. . . . (Many of us) manage to hide into our twenties a full realization that (we are) not like (them). *(pp. 15-16)*

Further, McDonald (1982) described "coming out" as a very difficult developmental process that may not be completed well into an individual's adult years.

Myers, Speight, Highlen, Cox, Reynolds, Adams, and Hanley (1991) identified the phases which members of marginalized groups must accomplish on their path to a positive self-identity, which they call the OTAID model (Optimal Theory Applied to Identity Development). Briefly, these phases include: 0) absence of conscious awareness, 1) individuation, 2) dissonance, 3) immersion, 4)internalization, 5) integration, and 6) transformation. In this very comprehensive model, the authors "provide a unifying system for understanding and conceptualizing the identity development process and describe the effect of oppression on self-identity" (p. 58).

Cass (1979) identified the specific developmental stages which gays and lesbians must accomplish: 1) identity confusion -- previously accepted heterosexual identity is questioned; 2) identity comparison – the possibility of a gay or lesbian identity is accepted; 3) identity tolerance -- the person seeks out others who are gay or lesbian, but public and private identities are kept separate; 4) identity acceptance -- gay or lesbian identity is accepted, and selective disclosure to other is begun; 5) identity pride -- the person immerses in gay and lesbian culture and rejects people with non-gay or non-lesbian identity and values; and 6) identity synthesis -- the person accepts his or her gay or lesbian orientation as one part of the person's identity. These stages are part of what is widely termed the "coming out to self" process. Myers, et al. (1991) acknowledged the work of Cass (1979) in expanding the scope of identity formation in a multicultural context.

Elliott (1993) described "coming out" as a unique process which differentiates gay men from other minority cultures in that they are probably the only group where the family of origin has to be informed about their membership status. This presents a powerful cohesive experience for gay males -- a rite of passage.

This cultural identity development process can take place over several years (O'Bear & Reynolds, 1985).

Table 1 Mean Age of Accomplishing the "Coming Out" Task for Gays and Lesbians

Task	Age of lesbians (in years)	Age of gay men (in years)
Awareness of homosexual feelings	13.8	12.8
Understood what homosexual was	15.6	17.2
Had the 1st same-sex sexual experience	19.9	14.9
Had first homosexual relationship	22.8	21.9
Considered self homosexual	23.2	21.1
Acquired positive gay identity	29.7	28.5
Disclosed identity to spouse	26.7	33.3
Disclosed identity to friends	28.2	28.0
Disclosed identity to parents	30.2	28.0
Disclosed identity professionally	32.4	31.2

It is important to note that there was a 16 year gap between awareness of same sex feelings and development of a positive gay or lesbian identity; 8 to 10 years between first awareness of same-sex feelings and self-labeling as homosexual; and 18 years from first awareness of one's orientation to coming out professionally

Finally, "coming out" is an important and necessary developmental task for anyone who is gay. Coleman, Butcher, and Carson (1984) provided a general explanation for developmental stages and the tasks associated with each stage.

> If developmental tasks are not mastered at the appropriate stage, the individual suffers from immaturities and incompetencies and is placed at a serious disadvantage in adjusting at later developmental levels -- that is, the individual becomes increasingly vulnerable through accumulated failures to master psychosocial requirements. . . . Some developmental tasks are set by the individual's own needs, some by the physical and social environment. Members of different socioeconomic and socio-cultural groups face somewhat different developmental tasks. *(p. 111)*

"Coming Out to Self:" A Developmental Task of Adolescence

Research has shown that "coming out to self" is an important developmental stage to accomplish successfully and that it is an important reflection of psychological health. Weinberg and Williams (1975) found that well-adjusted gay males 1) had rejected the idea that homosexuality was an illness, 2) had close and supportive associations with other gay males, and 3) were not interested in changing their sexuality.

Pope (1992) stated that this developmental task of discovery and acceptance of who we are and how we function sexually plays an important role, especially in adolescence. This is, however, also the time for many gay males when a denial of their differences with their peer group exists. Unfortunately, if the developmental tasks of sexual orientation identification are not accomplished during this critical time and are denied and delayed, then other tasks are also delayed causing an identification "chain reaction" and, thereby delaying other tasks such as relationship formation. It is very common for gay men who came out when they were substantially past adolescence to have all the problems associated with those of teenagers who have just begun dating. Once the critical period has passed in the developmental task, it may be very difficult or impossible to correct the psychological difficulties that occurred as a result of this.

On Disclosing Sexual Orientation to Others

Sexual orientation is generally not automatically visible (Goffman, 1983; Pope, 1995). Many gays are able to "pass" for a member of the majority culture, but still, at the most fundamental level of cultural identity formation, they are required to confront their sexual orientation. They remain a member of their own cultural minority group and possess special issues which must be addressed within their own minority, as well as the majority culture. Few gay males can be identified merely by appearance. This aspect of gay oppression, however, has its own insidious consequences. The decision to "come out," therefore, is a very important one for all gays.

For those minorities, in general, who can "hide" their membership and for sexual minorities, specifically, there are profound reasons to not hide from their family, friends, co-workers, and employers. For gays these include their own individual mental health, as well as three other categories: 1) personal reasons such as honesty, integration of their sexuality into every aspect of their life, recognition of who they are as a person, and support from those around them; 2) professional/political/societal reasons such as providing a role model for other gay males, desensitizing their co-workers and themselves toward the issue, and eliminating any fear of blackmail; and 3) practical reasons such as so that their domestic partner can get benefits, come to events, and in order to prevent slips of the tongue and embarrassment when it inevitably slips out in everyday conversation with co-workers. The most important reason, however, is the full integration of every aspect of who the person is into one fully functioning human being (Pope, 1992).

"Coming out to others" is a continuous process that has no end; gay males must make this decision to "come out" any time they meet a new person, in a new situation. Different ways to "come out" can be classified by who, when, where, and how. "Who" includes the decision of whom to tell and may include the person who is conducting the job interview, as well as the newly hired person's supervisor / manager/ evaluator, peers, or people they supervise. "When" is a decision of timing and may include: on the resume, during your job interview, on the first day of the new job, during the first weeks or months, much later when they get to know the person, or never. "Where" includes the decision to disclose to individuals one at a time or to many people in a group; however, if a group is chosen then another decision must be made regarding the type of group -- subordinate, peer, or supervisory. "How" is a style issue. Some gay males are more comfortable with a more subtle style while others want to make a stronger statement. Methods may include simply using the correct gender-specific pronouns when speaking of dates or love relationships, matter of fact statements of reality, or defiant announcements based on perjorative homophobic, racist, or sexist comments made in the workplace.

Pope and Schecter (1992) identified different methods of "coming out to others" which briefly include: 1) "the ACLU approach" – confronting oppression of all people wherever you find it, including especially homophobic comments; 2) "the Rock Hudson/Johnny Mathis approach" -- open about their sexual orientation in San Francisco where they visit, but not out in Los Angeles where they live and work; 3) "the Martina Navratilova approach" – simply using the correct gender-specific pronouns when speaking of dates or love relationships; and 4) "the Queer Nation approach" -- defiant announcement of sexual orientation in response to perjorative homophobic comments.

On Conducting an "Environmental Homophobia Assessment"

For the gay man, it may be important to determine if their fears of "coming out to others" are based on reality, on previous experiences, or on the person's own internalized homophobia. In order to determine this, an objective "Environmental Homophobia Assessment" must be conducted. There are two parts to this process where the environment must be objectively observed and analyzed for actual clues to 1) the general corporate/organizational climate -- for example, corporate/institutional anti-discrimination policy, gay/lesbian employees/student group, inclusionary or exclusionary language, such as are only "wives and husbands" invited to events; and 2) the attitudes of the specific department, manager, or co-workers toward sexual orientation issues -- for example, types of jokes which are told and tolerated, newspaper articles on the bulletin boards. The findings of this assessment can help you determine when a workplace, school, or any institution is safer.

On Passing as a Straight Man

Many gay men and some racial and ethnic minorities can "pass," but this is not a very effective method of creating a positive self-identity (Pope, 1995). In fact "passing" behavior is antithetical to creating a positive self-identity. The consequences of passing include lower self esteem (Berger, 1982) along with feelings of inferiority and the internalization of negative self-concepts (Weinberg & Williams, 1975). The cumulative effect of this devaluing of self and like-others is emotionally unhealthy (Fischer, 1972; Freedman, 1971; Weinberg, 1971).

On Oppression and Discrimination

Pope (1995) stated that gay men have historically faced discrimination in the following ways: lack of civil rights, secret or semi-secret lives, oppression, rejection or ostracism by their family of origin, societal censure, lowered self-esteem due to internalized homophobia, fear and reality of physical violence, and being the object of campaigns of hatred and vilification by right-wing political groups and fundamentalist religious groups.

Pope (1995) also stated that gay males and lesbians are also a psychological minority in the sense that lesbians and gay men were labeled as "diseased" by the psychological community until 1973 and the 7th printing of the *Diagnostic and Statistical Manual of Mental Disorders* (2nd ed.) (American Psychiatric Association, 1980, p. 380). This change was a result of a protracted professional discussion and which finally led to a membership vote on whether homosexuality *per se* was a mental illness. Gays and lesbians, therefore, are certainly a minority created by the psychological community from the prejudices of American culture.

On STDs and AIDS

Outside of Africa, gay men in the USA and around the world have been the group hardest hit by the acquired immune deficiency syndrome (AIDS) epidemic. The losses have been mounting for over 20 years. Gay men have lost their life partners, friends, extended family, mentors, and role models. We are a community devastated by the enormity of these losses. Those who remain alive struggle to get some perspective about all of this. Life has changed dramatically for all gay men since the beginning of this pandemic.

Gay men who are just now coming out generally have one of two reactions -- denial or fear. If the reaction is denial, they plunge headlong into the gay sex culture whether it be multiple partners, anonymous partners, sex in the parks, sex in the video booths, sex in the bars and bathes, sex clubs. They have the attitude that "it can't happen to me" or "I don't care." They missed the overt sexuality of the 1960s and 1970s. And they want to make up for what they perceive as "lost time."

If they react with fear, they are obsessed with "it." They may have read nothing on the subject, but they have seen plenty on television. They want no part of AIDS and do everything possible to make certain that they will not get it. This includes abstinence from any sexual encounter. When they do have sex (and this happens rarely), they practice what they think of as "total safe sex," including, but not limited, to requiring a condom and foam spermicide for oral sex, rubber gloves during sex, and no deep kissing without a rubber oral dam.

Obviously, neither of these approaches is ultimately satisfying. What we do see in those who have faithfully honored their losses is a maturity in perspective never seen in the gay male community previously. Those who have approached the AIDS epidemic realistically and practically have continued to live their lives, but with many behavioral changes. Gone are the days and nights in the steam bathes with multiple and anonymous sex partners, practicing rimming, swallowing, bare-backing, fisting, and any other sex act gay men had perfected. It was discovered that the bottom/receiver in anal sex was in greatest jeopardy of contracting the human immunovirus (HIV) and so gay men cautiously considered this practice. AIDS has put the gay community through changes.

The incidence of sexually transmitted diseases (STDs) in gay males peaked during the 1970s and 1980s. STDs have risen and fallen with the HIV incidence rates. Anonymous testing facilities for STDs preceded the HIV epidemic and laid the groundwork for the HIV testing confidentiality procedures. Recently, STD rates have begun to rise for younger gay males whose memory of HIV is intentionally or unintentionally clouded or nonexistent. STDs and AIDS are significant issues for all gay males whether they acknowledge this or not.

On Homoprejudice and Internalized Homoprejudice

Another issue of great importance for gay males is homoprejudice, that is, prejudice directed toward gay men, and it's obverse, internalized homoprejudice, prejudice directed by gay men inward toward themselves. Oppression oppresses; if you keep telling someone how bad, evil, and sinful they are, they will eventually begin to believe it, even though it is contrary to their own experiences and belief system.

Legal Issues

The legal issues which gay men may confront in their lives include: 1) discrimination in housing, employment, and other basic laws; 2) police entrapment; 3) sodomy laws; 4) intergenerational sex; 5) obscenity and pornography laws; and 6) marriage. Each of these are controlled by a maze of local, state, and federal statutes and court interpretations. Legal issues may impinge on a gay man's life in a variety of ways, especially if they are closeted.

Despite different opinions about homosexuality, the vast majority of Americans believe that gay and lesbian people should not be singled out for discrimination or denied basic human rights. A fundamental American value holds that every person should have an equal opportunity to a good job, a decent home, and a loving family.

Laws prohibiting discrimination against lesbians and gay men in employment and housing exist at local, state, and federal levels; they have been instituted through legislative statute and executive order. Recently, right-wing religious fundamentalists have taken to overturning such laws and policies through the referendum, where a statewide election is held over prohibiting such discrimination. Those opposed to such laws use code words like "special" rights instead of "human" or "civil" rights to try to take the humanity out of gay and lesbian persons, to try to place us on the fringe of society where we can be isolated and then disposed of. Gays and lesbians and our supporters have organized against such inhumane tactics and have carved a place for us at the American political table. Regular updates on such actions are included at http://hrc.org -- the web page for the Human Rights Campaign. Awareness of these issues are crucial for the gay males who are doing career planning or wanting to buy a house in a community.

When police pose as a gay man and try to get another gay man to have sex with them in a public situation, this is police entrapment. If a man is apprehended in this manner, his behavior may be reported in newspapers and other public media and he may have a police record for the first time in his life. This may be a crisis for this person. Because gay men are subject to discrimination if their sexual orientation is made public, they try to hide their sexual orientation and feel they cannot openly meet other gay men. Many of these men may be officially married to women, have children, and good jobs -- pillars in their communities. The cost to them is huge if they are caught. Yet their drive to have sex with another man is so great that they go to public places like restrooms or parks hoping they will not get caught. Police set out to trap these individuals into a sexual encounter for lewd and lascivious conduct.

Sodomy laws are laws which states have passed to not allow the insertion of a penis or other object into the mouth or anus of another person. These laws are not used exclusively against gay males and have been used against heterosexual individuals as well. Most of these state laws have been struck down by the privacy rights found in the U.S. Constitution (Hardwick vs. Bowers). Several states continue to have such laws, and they are used very selectively against its citizens.

Intergenerational sex is sex between two people of disparate ages, or more specifically, a minor person and an adult, with both minor and adult having different chronological definitions depending on the state. Also known as "pederasty," this sex between a younger man and an older man is illegal in all states. A complicated developmental psychological issue, legislators have attempted to simplify the issue by putting hard and fast age limits in place. This has had a detrimental effect on the lives of many young men and their older partners, who even as they profess their love for one another are registered as "sex offenders" and have their names broadcast on the internet. Power and sex are inextricably linked in our society. There is no effective way yet to sort these issues out fairly and justly to all parties.

In legislating the legality of published books, films, or videos, the United States Supreme Court has offered a "community standards" approach which allows the "community" to set its own "standards" as to the whether the publication is obscene or pornographic or of great value. This has caused for great inconsistency between one community and another. Gay men are consumers of such erotic literature and are subject to laws which regulate the sale or display of such material. When police raid any home, the first issue they always comment on is that they found "pornography." This is to show the public that the person was somehow "depraved" and beyond the normal boundaries of human behavior, when the truth is just the opposite. Erotic literature is used and collected by a large number of human beings.

Rankins and Pope (2000) reported that many lesbians and gay men are in committed, long-term relationships often taking on many of the responsibilities associated with civil marriage. Unlike legally married people, however, lesbian and gay people cannot share in the economic and legal benefits of civil marriage. Rights that married people take for granted, such as the ability to visit a sick or injured spouse in the hospital, are denied to gay and lesbian people. Because their committed relationships are not recognized by law, hospitals, and other institutions do not have to respect the basic human rights of gay and lesbian couples. Likewise, if one partner in a married couple is seriously ill and incapacitated, the other spouse should be able to make decisions regarding his/her care and guardianship. This basic right of guardianship is denied to gay and lesbian couples, because their committed relationships are not recognized under the law. If one partner is incapacitated and in the hospital, the other partner may not be allowed to visit or allowed to make basic health care decisions. Laws offering very limited rights have been termed "domestic partner" laws and have been adopted by many cities and one state (Vermont).

Sharon Kowalski and Karen Thompson shared a home in Minnesota and exchanged rings to show their commitment to each other. Their relationship, however, was not legally recognized. When Sharon was seriously injured in a car accident, the hospital refused to allow Karen to visit her. Karen was denied any information about Sharon's condition and was not allowed to make any decisions about the treatment of her loved one. She waited in anguish for hours in the waiting room not even knowing whether Sharon was dead or alive. Finally, a priest found out for Karen that Sharon had sustained a serious brain injury. Karen spent nine and a half years and over $300,000 fighting a court battle to win the right to visit, care for, and finally bring home the person she loved.

In Hawaii, two gay men were in a committed relationship for 20 years. One Friday night, one of the men had a stroke and was taken to the hospital. When his partner arrived, the hospital refused to let them see each other, even though the couple had a legal document stating their wish to make medical decisions for each other. When the man denied visitation finally got to speak to the hospital lawyers days later, they said, "You can pick his body up at the city morgue." His partner had died three days earlier.

The legal issues which are important for gay men in American society continue to change at an amazing rate. It is important to keep up to date on laws in your community as they apply to gay men and their families. Although most police departments in the U.S. no longer spend much time enforcing these laws, they remain on the books to be used selectively to silence this important sexual minority.

DEVELOPMENTAL STAGES OF LIFE AND GAY MEN

In the next section, we look at the developmental stages that gay men go through and at the specific issues which are addressed at each stage. Whether it is adolescence, adulthood, or the senior years, gay men have unique issues which must be addressed and understood by health care providers.

On Adolescence

In adolescence, young men begin to explore their sexuality. Although there is now socially an awareness within young persons and their social institutions that a same-sex sexual orientation may be a possibility, the possibility is still considered a negative one for most young male adolescents. Pope (2000)found that

> Everyone of the boys involved in school shootings during 1998-1999 were called "faggot," "wuss," "queer" and they were physically as well as verbally harassed (CNN Morning Live, 1999; Sullivan, 1998; Wilkinson &Hendrickson, 1999). "Jocks pushed them against lockers, (and) they yelled 'faggot' and 'loser' at them while they ate lunch in the cafeteria" (Wilkinson & Hendrickson, 1999, p. 50). This is the lexicon of adolescence in America. This verbal and physical harassment is designed to elicit conformity from those so targeted and security for the deliverer, "no matter how bad my life is, at least I'm not one of THEM." To be a boy or girl who is "different" from your peers' notions of what a male or female is supposed to do or be is to become the object of derisive comments challenging your sexual orientation. In the USA if you are a sensitive boy who cries at movies, or an athletic girl who wears jeans and no makeup, you are subject to whispers or catcalls from your peers. To be different during a time when conformity to your peer group is the norm is to be a target for verbal and physical harassment from that same group, especially about sexuality. *(Pope, 2000, p. 285)*

Adolescence is the stage at which most gay men should be coming out to themselves, yet because of the stressors associated with accepting one's sexual orientation, it may be a delayed, protracted process. David, a 19 year-old, gay male from Baltimore, wrote,

> ...actually, the term "coming out" is more than a bit confusing, because it isn't a single, momentous event, but a series of lengthy stages. Perhaps the most difficult part of this process is realizing and admitting "I am gay." In my case, there was a gradual awareness that I was different from everyone else. Realizing that I was attracted to my own sex didn't lead to feelings of pride and dignity. My first reactions were very negative, which was to be expected considering the pervasive stereotypes. *(Heron, 1983, p. 54).*

Many gay male adolescents have relationships with similar aged peers, but some also choose to develop strong, intimate relationships with older men who are stable emotionally and secure in their own sexual orientation. Christopher, a 17 year-old gay male from New Jersey, wrote,

> I did have one very short-lived romance in school (with a classmate), but we were doomed from the start. He was too uptight about being gay and I wasn't. But my first real affair was with a much older man, and he was a beautiful person. I grew so much from our relationship. He shared his experience with me, and his love, and I grew. He helped

me to like myself as I never did. I felt so good about myself and being myself that I decided no one was going to force me to be someone else, and thus I began to come out. *(Heron, 1983, pp. 19-20)*

Part of the process of a gay male coming to a full acceptance of who he is during adolescence is to reject himself and try to be something he is not. First he cries because he is different, because he cannot conform to those societal ideals that he once chose to live up to. Then, he tries to hide his feelings for his sake and the sake of those he loves. You try dating girls (more or some or once). He tries looking at naked photos in Playboy and getting aroused. Sometimes it works. He tries to force himself to be "normal" by trying anything considered "manly," like playing and really being "into" sports, reading books about cars and engines, hanging up centerfolds in his locker, finding Jesus and attending church and going fishing and hunting with his dad and grandpa. Finally, he decides to stop the foolishness and accept himself completely. He realizes and begins to appreciate that men can be many different ways including liking to dance, liking art, liking classical music and opera, liking to look at nature not just kill anything that moves in it, liking to write about feelings, and being able to cry at sad or happy movies.

On Adulthood

For the adult gay man who has been out to self for many years, the old Freudian axiom of what it takes for the mature man to have a successful life rings true: "love and work." These are the hallmarks of a mature life, of a happy and successful person, whatever your sexual orientation may be. Good career decision making, competent stigma management, and excellent relationship skills are the important skills for adult gay men. Counseling adult gay males is focused more around issues of sexuality than on anguish over their sexual orientation or wanting to change that orientation. The needs of individuals at different ages differ (Herr & Cramer, 1988). There are, however, some additional complications for gay males. Since the "coming out" process can begin at any age, not just adolescence, the energy required and the stress associated with that process can have different impacts depending on when it occurs. The tasks of self-concept reformation during the "coming out" process can be overwhelming.

Further, according to Elliott (1993), "the forces acting on a college student who has been out for only four years in the late 80s and early 90s are vastly different than those experienced by someone who has been out since the mid-1950s. The trauma of changing jobs and facing the possibility of self-disclosure to a whole new cadre of co-workers can be very stressful for the middle aged lesbian or gay person who was raised in a much more restrictive age" (p. 17).

On Being an Older Gay Man

Sexual issues for elderly people in general or for elderly gay men, specifically, are rarely addressed in the gerontological literature. Although there is increasing research on gay men in general, only a few research studies have been done on the aging gay male and even fewer on the aging lesbian female (Pope & Schulz, 1990).

Issues of sex and sexuality in aging adults of any sexual orientation are rarely addressed and, when they are, it is almost as if it must be done in whispers so as to not talk openly about the sex lives of this group. Somehow it is unseemly and shameful to discuss the sex lives of our parents or grandparents. Sexual functioning of the aging individual is one of the last taboos. It is as if they are not sexual or, if they are but don't discuss it, it will somehow disappear from our awareness.

> Tripp (1975) in his pioneering work on the antecedents of human sexual behavior discussed the origin of taboos on human sexual expression. Approved and disapproved forms of behavior translated into concepts of right and wrong are applied to every aspect of life. They affect the clothes one wears, the food one eats, the ways to which kindness and hostility are expressed -- and, most firmly of all, the kinds of sexual expressions that are deemed acceptable or unacceptable. No doubt the rigor of sexual mores stems, in part, from the unusually high emotion that accompanies sex. *(p. 4)*

The dearth of literature on sexual issues in the elderly is now becoming a crisis because of changes in American demographics. In 1993, 12% of the U.S. population were over age 65; however, it is estimated that, by the year 2025, that number will have risen to 20%. The fastest growing group of Americans is those aged 85 and older, according to current research (Human Capital Initiative,1993). If 4% to 10% of the United States population has a same sex orientation (Kinsey, Pomeroy, & Martin, 1948), then issues of older homosexuals will effect a substantial portion of our society. Therefore, counselors will have to work with older homosexuals, whether they like it or not, whether they are comfortable with it or not. These statistics speak to the need to address these issues now.

SEX IN LONG-TERM RELATIONSHIPS

How to have a satisfying long-term relationship and what the role of sex is in that relationship is the primary sexuality issue that adult gay men address. According to McWhirter and Mattison (1984), gay male relationships go through stages and with each stage attitudes toward sex change. The stages they identified included: 1) Blending (first year); 2) Nesting (second and third years); 3) Maintaining (fourth and fifth years); 4)Building (year six through year ten); 5) Releasing (year eleven through year twenty); and 6) Renewing (beyond year twenty).

During the Blending stage, gay males are romantically in love and the sex which generally has brought them together in the first place is tremendous in quality and quantity. Most couples find themselves sexually exclusive during this stage.

During Nesting, gay males are making a home together with a resultant decline in romantic, passionate love and a shift in the way they love each other. A decrease in the frequency of sex occurs and, for some couples, this creates serious problems, especially when one partner sees the decline as a loss of love not a shift. If they have not paired with a man who meets or approximates their physical or sexual ideal or both, there is a renewed interest in seeking extra-relational sexual activities.

During the Maintaining stage, gay males are beginning to establish traditions and allowing the individual to reemerge after the "cocooning" of the first two stages. McWhirter and Mattison (1984) reported that for all of the couples in their study, some outside sexual activity had begun by the end of this stage, always with the caveat to not get emotionally involved. Each partner experiences confusion over individual or mutual decline in intense sexual attraction to the other.

The Building stage is characterized by working together and by knowing what the other is thinking, which may lead to boredom and empty routines, but also can lead to increasing productivity with the security and complementarity of the growing relationship. Much of the erotic attraction is extinguished during this stage. There must be some resistance for sex to be passionate, but this stage is filled with way too much cooperation. With a decline in jealousy, more effective communication develops around having sex with others.

The Releasing stage for gay male couples is characterized by trusting, combining finances, a comfortable and well-managed home, illusions are gone, but the man they see is the real person with his endearing qualities and his imperfections. There are few illusions that the partner will somehow change, and boredom and monotony are the issues to be confronted. At the beginning of this stage, sex with each other has more caring, caressing, and cuddling to it, along with a greater acceptance of each other's more exotic sexual desires. At the end of this stage, there is a marked decrease in sexual frequency or even long periods of abstinence with each other, along with a decline in intensity and desire for most couples.

During the Renewing stage, gay male couples have achieved financial, emotional, and relationship security. There is a permanence in their relationship based on the lack of loneliness and security of companionship. An overall relationship renewal begins involving interest and enjoyment with each other and a return to more affection and tenderness. Sometimes this translates to sex; sometimes not.

McWhirter and Mattison (1984) reported that,

> The majority of couples in our study, and all of the couples together for longer than five years, were not continuously sexually exclusive with each other. Although many had long periods of sexual exclusivity, it was not the ongoing expectation for most. We found that gay men expect mutual emotional dependability with their partners and that relationship fidelity transcends concerns about sexuality and exclusivity. *(p. 285)*

The difficulty with sexual non-exclusivity was the cognitive and emotional dichotomy that most experienced when putting this concept into practice.

In principle, most accept the idea of sex play with others, but when their partner exercises the option, feelings of jealousy, fear of loss and abandonment, or just plain anger frequently erupt. Many men say they recognize their double standard. "It's OK for me to have sex with someone else because I know how I feel about you, but it's not OK for you to do the same thing." The undelivered communication in these cases is, "because I can't or don't really trust you." It is a heritage of male training in our culture. Many couples in the earliest years together linked faithfulness with sexual exclusivity, while couples with a longer history think faithfulness has little or nothing to do with sex (p. 255).

Sexual relationships outside of the primary relationships always take time and energy away from the primary one. It is the nature of all human relationships. As long as there are certain rules in the primary relationship, it may work. Such rules may include: 1) no sex with mutual friends; 2) sex is allowed at the baths, but no developing of friendships from that; 3) sex is ok only when one is out of town; 4) sex encounters with others must not interfere with the couple's customary or planned time together; 5) the primary relationship partner always comes first; 6) outside sex is permissible, but never discuss it; 7) no emotional involvement with sex partners is ever allowed; 8) outside sex is permitted at home in the partner's absence, but not in certain places, such as the couple's bedroom; 9) never sleep over at another person's house, always come home; 10) talking about it is expected, but it must be at least 48 hours after the sex took place.

For most adult gay men, maintaining the health of their primary relationship is the focus of their sexuality. Other gay men who have not been able to achieve a relationship may turn to paying other males for sex where they get some of their needs met for one night or to masturbation to relieve their sexual needs.

COUNSELING AND TREATMENT RECOMMENDATIONS

Herr and Cramer (1988), Pedersen (1988), and Sue, Arredondo, and McDavis (1992) discussed the role of the counselor in a multicultural society especially when dealing with individuals who are members of a minority culture different from their own. Herr and Cramer stated that it is very important for counselors who provide counseling to special populations to reduce the "stereotypes, discrimination, environmental barriers, and other forms of bias that typically impede the development of such groups"(p. 154). Further, in order to counsel such individuals, that is, members of a cultural minority, counselors must have some familiarity with the culture of that minority. Counselors must be familiar with the gay male culture, as well as the status of gays and lesbians within other multicultural communities if they hope to adequately serve their clients from the gay male community (Pope, 1991; Pope, Rodriguez, & Chang, 1992).

The American Counseling Association's multicultural counseling competencies and standards (Sue, Arredondo, & McDavis, 1992), along with the American Psychological Association guidelines on cultural sensitivity (Herr & Cramer,1988) both recommend multicultural guidelines for counselors. Counselors must be culturally aware of their own background and the values and biases which come from that, comfortable with the differences which may exist between the counselor and client, and be sensitive to specific circumstances which would indicate the need to refer a client to someone better able to fulfill that client's needs.

Counselors with gay male clients must become aware of that culture in order to be knowledgeable facilitators of that person's growth and development process. Elliot (1993) stated that counselors should become aware of the sociopolitical issues, specific knowledge, necessary information, and institutional barriers which confront gay male clients who are seeking counseling. Counselors must also be aware of the history, culture, ethics, jargon, and sense of community that define the gay male culture.

Recommendations for Working with Gay Men

Recommendation 1: Counselors must address the issues of gay male clients in a "matter of fact," non-judgmental way. When addressing any sexual issue with gay men, counselors must be comfortable themselves in talking about sexual behavior and sexual orientation. It is important to be "matter of fact," straightforward, and non-judgmental in tone and behavior. Gay clients will be particularly attuned to the nuances of how such issues are presented. They will look for the least sign of discomfort, hesitancy, or disapproval in voice or manner. They have been trained to be environmentally sensitive because they have had to assess external environments all of their life for prejudice, hatred, violence, or rejection directed toward them. This is particularly true for older gay men as almost all have grown up and discovered their sexual orientation in hostile environments.

Even a simple statement like, "Are you married?" indicates an assumption that all people are heterosexually-oriented since "marriage" is currently limited in almost all jurisdictions to male/female couples. A better phrasing might be, "Do you have a partner?" It is important not to assume that all clients are heterosexually-oriented, because that assumption can be reflected in communication, both verbal and nonverbal, to the patient. Such communication can cause a gay male client not to be open or trust the counselor so readily, which sets up a dynamic which is difficult to correct later.

Another important communication issue is the use of the phrase "sexual orientation" versus "sexual preference." "Sexual orientation" is generally a less negatively loaded term. Sexual preference connotes "choice" and the only choice that a gay man has is whether or not to be happy, which stems from acknowledging his innate sexual orientation. Most medical research indicates a genetic or hormonal basis for sexual orientation (Heston & Shields, 1968; Kinsey, 1941; LeVay, 1991; Money, 1988), it is both incorrect and insensitive to refer to "sexual preference."

Recommendation 2: Counselors must assess gay clients for identity development stage. The assessment of the identity development stage is important so that client issues are more sensitively and effectively handled. With accurate assessment comes the key to providing effective care for gay male clients.

For example, if a client is functioning at the "identity confusion" stage and the counselor is responding as if the person were at the "identity synthesis" stage, then there is crossed communication and generally miscommunication. The client is expecting more tolerance for ambiguity in the social presentation of who he is, while the counselor is expecting more integration of identity into all aspects of the client's life and is communicating in a very direct manner.

Lower levels of self-esteem are associated with the first stages of identity development and higher levels with acceptance of self at the later stages. Berger (1982) found that those who were less satisfied with their gay identity had more psychosomatic complaints than those who were experiencing high life satisfaction.

Recommendation 3: Counselors must have awareness of the gay male culture, acknowledging that there is such a thing as gay culture and that there are institutions which may be of support to gay clients. Pope (1995) summarized the different facets of gay culture in the United States and discussed such topics as gay ghettos (geographic living areas) in every major city, economic and social organizations in the community, cultural traditions, and familial rituals.

Counselors demonstrating an awareness of the gay culture are more easily trusted and accepted. It is important to become aware of the sociopolitical issues, specific knowledge, necessary information, and institutional barriers which confront gay male clients who are seeking help. Counselors must also be aware of the history, culture, ethics, jargon, and sense of community that define the gay male culture (Pope, 1995).

Having negative views toward sexuality in general or homosexuality in particular may negatively effect a counselor's level of care toward gay male clients. Awareness of this negative attitude is the first step; however, this is not enough to insure that these clients receive top quality, first class care for their medical and psychological issues. In order to provide such care to gay males, counselors much confront and overcome this prejudice.

For example, negative attitudes, such as fear of acquired immunedeficiency syndrome (AIDS) and sexually transmitted diseases (STDs) on the part of counselors can increase the health problems that clients may face. A counselor may not take these types of health issues into consideration when assessing the over all health of the client. Further, if the counselor thinks of an elderly gay male as asexual, he/she may not think to take proper precautions him/herself when dealing with the elderly patient who may be infected with AIDS or an STD.

Recommendation 4: Counselors must be arare of the discrimination that gay males face in society every day of their lives. The special needs of this cultural minority arise from the oppression and discrimination which have helped define the gay male community. The special needs include: the lack of civil rights, secret or semi-secret lives, rejection or ostracism by their family of origin, societal censure, lowered self-esteem due to internalized homophobia, fear and reality of physical violence, and being the object of campaigns of hatred and vilification by right-wing political groups and fundamentalist religious groups (Cooper, 1989). Sensitivity to this discrimination and the concomitant special needs will be rewarded with the development of higher levels of trust and openness from the client.

Further, because of the lack of legal support for non-married partners, gay male couples may have given each other limited power of attorney over medical and financial decisions. These documents are important for the caregiving partner as the legal "next of kin" may not have any real relationship to the client for a variety of reasons including disapproval of the individual's sexual orientation. We recommend that couples have such a document where none exists.

Recommendation 5: Counselors must be aware of the importance of sex for gay men. Gay men tend to be quite sexual throughout their lives (Berger, 1982; Kelly, 1977; Pope & Schulz, 1990; Vacha, 1985), which may be a direct result of their socialization into the dominant male sex role in America. It may also be a result of the particular institutions in the gay male subculture, for example, bars and baths, which foster these attitudes and provide a testing ground for their concomitant behavior. Even gay men who are hospitalized or institutionalized may want some level of sexual activity with other men or with themselves. Providing appropriate outlets for sexual activity is an important challenge for counselors.

Recommendation 6: Counselors must be flexible in understanding the types of sexual behaviors which gay male clients choose for themselves. The choice of appropriate sexual behavior for each client may be different, and the counslor's role is to be flexible in regards to helping the gay men express themselves sexually. Auto-erotic behavior (masturbation) may be quite fulfilling for many men, but others will want sex with a partner and find that more fulfilling; yet others may prefer the use of sex toys or multiple partners.

Encouraging social and artistic activities might also be useful for those who are less inclined to overtly meet their sexual needs. In this case, the goal is to channel this new sexual energy into creative activities (similar to the psychodynamic defense mechanism of sublimation). Such activities might include painting, sculpting, gardening, body building, writing, and others.

Recommendation 7: Counselors must have an attitude that sexual activity for gay male clients is positive. Sexual activity should be seen as facilitative, an aid to better emotional and physical health, not as something bad and negative. Depression is one of the problems for many gay men, and it is a factor in decreasing sexual appetite. As increased sexual activity or the precursors to such activity are observed, this can be noted as a positive behavioral response to the emotional and physical health of the individual.

SPECIFIC STRATEGIES FOR PROVIDING SERVICES

In this section, we identify specific interventions to use in addressing some of the issues raised in this chapter on sexuality counseling for gay men. These interventions are by no means meant to be exhaustive, yet they serve to highlight and illustrate some approaches for working with gay men. In the first sub-section, of an analysis of a common problem, that of a young gay man who is in the process of coming out to himself and accepting his sexual orientation as correct for him is presented. The second sub-section presents the case of Leon who is 38 years old, has just come out to himself, and now is developing his first same-sex relationship. Following a description of the client, we discuss some of the issues involved in the case.

Young gay man "coming out to self": The process of coming out is a difficult and elusive process which involves exiting from pervasive heterosexual expectations and developing a complex, new "self" in the face of widespread cultural stigmatization and discrimination (D'Augelli, 1994a, 1994b; Hershberger & D'Augelli, 2000). Many issues are important in this type of scenario including telling others and fears of rejection by family, friends, classmates, mentors, and the many important others in one's social network; parental conflicts; violence; veral harassment; physical attacks; worry about AIDS; relationships; etiology; dating skills; developing social support. Helping the young gay man identify which of these are particularly salient for him is the primary goal of this assessment.

Hershberger and D'Augelli (2000) reported that,

> A developmental approach to sexual orientation must take into account the individual's developmental status. This means that same-sex eroticism will be experienced, thought about, and expressed not only in different ways at different ages but also in ways that reflect the individual's physical, cognitive, emotional, and social development at a particular point in her or his life. *(p. 226)*

"Coming out" is a complex process which is always presaged by the questions: "How do you know?" or "Are you sure?" A bibliotherapy approach which includes reading books and searching online is a helpful intervention. Books for the adolescent include Alyson (1985), *Young, gay and proud!;* Fricke (1981), *Reflections of a rock lobster: A story about growing up gay;* and Munchmore and Hanson (1982), *Coming out right: A handbook for the gay male.* Books to inform include Weinberg (1971), *Society and the healthy homosexual;* Freedman (1971), *Homosexuality and psychological functioning;* and Altman (1971), *Homosexual: Oppression and liberation.* And finally, books to give to parents might include those by Clark (1987), *The new loving someone gay;* Griffin, Wirth, and Wirth (1986), *Beyond acceptance: Parents of lesbians and gays talk about their experiences;* Muller (1987), *Parents matters: Parents relationships with lesbian daughters and gay sons;* Silverstein (1977), *A family matter: A parents guide to homosexuality;* and Heron (1983), *One teenager in 10: Testimony of gay and lesbian youth.*

Online resources could include Indiana University's GLB Resources Center at http://www.indiana.edu/; the International Lesbian and Gay Youth Association (http://www.ilgya.org); Parents and Friends of Lesbians and Gays (http://www.pflag); Gay, Lesbian, and Straight Educators Network (http://www.glsen.org); Gay and Lesbian Teen Pen Pals (http://www.chanton.com/gayteens.html); National Resources for GLBT Youth (http://www.yale.edu/glb/youth.html); Oasis (teen magazine) (http://www.oasismag.com); Outright (http://www.outright.com); Out Proud, National Coalition for GLBT Youth (http://www.cybrespaces.com/outproud); The Cool Page for Queer Teens (http://www.pe.net/~bidstrup/cool.html); and National Gay and Lesbian Task Force (http://www.ngltf.org).

Dr. Mark Pope maintains several resources for "coming out" on his website (http://www.umsl.edu/~pope/) these resources include a list of historical figures who are gay, lesbian, or bisexual; books for GLBT youth to read; guidelines for coming out to parents; and guidelines to help school personnel respond to students when they disclose their sexuality. Another valuable resource for counselors is http://www.aglbic.org, the site of the Association for Gay, Lesbian, and Bisexual Issues in Counseling (AGLBIC)

Description of the Case of Leon

Leon, a 38 year old male, has returned to see his counselor two years after coming out. Back then, he came for counseling because he was becoming increasingly depressed, and it was in the second session that he suddenly blurted out, "I think I am gay." Over about a year of treatment he had made significant progress. He began to explore his local gay community, found sex exciting for the first time in his life, marched in a gay pride parade in New York, and developed a group of supportive gay friends. He left treatment when he began to feel more relaxed and confident about his identity, but before coming out at work or to his family. He returned to treatment with the following statement:

"I thought that I was OK now. I was not depressed and for the first time had a social life and fun things to look forward to. I've dated off and on and about a six months ago began a relationship with Paul. We get along great and I really believe that we love each other. Even though he is more experienced than I am, the sex is wonderful. So why am I back here? To put it in a nutshell, I am thinking about giving up all of this and going back in the closet. Paul is much more out than I am. His co-workers know he is gay, and his family is very much a part of his life. I was shocked when he wanted me to meet them, and I was even surprised that I was able to have a good time around them. They have taken me in almost like I am a family member. Over Christmas I went to Paul's office party and he introduced me as his boyfriend! That almost blew me away!

"So what's the problem? Well, I find myself more and more depressed. Paul wants me to move in with him, and I really want to do it. But, I can't. First, my family would find out about me, and I am sure that would be the end of my relationship with them. I don't want to hurt them so I have decided never to tell them. I am my mother's worst nightmare…a gay son! I cannot imagine sitting down with them and introducing Paul. They would throw both of us out of the house. And, I work for a company that is very conservative. Because my office is at home, my boss and sometimes my co-workers come by for meetings. How could I ever let them come into an apartment that I am sharing with Paul? I hear them making jokes about queers and fags, and I would just die if I thought they were laughing at me behind my back. I even think that my boss would fire me! Then what would I do?

"I am depressed because I really love Paul and can't imagine life without him. But he deserves to be with a man who can live like he does, and that will never be me. Help me figure out what to do!"

Leon has moved through many of the Cass's stages identified above. He has moved through identity confusion, and identity comparison and clearly has made it to identity tolerance. The counselor was probably right in agreeing to terminate the first therapeutic relationship, for Leon looked like he was headed for identity acceptance. Somewhere along the way, however, he seems to have regressed. Rather than begin to celebrate his new-found self, Leon has become depressed because of the threat of losing Paul and going back to the solitary and unhappy life he had two years earlier.

Analysis and Response to the Case of Leon

What might the counselor want to explore with Leon? Leon's internal homonegativity seems to have become projected onto his family and work place. Naturally, he believes both family and co-workers will reject him if he comes out. As he considers such a dire possibility, he once again feels shameful and afraid, feelings that had not plagued him in the past 18 months. However, encouraging him to take a look at both of these issues may just shut him down more. He is feeling very overwhelmed by such threatening prospects.

One approach might be to explore how he has communicated his feelings to Paul. Has he been able to talk about his fear in the safety of their relationship? Has he let Paul know how much he does not want to give him up? Have he and Paul discussed the practicalities of living together? Another way to explore these dynamics would be to encourage Leon to talk about individual family members who might be more open to the news that he is gay. Perhaps there is a cousin or other family member who would at least be willing to listen to him. Or, maybe there is some other way he and Paul can live together without his family knowing about their relationship. There might even be at least one co-worker who would be supportive of him. The goal would be to help Leon realize that part of the problem is his own fear, and the other part is that he overwhelms himself by imagining suddenly being out to everyone. The threat of such exposure shuts him down.

There are also issues of intimacy and relationship-building that Leon is likely to have never experienced before. It could be that his fear of getting closer to Paul might be expressed in such homonegative statements about his family and co-workers. Leon seems to be trapped between wanting more of a relationship with Paul but not able to make a commitment towards that and the potential rejection from his family and work. Helping Leon break down this challenge into acceptable steps would be the first step in supporting him as he sorts his feelings out. Most important would be for the counselor to be with Leon *exactly where he is* rather than to try to push him towards identity pride and synthesis. Leon may move through these challenges slowly, he might begin to move quickly, or he might shut down further. He will take steps when he is ready, and the first step has been his return for counseling to help him figure out where he is and where he wants to be. The gay-affirming counselor will encourage Leon but also sit with him patiently as he tries to set new goals for himself.

SUMMARY AND CONCLUSIONS

In this chapter we looked at the complexities in understanding sexual orientation, the various terms that are common in this area and, from a developmental perspective, gay male sexuality for adolescent, adult, and older gay males. We also addressed the implications for counseling with gay males, as well as a case study with our analysis of this case.

Sexuality counseling with gay men is a complicated area of mental health practice. From etiology to cultural identity development stages, we have only a rudimentary knowledge of gay men because of the recency of most research regarding this increasingly important social group. Gay men have all of the problems of being a male in American society with few of the rewards. In a sex-phobic society like ours, it is no wonder that the struggles of gay men, lesbians, bisexuals, and transgendered persons continue to be unresolved. Similar to race, ethnicity, gender, age, and other cultural issues, sexual orientation provides a rich tableau upon which an individual's sexuality is played out. Because sexual orientation is so primary to one's sexuality, it must by definition take a preeminent position in human sexuality counseling.

Finally, Croteau and Hedstrom (1993) described the process of counseling with members of socially oppressed cultural groups as "a process of flowing back and forth between recognizing and appreciating the similarities or common humanity of the individual and recognizing and appreciating the differences or uniqueness of the client's particular culture and social oppression" (p. 201). Beyond awareness of the information presented above, counselors are invited to use their gay male clients as teachers. Most gay men are more than happy to provide information about themselves and their communities and understand that most counselors have not received training in providing clinical services to gay men. Expressing respect and openness, asking questions about aspects of the gay male experience that are not understood, and understanding the negative and sometimes long lasting impact of oppression will enable counselors to build successful and effective relationships with gay male clients.

REFERENCES

Altman, D. (1971). *Homosexual: Oppression and liberation*. New York: Avon Books.

Alyson, S. (Ed.) (1985). *Young, gay and proud!* Boston: Alyson Publications.

American Psychiatric Association. (1980). *Diagnostic and statistical manual of mental disorders* (3rd ed.). WDC: Author.

Barret, B. (1998, December). Sexual orientation, sexual identity, and sexual behavior. *Counseling Today*, 24.

Barret, B. (1999, March). Conversion therapy. *Counseling Today*, 12.

Barret, B., & Logan, C. (2001). *Counseling gay men and lesbians: A practice primer*. Belmont CA: Brooks/Cole.

Barret, R. L., & Robinson, B.E. (1990, revised 2000) *Gay fathers*. San Francisco: Jossey-Bass.

Bayer, R. (1981). *Homosexuality and American psychiatry: The politics of diagnosis* (pp.221-239). New York: Basic Books.

Beiber, I. (1965). Clinical aspects of male homosexuality. In J. Marmor (Ed.), *Sexual inversion: The multiple roots of homosexuality*. New York: Basic Books.

Berger, R. M. (1982). *Gay and gray: The older homosexual man*. Boston: Alyson Publications.

Blumstein, P. & Schwartz, P. (1990). Intimate relationships and the creation of sexuality. In D.P. McWhirter, & S.A. Sanders (Eds.), *Homosexuality/ heterosexuality: Concepts of sexual orientation*. The Kinsey Institute series, vol. 2 (pp. 307-320). New York: Oxford University Press.

Boswell, J. (1980). *Christianity, social tolerance, and homosexuality*. Chicago: University of Chicago Press.

Boswell, J. (1995). *Same-sex unions in premodern Europe*. New York: Vintage Books.

Bullough, V. L. (1976). *Sexual variance in society and history*. New York: John Wiley & Sons.

Cass, V. (1979). Homosexual identity formation: A theoretical model.*The Journal of Homosexuality, 4*, 219-235.

Clark, D. (1987). *The new loving someone gay*. Berkeley, CA: Celestial Arts.

Coleman, E. (1982). Changing approaches to the treatment of homosexuality: A review. In W. Paul, J. D. Weinrich, J.C. Gonsiorek, & M.E. Hotvedt (Eds.), *Homosexuality: Social, psychological, and biological issues* (pp. 81-88). Beverly Hills, CA: Sage.

Coleman, J. C., Butcher, J. N., & Carson, R. C. (1984). *Abnormal psychology and modern life (7th ed.)*.Glenview, IL: Scott, Foresman and Company.

Cooper, C. (1989, April). Social oppressions experienced by gays and lesbians. In P. Griffin, & J. Genasce (Eds.). *Strategies for addressing homophobia in physical education, sports, and dance*. Workshop presented at the annual convention of the American Alliance for Health, Physical Education, Recreation, and Dance, Boston, MA.

Croteau, J. M., & Hedstrom, S. M. (1993). Integrating commonality and difference: The key to career counseling with lesbian women and gay men. *Career Development Quarterly*, 41, 201-209.

D'Augelli, A. R. (1994a). Identity development and sexual orientation: Toward a model of lesbian, gay , and bisexual development. In E. J.Trickett (Ed.), *Human diversity: Persepectives on people in context* (pp. 312-333). San Francisco: Jossey-Bass.

D'Augelli, A. R. (1994b). Lesbian and gay male development: Steps toward an analysis of lesbians' and gay men's lives. In B. Greene, & G. M.Herek (Eds.), *Lesbian and gay psychology: Theory, research, and clinical applications* (pp. 118-132). Newbury Park, CA: Sage.

Elliott, J. E. (1993). Career development with lesbian and gay clients. *Career Development Quarterly, 41*, 210-226.

Fischer, P. (1972). *The gay mystique: The myth and reality of male homosexuality*. New York: Stein & Day.

Freedman, M. (1971). *Homosexuality and psychological functioning*. Belmont, CA: Brooks/Cole.

Fricke, A. (1981). *Reflections of a rock lobster: A story about growing up gay*. Boston: Alyson Publications.

Goffman, E. (1963). *Stigma: Notes on the management of a spoiled identity*. Englewood Cliffs, NJ: Prentice-Hall.

Griffin, C. W., Wirth, M. J., & Wirth, A. G. (1986). *Beyond acceptance: Parents of lesbians and gays talk about their experiences*. Englewood Cliffs, NJ: Prentice-Hall.

Heron, A. (Ed.). (1983). *One teenager in 10: Writings by gay and lesbian youth*. Boston: Alyson Publications.

Herr, E., & Cramer, S. (1988). *Career guidance and counseling through the lifespan* (3rd ed.). Glenview, IL: Scott, Foresman and Company.

Hershberger, S. L., & D'Augelli, A. R. (2000). Issues in counseling lesbian, gay, and bisexual adolescents. In R. M. Perez, K. A. DeBord, & K.J. Bieschke (Eds.), *Handbook of counseling and psychotherapy with lesbian, gay, and bisexual clients* (pp. 225-247). Washington, DC: American Psychological Association.

Heston, L. L., & Shields, J. (1968). Homosexuality in twins: A family study and a registry study. *Archives of General Psychiatry, 18*(2),149-160.

Hirschfeld, M. (1935). *Men and women: The world journey of a sexologist*. New York: Putnam.

Human Capital Initiative. (1993). *Vitality for life: Psychological research for productive aging*. Washington, DC: American Psychological Association.

Isay, R. A. (1989). *Being homosexual: Gay men and their development*. New York: Farrar, Straus & Giroux.

Just the Facts Coalition. (2000). *Just the facts about sexual orientation & youth: A primer for principals, educators &school personnel*. Washington, DC: Author.

Kelly, J. (1977). The aging male homosexual. *The Gerontologist, 17,*328-332.

Kinsey, A. C. (1941). Homosexuality: A criteria for a hormonal explanation of the homosexual. *Journal of Clinical Endocrinology, 1*(5), 424-428.

Kinsey, A. C., Pomeroy, W. B., & Martin, C.E. (1948). *Sexual behavior in the human male*. Philadelphia: W. B. Saunders Company.

LeVay, S. (1991). A difference in hypothalamic structure between heterosexual and homosexual men. *Science, 253,*1034-1037.

LeVay, S. (1999). *Queer science*. New York: McGraw-Hill.

Lewes, K. (1988). *The psychoanalytic theory of male homosexuality*. New York: Meridian.

McDonald, G. J. (1982). Individual differences in the coming out process for gay men: Implications for theoretical models. *Journal of Homosexuality, 8*, 47-60.

McWhirter, D. P., & Mattison, A. M. (1984). *The male couple: How relationships develop*. Englewood Cliffs, NJ:Prentice-Hall.

Money, J. (1988). *Gay, straight, and in-between: The sexology of erotic orientation*. New York: Oxford University Press.

Money, J. (1990). Agenda and credenda of the Kinsey scale. In D. P. McWhirter, S. A. Sanders, & J. M. Reinisch (Eds.), *Homosexuality/heterosexuality: Concepts of sexual orientation* (pp. 41-60). New York: Oxford University Press.

Muller, A. (1987). *Parents matters: Parents relationships with lesbian daughters and gay sons*. Tallahassee, FL: Naiad Press.

Munchmore, W., & Hanson, W. (1982). *Coming out right: A handbook for the gay male.* Boston: Alyson Publications.

Myers, L. J., Speight, S. L., Highlen, P. S., Cox, C. I., Reynolds, A.L., Adams, E. M., & Hanley, C. P. (1991). Identity development and worldview: Toward an optimal conceptualization. *Journal of Counseling & Development, 70,* 54-63.

Nicolosi, J. (1991). *Reparative therapy of male homosexuals.* Northvale, NJ: Aronson.

O'Bear, K., & Reynolds, A.L. (1986). *Opening doors to acceptance and understanding: A facilitator's guide to presenting workshops on lesbian and gay issues.* Paper presented at the annual convention of the American College Personnel Association, San Francisco, CA.

Pedersen, P. (1988). *A handbook for development of multicultural awareness.* Alexandria, VA: American Counseling Association.

Pollack, W. (1998). *Real boys: Rescuing our sons from the myths of boyhood.* New York: Random House.

Pope, M. (1991, December). *Issues in career development for gay males and lesbians.* A paper presented at the Multicultural Counseling Conference, San Jose State University, Gilroy, California.

Pope, M. (1992). Bias in the interpretation of psychological tests. In S. Dworkin and F. Gutierrez (Eds.), *Counseling gay men &lesbians: Journey to the end of the rainbow* (pp. 277-292). Alexandria, VA: American Counseling Association.

Pope, M. (1995). The "salad bowl" is big enough for us all: An argument for the inclusion of lesbians and gays in any definition of multiculturalism. *Journal of Counseling & Development, 73* (3), 301-304.

Pope, M. (2000). Preventing school violence aimed at gay, lesbian, bisexual, and transgender youth. In D. S. Sandhu & C. B. Aspy (Eds.), *Violence in American schools: A practical guide for counselors* (pp. 285-304). Alexandria, VA: American Counseling Association.

Pope, M., & Chung, Y. B. (2000). From bakla to tongzhi: Counseling and psychotherapy issues for gay and lesbian Asian and Pacific Islander Americans. In D. S. Sandhu (Ed.), *Asian and Pacific Islander Americans: Issues and concerns for counseling and psychotherapy* (pp. 223-256). Commack, NY: Nova Science Publishers.

Pope, M., Rodriguez, S., & Chang, A. P. C. (1992, September). *Special issues in career development and planning for Asian gay men.* Presented at the meeting of International Pacific Friends Societies, International Friendship Weekend 1992, San Francisco, California, USA.

Pope, M., & Schecter, E. (1992, October). *Career strategies: Career suicide or career success.* Presented at the 2nd Annual Lesbian and Gay Workplace Issues Conference, Stanford, California.

Pope, M., & Schulz, R.(1990). Sexual attitudes and behavior in midlife and aging homosexual males. *Journal of Homosexuality, 20* (3/4), 169-177.

Rankins, M., & Pope, M. (2000, August). *Gay and lesbian marriage: The coming dawn.* A poster presentation at the 108th annual convention of the American Psychological Association, Washington, DC.

Roscoe, W. (1994). Strange country this: Images of berdaches and warrior women. In W. Roscoe (Ed.), *Living the spirit: A gay American Indian anthology* (pp. 48-76). New York: St. Martin's Press.

Rowse, A.L. (1977). *Homosexuals in history: A study in ambivalence in society, literature and the arts*. New York: Carroll & Graf Publishers.

Ruan, F.F. (1991). *Sex in China: Studies in sexology in Chinese culture*. New York: Plenum.

Sanders, S. A., Reinisch, J. M., &McWhirter, D. P. (1990). Homosexuality/ heterosexuality: An overview. In D.P. McWhirter, S. A. Sanders, & J. M. Reinisch (Eds.), *Homosexuality/heterosexuality: Concepts of sexual orientation*(pp. xix-xxvii). New York: Oxford University Press.

Silverstein, C. (1977). *A family matter: A parents guide to homosexuality*. New York: McGraw-Hill.

Socarides, C. (1968). *The overt homosexual*. New York: Grune & Stratton.

Socarides, C. (1973). Findings derived from 15 years of clinical research. *American Journal of Psychiatry,130*, 1212-13.

Sue, D. W., Arredondo, P., & McDavis, R. J.(1992). Multicultural counseling competencies and standards: A call to the profession. *Journal of Counseling & Development, 70*, 477-486.

Thorstad, D. (1974). *The Bolsheviks and the early homosexual rights movement*. New York: Times Change Press.

Tripp, C. A. (1975). *The homosexual matrix*. New York: McGraw-Hill.

Vacha, K. (1985). *Quiet fire: Memoirs of older gay men*. Trumansburg, NY: The Crossing Press.

Weinberg, G. II. (1971). *Society and the healthy homosexual*. New York: St. Martin's Press.

Weinberg, M. S., & Williams, C. S.(1975). *Male homosexuals: Their problems and adaptations* (rev. ed.). New York: Penguin.

Chapter 9

TRANSGENDER ISSUES IN COUNSELING

Janet H. Fontaine
Indiana University of Pennsylvania

INTRODUCTION

Only within the last ten to fifteen years have **transgender** issues acquired a forum in the wider counseling profession. Prior to the mid 1980s, the term *transgender* was not one in common usage. The term brought together a variety of gender variant issues under one rubric and created a community voice to bring its issues to the forefront of psychological practice.

The multifaceted nature of these issues and the level at which they challenge the clinician's beliefs require special consideration for those who provide care for such clients. Ethical practice requires both the exploration of a counselor's personal beliefs and education about gender diversity itself, but herein lies a problem. There is little available research data or other information on transgendered client issues and treatment. Only within the past four years have noteworthy contributions been made to the treatment literature for transgendered clients (e.g., Ettner, 1999; Israel & Tarver, 1997). In addition, the topic of gender variance has the potential to evoke such strong affective responses that the uninitiated counselor should probably explore client referral to those more experienced, rather than attempt to work through their own issues in the counseling moment. However, in many cases, such experienced counselors are unavailable and the choice is one of providing the best care possible versus no care at all.

This chapter helps to fill the noted informational void by providing a rudimentary introduction to transgender client issues. This introduction will assist counselors in understanding the needs of this underserved population. An essential first step is to gain familiarity with terms and concepts that define gender, sexual attraction, and gender variant populations

Gender's simplistic definition is one's biological sex with the typical method of assignment based on external genitalia. However, the general public has become more aware that this classification method can be more confounding than they have been led to believe. Within the gender variant community, *gender* is seen as a more complex term, involving the interplay of gender identity, gender expression, and physical sex characteristics. It is comprised of psychological, cultural, physiological and spiritual roles, emotions, and attributes that vary from culture-to-culture and person-to-person. Gender is the way a person interacts with the world. "It is mostly between our ears, not our legs" (K.Wilson, personal communication, September 8, 2001). **Gender identity** refers to a person's cognitive, innate sense of self as masculine or feminine. Gender identity is thought to be established within the first two years of development (Chodorow, 1987). For most people, biology and sense-of-self (gender identity) are congruent and unambiguous. Gender identity is believed to be beyond the conscious control of the individual, that is, one cannot simply "will" oneself to acquire an identity opposite to that of their biological gender.

Gender identity disorder (GID) was first listed in the *DSM-III* (APA, 1980) and supplants the older diagnostic category of transsexualism. According to the *DSM-IV* (APA, 1994), *GID* is characterized by "a strong and persistent cross-gender identification (not merely a desire for any perceived cultural advantages of being the other sex)... persistent discomfort with [one's biological] sex or sense of inappropriateness in the gender role of that sex;... and clinically significant distress or impairment in social, occupational, or other important areas of functioning" (pp. 537-538). **Gender dysphoria** is a persistent, intense distress with one's physical sex characteristics or their associated cultural role.

Gender role is comprised of behaviors that society associates with gender, that is, how society has "constructed" gender. These behaviors are culture specific and give rise to the societal labels of "feminine" and "masculine." *Gender role* constitutes how one presents one's gender to the world. As behaviors, they are under the conscious control of the individual. Thus, one can have the physical anatomy of a male, have a gender identity of a female, and dress and act in either venue.

Sexual orientation is the erotic and affectional attraction to another person, including erotic fantasy, activity, or behavior, and affectional needs. It usually does not come into issue until an individual is attracted to someone of the same gender. Individuals may have sexual orientations that are heterosexual, homosexual, bisexual, or asexual. Sexual orientation is believed to be beyond the conscious control of the individual. Sexual behavior, how one acts out sexually, on the other hand, is under conscious control. **Sexual identity** usually refers to an individual's self-definition of her/his sexual orientation.

As mentioned previously, the term *transgender* is a recent label and serves as an inclusive community term for all who tend to blur traditional gender boundaries, that is, anyone who transgresses gender. Under this umbrella falls a variety of gender variant persons and terms including **transsexuals, transgenderist, crossdressers, transvestites, drag queens or kings, intersexed/hermaphrodites, bigender** and **androgynous** individuals (Fontaine & Wilson, 2000). It includes a range and variation of gender conditions/ expressions, identities and roles, that challenge or expand the current dominant cultural values of what it means to be male or female. Since the term evolved from the community itself, it is the preferred term in working with gender variant populations (Leslie, Perina, & Maqueda, 2001). K. Wilson (personal communication, August 28, 2001) indicated **gender variance** as a more recent term. Differentiation of these groups is provided below.

Transsexuals are transgender individuals with the biological characteristics of one sex but who identify with the opposite gender (e.g., an individual who possesses the external genitalia of a man but experiences a female gender identity). A transsexual feels a need to change his/her physical sex characteristics to better fit her/his sense of gender identity. **MTF/FTM** refers to the direction of a sex or gender role change: male-to-female or female-to-male.

Without medical intervention, transsexuals typically experience intense gender dysphoria and feel an overwhelming desire to permanently fulfill their lives as members of the opposite gender (Israel & Tarver, 1997). They frequently experience a profound lack of congruence between mind (gender identity) and body (biological sex) and are most uncomfortable with the gender role that society expects based on their biological sex (Brown & Rounsley, 1996). There is no implicit sexual orientation or sexuality conveyed in the transgendered phenomena. Transsexuals may be sexually attracted to males, females, both, or neither and may present in either gender role depending on the circumstances. A *transgenderist* is an individual who lives in a transgender role without sexual reassignment procedures. Sometimes the term is incorrectly substituted for transgender.

Crossdressers represent a broad spectrum of gender role presentation, ranging from a single article of clothing to passing in the opposite sex role, from secret to public, and from very occasionally to full time. Crossdressing may or may not have an erotic association. Crossdressers may experience gender dysphoria to varying degrees and may be content to rely on crossdressing to express elements of their sense of gender. The psychiatric term *transvestite* is commonly considered offensive (but the abbreviation TV is often not). Israel and Tarver (1997) found that MTF crossdressers are generally heterosexual (attracted to women), although they may be attracted to men, both or neither. Most crossdressers do not identify fully as the opposite sex or desire to live full-time in a cross-gender role. While crossdressing behavior is under voluntary control, crossdressers may experience feelings of relief from tension and anxiety when afforded freedom to dress in accordance to their individual sense of femininity or masculinity.

Drag Queens/Drag Performers or **female impersonators** are biologically male individuals who crossdress typically for theatrical/performance purposes and may or may not identify as transgender. Their presentation is sometimes outrageous and challenges social gender stereotypes. The performer, RuPaul, falls into this category. *Drag Queen* is often a community term but is sometimes considered pejorative, implying prostitution. **Drag King** is the corresponding female-to-male term. While drag is often associated with being gay, no assumption of sexual orientation can be made as individuals may identify as heterosexual, gay or lesbian, asexual or bisexual.

Intersex and hermaphrodite are medical terms applied to individuals born with physical or hormonal attributes of both the male and female sex. These individuals are usually assigned a sex and associated gender role at birth by physicians based solely on their apparent anatomy (Israel & Tarver, 1997). Some, but not all of these individuals, self-identify as transgender later in life.

Bigender individuals identify with more than one point on the gender spectrum. For example, a biological male who lives part-time in both male and female roles with equal comfort might identify as bigender.

Androgynous individuals present with characteristics of both genders or of neither. Such things as gender neutral clothing, avoiding definition as male or female and utilizing androgynous mannerisms would define this group. Their idea is to challenge social stereotypes of gender appropriate behaviors and roles, and they fit anywhere along the continuum of sexual orientation and transgender categories.

While these definitions may provide clarity in differentiating relevant factors clients may present, the real challenge of working with gender variant individuals is in broadening traditional binary constructions of gender identity and sexual orientation. Mutually exclusive categories such as male or female, heterosexual or homosexual, become blurred when working with transgender clients, requiring the clinician to think outside the gender box to be effective.

HISTORY

Ettner (1999) stated that gender variant behavior (especially crossdressing) has been around "from the beginning of time" (p. 4). She presented a litany of historical, anthropological and sociological case data to support her contention: Old Testament references, **Joan of Arc**, the **Two-Spirit** traditions in Native American Cultures, and the **Mahu** in ancient Polynesia.

Within the United States, there have been several significant individuals who have called public attention to the issues and trials of transgendered people. In 1953, **Christine Jorgenson**, a former G.I. in the U.S. Military, made the popular press upon her return to the United States after sexual reassignment surgery in Europe. The "Christine operation" shocked the world and, for the first time, began large-scale legitimate professional discussion of transsexual issues.

In 1956, the first known U.S. **sex-reassignment surgery (SRS)** was conducted by Dr. Elmer Belt, through the encouragement of **Dr. Harry Benjamin**. Dr. Benjamin, the most significant 20th century figure in this country's transgender treatment and care, received his medical degree in his native Germany and immigrated permanently to the United States at the start of World War I. His interest in glandular functioning related to the aging process was broadened through a series of contacts with **Dr. Alfred Kinsey**. A case referred to Benjamin in 1948 from Kinsey's famous sex studies of an individual (Van) who wanted to change his sex, had a profound effect on Benjamin. His second referral from Kinsey effected his eventual concentration in transsexual treatment. By 1953, Benjamin had seen ten gender dysphoric patients; by 1965 he had seen over 300. Benjamin's (1966) pioneering work, *The Transsexual Phenomenon*, provided both the medical and transgender community with a voice in the larger treatment world and continues to be seen as one of the best medical and psychological reference books available for the transsexual community In 1979, the **Harry Benjamin International Gender Dysphoria Association (HBIGDA)** provided the treatment community with **Standards of Care for Gender Dysphoric Persons (SOC),** consisting primarily of the medical aspects of treatment that are still utilized today. These Standards, however, have recently come under harsh criticism for their pathologizing of transgender individuals and conservative criteria to qualify for SRS (Ettner, 1999; Israel & Tarver, 1997).

Although history records centuries of gender variant behavior and varying societal reactions, contemporary American society holds it in great disdain. Transgender individuals are the object of ridicule, outright contempt, and ostracization; and, even in the medical community, are victims of these attitudes as evidenced by the experiences of transactivist Feinberg (2001):

> I dread seeing a physician because of a lifetime of experiences. Five years ago, while battling an undiagnosed case of bacterial endocarditis, I was refused care at a Jersey City emergency room. After the physician who examined me discovered that I am female-bodied, he ordered me out of the emergency room despite the fact that my temperature

was 104F degrees. He said I had a fever 'because you are a very troubled person'. Weeks later I was hospitalized with the same illness in New York City in a Catholic Hospital where management insists patients be put in wards on the basis of birth sex. They place transsexual women who have completed sex-reassignment surgery in male wards. Putting me in a female ward created a furor.... These and other expressions of hatred forced me to leave... Had I died from this illness, the real pathogen would have been bigotry. *(pp. 897-898)*

Since the 1980s, many in the gender variant community have expressed concern over medical policies that impact it. Their current struggle balances issues of stigma in the psychological literature (similar to the homosexual community's struggle to remove sexual orientation from the *DSM)* with promoting the legitimacy and medical necessity of sex reassignment procedures that relieve the distress of gender dysphoria. Developing a nonjudgmental language of labels and concepts is also a goal. *DSM-IV-TR* (APA, 2000) maintains several mental illness diagnostic categories for gender variant behavior. Crossdressing **(Transvestic Fetishism)** is classified within the **Sexual Paraphilias.** By the very nature of this category, crossdressing becomes associated with criminal or harmful conduct in a very demeaning manner. Persons are pathologized and demonized simply because they do not conform to societal expectations of appropriate gender roles. One is tempted to ask, "Whose problem is it anyway?" Transgender advocates call for the right of the individual for self-identification/ definition and respect for that right by both the medical and psychological communities without pathologizing the behavior.

CULTURAL AND GENDER CONSIDERATIONS

Attempts to identify the prevalence of gender variance are similar to those of any sexual minority population subjected to societal persecution and harassment. Members remain hidden for their own protection. Traditional methods of estimating prevalence are based on clinical population data, that is, those individuals seeking medical and/or psychological treatment. The implicit problems with this approach are obvious. Burgess (1999) sees another major difficulty with epidemiological studies as the broad scope of the term "transgender." Depending on which subgroup of the transgender population studied, prevalence varies. A *Playboy* report of a British study, cited in Ettner (1999), indicated as many as 25% of the 5,000 males who responded said that they *crossdressed* at some time in their lives. Ettner (1999) believes a conservative estimate is that between 3%-5% of the population has some degree of *gender dysphoria.* Gainor (2000) estimated that *transsexuals* constitute .01% of the population. What is most consistent across studies of transsexuals seeking surgical reassignment, however, is the ratio of males to females. Evidence documents this ratio of *male-to-female (MTF)* versus *female-to-male (FTM)* cases to be approximately 2.5 - 3 MTFs to 1 FTM (Tsoi, 1988; Van-Kesteren, Gooren & Megens, 1996).

The issues with FTM transsexuals vary significantly from those of the male-to-female candidate. Ettner (1999) summarized research that indicated female-to-male transsexuals

...are psychologically better adjusted than their male-to-female counterparts...female-to-male transsexuals more commonly have stable partnerships, are more likely to engage in monogamous behavior, and are, overall, better integrated socially than male-to-female transsexuals. *(p. 117)*

The general underutilization of mental health services by people of color is historic (Sue & Sue,1999). Geographic accessibility, sociopolitical attitudes, and economic realities create barriers to service utilization, and transgender clients of color are no exception. Gainor (2000) indicated that little is known regarding transgender people of color. Most research on gender nonconforming people of color comes from studies of transsexuals and crossdressers in Asian and South American countries.

In one of the major counseling resources available for work with transgendered clients, Ettner (1999) neglected the topic of clients of color altogether. Israel and Tarver (1997), another major resource, dedicated but seven pages to the topic of cultural diversity. They do, however, provide Recommended Guidelines for Transgender People of Color (pp. 130-131). Their suggestions for psychological interventions include general good practice for dealing with all culturally diverse clients (e.g., discussion of whether racial and cultural differences will effect working together, obtaining informed consent in the language of "greatest fluency" of the client, consideration of the counselor's level of knowledge regarding the client's cultural background, etc.). Other considerations specific to transgender clients of color include consideration of the familial and traditional ethnic community perspectives on gender variance, sensitivity to the disproportionate incidence of HIV, and the compounded stressors resulting from dual minority status. They further suggested that counselors view both gender and racial identities as "integral aspects of an individual's identity" (Israel & Tarver, p. 131).

Transgender people of color must cope with the dual realities of racism and prejudice based on their gender identity and presentation. Depending on their ethnic community's emphasis on gender roles, the degree of this prejudice will vary. Similarly, differences due to generational factors or socioeconomic class may affect reactions. Israel and Tarver (1997) indicated that in African American, Asian, or Latin American cultures, heterosexual males and females will commonly stereotype gay males and lesbians as not being part of their ethnic community because they assume all people of color are or should be heterosexual. Many racial communities fail to distinguish between gender identity and sexual orientation

In such commonplace instances as completing a form, the transgender person of color is faced with polemic choices, dividing identities along both race or gender lines, much like a biracial person who must choose between racial identities. Building a positive self-image becomes more difficult as the individual must embrace both concepts (race and gender), yet each social group may place the individual in the position of having to declare her/his primary identity. Israel and Tarver (1997) found that even within the transgender community, the person of color is likely to experience racism.

DEVELOPMENTAL/DIAGNOSTIC FACTORS

Mallon (1999) stated that to understand the process of transgender identity formation, the counselor must be aware that traditional developmental models fail to address anything but a presumed heterosexual and unified/consistent gender identity. Using these traditional approaches implicitly places a transgender identity in a pejorative perspective.

Since a conceptual *treatment* framework rests upon the belief about the etiology of a disorder or condition, it is critical to understand the current status of the nature/ nurture controversy as it relates to gender variance. Thinking about the etiology of transgenderism has evolved from a purely psychological perspective to a biologically-based one as state-of-the-art medical and scientific technologies have become available to permit closer scrutiny of hormonal and prenatal fetal influences.

Early counseling approaches were focused on a "cure" for the individual, since the condition was viewed as a psychological disorder. Reparative therapies were the treatment of choice. Leslie, Perina and Maqueda (2001) indicated that the broader psychiatric model viewed transsexuality as an insufficient identification with the same-sex parent or overidentification with the opposite-sex parent in infancy or early childhood (i.e., too much mother and too little father).

Running parallel to approaches of psychological causality are endeavors aimed at finding a biological basis. Brain and hormonal research have yet to provide incontrovertible evidence of a biological basis. However, compelling clues come from the study of intersex babies, those born with mixed genitalia. Baby girls with this condition have an enlarged clitoris that is mistaken for a penis. Left untreated, by age 4 their appearance would begin to show signs of masculinity. When treated, surgically and with steroids, these infant girls are indistinguishable from other baby girls but, as they mature, they show behavior more typical of boys than girls, which persists longitudinally (e.g., tomboy behaviors) (Zucker, Bradley, Oliver, Blake, Fleming, & Hood, 1996). Thus the nurture, or psychosocial argument, is further cast in doubt.

Both approaches, however, begin with the premise of abnormality and thus seek an explanation for an apparent deviation from the norm. Today's medical and psychological communities officially maintain this pathology view as evidenced in the diagnosis of **Gender Identity Disorders (GID)** in the *Diagnostic and Statistical Manual of Mental Disorders, 4th Edition (DSM-IV)* (APA, 1994). In effect, these professions hold that the questioning of one's gender identity is, in and of itself, a form of mental disorder, regardless of whether the individual is otherwise leading a successful life or not. These mental health standards stigmatize transgender persons simply on the basis that they do not conform to society's notions of how a person should be and act. Until 1975, when the American Psychiatric Association depathologized and removed it from the *DSM*, homosexuality was viewed from this same perspective.

The fact that transgender clients experience psychological difficulties (e.g., depression, panic and anxiety attacks, substance abuse) is irrefutable, but whether the condition itself gives rise to these difficulties or whether these difficulties are due to societal messages and treatment is the question. Evidence is available for both sides of this argument (Buhrich & McConaghy, 1978; Cole, O'Boyle, Emory, & Meyer, 1997; Cohen, deRuiter, Ringelberg, & Cohen-Kettenis, 1997; Greenberg & Laurence, 1981; Murray, 1985).

Israel and Tarver (1997) hold the view that "having a transgender identity is not in and of itself pathologic" (p. 39) but do indicate that a person with gender issues may be vulnerable to a variety of mental health issues. Some may have adopted a mentally ill view of themselves due to the experience of life-long social ostracization and internalized shame.

Transgender clients, like others, may approach the mental health provider with a variety of agendas and issues. One of the more complex, from the counselor's viewpoint, is the dual role that the **HBIGDA Standards of Care** create for counselors. These Standards provide medical and psychological service providers with criteria upon which to base treatment decisions, for example, whether the transgendered person is a valid candidate for SRS. The SOC requirement of a recommendation from the client's mental health practitioner places the counselor in a **gatekeeper role**. According to the SOC, the mental health professional working with individuals with a gender identity disorder have the following responsibilities. They must:

A. accurately diagnose the individual's gender disorder according to either the DSM-IV or ICD-10 nomenclature;
B. accurately diagnose any co-morbid psychiatric conditions and see to their appropriate treatment;
C. counsel the individual about the range of treatment options and their implications;
D. engage in psychotherapy;
E. ascertain eligibility and readiness for hormone and surgical therapy;
F. make formal recommendations to medical and surgical colleagues;
G. document their patient's relevant history in a letter of recommendation;
H. be a colleague on a team of professionals with interest in the gender identity disorders;
I. educate family members, employers, and institutions about gender identity disorders;
J. be available for follow-up of previously seen gender patients. *(Ettner, 1999, p. 140)*

Items E, F and G are those which create professional role conflicts and place the counselor in a gatekeeper position; for without these letters, the transgendered client cannot obtain surgery. It is thus possible that a client may approach therapy with the sole purpose of obtaining this prized letter, with little or no intent of engaging in beneficial counseling.

For those not yet ready to even discuss their gender confusion, self-medication through the use of alcohol and drugs is a common escape method. The hatred, violence, discrimination, and internal shame and self-hatred experienced by some transgendered clients, as well as their own gender dysphoria, can be attenuated for the short term with such substances. The most recent study of the prevalence of substance abuse in transgender individuals (Clements, Marx, Guzman, Ikeda, & Katz, 1998) found that 55% of MTF individuals surveyed had been in alcohol or drug treatment sometime during their lifetime. The same study found that substance abuse played a significant role in high HIV prevalence in MTF transgender individuals. Of a sample of 515 transgender individuals, the study found 35% of MTFs , 63% of African-American MTFs, and 1.6% of FTM transgender individuals all tested positive for HIV. Reback and Lombardi (1999) reported that the drugs of choice by MTF transgender individuals were alcohol, cocaine/crack, and methamphetamine.

COUNSELING AND TREATMENT STRATEGIES

Little difference was found between TG clients and others who experience major life changes, relationship difficulties, or significant discrimination (Israel & Tarver, 1997). However, working with transgender clients entails special knowledge, considerations, and more active roles than with more traditional clients. Additionally, the types of gender identity issues incorporated under the rubric of gender variant/transgender clients defies a single treatment strategy or approach. Add to the particular client issue the diversity of sexual orientation, and one begins to comprehend the complexity of case conceptualization and treatment. Ettner (1999) claimed that counselors who treat gender variant clients would eventually come to appreciate this range of gender conditions and expressions.

Counselor Roles and Initial Therapy Considerations

Tideman (2001) identified several factors which complicate the counseling process specifically with transsexual clients seeking medical interventions. In some cases, as noted previously, counseling may not be voluntary. That is, HBIDGA SOC require individuals with gender identity disorders to engage in counseling and counselors to ascertain the client's readiness for hormone and surgical treatment. TG clients may simply be going through the motions in seeking treatment in order to get their ticket punched.

The multiple counseling relationships and roles inherent in the SOC treatment process also complicate therapeutic work. Eight different roles and overlapping relationships involved in working with transsexual clients were identified: counselor, educator, adversary (letters of referral for medical treatment turn counselor into an antagonist from whom the client must obtain a "go"), gatekeeper, physician (acting as if she/he were in the medical profession in making referrals for hormones, surgery, etc.), advocate, power broker, and keeper of the status quo ("How does a feminist therapist maintain a nonjudgmental posture when dealing, for example, with a man who dresses in the often outrageous 'femme' style that so many women abhor? How do I sit face-to-face with this individual human being who is suffering because of gender oppression – but doesn't care?") (Tideman, 2001, p. 193).

As an educator, counselors may need to provide clients with information about the nature of gender dysphoria, the difference between sexual orientation and gender identity, and even reassure the client that he/she did nothing to bring this condition upon him or herself. Many counselors may feel uncomfortable with such a directive, educational role, but such information can provide much short-term relief for the client as it helps to put the puzzle pieces together.

Ettner(1999) indicated that giving advice is often helpful for gender variant clients. As clients face the issues of coming out of the closet, counselor recommendations about employment and relationship transitioning and timing can be valuable in preserving the safety and livelihood of the TG person. In addition, counselors should be prepared to provide support and advocacy for their clients wherever needed. Clients may experience difficulties in getting their legal and medical needs met and the counselor's intervention may be of great assistance.

One of the more subtle roles the counselor may play with TG clients is that of **mentor** or **role model**. Depending on counselor gender and the direction of client transition, clients may utilize the counselor as a role model and incorporate many of the counselor's mannerisms and expressions into his or her own gender role behavioral repertoire.

Even prior to addressing these complex issues, working with gender variant clients raises several practical issues not typically considered when treating non-gender variant clients. The **privacy** of the counselor's physical environment (waiting and bathrooms) is an example. Providing a place where clients can feel comfortable and/or avoid unnecessary derogatory and awkward interchanges with others is a minimum accommodation. Leslie et al. (2001) provided some practical suggestions for creating comfortable environments for transgender clients and for clinical work with them. Although specific to transgender clients with substance abuse problems, some of their "do's and don'ts" may be generalized to broader, clinical, TG populations. They suggest using pronouns appropriate to the client's presentation, obtaining **clinical supervision** to work through client **countertransference** issues, and determining the sexual orientation of all clients, not just transgender ones. To enhance the environment, training staff on issues and permitting clients to use bathrooms based on their gender self-identity and gender role are further suggestions. Their suggestions for things not to do are also valuable. A partial list of their "don'ts" includes:

- ...project your **transphobia** [a strong and irrational fear of gender variant individuals] onto the transgender client.
- Never make the transgender client choose between hormones and treatment and recovery.
- Don't make the transgender client educate the staff.
- Don't assume transgender women or men are gay.
- Never allow staff or other clients to make transphobic comments or put transgender clients at risk of physical or sexual abuse or harassment. *(p. 97)*

Common Strategies

Given all of the above, however, there are certain commonalities of counseling approaches that can be recommended. The first of these is the transtheoretical concept of relationship quality. More than with any other type of client, the quality of counseling relationship established with TG clients is essential to the therapeutic process. Establishing trust is perhaps the foremost counselor task as a safe and conducive environment encourages the client to speak what he/she thinks is unspeakable and explore shame-based thoughts, feelings, and behaviors. Nonjudgmental attitudes, gender appropriate language, the avoidance of heterosexist assumptions, empathy, strict adherence to confidentiality, and respect for the dignity of the individual are the foundations of therapeutic work with all gender variant clients. Ettner (1999) indicated that "respect and empathy" provide clients with permission to grow into their new gender role.

Clinical Considerations

Transgender individuals often will initially seek assistance for an issue other than gender dysphoria or conflict. It is also possible that a TG client him or herself has been in such deep denial that she/he is not even aware of her/his gender identity issues and to recognize that gender conditions are largely self-diagnosed. Psychological difficulties such as depression, anxiety, relationship troubles, and substance abuse are typical presenting problems. The severity of these difficulties at intake, however, may be greater than nonTG clients, as many gender variant persons delay seeking psychological help, fearing treatment for one issue would necessitate dealing with their gender identity conflict for which they are not yet ready.

While working with clients on nongender related issues, counselors should be alert to any subtle or oblique reference that may point to a potential gender identity conflict. Skilled in masking their transgender conflicts from general society, transsexual clients typically present no external clues to their inner turmoil. If such behaviors as crossdressing are mentioned, they are typically done so in such a minimizing manner that the counselor may fail to comprehend the centrality of the issue to the client's identity and its relationship to the presenting problem. Thus, if a client presents with marital and/or substance abuse problems, casually mentioning occasional crossdressing, the counselor's prioritizing of treatment issues could be to first address the substance and relationship issues, relegating the crossdressing to a less critical status to be dealt with at a later time. This may or may not be a viable treatment strategy and, before embarking in this direction, it is good clinical practice to explore the level of compulsiveness of the crossdressing behavior and any accompanying gender identity conflict. The converse is also true, however. Focusing on gender issues with a client who presents with depression or family issues may be inadequate or even harmful treatment.

Crossdressing appears to be a common behavior for both transsexuals and those who self-identify as crossdressers/TVs. Often their **sexual fantasy** and **fetish behavior** histories are similar. For diagnostic purposes, counselors will find that although crossdressers never lose their desire to dress as the opposite sex, they possess no desire to alter their anatomy. An additional differential diagnostic criteria is age at onset of crossdressing. Transsexual cross gender identification typically begins in early childhood, while crossdressing feelings and behaviors for the TV usually begin at puberty.

Transgender clients often feel isolated, believing there are no others like themselves. Counselors should have knowledge of **community resources** and provide gender variant clients with information about available **support groups** and community organizations. The **internet** has also become a valuable resource to relieve isolation and connect transgender individuals and educate them on issues and resources. (Several electronic resources for both counselors and clients are provided in Appendix A.)

There is a disproportionate incidence of suicidal thoughts and attempts among transgender individuals (Israel & Tarver, 1997), and counselors should be particularly alert for those clients experiencing severe depression. Progress in counseling can catapult clients into deeper layers of self-exploration and self-loathing. Without sufficient support systems, clients may become emotionally flooded and overwhelmed with negative thoughts and feelings, viewing suicide as the only viable escape from their inner turmoil.

It is not uncommon for TG clients to abruptly terminate treatment after productive sessions. The client may feel he/she has achieved the necessary identity awareness and no longer needs further exploration. Although valid for some clients, for others it may represent **regression** into basic denial and avoiding further exploration of identity issues. Ettner (1999) suggested preventing such reversals by educating the client at the beginning of treatment to expect these tantalizing leanings toward termination.

The **network** of friends, relatives, partners, and children of gender variant clients is also often in need of counseling services. Many transsexual clients exploring medical interventions are in heterosexual marriages, and spouses commonly struggle with such issues as self-blame, grief, fear of separation and divorce, threats to loss of social and economic status, and extended family rejection. Parents face many of the same grief reactions to the loss of the son or daughter they believed they knew. It is also typical for parents to blame themselves for their child's "condition." Children of transsexual parents face a type of grief and mourning process. Anxiety about their own gender identity, the fear of being outed (as having a transsexual parent), and the consequent harassment and physical danger they are vulnerable to are practical issues which need to be addressed. In most cases, it is advisable to refer relatives, spouses, and significant others to another therapist to avoid conflicts of interest.

A major counselor responsibility in working with transsexual clients who desire SRS is the necessity for parallel forms of treatment – psychological and medical. The HBIGDA Standards of Care (1998) mandate an RLT or a period of psychological treatment for transgendered persons requesting medical services. Cross-sex hormones and surgical procedures can be obtained only after said psychological treatment and endorsement by the mental health practitioner. The first step in this SOC process is to obtain a diagnosis of Gender Identity Disorder, recommended to be obtained from an adult specialist in the treatment of GID (a counseling practitioner with a minimum of a master's degree, trained in the assessment of sexual disorders as well as GID, and involved in continuing education in the treatment of GID) (HBIGDA, 1998). This first phase is not necessarily therapeutic per se, but a necessary entry point for treatment. Medical referral is one of the more difficult counselor decisions and assistance from an experienced GID specialist is sound practice, and most types of physical interventions require this type of referral. Hormone treatment, sometimes a valuable tool in lessening levels of depression in some transsexual clients, requires such diagnosis and successful completion of a **Real Life Experience** (having the individual live in the new gender role for a prescribed period of time) or a minimum of a three-month period of counseling. Such physical interventions as electrolysis, however, are outside the medical domain and can provide the client with an initial step that may be effective in addressing the depth of gender dysphoric pain an MTF may be experiencing. Without appropriate training and education in the treatment of gender variant clients, however, many counselors may be at a loss as to what treatments, if any, are appropriate in the given situation. It is, therefore, incumbent on the service provider to seek consultation and supervision from clinicians experienced in treating gender variant clients and to obtain further training to ensure proper treatment is provided.

Treatment Goals

Self-acceptance is one of the major goals with gender variant clients. Working through client denial (God, don't make me be one of 'those'), and internalized shame and guilt are the beginnings of this long process. Gender variant clients have felt "different" for the majority of their lives, and their journey to understand this difference may have created a multitude of possible explanations ranging along a continuum from the least to the most socially unacceptable. For the transsexual client, there are no socially acceptable explanations or alternatives. Believing/having been taught that one is a "freak of nature" for most of one's life and being told in a variety of ways to "not be yourself" illustrates the level of clinical challenge the counselor faces inhelping a client work towards self-acceptance. Support, respect, encouraging the expression and exploration of long repressed conflictual gender identities, and contextualizing one's gender identity among the many identities an individual possesses are the skills and strategies needed in reaching this goal. Above all, "therapists must be very mindful of the goals of treatment: to help maximize success in work and in relationships, and to actualize one's full potential in life, while finding comfort in gender role and body" (Ettner, 1997, p. 127).

CASE STUDY

(Note: The client's male [Charles] and female [Cathy] identities will be used with fluidity in this section to match the gender-related issue being discussed. Additionally, a single case study cannot possibly capture the diversity within the transgender community and the reader is cautioned about generalizing from this case.)

Charles is a 56 year old attorney in the process of a divorce from his second wife of 14 years and a closeted, self-identified "transvestite" for more than 47 years. He has two children from his pervious marriage but has little contact with them as his former wife lives out-of-state and has "turned his children" against him. His legal practice is fairly successful and his standard of living is upper middle class. Charles maintains a traditional male role in his work life and identifies as "Cathy" in his transgender life.

Charles is a devout Catholic, having entered the seminary right after high school graduation. He left after12 years, one year short of ordination, due to an affair he had with a 20-year old woman who was "madly in love" with him. Within six months of leaving religious life, Charles met and married his first wife. He spent the next five years in education, teaching Spanish in New York and serving as a school administrator in Mexico City. Charles's first marriage ended after 12 years. In the late 1970s, he returned to New York where, four years earlier, he had trained for the police department, and was able to secure his old job back as a police officer. It was in New York that he met and married his second wife, again after a brief courtship. He was emphatic in stating that, at no time during his two marriages, did he ever disclose his crossdressing behavior to his wives and does not believe his gender variant behaviors had anything to do with his divorces as they were deeply closeted.

Charles's first experience with counseling was in the mid 1980s when he sought help to deal with his first wife's diagnosed manic-depressive episodes. During this treatment of approximately four months, focus remained on coping strategies with little self-exploration on Charles's part. Charles did inform his therapist of his crossdressing behavior but, according to him, the therapist "downplayed" it.

Not until approximately 15 years later, in late 1999, did Charles seek counseling again, this time at the suggestion of his second wife due to marital difficulties. He entered marital counseling to work on the relationship, seemingly stressed around money issues. He, again, mentioned his crossdressing to his therapist (at a time when his wife was not in the room) but had it relegated to an unimportant relationship issue. It wasn't until his wife decided the relationship could not be saved and separated from him after 9 months of couples counseling, and after a supportive counseling relationship in which Charles felt comfortable had already been established, that Charles had the courage to begin exploring his gender identity confusion. In retrospect, he recognized that his marriages had served to control his crossdressing behavior for once they ended, his need to crossdress intensified greatly. He said he never went out after work in his marriages because he was "afraid to be tempted."

During counseling to explore his gender confusion, his general developmental and gender variant history became crucial to examine. He indicated that up until that time, everyone "played [his] crossdressing down," that they didn't "understand how oppressive it was and how obsessive it was, more than [his] problems with alcohol." (He had developed an alcohol abuse problem during his first marriage, although he claimed neither of his wives ever saw him intoxicated.) Charles indicated that even in childhood he "always felt different" and had a hard time making friends, but had no understanding or labels for his feelings and behaviors. He always felt "one step off" and that he had "to put on an act" at all times just to fit in. As a child, he remembered being envious of girls at school who could wear pretty dresses and long hair. He had had long hair himself up until entering kindergarten and felt awkward once his mother had it cut. At the age of 15, he rented his first wig at a costume shop and several days later put on girls clothing, makeup and jewelry, and went downtown walking through stores, "enjoying every moment of being a girl." For the next three years, he lived out this fantasy as often as he could without being discovered by his family. At age 18, he "decided to run away and hide" from his fantasy, to "escape the woman inside" of him and believed the best way to do that was to join a Catholic seminary. During his 12 years in seminary, he engaged in no sexual activity of any type, using prayer to mediate his sexual desires and to "take away this evil spirit from my soul." He does remember, however, cutting his face out of pictures and pasting them on pictures of girls/women bodies in magazines. He also stated that when he would see a woman, "I would imagine myself in her body."

After leaving the seminary, Charles found his crossdressing impulses returned with greater intensity. He felt powerless over "the female personality inside of me." It was at that point that he met and married his first wife and, for the next eight years, was able to control his crossdressing. Toward the end of that relationship, while still a police officer in New York, he found himself "sneaking away" to towns outside the city so that he could dress as a woman.

During his second marriage to a woman he calls the "love of my life," he never crossdressed but could not eliminate his fantasies of being a woman. Charles said "whenever I had sex with my wives, I had a fantasy of being a woman – every single time."

For most of his adult life, Charles never "understood what was going on inside" of himself. While in New York, he frequented a local medical school library in search of articles that would help explain his feelings, fantasies and desires. At some point in his development, he settled on the term "transvestite" to explain his impulses and behaviors.

Work on clarifying anyone's gender identity is a slow, peel-the-onion-one-layer-at-a-time process and Cathy was no exception. A client's readiness to accept a transsexual identity is of utmost importance and, for many clients, it is a gradual, developmental process. The examination of Cathy's childhood memories of gender variant events and fantasies, exploration of her levels of gender dysphoria at various times in her life, and assessing the range of feelings she experienced when in each gender role were important touchstones in this process. Although Charles spoke mainly of crossdressing, self-identified only as a crossdresser, and indicated several protracted periods in his history when he did not crossdress, it seemed crucial to explore what levels of distress these abstinences created. Asking what would happen if a client stopped crossdressing assists in a differential diagnosis between CD and TS. Transsexuals are more able to forgo crossdressing for extended periods of time without the consequent anxiety and tension that crossdressers experience.

Several issues presented at the outset of counseling provided initial treatment direction. Charles repeatedly stated that he was "not attracted to men," and had had very satisfying sexual relationships with both of his wives which reflected his potential confusion around issues of gender identity and sexual orientation. He also expressed great distress at the recent increased intensity of his crossdressing desires. The information needed to differentiate sexual orientation and gender identity was integrated into clinical work centered around his acquiring greater acceptance/becoming less judgmental of his crossdressing feelings and behaviors. Community resources were provided to assist in his establishing a support network, as well as to provide places where he could crossdress and feel accepted.

During the months of counseling in which Cathy worked toward self-acceptance, comprehending and clarifying her gender identity issues, she also began to address her substance abuse problems. She joined AA and regularly attends meetings. A significant integrative benchmark was made when she began sharing her inner-most closeted secret with others - her AA sponsor and select members in the local TG community she had met. Because of her religiosity, Cathy found the concept that "God doesn't make mistakes" extremely helpful in becoming more self-accepting.

Cathy's counseling is on-going, not only for further gender identity clarification but also to provide support during the post-divorce period and with other life stress events. Currently, she still maintains separate roles in her work (Charles) and social life (Cathy) but is becoming more open with her female role, the one in which she feels the most comfortable. She has agreed to speak to several local college classes on transsexual issues and is becoming politically active in the TG community. Most recently, she has decided to explore the possibility of sex reassignment surgery and is hesitantly beginning to view and call herself a transsexual.

CONCLUSION

Transgender individuals are present in every strata of society: every race, every class, every culture, every age, and every sexual orientation. Evidence exists to document that gender variant individuals have been around in every era of recorded history. And, while gender variant clients have many of the same psychological stresses that more traditional clients may present, their treatment paradigm becomes more complex due to the potential need of parallel forms of treatment, the mix of gender identity and sexual orientation, and the depth and intensity of their pain and confusion.

Working with transgender clients should engender a multidisciplinary approach and familiarity with HBIGDA SOC. Medical, legal, and mental health professionals may need to work collaboratively in the best interest of the client. Electrolysis for MTFs, top surgery for FTMs, and hormone therapy concurrent with counseling may expedite relief of client distress. It is sound strategy to encourage the transgender client to explore and consider serviceable alternatives, rather than regard SRS as the only option. Suggestions, such as efforts to become more congruent in one's social or work lives, considering whether changes brought on with hormonal therapy meet one's needs, and weighing the cost/benefit ratio of each step in the transitioning process provide a valuable service to TG clients. K. Wilson (personal communication, March 18, 2000) indicated that past perspectives, even within the transgender community itself, allowed for few alternatives but to "take the train to its final destination" (i.e., SRS). More current thinking fosters the possibility of "getting off the train" wherever one decides one is comfortable (e.g., terminating treatment after breast augmentation surgery or hormone treatment). Clients may be forced to prioritize treatment decisions based on financial exigencies, and mental health concerns may take second billing to the need for physiological interventions.

Once clients have made the decision to transition, they typically experience a time urgency that the counselor needs to manage. Clients are faced with a multitude of choices and decisions which tax interpersonal, psychological, and financial resources. Ensuring a prudent examination of alternatives at each step of the process is sound clinical practice.

The transgender client him or herself may not be the only person in need of mental health services. Spouses, children, parents and/or coworkers may need assistance in coming to terms with the transgendered relative's choices and actions. Relationships which, under ordinary circumstances, could be relied upon for support and nurturance are typically severely strained and tested. Those close to the transgender client may need therapeutic support during the disclosure and transition processes.

Collaboration with other mental health workers can ensure that countertransference issues are addressed and that the counselor maintains an appropriate balance of therapeutic, social, political, and medical issues that surface.

REFERENCES

American Psychiatric Association. (1980). *Diagnostic and statistical manual of mental disorders* (3rd ed.). Washington, DC: Author.

American Psychiatric Association. (1994). *Diagnostic and statistical manual of mental disorders* (4th ed.). Washington, DC: Author.

American Psychiatric Association (2000). *Diagnostic and statistical manual of mental disorders* (4th ed., Text Revised). Washington, DC: Author.

Benjamin, H. (1966). *The transsexual phenomenon.* New York: Julian Press.

Bornstein, K. (1995). *Gender outlaw: On men, women, and the rest of us.* New York: Vintage Books.

Brown, M., & Rounsley, C.A. (1996). *True selves: Understanding transsexualism —for families, friends, coworkers, and helping professionals.* San Francisco: Jossey-Bass.

Buhrich, N., & McConaghy, N. (1978). Parental relationships during childhood in homosexuality, transvestism, and transsexualism. *Australian and New Zealand Journal of Psychiatry, 12*(2),103-108.

Burgess, C. (1999). Internal and external stress factors associated with the identity development of transgendered youth. In G.P. Mallon (Ed.), *Social Services with transgendered youth* (pp. 35-48). Binghamton, NY: Harrington Park Press.

Chodorow, N. (1987). Feminism and difference: Gender, relation, and difference in psychoanalytic perspective. In M. R. Walsh (Ed.), *The psychology of women: Ongoing debates* (pp. 249-264). New Haven, CT: Yale University Press.

Clements, K., Marx, R., Guzman, R., Ikeda, S., & Katz, M. (1998). *Prevalence of HIV infection in transgender individuals in San Francisco.* Unpublished manuscript. San Francisco, CA: San Francisco Department of Public Health.

Cohen, L., deRuiter, C., Ringelberg, H., & Cohen-Kettenis, P.T. (1997). Psychological functioning of adolescent transsexuals: Personality and psychopathology. *Journal of Clinical Psychology, 53*(2), 187-196.

Cole, C.M., O'Boyle, M., Emory, L.E., & Meyer, W.J. (1997). Comorbidity of gender dysphoria and other major psychiatric diagnoses. *Archives of Sexual Behavior, 26*(1), 13-26.

Ettner, R. (1999). *Gender loving care: A guide to counseling gender-variant clients.* New York: W.W.Norton & Company.

Feinberg, L. (2001). Trans health crisis: For us it's life or death. *American Journal of Public Health, 91*(6), 897-900.

Fontaine, J.H., & Wilson, K. (2000, March). *Multicultural counseling: Transgender issues for counselors.* Paper presented at the American Counseling Association National Convention, Washington, DC

Gainor, K.A. (2000). Including transgender issues in lesbian, gay, and bisexual psychology: Implications for clinical practice and training. In B. Greene, & G.L. Croom (Eds.), *Education, research, and practice in lesbian, gay, bisexual, and transgendered psychology: A resource manual* (pp. 131-160). Thousand Oaks, CA: Sage Publications.

Greenberg, R.P., & Laurence, L. (1981). A comparison of the MMPI results for psychiatric patients and male applicants for transsexual surgery. *Journal of Nervous and Mental Disease, 169*(5), 320-323.

Harry Benjamin International Gender Dysphoria Association (1998). *The Standards of Care for Gender Identity Disorders* (5th ed.). Retrieved from *http://www.hbig da.org/soc.html*

Israel, G.E., & Tarver, D.E. (1997). *Transgender care: Recommended guidelines, practical information and personal accounts.* Philadelphia: Temple University Press.

Leslie, D.R., Pcrina, B.A., & Maqueda, M.C. (2001). Clinical issues with transgender individuals. In USDHHA book, *A provider's introduction to substance abuse treatment for lesbian, gay, bisexual and transgender individuals* (pp. 91-98). Rockville, MD: U.S. Dept. of Health and Human Services, DHHS Publication #(SMA) 01-3498

Mallon, G.P. (1999). Knowledge for practice with transgendered persons. In G. Mallon (Ed.), *Social Services with transgendered youth (pp. 1-18).* Binghamton, NY: Harrington Park Press.

Murray, J.F. (1985). Borderline manifestations in the Rorschachs of male transsexuals. *Journal of Personality Assessment, 49*(5), 454-466.

Reback, C.J., & Lombardi, E.L. (1999). HIV risk behaviors in male-to-female transgenders in a community-based harm reduction program. *International Journal of Transgenderism, 3*(1&2), 58-67.

Sue,D.W., & Sue, D. (1999). *Counseling the culturally different (3rd ed.).* New York: John Wiley & Sons, Inc.

Tideman, J. (2001). *Sex and gender for psychologists.* Unpublished doctoral dissertation, Indiana University of Pennsylvania, Indiana, PA.

Tsoi, W.F. (1988). The prevalence of transsexualism in Singapore. *Acta Psychiatrica Scandinavia, 78*(4), 501-504.

VanKesteren, P.J., Gooren, L.J., & Megens, J.A. (1996). An epidemiological anddemographic study of transsexuals in the Netherlands. *Archives of Sexual Behavior, 25*(6), 589-600.

Zucker, K.J., Bradley, S.J., Oliver, G.,Blake, J., Fleming, S., & Hood, J. (1996).Psychosexual development of women with congenital adrenal hyperplasia. *Hormones and Behavior, 30*(4), 300-318.

APPENDIX A

On-line Resources for Clients – all contain numerous links to informational resources.

http://gicofcolo.org/links.html

http://gidreform.org/reference.html#links

www.isna.org (Intersex Society of North America)

www.ftm-intl.org (FTM International)

www.gpac.org (GenderPAC – an inclusive gender variant organization)

www.transgender.org/tg/ifge/index.html (International Foundation for Gender Education)

Resources for Counselors

Denny, D. (1992). Blanket requirement for real-life test before hormonal therapy: In our opinion inadvisable. *The American Educational Gender Information Service, Inc.*[On-line]. Available: *www.gender.org/aegis*

Denny, D., & Miller, C. (1997). The counseling needs of transgendered persons. *The American Educational Gender Information Service, Inc.* [On-line]. Available:*www.gender.org/aegis*

Harry Benjamin International Gender Dysphoria Association (1998). *The Standards of Care for Gender Identity Disorders* (5th ed.) [On-line]. Available: *www.hbigda.org/soc.html*

Vitale, A. (1996). Client/therapist conflict: *How it started and some thoughts on how to resolve it. Notes on gender transition.* [On-line]. Available: *www.avitale.com/* TvsClient

Chapter 10

What's Age Got to Do with It?

E. Christine Moll
Canisius College

During the 20th century, the population of older persons (age 65 and over) within the United States grew from 5% in 1930 to 13% in 1990. Scientific and medical advances contributed to the survivorship of many of our older citizens. In the early years of the 21st century an increase within the population of those age 65 and over will occur, in addition to the predominance of the **Baby-Boom generation** (individuals born between 1946 and 1964) moving towards pre-retirement and retirement years. Traditional social and medical services for older persons within our society are currently being stretched and new services, yet to be defined will be demanded (U.S. Bureau of the Census, 1999).

The U.S. Bureau of the Census (1999) reported that women outnumber men in post retirement years. In 1994, **AARP (American Association of Retired Persons)** anticipated that a woman's life expectancy extends over 19 years beyond that of an older man. Many of these women are widows, some are divorced, and others never married.

Older persons are a vibrant group within our society. AARP reports a membership of over 33 million individuals age 50 and over. AARP funds research, political involvement, education, and much more *(http://www.aarp.org/ar99/leadership.html*, 11/03/00). Yet, representations of older people within television, movies, and other media often show a more vulnerable, frail image of our elders. Even more rare is the portrayal of an older person as a romantic, or a sexual being (with the exception of the occasional advertisement for **Viagra** to aid men with **erectile dysfunction [ED]**).

The thought that sexuality is a part of being human and of intense interest to young and perhaps middle-aged people is not new. However, research concerning older individuals and sexuality somewhat reflects the **cultural cliches**. Much of the exploration and writing comes from the 1970s following the work of **Masters and Johnson**. As the older population grows, more current work is emerging slowly. **Cultural taboos**, myths, and a sort of secret code among the young not to speak to elders about sex might have formed an undercurrent for the gaps in our understanding about older persons and sex (Ade-Rider, 1990).

So do those 65 and over join a sort of sexless, neutered cohort? Can one expect that after submitting an application to AARP that one becomes sexless, or takes a vow of chastity? The topic of sex is not as taboo as it once used to be in society. However, the myth that sex is not for an older person appears to remain. Greeting cards lean towards promoting the myth with jokes about "being over the hill" and loss of sexuality. Some people appear to believe this about themselves. Personal history, culture, family traditions or rituals sometimes contribute to an individual believing that by some mythical age, perhaps 55 or 62, their sexual self evaporates or is eliminated (Schlesinger, 1996).

Conversely, can moving into one's pre- or post-retirement years be a time of rediscovering sex, one's sexuality, and sexual expression? Research also suggests that the discomfort about discussing sexual issues lies not so much with the population of those over age 65, but with those younger, including physicians, and social service providers (Ade-Rider, 1990; Pfeiffer, 1978; Starr & Weiner, 1981). Our responsibility in this new century is to move beyond the fiction, the forbidden thoughts, the taboos, and fallacies to acknowledge the truth and reality about the sexuality of the older members of society. In so doing it is possible to recognize the charm, the issues, and the dilemmas of sex later in life (Schlesinger, 1996). As professionals become more sensitive to the biopsychosocial health of older persons, we can also help senior citizens become more comfortable in expressing themselves as sexual beings.

This chapter explores the current issues related to sexuality and counseling older persons. Cultural considerations including **gender sensitivity** are discussed. Developmental factors relative to **gerontology**, sexual changes, institutional life, in addition to the positive and not so positive aspects of sexuality and aging are noted. Strategies for counselors to use in assessment and **intervention** with older persons and sexual issues are included.

BACKGROUND

A doctor was discussing heart surgery with his patient, a 78-year-old woman. He asked her how often she and her 80-year-old husband made love. She replied, "Oh, we make love every day. The doctor was amazed!

> "Do you mean you and your husband have sex every day?" he asked.
> "I think you misunderstand," she answered. "We have sex about once a week, but we make love every day." *(Gordon & Snyder, 1986)*

Gordon & Snyder (1986) reminded readers that as children and adolescents we might have had difficulty imagining our parents, as sexual beings. The concept that our grandparents were and are sexual beings is too overwhelming to consider. The notion that sexuality stops or is just not what it used to be remains even in the midst of scientific advances which include successfully returning John Glenn, a pioneer astronaut, to space in his seventies. Starr & Weiner (1981) recounted a discussion with medical students about sex and aging. One student asked "But how can I tell an elderly male patient to be excited about his wife when I think how unexciting it must be to think of and see flabby breasts, an unshapely body, and an old face?" When challenged to consider 30 or 50 years of marriage itself a "turn-on," the student admitted never considering such a thought. Another student admitted embarrassment at the thought of speaking to older patients about sex. He said, "Old people don't like to talk about something they don't do any more." Again, the instructors inquired how did he know such a thing and he shrugged and said, "Just assumed so! "(Starr & Weiner, 1981, p. 3).

Comfort (1972) confronted the lack of research regarding the sexuality of older persons. Comfort believed researchers failed to ask older people about their sexual activity because society presumed they had none, however, no one ever asked "the" question.

I recently received a personal email anecdote which illustrates society's assumptions. A minister decided to do something a little different on Sunday morning. He said, "Today congregation, I am going to say a single word and you are going to help me preach. Whatever word I say, I want you to sing whatever hymn comes to your mind."

The Pastor yells out, "Cross." Immediately the congregation started singing in unison, "The Old Rugged Cross."

The Pastor hollered out, "Grace." The congregation began to sing, "Amazing Grace."

The Pastor said, "Power." The congregation sang, "There is Power in the Blood."

Then the Pastor said, "Sex." The congregation fell in total silence. Everyone was in shock. They all nervously began to look around at each other, afraid to say anything. Then all of a sudden, way from the back of the church, a little old 87-year-old grandmother stood up and began to sing -- "Precious Memories."

The **stereotypes** of "dirty old man," "old fool," "old hag," or "biddy" and similar attitudes place older people in a position many choose not to fight. Many older people accept these attitudes as if living in a sexless portion of life designed by society. Many choose to remain silent about sexual concerns or issues for fear of being ridiculed, or being labeled as "abnormal," "dirty," "inappropriate," or "sick" by one's physicians, family, friends, and neighbors. They fear alienation. Our society continues to perpetuate the myth that by the time we are in our sixties, sex is not necessary, or for that matter possible. And, if we do "do it," senior-sex is not healthy and certainly not pleasurable (Gordon & Snyder, 1986; Schlesinger, 1996; Starr & Weiner, 1981).

CULTURAL AND GENDER CONSIDERATIONS

The AARP contingent of society and its sub-generations form a culture in and of themselves. However, within that culture of aging there are other diversities: gender, health & wellness, ethnicity, those living in the community or those living in institutional settings, sexual orientation, and socio-economic differences to name but a few.

The U.S. Bureau of the Census (1999) stated, "Among the U.S. elderly in 1995, women outnumbered men 3 to 2. At ages 85 and over, there were 5 women to every 2 men" (p. 3). The Bureau suggested that men are usually older than their wives, in addition to women having a higher life expectancy. These factors contribute to the higher proportions of elderly women living alone. Over 9 million people over age 65 live alone, and better than three-quarters of those are women. Almost 1 million people over age 65 live in nursing homes. The majority of nursing home residents are women over age 75.

As a whole, the economic situation for individuals age 65 and over appears to be improving in recent years. The U.S. Bureau of the Census (1999) reported that "in 1995, poverty rates for elderly Blacks (25 percent) and Hispanics (24 percent) were higher than the rate for elderly Whites (9 percent). Elderly women (across cultures) had a higher poverty rate (14 percent) than elderly men (6 percent)" (p.5).

The number of foreign-born older citizens within the United States has decreased from 20 percent in 1960 to 8.6 percent in 1994. This may be due to the deaths of the immigrants to the United States in the early 20th century. However, the "total foreign born population in the U.S. is growing much faster than the total U.S. population." In 1994, the largest proportions of foreign-born persons were from Latin America and Asia (U.S. Bureau of the Census, 1999, p.10). So, in 1960 about one of every three foreign born person was elderly, in 1994 only 12 percent of all foreign-born persons were older individuals.

In addition to gender, socio-economic, and cultural concerns, from 2010 to 2030 the Census Bureau projects a population explosion of persons 65 and over due to the Baby Boom Generation reaching their senior years. Individuals 65 and over will be most prominent and in need of quality services (U.S. Bureau of the Census, 1999).

DEVELOPMENTAL/DIAGNOSTIC FACTORS

Sixty (plus) and Sexy

Schlesinger (1996) suggested that in 1966 Masters and Johnson regarded their work about gratifying sex in the later years to be one of their most prominent pieces of research. Frankly, a person needs to be in good health and have an engaged and engaging partner. Sexually, both men and women can perform reasonably into one's 80s and beyond. However, one needs to recognize and not be alarmed by the physiological changes that can come to pass with aging. There is a **self-fulfilling prophecy** that can occur if one believes that with aging one loses **sexual effectiveness**. The adage created by Masters and Johnson, "If you don't use it, you lose it," materializes when an individual is duped by the "myth" of aging discussed earlier.

Starr and Weiner (1981) believe that older individuals are certainly "interested in sex, they also think about it, desire it, and engage in it when they can" (p.35). With retirement from one's job and demands of raising a family comes the time to be attentive to one's sexual drives and urges which have been a part of life. In a survey of individuals age 60 and older, one question presented by Starr and Weiner (1981) was, "Do you like sex?" Over 90% of the respondents "indicated a strong interest in sex"(p.36). Starr and Weiner (1981) reported that their respondents "said sex is the same or better now compared with when they were younger" (p.41). A few examples from Starr and Weiner include:

> (Divorced female, age 79) " Yes. Feeling of deep response and communication with my partner. Gives me a zest for life."
> (Single male, age 67) "Yes. Successful sex acts give one a feeling of satisfaction, relaxation, exhilaration and joy."
> (Married male, age 80) "Yes. I like sex because it is a feeling you do not forget."
> (Widowed female, age 73) "Yes. It's not only a biological experience, but in a way mystical – to feel one with another person, with the world."
> (Married male, age 88) "I love my wife and sexual relations."
> (Married male, age 69) "Yes, It's important to me. Like eating. Going to the theater, etc. A part of my life."

(Widowed female, age 67) "Yes. It makes me feel young and desirable—same as I felt years ago." *(pp. 37-39)*

Psycho-physiological Considerations

Starr and Weiner (1981) reported that for about a quarter of their respondents a decline in sexual response and feelings, especially for men, occurred. Many men reported erectile problems and believed that without an **erection** sexual activity was useless and thus withdrew from any sexual activity. Other respondents felt a loss of sexual activity because one or both partners withdrew from that part of their relationship as a result of fear, anxiety, lose of desire, or boredom. However, Starr and Weiner pointed out that these are issues that often begin in mid-life and are of a psychological nature more than a physiological problem.

For men, fear of **impotence, depression**, self-incriminating feelings of being undesirable, and lack of confidence can form a downhill spiral. Overall, sex **hormones**, especially **testosterone,** begins to decrease. This affects not only one's reproductive ability (although it is noted that men fathered offspring even at 100), it also affects other health processes: bone growth, cardiovascular function, etc. Men may begin to see their muscles sagging, their **testes** more limp, and major differences in their sexual responsiveness. A longer recovery time is necessary before another erection can be achieved in addition to a shorter **orgasmic period** (Weg, 1981). Naivete compounds fear. Many men panic when it takes more time to achieve an erection not understanding that this can be a part of one's aging. Therefore, embarrassed to seek medical advice or counseling, some men simply refrain from intercourse or sexual activity. Schlesinger (1996) related that few individuals understand that an older male can on occasion have an orgasm without **ejaculating**. If couples were aware of this, it could put them more at ease.

Attention is currently being given to men and the potential for prostrate cancer, which can cause **impotence** and **incontinence**. Men, beginning at age 50, are encouraged to obtain a **prostate-specific antigen (PSA)** level annually (Goldstein & Griswold, 1998).

One question to consider is, "Where is one's focus or life attitude; is the glass half empty or half full?" People are often tempted to concentrate on "loss" rather than potential gain. Physicians, counselors, and other human service practitioners working with older persons can assist in reframing sexual attitudes. Open, honest conversation initiated by the counselor can provide an atmosphere for the client to explore concerns, changes (real or perceived), and options for alternative expressions of intimacy.

Women also experience sexual problems in later life as a result of either organic or psychological origins. In addition to **menopause**, other psychosocial and physiological changes occur. Menopause, the loss of **ovulation** and the end of **menstruation,** brings on other changes within a woman's body.

"Skin elasticity decreases everywhere in the body, the breasts sag, the abdominal skin is often wrinkled…the muscles of the limbs show increasing lack of muscle tone, and the battle of various bulges may be underway" (Weg, 1978, p.53). And, if that does not sound sensually exciting, promising, and hopeful, a woman also experiences a gradual decrease in **estrogen** and **progesterone**, in addition to a gradual **atrophy** of the **genitalia**. Atrophy of the **vagina**, a result of the lack of natural **lubrication**, can lead to discomfort during sexual activity. And while a woman may experience **dyspareunia**, or painful intercourse at any age, it is particularly present in postmenopausal women (Weg, 1981). "Frequently women from five to ten years post-menses who experience infrequent coition—and infrequently mean once a month or less—and who do not masturbate with regularity, have difficulty in accommodating a penis during intercourse" (Runciman, 1978). **Hormone replacement therapy** can not only enrich sexual activity, but can protect against arterial degeneration, and **osteoporosis** in addition to improving memory and one's mood (Goldstein & Griswold, 1998; Weg, 1978, 1981).

However, a woman in collaboration with her primary care physician needs to be sensitive to the increased possibility that with hormone replacement therapy comes the risk of **breast cancer**. Therefore, regular self-examination, **mammograms**, and continued education are necessary. In the event that a woman is diagnosed with breast cancer, Goldstein & Griswold (1998) suggested "standardized treatment routines for breast cancer involving surgery, chemotherapy, and radiation tend to strip away individuality" (p. 325). Counselors need to be able to appraise an individual's perception and resiliency. How will such a disease affect her quality of life? Goldstein & Griswold proposed that "patient education materials be updated frequently and be gender, culture, and age sensitive" (p.325) to assist clients in making well informed, apropos decisions.

A woman may also experience **orgasmic dysfunction** later in life. Medical factors causing dyspareunia or **hormonal imbalances** may contribute to a woman's inability to experience an orgasm. However, psychological issues may also be present. Interpersonal issues between partners, depression, illness or lack of sexual interest on the part of one partner are but a few of the concerns facing older women. The lack or forfeiture of sexual interest on the part of some women may be attributed to societal fallacies. Two such misconceptions are that sex is somehow dirty, or not needed if one can no longer give birth to children (Goldstein & Griswold, 1998; Johnson, 1998; Schlesinger, 1996; Weg, 1978, 1981).

In addition to the gender-unique concerns, men and women share health concerns that can affect sexual activity or interest as they age. Late/Maturity onset **diabetes**, **high blood pressure**, **heart disease**, **arthritis**, the consequence of falls, and the aftermath of surgery are but a few that can occur. Others that may come as a surprise to those who do not interact or work with older individuals include: prescription drug interactions, or abuse, **alcohol abuse,** increased **venereal disease**, and **HIV** (Crisologo, Campbell, & Forte, 1996; Goldstein & Griswold, 1998; Johnson, 1998; Schlesinger, 1996; Weg, 1978, 1981; Whitbourne, Jacobo, & Munoz-Ruiz, 1996).

A variety of **prescription drugs** such as those for hypertension, diuretics used with heart patients, and psychotropics can interfere with potency and sexual interest (Weg, 1981). Often doctors fail to educate patients about the side effects of certain medications. In addition, older people, like their younger **counterparts,** enjoy social drinking. They may even use **alcohol** as a "night cap" unaware of the interactions alcohol may have with prescription medication. Weg (1981) suggested, "Alcohol in small amounts can in some cases lower sexual inhibitions" (p. 232) but warned against encouraging such behaviors on a regular basis. Boredom, depression, and isolation are noted causes for some older persons to increase drinking to the point of abuse (Weg, 1981; Whitbourne et al., 1996).

Depression in older persons often goes undiagnosed or is misdiagnosed. Feelings of inadequacy, distress, and failure often cause somatic symptoms such as sleep and appetite disturbances, memory loss, and pessimism that might also be symptomatic of other diseases (arthritis or Parkinson's). Older individuals may also be socially trained to mask depressive feelings in conversations with a doctor. An individual may be misdiagnosed as having early dementia (Goldstein & Griswold, 1998; Whitbourne et al., 1996). All of this may effect an older person's sexual interest and attitudes.

The older man or woman, despite what society may prefer to believe, may give way to extramarital relationships. Divorced or widowed individuals may feel comfortable pursuing sexual activity in less monogamous experiences to the point of being "risky" or foolish. Postmenopausal women, no longer overwhelmed about birth control, may not even consider using traditional protection such as condoms (Crisologo, Campbell, & Forte, 1996; Weg, 1981). In the 1980s over 10% of those diagnosed with **AIDS** were age 50 and over. Some of these may have contracted the virus in the early 70s and 80s from blood transfusions (Crisologo et al., 1996). However, in 1996, of the 68,000 plus individuals over age 13 years reported with AIDS, "7459 (11%) were over age 50 years; this proportion has remained stable since 1991. Of those over age 50 years, 48% were aged 50 - 54 years, 26% were aged 55 - 59 years, 14% were aged 60 - 64 years, and 12% were over 65 years" (CDC, 1998). The Center for Disease Control reported that between 1991-1996, for heterosexual men the incidence of the virus increased better then 95%. This increase was attributed to a rise in sexual contact or **injecting drug use (IDU)** as opposed to the reception of **blood transfusions**. Remarkably, for women the virus increased over 106% because of heterosexual contact and IDU. However, Crisologo et al. (1996) reported that little to no research is available regarding older persons with HIV or AIDS. They attribute the dearth of study to ageism, and the myth that older persons are asexual. Yet the risk is real and growing for both heterosexual and homosexual aging individuals.

Caregiving and Institutional Living

The word "**caregiving**" is but one term with diverse meanings when referring to elder care. The continuum extends from hired care aides to assist an older person in his/her home or a nursing care facility, to a younger family member, often a mid-life daughter, or daughter-in-law, to a partner or spouse. In the case when a life partner is the caregiver, often he or she is beleaguered with physical and/or emotional problems, frequently complicated by the stressful, overwhelming burden of caregiving. The endless needs of the ailing partner demanding extensive time and attention wears upon the caregiver's emotional well-being. There can also be adverse affects upon the infirmed person as well. In the worst-case scenario, elder abuse occurs when the caregiving becomes oppressive. "Elder abuse is most likely to occur when the caregiver has experienced a series of life crises, is an abuser of alcohol or drugs, is inexperienced at caregiving, has economic problems, and lacks support from other family members" (Whitbourne et al., 1996).

However, before the caregiving experience gets out of control, couples, perhaps with assistance from family members, may opt to **institutionalize** the older, ailing relative. Such a move not only can provide more professional care for the infirmed, but also is an effort to ease the burden on the caregiver (McFall & Miller, 1992). The role of a caregiver is changed, but in many ways not diminished. A different set of responsibilities emerges. Already emotionally drained from the in-home caregiving, healthy partners often feel guilty about having to place a loved one into an institution, in addition to continuing to have time constraints. Healthy partners often feel responsibility for the well being of their loved ones and also feel stressed to "make time" to visit the infirmed individuals. In contrast to the in-home care dilemmas, visiting a loved one in nursing care can be equally or even more stressful for the partner still living in the community.

As life demands that a life partnership change, many may not realize the implications of those changes. Not only does the communication, intimacy, and sexual expression modify, but living arrangement may as well. Even if the infirmed partner remains in the family home, circumstances can necessitate that the caregiver sleep in a different bedroom. Other individuals may require specialized care available in a hospital or nursing facility, thereby leaving the caregiver to continue living in the civic community alone, or with family members, but apart from his or her partner. In either case, intimacy and private time can be difficult to arrange.

Sexual expression is an essential way to communicate affection between life partners. These sexual interactions and communication patterns are worked out over time. Patterns of behavior, communication, needs and wants become second nature and familiar. Each understands the **sexual cues** of the other. The notion of **touch** as a means of communicating affection is important. The importance of touch is altered from couple to couple, and family-to-family. It is also important to note that the "situational factors including type of touch, location of touch, intensity, nature of the relationship, and the context in which the touch occurs, will strongly influence the perceived meaning of touch" (Kaplan, 1996, p. 282). The little research that is available does stress that older persons continue to need intimacy, affection, and touch in their lives. Such activity can promote self-esteem and well being, even in the midst of debilitating illness.

There is most certainly an impact on the sexual activity or behaviors of one living within nursing facilities. In addition to what physical ailments may be present, a progressive **dementia** is quite possible. However, there is an old saying, "Just because there is snow on the roof doesn't mean there isn't a fire in the furnace!" "Sexual desire often remains intact despite cognitively disabling illnesses" (Kaplan, 1996, p.283). It is lamentable that many residents in nursing homes do not receive general affection, ample touch, nor have sexual outlets to stimulate them and affirm their self worth. Once again, and perhaps more so, older people in nursing homes are seen as **sexless**. Yet, conversely, there is a distinct possibility that those with dementia may need intimacy even more so to affirm that they have not been cast aside to some hole in the wall and not remembered, but are indeed loved, cherished, and taken to heart.

Kaplan (1996) wrote, "The research that exists on sex…in nursing homes has tended to focus upon masturbation and/or sex among residents" (p.284). Little, if any, study is available regarding residents with spouses or partners living in the community and how their intimacy needs and urges as a couple are addressed.

When an older person's needs are not met at a nursing home, she/he may act out with inappropriate behaviors. These can be defined (but not limited too) aggressive behaviors such as "hugging, kissing, touching body parts, intercourse, making obscene gestures, and touching the body parts of another person" (Kaplan, 1996, p.235). This aggression is directed to caregivers and institutional staff.

The needs of the "well" partner/spouse living in the community can sometimes be ignored, or overlooked. The healthy partner may experience adverse situations that can be challenging to the most stable of individuals. A spouse with dementia may not remember his/her partner's name, or that some sexual activity did occur, and make demands for more.

The ailing individual is no longer physically attractive to his/her spouse. Another concern may be that the healthy partner may not know what sexual activity is and isn't possible and is embarrassed to ask a doctor or counselor in the nursing home. Conversely, it is entirely possible that some older persons may be relieved of their spousal sexual role as their partner moves into a nursing home and be content not to continue the sexual connection with his/her partner (Kaplan, 1996).

For those who would like privacy and time for intimacy within the walls of a nursing facility whether both are residents or a "mixed couples" (one living in residential care and the other in the community), nursing homes are generally not the most romantic environments. Privacy is practically unattainable. Patient rooms are built as a hub around staffing desks, doors cannot be locked, residents often live with a same sex roommate, and the halls are bustling with activity and noise. There is also the issue of the aromas: more than tinge of incontinence, both urine and stool exists, musty indescribable smells, and sanitizing cleaning agents permeate the air (Weg, 1981). This is not exactly today's understanding of "aroma therapy."

Weg (1981) suggested, "Most nursing homes in the United States follow a restricting morality defined by the Judeo-Christian tradition. All nursing homes in the United States follow a restricting genital **sexual morality** defined by governmental agencies" (p.174). However, Weg (1981) proposed that nursing homes are hiring staff with gerontological training. These counselors and recreational therapists are trained and sensitive to the sexual needs of the residents. However, an investigation of relevant research published within the past five years produced scant information regarding the topic of residential care and their efforts to address sexual needs. The majority of what is available addresses how nursing homes can help those residents with deviant sexual behavior.

Whether institutionalized in long-term care, or receiving short-term rehabilitation, or living an active and well life in the community, older persons have sexual desires and wishes. These cravings need not be the memories of an active sexual life from one's youth, almost seemingly in a different lifetime, but can be lived and fulfilled in the here and now. The older person with sexual needs is not the dirty old man or depraved biddy portrayed in jokes, but someone with the human right to express him or herself holistically.

COUNSELING AND TREATMENT

Case Studies

The following two cases demonstrate distinctly different situations about how older individuals can meet sexual needs.

While still in his 30's with approximately 10 years experience in private practice, Dave worked with a female client who was approximately 70 years old. Even today in retelling her story Dave smiles. She approached talking about the reason she had come to counseling with some trepidation. She quietly and haltingly told him that she was having a sexual problem. Based on the embarrassed tone in her voice and her nonverbal language, Dave assured her that he had professional training in sex therapy and it was certainly appropriate to talk about sex in counseling.

As she relaxed she shared with Dave that her husband had died approximately three years previously. However, she now had a male companion who was about 5 years younger than her. She was extremely perplexed about her sexual encounters with her new boyfriend. It seems she was unable to orgasm.

Dave apologetically assured her that it was important for him to ask in some detail about her sexual behavior. He explained that he needed to accurately understand what the problem might be. Apparently her husband was disabled and throughout their long marriage they had sex in the female superior position. Her new boyfriend and she only had sex in the traditional missionary position. It seemed self-evident that the problem lay in the mechanics of her sexual behavior with the new boyfriend. Dave launched into a short educational lecture on the biology and mechanics of sex explaining that it was not unusual for women to have difficulty experiencing an orgasm with the male on top. Indeed that for many women, the female superior position allows for better stimulation of the clitoris. Intrigued, she said that in her day no one ever talked about sex. She had no idea that the problem could be solved so easily. Encouraged, Dave went on to describe how penile penetration is actually the least stimulating experience for many women. He further explained that manual stimulation, oral stimulation, and especially stimulation with a vibrator were actually more likely to produce an orgasm.

She eagerly took in the information. As their discussion continued, Dave helped work on how she might talk with her boyfriend about trying different sexual positions. As Dave was beginning to terminate the counseling session, she said that she had one additional question. By this time they had a comfortable rapport and once given permission to talk about sex she was enthusiastically discussing the topic. She asked with a gleam in her eye and hope in her voice . . ."So, you don't sell those vibrator things? Do you?"

Dave reports his only response was a smile!

The counselor (Dave) in this case presentation appears to have comfortably bridged the generation gap between himself and his older female client. He allowed her the space and security to discuss her sexual concerns with growing comfort. He provided education, but with respect and regard, and affirmed the client's right to be sexually active in her older years. In so doing the client appears to be empowered not only within herself, but also with her new sexual partner.

Another colleague (Charlene) tells of an 83-year-old gentleman who was referred by his physician for counseling. In response to the counselor's "Tell me about you," Stan explained that he married later in life at the age of 33 to a wonderful woman. Both in the beginning, and as session continued, Stan often told stories of how he and his wife of 42 years loved to travel. He explained how she became frail during a long, gradual decline in her health. Their daughter visited often from her home in New York, however Stan was the primary caretaker. He remained in their Florida home after her death and managed his daily living activities reasonably well. Moreover, Stan worked as a van driver for an airline at the local airport four days a week. It was clear to the counselor that as he spoke of his many friends who were pilots, attendants, and mechanics he enjoyed the friendship and support he received while working.

In the years following his wife's death Stan also survived a minimum of five surgeries. These included the removal of a cancerous prostrate tumor, the insertion of a heart pace maker, the removal of aortic abdominal aneurysms, heart surgery to insert a new aortic value, and do a by pass, and finally the removal of a gangrenous gall bladder. His doctors admitted to him and his daughter that any one of these procedures could have killed him. He appeared proud to have mystified the doctors. And while Stan appeared to be clearly a "survivor," he confessed that he is impotent and deals with urinary incontinence. "Nothing works," he said with resignation. After the most recent health event, his physicians recommended that he move from Florida to Western New York to live with his daughter for support and extra care.

Stan sought short term counseling to support him in the transition from living independently to sharing life with his adult daughter. He reported they do well together, but that "she is her mother's daughter!" Stan told Charlene one day about his social life. He spends two days at the Senior Center. He gets a good meal there and enjoys playing cards or pool with the other gentlemen. There are many older women there, but Stan is not interested in any of them. He quickly stated "None of them are as patient as my wife...besides nothing works anymore!"

Stan appeared to accept his impotence, but would mention it now and again in conversation. So Charlene pursued what he meant by "nothing works." Stan explained about how the prostate surgery and the treatments that followed left him impotent. They discussed that one does not need to have intercourse to be sexually fulfilled. Charlene explored how else might Stan feel appreciated and accepted as a person and a man? And once again he asserted that no woman could be as patient or accepting as his wife!

However, he then gleefully shared how he manages to still enjoy a pretty woman now and then. He and his daughter frequent a neighborhood pub to meet neighbors and have a bite to eat. On Friday evenings, two women in their 40s come into the pub to play pool. They wear revealing sweaters, and have developed a flirtatious relationship with Stan. He reports that he enjoys pulling his chair up to a table near the pool table to watch "the girls" play pool. The women often invite Stan to play pool with them, or will simply visit with him while waiting for others to finish a game. He simply enjoys being affirmed, appreciated, and recognized as a vibrant male!

Permission to be affirmed and recognized as a "whole person" appears to be as necessary for older persons as for anyone throughout the life span. As counselors, like my colleague Dave, we may need to help our clients adapt to the aging process. This process includes many things, one's sexuality is but one of those elements of aging.

Stan and the woman from the previous case both seem to have a positive attitude about their sexual selves. Their interest is very much alive, not "retired," but a part of life. The two individuals here are "self aware" – each knows him/herself rather well. While they may come from a generation that did not speak of sexual behaviors as openly as it appears our society does today, each is aware of needs and desires. Stan accepts that his health has changed his abilities, and the death of his wife of 42 years changed his desire for a partner, but his interests are alive and well. He appreciates being hugged and having affection. The woman in search of a vibrator knew what she needed. Once she was able to freely discuss her concerns with Dave, she was eager to learn, and work to fulfill her sexual desires.

Additional Treatment Strategies

Counselors working with older persons need not only a strong orientation to the basic skills of counseling, but a knowledge base about the developmental, physical, emotional, and spiritual concerns of clients over sixty years old. A network of community resources to assist clients with the information they need to make good decisions is also helpful. Doctors knowledgeable about gerontology, in addition to social services, and organizations, which focus on particular chronic diseases, can broaden a counselor's effectiveness working with older clients. An index of local services, organizations, and physician groups with addresses and telephone numbers is important. An added bonus might be to have a few personal contacts within those services, and/or brochures of several resources available for clients.

In addition to traditional counseling techniques, relaxation techniques, the use of phototherapy, and exploring a client's leisure may also prove useful. People construct meaning from circumstances and belongings in their lives. Such things define who they are and their history (Weiser, 1990). What people take into the core of their being to construct meaning comes via the five senses: touch, hearing, seeing, smells, and taste. Weiser (1993) defined these things as "filters of meaning" (p. 84). The use of phototherapy, relaxation techniques, and leisure can tap into a person's senses in a non-threatening and meaningful way.

Conventional relaxation techniques, such as deep breathing, guided imagery, and stretching/exercise might be helpful for some clients discussing sexual concerns with a counselor. Older clients who are exploring dating for the first time in many years, either after the death of a life partner, or divorce, may be apprehensive about the "dating scene" today. Twenty-five or even 40 years may have lapsed since the client has had to "think about" dating. A client may report that their hands are clammy, the heart races, and they may even feel giddy. A client may or may not be able to articulate that she/he feels like a "kid again" or adolescent. Such feelings may be uncomfortable for a 50, or 60, or 75-year-old man or woman. Helping the client relax, breathe, and imagine being on a date, the conversation that could occur, and the conclusion of the date can help the person ease back into courtship.

Burlew (1989) discussed the use of a Life-Long Leisure Graph as a "tool to help counselors investigate client leisure needs...based on the concept that people satisfy their psychological needs through both work and leisure activities" (165). If one's psychological concerns are fulfilled, then one's quality of life is increased. Many older persons are retired or work part time. Exploring a client's leisure activities over her/his lifetime can not only provide a vehicle to identify the client's priorities and values, but may also help in addressing one's psychosexual concerns. In discussing leisure, a client may learn of ways to meet others socially, thus opening a door for relationships: friendships, or connections that are more intimate. If a client can no longer physically do what she/he enjoyed during youth, discussion might explore how the client can adapt or find alternative outlets along the same interests. Older persons might be able to overcome real or perceived barriers and increase their life satisfaction through exercise and leisure activities.

Common photos taken of traditional family events, vacations, or gatherings "can be conceptualized as metaphorical markers indicating meaningful experiences and emotions. They act as 'footprints' showing where we have been, emotionally, as well as physically, and where we might be heading" (Weiser, 1990, p. 86). Snapshots provide a bridge to span a client's life. A moment was frozen in time. A client might be able to recall thoughts and emotions about that moment when she/hc reexamines photographs in a safe environment with the counselor. Photographs can rekindle lost memories, beliefs, and/or facts inside a person. In the conversation between a counselor and an older client, traditions, relationships, and values are often shared. A counselor can learn about the client's self image and internal scripts about life's "shoulds" and "ought to be's." Discussion can follow about what was not right or flawed at that historical moment, how is that moment similar to the present, and how might the person "fix" it in the present.

Family albums and/or collages of magazine photos can initiate conversation about a client's sexual concerns. Feelings about attractiveness, sensuality, and arousal in one's past and now one's present might be explored. The counselor not only observes the clients viewing the pictures, but also becomes a "time witness" and perhaps a "silent witness" in a journey with the client through time. The process can be rewarding to both.

Fryrear & Corbit (1992) recommended that photos could be used successfully in group therapy as well. Working with a group of older persons discussing not only sexual issues, but issues of aging, counselors can use phototherapy to help the participants identify what constricts them. Fayrear and Corbit (1992) delineated an activity to assist group participants in identifying and changing personal constrictions. The counselors leading the group encouraged the members to identify and discuss personal obstacles (real or perceived). Participants were then invited to model her/his own constriction (need for perfection, fear of failure, and/or need to be in control). Photographs were taken as each acted out their concern. The participants were encouraged to assist one another in finding humorous solutions to change the obstacles in each other's lives. Again, photos were taken to capture group members conquering their issues in humorous ways. These helped group members discover that therapy can be fun, and in laughing at their own dilemmas, members gained perspective, and actually found that some of the self-imposed barriers were eliminated.

CONCLUSION

To paraphrase (a 60+-year-old rock & roll legend) Tina Turner's "What's love got to do with it" – we ask, "what's AGE got to do with it?" And, like Tina's response in the song, we sing out "nothin' absolutely nothin'!!" As baby boomers move into their (our) older years perhaps the image of people losing a sex drive, or losing sexuality will change.

One's sexual nature is as different from another's in one's older years as during one's youth or midlife. Individuals need to be assisted in knowing themselves, knowing their bodies, their needs & desires, and be empowered to experiment a variety of ways to meet those needs. Counselors working with older individuals need not be put off, or dumbfounded by their need to discuss sexual issues. Rather, much can be learned from older clients in the exchange of therapeutic conversations. We can help our client break the stereotypes, move away from the "jokes" and assist our clients in shaping the environment to meet their needs. They, with perhaps our assistance, will be empowered to discover their own solutions, and options proactively for their own lives.

REFERENCES

AARP. (1994). *A profile of older Americans: 1994*. Washington, DC: Author.

Ade-Ridder, L. (1990). Sexuality and marital quality among older married couples. In T. H. Brubaker (Ed.), *Family relationships in later life: Second edition* (pp. 48-67). Newbury Park, CA., Sage Publications, Inc.

Burlew, L. (1989). The life long leisure graph: A tool for leisure counseling. *Journal of Career Development, 15*(3), 164-172.

Centers for Disease Control and Prevention United States. (January 23, 1998). AIDS among persons aged > 50 years. *Morbidity and Mortality Weekly Report.* Retrieved on January 15, 2001, from *http://www.thebody.com/cdc/mmwr472.html*

Comfort, A. (1972). *The joy of sex*. New York City, NY. Crown

Crisologo S., Campbell, M.H., & Forte, J.A. (1996). Social work, AIDS and the elderly: Current knowledge and practice. *Journal of Gerontological Social Work, 26*(1/2), 49-70.

Fryrear, J., & Corbit, I. (1992). *Photo art therapy: A Jungian perspective*. Springfield IL: Charles Thomas.

Goldstein, M.Z., & Griswold, K. (1998). Gender sensitivity in health care for elderly men and women. *Psychiatric Services, 49*(3), 323-325.

Gordon & Synder. (1986). *Personal issues in human sexuality*. Boston, MA: Allyn & Bacon.

Johnson, B.K. (1998). A correlational framework for understanding sexuality in women age 50 and older. *Health Care for Women International*, 19, 553-564.

Kaplan, L. (1996). Sexual and institutional issues when one spouse resides in the community and the other lives in a nursing home. *Sexuality and Disability, 14*(4), 281-293.

McFall, S., & Miller, B.H. (1992). Caregiver burden and nursing home admission of frail elderly persons. *Journal of Gerontology: Social Sciences, 47*, S73-S79.

Pfeiffer, E. (1978). Sexuality in the aging individual. In L. Solnick, (Ed.), *Sexuality and aging* (pp. 26-32). CA; University of Southern California Press.

Runciman, A. P. (1978). Sexual problems in the senior world. In L. Solnick, R. (Ed), *Sexuality and aging* (pp. 78-95). CA: University of Southern California Press.

Schlesinger, B. (1996). The sexless years or sex rediscovered. *Journal of Gerontological Social Work, 26*, 117-131.

Starr, B., & Weiner M. (1981). *The Starr-Weiner report: On sex & sexuality in the mature years*. Briarcliff Manor, NY: Scarborough House.

U.S. Bureau of the Census. (1999). *Aging in the United States: Past, present, and future*. Retrieve from *http://www.census.gov/ipc/prod/*

Weg, R. B. (1978). The physiology of sexuality in Aging. In L. Solnick (Ed.), *Sexuality and aging* (pp. 48-65). CA: University of Southern California Press.

Weg, R.B. (1981). *Sexuality in the later years: Roles and behavior*. New York, NY: Academic Press.

Weiser, J. (1990). More than meets the eye: Using ordinary snapshots as tools for therapy. In T. Laidlaw, C. Malmo, & Associates (Eds.), *Healing voices: Feminist approaches to therapy with women* (pp. 83-117). San Francisco: Jossey Bass.

Weiser, J. (1993). *Photo therapy techniques: Exploring the secrets of personal snapshots and family albums* (1st ed.) Vancouver: PhotoTherapy Centre Press.

Whitbourne, S.K., Jacobo, M., & Munoz-Ruiz, M.T. (1996). Adversity in the lives of the elderly. In R.S. Feldman (Ed), *The psychology of adversity* (pp.160-181). Amherst, MA: University of MA Press.

Chapter 11

HIV AND SEXUALITY

Jennifer Walker

Saint Louis University

BACKGROUND

Between 1979 and 1981, anecdotal reports of unusual diseases (**Kaposi's sarcoma** and **pneumocystis carinii pneumonia**) affecting gay men began to surface (Weitz, 1992). Because the original cases were all gay men, the new disease was referred to as Gay Related Immune Disorder, or GRID. Soon non-homosexual groups began to become infected with this disease, thus the CDC officially named the disease Acquired Immune Deficiency Syndrome, or AIDS, in September 1982 (Weitz, 1992).

Human immunodeficiency virus (HIV) must be present in order for someone to develop AIDS. After the initial infection, the virus enters the bodies CD4 cells and becomes dormant, often for as long as ten years or more (Pohl, Denniston, & Toft, 1990). The process of changing from HIV negative status to HIV positive status is termed seroconversion. Prior to 1993, the CDC defined AIDS as the manifestation of one or more of the following illnesses:

1. **Opportunistic infections**, including Pneumocystis carinii pneumonia and **Cytomegalovirus** (CMV)
2. **Neoplams,** including lymphomas and Kaposi's sarcoma
3. Neurologic abnormalities, including forgetfulness, balance problems and leg weakness
4. **Wasting**, the loss of large amounts of weight.

The revised 1993 defintion included the criterion of a CD-4 count below 200, regardless of any opportunistic infection, and added cervical cancer to the list of diagnostic criteria (Kain, 1996).

The following statistics are taken from the 2001 HIV/AIDS Surveillance Report. As of June 2001, there were 134,845 female adolscents and adults with AIDS in the U.S. By ethnicity, 58% are Black, 19.6% are Hispanic, and 21.6% are White. For White females, 42%

contracted AIDS through injecting drug usage, 40% through heterosexual contact, 6% by transfusion, and for 12% the transmission risk was not reported or identified. For Black females, 40% contracted AIDS through injecting drug usage, 39% through heterosexual contact, 2% through transfusion, and for 19% the transmission risk was not reported or identified. For Hispanic females, 39% contracted AIDS through injecting drug usage, 47% through heterosexual contact, 2% from transfusions, and for 11% the risk was not reported or identified.

As of June 2001, 649,186 adolescent and adult men in the U.S. have AIDS. By ethnicity, 47% of these males are White, 34% are Black, and 18% are Hispanic. For White males, 74% of males contracted AIDS through having sex with other males, 9% through injecting drug usage, 8% through having sex with males and injecting drug usage, 1% through hemophelia, 2% through heterosexual contact, 1% through transfusion, and for 4% the risk of transmission was not reported or identified. For Black males 39% contracted AIDS through having sex with other males, 33% through injecting drug usage, 7% through having sex with other males and injecting drug usage, 8% through heterosexual contact, 1% through transfusions, and for 13% the risk was not reported or identified. For Hispanic males, 42% contracted AIDS through having sex with other males, 35% through injecting drug usage, 7% through having sex with other males and injecting drug usage, 6% through heterosexual contact, 1% through transfusions, and for 9% the risk was not identified or reported.

As of June 2001, 104,050 males (children, adolescents, and adults), are diagnosed with HIV in the U.S. By ethnicity, 43% are White, 46% are Black, and 9% are Hispanic. There are 145,753 females (children, adolescents, and adults), diagnosed with HIV in the U.S. By ethnicity, 43% are White, 46% are Black, and 9% are Hispanic.

The statistics reported on AIDS include those individuals who have had an opportunistic disease and now are considered having full-blown AIDS; the statistics for HIV+ include those individuals who have not had an opportunistic disease, but have only tested positive for HIV. For reporting purposes, the two categories are separate and individuals fall only into either the AIDS or the HIV+ category.

Despite these alarming figures, medical advances are making a positive impact in the battle against HIV and AIDS. Between 1995 and 1997 the AIDS death rate declined by 62 percent and there was a 30 percent drop in the rate of hospitalizations (CDC Media Relations, 1999). The aggressive use of **antiretroviral therapy** is largely credited with the reduction in the AIDS death rate.

The following terms, defined here, will be used throughout this chapter:

- **Human Immunodeficiency Virus (HIV):** An unusual type of virus that is almost impossible for the body to eliminate. HIV is a retrovirus that destroys the part of the immune system that ordinarily fights viruses.
- **Acquired Immune Deficiency Syndrome (AIDS):** When an individual's CD4 count falls below 200 or he or she is diagnosed with one or more opportunistic diseases (such as Kaposi's Sarcoma or Wasting Syndrome).
- **Opportunistic Infections:** infections caused by generally innocuous microbes that take advantage of the suppressed immune system in the HIV+ person (Kain, 1996).
- **Antiretroviral Medication:** This includes protease inhibitors and reverse transcriptase inhibitors. This "drug cocktail" decreases the HIV viral load in both

genders, though side effects are possible (Morbidity and Mortality Weekly Report, 1998).

- **Cytomegalovirus**: A herpes virus that affects different parts of the body, and can cause blindness (Kain, 1996).
- **Kaposi's Sarcoma (KS):** An illness characterized by abnormal growth of blood vessels that develops into purplish or brown lesions. KS is the most common tumor associated with AIDS, particularly in gay men. When it affects internal organs it can cause stomach problems, coughing, and shortness of breath.
- **HIV Wasting Syndrome:** A loss of 10 percent or more of body weight with no other explanation than HIV infection.
- **Seroconversion:** When a person exposed to an infectious agent such as HIV develop antibodies to that agent, seroconversion has occurred.
- **Sero-concordant**: A couple who are both HIV positive.
- **Sero-discordant**: A couple consisting of one person who is HIV positive and one person who is HIV negative.

This chapter addresses a broad range of issues, including the effects of gender and ethnicity and HIV/AIDS, children with HIV/AIDS, issues for those with HIV/AIDS in rural areas, coping, long term survival, and existential factors. Counseling issues, including ethics will be discussed, as well as a case study, including counseling interventions and implications.

HIV/AIDS: CULTURAL AND GENDER CONSIDERATIONS

Women with HIV and AIDS

Although AIDS is decreasing in men, rates in women, especially women of color, continue to climb rapidly. While overall AIDS deaths in 1996 in the U.S. declined by 15 percent for men, they increased by 3 percent for women (Waters, 1997). Between the years of 1987 and 1992, AIDS cases in women in the U.S. increased by more than 1000 percent (Cohan & Atwood, 1994). AIDS rates in African American women are 15 times those in white women, while rates in Latina women are 6 times higher (Kaplan, Marks, & Mertens, 1997). Originally AIDS was thought to affect only gay men, thus research has focused primarily on issues affecting gay men with HIV and AIDS. Women with HIV have been largely ignored in the research, and have virtually been excluded from clinical trials (Cohen & Alfonso, 1997; Grove, Kelly, & Liu, 1997; Kaplan et al., 1997; Lawless, Kippax, & Crawford, 1996; Sherr, 1996; Weitz, 1993). Most of the women with AIDS in the U.S. live in poverty (Ward, 1993). While gay men with HIV and AIDS have been able to form supportive groups and networks, women with HIV and AIDS, who tend to be more geographically isolated and disparate, have not formed these networks as readily.

Women with HIV and AIDS face a number of difficult issues, including caregiving demands, which may preclude them from engaging in self care, social stigma, and the decision to disclose about their HIV status. Women may face enormous guilt as well, if one of their children is infected with HIV.

Effects of AIDS Stigma

Women have been viewed as "vectors" of transmission for the HIV virus, and "victimizers" if they are pregnant or have infected children. Lea (1994) noted that "They also encounter the stigma that only promiscuous women catch the disease and they deserve to be punished for their wanton behavior"(p. 493). One study found that women clearly feel more stigmatized than men and this may be because HIV services tend to be geared toward gay men (Green, 1996). The AIDS stigma may produce feelings of shame in women with HIV and AIDS as they internalize societal dictates. This stigma may keep women with HIV and AIDS from accessing services, including medical, counseling, or psychosocial support. Some women may fear that if they go to an AIDS center their children may be stigmatized, even if not infected. AIDS service agencies need to recognize how AIDS stigma can deter women with HIV and AIDS from accessing the services that will give them a better quality of life.

Women as Caregivers

Traditionally, women have taken on the caregiving role in our society. This role can become exceedingly difficult for the woman caring for a husband or boyfriend who may be ill, as well as caring for her children (who may also be sick with AIDS). All of the caregiving expectations a woman with HIV or AIDS faces may prevent her from seeking services for her own care, which will compromise her immune system. Bennett, Casey, and Austin (1996) noted that women who have infected a child may overcompensate by either overprotecting the child or being overly permissive. A woman caring for an infected partner may come to the realization that after having provided support for her partner, she may be left alone to face the disease. Social support may serve to buffer women with HIV and AIDS from the negative effects of stress (Lea, 1994).

Social Support and Coping

Women with HIV and AIDS need social support to cope with feelings and to lessen the alienation and isolation they may experience as a result of AIDS stigma. Women also need to inform partners or potential partners of their seropositive status and engage in safer sex practices. This can be a frightening proposition as women may fear rejection by partners. Support groups can provide a safe atmosphere for women to practice disclosing to partners their HIV+ status.

Lafond, Mensah, & Badeau (1992) stated that negotiation of safer sex practices may be difficult for women who are victims of violence, have little knowledge about HIV transmission, and who are afraid to destroy the spontaneity of sex. Cultural factors may interfere with safer sex practices as well. African American women may not perceive themselves as being at risk if they ascribe to the myth that AIDS is a gay white man's disease (Land, 1994). Kain (1996) noted that "The still prevalent misperception that women only become HIV infected if promiscuous often colors women's decisions to share their HIV positive status"(p.33). Disclosing about her seropositive status is one of the most difficult decisions a woman with HIV or AIDS may face. While nondisclosure may prevent some negative consequences, there may be a double edged sword in that it decreases opportunities for social support (Simoni, Mason, Marks, Ruiz, Reed, & Richardson, 1995).

Evidence suggests that when women with HIV or AIDS become more symptomatic, they may hide their emotions from their family (Schiller,1993). However, one study found that women with HIV have larger and more supportive social networks than do men (Green,

1996). Women with HIV and AIDS have a significant need for positive social support. If unable to obtain this from family or friends, they can derive social support from a derived "family"—members of a woman's support group.

Sex Workers

Female sex workers have been viewed as being reservoirs of infection who readily spread HIV to their customers. Studies indicate that primarily I.V. drug using prostitutes are HIV infected. Darrow, Boles, & Cohen (1991) found that in San Francisco 1.8 percent of non-injection drug using prostitutes were HIV positive, as compared to 15 percent of injection drug using female sex workers. For street prostitutes, a slow night or violence may influence their decision to succumb to a client's wishes and not use a condom (Jackson & Highcrest, 1996). In addition to inconsistent condom usage, Barnard (1993) found that close to 30 percent of street prostitutes interviewed had at least one incident of condom failure in the previous month.

Sex workers may be more in danger of HIV infection in their private lives. Even when their husband or boyfriend is suspected of being infected, there may be resistance to condom usage because of the association with work (Jackson & Highcrest, 1996).

Female I.V. Drug Users

Women who inject drugs may be most vulnerable to HIV infection. Injecting drugs alone increases susceptibility to HIV because of immunosuppression (Mientjes, Miedema, van Ameijden, van den Hoek, Schellekens, Roos, & Coutinho, 1991). Additionally, female I.V. drug users who are under the influence of drugs are unlikely to give much thought to safer sex practices. If these women are sharing needles with their primary partner, they may believe there is little merit in taking other protective measures, such as a condom (Klee, 1996). Researchers (e.g., Rosenbaum & Murphy, 1990) have noted the difficulty in outreach and treatment for female I.V. drug users who face excessive stigma. Additionally, these women may fear that if they access help, their children will be taken from them.

Men with HIV and AIDS

Men, particularly gay men, have been dealing with the AIDS epidemic since the discovery of the virus in 1981. Men with HIV and AIDS face a number of issues, including stigmatization, which may be compounded if they are forced to "come out" about their sexual orientation as they reveal their HIV status. Homosexual men in particular may have witnessed the decimation of their communities due to AIDS. The experience of multiple losses can produce trauma similar to that experienced in war and natural disasters. As gay men watch friends die by the dozens, death anxiety may surface as they fear their own mortality. Gay men may be perceived by some as "deserving" their disease as God's punishment for being gay. Heterosexual men with HIV and AIDS may be reluctant to disclose their HIV status for fear they will be perceived as homosexual. In this section social support, sexuality, and bereavement around multiple losses will be discussed.

Social Support and Sexuality

Gay men with HIV and AIDS have readily formed supportive networks and groups to deal with the effects of HIV. Gays and lesbians, infected or not, are more likely to turn to friends than family for support (Catania, Turner, Choi, & Coates, 1992; O'Connor, 1997). A different dynamic is apparent in I.V. drug users with HIV and AIDS. Relationships between addicts are marked by theft and distrust and are generally not reciprocal or supportive (Grummon, Rigby, Orr, Procidano, & Reznikoff, 1994). Some gay men move back to their home towns if they begin to experience physical deterioration. While peer support seems to be available in the short term, family support may be more continuous (Grummon et al.,1994).

Kain (1996) noted that for gay men with HIV and AIDS, dynamics in relationships will vary between sero-concordant couples and sero-discordant couples. For sero-concordant couples, issues of trust, anger and guilt may arise as the couple grapples with who infected whom. The partner who is sicker may experience anxiety as he fears his partner will be unable to care for him. In sero-discordant couples, the HIV+ partner may envy and resent his HIV- partner, while the negative partner may experience guilt. Sero-discordant couples will likely fear the possibility of HIV transmission to the negative partner. The negative partner may experience anticipatory grief and struggle with whether to remain in a relationship which may end in the death of his partner.

Men with HIV and AIDS need to learn to adopt safer sex procedures. Feelings of loss can result when these men give up former sexual activities and adopt new "safer" activities (Kain, 1996). If men with HIV and AIDS have internalized some of the stigma laden messages about the virus, they may be unable to have a satisfying sexual relationship because they feel "dirty." I.V. drug users may be more likely to spread the virus if their drug use precludes them from being cautious with sex or needle sharing. Faced with the immediate threat of police confrontation or violence from a drug dealer owed money, I.V. drug users may not perceive the risk of HIV transmission to be important (Harvey, Strathdee, Patrick, Ofner, Archibald, Eades & O'Shaughnessy, 1998).

Bereavement and Multiple Losses

Gay men with HIV and AIDS are often forced to contend with the deaths of many of their friends and possibly lovers. Since gay men with HIV and AIDS tend to be younger, they are not developmentally prepared for certain tasks related to multiple losses—such as planning for funerals (Nord, 1998). Survivor guilt can be a product of multiple losses as these men question why they are still alive. Kain (1996) observed that "living in a state of multiple loss challenges people to find meaning in the face of absurdity"(p. 226). Diagnostically, these men may experience depression, numbing, suicidal ideation, labile and explosive emotions, outbursts of rage, and symptoms of Post Traumatic Stress Disorder (O'Connor, 1997). The advent of new treatments such as Protease Inhibitors casts a more hopeful light on AIDS survival, which may diminish the phenomena of multiple losses. However, Nord (1998) suggested that "...raised hopes create the potential for crushing disappointments"(p. 236).

Ethnicity and HIV/AIDS

HIV infection is disproportionately represented in people of color of both genders. Clinicians need to be particularly sensitive to cultural factors when working with cultural minorities with HIV or AIDS. Folk healing practices may be practiced by Hispanics, and for Native Americans, the connection to nature and natural healing methods may be paramount.

Some people of color may not believe they are at risk for HIV transmission if they view it as a "gay man's disease." Due to sanctions against homosexuality in many cultures, secretive homosexual activity by men of color may place many uninformed women at risk (Dicks, 1994). HIV infected minority group members are more likely than are Whites to access medical treatment later in the disease course when treatments are less effective (Easterbrook, Keruly, Creagh-Kirk, Richman, Chaisson, Weisfuse, & Thomas, 1991). There is a mistrust of the white medical establishment on the part of many minority groups due to historical events, such as the infamous Tuskeegee experiments. Intervention efforts are needed to prevent the prediction that in the 21st century AIDS will become the leading cause of death among minority women of childbearing age (Land, 1994).

Carballo-Die'guez (1989) noted that in counseling, Hispanic clients do not discuss folk beliefs for fear of not being taken seriously. Counselors should explore these beliefs in a culturally sensitive manner. Suarez, Raffaelli, & O'Leary (1996) identified common reasons for practicing folk healing including the attainment of physical relief, spiritual or emotional relief, and to ward off evil. Use of culturally meaningful healing practices may provide HIV-infected Hispanics with more of a sense of mastery and control over their disease.

The stigma against homosexuality may be particularly prevalent in the black community. This stigma may prevent Black gay men from taking precautions to protect themselves or others against HIV infection (Rose, 1998). Some professionals (Quinn & Thomas, 1994) have noted lower levels of HIV/AIDS knowledge in minority communities, as well as the fact that minority gay men may not benefit as directly from service and support organizations initially developed to serve the gay White subculture (Siegal & Raveis, 1997). AIDS service organizations need to employ diversity in hiring practices to reflect the clients they serve. The Hispanic emphasis on masculine pride may encourage traditional men to have multiple sexual partners and use condoms less frequently. Hispanic women who adhere to traditional sex roles may be less willing to engage in protective sexual behaviors, such as inquiring about AIDS (Hines & Caetano, 1998).

DEVELOPMENTAL FACTORS

Children with HIV and AIDS

Children infected with HIV face a number of critical issues including the enormity of the AIDS stigma, the possible loss of one or both parents, and the possibility of their own early death. Currently between 72,000 and 125,000 children and adolescents in the U.S. have lost their mothers to HIV/AIDS (Levine, 1996). Because so many of these children have lost their mothers and/or are orphaned, a huge toll is being exacted on the foster care system in our country.

The demographics of HIV/AIDS in children mirror demographics found in women with HIV/AIDS. About 75 percent of children with HIV come from African American and Hispanic families. Trends in HIV infection for children are rapidly changing. Historically children with HIV were infected either by their mothers during pregnancy or through blood transfusions. However, in the future we will likely see school age children and adolescents becoming infected through heterosexual or homosexual activity or through injection drug use (Brewer & Parish, 1998).

Physiological Symptoms/Emotional Responses

Children who acquire HIV in vitro are at a higher risk for developmental delays, slowing of motor functions, and impairment of cognitive functioning (Levenson & Mellins, 1992). Children with HIV often experience impaired brain functioning, which will manifest in attention problems, problems in verbal expression, motor coordination, and language skill. As HIV progresses, apathy, cognitive impairment, reduced speech and memory problems may occur (Olson, Huszti, & Parsons, 1997). Children may experience anger, depression, grief, loss, and isolation due to societal rejection (Olson et al., 1997).

Developmentally, children younger than five may not have an understanding of death as being permanent. It is important for those working with children to assess their understanding of death. Children who lose one or both parents to HIV will be affected profoundly. If relevant, children need to be given concrete information about future living arrangements (Olson et al., 1997).

Bereavement and Loss

Children and adolescents with HIV and AIDS will be profoundly affected after the loss of a parent. Mourning for these children is complicated by the fact that they may lack the vocabulary and social skills needed to fully comprehend death or experience mourning (Ward-Wimmer, 1997). Children can be helped to understand death through the use of play and books about death (Olson et al., 1997). It is important for children to be allowed to mourn in their own way and for teachers and counselors to be aware of culturally significant rituals (Brewer & Parish, 1998). Children and adolescents who are allowed to fully experience their feelings of loss will be the best equipped when dealing with their own chronic illness. Children and adolescents with HIV and AIDS who lose a parent may experience survivors' guilt—why was it he/she and not me who died? It is important for these children to find meaning in these existential dilemmas.

Disclosure of HIV

Historically, disclosure of HIV and AIDS in children or adolescents has resulted in extreme stigmatization including refusal to let children attend public school, and an incident in which a family's house was burned down. While the reluctance to disclose a child's HIV status is easily understood, the stress associated with withholding the HIV status is tremendous (Wiener, Heilman, & Battles, 1998). Information about HIV should be given to children over time in a developmentally appropriate manner, and children need to know that there are ways to cope with the disease and lead a happy life (Olson et al., 1997). Selective disclosure to trusted persons may be the most appropriate way for a family dealing with HIV to access the social support they need.

DIAGNOSTIC FEATURES AND COUNSELING ISSUES

Coping with HIV in Adults

Individuals diagnosed with HIV who had good coping skills prior to diagnosis tend to cope better with HIV than those who had poor coping skills prior to diagnosis. People with HIV and AIDS who are drug users may increase their drug usage as a means of coping. Substance abuse can result in impaired judgement and increase the propensity to engage in unsafe sex. Some have suggested that persons from ethnic minority groups cope less well with health problems (Schmidt, McKirnan, & Tranmer, 1990). Persons newly diagnosed with HIV will likely be in a state of mourning for the loss of their health and possibly a loss of their "in the closet" status. With the advent of antiretroviral medication including **Protease Inhibitors**, AIDS may have become a chronic manageable illness. However, the medication is expensive and may not be available to all, and the effect of the new medications on people of color and women's survival rates is unclear. This section will focus on resilience and personal control, as well as coping.

Individuals with HIV and AIDS may have witnessed scores of friends in their 30s or 40s die—a developmentally premature occurrence. Persons coping with HIV and AIDS may have to resolve developmental issues that usually occur in much older people. Erik Erikson has identified the final developmental stage of life as integrity versus despair, in which older people conduct a life review. Those with HIV and AIDS may need to do their life review at a much younger age and may despair at what they have failed to accomplish in their young lives. Tunnell (1989) noted that therapists can point out ways in which the person's life has been valuable and encourage him/her to live in the present in ways which provide integrity.

Some have noted that it is adaptive for those with HIV/AIDS to have an attitude of acceptance (Gloerson, Kendall, Gray, McConnell, Turner & Lewkowicz, 1993), while others have found that, at least among gay men with AIDS, realistic acceptance of future debilitation and mortality predicted decreased survival time (Reed, Kemeny, Taylor, Wang, & Visscher, 1994). So, while it may be adaptive to accept that one has a chronic illness, the acceptance of the disease as an automatic death sentence may be detrimental, and in fact hasten death. One factor identified by many is that of a "will to live" and a "fighting spirit" which has been found in **long-term survivors** of AIDS.

Resilience and Long-Term Survival

A phenomenon in the 1980s was noted as some people with AIDS seemed to survive much longer than others. These "long-term survivors" were defined by the Centers for Disease Control as those living three or more years subsequent to an AIDS diagnosis. Long-term survivors may differentiate themselves by actively coping with their difficulties, as well as cognitively reframing the stress and hardships they endure. In a sample of 53 male long term survivors, Rabkin, Remien, Katoff & Williams (1993) found that:

> Nearly all experienced one or more episodes of life-threatening illness, the majority were unable to work, and many originally had been led to believe that they only had months to live. Despite this...nearly all maintained the conviction that good times lay ahead and that their lives were worthwhile. (p. 166)

What is it that differentiates those who are resilient in the face of HIV and AIDS from those who are not? Barroso (1997) noted that long-term AIDS survivors do not make AIDS the sole focus of their lives, tend to re-prioritize their lives and goals, have a positive attitude, and derive satisfaction from helping others with HIV and AIDS. Long-term survivors or persons who are resilient in the face of AIDS can serve as positive role models in support groups and in turn feel rewarded as they help others. One factor that may contribute to adaptive coping skills for people with HIV and AIDS is a sense of mastery or control over the disease.

Personal Control

It is helpful to have perceived control when the situation is objectively controllable, but this belief is maladaptive when control is impossible (Thompson & Spacapan, 1991). For people with HIV and AIDS, the ambiguity of their disease and its progression can make achieving a sense of control difficult. Jue (1994) revealed that long-term survivors tend to focus on the aspects of a situation that they can control, rather than obsessing about circumstances beyond their control.

Griffin and Rabkin (1998) found in a largely minority sample of women and men with AIDS that perceptions of control over the day to day course of the illness was associated with psychological adjustment. They also noted that beliefs in personal control became more important as one's health status became more uncertain. Others, however, have suggested that maintaining beliefs of personal control over a chronic illness may be maladaptive because of the helplessness created by personal failure to positively impact the disease (Burish, Carey, Wallston, Stein, Jamison, & Lyles, 1984). So, in the face of the unpredictable course of AIDS, is a belief in personal control desirable in persons with HIV and AIDS? Clearly, more research is needed in this area. One study (Taylor, Helgeson, Reed, & Skokan, 1991) did find that even with advanced stage AIDS patients, feelings of personal control allow them to cope with less psychological distress and enjoy a higher quality of life. A belief in personal control may be empowering for many with HIV and AIDS, as long as the belief is tempered with reality.

Existential Dilemmas and Meaning Making

People with HIV and AIDS face a number of existential dilemmas beginning with the need to get the most out of the remainder of their lives. They may be grappling with survivor's guilt if they have seen loved ones die with AIDS. HIV+ mothers may feel guilty about the prospect of leaving their children behind if they die. Persons with HIV may question their sexuality—will they choose to be celibate, to engage in safer sex methods? What about the potential rejection they may face from a prospective lover who is told they are HIV+? Could they deal with the guilt of infecting someone else with HIV?

Quality of life will likely be a significant issue for most with HIV and AIDS. Those who formerly had unhealthy lifestyles, such as sex workers or I.V. drug users, may choose to develop more productive lifestyles. People with HIV and AIDS who experience severe side effects from drug treatments may decide to discontinue their medication to create a better quality of life. They need to know the consequences of their decision in order to make an informed choice. Conversely, some people with HIV and AIDS may begin to feel well enough because of their drug regimen that they want to return to work. These individuals need to look at insurance coverage issues, as well as possible retraining.

Some people with HIV and AIDS create meaning in their lives by being able to give to others with HIV (Rose, 1998). One means of doing this could be in support groups. Yalom (1985) has talked about the importance of altruism in support groups, where members give to others with no thought of reward. One study of women living with AIDS found that finding their meaning in life assisted these women with healing and growth (Dunbar, Mueller, Medina & Wolf, 1998). Women with HIV who choose to do public speaking about their disease and who educate other women about HIV and AIDS described feeling a deep sense of fulfillment (Chung & Magraw, 1992).

Living with HIV/AIDS in Rural Areas

The majority of research in the area of HIV and AIDS has focused on urban samples. Rates of HIV infection are rapidly increasing in rural areas. Between 1989 and 1994 the percentage increase in AIDS among rural men through sexual contact with other men was 69 percent, while the increase in the same category in urban areas was only 19 percent (Shuff, 1997).

The AIDS stigma may be particularly prevalent in rural areas if there is a lack of HIV education available. If persons with HIV and AIDS feel like "everybody knows everybody else's business" in their rural community, fear of breaches in confidentiality may be extreme. These individuals may be reluctant to join support groups because of fears of confidentiality breaches. Many with HIV and AIDS in rural areas have difficulties accessing AIDS related services because of transportation problems (Heckman, Somlai, Peters, Walker, Otto-Salaj, Galdabini, & Kelly, 1998; Mancoske, 1997; O'Rourke & Sutherland, 1998; Walker, 1999). Telephone linked support groups are one way to overcome transportation barriers in rural areas.

COUNSELING AND TREATMENT STRATEGIES

Because many people with HIV and AIDS have been marginalized all of their lives, it is absolutely imperative for counselors to treat them with unconditional positive regard. Counselors who have unresolved issues with homosexuals, I.V. drug users, or sex workers need to address their unfinished business prior to working with this population. Counselors who choose to work with this population also need to feel comfortable with their own mortality, and issues around death, dying, and chronic illness. Counseling people with HIV and AIDS can be incredibly uplifting and rewarding. Counselors may witness wondrous fortitude in their clients, but they also may feel powerless if they see their clients die. Counselors whose caseload consists solely of people with HIV and AIDS need to be vigilant in order to prevent burnout. This section will address various treatment strategies, ethical dilemmas, support groups, and will present a case study, including treatment interventions.

Ethics and HIV

Counselors working with people with HIV and AIDS may face ethical dilemmas. The primary ethical principle is nonmaleficence, or do no harm. In the groundbreaking case *Tarasoff v. Regents of the University of California* (1976) it was stated that if a client threatens to harm another party, it is appropriate for counselors to breach the client's confidentiality in order to warn the intended victim. If a client with HIV or AIDS is having unprotected sex with another individual and that person does not know their HIV status, the client *is* acting irresponsibly, but there is no "smoking gun." That is, unprotected sex with another party does not necessarily guarantee transmission of HIV, the party engaging in unprotected sex with the client must know of the risk of HIV transmission, and HIV disease is not necessarily fatal. Counselors in this situation face the unenviable task of deciding whether to breach the client's confidentiality, which may precipitate social ostracism, or to protect the client, thus endangering those who may become HIV infected unknowingly.

The American Counseling Association revised the ethics code in 1995 so that a counselor who has confirming information that a client has a fatal and contagious disease is justified in disclosing information to an at risk third party. Some (e.g., Cohen, 1997) have noted the ambiguity in this statement. Others have advocated using a series of steps with clients who are having unprotected sex and not informing partners. Clients should be informed of the limits of confidentiality, then encouraged (over a series of sessions) to inform their partners of their HIV status. If the client refuses to do so, the counselor needs to decide if she/he should directly warn the potential victim, or if the person is unknown, report the client to the state public health department (Erickson, 1993).

With respect to children, Brewer and Parish noted that the *Tarasoff* case and other related legislation seldom compels a school counselor to disclose information about an HIV infected person in school. At times the ethical guidelines may be at odds with official school policies which put school counselors in a difficult position. For example, if a school counselor informs the parents of the student's HIV status, other behaviors such as drug use, sexual activity, and sexual orientation may be revealed, further complicating the situation (Cobia & Carney, 1998). School counselors can empower their clients to disclose their positive status to parents through the use of role playing. Students need to be prepared for reactions of anger and shock on the part of their parents (Cobia & Carney, 1998).

Support Groups

Support groups can be helpful for people with HIV and AIDS for a number of reasons. In many HIV/AIDS support groups, practical issues such as medical treatments, medication, and funding sources are regularly discussed. Benefits from group participation include sharing feelings, relief from feeling alone, and obtaining information on treatments (Kalichman, Sikkema, & Somlai, 1996). Support groups can provide a social support network for people with HIV and AIDS, many of whom may have little social support. Support groups provide an opportunity for members to learn from each other and to receive constructive feedback. Modeling can be a powerful factor in HIV/AIDS support groups as long term survivors or those who are resilient demonstrate a positive attitude and coping skills for others. It is important for group leaders to facilitate an attitude of acceptance and tolerance in HIV/AIDS support groups. Members, many of who are from marginalized groups, may be particularly sensitive to slights.

Some believe that homogenous groups are the most efficacious for people with HIV and AIDS. A homogenous group may consist of only those diagnosed with HIV. A more heterogenous group could consist of people with HIV, people with AIDS, and HIV-caregivers. With respect to heterogenous groups, Burke, Coddington, Bakeman, & Clance (1994) stated, "Members who are not similar to others in the group-either with respect to their HIV status or the length of time they have known their status-are more likely to leave the group early." (p.129)

Walker (1999), in a study of rural women with HIV and AIDS, reported that a study participant felt uncomfortable as the only woman in a support group consisting of men, and subsequently terminated from the group.

Group facilitators cannot guarantee confidentiality on the part of the members, but it is imperative that a norm of confidentiality be set and maintained throughout the life of the group. Confidentiality is particularly important for people with HIV and AIDS, who could face painful ostracism if their IIIV status was revealed. Some people with HIV and AIDS may have adverse experiences in groups, if they feel the focus on illness is depressing or witness the physical decline of other members (Kalichman et al., 1996). If support groups are not having an advantageous effect, perhaps the member should be seen individually.

Theoretical Framework/Strategies

Many theoretical frameworks may be helpful in working with people with HIV and AIDS. However, an Existential framework may be particularly helpful for those who are dealing with issues such as quality of life, the ramifications of chronic illness, and making the most of one's life. Existentialists focus on choices and responsibility in client's lives. People with HIV and AIDS can be encouraged to make better choices in their lives, which may include employing safer sex methods and deciding to give up alcohol and/or drugs.

Eversole (1997) noted that counselors working with clients with HIV need to "bend the frame" of traditional counseling approaches. This could involve demonstrating the use of a condom with a dildo, a skill not taught in most counseling programs. Counselors may need to engage in more case management and client advocacy with this population, particularly for newly diagnosed clients, who may get discouraged if they encounter systemic obstacles.

Clients with HIV and AIDS may have substance abuse issues that are a primary concern. Kain (1996) suggested that recovery issues may need to take precedence over HIV adjustment issues. HIV+ substance abusers may remain in denial throughout the course of their disease process. Counselors need to determine whether a substance abusing client needs treatment initially, as well as follow-up treatment, which can include twelve step programs. Clients who have severe substance abuse problems not only place their own lives at risk (and may be unable to follow complicated antiretroviral drug regimens) but also risk infecting others while they are under the influence.

If specific behavioral changes are desired, cognitive behavioral techniques can be employed. Strategies to prevent the transmission of HIV include determining antecedents to risky behavior, assertiveness, and terminating sex when it becomes unsafe (Roffman & Downey, 1997). Kain (1996) stated that the cycle associated with CD4 counts can produce extreme anxiety and irrational thoughts such as "My CD4 cell count was 150 last month and dropped to 100 this month; in two more months I'll be dead" (p. 121). In this situation, clients need to be provided with accurate medical information, such as the fact that CD4 cell drops are not linear. Cognitive behavioral strategies such as gently disputing clients' irrational thoughts and teaching them to substitute more rational thoughts can be helpful.

Counseling Children and Adolescents with HIV

Children and adolescents with HIV may have experienced losses, such as a parent or sibling, and may come from families with substance abuse issues. It is important for counselors to have an understanding of substance abuse and its impact on family dynamics (Ward-Wimmer, 1997). Children who have lost a parent may have intense feelings of abandonment. These children need to be provided with concrete information about future living arrangements and changes in schools or neighborhood (Olson et al., 1997).

Cobia and Carney (1998) stated, "Play therapy may provide children with the opportunity to express their emotions related to fear of death, sense of vulnerability, changes in physical health, and concerns about acceptance from peers and family members" (p. 43). Children who experience behavioral distress associated with medical procedures can be taught behavioral techniques, such as deep breathing or distraction (Olson et al., 1997). It is important for counselors to empower children in the counseling process by giving them lots of choices.

Counselors need to continually assess the level of depression and risk of suicide in children and adolescents with HIV. For adolescents, disclosure of HIV status may prompt the decision to reveal their sexual orientation. Adolescents who reveal that they are homosexual and experience subsequent rejection and discrimination may encounter overwhelming feelings of sadness and hurt.

HIV+ adolescents, who tend to engage in egocentric thought processes, may be unlikely to use condoms. Some (Olson et al., 1997) have found that the adolescents with the highest number of sexual partners are least likely to report using condoms. Counselors need to assess the adolescent's understanding of safer sex practices and need for education around HIV transmission. While school based HIV/AIDS education programs are often opposed because it is feared this information will make adolescents more sexually active, research shows just the opposite to be true—adolescents who received this education were less likely to engage in sex (Olson et al., 1997).

Current Trends

Two HIV/AIDS treatment professionals, one from a large urban area, and one from a rural area were interviewed. According to Keville Ware, who works in an urban setting primarily with gay men, there is a negative side to getting healthier for some. After about one year of being on antiretroviral medication, many of his clients experience rage, depression, relapse, and sexual acting out. Keville feels that these are repressed feelings due to survivor's guilt and multiple loss, and equates their experience (of losing so many friends to AIDS) to Holocaust survivors. Keville sees these emerging repressed feelings particularly in long term survivors. Keville stated that he sees more positive effects of antiretroviral medication in white men, and that African American men seem to have more limited awareness of treatments, and don't seek treatment until late in the disease process. Keville runs two HIV support groups and notes that the effects of the new medications have changed the course of the groups dramatically, members are dealing more with life issues such as returning to work. Additionally, Keville notes that some clients stop taking medications, and that there are unresolved emotional issues for those in the gay community (Keville Ware, personal communication, August 1, 1999).

Blain Naramore, who works for an agency that services many rural counties, stated that he is seeing positive effects of antiretroviral medication in men, women, and people of color. Blain stated that men in the rural areas often refuse to use condoms because it is not "manly." Blain said that he knows of five couples, all of whom refuse to use safer sex methods, even when [the woman] knows her husband is HIV+. Blain noted that three of these women have become HIV infected by their husbands. He has seen a recent increase in HIV in unmarried, pregnant, young women and adolescents. He noted that these women and adolescents are embarrassed about their diagnosis. Blain stated that if pregnant women follow the drug regimen, their babies are usually HIV negative. He noted that acceptance of the disease is very difficult for some of his clients who previously ascribed to the myth that only gay men get HIV. Blain stated that his clients don't seem to have any problem accessing the expensive antiretroviral medications, due to funding sources. He observes that HIV infection is increasing in women in rural areas, but decreasing in gay men (Blain Naramore, personal communication, August 5, 1999).

CASE STUDY

Conseula, 28, is an HIV positive, second generation, Hispanic American mother of 2 daughters, Angelica and Hortencia, nine and ten. Both of her daughters are HIV negative. Conseula and her daughters live in a town of 10,000 people. Conseula's husband, Ernesto, died six months ago after a year-long battle with AIDS. Conseula had been unaware of Ernesto's extramarital homosexual relationships, and was unknowingly exposed herself. Though Ernesto had symptoms of HIV such as weight loss, night sweats, swollen lymph nodes, and severe fatigue, he did not seek treatment until the disease had progressed to the late stages of AIDS. Conseula has been diagnosed as HIV+ for 18 months, but her doctor says it is likely that she has been positive for a number of years. She is currently on antiretroviral medication.

For several months, Conseula has had insomnia, crying bouts, and has had to ask her mother for help with her daughters from time to time. Conseula has a part time job as a sales clerk, and relies on public assistance for food stamps and her rent. Her caseworker referred her to the local community mental health agency. Conseula is reluctant and somewhat ashamed to be seeking counseling, because in her culture help is generally sought within the family.

Conseula is estranged from an older sister, Lupe, a medical technologist at a local hospital, because Lupe told several colleagues about Conseula being HIV+. Conseula is terrified about her diagnosis being revealed and subsequent ostracism. Several of Conseula's aunts, uncles, cousins, and some of Ernesto's family who live nearby have turned their back on her since her HIV diagnosis. Conseula says she feels dirty and ashamed that she has this disease, and embarrassed because of her husband's infidelity with other men.

Counseling Strategies for the Case of Conseula

Caitlin, a Licensed Professional Counselor, notes that Conseula has major depression, bereavement issues, and severe guilt because "she doesn't want her daughters to be alone when she dies from AIDS." Caitlin ascertains that Conseula's social support system is limited, her mother lives in town and is supportive, and a neighbor helps Conseula with transportation, since she doesn't own a car.

Caitlin informs Conseula about an HIV/AIDS support group at the center. Conseula seems to be reluctant to participate in the support group because she fears that someone will inform others about her diagnosis. Due to inadequate transportation Conseula can only come to see Caitlin twice monthly. Caitlin agrees to visit Conseula at her house for counseling twice monthly, as well. Caitlin gives Conseula phone numbers for two other HIV positive women. Conseula is referred to a psychiatrist, who places her on anti-depressant medication.

Caitlin encourages Conseula to grieve her multiple losses—including her husband, her health, and feelings of anticipatory loss for her daughters who she fears will be left alone. Caitlin provides Conseula with some information related to treatments for HIV, and helps her to view her HIV infection as a chronic manageable illness rather than necessarily a terminal one. Conseula continues to fear that she will leave her daughters and that they will not remember her. Conseula and Caitlin decide to make some videotapes for Hortencia and Angelica, in the event of Conseula's death. Caitlin videotapes Conseula as she discusses issues with her daughters such as dating, and each child's special qualities and strengths. Conseula also begins to keep a daily journal.

Caitlin notices that Conseula's depression has decreased, and she is accessing a social support network. She continues to respond well to the antiretroviral medication she is taking. When Caitlin provides home counseling to Conseula she often involves Conseula's mother and daughters in the sessions. This helps Conseula's family to gain some insight into her illness, as well as ways in which they can support her. These conjoint sessions also allow Conseula's family to express their feelings. Angelica and Hortencia express that they miss their father and fear the same fate awaits their mother. Caitlin has noticed in herself profound feelings of sadness during some of the sessions when Conseula discusses her daughters. During clinical supervision Caitlin comes to realize that she is experiencing countertransference with Conseula because Conseula's daughters are close in age to Caitlin's son and daughter.

Follow Up

Caitlin needs to continue to help Conseula resolve her grief and loss issues, assess her mood, social support network, and coping skills. Although Conseula has made some friendships with HIV positive women, Caitlin may want to discuss with Conseula whether to reconsider the support group in the future. If at some point Conseula wants to date, Caitlin will likely use cognitive behavioral techniques such as rehearsal to practice safer sex negotiation skills. Caitlin is self aware enough to realize that she is having countertransference feelings, and has addressed this in supervision. She will want to remain attuned to further feelings of this nature.

CONCLUSION

Since the discovery of HIV in 1981, the demographics of those who are infected with the disease have changed dramatically. Currently, groups in which HIV infection is increasing most rapidly include women, people of color, and adolescents. Unfortunately, the myth that HIV and AIDS only affects gay men has influenced some to continue high risk activities, which could lead to HIV infection. Women with HIV and AIDS may let their caregiving needs preclude self care. People with HIV and AIDS of both genders are in need of a coping skills and social support networks. Disclosure of HIV status can be very difficult, and may result in ostracism. Gay men who disclose their HIV status may be forced to disclose their, formerly, hidden sexual orientation as well. Children with HIV and AIDS will likely face many losses, including loss of a parent.

Antiretroviral medication has made an impact upon the quality of life for many with HIV and AIDS. Early anecdotal reports suggest that many are benefitting from these new medications. More research is needed to ascertain the physical, emotional, and quality of life effects of antiretroviral medications. Research also needs to examine the availability of antiretroviral medications.

Trends suggest that gay men, especially long term survivors, may experience an upheaval of emotions as long repressed multiple losses come to the surface. These men have lost so many friends that their emotional state may mimic that of war survivors. They may have intense survivor's guilt as they question why friends who have died didn't have access to new drug treatments. Clinicians must be vigilant in assessing these clients for clinical depression or suicidal ideation.

Women and people of color tend to seek treatment later in the HIV disease course. Proactive efforts are needed to empower these groups to access diagnosis and early treatment. Qualitative research studies could examine the perceptions of people of color related to HIV/AIDS and how these perceptions influence the accessibility of treatment or prevention. Findings from studies such as this could, in turn, be used to improve prevention and community outreach efforts with people of color. People with HIV and AIDS who live in rural areas may face great stigma if HIV/AIDS education is lacking in that area. Transportation may be one obstacle to rural people with HIV accessing medical and counseling services. More research is needed around particular issues or obstacles that those living in rural areas encounter.

People with HIV and AIDS can derive many benefits from individual counseling or support groups. Support groups provide universality, or a sense of not being alone with the disease, as well as an opportunity to gather important medical information. Support groups may not be appropriate for every person with HIV and AIDS, due to fears of confidentiality breaches. Clients can practice safer sex negotiation skills in counseling. Counselors working with people with HIV and AIDS need to be self aware to prevent countertransferences from occurring. Counselors can help people with HIV and AIDS to reframe thinking about AIDS as a terminal illness to a chronic one, and can encourage them to return to working if their health is good. Research in this area could focus on the relationship between quality of life and participation in support groups. Another area in which research is needed is related to group composition. Can clients benefit equally from groups with members with similar diagnoses, as well as more heterogenous groups (such as clients with HIV, AIDS, and HIV-caregivers)?

REFERENCES

American Counseling Association. (1995). *Code of ethics and standards of practice.* Alexandria, VA: Author.

Barnard, M. (1993). Violence and vulnerability: Conditions of work for streetworking prostitutes. *Sociology of Health and Illness, 15(5)*, 683-705.

Barroso, J. (1997). Reconstructing my life: Becoming a long-term survivor of AIDS. *Qualitative Health Research, 7(1)*, 57-74.

Bennett, L., Casey, K., & Austin, P. (1996). Issues for women as carers in HIV/AIDS. In L. Sherr, C.Hankins, & L.Bennett, (Eds.), *AIDS as a gender issue: Psychosocial perspectives.* London: Taylor & Francis.

Brewer, L.K., & Parish, M.T. (1998). Children and HIV: Concepts and strategies for teachers and counselors. In L.L. Palmatier (Ed.), *Crisis counseling for a quality school community: Applying William Glassers' choice theory* (pp. 269-303) Washington, DC: Taylor & Francis.

Burish, T., Carey, M., Wallston, K., Stein, M., Jamison, P., & Lyles, J. (1984). Health locus of control and chronic disease: An external orientation may be advantageous. *Journal of Social and Clinical Psychology, 2,* 326-332.

Burke, J.M., Coddington, D., Bakeman, R., & Clance, P.R. (1994). Inclusion and exclusion in HIV support groups. *Journal of Gay and Lesbian Psychotherapy, 2(2)*, 121-130.

Carballo-Die'guez, A. (1989). Hispanic culture, gay male culture, and AIDS: Counseling implications. *Journal of Counseling and Development, 68,* 26-30.

Catania, J.A., Turner, H.A., Turner, H.A., Choi, K., & Coates, T.J. (1992). Coping with death anxiety: Help seeking and social support among gay men with various HIV diagnoses. *AIDS, 6(9)*, 999-1005.

CDC Media Relations Releases. (June 8, 1999). Retrieved from http://www.gov/od/oc/media/pressrel/r990608.htm

CDC. (1998, April 24). *Morbidity and Mortality Weekly Report, (47),* 43-82.

Chung, J.Y., & Magraw, M.M. (1992). A group approach to psychosocial issues faced by HIV-positive women. *Hospital and Community Psychiatry, 43(9)*, 891-894.

Cobia, D.C., & Carney, J.S. (1998). Children and adolescents with HIV disease: Implications for school counselors. *Professional School Counseling, 1(5)*, 41-45.

Cohan, N., & Atwood, J.D. (1994). Women and AIDS: The social constructions of gender and disease. *Family Systems Medicine, 12(1)*, 5-20.

Cohen, E.D. (1997). Ethical standards in counseling sexually active clients with HIV. In J. Lonsdale (Ed.), *The Hatherleigh guide to ethics in therapy* (pp. 211-233). New York, NY: Hatherleigh Press.

Cohen, M.A.A. & Alfonso, C.A. (1997). Women, sex, and AIDS. *Intenational Journal of Mental Health, 26(1)*, 99-106.

Darrow, W., Boles, J., & Cohen, J.B. (1991). HIV seroprevalence trends in female prostitutes, United States: 1986-1990. *VII International Conference on AIDS, Florence, Italy.*

Dicks, B.A. (1994). African American women and AIDS: A public health/social work challenge. *Social Work in Health Care, 19(*3/4), 123-143.

Dunbar, H.T., Mueller, C.M., Medina, C., & Wolf, T. (1998). Psychological and spiritual growth in women living with HIV. *Social Work, 43(*2), 144-154.

Easterbrook, P.J., Keruly, J.C., Creagh-Kirk, T., Richman, D.D., Chaisson, R.E., & Moore, R.D. (1991). Racial and ethnic differences in outcome in zidovudine-treated patients with advanced HIV disease. *Journal of the American Medical Association, 266,* 2713-2718.

Erickson, S.H. (1993). Ethics and confidentiality in AIDS counseling: A professional dilemma. *Journal of Mental Health Counseling, 15(*2), 118-131.

Eversole, T. (1997). Psychotherapy and counseling: Bending the frame. In M.G. Winiarski (Ed.), *HIV mental health for the 21ˢᵗ century* (pp. 23-28). New York: New York University Press.

Gloerson, B., Kendall, J., Gray, P., McConnell, S., Turner, J., & Lewkowicz, J.W. (1993). The phenomena of people doing well with AIDS. *Western Journal of Nursing Research, 15(*1), 44-58.

Green, G. (1996). Stigma and social relationships of people with HIV: Does gender make a difference? In L. Sherr, C. Hankins, & L. Bennett (Eds.), *AIDS as a gender issue: Psychosocial perspectives* (pp. 46-63). London: Taylor & Francis.

Griffin, K.W., & Rabkin, J.G. (1998). Perceived control over illness, realistic acceptance, and psychological adjustment in people with AIDS. *Journal of Social and Clinical Psychology, 17(*4), 407-424.

Grove, K.A., Kelly, D.P., & Liu, J. (1997). "But nice girls don't get it": Women, symbolic capital, and the social construction of AIDS. *Journal of Contemporary Ethnography, 26(*3), 317-337.

Grummon, K., Rigby, E.D., Orr, D., Procidano, M., & Reznikoff, M. (1994). Psychosocial variables that affect the psychological adjustment of IVDU patients with AIDS. *Journal of Clinical Psychology, 50(*4), 488-502.

HIV/AIDS Surveillance Report. (2001). *13,(*1).

Harvey, E., Strathdee, A., Patrick, D.M., Ofner, M., Archibald, C.P., Eades, G., & O'Shaughnessy, M.V. (1998). A qualitative investigation into an HIV outbreak among injection drug users in Vancouver, British Columbia. *AIDS Care, 10(*3), 313-321.

Heckman, T.G., Somlai, A.M., Peters, J., Walker, J., Otto-Salaj, L., Galdabini, C.A., & Kelly, J.A. (1998). Barriers to care among persons living with HIV/AIDS in urban and rural areas. *AIDS Care, 10(*3), 365-375.

Hines, A.M., & Caetano, R. (1998). Alcohol and AIDS-related sexual behavior among Hispanics: Acculturation and gender differences. *AIDS Education and Prevention, 10(*6), 533-47.

Jackson, L.A., & Highcrest, A. (1996). Female prostitutes in North America: What are their risks of HIV infection? In L. Sherr, C. Hankins, & L. Bennett (Eds.), *AIDS as a gender issue: Psychosocial perspectives* (pp. 149-162). London: Taylor & Francis.

Jue, S. (1994). Psychosocial issues of AIDS long-term survivors. *Families in Society: The Journal of Contemporary Human Services, 75*(6), 324-332.

Kain, C.D. (1996). *Positive HIV affirmative counseling.* Alexandria, VA: American Counseling Association.

Kalichman, S.C., Sikkema, K.J., & Somlai, A. (1996). People living with HIV infection who attend and do not attend support groups: A pilot study of needs, characteristics, and experiences. *AIDS Care, 8*(5), 589-599.

Kaplan, M.S., Marks, G., & Mertens, S.B. (1997). Distress and coping among women with HIV infection: Preliminary findings from a multiethnic sample. *American Journal of Orthopsychiatry, 67(*1), 80-91.

Klee, H. (1996). Women drug users and their partners. In L. Sherr, C. Hankins, & L. Bennett (Eds.), *AIDS as a gender issue: Psychosocial perspectives* (pp. 163-176). London: Taylor & Francis.

Lafond, J.S., Mensah, M.N., & Badeau, D. (1992). Women and AIDS: Reality of myth. *Canada's Mental Health, 4(*4), 23-25.

Land, H. (1994). AIDS and women of color. *Families in Society: The Journal of Contemporary Human Services, 75*(6), 355-361.

Lawless, S., Kippax, S., & Crawford, J. (1996). Dirty, diseased and undeserving: The positioning of HIV positive women. *Social Science and Medicine, 43(*9), 1371-1377.

Lea, A. (1994). Women with HIV and their burden of caring. *Health Care for Women International, 15,* 489-501.

Levenson, R.L., & Mellins, C.A. (1992). Pediatric HIV disease: What psychologists need to know. *Professional Psychology and Practice, 23,* 410-415,

Levine, C. (1996). Children in mourning: Impact of the HIV/AIDS epidemic on mothers with AIDS and their families. In L. Sherr, C. Hankins, & L. Bennett (Eds.), *AIDS as a gender issue: Psychosocial perspectives* (pp. 197-214). London: Taylor & Francis.

Mancoske, R.J. (1997). Rural HIV/AIDS social services for gays and lesbians. *Journal of Gay and Lesbian Social Services, 7(*3), 37-52.

Mientjes, G.H.C., Miedema, F., van Ameijden, E., van den Hoek, A., Schellekens, P., Roos, M., & Coutinho, R.A. (1991). Frequent injecting impairs lymphocyte reactivity in HIV positive and HIV negative drug users. *AIDS, 5,* 35-41.

Naramore, B. (August 5, 1999). Service Team Leader, Special Health Resources of East Texas, Longview and Tyler, Texas.

Nord, D. (1998). Traumatization in survivors of multiple AIDS related loss. *Omega, 37(*3), 215-240.

O'Connor, M.F. (1997). Treating gay men with HIV. In M. O'Connor, & I.D. Yalom (Eds.), *Treating the psychological consequences of HIV* (pp. 73-116). San Francisco: Jossey-Bass Publishers.

Olson, R.A., Huszti, H., & Parsons, J.T. (1997). Treating pediatric and adolescent HIV. In M. O'Connor, & I.D. Yalom (Eds.), *Treating the psychological consequences of HIV* (pp. 73-116). San Francisco: Jossey-Bass Publishers.

O'Rourke, J.K., & Sutherland, P.S. (1995). Negotiating HIV infection in rural America: Breaking through the isolation. In S.A. Cadwell, R.A. Burnham, & M. Forstein (Eds.), *Therapists on the front line: Psychotherapy with gay men in the age of AIDS* (pp. 363-378). Washington, DC: American Psychiatric Press, Inc.

Pohl, M., Denniston, K., & Toft, D. (1990). *The caregiver's journey: When you love someone with AIDS.* Hazeldon: HarperCollins Publishers.

Quinn, S., & Thomas, S. (1994). Results of a baseline assessment of AIDS knowledge among Black church members. *National Journal of Sociology, 8,* 89-107.

Rabkin, J.G., Remien, R., Katoff, L., & Williams, J.B.W. (1993). Resilience in adversity among long-term survivors of AIDS. *Hospital and Community Psychiatry, 44(2),* 162-167.

Reed, G.M., Kemeny, M.E., Taylor, S.E., Wang, H.J., & Visscher, B.R. (1994). Realistic acceptance as a predictor of decreased survival time in gay men with AIDS. *Health Psychology, 13(4),* 299-307.

Roffman, R.A., & Downey, L. (1997). Cognitive-Behavioral group counseling to prevent HIV transmission in gay and bisexual men: Factors contributing to successful risk reduction. *Research on Social Work Practice, 7(2),* 165-186.

Rose, S. (1998). Searching for the meaning of AIDS: Issues affecting seropositive Black gay men. In V.J. Derlaga, & A. Barbee (Eds.), *HIV and social interaction* (pp. 56-82). Thousand Oaks, CA: Sage Publications.

Rosenbaum, M., & Murphy, S. (1990). Women and addiction: Process, treatment and outcomes. In E.Y. Lambert (Ed.), *The collection and interpretation of data from hidden populations* (pp. 120-127). National Institute on Drug Abuse Research Monograph 98. rockville, MD: U.S. Department of Public Health.

Schiller, N.G. (1993). The invisible women: Caregiving and the construction of AIDS health services. *Culture, Medicine, and Psychiatry, 17(4),* 487-512.

Schmidt, M., McKirnan, D.J., & Tranmer, P.A. (1990). Neuropsychological, emotional and social components of functional status among minority inner-city PWAs. Sixth International Conference on AIDS, San Francisco (abstract).

Sherr, L. (1996). Tomorrow's era: Gender, psychology and HIV infection. In L. Sherr, C. Hankins, & L. Bennett (Eds.), *AIDS as a gender issue: Psychosocial perspectives* (pp. 16-45). London: Taylor & Francis.

Shuff, M. (1997). Rural practice. In M.G. Winiarski (Ed.), *HIV mental health for the 21st century* (pp. 9-31). New York: New York University Press.

Siegel, K., & Raveis, V. (1997). Perceptions of access to HIV-related information, care, and services among infected minority men. *Qualitative Health Research, 7(1),* 9-31.

Simoni, J.M., Mason, H.R.C., Marks, G., Ruiz, M.S., Reed, D., & Richardson, J.L. (1995). Women's self disclosure of HIV infection: Rates, reasons, and reactions. *Journal of Consulting and Clinical Psychology, 63(3),* 474-478.

Suarez, M., Raffaelli, M., & O'Leary, A. (1996). Use of folk healing practices by HIV-infected Hispanics living in the United States. *AIDS Care, 8(6),* 683-690.

Tarasoff v. Regents of University of California, 17 Cal.3d 425, 131 Cal.Rptr. 14, 551 P.2d 334 (1976).

Taylor, S.E., Helgeson, V.S., Reed, G.M., & Skokan, L.A. (1991). Self-generated feelings of control and adjustment to physical illness. *Journal of Social Issues, 47(*4), 91-109.

Thompson, S.C., & Spacapan, S. (1991). Perceptions of control in vulnerable populations. *Journal of Social Issues, 47*(4), 1-21.

Tunnell, G. (1989). *Complications in working with AIDS patients in group psychotherapy.* New York: New York University Medical Center. (ERIC document Reproduction Service No. ED 347 166)

Walker, J. (1999). Rural women with HIV and AIDS and their care providers: Perceptions of service accessibility, psychosocial and counseling issues. *Unpublished manuscript.*

Ward-Wimmer, D. (1997). Working with and for children. In M.G. Winiarski, (Ed.), *HIV mental health for the 21st century* (pp. 190-205). New York: New York University Press.

Ward, M.C. (1993). A different disease: HIV/AIDS and health care for women in poverty. *Culture, Medicine and Psychiatry, 17(*4), 413-30.

Ware, K. (August 1, 1999). HIV/AIDS Program Coordinator, Montrose Counseling Center, Houston, Texas.

Waters, M. (1997). *Report from the National Conference on Women and HIV.* Retrieved from: *http://www.ama-assn.org/special/hiv/newsline/ conferen/women/womclin.htm*

Weitz, R. (1992). *Life with AIDS.* New Brunswick, New Jersey: Rutgers University Press.

Weitz, R. (1993). Powerlessness, invisibility, and the lives of women with HIV disease. *Advances in Medical Sociology, 3*, 101-121.

Wiener, L.S., Heliman, N., & Battles, H.B. (1998). Public disclosure of HIV: Psychosocial considerations for children. In V.J. Derlaga, & A. Barbee (Eds.), *HIV and social interaction* (pp. 193-217). Thousand Oaks, CA: Sage Publications.

Yalom, I.D. (1995). *The theory and practice of group psychotherapy* (4th ed). New York: Basic Books.

Chapter 12

SEXUALITY COUNSELING IN ADDICTIONS

Michael D. Loos
University of Wyoming
Mary L. Loos
Attorney at Law

Alcohol acts on the sexual instinct by removing the resistances and increasing the sexual activity. These facts are generally known, but their real nature is not inquired into as a rule. *(Karl Abraham, 1908)*

We all have sex problems. We'd hardly be human if we didn't. What can we do about them? *(Alcoholics Anonymous, 1939, p. 69)*

BACKGROUND

Drug addictions influence all communities and populations. It is not a question whether counselors will come into contact with men and women who have experienced the adverse consequences of addiction; it is more a matter of when they will be faced with providing counseling services to this special needs group. Much will depend upon the rates and incidences of substance abuse in any given community. Counselors wishing to serve any given community must do so with an understanding and respectful focus on the particular ethnic, cultural, and lifestyle makeup of the community. We encourage counselors to use the practical guides of Ridley (1995) and Atkinson, Morten, & Wing Sue (1989) when working with diversity issues in the chemically-dependent. Also, Buelow & Buelow (1998) offer some excellent guidelines.

In this chapter we focus on the broad area of sexuality issues for which the recovering population may seek counseling assistance. Deferring to brevity, no attempt is made to be exhaustive of the material on physical/medical issues related to addiction and sexuality. These problems produce a gamut of issues better left to physicians specializing in the treatment of medically-related sexual dysfunction. We address, however, some counseling needs associated with these disorders as they influence relationship and intimacy in recovery.

The primary emphasis is on specific counseling issues men and women face rather than a focus on the disorders that precipitated or promoted the issues. A final reason for limiting the scope of this chapter is to avoid overwhelming the counselor with the "how" or "what" happened to the client; rather, attend to the client's need for clarity and resolution necessary for the "letting go" of the past requisite to "giving themselves" to a new way of living.

The core issues of the chemically-dependent person's problems with sexuality stem from his/her selfish, dishonest, inconsiderate, injurious and unjustifiable suspicions or bitterness in regard to relationship behavior. The authors blend personal and professional experiences with current literature in the field to address this most salient, but seldom adequately addressed, feature in addictions recovery, adversely affecting many individuals with an earnest desire for healthy, peaceful, long-term recovery.

Definitions

Before examining the many aspects or issues of sexuality counseling with this special needs population, some important concepts are defined. When we talk about "**addiction**," being a process, it is a complex **bio-psycho-social-spiritual** problem. There may be, in fact, **genetic** as well as **neurochemical** overlays (DuPont, 1997). We recommend that the reader view the contents of this chapter through this lens, for if viewed from a different clinical orthodoxy, some of what is stated will be potentially misunderstood or distorted. Diversity in orthodoxy is appreciated, and we acknowledge there are many ways of looking at the population of chemically-dependent. For the purposes of this chapter, we request that the reader suspend his/her own clinical orthodoxy, ideas, or biases in favor of the authors'. Then, after reading and digesting the content, integrate the material with your preferred orthodoxy.

The use of the term "**active addiction**" means the current use of mood-altering substances with adverse consequences, and also refers to "**practicing one's addiction**." "**Abstinence**" refers to the condition of people when they are "clean and dry," or not currently using mood-altering substances. It is understood and accepted that there exists neurochemical and "**brain reward**" influences for days, weeks, and maybe months after cessation of use (DuPont, 1997; National Institute on Drug Abuse [NIDA], 1999).

"**Recovery**," an ongoing process, involves the willingness to identify maladaptive behaviors and to recognize and accept the need to make significant changes in thinking, feelings, and behavior, along with some fundamental alterations in core beliefs and values. "**Sobriety**" refers to the daily living of this "new" way of life by the chemically-dependent person in recovery, with the accompanying benefits of a sense of ease, peace, and serenity. Abstinence is often mistaken for sobriety, and the terms have been used interchangeably throughout the research literature. However, we believe that while continuous abstinence is necessary for many recovering individuals to achieve sobriety, the term sobriety encompasses much more than mere abstinence.

> We are going to know a new freedom and a new happiness. . . . We will comprehend the word serenity and we will know peace. . . . Our whole attitude and outlook upon life will change. *(Alcoholics Anonymous, 1939, p. 84)*

As noted in the above passage, it would be incorrect for the practitioner to assume that mere abstinence is sufficient for recovery. Effective long-term recovery is contingent upon the adoption of a set of life skills and coping skills acquired from the practice of a different manner of living.

A "**sponsor**" is a recovering addict's/alcoholic's guide to learning how to practice the 12 Steps in daily living. The **12 Steps** of most recovery programs have been based on the 12 Steps of Alcoholics Anonymous, and are considered a guide for successful living in daily recovery from alcoholism and other addictions. **Sponsorship** usually involves a one-on-one relationship between a person seeking guidance from a person who has demonstrated successful maintenance of sobriety. Generally speaking, sponsors have several years of continuous sobriety, and **sponsees** (individuals seeking sponsorship) may have little experience or may be returning after a relapse of use with his/her drug of choice/self administration. Sponsorship differs significantly from counseling.

"**Counseling**" involves an examination of deeper issues that adversely affect relationships, and is usually conducted by a credentialed professional. We believe that both sponsorship and counseling are essential for effective, long-term recovery from addiction.

"**Sex**" refers to sexual intercourse, the biological function, whether for the purpose of procreation or simple physical intimacy, without regard to whether it is heterosexual or same-sex engagement. Our intended use of the term "**relationship**" is based on a care perspective, that is, a willingness to communicate, share, give recognition, provide acknowledgment, and includes casual friendship. "**Intimacy**" differs from relationship in the level of willingness of one to be deeply committed to a common experience of knowing and sharing oneself with another who is likewise committed to knowing and sharing himself/herself. Intimacy includes higher levels of honesty, expression, expectation, and envisions a more intense state of being than a mere involvement in relationship.

Short Historical Perspective

Although there have been studies on the nature of addiction and other studies on the topics of sexuality and intimacy, the recent research on the effects of addiction on sexuality is generally limited. The focus tends to be on physical dysfunctions, on related issues such as sexual assault, or on sexually transmitted diseases. Little is found regarding addiction and intimacy. Over several decades, extensive growth of the knowledge base about addiction and changes in public perceptions and expressions of sexuality have provided for significant opportunities for research about the impact of substance abuse on relationship behavior.

The post-WWII era of the 1950s brought troops home, and with their return a rise in alcohol and nicotine consumption with associated problems of both a social and legal nature. Illegal narcotic use was at a low during the war years, but fear of the resumption of illicit use fostered federal and state legislation to restrict distribution and enhance penalties for illicit use (Musto, 1997).

The 1960s saw a shift in emphasis from criminality and prosecution to public health and treatment, with the advent of community mental health center programs and the introduction of methadone. During this period, alcohol and drug treatment gained political favor, resulting in civil commitments as an alternative to prison for those who were addicted. By the end of the 1960s, addiction again was viewed as associated with crime and criminal sanctions and enforcement became national policy (Musto, 1997). The conduct of the chemically-dependent when under the influence, generally associated with inappropriate relationship behavior, was the impetus behind this movement.

The 1970s saw a worsening of the drug situation attributed to "ghettoization" (Johnson & Muffler, 1997) and attendant, indiscriminate sexual behaviors to obtain drugs. Policy followed by the mid-1970s that prompted the harm reduction philosophies of today. It was during this tenure that the primary focus was on illicit substances to the exclusion of alcohol, tobacco and prescription medications. In our opinion, the elimination of substance abuse and addiction is unlikely, and the 1970s' legislative efforts supporting control of abuse via law enforcement are equally unattainable (Musto, 1997). Additionally, it was during this era that **iatrogenic** (physician-introduced) addiction became a notable problem.

The 1980s and 1990s witnessed continued, widespread use and abuse of mood- and mind-altering substances. Research on alcohol and drug addiction issues in this era was prolific. Unfortunately, also during this time of increased use and study, there was a corresponding reduction in expenditures for treatment and rehabilitation. In deference to funding the "war on drugs," the bulk of monetary support went to interdiction and criminal justice, this in spite of rhetoric to the contrary. In the past decade more than two-thirds of the federal budget previously earmarked for substance abuse issues has been directed away from treatment (Musto, 1997). This movement away from the public health model to a legal, moral model is predominant today, suggesting a societal attitude of drug intolerance.

The late 1980s and 1990s also heralded the rise of HIV/AIDS, hepatitis-C, and increasing sexually-transmitted diseases, typically associated with intravenous drug usage and indiscriminate sexual conduct and unprotected sexual contact. This adds a new dimension to legislated drug abuse control (i.e., the criminalization of pregnancy) (Rosenbaum 1997)) and the treatment of individuals seeking recovery.

The mid- to late-1990s gave us "generation X," and the live fast, die young, stay pretty proponents. Body-piercing and tattoos are about finding an identity different from that of the previous generation. Continued debate over legalization or decriminalization demarcates the era, as does increasing alarm about alcohol and tobacco. Alcohol and tobacco are now considered "dangerous" substances, like the "harder drugs" of heroin, cocaine and amphetamines (Musto, 1997). The current status of alcohol and tobacco is found objectionable to many people who would still prefer to view these substances as socially tolerable, if not acceptable. Increased public concern over domestic violence and sexual assault associated with substance abuse has become a hallmark of the time.

The 1990s also saw public policies that were more restrictive regarding needle sharing and unprotected sex, unconscionably so, relative to the proliferation of sexually-transmitted diseases. On the other hand, we believe that it seems more sensible to endorse programs and policies supportive of individuals seeking healthy long-term recovery from addiction than to champion divergent political ideologies and symptom abatement at the cost of human lives.

Myths and Realities

At this point it would be helpful to examine some of the myths and realities associated with mood-altering substances and sexuality: sex, relationships, and intimacy.

Values typically attached to the use of alcohol and other drugs are both positive and negative. There is truth to the perception that use of substances provides social ease, relaxation, decrease in stress, and an effective way to alter mood. Current beliefs include the medicinal value of moderate use of alcohol, "a glass of wine" to improve heart health or facilitate sleep, among other "curative" effects.

Some of the positive perspectives become negative issues, as with the use of substances to enhance masculinity or femininity, or to increase sophistication, and to improve social, psychological, and sexual functioning. For example, the above uses could be to disguise feelings of failure, inadequacy or insecurity; promoters or indications of success; extrinsic factors of control; as a coping strategy to deal with life (Brown, 1995). The differences between the positive and negative positions are denoted by using substances responsibly during celebratory activities versus solution-seeking (relief, self-treating) and problem-oriented (abuse, dependence, addiction) use behaviors.

Loss, or anesthetizing, of inhibitions is both reality and myth. The myth promotes the illusion that one is more socially graced, articulate, physically attractive, and sexually competent. The reality is the loss of inhibition promotes indiscriminate sexual behavior and resultant sexual problems, primarily loss of personal control and temporary incapacitation of higher cortical functioning, resulting in impaired reasoning and judgment. Some consequent physical problems include erectile dysfunction, premature ejaculation, inorgasmia, vaginosis, enhanced desire but loss of function, or **sexual trauma**. Sexual trauma includes emotional abuse, physical abuse, economic abuse and sexual abuse (Skrip & Kuntzman, 1991). Substance abuse is often associated with sexual trauma, including additional symptoms such as self-doubt, low self-esteem, role confusion, depression, feelings of isolation and despair, perceived helplessness, eating disorders, dissociation, somatization, anxiety, extreme difficulties with trust and intimacy, and suicidal ideation or intent (Wadsworth, Spampneto & Halbrook, 1995).

Sexual Behaviors and Problems

As previously stated, the host of physical sexual difficulties associated with long-term, chronic use of alcohol and other drugs are expanded upon in this chapter except as related to the psychosocial problems associated with addiction. These problems should be recognized and addressed or referred, as appropriate under the circumstances, by the counselor as a member of a multi-disciplinary treatment team.

Rather, the chapter includes the issues of rape, incest, guilt, shame, remorse associated with sexual conduct and misconduct, loss of control issues, developmental issues related to sexuality and addictions, issues of intimacy in relationships, and resistance/reluctance issues associated with risk and trust in developing healthy relationships. Attention is focused on the female and male experience in the adult population, and will embrace the dominant heterosexual as well as alternative lifestyles.

CULTURAL CONSIDERATIONS

Substance abuse has a devastating impact on all the diverse populations of American communities. Despite increased efforts to study drug abuse in special populations, little is known about the relationship between race or ethnicity, and the effects of substance abuse and its treatment (John, Brown & Primm, 1997). As might be expected, with the paucity of research, the impact of the use and abuse of substances on sexuality issues is likewise under-addressed.

What is known, for example, is the alarming frequency of HIV/AIDS in the African American population as compared to the incidence for whites or Hispanics. The African American population is disproportionately over-represented among total adult AIDS cases, female AIDS cases, and pediatric AIDS cases because of bias in research methodology. Nevertheless, this represents a significant sexuality counseling issue among members of this population. Little is known about the incidence and prevalence of sexual trauma, save for female substance abusers who engage in sexual behavior in exchange for drugs of choice. Again, there is a question of bias in data collection (John et al., 1997).

Among Hispanic people who reside in the United States, substance abuse is a major problem. As with other populations, limited literature exists with respect to etiology and impact of addiction, let alone specifics regarding the impact of substance abuse on sexuality. What is known is that substance abuse among young Hispanic women is on the rise. Personal and sexual issues must be addressed sensitively with respect for family networks and cultural norms, such as dignity, respect and love, the three core values of Hispanic culture (Ruiz & Langrod, 1997). What is also evident in the literature is the engagement in sexual activity predisposing exposure to HIV/AIDS at a significantly higher level than the white population.

American Indian populations have had limited exposure to substances other than alcohol principally because of their historical position as a subsistence society (Westermeyer, 1997). Alcohol continues to be the substance of choice, with intoxication as the goal of use. It is important to know that the native American norm for alcohol is abstention, rather than promotion of use. The stereotypic pattern of alcohol abuse includes rapid drinking over a prolonged period, with drunkenness as the aim (Weisner, Weibel-Orlando & Lang, 1984). Concerning sexuality and related issues, exhibitions of violence and indiscriminate sexual contact are the most common occurrences in this population. Cultural pride and revivalism must be attended to as important components of treatment.

The population of Asian Americans, like the American Indian, includes many subgroups, that is, Chinese, Filipino, Japanese, East Indian, Korean, Vietnamese, Thai, and others. The same population also contains members of all of the world's great religions, a factor that will weigh heavily on the choice of approaches to problems of a sexual nature as related to substance abuse. Issues of loss of personal control, personal shame, family shame, and selfishness will be difficult issues to address from a cultural perspective, as these characteristics embody opposing values to the cultural norm. Family counseling approaches are preferred and attention must be given to issues around abandonment of the client by the family if family members sense failure (Westermeyer, 1997).

DEVELOPMENTAL AND DIAGNOSTIC FACTORS

Women

While physiological factors may account for some of the gender differences in substance abusers, other factors include psychological and socioeconomic attitudes. Females often are faced with conflicting societal values and expectations, and experience certain prejudices and discrimination (Jacobson, 1987). Many of the same factors that contribute to active addiction in women affect their sexual lives and satisfaction in recovery.

Although sexual trauma is not necessarily part of every dysfunctional family system, some recovering women have experienced some form of sexual trauma that should be addressed by a competent professional. Other related topics include being viewed merely as another's sex object, loss of control over choice whether to engage in sexual activity, and resisting or holding back the enjoyment of sexual encounters (Wills-Brandon, 1989; Woititz, 1985). Greater social stress related to changing sex roles, engaging in previously male-dominated roles, for example, paid work outside the home and being single heads of households (Jacobson, 1987), should also be considered.

Many of the problems identified as sexually-related are rooted in risk and trust issues. Female substance abusers are often more likely to be victims of alcohol-related aggression, including date rape (Perez, 1994). When forcible rape involves someone the victim knows (date, marital, group or gang rapes), the victim is less likely to report the incident. A recovering addict who is also a recovering rape victim may struggle with her views of herself and the world, views that have been altered, perhaps shattered, by the experience. If her view of herself incorporates self-blame or places fault on external forces for the occurrence, she may have a decidedly more difficult process of recovery. On the other hand, a woman who perceives some sense of control over her future is usually more successful in her recovery process (Miller, 1999). This reasoning may also apply to incest and other sexual abuse survivors.

Whereas males are more likely to leave their alcoholic partners, most females remain with their alcoholic mates. Women are often economically dependent and feel they cannot risk leaving, even in quite desperate situations (Roth, 1991). Again, these experiences can create reluctance for a recovering woman to risk trusting others again, particularly males. Negative experiences present basic security and autonomy issues for which the female client will need counseling.

Reports show the need to provide more education to females of child-bearing age about the risks and consequences not only of drug use but also of alcohol consumption during pregnancy. For example, research regarding the use of drugs during pregnancy reveals increased risks associated with miscarriage, ectopic (tubal) pregnancy, stillbirth, low weight gain, anemia, thrombocytopenia, hypertension, among a myriad of still more medical problems (NIDA, 1999). Fetal alcohol syndrome (FAS) and babies with fetal alcohol effects (FAE) or alcohol-related birth defects are preventable birth defects (Mayo Foundation for Medical Education and Research, 2000). While FAS is not curable, it can be completely prevented. FAS is prevalent in the African-American community (CDC, undated brochure).

Another significant sexual health issue includes the risks of sexually transmitted diseases (STDs) and HIV/AIDS. Sixty percent of college women who acquired an STD (including HIV) were under the influence of alcohol at the time of intercourse (National Clearinghouse for Alcohol and Drug Information [NCADI], undated brochure). AIDS is identified as the fourth leading cause of death among women ages 15 to 44 years of age, with approximately two out of every three female AIDS cases related to injection drug use. HIV infection can cross the placental barrier in infected pregnant drug users; in the United States, 54% of pediatric AIDS cases are related to the mother's use of injected drugs or the mother engaging in unprotected sexual activity with an (infected) injection-drug user. Evidence suggests that pregnant drug users may transmit hepatitis C virus to their unborn fetuses, increasing the risk of maternal transmission of HIV to unborns. With respect to preventive interventions and risk reduction of HIV infection in females, NIDA (1999) reported that counseling in an office setting was more effective than information provided on the street (NIDA, 1999).

Educating recovering women regarding their own sexual response cycle, including desire-excitement-orgasm-resolution (climax), may be a necessary component of treatment. Many alcoholics and addicts have engaged in substance abuse to mask or numb their feelings, including, and in some instances especially, those of a sexual nature. For some, sex became a barter system, a way to obtain the drugs of choice, or to keep the peace in the household. Sexual activity for chemically-dependent women has seldom been for achievement of true intimacy with another individual.

Even when they are in recovery from their own addiction, many women repeatedly choose the same types of individuals with whom to again engage in a relationship. This is an indication that counseling should be directed toward underlying reasons for her selection of a potential partner. Perhaps she is not comfortable with others who treat her respectfully. Maybe she says they are not as "fun" or as "interesting." Avoiding honest, well-meaning, respectful men is a relapse issue. The recovering addict in treatment engaging in old relationship patterns may be recreating past situations in which she felt more comfortable, that is, those she felt she had more control over. Unfortunately, those past situations often involved abusive relationships. Maybe she is looking for a challenge, to make someone over, save her partner from him/herself, or just feels more "alive" in crisis situations. Avoiding the opportunity for growth through recreating or reliving prior bad experiences is unproductive. Relapse potential should be taken seriously in this setting, and relapse prevention treatment must augment other counseling issues.

If the recovering female in counseling continues to make progress in recovery and her partner does not seek treatment, she may realize the need to make a difficult decision, whether to remain in the relationship. She may seek advice or support regarding her decision to remain or leave. Understanding that she is not responsible for another's recovery is important.

Men

Addictions treatment forced many men to engage in counseling, an elective opportunity that was generally dismissed until entry into a treatment setting. This is changing today as more men are seeking the benefits of counseling (Kupers, 1993). Men were encouraged to discuss issues they previously felt unable or unwilling to examine; but now, in the face of the pain of addiction recovery, were supported to discover and divulge. Age-old issues of a question of adequacy and independence seemed set aside, although the counselor still had to address the resistance and reluctance of the client as manifested in the demonstration of power and control.

Some key problems for recovering men in counseling include: an inability to express emotion; self-esteem issues; lack of respect for women; fears of abandonment, betrayal, or rejection in relationship; lack of honesty in relationship, as evidenced by feelings of jealousy and actions of infidelity; sexual orientation and sex-role identity; fear of intimacy; performance anxiety; and sexual trauma as either perpetrator or victim (Ackerman, 1993; Coleman, 1987; Colgan, 1990; Evans & Schaefer, 1987; Miller, 1999; NIDA, 1999; Urqiza & Capra, 1990).

First, and foremost, is working with the male client toward learning to identify feelings accurately, claim ownership of the emotion, elect appropriate options for expression and related behavior. Helping men understand their feelings is best approached in a psycho-educational manner. The senior author's approach is to simplify feelings by labeling them in a rudimentary fashion, synthesizing them into six basic emotional expressions of happy, sad, hurt, ashamed, scared, embarrassed, and angry. Effort is directed at facilitating an understanding that many expressions of emotion, other than happy, appear on the surface to resemble anger. This promotes a deeper examination of the client's issues by encouraging him to explore feelings in a knowledgeable and emotionally secure manner (Hutchins, 1979, 1984; Mueller, Dupuy, & Hutchins, 1994; West, Hutchins, & DeVilbiss, 1996). Discovering one's emotional self in this fashion provides both support and structure to the newly recovering, conditions essential for successful treatment (L'Abate, 1992). It is only through the self-examination, discovery, and disclosure process that the client gains comfort with feelings/emotions, preparing him for the intense work on self and other relationships to follow. Without this fundamental preparation, counseling about issues of sexuality, relationship, and intimacy would become too emotionally overwhelming, emotionally painful, and emotionally threatening; something to be avoided, not addressed.

The enhancement of personal esteem, worth, and status is equally important as requisite to sexuality counseling with the chemically-dependent male. It is difficult for a client to experience success in a relationship if he is unable to establish a secure, genuine relationship with himself. Many men, male substance abusers in particular, find themselves uncomfortable and confused about matters of relationship and intimacy (Ackerman, 1993), or are prone to feelings of inadequacy and, therefore, need to dominate in relationship (Kupers, 1993). Perhaps chemically-dependent males, more than their non-chemically-dependent peers, experience problems with nurturance and attachment to a more intense degree. Substance abuse then becomes a poor, but readily available, source of self-treatment in the absence of satisfaction for the basic need to love, be loved, and be respected for being alive. Men in treatment need help understanding that they are not alone with this struggle for self-acceptance. This struggle offers both support and hope that counseling could make a difference in their lives. Through identification and resolution of basic security issues, the invitation is accepted to develop risk and trust behaviors necessary for engaging in discussions about more intimate relational issues.

When fear and doubt as residuals of failed relationships with self and others prevail, men appear unable to move beyond their projections. They may express a fear of the possibility of abandonment, betrayal, and rejection in developing relationships, whether with other men or women. Incapacitated by the reality of the past, coupled with their inability (or unwillingness) to muster the courage to risk participation here and now, men typically seethe with adolescent jealousy and resentment, or resort to isolation and loneliness as coping strategies. Counseling interventions at this point might focus on what is necessary for the client to "abandon" (or let go of) the past in order to accommodate room for the future of "the here and now." Usually, the historical examination of failed relationships is a good place to start. This is particularly true if the client has developed an understanding of attending to his role in the loss of relationship, no longer content to entertain the unproductive focus on how the other party was at fault. Accepting the pain of being forthright, owning the responsibility of his part in the loss and recognizing the importance of making changes based on what he has discovered become the focal points of counseling interventions.

Honesty and personal responsibility are essential for finding and maintaining healthy relationships. Honesty is also something with which many recovering men have extraordinary difficulty. As denial was the primary characteristic allowing him to exist with himself, let alone others, genuineness and openness are difficult to nurture. With the chemically-dependent, merely discovering the facts or truths is insufficient in developing the capacity for honesty with self and others. For many men with addictions, honesty is to be avoided as it interferes with business, pleasure, control, "getting ahead," and the presumed competitive nature of all men's relationships. In counseling, attention must be paid to the development of the "feminine" side of the client, his capacity for warmth, sensitivity, tenderness, compassion, vulnerability, and connection. Toughness, though championed by many men, becomes a dangerous ally for many men in recovery from addiction because it establishes the scenario for him to again be self-deceiving, denying the nature of his inner, true self; portraying a false sense of self as a protective action; and building all new relationships on a foundation of incredulity and dishonesty. The counselor must challenge the client to see his error of reason and to nourish insight until it results in his behavior change. Men are not limited in the capacity to form healthy relationships nor in the capacity to love; men are only reluctant in giving themselves to the experience of both (Ackerman, 1993). Additionally, counselors having reached this level of relationship with the client can now work with him to employ his newly found capacity to give himself to others, understand and communicate in relationships, and listen to himself and others, without fear of rejection in relationship (Ackerman, 1993; Kupers, 1993).

Having successfully developed this foundation, men can now attempt to deal with the primary sexuality related issues in recovery. Not all men are comfortable with themselves as men in the way they have been educated about manhood; nor are some men at ease with only the masculine side of themselves as they have seen modeled by the significant men around them throughout their lives. Some of the more troubling issues in recovery for men are their resolution of sexual victimization or trauma, sexual orientation, and sex-role identification.

Sexual abuse issues include incest and rape as a male victim; or sexual abuse and rape as a male perpetrator. Either, or both, of these issues provide a challenge to the counselor who works with this population. The major characteristics are feelings of shame, guilt, remorse, rejection, and homophobia (Miller, 1999). Counselors must be sensitive when processing these experiences with men, manifesting a caring attitude and demeanor during and after disclosures about events and stories. As might be expected, there is nearly twice the prevalence of abuse in female victims than male and, therefore, little research exists regarding how to best (to) counsel the male victim. Quite the contrary is true in the case of perpetration. According to Miller (1999), counselors, unless specially qualified to work with male perpetrators, should consult with those trained to work with sexual abuse perpetrators, usually a multi-disciplinary team. Counselors must not let the focus of addiction to act as an excuse for the client's behavior.

Sexual orientation is described by Cabaj (1997) as based in desire, not behavior; to be in relationship, physically and emotionally, with members of the same gender. Perhaps as many as one-third of the gay population experience difficulty with alcohol and other drugs (Eliason, 1996). This suggests that counselors will likely be addressing such critical issues as homophobia, discrimination, and harassment with some, if not most, male clients. The heterosexual counselor needs to integrate orientation issues into the counseling plan if counseling is to be successful. It is also important to note that gay men have been talking about gender issues for a long time primarily because of oppression and a continuance of pejorative references. Some major issues to be addressed will include fears of oppression, harassment, and legal intercessions. Abandonment, betrayal, and societal stressors impinge on healthy relationship building. Supporting lifestyle choice and developing a genuine connection with the client become more important for successfully working with the gay client, helping him incorporate new coping strategies and learning to be constructively assertive.

Sex-role identification issues are also a prevalent theme in working with males regarding sexuality issues. Folded into this discussion must be not only a list of expectations that go with traditional male roles, but an examination of how these roles have changed within the culture of community, as well as a description of what might be expected if the client is to change his relational style. A movement away from the superior/subordinate, victor/vanquished model of male modeling can enhance the client's gravitation toward developing intimacy in relationship (Kupers, 1993).

Fear of intimacy is a target issue in addictions recovery. According to Ackerman (1993), intimacy is emotional bonding that begins with knowing, accepting, and liking oneself. In the chemically-dependent male, strides are needed to accentuate the importance of negotiating a healthy relationship with himself before embarking on the journey of intimacy with others. Threats to intimacy include an inability to express emotion accurately, fears of spending time with another in shared experiences, creating depth in personal/interpersonal communications/exchanges, exclusivity, fear of rejection, and an inability to risk or trust that promotes a need to control. Effective sexuality counseling includes a thorough examination of the impact of these conditions on the client before engaging in an intimate relationship.

COUNSELING STRATEGIES

From the senior author's perspective, counselors are, in general, well prepared to address many of the attenuate issues that the chemically-dependent population brings to treatment. There is, however, an orthodoxy shift that the counselor must be aware of, and be prepared to make.

In working with this population, counselors may be in the unfamiliar, uncomfortable position of being more direct, more immediate, and more confrontational with a client than in more traditional settings with non-chemically-dependent clients. Treatment approaches are typically more structured and supportive of abstinence from mood-alterers while primary care occurs, and emphasis on follow-up more structured and community-focused than to what counselors may be accustomed. A focus on feelings, not just behaviors, is critical. The more integrative the counselor is with his or her counseling approach, the greater the likelihood of successful interventions.

The chemically-dependent client comes to any level of clinical service not only with his/her addiction issue, he/she comes with a plethora of mental, emotional, behavioral, and values problems as well; many may pre-exist chemical abuse and dependency; some may have occurred as a consequence of addiction; others will originate as a result of treatment. Historically, primary interventions have included some form of the 12 Steps of Alcoholics Anonymous. The importance of finding and using 12-Step programs as adjunctive to traditional modes of counseling has been widely accepted and emphasized (DuPont, 1997; Miller, 1999; Buelow & Buelow, 1998; Nace, 1997). However, the 12 Steps have let some people down with a formulaic approach in trying to address the multiplicity of problems that people bring with them in seeking long-term, effective recovery. Individuals who present for treatment with some observable behavior indicative of a sexual problem may find, or have found, the 12 Steps inadequate to support resolution. Yet attempting to resolve sexuality issues without a blend of traditional counseling and 12-Step reference would be contraindicated, especially if community-based support groups are integral to long-term, comfortable sobriety.

Other before, during, and after recovery issues include resistance and reluctance issues. The chemically-dependent client will generally resist doing what he/she may really need to do to get better. This reluctance is usually based on his/her fears, generally associated with the guilt, shame and remorse of past conduct, promoting resistance and reluctance to change, becoming an impediment to open, honest, sober sex or intimacy.

Developmentally, there are several focal issues with which to deal in recovery including re-examining risk/trust dimensions, autonomy versus dependence, ego identity versus role confusion, intimacy versus isolation, and generativity versus self-absorption (Erikson, 1963). Without exception, the chemically-dependent client experiences conflicts in most, if not all, of these areas. Similarly, the counselor must be prepared to facilitate individual client growth through risk and trust activities, providing a fertile environment in which the client can practice healthy development. One of the best practices from which the senior author has experienced greatest client growth comes from an adequate psychosocial education; an education that includes information not only about the disease process of addiction but some of the important developmental life areas adversely affected by alcohol and drug abuse/addiction. Autonomy and the intimate relationships the client has with him/herself and with others, essential for successful recovery must be examined as they are.

CASE STUDIES

Case Study: Female

Tiffany participated in the family sessions while her husband, Brandon, was in treatment for alcoholism. Additionally, she attended Al-Anon meetings and a weekly open AA meeting with Brandon during the first six months after he completed treatment and attended AA. Tiffany wanted to be supportive of Brandon's efforts to maintain sobriety. When Brandon's drinking was no longer an issue, it became clear that Tiffany had substance abuse problems of her own that needed to be addressed. The problem reached the point that it threatened her long-term relationship with Brandon. Tiffany did not want this relationship to end. Brandon promised to be as supportive in Tiffany's attempts to recover as she had been in his.

However, Tiffany felt that she could not take the time off from her new full-time job to go through a treatment program. Also, money was tight for them, as Brandon's sponsor insisted that he not return to work until he had achieved six months of recovery. Though Brandon had recently started a new job in his profession, Tiffany did not want to create additional financial burdens by not working while she was in a treatment facility, usually a 28-day stay.

So Tiffany opted to attend AA meetings after work every day and on weekends. She also attended a few other recovery meetings on occasion, including Narcotics Anonymous (NA), Al-Anon, and Adult Children of Alcoholics (ACOA). Tiffany assessed herself as having many addictions, including alcohol, prescription drugs, and sex and love addiction. She did not attend any Sex Addicts Anonymous (SAA) or Sex and Love Addicts Anonymous (SLAA) meetings at first because she did not know of any meetings in her area. When she became aware of a sex addicts meeting in the area, she decided not to go because she heard it was mostly made up of men; she did not want to speak openly about her sexual addiction to a group of men, fearing the potential come-ons and possible relapse into inappropriate sexual behavior. Tiffany valued her current relationship with Brandon and did not want to take any chances of losing it, even if she had to "white-knuckle" her way into recovery, as she put it. Of all the meetings she attended, she felt most comfortable with women's AA groups and AA discussion groups (men and women). Eventually, she stopped going to NA and ACOA, as she did not feel the groups she attended were as healthy for her as the AA meetings that she was most comfortable attending. She said she felt the members acted as if their problems were unique or they blamed others (parents) for their troubles in relating with the world around them normally. She only went to a few Al-Anon meetings, feeling more comfortable with addressing her own recovery issues than focusing on Brandon's alcoholism and recovery and how his problems affected her as his spouse. She also said that she felt more welcome, more a "part of" or that she "belonged in" the AA recovery groups than she did in any of the other 12-Step programs. Early in her sobriety Tiffany recruited a female sponsor and followed all of the suggestions her sponsor gave her. Tiffany felt that she could address all of her addictions successfully with the principles she learned in AA and in working closely with her sponsor.

Tiffany was in continuous recovery for about two years and five months when she began to feel that she was not happy and she was unable to achieve the high goals she had set for herself (perfectionism and unrealistic expectations consistent with early recovery where people throw themselves into a new life, too much, too soon). She had started back to college, taking two courses at night after working all day as a secretary. She was in her third year of undergraduate study, and felt that she still had many years left to attend, going only part-time. Until the last three months, she attended three to five meetings a week. Brandon was offered a better job, so the two of them relocated to another city about sixty miles away. Shortly after Tiffany and Brandon relocated, Brandon was offered an even better position and higher salary to return to his previous employment. Tiffany realized that they would soon move again. Tiffany did not want to make more friends in AA in the town where she was residing temporarily, only to have to leave them so soon. (Excuses are common, plausible, and sometimes sound reasonable.) Therefore, to avoid the pain of leaving new friends, she simply stopped going to any more meetings. She stopped calling her sponsor on a daily basis the last couple of months, and did not have regular contact with her sponsor during this time.

Although she and Brandon still were very much in love, she was so unhappy with the rest of her life that she began to fantasize about various means of suicide. Her depression grew until one night Brandon approached her with an intervention strategy. He told her that he knew she was unhappy; that he knew, from being a recovering alcoholic himself, that she was devising a plan for a way out of her sadness; and he offered to help her find a way to achieve fulfillment in her life instead. He suggested that she look into going into a treatment program to discover what she may feel she missed by only attending AA to achieve recovery. He started going to Al-Anon to learn to detach with love, so he would not enable her to death. Brandon was very supportive and vowed to stand by her through this problem, no matter what it took or how much it cost them. Tiffany promised to call her sponsor and check with her doctor about treatment the next morning.

Tiffany's sponsor directed her to meetings, which they attended together. Her primary care physician referred her to a psychiatrist, where she sought counseling for treatment of depression and floating anxieties she was experiencing. Tiffany's psychiatrist asked a series of questions to evaluate her emotional state. Tiffany and her psychiatrist met for an hour twice each week for several months. Tiffany's doctor prescribed anti-depressant medication. She was encouraged to maintain regular contact with her sponsor and directed to resume attending meetings regularly.

Tiffany followed through with everything as she was instructed by her physician and her sponsor. She wrote about her feelings and kept a dream journal, to explore some of the hidden meanings in her unconscious state, as much as she could recall them. She contracted with her counselor not to jump off the roof of the building where she worked or otherwise harm herself. Tiffany agreed to call her sponsor before she took a drink, if she were so tempted, or if she just needed to talk to someone. She agreed to attend ninety meetings in ninety days, just as she had done when she first attended AA.

The anti-depressant medication provided relief from her psychological symptoms for awhile. After a few months on the medication, however, she complained of a lack of sexual feelings, and felt it interfered in her love life with Brandon. Her doctor allowed Tiffany to discontinue use of the drug under supervision, and helped her work through the mental and emotional anxieties that returned.

At some point, Tiffany realized that there was a trade-off between experiencing all of her feelings or numbing them. She reconciled herself to feeling all of her emotions, bad and good. She believed that by experiencing her emotions, she could get in touch with her body and herself. Tiffany began to remember childhood traumas, including abuse, which she related to her counselor; together they worked through the issues to find a solution.

Tiffany began re-parenting herself. When Brandon was out of town on a work-related trip, Tiffany went to the zoo, taking along only her invisible-to-the-rest-of-the-world ten-year-old self. She sat in the front row at the dolphin show so she could get splashed. Tiffany bought herself an ice cream with real sugar, not the diet kind she usually ordered. She rode the train around the park. She visited the ladies' rooms around the park often because she was so embarrassed to cry in public. Tiffany felt these were good signs, simultaneously feeling the deprivation of her childhood and gratitude for the opportunity to fill the void. She bought herself a toy bear at the gift shop before she left the zoo.

When Tiffany related these experiences to her counselor, she was encouraged to try more activities that she felt she missed in her childhood. She was also encouraged to continue to journal about the experiences and the feelings that arose from them. She learned to cope with the feelings of over-responsibility demanded of her in her youth as the eldest child in her large family. Tiffany learned she did not have to drink or drug to deal with her past hurts and fears.

As Tiffany developed trust and respect for her counselor, she divulged some of the sexual problems she was experiencing. She began to read about sexual dysfunction and learned about her own body's response. Tiffany invited Brandon to participate in a couple of sessions with her counselor. They discussed her orgasmic difficulties that she had experienced even before being placed on the anti-depressant. Together, they patiently worked through Tiffany's sexual disorder. The sex that Tiffany had considered ordinary in the acting-out phase of her sexuality occurring before her committed relationship to Brandon had become a dead weight in her relationship with him. Tiffany sensed there was a more satisfying relationship available for them if she could work through her historical sexual issues.

Together Tiffany and Brandon developed a highly spiritual connection that transcended anything Tiffany had ever experienced before. She spoke glowingly about the relationship, even when sexual activity was not consummated between them. She learned to express herself emotionally, as well as sexually with Brandon. Tiffany learned about her own responsibility in exercising her sexual powers, and thereby became a confident sexual partner. She made much progress and then asked her counselor for a goodbye session.

Tiffany's counselor, her sponsor and perhaps most important, her husband, all provided a safety net for Tiffany. With their encouragement and support, she was able to develop areas of her life previously unknown to her and transcended even her own high expectations in achieving personal fulfillment.

Tiffany has maintained her sobriety to this day, and continues periodically to seek therapy for issues as they arise for her. Often she can define the problem, get resolution for it, and return to her happy life within as few as five counseling sessions. This speaks well of her commitment to her own psychological health, and is also a tribute to her counselor's ability to help her in resolution, and to her entire support network.

Case Study: Male

Quick to assert that he was not an alcoholic, Brandon reported on intake and during his psychosocial history that he remembered that the first time he used alcohol with his friends, he drank too much, blacked out, and was brought home by the police. Vowing never to drink again, six weeks later, Brandon reported that he drank too much and failed to remember what had transpired during the evening. He knew only that he had been picked up by the police and questioned about a violation of curfew, destruction of property, obstructing justice, and public profanity directed at a law enforcement officer. A repeat of this history resulted in a third alcohol-related offense for which he was not caught, grand theft auto. Brandon said that this all occurred during his adolescence, age 13-15 years.

Brandon's family history was positive for addiction to alcohol and prescription drugs. Clearly by age 13, Brandon's use of alcohol produced problematic results, including a loss of control of how much he would drink; that, in spite of adverse consequences, he would continue to use; and he was experiencing **blackouts**, memory loss of events that occurred while he was under the influence of alcohol and other drugs. Though indications were present that addiction to alcohol was probable, Brandon continued to deny the problem because he exerted rigid controls in his life, avoiding the problems that formerly were significant in his life.

Brandon stated that while in college he did use alcohol and other drugs but never with ensuing problems of the immediate-consequence type. He did say, however, that every time he drank, he "broke out drunk." Brandon's answer to this dilemma was to not drink, a pledge to which he directed an enormous amount of energy. Not using a mood-altering substance left Brandon feeling vulnerable to emotions he was unable to identify or express, or unwilling to "feel through." It was during his junior year in college that Brandon "discovered" amphetamines, marijuana, and LSD. The use of these substances was rewarding in that the drugs, in Brandon's words, "allowed me to feel different, socialize with ease, express myself" without hesitancy or fear. Moreover, Brandon reported that he never found himself in trouble as a result of using these drugs.

Brandon married his high school sweetheart during his senior year in college. Brandon and Marie had dated for over six years and thought that they could handle the rigors of school and relationship with little difficulty. After graduating from college they headed east for graduate study. Marie was given to work, not school, and supported Brandon and herself, Brandon supplementing that income with an assistantship and a job as a motel manager. There were some difficult times, mostly associated with Brandon wanting to spend time with his cohort of graduate students, and Marie wanting Brandon to spend less time with books and school.

During these years Brandon continued to use illicit substances with some regularity, contributing to the stress on his and Marie's relationship. With a failing marriage at hand, Brandon and Marie agreed to revive their relationship, the outcome being conception, pregnancy, and birth of a son. The newfound responsibilities of fatherhood and parenting put a damper on the frequency of Brandon's illicit substance use. This occasion prompted his return to primarily using alcohol, viewed as a more "acceptable" drug, but never the cessation of use. As marital discord prevailed, Brandon admittedly increased his consumption of both alcohol and other drugs.

When asked about the marriage, Brandon responded that the attempt to salvage the relationship failed, mostly by his inability to give himself to Marie. Brandon clarified this by saying he just did not want to remain in a committed relationship with someone with whom he shared little in common, from whom he felt detached, and by whom he felt devalued. Alcohol and marijuana were the only substances used during this period but not to the extent that someone would notice that a problem with use existed. Brandon prided himself on his ability to hide just how important altering his mood had become, almost as valuable as the air he breathed.

As could be expected, Brandon's marriage ended in a rather ugly divorce, replete with allegations of illicit drug use, infidelity, alienation of affection, and any other "slanderous jealousies" each could sling at the other. What Brandon said really hurt him the most was that she promised that she would never allow him to see their son again. According to Brandon, this became a reality although the courts were generous in awarding him legal visitation with his son.

Unhealed from the pain, sadness, and fears associated with his recent divorce, Brandon, some six months later, met and married another woman, a divorcee with two children. Predictably, this relationship worked well for awhile, addressing Brandon's "neediness" for attention, affection, and nurturance. Equally calculable was the certain demise of this relationship; the end of this relationship was principally due to Brandon's continued use of substances. Brandon continued to use substances to obtain relief from the stressors of his daily life, the amelioration of feelings of loneliness, lack of esteem and sense of worth, and the dread of repeating his past relationship experiences. In this second marriage, Brandon admitted that he "was unfaithful," participating in several extramarital affairs, always when under the influence. Trying to address his guilt, Brandon passed these indiscretions off as "looking for something that was missing" in his life. Brandon sought his first treatment for alcoholism in the final months of this marriage. He reported that he knew that his feelings and behavior were seriously out of order and that it was related, in part, to his alcohol consumption, something with which he could no longer hide, explain, or cope.

After spending a month in treatment, Brandon returned to his family, looking better, acting more responsibly, willing to remain clean and dry and engage with members of family and community. On the inside, Brandon stated that it was like he was dying; most often unable to express his feelings to his partner and, on occasion, unwilling to take the risk to share for fear of emotional pain or reprisal in the form of some indignation. It did not take long for the inevitable to happen. During the one attempt at disclosing to his partner what he really experienced intrinsically, his mate scoffed, "If that's how you really feel, what are you still doing here?" Brandon packed a small suitcase, walked out and never went back. Brandon, when confronted with emotional stress in relationships, would pick up and leave, solving the immediate problem and retaining his posture of avoiding dealing with feeling issues.

Not as grief-stricken by the termination of a second relationship, though noticeably in more difficulty with alcohol, Brandon opted to abandon life, preferring isolation, superficial relationships, and limited responsibilities as a lifestyle. When in relationships, Brandon proclaimed that he was emotionally abusive, often derisive with his tongue, but never in other fashions. He commended himself on his willingness to be a partner in the handling of extrinsic duties as a mate. Also, Brandon confided that he was generally not very good at being honest about his feelings regarding his emotional needs. His decision to remain unmarried came readily and was cleverly disguised as responsible. Again, Brandon found refuge in self-deception.

Following an injury that left Brandon homeless, he entered yet another relationship, this time with someone who would drink, drug, and embark with him on his crusade to prematurely end life, death by alcoholism. What Brandon did not expect was to be unaccepting in his partner of the very behaviors that he emulated for many years. Another unanticipated occurrence was the lack of willingness of this new partner to sit idly by and watch Brandon kill himself. Instead, this partner gave Brandon the option of treatment or the highway; someone Brandon was not expecting to appear in his life; a mate who wanted to be in relationship and would take risks to ensure its survival.

Brandon entered treatment for alcoholism and drug dependency, preferring to "get better than get gone." Something "miraculous" happened in the first few hours of treatment that impacted Brandon in such a way as to alarm the staff and residents of the treatment center. Brandon's new partner was equally shaken by the changes that occurred within a few hours.

In a literal sense, *everything* about Brandon was different, according to all who knew him. Brandon has not found it necessary to use alcohol or other mood-altering substances since that day. This is not to mean Brandon did not have to work on issues. It means only that the willingness was there to attend to the task along with the complimentary absence of resistance and reluctance to experience the emotional upheaval so rigorously avoided in the past.

Brandon addressed in counseling his longing to be whole, to be a part of. He focused, with the help of his counselor, on the emotional fears harbored for years. Issues of adequacy, security, esteem, worth, and status were examined, discovered, and disclosed in the safety of the counseling arena. Self-awareness and self-forgiveness were championed, not at the expense of maintaining dignity. The counselor worked with Brandon to develop skills in relationship building, coping, and living life on life's terms. Integral to traditional counseling, the treatment staff encouraged sponsorship and attendance at community-based support meetings of Alcoholics Anonymous.

In sobriety, Brandon has worked tirelessly to mature emotionally and spiritually, particularly in relationships: with himself, his partner, and others in his life. Likewise, Brandon found it necessary to improve his relationship with a power greater than himself. Brandon married the woman who gave him the choice of alcohol or her. She, too, entered a recovery program. As a couple, both she and Brandon have had many issues through which to wade, most of those dealing with sexuality issues such as risk and trust in relationship; sexual fidelity; emotional honesty; selfish and self-centered behaviors that threaten emotional security; respect; and intimacy. Comfort with intimate issues would not have been possible without effective interventions during treatment and their commitment to ongoing recovery, including counseling, when indicated.

SUMMARY: SEXUALITY COUNSELING AND ADDICTION

Major Issues

For women, factors that must be examined in some detail with the help of the counselor include the following:

    Physiological, psychological, and socioeconomic determinants
    Social stressors related to sex role identity
    Sexual trauma and sexual dysfunction
    Risk and trust issues that adversely affect relationship and intimacy
    Self-esteem, worth, and status concerns
    Partner selection problems
    Sexual infidelity
    Emotional security and autonomy issues
    Intimacy issues
    Child-bearing factors as related to FAS/FAE and sexually transmitted diseases
    Sexual response cycle and previous sexual encounters, and body image issues
    Sexual orientation issues.

Many women find it uncomfortable to discuss the above issues in an open setting such as an Alcoholics Anonymous meeting, even with the encouragement of a sponsor and in a supportive group environment. Though essential to effective, long-term recovery, the formulaic approach of the 12-Step meetings is generally insufficient and non-conducive to women's work.

For men, some of the factors to be addressed remain the same but are different in manifest expression. Similar to their female counterparts, many men find it too embarrassing to reveal their innermost selves in the group setting of an Alcoholics Anonymous meeting. Some of this embarrassment is associated with an unhealthy ego, some with the presence of peers and members of the opposite sex. Sharing intimate details promotes overwhelming shame, guilt, or remorse and the notion that the chemically-dependent male will not be accepted by the group, left alone to attempt recovery without help. Men's work includes the following:

Inability to identify and express emotions appropriately
Self-esteem, worth, and status issues
Lack of respect for women
Fears of abandonment, betrayal, or rejection in relationships
Lack of honesty
Manifest anger, jealousy
Sexual infidelity
Sexual orientation issues
Sex role identity problems
Fear of intimacy
Nurturance and attachment concerns
Sexual trauma.

Conclusions

Counselors who work with addictions clients on sexuality issues, though generally well prepared to address most traditional concerns or problems, must first break through counselor resistance to modify or shift personal orthodoxy in order to reach the degree of empathy necessary to achieve positive clinical outcomes. This shift usually involves being more immediate, more directive, and more confronting than is typical in most counselor preparatory programs. A second concern in working with this population is the ability of the counselor to set aside personal bias, judgment, and opinion and be sensitive to the existence of myriad problems that lay beneath the surface issues of intoxication and behavior problems.

Sexuality issues must be viewed in a more expansive manner than merely observable behaviors that suggest some apparent problem. For the chemically-dependent client, outward behavior is seldom representative of the inner dynamics and conflicts. Much like the maligned anger response, anger in the chemically-dependent is more than likely an inappropriate expression of either emotional pain, sadness, embarrassment, or fear. Although it looks like anger, it may not be simply anger; perhaps a more debilitating condition such as an attachment disorder may be at work and mistaken for angry acting out.

Leaping from symptom to diagnosis with the chemically-dependent may present some difficult, and embarrassing, periods, particularly with sexual issues. Though sexual trauma is an all too frequent occurrence, it may not be what one "expects" to discover. Nor would the senior author suggest the counselor tackle these issues too early in the treatment and recovery process. Some clients take the "flight to health" to avoid dealing with the issue; others may abandon treatment prematurely for the same reasons.

The focus preferred is to enter the client's world in an area of deficient expertise, the area of emotions, understanding that one of the primary reasons to use/abuse substances is to alter how one feels. Many problems experienced by the client are related to an inability to engage in healthy relationships with self, others, life. The role emotion plays in a relationship evolves in time with effective counseling, setting the stage for the counselor to move with the client in his/her experience. Only from the inside can the client recover.

Germane to sexuality counseling with this population are issues around esteem, worth, status, relationship, and intimacy, as related to past and projected future. Working with a client in discovering areas of intrapersonal and interpersonal changes so as not to repeat a rather disruptive history is both challenging and immensely rewarding. The authors cannot more heartily recommend a specialty practice in this area.

As with all counseling, the counselor is guided by acquisition of a body of knowledge, by supervised practice of skills in the use of evidenced-based techniques and strategies, and some form of demonstration of competence in using that body of knowledge successfully with clients served. Just as we are prepared to practice, we are held accountable, in some fashion, for qualified practice and protection of the public we serve. Ethical and legal practice is prominent in our delivery of care.

Research Directions

Effective clinical outcome studies based on community indicators are sorely needed. We have examined client-counselor variables and client-program variables long enough. We have developed many good programs without deriving good clinical outcomes. Are there existing community-based indicators that suggest treatment for addictions really does provide a significant positive impact on community, something people can see that supports claims of efficacy?

Evidenced-based strategies, though long researched, are a fairly recent addition to current clinical practice. More of this type of research is necessary, perhaps with an interest in how some symptoms may be, in fact, by syndromes, best treated in longer-term counseling relationships. In the recent past we may have been opting for symptom abatement at the expense of long-term quality care of the client. Can we move from a symptom treatment approach to a more client-centered care that is respectful of client need?

Additional studies on the neurobiology of addiction are forthcoming, hallmarking a need to enhance the quality of training and expertise of the next generation of addiction counselors. We must market deliberately to attract more practitioners to this area of service and develop specialty tracks to accommodate their interests. The preparation of scientist-practitioners looms large when one considers the ever-increasing body of knowledge already stretching our capability to develop and update training practice, and to have adequate personnel resources to educate and train them. How can we best attract, develop, and train the number of addiction counselors necessary for the coming years?

REFERENCES

Abraham, K. (1994). The psychological relations between sexuality and alcoholism. In J. D. Levin & R. H. Weiss (Ed.), et al. *The dynamics and treatment of alcoholism: Essential papers* (pp.53-59). Northvale, NJ: Jason Aronson, Inc.

Ackerman, R. J. (1993). *Silent sons: A book for and about men.* New York, NY: Fireside.

Anonymous. (1939). *Alcoholics anonymous.* New York, NY: Alcoholics Anonymous World Services, Inc.

Atkinson, D. R., Morten, G., & Wing Sue, D. (1989). *Counseling American minorities: A cross-cultural perspective.* Madison, WI: Brown & Benchmark.

Brown, S. (Ed.) (1995). *Treating alcoholism.* San Francisco, CA: Jossey-Bass.

Buelow, G. D., & Buelow, S. A. (1998). *Psychotherapy in chemical dependence treatment: A practical and integrative approach.* Pacific Grove, CA: Brooks/Cole Pub. Co.

Cabaj, R. P. (1997). Gays, lesbians & bisexuals. In J. H. Lowinson, .R. Ruiz, R.B. Millman, & J.G. Langrod (Eds.), *Substance abuse: A comprehensive textbook,* (3rd ed.). Baltimore, MD: Williams & Wilkins.

Centers for Disease Control and Prevention. (n.d.). *I never thought I'd get pregnant.* Atlanta, GA: Author.

Coleman, E. (1987). Child physical and sexual abuse among chemically-dependent individuals. *Journal of Chemical Dependency Treatment, 1,* 27-38.

Colgan, P. (1990). Dimensions of pleasure: Sexuality, men and counseling. In D. Moore, & F. Leafgren (Eds.), *Problem-solving strategies and interventions for men in conflict* (pp. 57-71). Alexandria, VA: American Association for Counseling & Development.

DuPont, R. L. (1997). *The selfish brain: Learning from addiction.* Washington, DC: American Psychiatric Press.

Eliason, M. J. (1996). *Who cares?: Institutional barriers to health care for lesbian, gay and bisexual persons.* New York, NY: National League for Nursing.

Erikson, E. (1963). *Childhood and society.* New York, NY: Norton.

Evans, S., & Schaefer, S. (1987). Incest and chemically-dependent women: Treatment implications. *Journal of Chemical Dependency Treatment, 1,*141-173.

Hutchins, D. (1979). Systematic counseling: The T-F-A model for counselor intervention. *Personnel and Guidance Journal, 57,* 529-531.

Hutchins, D. (1984). Improving the counseling relationship. *The Personnel and Guidance Journal, 62,* 572-575.

Jacobson, G. (1987). Alcohol and drug dependency problems in special populations: Women. In R. E. Herrington, G. R Jacobson, & D. G. Benzer (Eds.), *Alcohol and drug abuse handbook* ((pp. 386-404). St. Louis, MO: W.H. Green.

John, S., Brown, Jr., L. S., & Primm, B. J. (1997). African Americans: Epidemiologic, prevention, and treatment issues. In J. H. Lowinson, et al. *Substance abuse: A comprehensive textbook*, (3rd ed., pp. 107-117). Baltimore, MD: Williams & Wilkins.

Johnson, B. D., & Muffler, J. (1997). Sociocultural determinants and perpetuators of substance abuse. In J. H. Lowinson, et al. *Substance abuse: A comprehensive textbook*, (3rd ed.). Baltimore, MD: Williams & Wilkins.

Kupers, T. A. (1993). *Revisioning men's lives: Gender, intimacy, and power*. New York, NY: The Guilford Press.

L'Abate, L. (1992). Major therapeutic issues. In L. L'Abate, J. E. Ferrar, & D. A. Serritella (Eds.), *Handbook of differential treatments for addictions* (pp. 5-19). Needham Heights, MA: Allyn Bacon.

Mayo Foundation for Medical Education and Research. (2000). *Fetal alcohol syndrome*. Retrieved from http://www.mayohealth.org

Miller, G. A. (1999). *Learning the language of addiction counseling*. Needham Heights, MA: Allyn & Bacon.

Mueller, R., Dupuy, P., & Hutchins, D. (1994). A review of the T-F-A counseling system: From theory construction to application. *Journal of Counseling & Development, 72*, 573-577.

Musto, D. F. (1997). Historical Perspectives. In J. H. Lowinson, R. Ruiz, R.B. Millman, & J.G. Langrod (Eds.), *Substance abuse: A comprehensive textbook*. (3rd ed., pp. 1-9). Baltimore, MD: Williams & Wilkins.

Nace, E. P. (1997). Alcoholics anonymous. In J. H. Lowinson, R. Ruiz, R.B. Millman, & J.G. Langrod (Eds.), *Substance abuse: A comprehensive textbook*. (3rd ed., pp. 383-389). Baltimore, MD: Williams & Wilkins.

National Clearinghouse for Alcohol and Drug Information. (n.d.). *Healthy women/healthy lifestyles: Here's what you should know about alcohol and other drugs*. Retreived from http://www.health.org/pubs/healwom/index.htm

National Institute of Drug Abuse. (1999). Drug abuse and addiction research: The sixth triennial report to Congress. Retrieved from http://www.nida.nih.gov/STRC/Role6.html

Perez, J. F. (1994). *Counseling the alcoholic woman*. Muncie, IN: Accelerated Development.

Ridley, C. R. (1995). *Overcoming unintentional racism in counseling and therapy: A practitioner's guide to intentional intervention*. Thousand Oaks, CA: Sage Publications.

Rosenbaum, M. (1997). Women: Research and policy. In J. H. Lowinson, R. Ruiz, R.B. Millman, & J.G. Langrod (Eds.), *Substance abuse: A comprehensive textbook* (3rd ed.). Baltimore, MD: Williams & Wilkins.

Roth, P. (1991). *Alcohol and drugs are women's issues*. Metuchen, NJ: The Scarecrow Press, Inc.

Ruiz, P., & Langrod, J. G. (1997). Hispanic Americans. In J. H. Lowinson, R. Ruiz, R.B. Millman, & J.G. Langrod (Eds.), *Substance abuse: A comprehensive textbook*, (3rd ed., pp. 705-711). Baltimore, MD: Williams & Wilkins.

Skrip, C., & Kuntzman, K. (1991). *Women with secrets: Dealing with domestic abuse and childhood sexual abuse in treatment.* Center City, MN: Hazelden.

Urqiza, A. J., & Capra, M. (1990). The impact of sexual abuse: Initial and long-term effects. In M.Hunter (Ed.), *The sexually-abused male: Prevalence, impact and treatment.* Vol. 1. pp. 105-135. Lexington, MA: Lexington Books.

Wadsworth, R., Spampneto, A. M., & Halbrook, B. M. (1995). The role of sexual trauma in the treatment of chemically dependent women: Addressing the relapse issue. *Journal of Counseling & Development, 73*(4), 401-406.

Weisner, T. S., Weibel-Orlando, J. C., & Lang, J. (1984). Seniors drinking, white man's drinking, and tee-totaling: Drinking levels and styles in an urban American Indian population. *Journal of Studies on Alcohol, 45*, 237-250.

West, P. L., Hutchins, D. E., & DeVilbiss, D. W. (1996). The T-F-A model and the substance abuse client: A case study. *Journal of Addiction and Offender Counseling, 16*(2), 34-49.

Westermeyer, J. (1997). Native Americans, Asians, and new immigrants. In J. H. Lowinson, R. Ruiz, R.B. Millman, & J.G. Langrod (Eds.), *Substance abuse: A comprehensive textbook*, (3rd ed., pp. 712-715). Baltimore, MD: Williams & Wilkins.

Wills-Brandon, C. (1989). *Is it love or is it sex? Why relationships don't work.* Deerfield Beach, FL: Health Communications, Inc.

Woititz, J. G. (1985). *Struggle for...intimacy.* Pompano Beach, FL: Health Communications, Inc.

SECTION 3
SEXUAL PROBLEMS AND TRAUMA

Chapter 13

COUNSELING FOR SEXUAL COMPULSION/ADDICTION/DEPENDENCE (SCAD)

Larry D. Burlew
University of Bridgeport
Al Barton
Piney Ridge Center

BACKGROUND

Sexual compulsivity, **sexual addiction**, and **sexual dependence** are three labels commonly applied to the problematic sexual behaviors of a heterogeneous group of men and women. However, many other labels exist to describe this particular sexual problem to include **sexual impulsivity**, **erotomania**, **hypersexuality**, **nymphomania** (for females), **satyriasis** (for men), **Don Juanism**, **hyperlibido**, and **erotophilia**. In the United States, the controversial "sexual addiction" movement has received public attention through popular media publications and television programs. Carnes (1991, 1994) reported that as much as 6% of the American population exhibits sexual compulsive or addictive behaviors. He also reported an 80% growth in the members of 12 Step, sex addiction, support groups in a ten-year span. A sizable industry of sexual compulsive treatment professionals and institutions has evolved in response to the phenomenon. Sex addict-specific treatment centers exist in Minnesota and Arizona. A journal, *Sexual Addiction and Compulsivity*, publishes articles specific to the field, and annual conferences are sponsored by the **National Association of Sexual Addiction and Compulsivity**.

The current authors prefer the acronym SCAD (Sexual Compulsion/Addiction/ Dependence) in referring to this disorder because there are several views on what it should be called. Wolfe's (2000) definition of compulsive love/sex behavior fits our concept of SCAD: "…existing when people do not and seem unable to curb, modify or control their sexual or relationship behavior, even when they are aware of actual or potential **self-defeating** social, medical, and/or financial consequences" (p. 236). Individuals with SCAD (here on in referred to as clients) use sex as a behavioral/cognitive response to emotional pain, anxiety, and depression (**Myers**, 1995). In the process, they objectify people or objects as a means to their next "fix;" are rarely reassured of their worth, even if an adult-to-adult sexual encounter occurs; may impulsively rely on **sexual abuse** for feelings of power; and struggle with true **intimacy** in healthy, sexual, adult-to-adult relationships.

Despite the abundance of information, clinical impressions and support services, no specific clinical diagnosis of sexual compulsion or addiction exists in the ***DSM-IV*** (APA, 1994). Legally, sexual obsessions or compulsions are not disabling conditions protected by the law and the **Americans with Disabilities Act** of 1991 (see Moskowitz, 1994). More specifically, a professional controversy exists in relationship to sexual compulsivity. Many authors (e.g., Arteburn, 1991; Cordasco, 1993; Pincu, 1989) conceptualize problematic sexual behavior within a medical model. Within this framework, it might be considered some form of an **impulse control disorder**. Others (e.g., Kaplan, 1996; Peele, Brodksy, & Arnold, 1991; Satel, 1993; Speziale, 1994; Walters, 1996) subscribe to an addictive sexual behavior concept. This framework suggests that the sexual addict uses sex to reduce psychological distress and experience a "high" of sorts. Levine and Troiden (1988) asserted there is no sexual addictive or compulsive behavior, but that these behaviors are better characterized as a learned dependence on sexual behavior to feel better. Apt and Hulbert (1995) also ruled out the addiction theory in favor of what they call "**sexual narcissism**," a term describing a person who is preoccupied with sex, but is unable to integrate sex and intimacy.

To include the continuum of theoretical models describing this particular sexual problem, we use the term sexual compulsion/addiction/dependence (SCAD). Some individuals use "**sexual addict**" or "**sexual compulsive**" exclusively, yet clients may benefit from either term in a self-conceptualization of their problems. Developmentally SCAD clients learn to cope with difficult feelings through sexual outlets such as frequent **masturbation**, **promiscuity**, constant **sexual daydreams** or thoughts, or using **pornographic** materials to become physiologically aroused. These clients use sexual activity as an anxiety reducer for stressful situations and experience uncontrollable sexual behavior or cognitions that ultimately lead to subjective distress, social or occupational impairment, or legal or financial consequences (Cordasco, 1993; Pincu, 1989; Black et al., 1997).

Historical Perspective

Though the phenomenon was described clinically more than one hundred years ago, more frequent publications about SCAD began in the early 1980s. Kraft-Ebbing (as cited in Myers, 1995) is the first known clinician to mention SCAD. As early as the late 1800s, he described patients whose sexual behavior and sexuality were in their thoughts and feelings, consuming any other goals and whose sexual enjoyments were impulsive and **insatiable**. His ideas accurately describe the SCAD behaviors of some clients. Colloquial historical terms such as "nymphomaniac," "Don Juan," and "**Casanova Complex**" are also used to describe elevated sexual behavior. Clients may use one of these colloquial labels, though the popularity of "sexual addict" has likely touched most people who are uncomfortable with their sexual behavior, so they may label themselves as such. The term "sexual addiction" was coined by a chapter of **Alcoholics Anonymous** in the 1970s (Apt & Hulbert, 1995; Augustine Fellowship, 1986). Patrick Carnes (1983, 1989, 1991) popularized problematic sexual behavior as an addictive disease in both lay and scholarly literature. Carnes is perhaps the best-known figure in the field and is a regular presenter and spokesperson for sexual addictions.

Definitions of sexual addiction in **popular media** can be vague and sensational. It has been popularly viewed as some life-threatening obsession with sex; pathological relationships that endanger self or others; a never ending compulsive search for sex and romance; or obsessive entrapment in relationships characterized by personal neediness and **hyper-dependency** (Carnes, 1991; Griffin-Shelly, 1994). Those with strong religious beliefs posit that the sexual addict's goal is to achieve constant sexual pleasure and is, therefore, a **sin** against God (Arteburn, 1991; Roberts, 1995).

As a clinical term, sexual addiction has been criticized as conceptually incorrect, as narrowly defining sexual behavior, often ignoring non-sexual relevant issues in therapy, and economically exploitative. Some professionals do not believe that people can be addicted to sexual behavior; rather they conceptualize compulsivity as a learned dependence on sexual behavior to meet one's needs (Coleman, 1987; Levine & Troiden, 1988; Walters, 1996). Practitioners are concerned that significant mental health issues such as **relational problems**, **depression**, **paraphilias**, and **conflict** with societal expectations get subsumed in the treatment of "sexual addiction," rather than explored as separate issues requiring specialized treatment strategies (Speziale, 1994). Additionally, sociological and economic factors surface as criticisms in the treatment of SCAD clients. Allgeier (1996) and Levine and Troiden (1988) argued that addiction diagnoses have social, monetary, and political agendas. These criticisms are hard to refute in the wake of a sizable industry of popular literature, twelve step groups, specialized therapists and treatment centers for SCAD.

Social constructivist theorists (e.g., Levine & Troiden, 1988; Walters, 1996) explain that terms like sexual addict or sexual compulsive are socially created labels for **deviant** sexual behavior. They believe that humans create their meanings in the absence of objective truths. Since no genetic or biological basis for SCAD has been proven (perhaps an objective truth), then society will continue to define right and wrong sexual behavior. The controversy existing around SCAD may stem from different groups' definition of deviant sexual behavior; some attempting to prevent a "**repathologizing**" of **erotic** behavior that flowered in the late 60s and 70s, while others rigidly stick to the concept that only sex within a **heterosexual** marriage is normal (Wolfe, 2000).

Kaplan (1996) and Goodman (1993) view sexual compulsion from a **psychodynamic** perspective. Behavior is not pathology inherently, but is rather a wrong mean to a right end. For Kaplan, the main difference between a paraphilia and sexual obsession is that childhood trauma is eroticized into paraphilia while people with sexual obsessions focus their pain on another person. The psychodynamic perspective has clinical significance and merit, but may be difficult to validate empirically.

CULTURAL/GENDER CONSIDERATIONS

Demographic research on SCAD suggests that it predominately occurs in males with college and graduate degrees (Black et al., 1997; Carnes, 1991; McKenna, 1992). Most age demographics of SCAD portray a phenomenon of the young, varying from age eighteen (Black, et al.) to forty (Carnes, 1991). Religious affiliation seems to play a peculiar role in SCAD. McKenna noted that religious figures such as **priests**, **ministers**, and **rabbis** have a high rate of SCAD. Relational and marriage status varies extremely in self-identified SCAD clients (Schneider, 1991).

In terms of developmental history, research varies with regard to the etiology of SCAD. In a study of 900 sexual addicts, Carnes (1989) found that an extensive number of his subjects had rigid or disengaged family systems, and childhood emotional and/or sexual abuse. However, Carnes's incidence of sexual abuse findings contrast sharply with those of Kafka and Prentky (1997) who only found that 28% of their sample of 60 sexual compulsives had a history of childhood abuse. Schneider (1991) believed that rigid family systems exclude discussions of sex and sexuality, ill-quipping children with accurate sexual information.

American **cultural norms** and **values** are often discussed in reference to SCAD. Many **Christian** writers who reference SCAD feel that **sexual deviancy** is part of a culture that is **morally bankrupt** (e.g., Arteburn, 1991; Roberts, 1995). Regardless of religious affiliation or lack there of, there seems to be an agreement that culture influences the prevalence and perpetuation of SCAD. Carnes (1991) and Peele et al. (1991) cited such factors as: convenience-oriented culture that believes in quick fixes to reducing anxiety; a reliance on technology that encourages easy solutions; an emphasis on entertainment and escapism that confuses meaning; a belief in the healing of sex to cure our negative feelings; disrupted family lives that contribute to feelings of abandonment; and a highly stressful culture that contributes to anxiety in the discussion of SCAD. Further research that includes a **diversity** dimension may drastically alter the thinking and conceptualization of SCAD.

Levine and Troiden (1988) asserted that SCAD is both conduct and belief systems that simply violate cultural definitions of what is normal. They argue that the concepts of sexual addiction and compulsion constitute an attempt to "re-pathologize forms of erotic behavior that became acceptable in the 1960s and 1970s" (p. 349). Therefore, a therapist's own values and cultural beliefs may impact a diagnosis of SCAD. For example, Hecker et al. (1995) found that single male and female clients were labeled sexual addicts more often than their married or monogamous counterparts. Additionally, in their study, religious male therapists tended to label clients as sexual addicts more often than either religious females or nonreligious males. As counselors, knowing one's sexual and philosophical beliefs is one way to prevent applying haphazard labeling and limited treatment to clients.

Diversity issues are rarely discussed in the SCAD literature. Two populations mentioned are **African Americans** (Saulnier, 1996) and **gay men** (Black et al., 1997; Irons & Schneider, 1996; Pincu, 1989). Interestingly, both groups are **minority** populations and, therefore, any discussion of sexual behavior must also include discussions of **racism**, **homophobia**, and **socioeconomic status**. Sexual compulsion in Black males may be fostered by the relative ease to be sexual without financial expenditure, along with cultural values that equate sex with power in a population whose power has been taken away.

Although gay men have high incidences of treatment for sexual compulsion, Irons and Schneider cautioned labeling promiscuous, gay, sexual behavior as SCAD. Quadlund (as cited in Black et al.) completed a study comparing 30 gay men who described themselves as sexual compulsives with a control population. Quadlund found only two differences between the groups: the compulsive group reported greater numbers of sexual partners and the tendency to have sex in public places. These empirical differences lend credence to a social constructionist perspective on sexual compulsion and addiction where the dominant group defines culturally acceptable sexual behavior. From a gay male perspective, these differences could be acceptable forms of sexual behavior and viewed as alternative forms of sexual expression. Labeling gay, male, sexual behavior as SCAD comes dangerously close to Levine and Troiden's (1988) assertion that SCAD merely **marginalizes** and pathologizes alternative forms of sexual behavior, labeling them as deviant by historical standards of "normal" sexuality.

Women's issues around SCAD literature have been discussed in works by Kasl (1989), Carnes (1989), Roberts (1995), Saulnier (1996), The National Council on Sexual Addiction and Compulsivity (n.d.), and Ross (1998). Black et al. (1997) mentioned that sexuality in American culture is defined from a masculine perspective. Roberts's text, *For Women Only, Dealing with Love Addiction and Sexual Issues*, is a short text with more of a testament and personal narrative of the experience following a 12-Step recovery program. Saulnier, however, cautions against the use of 12-Step recovery programs for women and minorities like African Americans, Hispanics, lesbians and gays, and poor people. While part of the reason for the popularity of 12-step programs is because they're normally free and readily available, she wrote, "This [12-step programs] may actually be a functional model for some people, for example, those who have been given to believe that they are responsible for controlling the world and everything in it, that is: white, mainstream, heterosexual men – the people for whom the program was designed" (p. 95). Women and minorities may need group models that do not focus almost entirely on individual change, but rather include pertinent topics like social change and the realities of societal oppression.

According to Carnes (1991), gender issues that contribute to SCAD focus on the barriers that women have overcome in the sexual sphere, such as birth control, freedom to pursue sexual relationships and the inherent power of sexuality, and the female bodily changes (e.g., menarche, abortion, menopause, or pregnancy) that could be construed as the catalytic events that can contribute to SCAD behavior(s)/act(s). These arguments essentially say that women can behave similarly to men, and thus be more prone to SCAD. By pointing out these dimensions, Carnes leaves open the critique that if women were not sexually liberated they would be less at risk to become sex addicts. Kasl (1989), on the other hand, discusses women's sense of co-dependence, power and control issues, addictive relationships, and questions around sexual and romantic behaviors as critical issues that have always existed for women. In some ways, she suggests that women's models of recovery must be based on relationship models.

DIAGNOSTIC FACTORS/MENTAL HEALTH ISSUES

Counselors must be careful not to pathologize sexual behavior in general that "feels" like deviant sex to the counselor him/herself. For example, is a client who consistently masturbates three times a day, when he/she wakes up, when arriving home from work, and before going to sleep at night, experiencing SCAD? The answer to that is not necessarily. A counselor should not make such an assessment without understanding (a) the sexual behavior in the context of the individual's life; (b) the client's perception of the masturbation; and (c) if any **adverse consequences** and/or risks are occurring due to such behavior. Listen carefully to the client's story beginning with the presenting issues to determine how masturbation fits into his/her life.

The above client may explain that he/she is very depressed over the ending of a 15 year relationship. Only two **significant relationships**, a marriage of 20 years and this **partnership** of 15 years, have occurred for the client who is now 55. The client describes him/herself as a highly sexual person who enjoyed frequent and intimate, **monogamous**, sexual relationships with these two partners. The client is feeling "old" and unsure how to begin "dating again" at 55 and, because of **AIDS**, for the time being prefers masturbation to satisfy sexual urges. He/she believes that another long-term significant relationship will occur in the future. Without hearing the client's full story and the sexual behavior within that context, a counselor might erroneously conclude that SCAD is an issue. This client might even be using masturbation as a means to abate the feelings of depression, but that is not necessarily negative or unhealthy and other symptoms should be present before diagnosing a client with SCAD.

The Cycle of SCAD

Clients with SCAD experience a cycle that leads to their compulsive sexual behavior(s), even though they may not initially identify the cycle. Both Carnes (1992) and Kasl (1989) identified the cyclic nature of SCAD. Helping clients identify the **SCAD cycle** during treatment is important. Understanding the SCAD cycle makes them realize that SCAD is not an isolated behavior, like spending 8 hours on the **Internet** searching for the right masturbation partner. Rather, SCAD is a process that "kicks in" sometimes hours before the sexual behavior itself occurs. The senior author uses the labels described below when working with SCAD clients.

*Phase 1: **The Trigger***. Similar to **drug addiction**, the trigger for SCAD clients is any person, place, situation, thought, or thing that starts the cycle. This might be having time alone and feeling bored; being "put down" in some way; seeing a person who you think is attracted to you; going to the room in the house where the sexual behavior typically occurs (e.g., in the bathroom); seeing the binoculars that might be used in **voyeurism**; or having thoughts about not being attractive enough. Kasl (1989) wrote that at some point a "[**cue**] shuts down her healthy self, creates a trance-like state, and takes control" (p. 21). The trigger is this cue, and the cue might be a fight with a spouse. The **trance** occurs as the individual avoids dealing with strong emotions, as well as an argument. Or, the trigger might be the binoculars that are now clearly associated with the cycle and ultimate sexual behavior.

*Phase 2: **The Craving***. This is the psychological response to the trigger, occurring before the actual "**sex seeking**" behaviors begin. Craving is the psychological need that motivates the SCAD client to become involved in the addictive sexual behavior. SCAD clients become preoccupied (Carnes, 1992) at this point and are internally "driven" or "punishing" in their thinking depending on the trigger. Some clients actually recognize that they've been triggered and have thoughts like, "Don't do this. You know it won't help. Why are you thinking this way?" Others might think, "I want this. I deserve this. It's the only way to make me feel better, or whole, or like a human being." Yet, another might think, "I'm a terrible shit for fighting with my husband all the time. It's all my fault." While the thoughts assume any form, they are usually exaggerated, oftentimes involve **irrational beliefs** and **cognitive distortions**, and are difficult to control. Most importantly, the thoughts are related to the craving in some way, which ultimately is screaming, "I want; I need."

*Phase 3: **Sex Seeking Behavior***. Craving becomes materialized in this phase; going from thoughts and needs to actions leading up to "**scoring**," which is being involved in the SCAD sexual behavior(s) itself. Therefore, any actions that lead to the sexual behavior(s) are included in this phase. We have heard drug addicts explain this as a "psychological high"…the seeking, not finding, the thrill of seeking again, almost copping but not, then seeking again, and finally copping. SCAD clients experience the same phenomenon. One midlife SCAD client said, "In some ways, all the preparation, getting 'dolled' up, telling myself that I still looked like a 30-year-old, getting in my car, and finally stepping through the door of a bar sometimes was more exciting then the sex itself, which usually wasn't that great." Carnes (1992) called this the **"ritualization"** phase and claimed that it was "the addict's own special routines which lead up to the sexual behavior" (p. 9).

Phase 4: Scoring. This is the engagement in the preferred or sexual act(s) of choice. The SCAD client has been psychologically high in the sex-seeking phase, but now actually "cops" by physically being involved in the sexual act(s) itself. Scoring varies from groping a person in the subway, to flashing someone on the street, to being involved in "golden showers," to spending an inordinate amount of time in the bathtub fantasizing about the ideal sex partner, to giving oneself enemas while masturbating. It is the SCAD client's perception that he/she has "scored" that defines what is actually the SCAD sexual behavior/act of choice.

*Phase 5: **Emotional/Physical Consequences***. Kasl (1989) referred to this phase as the **"hangover,"** and like a hangover the good times are over and the SCAD client feels the "pain" of scoring. This pain might be psychological with shameful feelings related to thoughts like "it wasn't enough" or "I'm right back to where I started" or "I feel dirty because I did it again." Or, the pain might occur as a physical reminder that the problem the SCAD client tried to avoid still exists, for example, the boss calling saying that you're late to work, and she's still expecting the overdue report on her desk. Or, it might be a partner demanding that an argument from the night before be finished. Depending on the nature of the scoring, there might also be **legal consequences** if the SCAD client got caught soliciting prostitutes or health worries about contracting **HIV** due to having **unprotected sex**. However, what ultimately happens? The SCAD client begins to experience anxiety, worry, apprehension and tension, which lead to Phase 1 and a familiar way of coping with tension via the SCAD cycle.

Behaviors

The range of SCAD behaviors is varied. Goodman (1992; 1993) cautioned that the problem for SCAD clients is neither specific behavior nor how often sexual activity occurs, but rather how it affects the life and system around an individual. Crucial for SCAD clients is reaching an understanding of how their sexual behavior relates to or affects their functioning (Carnes, 1991, 1998; Goodman, 1993; Pincu, 1989). Books designed for mass audiences are filled with anecdotes and case histories of **sexual excess** including excessive masturbation, **prostitution, extramarital affairs**, paraphilias, dangerous encounters, fantasy sex, seductive role sex, **intrusive sex, anonymous sex**, trading sex, pain exchange, exploitative sex, and **multiple partnerships** (e.g., Arteburn, 1991; Carnes, 1991, 1998; Roberts, 1995). Carnes (1991) felt that certain types of sex are addictive-prone. This includes sex that is exploitative of others, non-mutual, objectifies another, unsatisfying, shameful, and fearful.

Black et al. (1997) reported that only three studies into the behavior of SCAD persons had been reported as of their work. Research into the behaviors of SCAD has largely focused on the distinction between paraphiliac and non-paraphilia sexual behavior. Kafka and Prentky (1997) coined the term "paraphilia related disorders" to describe sexual disorders that meet all criteria for paraphilia, but are not considered socially deviant. This division is evidenced by

Black et al. (1997) and Carnes's (1994) list of compulsive behavior categories: compulsive "**cruising**" (searching for) and relations with multiple partners; compulsive fixation on unavoidable partner; compulsive masturbation; compulsive multiple love relationships and compulsive sexuality within a relationship; voyeurism; **exhibitionism**; intrusive or inappropriate sex; anonymous sex; trading sex (includes filming or photographing); paying for sex; and pain exchange.

The above categories, especially Carnes's categories, have been adopted in other studies of SCAD (e.g., Irons & Schneider, 1996; Schneider, 1991). Although their lists concur on many behaviors, Black et al. (1997) found that no paraphiliac behavior, including exhibitionism, **sadism**, **telephone sex**, **transvestitism**, or **fetishism**, occurred in more than 6% of the respondents in their study of SCAD populations. A shortcoming in this study was the deliberate exclusion of **illegal behavior** in the questionnaires administered to subjects. Research that included illegal sexual behavior might reveal different findings. Kafka and Prentky (1997) studied 30 men who considered themselves as SCAD and found that the division between paraphiliac and nonparaphiliac behavior was even, thus lending credence to Carnes's assertion that SCAD clients have paraphiliac disorders.

Other presenting behaviors common to SCAD that a clinician might overlook include sexual humor, seductivity, inappropriate dress, moralizing sexual issues, judgmental religion, sexual dysfunctions, "polar-achievers" (over- or under-achievers), and patterns of short-term relationships or on-line computer SCAD (Bingham & Piotrowski, 1996; Carnes, 1991). **Substance use** or other addictions may occur with SCAD. Goodman (1992; 1993) believed in an underlying disease process common to all addictive disorders, and reported **multiple addiction** rates of 50% in clients. These rates of substance abuse and SCAD are validated by other researchers (e.g., Cordasco, 1993; Irons & Schneider, 1996; McKenna, 1992).

Counselors should be aware that their clients' sexual behavior might not remain static or constant. Cyclical or ritualistic behavior, reminiscent of the *DSM-IV* diagnosis Obsessive-Compulsive Disorder may be found in some SCAD clients (Carnes, 1989; McKenna, 1992). Periods of escalating and de-escalating sexualized behavior have also been documented by researchers (Black et al., 1997; Carnes, 1991; Kasl, 1989). For example, in Black et al.'s study of 36 self-identified sexual compulsives, 78% reported periods of no compulsive sexual behavior at times in their lives.

Affective and Cognitive Symptoms

How SCAD clients feel (affective states) or what they are thinking (cognitive states) is mostly reported by clinical impressions. They may exhibit grief, rage, shame, disappointment, loneliness, depression, out of control, or have feelings of low self-esteem (Carnes, 1991; Cordasco, 1993; Goodman, 1993). Additionally, SCAD clients may experience anhedonia, anxiety, depression, or manic-depressive features (Black et al., 1997; Goodman, 1993). Researchers tend not to list the positive features that SCAD clients experience which could create an ambivalence to cease SCAD behaviors.

Most literature cites cognitive distortions as common in SCAD clients (Carnes, 1991; Cordasco, 1993; McKenna, 1992). They may express self-loathing, fears that they cannot be loved as well as perfectionism and unworthiness. These clients may defend their cognitive distortions through a number of mechanisms such as minimizations, rationalizations, projection, intellectualizations, and detachment (Griffin-Shelly, 1994). The **denial** of a problem is a central SCAD cognition, which is prevalently supported in the literature of **Sexual Addicts Anonymous (SAA)**, **Sexual Compulsives Anonymous (SCA)**, **Sexaholics Anonymous (SA)**, and **Sex and Love Addicts Anonymous (SLAA)** (Goodman, 1993; Griffin-Shelly, 1994; McKenna, 1992; Pincu, 1989).

COUNSELING AND TREATMENT STRATEGIES

The following counseling and treatment recommendations are not a panacea for every issue a SCAD client presents during the counseling process. As with any client, related or concurrent issues will be identified requiring interventions that must be added to the treatment plan. Also, a client's presenting problem may be depression or feelings of inadequacy or relationship problems and then the issue of SCAD surfaces as the client's story unfolds. In these cases, a client may conceptualize his/her major problem as feelings of inadequacy and view the SCAD activities as the behavioral consequence of the feelings of inadequacy. It is important for a client to choose the focus of his/her own therapy to make it truly meaningful and productive. However, a client needs help in identifying all issues related to the identified problem(s) and in understanding that those issues must be concurrently treated.

SCAD clients can benefit from an **existential counseling** approach. Oftentimes these clients feel that their sexual behavior and their lives are out of their control. Therefore, having them identify the focus of their treatment begins a process of regaining control of their lives. A SCAD client may identify his/her primary problem as low self-esteem with the contributing issues of SCAD evidenced by a paraphilia, substance abuse issues, a history of low-paying employment, and chronic headaches. The client may even identify another issue as the primary problem (e.g., SCAD) as his/her therapy progresses. However, if he/she doesn't, then establish specific treatment strategies for each contributing issue while framing it around the low self-esteem.

Counseling strategies are recommended below to address the issue of SCAD. The senior author, L. Burlew (here on in referred to as "I"), uses an existential approach in working with SCAD clients. Existential counseling allows for flexibility in choice of techniques and strategies based on the client's problems. As an existential counselor, a treatment plan is developed using the following concepts: finding **meaning** and living **authentically**, taking **responsibility** in life choices, developing **"I-Thou" relationships**, and understanding **death** as urgency in living. The concepts create a framework to directly confront and "attack" SCAD behaviors. (For individuals less familiar with existential counseling concepts, the following resources will be helpful: Victor Frankl's [1984] *Man's Search for Meaning*; or Gerald Corey's [2001] chapter on Existential Counseling or Frank's [1999] chapter in Capuzzi and Gross's text, *Counseling and Psychotherapy*.)

Assessment

Before any treatment begins, an accurate **assessment** and **diagnosis** of the client's problem(s) must occur. As mentioned previously, **misdiagnosis** of SCAD might occur when a counselor's values and beliefs about sexuality and sexual behavior rigidly adhere to the dominant culture's perspective on acceptable sexual behavior. Therefore, counselors must be careful not to pathologize alternative forms of sexual behavior. Similarly, they must be careful not to overlook sexual behavior that fits the criteria for SCAD based on a culture or worldview that is different from America's.

Model an "I-Thou" relationship during the assessment process by creating a safe environment for the client to openly share his/her experiences through appropriate problem exploration. Unless the client is harming self or others, it is the client's responsibility to make meaning of his/her experiences and evaluate them as positive, negative, or neutral. The counselor, however, should confront any behavior that is causing the client negative consequences (thus confronting **denial** and/or **resistance**); that is exaggerated by rigidly identifying with common labels promoted by the media (**catastrophizing** as Albert Ellis might say); or that is causing problems with cultural differences in terms of appropriate sexual behavior.

Effective problem exploration allows the counselor and the client to determine if SCAD is an accurate diagnosis. Through an interview, Cooper (as cited in Hannah, 1998) described criteria for SCAD. Cooper said, "These are people who have problems with sexuality and use it in **self-destructive** and maladaptive ways. There are five criteria for compulsive sexual behavior: 1) Denial – some way of convincing yourself that it's okay to do what you're doing. 2) Persistent desire to stop or **control** the behavior. 3) Expenditure of a great deal of time on the sexual activities. 4) Consequent reduction of important social, occupational or recreational activities. 5) Continuation of the sexual activity despite the adverse consequences or significant risks" (p. 109).

Wolfe (2000) also addressed the need for assessment and listed 10 questions that can be used specifically as an assessment tool for both SCAD and love/relationship compulsivity. The questions target specific thoughts, feelings, and actions that indicate the client might be experiencing SCAD, and they are "directed at determining the extent to which the presenting complaint is potentially or actually self- and/or other-defeating" (p. 239). The questions are a guide, and the counselor must use his/her astute clinical judgement to work with the client on a realistic assessment for SCAD. Wolfe's questions are listed below (anything in parenthesis was added by the current author).

1. Do you, or others who know you, find that you are overly preoccupied or obsessed with sexual activity [love relationships]?
2. Do you ever find yourself compelled to engage in sexual [love relationship] activity in response to stress, anxiety, or depression?
3. Have serious problems developed as a result of your sexual [or love relationship] behavior, such as job or relationship loss, contracting or spreading sexually transmitted diseases or other illness, experiencing or causing injuries, or getting charged with sexual offenses?
4. Do you feel guilty and ashamed about some of your sexual [or love relationship] behaviors?
5. Do you fantasize or engage in any unusual or what some would consider "deviant" sexual behavior [love fantasies]?
6. Do you find yourself constantly searching or "scanning" the environment for a potential sexual [or love] partner (or an opportunity to engage in behavior perceived as sexually oriented)?
7. Do you ever find yourself sexually [or romantically] obsessed with someone (or some thing) who is not interested in you or does not even know you?

8. Do you think your pattern of masturbation (or any other behavior perceived as sexually oriented and/or motivated) is excessive, driven, or dangerous?
9. Have you had numerous love [or sex] relationships (or sexually oriented experiences) that were short-lived, intense, and unfulfilling?
10. Do you feel a constant need for sex or expressions of love in your sexual [or love] relationships? *(p. 239)*

Counselors must also be aware of the **cultural implications** when assessing for SCAD. For example, Suren is a 20 year-old college student from **India** attending college in America. Currently, he is a junior, is in a year-long, sexually monogamous relationship, and has had two other girlfriends. Each girlfriend was American, and he has had sex with each of them. He reports to the counselor that he is a **sex maniac** because in his country, he would never be allowed to have sexual relations before marriage. He is concerned that when he goes back to India, he won't be able to get "sex" off his brain.

Is Suren experiencing SCAD? Does he meet specific criteria for an assessment of SCAD? These questions can only be answered based on the culture and worldview through which you are processing the criteria for SCAD. Therefore, a **bicultural** assessment might be helpful to Suren: one using an American worldview for young adults in college and another for an Indian worldview for young adults. Ultimately, Suren must determine what his sexual behavior means to him, regardless of whether or not he's in America or India, and how comfortable he is with that based on his own beliefs and values.

Treatment becomes more complex though because Suren might want to work within a framework of **acculturation** and learn to become comfortable with American norms regarding acceptable sexual behavior for young adults. On the other hand, he may choose to operate from an Indian worldview and then must learn to articulate to potential girlfriends his discomfort with **sexual intercourse** before marriage and find partners who hold similar values. Whichever path Suren chooses, he must ultimately believe he can return to India and control his sexual desires and behavior in a country with more restrictive sexual norms.

Clients may fit the criteria for SCAD, report to counseling feeling like there are sexual problems, and still not identify with a diagnosis of SCAD. It is enough that the client realizes controlling his/her sexual behavior has become a problem. A counselor can still begin educating the client about SCAD, typically by describing the cycle of SCAD. The more a client identifies him/herself with SCAD symptoms and feels unhappy with this personal reflection, the more urgent the need for change becomes. However, don't expect every SCAD client who identifies with the SCAD cycle and symptoms to feel an urgency to change.

Finding Meaning

From an existential perspective, finding meaning is "seeking something to satisfy an intrinsic need," is a "motivational force in people," and "gives people a reason for the routines of their daily lives" (Vontress, Johnson, & Epp, 1999, pp. 48-49). Clients who self-refer with issues of SCAD already decided that their sexual behavior is not meeting their intrinsic needs, and is "controlling" their daily routines through an unwanted motivation to seek sexual activity that produces negative consequences. Therefore, they already know they are living inauthentically because they desire something else. Some professionals (e.g.,

Allgeier, 1996) recommend that such clients must admit that they are sex addicts and out of control; others (e.g., **Dolan**, 1990) suggest that they have to admit that they have a problem.

I, on the other hand, do not believe that SCAD clients have to say, "I am a sex addict" unless they prefer to describe themselves as such. Rather, I ask them to identify several activities in their daily SCAD routines. A client (let's call him Jack) might list the following:

A. Spending long periods of time away from my family in a day.
B. Hanging out in bookstores desperately trying to get a **blowjob**.
C. Afterwards, washing my **genitals** compulsively until I'm raw.

Then, I ask Jack what feeling comes to mind for each activity, as well as any body response. Next to each item Jack might list the following:

A. Guilt; pain in my neck
B. Desperate; legs get tired standing around
C. Dirty and worried; genitals hurt after the washing

Sometimes, **guided visualization** helps a client who can't identify the feeling or body response. Even if the feeling and body responses are identified, I still want Jack to get in touch with them by closing his eyes and imagining that, for example, he's standing around the bookstore trying to "score" a blowjob. This exercise intensifies the body's response to the SCAD behavior and enhances the discussion of the questions to follow.

The following questions help SCAD clients like Jack tap into the inner meaning (or lack of) of his current sexual activity. I ask what message his inner self is sending about the SCAD behaviors based on his re-experienced feelings and body responses, and Jack will most likely say something like, "This doesn't feel good;" or "This is awful and disgusting." Then I ask, "If something is really important and meaningful to you, like your (let's say child), would you be sending yourself such messages?" Inevitably, the answer is, "Of course not." Once this point is reached, then the SCAD client can admit that his/her sexual behavior is not meeting his/her intrinsic needs, thus it is not meaningful. Finding true meaning then becomes the focus of therapy.

Most likely counselors will work with clients who have been referred to counseling specifically for SCAD due to legal problems or to negative consequences from work or family life. One client (Fred), who was referred to counseling by his father, claimed, "I like having sex with **prostitutes,** and I like going to bookstores for anonymous sex." He worked for his father, had charged $100,000 of unsubstantiated business expenses to the business, was "sweating more than usual," and feared that he might have AIDS. He disclosed some of his sexual behavior to his father, yet had disclosed nothing to his wife of many years. He worried that she might have HIV if he tested positive.

Fred believed that his SCAD activities "satisfied an intrinsic need" because he related to the physical pleasure and stress release that the sex produced. He identified with the SCAD cycle but frequently intellectualized in defense of his sexual activities. He claimed that his sexual behavior was the "bad boy" part of himself that his mother and father had staunchly prohibited in his Catholic upbringing.

In this case, Fred was identifying with the "positive" aspects of the SCAD routines; therefore, I asked him to share anything negative about his SCAD activities. Fred listed the following:

A. Uncontrollable spending on prostitutes leading to illegal use of company funds.
B. Unprotected sex with multiple partners, which put himself and his wife in danger of contracting HIV.
C. Strong fear of death now that he might be having symptoms of HIV.

Fred added the following feelings and body responses in relationship to the above activities.

A. "Terribly" guilty that he had let his father down, put the company business potentially in financial difficulty, and afraid that his father might put him in jail. He felt this through bad headaches, neck aches, and day sweats.
B. Again, "terrible" guilt that he might have "killed" both himself and his wife and afraid that if he told his wife, she would **divorce** him. He felt this through strong, painful, heart palpitations, sporadic **impotence** with his wife, and sometimes **night sweats**.
C. "Dread" of how he would answer for his behavior to God. He felt this through restlessness at night, which sometimes created an inability to sleep.

I refer to Fred's experience as an **existential paradox** or a paradox of meaning. While he focuses on the positive aspects of his SCAD routines and believes that they are meaningful to him, his body and soul are clearly sending opposing messages. Clients are often confused about this paradox and ask questions like, "How can something that seems meaningful to me feel so awful?" Sometimes individuals act out of habit or not knowing any other way to satisfy their needs. They ignore the strong messages sent by the inner self that their behavior is not acceptable or not really meeting their most important needs. Therefore, they continue with their behavior, live with the uncomfortable suffering from the existential paradox, and forego the search for true meaning.

Fred can be helped by explaining the existential paradox that while his SCAD routines produce some physical, external pleasure, they also produce strong emotional and **psychosomatic distress**. Then, ask him, "If something was really important and meaningful to you, like one of your children, would your being, your inner self be sending such distress?" Even Fred had to agree with the logic and was willing to begin searching for true meaning without the SCAD activities.

Living Authentically

This aspect of treatment involves the client knowing him/herself well enough, his/her own values and beliefs, to live true to self and not in "**bad faith**" (or according to the values and beliefs of others). The client identifies intrinsic needs and sets **goals** for the here and now to meet those needs. The identified needs must be meaningful enough to motivate the client to accomplish the established goals.

Using the client Jack as an example, goals can be established in two ways. While stopping the SCAD cycle is ultimately an outcome, it in itself is too complex and overwhelming as a single goal. Rather, as a first method for setting goals, search for meaning from the client's original list of significant SCAD activities. For example, in Jack's case, one goal might be, "Spending long periods of time with my family." In order to accomplish this, he must stop going to bookstores for sex. The counselor might also ask Jack to identify activities that will help him feel "clean," rather than "dirty and worried;" he might say, "If I lived a good, decent life and did things I felt proud of." Jack needs help in understanding that he is already doing some things of which he can be proud. This activity prevents him from catastrophizing or believing that everything he has done is "dirty," thus trying to help Jack not feel completely hopeless. However, one goal can be to substitute activities of which he can be proud for the time normally spent in bookstores. Another goal can be to use some of that time to always be at home for family dinners.

As a second method for setting goals, help the client identify what he/she is ultimately getting from the routine sexual activity(ies) itself. I use the **Gestalt empty chair** technique as one strategy to do this. In Jack's case, one chair might be the "blow job self" and the other chair might be the "dirty worried self." From the dialoging an intrinsic need like, "I feel worthwhile because so many people want me" might be identified. In which case, Jack can set a goal of ways to feel worthwhile in place of multiple sex partners.

Additionally, from this technique, other significant information might arise like, "I don't have to be involved with any of these people; I don't have to take responsibility for them." This information can lead to insights for Jack like he is interacting with these anonymous sex partners, yet treating them like objects or as "I-It" encounters. Treatment strategies can be developed to help Jack relate to his interpersonal environment from an "I-Thou" perspective. If he wants to have "I-Thou" encounters, then he will stop having anonymous sex in bookstores.

Taking Responsibility

Once meaningful goals are established, clients need help to take responsibility for making choices and for taking action to achieve those goals. The choices involve any strategies necessary for the client to make change and responsibly take action on those strategies. Without taking action, a client saying, "I want to spend more quality time with my husband," doesn't mean anything if she takes no action. As she actually spends more time with her husband, then she is accomplishing her goal.

This aspect of counseling takes great courage for SCAD clients. First, reaching their goals requires dealing with the SCAD cycle because it has been a significant part of their behavior, thoughts, feelings and coping mechanisms for much of their lives despite negative consequences. Second, they must learn new behaviors and skills that were probably overlooked and underdeveloped, as well as engage in their **interpersonal** and **intrapersonal** worlds in unfamiliar ways. Finally, the familiar "SCAD self" will be replaced with new, more meaningful, functional aspects of the self. This replacement might feel like a form of death with the concomitant grieving that normally occurs with such change.

Treatment Considerations

The treatment considerations reviewed below are in no particular order. And, ultimately clients must choose and act on those aspects of treatment they believe will help them reach their goals. The treatment considerations are compiled from my own experiences with SCAD clients, as well as from the current literature.

In order to reach their goals, SCAD clients must make decisions about their sexual activities. In terms of sexual behavior, the goal for SCAD clients is to control undesirable sexual activities rather than completely give up all sexual behavior. However, **abstinence** is usually the recommended approach to begin this process (e.g., Ross, 1998). My experience is that most clients readily agree to abstinence, but relapse pretty quickly unless they are intensely attacking the SCAD cycle. Relapse is not a negative experience in treatment; rather the reality of their diagnosis becomes clear, and they realize that treatment involves more than attempted **celibacy**. The following treatment strategies are useful to help clients with abstinence.

A. Some SCAD clients may want **inpatient** treatment to help them stop their out of control sexual behaviors. Be ready with the names and locations of inpatient treatment facilities.

B. If they continue with **outpatient** treatment, then more than one session a week is required. Additionally, signing a written, **behavioral contract** clearly identifying the undesirable sexual behavior they intend to abstain from helps.

C. **Support groups** like Sexual Compulsives Anonymous or Sex Addicts Anonymous with 12-step programs can be helpful during the early stages of treatment. Working the 12-step program with **sponsorship** from another SCAD individual helps clients when their craving is at its worst. Know the locations of SCA or SAA meetings and attend a couple of meetings with clients if necessary. Avoid any 12-step groups that **discriminate** against minority populations like homosexuals (Jenish, 1991; Saulnier, 1996). Additionally, considering Saulnier's beliefs that the 12-step models were "made for white, mainstream, heterosexual men" (p. 95), other types of support groups may be more appropriate for women and minorities. In which case, a homogeneous support group focused on a related issue (e.g., relationship problems; sexual problems; general addiction) or on SCAD itself may be of greater benefit for women and minority clients. The counselor can suggest that the SCAD client seek a group member who can function much like a sponsor would function in a 12-step program.

SCAD clients struggle with abstinence from the undesired sexual behavior(s) during the early stages of treatment. Initially, it may even help for the client to refrain from any sexual behavior. However, whatever choices are made, it helps if they make sense to the client. If a client's goal is to spend more time with his family, then he should be able to articulate how abstinence contributes to that goal. Then, abstinence takes on a special meaning to the client and, as he spends more time with his family, he identifies the significance of that choice.

A natural outcome of choosing abstinence or reduced sexual activity is that clients have to deal with the SCAD cycle. Like a drug addict, they experience **withdrawal** symptoms. They can experience anxiety, depression, nervousness, persistent worry, and insecurity (e.g., "Maybe I can do it one more time, then that will be it."). They can be irritable, express anger, seem resistant to therapy, seem to reject help from their natural support groups, and blame others for all their problems. It is important that everybody involved with the client be patient, supportive, and understanding, while firmly reinforcing the choices (e.g., abstinence) he/she is making.

Breaking the SCAD cycle takes time yet must happen for clients to reach their newly formed goals. The cycle is the barrier keeping them from finding and fulfilling "meaning" in their lives at this time. I don't reinforce the idea promoted by 12-step programs that once a SCAD individual, always a SCAD individual, which becomes the label of a "**recovering** sex addict." Rather, I reinforce the idea that each day the client acts responsibly in working on his/her goals, then he/she is that much closer to living a meaningful life without the SCAD cycle.

Many treatment strategies have been recommended in helping clients deal with the SCAD cycle, so it is impossible to include a comprehensive list. The strategies below provide some direction in working with a client on the SCAD cycle. The counselor and SCAD client must work together to apply these strategies (or any others) that make most sense to the client's SCAD behavior and life.

A. Learning more about the SCAD cycle helps clients realize that SCAD is a process, not just sexual behavior. Reading books like Charlotte Kasl's (1989) *Women, Sex, and Addiction: A Search for Love And Power* or Patrick Carnes's (1991) book, *Don't Call It Love: Recovery from Sexual Addiction*, gives clients greater insight into the addiction process. Again, joining an appropriate 12-step program might also be useful as part of their education.

B. Attacking the cycle so that clients don't give into their sexual compulsions is important in terms of taking responsibility for their actions. What are the triggers that begin the cycle? If clients can't identify their triggers, then have them keep a **journal**. Once triggers are known, clients must learn to identify when a trigger "kicks in" (i.e., what feeling, body reaction, or thought signals that a trigger is occurring). If the trigger involves a thing, like pornographic material, then "**eradicate**" it with an elaborate **ritual**. A client might bring the pornography to my office, burn it in a trashcan, and process any feelings of loss that occur. However, also process the good feelings related to the challenges that come with giving up the trigger. On the other hand, if it's a thought, then **cognitive restructuring** is appropriate to eradicate the irrational thinking. Whether it's a person, place, situation, thought, or thing, I help the client "eradicate" the trigger. In the case of a situation (e.g., argument with a boss) or person (e.g., parent) what gets "eradicated" is the old behavioral response to the trigger.

C. In conjunction with individual counseling, **group therapy** for SCAD clients is helpful because group members support each other during this "eradication" process. Additionally, members help each other to not fall into the old pattern of "keeping isolated." Being isolated is a way that others are less likely to find out about and, probably interfere with, the SCAD sexual behavior. In group, they can also practice healthy interpersonal skills, set boundaries, role-play new ways of solving problems, etc. (Allgeier, 1996; Dolan, 1990; Gideonse, 1998; Haugh, 1999; Jenish, 1991; Morris, 1999).

D. SCAD clients work on eradicating triggers, but they still deal with the craving. As they learn to productively deal with physical triggers, they still experience their own psychological trigger that simply tells them "to have sex." To deal with the craving I combine **cognitive therapy** to attack irrational beliefs or desires with some aspects of **Morita Therapy** (see Burlew & Roland, 1999). Cognitive therapy strategies are useful for attacking irrational beliefs and substituting old core beliefs with new, more productive beliefs (Apt & Hulbert, 1995; Carnes, 1991; Myers, 1995; Wolfe, 2000). Morita Therapy originated in Japan with the belief that people have no control over their emotions and thoughts, so accept that they exist and act responsibly in spite of feelings and thoughts. Clients can make daily lists of what they are responsible to do that day and take action to complete those things. When a craving occurs, the client mentally says, "I am craving, and I know I can't control that feeling." Then, the client immediately gets involved with something on his/her list; or as in the 12-step model, the client calls a friend or sponsor and meets for coffee. However, from a Morita Therapy perspective, while having coffee, talk about something other than the craving.

E. Finding natural "highs" and true "joys" in life are important for SCAD clients in working through "sex seeking behavior" (Phase 3) and actual "scoring" (Phase 4). Old routines are substituted with behaviors leading to the accomplishment of newer, more meaningful goals. SCAD clients need help in identifying the "joy" of being involved in that life meaning (e.g., finding other ways of feeling worthwhile) instead of the sex seeking behavior or actual sex acts themselves. Two areas of importance at this point are: 1) taking risks to act on goals; and 2) learning new skills to accomplish the goals. Many therapeutic strategies are necessary at this time. Some examples include: **relaxation training**; psychoeducational lectures and workshops; training in social skills, **assertiveness**, **conflict resolution**, **anger**, **problem solving**, and **decision making** (Apt & Hulbert, 1995; Carnes, 1991; Myers, 1995; Wolfe, 2000). Basically, SCAD clients need help in reaching their goals by developing the skills that were underdeveloped due to all the time spent on seeking sex. Additionally, these clients need continual reinforcement and support from the counselor, their friends, and family to practice and incorporate new skills into their new self.

F. Eventually, SCAD clients will incorporate healthy sexual behavior into their lives. Ross (1998) suggested that a SCAD client must "learn how to be sexual in ways that honor her [his] body, mind and spirit" (p. 50). If a significant other is involved, then that person can be involved in the treatment process. Sometimes, the couple must be referred to a **sex therapist** to work on all aspects of their sex life. For SCAD clients who are single, I recommend learning to **date** all over again and sometimes **psychoeducational workshops** around this topic are helpful. Learning to date, instead of immediately becoming involved in sexual behavior, teaches SCAD clients to develop **intimacy** before sexual activities.

G. The "emotional/physical consequences" of no longer engaging in the SCAD activities will cause symptoms similar to Phase 5 of the SCAD cycle. Clients begin withdrawal and may feel like they have a "hangover." As an existentialist, I believe these consequences are a natural part of existential anxiety or the struggle to live life differently from before, thus dealing with the unknown. Depending on what the consequences are, I may use relaxation training or aspects of Morita Therapy.

Support groups are helpful at this time. Some clients may need help in dealing with depression and should be assessed to see if antidepressants would help. Myers (1995) suggested **serotonin reuptake blockers**, which are also sexually inhibiting medications as well. Some clients may need to explore family background and confront the origins of the SCAD behavior, particularly related to early family trauma, abuse, and neglect (Carnes, 1991; 1992; 1998; Dolan, 1990; Morris, 1999). Morris suggested clients write **autobiographies** about these early traumas and the "repercussions" to their lives.

Helping clients attack the SCAD cycle is a complex process that involves many intervention strategies. While attacking the cycle, clients also work on enhancing their life skills to successfully accomplish their new life goals. Simultaneously, these clients may be working on **cross-addiction** issues related to drugs, alcohol, food, or work (see Carnes, 1991).

Developing "I-Thou" Relationships

SCAD clients deal with people as objects or experience "I-It" relationships. A large part of treatment involves helping SCAD clients develop "I-Thou" relationships, **boundary setting**, **communication**, and intimacy. Some suggested strategies are listed below, even though many strategies exist for effective **relationship building**.

A. Developing a sense of "I-Thou" relationships is important. Having the client **interview** people he/she respects as being good in relationships may help the client develop a list of characteristics or skills that are exhibited in healthy, adult-to-adult sexual relationships. Guided imagery about how the client wants to be in intimate relationships is an interesting strategy. **Bibliotherapy** about connected relationships is informational to a person lacking relationship skills. In any of these strategies, the client should list relationship characteristics and new relationship skills that he/she has not mastered but is willing to try. Additionally, these clients need help in being less **egocentric** and more **sociocentric** when involved in interpersonal relationships.

B. **Family counseling** and/or couples work is recommended (Allgeier, 1996; Apt & Hulbert, 1995). Morris (1999) believes that the family can "help the addict get even clearer about his [her] problems" (p. 70). More importantly, family members can explore how they are **enabling** clients to continue in I-It relationships with them. Friends can even be included. Again, support groups are helpful for clients to role-play new ways of being in relationships.

C. SCAD clients objectify people by seeing them only as a means for their **sexual gratification**. Even their significant others are objects in some ways because they keep many aspects of their lives "secret." Practicing some of the strategies above to develop healthy relationships helps SCAD clients relate to their significant others as true intimates, thus as I-Thou relationships. They also need help in developing friendships at an intimate level, as opposed to only viewing new acquaintances as potential sex partners. Strategies such as **modeling** friendship behaviors and

educating clients about effective decision-making related to when couples decide to have sex are helpful.

D. **Body image, massage,** and **movement therapy** (Gideonse, 1998; Morris, 1999) help SCAD clients appreciate their physical body as something **sacred**, to be proud of, and to be shared with an intimate loved one. So much **shame** has been attached to their sexual activities and how they use their bodies, that new levels of **self-esteem** and **respect** must be developed about their own body image.

If SCAD clients are successful in developing I-Thou relationships, then using people only for their sexual pleasure becomes more difficult. They may also decide to make amends to friends and family members whom they have injured with their SCAD activities. Finally, they will eventually develop more meaningful friendships.

Understanding the Existential Concept of Death

Vontress et al. (1999) claimed that "only one who is aware of death lives intensely" and "those who accept eventual death are decisive, can make choices, and are more likely to implement them, for they realize that their days are numbered" (p. 51). Integrated throughout the existential counseling process with SCAD clients is the concept of loss. They lose their old way of being, their old sexual behavior and rituals, and their old way of looking at themselves and others. In some sense, there is a death of self. Listed below are a couple of strategies that help SCAD clients realize the urgency of making responsible choices and implementing or acting on those choices to reach their goals, thus to find meaning in their lives.

A   Through the losses they experience (and maybe even the **loss** of some significant people in their lives), identify this as a **grieving** process much like one experiences in a death. Discuss death openly and use exercises like **writing** their own **eulogy** to identify what they project as their most significant life accomplishments. Help them see the urgency in working toward these accomplishments because death is inevitable. Reinforce the idea of accomplishing as much as they can each day because nobody knows when they will actually die.

B. Organizing rituals discussed earlier to eradicate triggers is important to grieve and bring closure to the SCAD part of their lives. They can even draw a picture (i.e., **art therapy)** of the negative aspects of their SCAD selves and burn them, while saving the positive life skills (e.g., creativity) that evolved with the SCAD behavior. They might even develop a **rebirth** ritual to signify the beginning of a new self that responsibly chooses and implements activities that lead to the meaning in their lives and to healthy, intimate, sexual and friend relationships based on I-Thou interactions.

CASE STUDY

Case of Eva

Eva, a 59-year-old businesswoman, owns an import/export business, which she inherited from her father. She describes herself as "somewhat successful." She is the only child of a middle class, Caucasian family. She feels closer to her father, who is now deceased, because he was an "exciting, charming man," while her mother is a "whiney, sexless being." She still financially supports her mother. Her father started the business, and she could have made it into a million-dollar company, but her "mind" wasn't always in the right place. It seems that her "love life" took precedence over business.

Eva says, "I was always precocious and started having sex when I was about 12 years old." At 12, she looked like she was 18 and at 14 she looked 25. She eloped at 14 with a 30-year-old man, a customer of her father's, but her father had this marriage annulled. She married a second time when she was about 23. Throughout the marriage, she had sexual affairs with other men. Her husband wanted her to go into therapy because he couldn't stand the constant "cheating." The more he "whined," the more she ran around.

About a year into the marriage, her second husband killed himself. He left a note blaming her. While this was a huge family scandal and she does feel a "twinge" of guilt, she admits she was going to leave him anyway. She never married again, but has had numerous relationships, none lasting more than 7 or 8 months. She normally ended the relationships. Sometimes the man discovered that she was sleeping with other men. Other times, she just became bored or the man "wasn't as attentive as before." On a few occasions, a man caught her in bed with somebody else and "roughed" her up and that frightened her enough to break off the relationship.

Eva self-reported to counseling because Allen, her 39 year old boyfriend of 8 months, broke up with her and won't interact with her until she "gets mental help." She "thinks" she loves Allen and is upset that her typical sexual behavior is ruining "yet another relationship." Eva believes Allen doesn't know about the "frequent" sexual activities that occur while she's on business trips. She believes that he is suspicious, however. She feels terrible about her behavior and has lied to Allen many times about why she wasn't in her room all night. But, she hasn't been able to stop. During business meetings, she "wines and dines" customers and frequently ends up having sex with a stranger. She says, "The alcohol makes me forget that I'm in a relationship. I'm flirtatious anyway, so when a man makes a move and I've been drinking, I don't say no." She feels flattered, but doesn't feel completely "desirable or wanted" until she's in bed with the guy. She is worried about getting AIDS and giving it to Allen, even though she thinks she "practices safe sex." The sad thing to her is that the sex is never that "great," and she always masturbates afterwards with a vibrator to achieve an orgasm.

Unfortunately, from a very early age, she always masturbated after sexual intercourse to achieve an orgasm. With Allen, she tried to make masturbating after sex exciting to him as well. However, after a few weeks of this, he claimed it made him feel inadequate. So, she waits until he falls asleep, and then goes into the bathroom to masturbate. She also masturbates several times during the day and hides this from Allen because he feels pressured" that she wants "to fuck," because he isn't providing enough. She never thought of this as a problem, even though she knows that the frequent masturbation has caused "difficulties" in her life. When she has the "urge," it doesn't matter where she is or what she's doing, she has to "take care of it."

No matter how many times she masturbates or how many times in a day she "fucks," she always feels incomplete. Even with Allen, she feels like something is missing. That's why when they go out drinking together, she "flirts with every man in the bar," even though this makes Allen very angry. She's explained to him that she's just "being friendly" and that he shouldn't be jealous. However, she knows that if Allen weren't with her, she'd go to bed with one of the men.

She's been to therapy for this feeling of emptiness and is tired of "shrinks" telling her that she's "fucked up" because of her father and mother. She especially doesn't like them suggesting that her father must have sexually abused her. She adamantly states that her father never sexually molested her and, that while she was close to him, she never even daydreamed about having sex with him. She has tried every type of sexual behavior one can think of, but it never "fills the hole."

Allen isn't the first man who wanted her to change, as evidenced by her second husband. With other boyfriends, she tried "being faithful" and that lasted about a week. She likes saying to herself, "Men can do it and it's okay, so what's wrong with a woman having a boyfriend and screwing around." Saying this to herself helped when she was younger, but now she is worried that she still hasn't "settled down" and it's "harder to attract men." Although she has had plastic surgery 3 times and looks like a 30 year-old woman, she feels "older" and fears being a lonely old woman at 70. She wants to believe she can "fall in love" and be committed to one man. She hopes Allen is that man, but isn't sure how to go about it.

Counseling and Treatment Strategies for Eva

I will cover each aspect of the existential approach discussed above. However, before I do, try applying the existential approach yourself to Eva's case. You might start by considering the questions below.

1. Using either Cooper's (as cited in Hannah, 1998) five criteria for compulsive sexual behavior or Wolfe's (2000) ten questions for sexual compulsion/addiction, assess whether or not Eva has a diagnosis of SCAD?
2. How will you help Eva find meaning in her life based on her previous SCAD activities?
3. How will you help Eva live authentically to identify goals that are meaningful to her now?
4. What strategies will you use to help Eva act responsibly to achieve her goals and to break the SCAD cycle?
5. Is Eva living in I-Thou relationships?
6. Is the concept of death evident in Eva's case?

From an existential counseling perspective, Eva is intricately involved in all aspects of her treatment plan. In this case, Eva would be present as we worked through each aspect of her case. Therefore, consider this as an exercise in learning to apply strategies for a diagnosis of SCAD.

1. Assessment

To be brief, I will use Cooper's criteria to assess for a SCAD diagnosis. Eva is not in denial that her sexual activities are causing problems in her current relationship or that her "love life" has had an impact on her business activities. She rationalizes that men "aren't monogamous" so why should she be, which probably allows her to feel less guilty about her activities. She denies that her frequent masturbation is a problem, even though it has caused "difficulties" in her life and is causing problems in her relationship with Allen.

In the past, Eva has tried to be monogamous but "that lasted for about a week or so." She also claims that she "hasn't been able to stop having sex with men" when on business, even though Allen is suspicious and she lies to him about this. More importantly, she suggests that she "loves Allen and is disturbed that her typical sexual behavior is getting in the way of yet another relationship," but hasn't changed her SCAD behavior.

Eva uses language suggesting she spends a great deal of time involved in the SCAD cycle. Examples include: "mind wasn't always in the right place" (thus must be on SCAD); "love life took precedence over business;" constant cheating; frequent sexual escapades; lied many times; frequently ends up having sex with someone; always masturbates afterwards; frequent masturbation; and flirting with every man in the bar (which takes time and energy away from Allen). Eva herself would admit that she is always on the "alert" for an indication that a man is interested in her or that she's interested in him or that she's just "horny."

Although not as evident in the case description, Eva's life revolves around business trips that give her the opportunity to be away from Allen, to conduct business, often over drinks, and to meet other men. Traveling takes time away from her relationship with Allen. Sometimes, while on these trips, she misses her business appointments due to a hangover or to extra time spent with a man. When not on a trip, she goes to the office during the day, and spends time with Allen at night, usually going to a club or bar. Friends are not mentioned, even though I suspect she spends no or little time with friends and rarely spends time with her mother.

Eva does identify adverse consequences or significant risks due to her SCAD activities. Her business could have been more successful. She drinks too much. She picks up "strange" men, and she is afraid of getting AIDS. Some of her boyfriends were "rough" with her when they found her sleeping with another man. She still doesn't have a committed relationship in which she only has sex with the one man. She still feels "incomplete." She fears being a "lonely old woman at 70." And she takes risks when masturbating because it doesn't "matter where she is or what she's doing, she has to take care of it."

Based on Cooper's criteria, my diagnosis is that Eva is experiencing SCAD. She exhibits the following: 1) some denial exists; 2) she has tried to stop the SCAD activities in the past with no success; 3) a lot of her time and energy is spent on SCAD activities; 4) her SCAD activities have impacted her social, occupation, and recreational roles; and 5) she has taken risks, experienced negative consequences, and continues with her SCAD routines.

On the other hand, don't assume that every client who has multiple sex partners and masturbates frequently is experiencing SCAD. If Eva dated, had sex with different men, then got involved in a long-term, monogamous relationship, and could remain monogamous, then SCAD might not be indicated. Or, if she were in a long-term relationship where both agreed to "**swing**," but she felt emotionally committed to her partner the diagnosis of SCAD might not be appropriate. Even frequent masturbation does not indicate SCAD if it's not causing risky behavior or if she likes achieving orgasms that way. Also, she might be achieving orgasms with her male partner and still masturbate for additional pleasure. Listen to the client's story carefully when discussing sexual behavior and make sure your own values don't influence the outcome of the assessment.

2. Finding Meaning

The SCAD diagnosis is shared with Eva and, most likely, Eva will want more information about SCAD. Eva can learn more about the SCAD cycle by reading books like Charlotte Kasl's (1989) *Women, Sex, and Addiction: A Search for Love and Power* or like Patrick Carnes's (1992) *Out of the Shadows: Understanding Sexual Addiction*. She can then examine her own life in relationship to the symptoms of SCAD.

Help Eva identify her SCAD routines. Her list might include behaviors that have not yet been mentioned. However, her list might include:

A. Sleeping with different men while on business trips.
B. Excessive flirting when out with Allen.
C. Masturbating regardless of the consequences.

The feeling and body responses corresponding to each behavior can then be identified. Those feelings and body responses might be:

A. Shame, fear of maybe getting AIDS, and a feeling of being dirty for lying to Allen, evidenced through frequent headaches and always wanting to shower.
B. Stupid, knowing that Allen gets furious over her flirting, yet excited because he obviously thinks of her as "his woman;" the stupid feeling gets evidenced as a dullness in her head and the excitement as a "prickly" feeling that runs down her back.
C. A panic feeling (when not able to masturbate) and a feeling of emptiness related to masturbation; she feels panic in her chest with almost a heavy breathing reaction and the emptiness is in her stomach like "never filling a hole."

Eva will realize the message from her inner self is that ultimately the SCAD behaviors "aren't good" for the most part, thus not really meaningful to her. The "exciting" feeling over Allen getting angry about her flirting is an existential paradox because it does feel "positive" to her. However, the negative consequence of the positive feeling (i.e., excitement) is to lose Allen. So, she can choose to stop the continuous flirting (a SCAD behavior for her) and find other ways to make her life exciting. When Eva determines that the SCAD routines are not really meaningful to her, then she will be challenged with living authentically and finding true meaning in her life.

3. Living Authentically

Eva will establish goals based on her SCAD routines, and additional goals will be determined as she progresses through therapy. Eva might contract to (a) quit masturbating so frequently; (b) quit sleeping with other men while on business trips; and (c) quit flirting when out with Allen. Relapses might occur unless the inner meaning of what she is trying to accomplish with those behaviors is discovered.

Using the Gestalt empty chair technique helps Eva gain insight to different dimensions of herself. For example, one chair might be her "flirting self" and the other chair might be her in relationship with Allen. Ultimately, she might discover that she has a fear of not being desirable or of being unwanted. She might realize that she felt unwanted as a child by her mother and learned that men were easier targets to fulfill her need to be desired and wanted. Therefore, one treatment goal would be to identify ways to feel wanted besides flirting and having intercourse with many men. With masturbation, the message might be that she can't rely on anybody else but herself to satisfy her needs. A second treatment goal can be learning to rely on others to satisfy her needs and to identify other needs besides only sexual needs.

Other goals will surface from discussions about Eva's SCAD activities and other aspects of her life. As mentioned above, Eva might immediately contract to not have sex with other men when on business trips, because it supports living in a committed relationship with Allen and allows her time to develop the "successful" business she knows she can establish. However, being responsible and acting on such a goal is another major challenge that requires her to deal with the SCAD cycle.

4. Taking Responsibility

At this point, I must help Eva to be responsible and take action in achieving her goals. New life skills may have to be learned. For example, if she is to depend on others to satisfy some of her needs, rather than doing everything herself, then she may have to learn the skill of trust. Don't overwhelm Eva by having her immediately relinquish all control. Rather, start on a smaller scale and simply say, "Tomorrow, what could you give somebody else to do that you would normally take care of?" Giving one of her duties to an employee may be a good place to start. Once she accomplishes the smaller goal, process it in the counseling session. Connect the action to the "joy" of allowing somebody else do something for her, rather than having to do everything for herself. Eventually these actions will return to her SCAD activity of masturbation and the ability to trust Allen to satisfy her. This might lead to seeing a sex therapist who can work with her and Allen on their sexual activities, **sexual self-esteem**, and **sexual communication**.

Ultimately, Eva will address the SCAD cycle during this phase of treatment. I can't go through all the suggestions for this aspect of treatment, but several factors seem critical at this point. First, Allen should be included in her treatment if he is in agreement. Because he made therapy a condition of continuing their relationship, I assume he will be involved. If involved, then Eva will most likely disclose the history of her affairs during business trips. I can only hope that Allen will remain in treatment with her after that. Second, Eva will most likely contract for abstinence from sexual behavior outside of her relationship with Allen. Two factors might help her achieve this: a) only go on the most critical business trips; let another employee do the noncritical ones; and b) abstinence from drinking on trips which requires an alcohol abuse assessment. (I will assume for the time being that Eva is not cross-addicted and that alcohol is only a trigger for her.) Third, she and Allen need to avoid the major places (i.e., bars and clubs) where she drinks and flirts and replace that with places and activities that help develop intimacy in the relationship. Finally, the SCAD cycle must be clearly identified, triggers eradicated, etc. through all the steps mentioned earlier.

5. Developing "I-Thou" Relationships

Much of Eva's SCAD behavior centers on treating people as objects or being involved in "I-It" relationships. Her attempts to fill the "hole" with multiple sex partners suggest that she doesn't care about their needs because they are objects to be used to reach an unreachable goal. She forever feels **empty** and probably **lonely**. In some ways, that emptiness is a quest to answer the question, "Who am I," which she probably never addressed due to her constant search for sex with men.

One way to begin this aspect of treatment is to concentrate on herself. Who is she besides a woman who defines herself by her sexual conquests of men? If that aspect of her is "dying," then what does she have to offer in the "I" part of a relationship? This might require **personality testing** (e.g., administering the **Myers Briggs Type Indicator**, MBTI) and exploring qualities she likes and dislikes about herself. It will require identifying new **leisure** activities that are satisfying to her, some that she can do alone and some that she can enjoy with others. It will also require helping her learn about people and what qualities she looks for in friends. From my perspective, a big part of filling the hole is helping her develop a sense of self.

As she learns more about herself, Eva can begin working on other relationships in her life. Allen loves her and seems available to work with her on an intimate loving relationship. **Couples counseling** is recommended to help Eva develop true intimacy skills, and to help both of them learn new **relationship skills**, such as communicating truthfully and effectively. Additionally, she might work on an intimate relationship with her mother, the initial source of her unwanted or unloved feelings. Currently, she treats her mother as a complete object, someone to financially support but not have any relationship with. This, of course, is the opposite of what the young child wanted. Family counseling is recommended if Eva's mother is willing to attend. Or, if Eva does not want to be in counseling with her mother, then helping her learn to live with her mother in an "I-Thou" relationship might heal old wounds. Guided imagery might help in determining the ideal daughter/mother relationship at midlife and older adulthood. Ask questions like, "What type of activities might a midlife daughter do with her older adult mother;" "What might they talk about;" and "How might that daughter be involved in the physical care of her mother?" Bibliotherapy is helpful with books about mother and daughter relationships.

Finally, Eva needs help in viewing people, particularly men, as potential friends rather than as sex partners. Most likely, Eva will not attend SAA meetings, so the next strategy is to recommend group counseling for individuals struggling with intimacy or relationship issues. Cognitive restructuring (part of the SCAD cycle treatment) will be helpful because she probably responds to men with thoughts like "does he want me" or "can I get him to bed," rather than thoughts like "he might be an interesting man to get to know as a friend."

6. Understanding the Existential Concept of Death

The concept of death can easily be introduced to Eva because she fears contracting AIDS, a terminal disease. Similarly, she is losing Allen, which can be conceptualized as a death. These situations can help her realize how short life can be and that there is an urgency to accomplish her goals.

In accomplishing her goals and ultimately eradicating the SCAD behaviors, she is losing the "hole" that runs her life. No matter how many sexual encounters she has or how many times she masturbates the "hole" is never satisfied. However, it has been her life. Having a

death ritual for that part of herself helps her grieve while relinquishing behavior, like sex with many men, that seems positive to her. She might draw a picture of the "hole" and do a collage representing the various aspects of her behavior and activities that she likes and dislikes. When she's ready, she can either tear it up or burn it as a way of saying goodbye. Then, she can do a **rebirthing ritual** to welcome in her new self. She can complete another collage that includes characteristics of her old self that are healthy for her (e.g., being an achiever), while adding new characteristics that she's developing or learning (e.g., trust). The collage will blossom as she grows and learns new things about herself.

SUMMARY

SCAD is a complicated sexual problem taking on many shapes and forms that is affecting as much as 6% of the American population (Carnes, 1991, 1994). One SCAD client may spend hours involved in sexual daydreams and rituals and is frustrated at wasting so much of his/her day on these activities. On the other hand, another SCAD client may be involved in multiple, risky, anonymous sexual contacts that cause shame plus difficulties in his/her work and social roles. In any case, counselors must carefully listen to a client's story and make a **value-free assessment**. It is too easy for counselors to use their own values and beliefs about "appropriate" sexuality when it involves a diagnosis like SCAD.

The treatment for SCAD clients is complex as can be seen from the case of Eva (and we only highlighted aspects of the treatment for brevity purpose). However, counselors must not shy away from treating SCAD clients, even though a team approach may be necessary. In Eva's case, for example, we might work with a certified sex therapist, a family counselor, a business consultant, and a recreation specialist. As appointments occur with the other specialists, then she processes the experiences or insights with the primary counselor. If Eva were cross-addicted, then alcoholism becomes part of the treatment plan, and another addiction's expert might become part of the team. She might attend Alcoholics Anonymous (AA) or a support group for people with relationship problems. And, other types of personal issues might surface; for example, she might have an adult form of Attention Deficit Hyperactivity Disorder (ADHD) or she might be a **workaholic**. As treatment progresses, each of these issues needs to become part of the treatment plan.

SCAD clients can be successful in modifying compulsive sexual behavior that has become problematic to them. Even clients referred for SCAD behaviors or activities can change. However, all SCAD clients need counselors who are nonjudgmental, knowledgeable about SCAD, and comfortable dealing with sexual language, activities, and behavior without overlooking other non-sexual relevant issues in therapy.

REFERENCES

Allgeier, A.R. (1996). Sexual addiction: Disease or denigration? *Journal of Sex Research,* *33*(2), 166-167.

American Psychiatric Association (1994). *DSM-IV.* WDC: Author.

Apt, C., & Hulbert, D.F. (1995). Sexual narcissism: Addiction or anachronism. *Family Journal, 3*(2), 103-108.

Arteburn, S. (1991). *Addicted to love*. Ann Arbor, MI: Servant Publications.

Augustine Fellowship. (1986). *Sex and love addicts anonymous*. Boston, MA: Fellowship-Wide Services.

Bingham, J.E., & Piotrowski, C. (1996). Online sexual addiction: A contemporary enigma. *Psychological Reports, 79*(1), 257-258.

Black, D.W., et al. (1997). Characteristics of 36 subjects reporting compulsive sexual behavior. *American Journal of Psychiatry, 154*(2), 243-249.

Burlew, L.D., & Roland, C.B. (1999). Eastern theories. In D. Capuzzi & D.R. Gross (Eds.), *Counseling & psychotherapy* (2nd ed., pp. 379-412) (pp. 379-412). Upper Saddle River, NJ: Prentice-Hall, Inc.

Carnes, P.J. (1983). *Out of the shadows: Understanding sexual addictions*. Minneapolis, MN: Compcare.

Carnes, P.J. (1989). *Contrary to love: Helping the sexual addict*. Minneapolis, MN: Compcare.

Carnes, P.J. (1991). *Don't call it love: Recovery from sexual addiction*. New York: Bantom.

Carnes, P.J. (1992). *Out of the shadows: Understanding sexual addiction* (2nd ed.). Center City, MN: Hazeldon.

Carnes, P.J. (1994). *27 tasks for changing compulsive, out-of-control and inappropriate sexual behavior: Therapist's guide*. Plymouth, MN: Positive Living Press.

Carnes, P.J. (1998). The obsessive shadow. *Professional Counselor, 13*(1), 15-17, 40-41.

Coleman, E. (1987). Sexual compulsivity versus sexual addiction: The debate continues. *SIECUS Reports, 14*(6), xxx.

Cordasco, C.F. (1993). Sex addiction. *North Carolina Medical Journal, 54*(9), 457-460.

Corey, G. (2001). *Theory and practice of counseling and psychotherapy* (6th ed.). Belmont, CA: Wadsworth.

Dolan, B. (June 4, 1990). Do people get hooked on sex? *Time, 135*(23), 72.

Frank, M.L.B. (1999). Existential theory. In D. Capuzzi & D.R. Gross (Eds.), *Counseling & psychotherapy* (2nd ed., pp. 151-178). Upper Saddle River, NJ: Prentice-Hall, Inc.

Frankl, V. (1984). *Man's search for meaning*. New York: Washington Square Press.

Gideonse, T. (1998, May 26). All sex, all the time. *Advocate* (Issue 760). 24-34.

Goodman, A. (1992). Diagnosis and treatment of sexual addiction. *Journal of Sex and Marital Therapy, 18*(4), 302-314.

Goodman, A. (1993). Diagnosis and treatment of sexual addiction. *Journal of Sex and Marital Therapy, 19*(3), 225-251.

Griffin-Shelly, E. (1994). *Adolescent sex and love addicts*. Westport, CT: Praeger.

Hannah, J. (1998, March 30). They gotta habit. *People, 49*(12), 109-112.

Haugh, R. (1999). The fix for a fixation. *Hospitals & Health Networks, 73*(2), 32-35.

Hecker, L.L., et al. (1995). The influence of therapist values, religiosity, and gender in the initial assessment of sexual addiction by family therapists. *American Journal of Family Therapy, 23*, 261-72.

Irons, R., & Schneider, J. (1996). Differential diagnosis of addictive sexual disorders using the DSM-IV. *Sexual Addiction and Compulsivity, 3*, 7-21.

Jenish, D. (1991, January 21). Obsessed with sex. *Maclean's, 104*(3), 44-45.

Kafka, M.P., & Prentky, R. (1997). Compulsive sexual behavior characteristics. *American Journal of Psychiatry, 154*(11), 1632.

Kaplan, H.S. (1996). Erotic obsession: Relationship to hypoactive sexual desire disorder and paraphilia. *American Journal of Psychiatry, 153*(JulySupplement), 30-41.

Kasl, C.D. (1989). *Women, sex, and addiction: A search for love and power.* New York: Ticknor & Fields.

Levine, M., & Troiden, R.R. (1988). The myth of sexual compulsivity and sexual addiction. *Journal of Sex Research, 25*, 247-363.

McKenna, C.A. (1992). *Love, infidelity, and sexual addiction.* St. Meinrad, IN: Abbey Press.

Morris, B. (1999, May 10). Addicted to sex. *Fortune, 139*(9), 66-76.

Moskowitz, E. (1994). In the courts. Rulings that neither obesity, sexual obsession, nor tobacco smoke allergy amount to disabling conditions protected by the law. *Hastings Center Report, 24*, 4.

Myers, W.A. (1995). Addictive sexual behavior. *American Journal of Psychotherapy, 49*(4), 473-84.

National Council on Sexual Addiction and Compulsivity (n.d.) *Women and sex.* Atlanta, GA: Author. Retrieved March 14, 2002 from http://www.ncsac.org

Peele, S., Brodsky, A., & Arnold, M. (1991). *The truth about addiction and recovery.* New York: Simon and Schuster.

Pincu, L. (1989). Sexual compulsivity and gay men: Controversy and treatment. *Journal of Counseling & Development, 68*, 63-66.

Roberts, D. (1995). *For women only: Dealing with love addiction and sexual issues.* Gresham, OR: East Hill Church.

Ross, C.J. (1998). Controlled by desire. *Professional Counselor, 13*(1). 21-22, 48-50.

Satel, S.L. (1993). The diagnostic limits of addiction. *Journal of clinical Psychiatry, 54*(6), 237.

Saulnier, C.F. (1996). Images of the twelve-step model, and sex and love addiction in an alcohol intervention group for Black women. *Journal of Drug Issues, 26*(1), 95-145.

Schneider, J. (1991). How to recognize the signs of sexual addiction. *Postgraudate Medicine, 90*(6). Retrieved March 14, 2002 from *http://www.ncsac.org/article.html/.*

Speziale, B.A. (1994). Marital conflict versus sex and love addiction. *Families in Society, 75*, 509-512.

Vontress, C.E., Johnson, J.A., & Epp, L.R. (1999). *Cross-cultural counseling: A case book.* Alexandria, VA: American Counseling Association.

Walters, G.D. (1996). Sexual preoccupation as a lifestyle. *Sexual and Marital Therapy, 11*(4), 373-382.

Wolfe, J.L. (2000). Assessment and treatment of compulsive sex/love behavior. *Journal of Rational-Emotive and cognitive-Behavior Therapy, 18*(4), 235-246.

Chapter 14

Counseling Adult Survivors of Childhood Sexual Abuse

Catherine Buffalino Roland
University of Arkansas

Academic programs that have as a core purpose the educating and training of counselors are usually driven by the idea of theory blending into practice. The specific clinical courses that typically occur in the latter part of a counselor preparation program, such as practicum or internship, rely on the student's ability to synthesize the didactic course material as a base for clinical practice. Although counselor preparation programs attempt to include many of the major specialty areas via coursework, all of the issues that an intern or practicum student might encounter cannot possibly be addressed during required coursework in any given program. The brief scenario that follows depicts a situation in which a counselor trainee is addressing her group supervision class. The student, Melissa, has encountered a client at her site for whom she feels unprepared and nervous, and seems to be unable to integrate the knowledge of counseling theory with the techniques necessary to establish a beginning counseling relationship. The client presented by Melissa is a 38 year-old woman who presented as an **adult survivor of childhood sexual abuse**.

Scenario

As the seven internship students gathered for their third meeting of the semester, Melissa asked to present a tape. Melissa seemed upset and confused about sharing the tape, which would be critiqued by her peers and the instructor. As the tape was inserted into the VCR, Melissa explained," I just never thought I'd get a client with this issue so early in this course experience – I have no idea what to do."

The tape revealed Melissa's discomfort with this client. Melissa was visibly uneasy and removed, and seemed shocked at what she was hearing from her client. The group discussion that followed the viewing of the tape was very telling. It was evident that each of the seven internship students in the class was uncomfortable with the topic of sexual abuse, and several confided that sexual abuse was the one topic they had hoped to avoid. The students were asked about the unit that dealt with sexual abuse that was included in their required Crisis Counseling class, and the majority of them revealed that, while they had gotten some information, they were not at all comfortable or confident that they could assist a client who was an adult survivor of sexual abuse. There were simply too many issues to be dealt with in Crisis Counseling to cover sexual abuse in depth. Melissa revealed that "her own issues" had surfaced as a result of seeing the client the first time, and that she would be returning to personal counseling to deal with them. The students then asked if we might take a few days to learn more about this important topic that was certain to be among the most presented from clients.

* * *

The previous scenario is fairly typical in counselor preparation programs, and occurs in classroom discussion as well as in clinical courses. With factors such as number of required hours, various state licensing requirements, and the specific interest areas of faculty, it would be impossible for all of the important and current issues within the discipline of counseling to be adequately addressed in a Master's in Counseling program. There are currently many more specialty courses included in counselor preparation programs than ever before, such as courses in family counseling, addictions, case management, crisis counseling, diversity/multicultural counseling, and human sexuality.

This chapter will assist in the preparation of counselors to work with a large segment of the population, adult survivors of childhood sexual abuse. It is hoped that the information included in the chapter will be helpful in synthesizing the didactic, practical, and emotional aspects of counseling this **special population** of adult survivors, whose sexual functioning and mental health may have been affected by the trauma.

BACKGROUND

The incidence of child sexual abuse has been well documented for over thirty years. The interest in the issue of sexual abuse as a mental health concern has grown relatively quickly, in the counseling of children, adolescents, and the population focused on in this chapter, adults who have experienced sexually abusive situations and contacts as children and adolescents.

The term **sexual abuse** is used throughout this chapter, and incorporates the essence of the terms sexual abuse and **incest.** Although the two terms have at times been used interchangeably, the term sexual abuse is slightly broader in nature. It encompasses all types of sexual abuse, not only familial incest, which was considered in the past to be the only incestuous relationship for many years (Bass & Davis, 1988; Courtois, 1997; Finkelhor, Hotaling, Lewis & Smith, 1990). Included in the chapter are the different types and categories of what is considered to be sexual abuse, and behavior that could be considered sexually abusive.

The impact that child sexual abuse has had on the mental health and sexual functioning of adult survivors leads to the impact it continues to have on practicing counselors and counselors-in-training. Children and adolescents who were sexually abused during the mid-seventies through the mid-nineties are now the women and men who seek counseling, and present as adult survivors of child sexual abuse. Current estimated incidences of sexual abuse that occurred during childhood or adolescence of adults are twenty-eight percent to thirty-three percent of women, and twelve percent to eighteen percent of men (Courtois, 1995; Morrow & Smith, 1995; Wyatt, Loeb, Solis, Carmona, & Romero, 1999). Within in-patient, clinical populations, rates of reported childhood sexual abuse by adult women range from thirty-five percent to seventy-five percent; the range for adult men within clinical populations has been reported between fourteen percent and twenty-five percent (Briere & Runtz, 1989; Polusny & Follette, 1995). Many incidences of sexual abuse remain underreported; both women and men who presented with unwanted past sexual experiences during childhood or adolescence also reported that the abuse was kept secret, sometimes for the duration of childhood and adolescence, or longer, from everyone (Blume, 1990; Schreiber & Lyddon, 1998). While exactly how many adults have actually been sexually abused as children or adolescents is not definiteve, it remains clear that the survivor population is large, it is growing and, therefore, it is necessary for counselors to gain knowledge and develop expertise about adult survivors in order to offer competent, ethical counseling services.

The incidence of adults experiencing aftereffects of childhood or adolescent sexual abuse is by no means new or modern. Perhaps one of the most poignant and telling discoveries concerning sexual abuse was recorded by Freud in *The Aetiology of Hysteria*, where he wrote: "I put forward the proposition...that at the bottom of every case of hysteria will be found one or more experiences of premature sexual experience, belonging to the first years of childhood" (Freud, 1959, p. 198). At the time, hysteria was the label assigned to women who demonstrated psychological and somatic symptoms that had not comfortably fit into other diagnoses, and were typically focused on issues of sexuality and sexual intimacy. Through his work with adult women who presented as hysterical, Freud put forth the view that the sexual experiences related by the women were unwanted and perpetrated by their fathers. A panic ensued in the European psychoanalytic community as a result of Freud's assertion (Courtois, 1988; Miller, 1984).

Freud eventually abandoned his theory and replaced it with what we know as the Oedipal theory, which completely altered educational thought and clinical practice concerning incest. Basically, the Oedipal theory postulated that the complaint by a child about parental sexual coercion was based in that child's fantasy, not reality. The perpetrating adult was then exonerated, therefore allowing the incest to continue (Courtois, 1988). For several decades, society denied the reality of sexual abuse and that has greatly influenced the psychiatric, medical, and mental health communities. Armstrong (1978, 1982) termed that period of the Oedipal theory as the "Age of Denial" and was among those who later helped illuminate the existence of sexual abuse and incest in society (Courtois, 1988; Courtois & Watts, 1982).

Several early researchers and clinicians contributed to the conceptualization of incest as a reality to be considered in the clinical realm, as well as those who continued the research during the 1980s and 1990s. While it is impossible to list all of them, the counselor or student interested in an historical perspective of the clinical aspects of sexual abuse should become familiar with the following: Armstrong (1978, 1982); Briere (1992, 1996); Briere and Runtz (1986, 1989); Finkelhor (1978, 1984, 1986); Goodwin (1982); Miller (1981, 1984); Rush (1977, 1980); and Tsai, Feld-man-Summers & Edgar (1979). Two women who were early contributors and are also current contributors to the field, and known as experts in the area of sexual abuse counseling are Suzanne Sgroi (1978, 1982, 1988, 1989) and Christine Courtois

(1979, 1988, 1997, 1999). I recommend that counselors and students interested in working with adult survivors read a some of this work from these clinicians/researchers as a first step in learning about this population.

SEXUAL ABUSE: DEFINITIONS AND DESCRIPTIONS

The categories, characteristics, and possible aftereffects of sexual abuse are concepts relevant to understanding the client who presents as an adult survivor. Although some definitions vary from researcher to researcher, listed in this chapter are terms and conditions that are broadly and generally agreed upon.

In the past, the terms incest and child sexual abuse have, at times, been separated in definition by the **familial** link between the **perpetrator** and the child or adolescent. More recently, the term sexual abuse has been used to encompass a broader spectrum of abuse, which includes both familial incest and the sexual abuse of a minor by a non-family member (Blume, 1990; Elliott & Briere, 1992; Polusny & Follette, 1995).

Sgroi, Bleck and Porter (1982) gave the following definition of child sexual abuse:

Child sexual abuse is a sexual act imposed on a child who lacks emotional, maturational, and cognitive development. The ability to lure a child into a sexual relationship is based upon the all-powerful and dominant position of the adult or older adolescent perpetrator, which is in sharp contrast to the child's age, dependency, and subordinate position. Authority and power enable the perpetrator, implicitly or directly, to coerce the child into sexual compliance. *(p. 9)*

To further support this broader definition of sexual abuse, and to incorporate the familial aspect into the terminology, several researchers have asserted:

Sexual abuse is both **intrafamilial** and **extrafamilial**; substantial overlap exists between the two types, although it is generally acknowledged that incestuous abuse is more psychologically complicated due to familial bonds and patterns of attachment/dependence between the child and the caretaker/abuser. *(Cole & Putnam, 1992; Courtois, 1988, 1999; Freyd, 1996; Herman, 1981)*

Counselors interested in the specialization of family counseling should be particularly knowledgeable about the issue of sexual abuse. Family dynamics are played out in session, as well as in life outside the session, and the adult survivor brings all of her or his past **sexual trauma** into the family or couples counseling relationship. Although an initial reason stated for seeking counseling may not be issues of sexual abuse, but rather the more typical issues of sex and intimacy, the adults in the family or adult partners who are survivors bring those dynamics into the process, and into the **family system**. The aftereffects of childhood sexual abuse for the adult family member are played out in a variety of emotional and behavioral ways, and the family counselor must be aware of the signals indicating those dynamics (Kempe & Kempe, 1984; Roland, 1992).

CATEGORIES OF ABUSE

Natural, developmental behaviors between peers that may have appeared sexual in nature were perhaps not necessarily abusive, and may have been a result of childhood curiosity or experimentation. It remains murky, however, when attempting to separate actual sexually abusive situations involving a power or coercive struggle, and the more spontaneous, natural behaviors of childhood or adolescence. When the issue of power is involved, the position of the peer or adult in authority may be confusing to the victim, and it may have been communicated that the sexual behavior is appropriate. "It is impossible to overemphasize the significance of the exploitation and misuse of accepted power relationships when assessing the impact of sexual abuse...." (Sgroi et al., 1982, p. 13). Below are specific categories of sexual abuse, suggested mainly by Courtois (1988), which are fairly well accepted in the mental health community as helpful in conceptualizing a case.

Abusive vs. Nonabusive

Factors to consider are participant age, mutual consent, participants' reactions to the event, and the power differential. It is important to note that, "the aftereffects of incest do not determine whether it was abusive or not...on the other hand, incest which is of the nonabusive type is not always benign and can cause later distress" (Courtois, 1988, p.21).

Relatives by Blood, Marriage or Involvement

Factors to consider are sexual contact between relatives with genetic ties, relatives who have ties through marriage or adoption, or individuals who are tied to the family due to involvement such as foster parent or live-in lover.

Nuclear and Extended Family

Factors to consider are sexual contact between a parent and a child, or a child and her or his siblings. The extended family is made up of all other family members not in the nuclear category, and typically not living in the home with the child.

Cross-generational

Factors to consider are sexual contact between a minor child and a person of significant difference in age, which could be within the nuclear family or the extended family, or someone who is in the parental role.

Peer Abuse

Factors to consider are sexual contact between individuals who are close in age, such as siblings, cousins, and half-siblings, provided that there is a power differential, which could manifest in various ways, such as captain of a school team, or head Boy Scout.

Opposite-sex/Same-sex

Factors to consider are numbers of males initiating abuse toward females, and that male abuse toward females is typically more traumatic, due to the degree and often the duration. Females tend to abuse males more frequently than they do females, and "...only about 5% of all sexual abuse of girls and about 20% of all sexual abuse of boys is perpetrated by older females" (Russell, 1986, p. 308).

Sexual abuse between individuals of the same sex is reported as more frequent between boys than girls, and is probably underreported. Of note is that same-sex abuse does not indicate homosexuality of the perpetrator. "The incest may instead represent a traumatic reenactment of the perpetrator's own sexual molestation at a particular age, as well as symbolic identification with the victim... traumatic stress response and a narcissistic choice, rather than a homosexual one" (Courtois, 1988, p. 25).

Multiple Sexual Abuse

Things to consider are the number of individuals who have abused the child or adolescent, as well as the number of victims being abused by the perpetrator concurrently or in sequence. In families, it frequently occurs that several if not all of the children have been sexually abused, often by the same perpetrator. It is also not infrequent to hear of a child who has been sexually abused by more than one perpetrator within one family unit.

Sexual abuse has many configurations, and each new case has the potential of unveiling a dynamic that was unconsidered before. It is necessary for the counselor to use all of the basic skills during the initial conceptualization period, so as not to appear shocked, disgusted, or judgmental. The underlying, consistent information to keep in mind and on which to concentrate is that any adult client having survived sexual abuse is a victim of trauma, and has most likely experienced pain, confusion, guilt and shame in some form. The category or type of abuse the client has undergone is not nearly as important to the clinical process as is the counselor's ability to empathize with, and believe in the magnitude of that trauma

THE PATTERN OF ABUSE

There are various patterns of intrafamilial and extrafamilial sexual abuse, and it may be prudent to consider that there are no specific, set formulas of how and when abuse takes place and in what logical order. It can be helpful, however, to review a pattern of occurrence in sexual abuse that was formulated by Sgroi, Blick and Porter (1982), and further conceptualized by Courtois (1988, 1999). The suggested phases of abuse are helpful in providing the counselor and student a framework from which to begin conceptualizing cases involving adult survivors of sexual abuse.

Engagement Phase

This phase includes the access and opportunity for abuse, the relationship of the individuals, and whatever inducements are offered by the perpetrator. The perpetrator usually has ready access, is known to the victim and the family, and has private time at request or by schedule.

Sexual Interaction Phase

The activities become more sexual in nature, including a scale of sexual behavior that may range from exposure to penetration. The activities may vary, and there is usually an escalation of sexual behavior. The progression during this phase has no set duration, no set schedule and no specific behaviors attached.

Secrecy Phase

It is during this time that the abuse is concealed, and as a result of the concealment, can be continued and even escalated. In order to ensure the secrecy, the perpetrator may resort to violence or threats, or more typically, the use of emotional coercion. Some examples might be to tell the child or adolescent that she or he will never be believed, or that if the story were told, the abuser will kill himself or herself, or at the least, be banished from the family. The terrorizing of the victim is usually effective and long-term in keeping the secret. In counseling survivors, it is important to remember that many individuals have not moved from this stage as children or adolescents, and have kept the secret until it has become no longer psychologically or spiritually possible to do so.

Disclosure Phase

This phase encompasses the "telling" of the secret, either by accident from getting caught in the act or someone else admitting suspicions, or by design of the victim. Disclosure of childhood sexual abuse by an adult is a difficult, heartwrenching process. Embarrassment, loyalty to family and friends, and fear of disbelief are some of the overriding factors in adult survivors not disclosing past abuse until they have felt safe within an accepting counseling relationship.

Suppression Phase

This phase, no matter when it occurs, includes denial and minimization of the abuse. Families, friends, spouses, partners, and sometimes children contribute to the suppression of the information about past abuse. For the adult, the denial of the family, often coupled with hostility and disgust, can cause a family rift so deep that it may be irreparable, leaving the adult survivor alone and isolated (Roland, 1992). Adults who were traumatized as children or adolescents can at times succumb to these pressures, and it is vital that a talented, empathic, knowledgeable counselor work with the adult survivor to support and encourage growth and strong self-esteem.

A challenge for the counselor in treating the adult survivor is to be aware of the phases of abuse from the past, and that for many clients, the past has not been 'finished' or even confirmed. To understand the client's experience as a child or adolescent within the family system allows the counselor to gain insight into the burden carried by the survivor, and the length of time the burden has been carried as part of that same family system, for every segment of development. Courtois (1988) emphasized, " In our society, the family is seen as the protected place, a place of safety and security which nurtures the growth and development of immature children...Abuse within the family therefore contradicts everything a family should be" (p. 32).

CULTURAL/GENDER CONSIDERATIONS

Counselors must be aware of any **cultural components** presented when working with adult survivors. As in all counseling, awareness, understanding and empathy are vital to the process of counseling those different from us; self- acknowledgement of any personal bias around culture is primary before the counselor can begin to deliver best services (Capuzzi & Gross, 1999). Although persons from diverse cultural and ethnic groups may have been influenced by their background, they should not be completely defined by them. Diverse groups often hold beliefs about relationships and roles, child rearing, moral values, and the family that differ from mainstream Western thinking, and counselors must consider those factors when working with survivors who are culturally or ethnically different (Thomas, 1992). Following are several examples of how cultural diversity impacts the counseling of adult survivors.

Sexual intimacy may be a good illustration of an issue impacted by a cultural consideration when the adult survivor is from a diverse group. In the treatment of a woman who is Asian or of Asian descent, as in Vietnamese, the counselor should be aware that in the client's world, the woman grew up in a culture that prizes the virginity of a young woman. If that client presents with sexual intimacy issues resulting from childhood or adolescent sexual abuse, she is likely carrying the added burden of loss of chastity, shame, and banishment from family, as well as low self-esteem due to her perceived failure as a Vietnamese woman (Mollica & Son, 1989). "In the Vietnamese culture, virginity is associated with conduct or behavior. This virtue emphasizes that a woman is forbidden to have any sexual relationships outside her marriage...she must remain chaste...Therefore a Vietnamese woman's value is synonymous with...virginity. Without her virginity a woman has no worth" (Mollica & Son, p. 372). Given this perception, the survivor of Asian descent may indeed suffer from issues of sexual intimacy, especially if the sexual trauma took the form of penetration, robbing her virginity from her at an early age. Although the loss of chastity was not her fault, the woman may carry that guilty secret for many years, therefore preventing any closeness or profound intimacy in her relationships.

Sometimes gender issues intersect with cultural components. The male/female roles expected and revered in that culture are strong, respected, and are an integral part of everyday life and may, therefore, be threatening to the survivor, causing further trauma. A Western - cultured survivor may react to the occurrence of past sexual abuse within the societal context that sexual abuse is a crime and punishable. A non-Western survivor living in the U.S., although somewhat protected by the legal system, may react in a way more characteristic of the culture of her people, accepting the sex-role mores and values inherent in that culture. Since many Asian Americans restrain their emotions within their cultural value of constraint (Robinson & Howard-Hamilton, 2000; Uba, 1994), counselors may find it difficult to explore the impact of the abuse within a timeframe experienced with non-Asian clients, which would require great patience and understanding.

The Latino/a culture is one in which the implications of childhood and adolescent sexual abuse intertwine with gender issues. The Latino/a population is the fastest growing group in the United States (Stavans, 1995), and the likelihood of counselors working with survivors of Latino/a descent is increasing. The counselor should take into consideration the traditional gender roles of **marianismo** for women, which refers to their spiritual superiority, and their closeness after marriage to the Virgin Mary, and **machismo** for men, which refers to them as providers of the family with honor and dignity, as well as physical dominance (Becerra, 1988; Robinson & Howard-Hamilton, 2000). The strong bond to Catholicism and family can place a burden on the adult survivor. To admit past sexual abuse may cause a great rift in the family, generating disharmony among members, and it may seem to the Latino/a survivor that silence is the best path, even through the silence may generate significant levels of guilt and shame. Values of respect, trust, dignity, and loyalty to family are basic within the Latino/a culture (Arrendondo, 1992; Comas-Diaz, 1993), and uncovering or announcing the "sin" of early, unwanted sexual contact could cause the adult survivor to keep the secret as long as possible so as not to disrupt the family system.

Cultural communication issues may be relevant in counseling the Latino/a population as well. Once the adult survivor makes the decixion to seek counseling, the process may appear to the counselor as slow and somewhat fraught with avoidance. This may be a result of the client's typically quiet manner and inherent hesitancy to be open with strangers. "Many Latinos tend to speak softly, avoid eye contact when listening to or speaking with persons perceived as having high status, and interject less" (Robinson & Howard-Hamilton, 2000, p. 40). The counselor may find it necessary to alter her or his style with respect to the diversity of the individual client in terms of communication and feedback.

Gay, lesbian and bisexual individuals presenting with issues of sexual abuse have an immediate challenge when seeking counseling: to find a counselor who is not homophobic, and who is knowledgeable, accepting and respectful. The myth that the occurrence of childhood or adolescent sexual abuse may be at the root of a person's sexual identity is just that -- a myth. There is no compelling evidence in support of the notion that past sexual abuse is the cause of an individual being lesbian, gay or bi-sexual. For some women, the aftereffects of sexual abuse may include a deep fear of men, viewing all men as potential abusers. The decision to steer clear of males by some women is often a result of loss of trust and terrorization from past sexual contact, but the sexual identity of the survivor is not determined by the occurrence of past abuse (Courtois, 1988).

Given the gender-specific research on prevalence of sexual abuse experiences of adult women, it may be more likely for a lesbian couple, as two women, to have included in their dyad an adult survivor of sexual abuse (Brown, 1995; Perez, DeBord, & Bieschke, 2000). In addition to the societal pressure of marrying traditionally and bearing children, lesbian survivors carry the symptoms and aftereffects of the abuse, sometimes causing a more intense, faster engagement in the counseling process, for which the counselor may not be prepared. Issues of low self-esteem and self-hate that may have plagued many lesbians as a result of their sexual identity may be intensified by admitting the past sexual abuse, and subsequent introspection throughout the counseling process.

Gay and bisexual men may underrepresent and play down past sexual abuse due to societal stereotypes, such as "men don't complain," " men must be stoic," and " men don't go to counseling" to name a few. Citing Lew (1988), Perez et al. (2000) suggested that:

> American culture allows little room for men to be considered victims and that early sexual experiences for men are often viewed as a demonstration of masculinity…inappropriate or abusive sexual experiences may not be labeled as such by gay men or may be associated with tremendous shame or confusion about how the experience affected their sexual identity development" *(p. 289).*

IMPACT OF ABUSE ON ADULT SURVIVORS

Sexual abuse has a profound effect on adults victimized as children or adolescents. Throughout the life span of an adult survivor, the negative impact of sexual abuse may have permeated all segments of the developmental process, including personality, sexual functioning, relationships, intimacy, career choice and general life satisfaction, to mention a few. The incidence of severe aftereffects and **symptomatology** varies among individuals who were sexually abused. Indeed, some report no profound aftereffects, however, it is generally known that adults who were sexually abused during childhood or adolescence report many serious symptoms, and many seek counseling on a regular basis, more than one time during their adulthood (Briere & Runtz, 1986; Courtois, 1988; Kluft, 1994). Browne and Finkelhor (1986) suggested that long-term aftereffects and the symptoms that resulted from the abuse were those that developed two or more years after the initial abuse occurred. Adult survivors may experience the effects and memories of sexual abuse for many years post-abuse, indeed for most of their lives.

The controversy around **false memory** and accusations of sexual abuse has tempered some of the strides made on this issue (Brown, 1996; Seligman, 1997). Counselors are responsible for familiarizing themselves with the ethical and professional issues concerning memory and abuse, while remaining true to the standards of practice for counseling, that is, giving the client the best service and ultimate respect possible. Sometimes, when working with an adult survivor who suspects, even "knows" that abuse occurred, but has no specific memory, the memories may be nonexistent and seem just too difficult for the client (Courtois, 1999; Krystal, 1995; Roland, 1993). The specifics are not as important as the client's fears, emotions, and any symptoms that have manifested. Those interested in the historical and clinical aspects of memory applied to sexual abuse should consult Courtois's (1999) *Recollections of Sexual Abuse: Treatment Principles and Guidelines.*

Clinicians and researchers have categorized the symptoms and aftereffects of sexual abuse. Courtois (1988) offered six general categories, which were emotional, perceptual, physical, sexual, interpersonal and social. Briere and Elliott (1994) suggested that the effects be divided into six different categories: posttraumatic stress, cognitive distortions, emotional pain, avoidance, impaired sense of self, and interpersonal problems. Below is a brief conceptualization that has combined the suggestions of Courtois (1988), and Briere and Elliot (1994), with my own experience of treating adult survivors for many years.

The *DSM-IV-TR* (APA, 2001) category of **Post-Traumatic Stress Disorder** included sexual abuse as a diagnostic feature under PTSD. However, not every client who presents as an adult survivor has had a diagnosis of PTSD, but rather it is simply an indication of the possible severity of the symptoms and aftereffects of abuse on adults. Rather than concentrating on the diagnostic implications, counselors might concentrate on the story told in the first few sessions, to gain insight into the symptoms, if any are emerging. Recent research alludes the connection between long-term posttraumatic symptoms to past childhood abuse, especially in women (Lindberg & Distad, 1985; Saunders, Villeponteaux, & Lipovsky, 1992). Therefore, students and counselors working with survivors might consult the *DSM-IV* (APA, 1994) and become familiar with the specific criteria mentioned for PTSD.

The **emotional effects** of sexual abuse for adult survivors may include feelings of apprehension, fear, anger, anxiety and depression, and can plague survivors for many years. In the research reported on long-term clinical effects, depression, or major depression, can be chronic, and may include self-damaging behaviors and suicidal tendencies (Browne & Finkelhor, 1986; Courtois, 1988). The perceived helplessness of the survivor, often a result of chronic sadness and loss, contributes to the feelings of powerlessness and numbness.

The **behavioral effects** may include activities that have been self-harming, such as addictions to alcohol, drugs, or exercise, or sexual acting out. The development of an **eating disorder**, such as **anorexia nervosa** or **bulimia nervosa** (Courtois, 1988), may , in some circumstances, be another aftereffect, although no definitive research has highlighted a solid link (Wonderlich, Brewerton, Jocic, Dansky & Abbott, 1997). However, the emergence of a full-blown eating disorder has manifested more often in female adult survivors than in many other groups studied (Everill & Waller, 1995, Mallinckrodt, McCreary & Robertson, 1995). At the least, a causal link has been established between past childhood or adolescent sexual abuse and eating disorders, most especially bulimia nervosa (Mallinckrodt et al., 1995; Rorty, Yager, & Rossotto, 1994).

Dissociation is a behavior long associated with the effects of sexual abuse among adult survivors (van der Kolk & Kadish, 1987). Dissociation "permits the isolation of a traumatic experience until the individual is better able to deal with it" (Kennerley, 1996, p.325). Briere and Elliott (1994) offered a definition of dissociation that is helpful in counseling clients who present with general dissociative behaviors:

> Dissociation can be defined as a disruption in the normally occurring linkages between subjective awareness, feelings, thoughts, behaviors, and memories, consciously or unconsciously invoked to reduce psychological distress…Examples include (1) derealization and depersonalization; (2)…disengagement; (3) alterations in bodily perception; (4) …numbing; (5) out-of-body-experiences; (6) amnesia for painful abuse-related memories; and (7) multiple personality disorders. *(p. 59)*

Being able to distinguish between behaviors that appear dissociative in nature, and a more clinical diagnosis of **Dissociative Identity Disorder** (DID), formerly known in general as Multiple Personality Disorder is important. DID is listed as a *DSM-IV* (APA, 1994) category that includes sexual abuse as a diagnostic feature. A paradox is centered around the DID diagnosis and how it might effect sexual abuse survivors in terms of level of acceptance and belief for "the story" of abuse. Movies have been made about persons with multiple personalities, and indeed popular talk-show hosts have invited many multi-personalitied adults to discuss the relative truth of their claims of being more than one person. The media attention has served as an impetus to tease and demean the integrity of those individuals presenting with DID in the clinical setting. Although it may at times be difficult to imagine someone with more than one personality, Ross (1997), a respected author on DID and MPD, has stated:

> People with DID do not have more than one personality. However, DID is a real disorder that can be treated...Debates about whether or not DID is real are meaningless...not believing in DID is like not believing in hallucinations...psychiatrists grasp the fact that hallucinations and delusions are not real, and understand that they are real psychotic symptoms. *(p. 62)*

The effects of sexual abuse on **personal esteem** may include consistently negative or low self-esteem, incorporating guilt and shame as part of the client's self-perception. The task of developing a sense of self may be interrupted or possibly even halted by one or more incidents of unwanted sexual contact, and can lead to long-term esteem impairment(Cole & Putnam, 1992). Negative perceptions of the self may manifest as feeling apart from the group or the family, feeling inadequate, self-hate, extreme introversion, or feeling unable to succeed in any endeavor. Low self-esteem can impact on the basic developmental life stages and how one moves through them. Impaired or skewed body image is a common effect of childhood or adolescent sexual abuse, directly contributing to issues of low self-esteem and negative self-perception, and may be a preliminary link to the development of an eating disorder, or other self-harming behaviors (Courtois, 1988; Daniluk, 1998; Simonds, 1994).

The **interpersonal effects** of sexual abuse may include relationship difficulties, fear of abandonment, distrust of others, difficulty developing and sustaining intimacy, commitment issues, parenting concerns, and being open emotionally. Multiple marriages or partnerships, or few if any committed relationships can be effects of sexual abuse as well (Briere & Elliott, 1994; Courtois, 1988). Difficulty relating to children, parents, and persons in authoritative roles may be a result of sexual abuse experienced as a child or adolescent, which can leave each set of relationships conflicted and fraught with ambivalence.

The effects of childhood or adolescent sexual abuse on the adult survivor in the area of **sexual functioning** can be many. With regard to the physical aspect of sexual functioning, an issue often presented in counseling couples concerns the inability or non-desire to perform. Briere and Elliott (1994) related, "Because childhood sexual molestation is likely to create an association between sexual stimuli and invasion or pain, many adults molested as children report fear or anxiety-related difficulties during sexual contact" (p. 58).

The sexual development of children is, at times, tenuous and unpredictable when sexual abuse has been introduced. Sometimes the behavior seen in childhood has continued through adulthood, and may include, for example, sexual promiscuity or sexual celibacy, problems with orgasm, violent sexual practices, sadness or extreme guilt after sex, or physical illness (Briere & Elliott, 1994; Courtois, 1988; Wyatt, Newcomb, Reederle, & Notgrass, 1993).

COUNSELING STRATEGIES

There are numerous clinical issues associated with counseling survivors, therefore, it is impossible to assign strategies and interventions even to those mentioned in this chapter. This section presents an overview of several strategies that have been used with reported positive outcomes. Both group counseling and individual counseling is effective with survivors over the years; group counseling is reported as highly effective in working with adult survivors who possess clear knowledge and recollection of childhood or adolescent sexual abuse (Webb & Leehan, 1996). Information on both modalities is provided in this section.

ESTABLISHING THE COUNSELING RELATIONSHIP

The **counseling relationship** plays a vital role in working with survivors. Using a combination of the **Relational Model** (Jordan, Kaplan, Miller, Stiver, Surrey, 1991) and the **Person-Centered** theory of counseling (Hazler, 1999; Rogers, 1951, 1961), the atmosphere must be open, accepting, and non-judgmental. How does this happen? A strategy to encourage the emergence of a positive counseling relationship involves, 1) discussing with the client early on the amount of specific knowledge she or he has about trauma in general and the specific abuse as well; 2) assessing for symptoms as perceived by the client at the beginning stages of counseling and how they may have manifested; 3) discussing the expectations on the part of both the client and counselor in terms of the counseling relationship and what is expected (for example, emergency calls and appointments); 4) discussing the responsibilities of both the client and counselor to maintain an open, mutual, balanced counseling relationship; and 5) agreeing on initial goals for a specified period of time, which all form a contract or agreement (Courtois, 1999). This can be accomplished through traditional talk-therapy within a relatively short period of time. This strategy helps establish the necessary **therapeutic alliance** from which counseling may grow and progress. The style and personality of the counselor is an important aspect of the process, and may have more to do with the outcome than any set of techniques used. Courtois (1988) offered the following as basic to the initial process of working with survivors:

> It is important...to maintain a stance of openness and acceptance...it is advisable that s/he (counselor) be active and open in engaging the client. The nonresponsive, abstinent therapist is often perceived as judgmental and unavailable. Such a position recreates dynamics from the past, making it almost impossible for the client to disclose and to engage in self-exploration. *(p. 169)*

VISUALIZATION/GUIDED IMAGERY

Visualization may be introduced into the counseling process only after a positive, trusting therapeutic alliance is formed. Most effective results from visualization techniques seem to occur after at least several months into the process, when the bonding between the client and the counselor is firm and trusted (Roland, 1993). Inner child work, (Davis, 1991; Whitfield, 1987) is helpful in the process of reframing negative thoughts and perceptions. The use of inner child visualizations may assist the client in reclaiming and retaining important connectedness with the true self (Miller, 1981). Jung (1954) suggested that visualizations are a way to approach the inner child, as a "genuine attempt to get at something necessary: the universal feeling of childhood innocence, the sense of security, of protection, of reciprocal love, of truth..." (p. 32).

The reframing of negative or painful images and skewed perceptions is important to the process of counseling survivors, and can be used around issues of low self-esteem, self-hate, self-blame, and body awareness/image. Visualization through guided imagery is helpful in the exploration of the etiology of an impaired image, leading to the possible reframing of that image. To provide a sense of hope and empowerment for the client, a visualization is suggested that would include the client choosing the age of the child (him or herself) for the imagery. Houston (1982) developed a general visualization called "Meeting Your Inner Child," which can be used as a basis for several structured exercises. The client's choice of the age of the visualized child holds some importance; typically the age chosen corresponds with the age or period of abuse or greatest fear. After asking the client to close her or his eyes and "see yourself as a child," the client is asked to "picture yourself" at a specific place that is warm, comfortable, and nonthreatening for the child (Houston, 1990). The counselor then asks the client to literally extend an open hand in the session, asking the visualized child to walk toward it and touch it when she or he is comfortable. Once the physical contact is made, the client is asked to visualize a conversation with the child, getting to know her or him. The client is asked to notice the physical characteristics of the child as imagined, and to appreciate all those she or he sees. Through the process of befriending the child, the client may gain a sense of how small and vulnerable the child appears, assuming the role of protector and champion. The physical appearance of the child is discussed at this point, since the impaired body perception of the client as adult may be in contrast to the image of the child. The reframing of the current image is encouraged by the visualized conversation and time spent with the inner child who looks and seems different than the client. The two time periods, then and now, hopefully converge into a more realistic view of body image and the self.

GROUP COUNSELING

There is consensus abut the efficacy of group counseling for adult survivors of sexual abuse (Hazzard, Rogers & Angert, 1993; Richter, Snider & Gorey, 1997; Westbury & Tutty, 1999). There are, of course, many models of group counseling, with numerous studies reporting group techniques that have been effective with survivors. Webb and Leehan (1996) suggested six basic goals to facilitate the healing process in a group setting for survivors. They are summarized in general below, and can be used for various group modes with the population:

1. To break down the sense of isolation of the members.
2. To provide a safe, supportive environment in which to share and explore feelings, as well as try out new behaviors.
3. To provide a consistent, dependable environment where members learn to trust other members of the group, as well as themselves.
4. To provide a setting for group problem-solving.

5. To encourage members to share deep emotions that may have been repressed, so that the fear of experiencing emotions dissipates.
6. To provide a setting for practicing interpersonal communication skills. *(p.53)*

CASE APPLICATION

The Client

Heather is a 42 year-old female of Irish-American descent. The youngest of two children, she was raised with her parents and her older brother, Jeremy, in a major Northeastern city. She has been married to her husband Ben for 22 years; they have one son, Brandon who is 19 and lives 200 miles from home. Heather has a degree in business and works as a computer programmer at a small firm; Ben is a professor at a nearby university. Heather presents as tired, depressed, and announces that she has not eaten in two days because she was on a diet to lose 20 pounds. She did not appear overweight.

Presenting Problem

Heather and Ben have been having frequent arguments concerning their intimate relationship -- she reported that they have not been sexual in several months, and that Ben told her that he was unhappy with that arrangement. During the first session, Heather revealed that she had been sexually abused between the ages of 6 and 10, by her uncle John, now deceased, and two neighborhood boys who were older. Her memory of the abuse was evident, and she shared that she had been in counseling for a year when she first got married, 22 years ago. Heather said she went to counseling at that time because, being a virgin when she married Ben, she was disappointed that when she did consummate the relationship, she was disinterested and tense. In fact, she admitted that although she and Ben seemed to have a good "sex life" she never really enjoyed it, and felt sad many times after. She had not ever told Ben this.

Heather had recently experienced depression and anxiety, and was unhappy with the weight she had gained over the past 5 or 6 years. She related that she felt her "body was failing her" and that she was "dumpy and not attractive anymore." "I feel like I did when I was 10!" was the last thing she said before she burst into tears.

Heather's Family History

Heather's family was originally from the Midwest, and moved to the Northeast when she was 6 years old. At that time, Heather's uncle John, her father's brother, lived with the family for a number of years, giving him access and opportunity for the abusive situation. Heather's mother was out of the home a lot, working in a local bank, while her father worked out of town often as a salesman. Her older brother, Jeremy, left home at 18 and never returned; she hears from him infrequently.

Heather's mother died four years ago of cancer after a long battle, and her father died the following year. Heather told her mother about her uncle abusing her, but was not believed.

She never told her father or her brother for fear of rejection. Her father was an only child, and there were no relatives close on his side of the family. Her mother's sister Emily, Heather's aunt, and Heather were reported as being close.

Heather's Life

Heather works a lot, often until late hours. She reported that Ben and she argue often, mostly about their intimacy issues, and that he told her recently that he wanted a separation. She revealed that her picture of herself was dumpy, unattractive, and fat, and that she felt out of control and "running in circles" with work and the home up keep.

Her son, Brandon, does not visit home often, and she fears it is due to the fights she and Ben have, usually in his presence. She said she misses her son and, although they speak on the phone frequently, she is worried Brandon will vanish like her brother Jeremy did.

Heather has been referred to counseling by her gynecologist, with whom she has shared her past abuse, and consulted about her low sexual drive and depression. Rather than prescribing any medication for the depression, the physician referred her to a clinician specializing in counseling survivors.

A Guided Visualization with Heather

As mentioned earlier, inner child work can, at times, be valuable in uncovering negative perceptions of self, and then reframing those perceptions. Below is an abbreviated description of an intervention for the counselor to use with Heather and her beginning battle with low self-esteem and impaired body image.

Counselor: Heather, I invite you to close your eyes, and place both feet squarely on the floor to ground you. Now, with your eyes closed, choose an age you wish to see your inner child, and let me know when you have.

Heather: I would like to visit my child at age 10 if I could.

Counselor: Heather, visualize yourself at age 10. What do you look like? How tall are you, what color is your hair, what length is it? Can you picture your favorite outfit if you had one?

Heather: Oh yes! I loved that light green shirt and tan skirt my mother got me at Macy's, I felt so grown up in it. Hair – well, it was pretty long then I think, and I always wore it in a braid or pigtails, Mother never liked it stringy. Yea, it was pretty nice, having all that hair, and the natural blond was so soft. Tall? I was almost this tall, so about 5'3" – always tall as a young kid, short now!!

Counselor: O.K., it sounds like a clear picture you've got there -- complete. Now Heather, please extend your arm and open your hand to the child you see. (She does that). Ask Little Heather to look at you, then ask her to come closer, and touch your hand when she's ready and comfortable. (About 40 seconds passes). Is she walking towards you?

Heather: Oh, yes! She's almost there – she's so pretty, and she is smiling at me. She is almost, yes, we are touching…(Heather stops because she is weeping quietly).

Counselor: What would you like to say to Little Heather? What do you notice about her? You can go on and talk with her when you are ready, no hurry.

Heather: I want to tell her she is pretty and sweet, and innocent. And I want to show her how pretty she is! She doesn't have to be sad, I'll take care of her…and I know she loves me too! And her hair is beautiful; she's smiling!

Counselor: She's smiling at you now? Is she closer?

Heather: Oh, yes, she's right here, she's looking at me and squeezing my hand.

Counselor: Heather, does it seem like Little Heather likes you? That she thinks you are pretty? Is she pleased to see you?

Heather: (Silence for about 20 seconds) Well, I don't know, I guess so – she's looking at me like she does!

Counselor: Heather, its time to say good bye to Little Heather for today. How would you like to do that?

Heather: (Takes a big breath and waits a few seconds) Honey, I'll come to see you soon, and then we can talk more. I love you, I love you…and I'll take care of you (she is weeping again).

Heather is asked to open her eyes when ready, and focus on the floor for a few seconds to get centered with the space and time. Then we discuss how the image of her inner child is similar to how she is an adult, and how it is different. The contrast is not the focus, the similarities are, so that the positive feelings with which she left Little Heather in the visualization translate to possibly reframing her negative perceptions of herself as an adult. There is clearly much more to work on with this issue; the abbreviated visualization is an illustration of the power of inner child work and reframing perceptions that can be effective with survivors. Although visualization can be facilitative to this process, counselors are urged to be experienced with the population and use caution. Survivors may experience emotions not known prior to the visualization, and polarities in behavior may be observed An empathic, knowledgeable counselor can guide the client out of the visualization so that the unexpected feelings may be dealt with (Ratican, 1992; Roland, 1993).

REFERENCES

American Psychiatric Association (2001). *Diagnostic and statistical manual of mental disorder* (4th ed.). Washington, DC: Author.

Armstrong, C. (1978). *Kiss daddy goodnight: A speak out on incest.* NY: Hawthorne Books.

Armstrong, C. (1982). The cradle of sexual politics. In M. Kirkpatrick, (Ed.), *Women's Sexual experiences: Explorations of the dark continent* (pp.109-125). N.Y: Plenum.

Arrendondo, P. (1992). *Latina/Latino value orientations: Tape 1. Cultural considerations for working more effectively with Latin Americans.* Amherst, MA: Microtraining and Multicultural Development.

Bass, E., & Davis, L. (1988). *The courage to heal: A guide for women survivors of child sexual abuse.* NY: Harper & Row.

Becerra, R.M. (1988). The Mexican American family. In C. Mindel, R. Habenstein, & R. Wright (Eds.), *Ethnic families in America: Patterns and variations* (pp. 141-159). NY: Elsevier.

Blume, J. (1990). *Secret survivors*. NY: Wiley.

Briere, J. (1992). *Child abuse trauma: Theory and treatment of the lasting effects.* Newbury park, CA: Sage.

Briere, J. (1996). *Therapy for adults molested as children: Beyond survival* (2nd ed.). NY: Springer Publishing.

Briere, J., & Elliott, D.M. (1994). Immediate and long term impacts of child sexual abuse. The Future of Children, 4, 54-69.

Briere, J., & Runtz, M. (1986). Suicidal thoughts and behaviors in former sexual abuse victims. *Canadian Journal of Behavioral Science, 18,* 413-423.

Briere, J., & Runtz, M. (1989). The Trauma Symptom Checklist (TSC-33): Early data on a new scale. *Journal of Interpersonal Violence, 4,* 151-163.

Brown, L. (1995). Therapy with same-sex couples: An introduction. In N.S. Jacobson, & A.S. Gurman, (Eds.), *Clinical handbook of couple therapy* (pp. 274-291). NY: Guilford.

Brown, L.S. (1996). Politics of memory, politics of incest: Doing therapy and politics that really matter. In S. Contratto, & M.L. Gutfreund, (Eds.), *A feminist clinician's guide to the memory debate* (pp. 5-18). NY: Haworth.

Browne, A., & Finkelhor, D. (1986). Impact of sexual abuse: A review of the literature. *Psychological Bulletin, 99,* 66-77.

Capuzzi, D., & Gross, D.R. (1999). Achieving a personal and professional identity. In D.Capuzzi, & D.R. Gross, (Eds.), *Counseling and psychotherapy: Theories and interventions* (pp. 23-42). Upper Saddle River, NJ: Merrill/Prentice Hall.

Cole, P., & Putnam, F. (1992). Effect of incest on self and social functioning: A developmental psychopathology perspective. *Journal of Consulting and Clinical Psychology, 60,* 174-184.

Comas-Diaz, L. (1993). Hispanic Latino communities: Psychological implications. In D. Atkinson, G. Morton, & D.W. Sue, (Eds.), *Counseling American minorities: A cross-cultural perspective* (pp. 245-263). Madison, WI: Brown and Benchmark.

Courtois, C.A. (1979). Characteristics of a volunteer sample of adult women who experienced incest in childhood and adolescence. *Dissertation Abstracts International, 40A*, Nov. – Dec., 3194 – A.

Courtois, C.A. (1988). *Healing the incest wound: Adult survivors in therapy*. NY: W.W. Norton.

Courtois, C. (1995). Walking a fine line: Isues of assessment and diagnosis of women molested in childhood. In C. Classen (Ed.), *Treating women molested in childhood* (pp. 1-35). San Francisco: Jossey-Bass.

Courtois, C.A. (1997). Healing the incest wound: A treatment update with attention to recovered memory issues. *American Journal of Psychotherapy, 51,*464-496.

Courtois, C.A. (1999). *Recollections of sexual abuse: Treatment principles and guidelines*. NY: W.W. Norton.

Courtois, C.A., & Watts, D. (1982). Counseling adult women who experienced incest in childhood and adolescence. *Personnel and Guidance Journal, 60,* 275-279.

Daniluk, J.C. (1998). *Women's sexuality across the life span: Challenging myths, creating meanings.* NY: Guilford.

Davis, L. (1991). *Allies in healing.* NY: Harper Perennial.

Elliott, D.M. & Briere, J. (1992). Sexual abuse trauma among professional women: Validating the Trauma Symptoms Checklist – 40 (TSC-40). *Child Abuse & Neglect, 16,* 391-398.

Everill, J.T., & Waller, G. (1995). Reported sexual abuse and eating psychopathology: A review of the evidence for a causal link. *International Journal of Eating Disorders, 18,* 1-11.

Finkelhor, D. (1978). Psychological, cultural and family factors in incest and family sexual abuse. *Journal of Marriage and Family Counseling, 4,* 41-49.

Finkelhor, D. (1984). *Child sexual abuse: New theory and research.* NY: Free Press.

Finkelhor, D. (1986). *A sourcebook on child sexual abuse.* Beverly Hills: Sage.

Finkelhor, D., Hotaling, G., Lewis, I.A., & Smith, C. (1990). Sexual abuse in a national survey of adult men and women: Prevalence, characteristics, and risk factors. *Child Abuse & Neglect, 3(1),* 19-28.

Freud, S. (1959). The aetiology of hysteria. In J. Riviere, (trans.), *Sigmund Freud: Collected papers, Volume 1* (pp. 183-219). NY: Basic Books.

Freyd, J.J. (1996). *Betrayal trauma: The logic of forgetting childhood abuse.* Cambridge, MA: Harvard.

Goodwin, J. (1982). *Sexual abuse: Incest victims and their families.* Littleton, MA: PGS Publishing.

Hazler, R. J. (1999). Person-centered theory. In D. Capuzzi, & D.R. Gross, (Eds.), *Counseling and psychotherapy: Theories and interventions* (2nd Ed.) (pp. 179-201). Upper Saddle River, NJ: Merrill/ Prentice Hall.

Hazzard, A., Rogers, J., & Angert, L. (1993). Factors affecting group therapy outcomes for sexual abuse survivors. *International Journal of Group Psychotherapy, 43,* 453-468.

Herman, J.L. (1981). *Father-daughter incest.* Cambridge, MA: Harvard University Press.

Houston, J. (1982). *The possible human.* Los Angeles, CA: Jeremy Tarcher.

Houston, J. (1990). Recalling the child. In J. Abrams, (Ed.), *Reclaiming the inner child* (pp. 248-251). Los Angeles, CA: Jeremy Tarcher.

Jordan, J.V., Kaplan, A.G., Miller, J.B., Stiver, I.P., & Surrey, J. (1991). *Women's growth in connection: Writings from the Stone Center.* NY: Guilford.

Jung, C.G. (1954). *The practice of psychotherapy: Collected works (Vol. 16).* Princeton. NJ: Bollinger.

Kempe, R., & Kempe, H. (1984). *The common secret.* NY: W.H. Freeman.

Kennerley, H. (1996). Cognitive therapy of dissociative symptoms associated with trauma. *British journal of Clinical Psychology, 35,* 325-340.

Kluft, R.P. (1994). Treatment trajectories in multiple personality disorder. *Dissociation, 7,* 63-76.

Krystal, H. (1995). Trauma and aging: A thirty-year follow-up. In C.Caruth (Ed.), *Trauma: Exploration in memory* (pp. 76-99). Baltimore, MD: The Johns Hopkins University Press.

Lew, M. (1988). *Victims no longer*. NY: Harper & Row.

Lindberg, F. H., & Distad, L. J. (1985). Post-traumatic stress disorders in women who experienced childhood incest. *Child Abuse & Neglect, 9*, 329-334.

Mallinckrodt, B., McCreary, B.A., & Robertson, A.K. (1995). Co-occurrence of eating disorders and incest: The role of attachment, family environment, and social competencies. *Journal of Counseling Psychology, 42* (2), 178-186.

Miller, A. (1981). *The drama of the gifted child*. NY: Basic Books.

Miller, A. (1984). *Thou shall not be aware: Society's betrayal of the child*. NY: Farrar, Straus, Giroux.

Mollica, R.F., & Son, L. (1989). Cultural dimensions in the evolution and treatment of sexual trauma. *Psychiatric Clinics of North America, 12 (2),* 363-380.

Morrow, S.L., & Smith, M.L. (1995). Constructions of survival and coping by women who have survived childhood sexual abuse. *Journal of Counseling Psychology, 42*, 24-33.

Perez, R.M., DeBord, K.A., & Bieschke, K.J. (2000). *Handbook of counseling and psychotherapy with lesbian, gay, and bisexual clients*. Washington, DC: American Psychological Association.

Polusny, M.A., & Follette, V.M. (1995). Long-term correlates of child sexual abuse: Theory and review of the empirical literature. *Applied & Preventive Psychology, 4*, 143-166.

Ratican, K. (1992). Sexual abuse survivors: Identifying symptoms and special treatment considerations. *Journal of Counseling & Development, 71*, 33-38.

Richter, N., Snider, E., & Gorey, K.M. (1997). Group work interventions with female survivors of childhood sexual abuse. *Research in Social Work Practice, 7*, 53069.

Robinson, T.C., & Howard-Hamilton, M.F. (2000). *The convergence of race, ethnicity, and gender*. Upper Saddle River, NJ: Merrill/Prentice Hall.

Rogers, C. (1951). *Client-centered therapy*. Boston: Houghton Mifflin.

Rogers, C. (1961). *On becoming a person: A therapist's view of psychotherapy*. Boston: Houghton Mifflin.

Roland, C.B. (1992). Treatment techniques for families with survivors of childhood sexual abuse. *Louisiana Journal of Counseling & Development, 3*, 3-9.

Roland. C.B. (1993). Exploring childhood memories with adult survivors of sexual abuse: Concrete reconstruction and visualization techniques. *Journal of Mental Health Counseling, 15*, 363-374.

Rorty, M., Yager, J., & Rossottao, E. (1994). *Childhood sexual, physical, and psychological abuse in bulimia nervosa. American Journal of Psychiatry, 151*(8), 1122-1127.

Ross, C.A. (1997*). Dissociative identity disorder: Diagnosis, clinical features, and treatment of multiple personality* (2nd Ed.). NY: John Wiley.

Rush, F. (1977). The Freudian cover-up. *Chrysalis, 8*, 31-45.

Rush, F. (1980). *The best kept secret: Sexual abuse of children*. Engelwood Cliffs, NJ: Prentice Hall.

Russell, D.E.H. (1986). *The secret trauma: Incest in the lives of girls and women*. NY: Basic Books.

Saunders, B.E., Villerponteaux, L.A., & Lipovsky, J.A. (1992). Child sexual assault as a risk factor for mental disorders among women: A community survey. *Journal of Interpersonal Violence, 7*, 189-204.

Schreiber, R., & Lyddon, W. (1998). Parental bonding and current psychological functioning among childhood sexual abuse survivors. *Journal of Counseling Psychology, 45*, 358-363.

Seligman, S. (1997). Discussion: Clinical techniques and the political surround: The case of sexual abuse. In C. Prozan (Ed.), *Construction and reconstruction of memory: Dilemmas of childhood sexual abuse* (pp. 207-222). Nashville, NJ: Jason Aronson.

Sgroi, S.M. (1978). Comprehensive examination for child sexual assault: Diagnostic, therapeutic and child protection issues. In A.W. Burgess, A.N. Groth, L.L. Holstrum, & S.M. Sgroi (Eds.), *Sexual assault of children and adolescents* (pp. 254-275). Lexington, MA: D.C. Health.

Sgroi, S.M. (1982). *Handbook of clinical intervention* in *child sexual abuse*. Lexington, MA: Lexington Books.

Sgroi, S.M. (1988). *Vulnerable populations: Evaluation and treatment of sexually abused children and adult survivors*. Lexington, MA: Lexington Books.

Sgroi, S.M. (1989). *Vulnerable populations: Sexual abuse treatment for survivors, adult survivors, offenders, and persons with mental retardation*. Lexington, MA: Lexington Books.

Sgroi, S.M., Bleck, L.C., & Porter, F.S. (1982). A conceptual framework for child sexual abuse. In S.M. Sgroi (Ed.), *Handbook of clinical intervention in child sexual abuse* (pp. 9-38). Lexington, MA: Lexington Books.

Simonds, S.L. (1994). *Bridging the silence: Nonverbal modalities in the treatment of adult survivors of childhood sexual abuse*. NY: Norton.

Stavans, I. (1995). *The Hispanic condition: Reflections on culture and identity in America*. NY: Harper Perennial.

Thomas, N.J. (1992). Cultural considerations in assessment and treatment of child sexual abuse: A commentary. *Journal of Child Sexual Abuse, 1(3)*, 129-133.

Tsai, M., Feldman-Summers, S., & Edgar, M. (1979). Childhood molestation: Variables related to differential impacts on psychological functioning in adult women. *Journal of Abnormal Psychology, 88,(2)*, 407-417.

Uba, L. (1994). *Asian Americans: Personality patterns, identity, and mental health*.NY: Guilford.

van der Kolk, B.A. & Kadish, W. (1987). Amnesia, dissociation, and the return of the repressed. In B.A. van der Kolk (Ed.), *Psychological trauma* (pp. 173-191). Washington, DC: American Psychiatric Press.

Webb, L.P., & Leehan, J. (1996). *Group treatment for adult survivors of abuse*. Thousands Oaks, CA: Sage.

Westbury, E., & Tutty, L.M. (1999). The efficacy of group treatment for survivors of childhood abuse. *Child Abuse & Neglect, 23*, 31-45.

Whitfield, C. (1987). *Healing the child within.* Deerfield Beach, FL: Health Communications.

Wonderlich, S.A., Brewerton, T., Jocic, Z., Dansky, B.S., & Abbott, D.W. (1997). The relationship of childhood sexual abuse and eating disorders. *Journal of the American Academy of Child & Adolescent Psychiatry, 36(8),* 1107-1116.

Wyatt, G.E., Loeb, T., Solis, B., Carmona, J., & Romero, G. (1999). The prevalence and circumstances of child sexual abuse: Changes across a decade. *Child Abuse & Neglect, 23*, 45-60.

Wyatt, G.E., Newcomb, M., Reederle, M., & Notgrass, C. (1993). *Sexual abuse and consensual sex: Women's development patterns and outcomes.* Newbury Park, CA: Sage.

Chapter 15

Counseling Sexual Abuse and Rape Victims

Mary B. Ballard and Hunter D. Alessi

Southeastern Louisiana University

Background

Historical Perspective

For centuries, myths about **sexual assault** have influenced the way victims are perceived and treated. In some primitive societies rape was not a crime, but a means of acquiring a wife (Feagan, 1992). Ancient Mosaic law placed a price on potential brides whose virginity was intact. However, if the girl was found not to be a virgin, her price was lowered, and her father would be compensated for his devalued property by being allowed to rape the women in the family of the man who had "stolen" the daughter's virginity. Chattel theory, which views the woman as property and virginity as a commodity, persists to this day as evidenced in myths that place blame on the victim (Holzman, 1994).

Two misogynistic images of women influenced both legal and societal actions toward rape victims: woman as temptress and woman as liar (Largen, 1988). Despite overwhelming evidence in the literature that rape is a crime of violence rather than passion (e. g., Harney & Muehlenhard, 1991), it is not uncommon for rape victims to have some of the blame and responsibility placed upon them (Matheny & Michels, 1989; Raitt & Zeedyk, 1997). Additionally, various religious tenets have perpetuated the myths that continue to impede treatment and recovery of clients who have been sexually assaulted. Young (1993) recounted stories from Roman Catholic literature about women who attained sainthood by choosing death rather than submitting to rape. Some Talmudic teachings assign blame to the victim, because it is assumed that she would have been rescued if she had cried for help (Young).

In the past 30 years, professionals have studied the types of reactions and behaviors exhibited by women who have been raped, seeking to outline effective ways of combating sexual violence. Even so, counselors working with women who have been sexually assaulted continue to face the challenge of not only treating problems resulting from a traumatic stressor, but also with facilitating the alleviation of concurrent feelings of guilt and shame (Davis & Breslau, 1994).

A major study by Burgess and Holmstrom (1974) identified a series of discrete, observable, and consistent reactions to rape, which they labeled **Rape Trauma Syndrome (RTS)**. In fact, current legal practice describes RTS as a "type of **post-traumatic stress disorder (PTSD)** by women who have been raped,"(Hackman, 1995, p. 455), with symptomology consistent with the diagnostic criteria for PTSD (Feagan, 1992).

It is now widely accepted that PTSD is a common consequence of rape, and that rape victims often meet the criteria for PTSD (Kilpatrick, Edmunds, & Seymour, 1992; Rothbaum & Foa, 1992; Rothbaum, Foa, Riggs, Murdock, & Walsh, 1992; Resick, & Markaway, 1991). Furthermore, numerous research studies confirm the high incidence and prevalence of rape (Koss, Gidycz, & Wisniewski, 1987; Russell, 1984; Kilpatrick, Saunders, Veronen, Best, & Von, 1987), suggesting that female rape victims may comprise the largest single group suffering from PTSD (Calhoun & Resick, 1993).

Counselors must have an understanding of the societal, legal, emotional, and physiological effects on the lives of women who have been sexually assaulted. In order to begin this process, there must first be a common language specifying precise terminology, so that the cumulative difficulties that arise from narrow definitions and esoteric labels are avoided during the counseling process.

General Overview of the Topic with Related Definitions

Sexual assault can be defined as "any unwanted sexual contact" (Louisiana Foundation Against Sexual Assault [LaFASA], 2000, p. 10), and may include rape, attempted rape, child sexual abuse, sexual harassment, and the use of sexually explicit language that elicits fear. Furthermore, it may involve male or female perpetrators, male or female victims, acquaintances, family members, friends, or strangers. This chapter focuses upon counseling women who have been sexually assaulted and who experience trauma-related symptoms of distress, including intense fear, helplessness, or horror.

Although there have been numerous attempts to delineate types of sexual assault (e.g., stranger rape, acquaintance rape, date rape, sexual battery), the common thread in most widely-accepted definitions is the occurrence of non-consensual sexual contact. Most sexual assaults are reportedly committed by someone known by the victim such as a husband, partner, friend, or relative.

A study by Koss, Koss, & Woodruff (1990) found that only 17% of reported rapes were perpetrated by strangers, and that 1 adult woman in 24 was sexually assaulted during a one-year period. However, more than 90% of the victims did not report the incident to police, and more than one-third of the women raped did not discuss their experience with anyone during the year following the assault.

Many rapes are not immediately reported because of fear, shame, and/or guilt (Matheny & Michels, 1989). Further obscuring the disclosure of sexual assault is the ambiguity of what constitutes rape. Often, victims do not identify their experience as a rape, particularly when the assailant is not a stranger (Calhoun & Resick, 1993).

Although women who have been sexually assaulted may experience a variety of problems, a large number of studies confirm that many victims display symptoms consistent with a diagnosis of PTSD (Barker-Collo, Melnyk, & McDonald-Miszczak, 2000; Petrak & Campbell, 1999; Resick & Calhoun, 1996; Rothbaum & Foa, 1992).

Rothbaum and others (1992) found that 94% of rape victims exhibited symptoms of PTSD approximately one week following the assault, and that 50% met the criteria after 12 weeks. In a 1987 study (Kilpatrick et al., 1987), 57% of the women who had been raped at some point in their lives developed symptoms of PTSD. Based on findings by Kilpatrick et al. (1992), it is believed that 31% of rape victims develop PTSD compared to 5% of non-victims.

There are clearly counseling implications for practitioners working with female clients who experience depressive or anxious behaviors. Rape has all of the elements of a traumatic stressor; even if no overt threats are made, women frequently view the experience as life-threatening (Raitt & Zeedyk, 1997). Clients who exhibit avoidance or numbing behaviors, flashbacks or nightmares, increased arousal, anxiety disorders, depression, or substance abuse may benefit from treatment for rape-induced PTSD (Calhoun & Resick, 1993).

CULTURAL/GENDER CONSIDERATIONS

A survivor's experience of rape and sexual assault is shaped and defined by the culture to which she belongs (Holzman, 1994). The meaning a woman assigns to the trauma, her decision about whom to tell and when, and her willingness to seek counseling afterward are determined by her culturally influenced values and beliefs about rape and sexual assault. In the United States the dominant culture has historically embraced a set of beliefs that makes the recovery process for survivors particularly difficult. These include: (a) it is impossible to rape a woman who does not want to be raped; (b) women say "no" when they really mean "yes;" (c) masculine men are aggressive and forceful, while feminine men are gentle and compliant; (d) women are responsible for sexually arousing men and should therefore provide them with sexual release; (e) women who are raped are usually responsible in some way (i.e., style of dress or flirtatious behavior); and (f) rape victims are always women (LaFASA, 2000).

If a survivor is seeking help within a system comprised of family, friends, law enforcement officials, and community health agencies who submit to these false assumptions, she will not likely get the support she needs. Counselors working with survivors must not only be free of these biases themselves, but must also be aware of their existence in others and how that might affect the treatment strategy. All too often a victim of rape or sexual assault becomes discouraged when the police or medical examiners fail to acknowledge the seriousness of the crime; the negative verbal and nonverbal demeanor of some authorities can be frightening and certainly discouraging. Therefore, the survivor may fear she has not been taken seriously and elect not to seek further assistance.

In addition to the damaging beliefs of the dominant culture, many survivors are also confronted with the additional myths of their traditional cultures. For example, African-American women often hesitate to report rape or sexual assault to the police for fear of being judged as prostitutes or willing participants (Wyatt, 1992). Since African-American women were raped repeatedly as slaves, the assumption developed that they were not refusing the sexual advances of men and, in fact, enjoying such behavior. Unfortunately, this stereotype still exists today with African-American women being suspected by certain investigating authorities of inviting the sexual crimes committed against them (Wyatt). Asian-American women also suffer from harmful stereotyping. Because Southeast Asia is home to a booming sex tourism business, Asian-American women are often characterized as sexually exotic and completely focused on satisfying the sexual desires and fantasies of men (Holzman, 1994). Therefore, it is easy to understand why these women may be reluctant to report a sexual crime.

Women from other countries who are raped may have a different experience with this trauma than American women based on the culture in which they live. For example, in many Southeast Asian communities where traditional cultures prevail, virgins who are raped are considered defiled and unworthy of a husband other than their rapist. Therefore, they will marry their rapist, who is not considered a criminal, as a means of securing a life-long partner. Other women who are raped in these communities are faulted by their families for bringing about such shame and disgrace. To protect their family's status in the community, they are often forbidden to share the rape experience with anyone. Therefore, these women are resigned to live with the secret of what has happened to them (Holzman, 1994).

Perhaps one of the most harmful beliefs of our dominant culture is that only women can be victims of rape. Nine percent of the rape victims in the United States are male (LaFASA, 2000). However, societal myths about male and female gender roles and attitudes prevent most of these men from ever reporting the trauma or seeking treatment (McCann & Pearlman, 1990). Afraid of ridicule and humiliation, most male survivors refuse to talk about what happened to them with family, friends, police, or community health agencies. Our society falsely assumes that male rape takes place primarily in prisons and within the homosexual community. Aware of this myth, heterosexual males often interpret rape as an assault against their "manhood" and fear being labeled homosexual (McCann & Pearlman). Therefore, they remain silent and suffer alone without ever disclosing the trauma to anyone (Isley, 1991).

Men who have been raped tend to cope with feelings of guilt, anger, shame and depression by presenting as controlled, stoic, and perfectly "put together" (Isley, 1991). However, they pay a high price for these rigid responses, suffering from the same PTSD symptoms as women. Unfortunately, men remain less likely to seek treatment than women, thus becoming more prone to other problems like substance abuse, depression, and suicide (Isley). For those that do seek counseling, it is typically to discuss a problem not related to the rape; the rape may be disclosed later as a result of the counseling process (Isley). Research is lacking on treatment strategies for men, primarily because of under-reporting, so little is known. More work needs to be done with this population.

While it is important not to stereotype the rape or sexual assault experience of any one member of a particular group, it is wise for the counselor to be aware of the different cultural beliefs that do exist. Armed with this information, the counselor is better prepared to assist the client with any such issues that might arise in counseling.

DIAGNOSTIC FACTORS/MENTAL HEALTH ISSUES

Specific Issues Related to the Topic

Riggs, Rothbaum, and Foa (1995) indicated that in the immediate aftermath of a rape, 94% of the victims had symptoms which met the Diagnostic and Statistical Manual of Mental Disorders, 4th edition, (DSM-IV) (American Psychiatric Association, [APA], 1994) criteria for PTSD; three months post-trauma, 47% of rape victims continued to exhibit symptoms indicative of PTSD (Riggs, Rothbaum, & Foa, 1995; Rothbaum et al., 1992). Other researchers found the incidence of PTSD in sexual assault victims to be 32% (Resnick, Kilpatrick, Dansky, Saunders, & Best, 1993), 57% (Kilpatrick, Saunders, Veronen, Best, & Von, 1987), 70% (Bownes, O'Gorman, & Sayers, 1991), and 80% (Breslau, Davis, Andreski, & Peterson, 1991). Symptoms must be present for at least one month in order to assign a diagnosis of PTSD. Otherwise, the counselor would want to peruse the criteria for acute stress disorder (ASD), which parallels the symptoms of PTSD with the exception that the duration is less than one month (APA).

Apparently, some women develop PTSD following a sexual assault, while others do not (Zoellner, Foa, & Brigidi, 1999). Moreover, Foa & Rothbaum (1998) reported that although the majority of victims meet the criteria for PTSD immediately following an assault, PTSD is seen in fewer than half of the victims after several months. Various risk factors have been identified as contributing to the development of chronic PTSD including type of rape (Koss & Harvey, 1991), delayed reporting and treatment (Stewart, Hughes, Frank, Anderson, Kendall, & West, 1987), minimal social support, history of maladaptive coping mechanisms (Matheny & Michels, 1989) and age of victim (Thornhill & Palmer, 2000).

Types of rape may be characterized by the relationship between the victim and offender (stranger vs. acquaintance), or the severity of the assault (degree of physical violence, number of assailants, threat-to-life). Comparisons between stranger and acquaintance rape found no significant differences in the levels of psychological distress (Hassel, 1981; Koss, Dinero, Seibel, & Cox, 1988). Mixed results have been reported on the extent of violence associated with sexual assault. Sales, Baum, & Shore (1984) found no effect of severity, but others report consistent associations between severity of the rape and victim reactions (Cohen & Roth, 1987; Gidycz & Koss, 1990; Resnick et al., 1993).

There is often a reluctance to report sexual assault for a variety of reasons. There may be a fear of retribution by the assailant, failure to conceptualize the assault as a rape, shame, guilt, or fear of public humiliation (Koss & Harvey, 1991; Matheny & Michels, 1989). Delaying reporting and treatment may exacerbate symptoms and lead to an increased risk of PTSD, as well as substance abuse, suicide, and other manifestations of psychological decompensation.

Because most rape victims feel isolated, a social support system can alleviate traumatic symptoms, while lack of support or equivocal support may foretell a poor prognosis (Barlow, 1993; Matheny & Michels, 1989). However, studies on the role of social support in the development of PTSD are inconclusive. Some studies provide credence to the view that positive social support facilitates recovery from sexual trauma, while others suggest that negative but not positive support is associated with improvement (Zoellner, Foa, & Brigidi, 1999).

Maladaptive coping responses are predictive of greater distress in response to rape (Matheny & Michels, 1989). Some of these responses are the result of preexisting mental health problems, while others include drug and alcohol abuse, and suicidal ideation (Koss & Harvey, 1991). Jones and Barlow (1992) suggested that biological vulnerability associated with other anxiety disorders may explain the development of PTSD.

Thornhill and Palmer (2000) contend that more psychological pain is experienced by married women of reproductive age than older and/or unmarried victims. However, others report that demographic variables are not predictive of post-trauma resolution (Koss & Harvey, 1991), and that middle-aged women suffer significant feelings of shame and worthlessness (Matheny & Michels, 1989).

Despite the lack of consensus regarding the development of PTSD in rape victims, there are clear indicators of risk factors which counselors can evaluate in individual clients. It appears that the prior history of the client and the presence or absence of adaptive coping mechanisms are important determinants of a positive or negative adjustment to the trauma.

Diagnostic Symptoms

Rape-induced trauma reactions will vary depending on the extent to which the individual was harmed, as well as the client's ability to utilize effective internal and external support. After a sexual assault, it is important to continually assess the client's mental status in order to differentiate between a normal reaction to trauma and ASD or PTSD (Foa & Rothbaum, 1998).

Moderate symptom severity is a normal and expected reaction to a major trauma, but most people will recover over time. Although they will remember the event(s), they are able to resume normal lives with adaptive social and occupational functioning. It has been postulated that these individuals are able to process the trauma effectively, a term described as "emotional processing" (Foa & Rothbaum, 1998, p. 73). Simply stated, emotional processing occurs when realistic and appropriate meanings are applied to the assault. The individual is able to attribute responsibility to the perpetrator, absolve herself from blame, and resume normal life activities without undue fear or anxiety.

When adequate emotional processing does not occur following a traumatic event, the client may develop a severe reaction which may include general anxiety, depression, social anxiety, sexual difficulties, PTSD symptoms, and ASD symptoms. Although all clients do not develop symptoms that meet the *DSM-IV* (APA, 1994) criteria for PTSD, counseling which addresses PTSD will often alleviate the other reactions as well (Foa & Rothbaum, 1998).

Because the diagnosis of PTSD cannot be assigned until symptoms have been present for at least one month, it may be necessary to assess the recent trauma victim for ASD. According to Barlow (1993), the majority of rape victims probably meet the criteria for ASD, and making this diagnosis may enable a victim to receive needed treatment immediately. Since some studies indicate that ASD is predictive of later PTSD (Koopman, Classen, & Spiegel, 1994), early treatment for dissociative or emotional reactions could facilitate reduction of symptoms and a return to a normal life for the client.

The *DSM-IV* (APA, 1994) diagnostic criteria for ASD and PTSD are found in Tables 1 and 2, respectively. An important component of both disorders is that the traumatic event which precipitates the symptoms must involve either actual or threatened death or serious injury, which is a widely reported response to sexual assault (Foa & Rothbaum, 1998).

The symptoms of both ASD and PTSD are nearly identical, each being characterized by re-experiencing, avoidance, and increased arousal. The salient difference between the two disorders is the time of onset and duration of symptoms. In order to confirm a diagnosis of ASD, the disturbance must occur within 4 weeks of the traumatic event. Conversely, PTSD symptoms must be present for more than 1 month, precluding this diagnosis until more than 4 weeks have passed following the trauma.

Re-experiencing of the event is often considered the distinctive feature of both ASD and PTSD (Calhoun & Resnick, 1993). Some ways in which the trauma is said to be re-experienced are recurrent and persistent recollections, distressing dreams or nightmares, flashbacks, dissociation, and psychological or physiological distress upon exposure to stimuli which are reminiscent of the event. Essentially any stimulus associated with an assault can trigger a flashback. For example, a women who developed an aversion to birds recalled that she could hear birds chirping as her assailant held a knife to her throat while he raped her.

Table 1 Diagnostic Criteria for 308.3 Acute Stress Disorder

A. The person has been exposed to a traumatic event in which both of the following were present:
  (1) the person experienced, witnessed, or was confronted with an event or events that involved actual or threatened death or serious injury, or a threat to the physical integrity of self or others
  (2) the person's response involved intense fear, helplessness, or horror
B. Either while experiencing or after experiencing the distressing event, the individual has three (or more) of the following dissociative symptoms:
  (1) a subjective sense of numbing, detachment, or absence of emotional responsiveness
  (2) a reduction in awareness of his or her surroundings (e.g., "being in a daze")
  (3) derealization
  (4) depersonalization
  (5) dissociative amnesia (i.e., inability to recall an important aspect of the trauma)
C. The traumatic event is persistently reexperienced in at least one of the following ways: recurrent images, thoughts, dreams, illusions, flashback episodes, or a sense of reliving the experience; or distress on exposure to reminders of the traumatic event.
D. Marked avoidance of stimuli that arouse recollections of the trauma (e.g., thoughts, feelings, conversations, activities, places, people).
E. Marked symptoms of anxiety or increased arousal (e.g., difficulty sleeping, irritability, poor concentrations, hypervigilance, exaggerated startle response, motor restlessness).
F. The disturbance causes clinically significant distress or impairment in social, occupational, or other important areas of functioning or impairs the individual's ability to pursue some necessary task, such as obtaining necessary assistance or mobilizing personal resources by telling family members about the traumatic experience.
G. The disturbance lasts for a minimum of 2 days and a maximum of 4 weeks and occurs within 4 weeks of the traumatic event.
H. The disturbance is not due to the direct physiological effects of a substance (e.g., a drug of abuse, a medication) or a general medical condition, is not better accounted for by Brief Psychotic Disorder, and is not merely an exacerbation of preexisting Axis I or Axis II disorder.

Note. From *Diagnostic and statistical manual of mental disorders* (4th ed.) (p. 431-432), by American Psychological Association, 1994, Washington, DC: Author. Copyright 1994 by the American Psychological Association. Reprinted with permission.

Table 2 Diagnostic Criteria for 309.81 Posttraumatic Stress Disorder

A. The person has been exposed to a traumatic event in which both of the following were present:
   (1) the person experienced, witnessed, or was confronted with an event or events that involved actual or threatened death or serious injury, or a threat to the physical integrity of self or others
   (2) the person's responses involved intense fear, helplessness, or horror.
   Note: In children, this may be expressed instead by disorganized or agitated behavior
B. The traumatic event is persistently reexperienced in one (or more) of the following ways:
   (1) recurrent and intrusive distressing recollections of the event, including images, thoughts, or perceptions. **Note:** In young children, repetitive play may occur in which themes or aspects of the trauma are expressed.
   (2) recurrent distressing dreams of the event. **Note:** In children, there may be frightening dreams without recognizable content.
   (3) acting or feeling as if the traumatic event were recurring (includes a sense of reliving the experience, illusions, hallucinations, and dissociatative flashback episodes, including those that occur on awakening or when intoxicated).
   (4) intense psychological distress at exposure to internal or external cues that symbolize or resemble an aspect of the traumatic event.
   (5) physiological reactivity on exposure to internal or external cues that symbolize or resemble an aspect of the traumatic event.
C. Persistent avoidance of stimuli associated with trauma and numbing of general responsiveness (not present: the trauma), as indicated by three (or more) of the following:
   (1) efforts to avoid thoughts, feelings, or conversations associated with the trauma
   (2) efforts to avoid activities, places, or people that arouse recollections of the trauma
   (3) inability to recall an important aspect of the trauma
   (4) markedly diminished interest or participation in significant activities
   (5) feelings of detachment or estrangement from others
   (6) restricted range of affect (e.g., unable to have loving feelings)
   (7) sense of a foreshortened future (e.g., does not expect to have a caeer, mariage, children, or a normal life span)
D. Persistent symptoms of increased arousal (not present before the trauma), as indicated by two (or more) of the following:
   (1) difficulty falling or staying asleep
   (2) irritability or outbursts of anger
   (3) difficulty concentrating
   (4) hypervigilance
   (5) exaggerated startle response
E. Duration of the disturbance (symptoms in Criteria B, C, and D) is more than 1 month.
F. The disturbance causes clinically significant distress or impairment in social, occupational, or other important areas of functioning.

Specify if:

Acute: if duration of symptoms is less than 3 months

Chronic: if duration of symptoms is 3 months or more

Specify if:

With Delayed Onset: if onset of symptoms is at least 6 months after the stressor

Note. From *Diagnostic and statistical manual of mental disorders* (4th ed.) (p. 427-429), by American Psychological Association, 1994, Washington, DC: Author. Copyright 1994 by the American Psychological Association. Reprinted with permission.

Persons with either ASD or PTSD exhibit avoidance of situations or circumstances which evoke memories of the trauma. They may avoid thinking about the event, and they become numb to their own emotions. One aspect of emotional numbing is a failure to enjoy sex. An inability to recall aspects of the trauma (such as the appearance of the perpetrator) is a common avoidance reaction, as are efforts to stay away from places or people that evoke painful recollections. Some victims have severe avoidance reactions, such as one woman who became agoraphobic for several years after being raped, and was unable to leave her house (Calhoun & Resick, 1993). Avoidance behaviors may create problems with interpersonal relationships, and may engender conflicts in the family, social, or occupational environments.

Symptoms of increased arousal which are evidenced by those with ASD or PTSD include sleep difficulties, irritability, trouble concentrating, restlessness, hypervigilance, and an exaggerated startle response. Irritability may evolve into hostility, which will have more negative consequences in relationships at home and at work. Difficulty in concentration may affect school work or job effectiveness. Restlessness, hypervigilance, and the exaggerated startle response can increase a woman's perception that something is physically wrong with her, escalating feelings of helplessness and hopelessness.

Women who meet the criteria for PTSD as a result of sexual assault commonly feel shame and guilt. They may also experience self-destructive and impulsive behavior such as promiscuity or drug use. In fact, individuals with PTSD are at increased risk for Panic Disorder, Agoraphobia, Obsessive-Compulsive Disorder, Social Phobia, Specific Phobia, Major Depressive Disorder, Somatization Disorder, and Substance Abuse Disorder (APA, 1994).

COUNSELING AND TREATMENT STRATEGIES

Counseling survivors of rape and sexual assault require immediate and long-term treatment strategies. Crisis counseling is necessary immediately following the rape, when the crime is being reported and the medical exams are being conducted. Once the initial crisis has passed, long-term strategies are needed to help the survivor successfully manage her emotional and physical reactions to the trauma. Long-term treatment methods for counseling survivors of rape and sexual assault lack broad-based empirical support concerning their effectiveness. Limited studies have been conducted on a variety of interventions designed to alleviate the symptoms of ASD and PTSD, but more thorough research needs to be done. The treatment strategies presented here represent those most strongly supported by the existing literature. It should be noted that none of these long-term approaches have consistently proven superior over the others in treating the survivors of sexual trauma. A crisis counseling approach will first be discussed, followed by the long-term intervention strategies of stress inoculation training, prolonged exposure, and cognitive processing therapy.

Crisis Counseling

Counselors at rape crisis centers are often the first professionals contacted by survivors. A series of steps needs to be followed in the immediate aftermath of a rape to insure the health and safety of the survivor, as well as the eventual arrest and prosecution of the perpetrator. Responding to questions from police and hospital personnel can be overwhelming during this time of emotional and physical distress. The counselor can assist the survivor in this process by providing important information and on-going support. What follows is a series of steps that the crisis counselor can utilize when contacted by the rape survivor.

1. Get to a safe place as soon as possible. If survivors are still in a dangerous area, they should immediately go to the house of a family member, friend, or neighbor, or go directly to the police station, the hospital emergency room, or the rape crisis center.
2. Do not disturb the evidence. Survivors should be told not to change clothes, use the bathroom, comb their hair, take a shower, brush their teeth, douche, or anything else that would destroy potential evidence until after a medical exam.
3. Seek medical assistance. Whether or not survivors intend to prosecute, they should be encouraged to get a medical and internal gynecological exam as soon as possible. Serious injuries, both internal and external, may exist, along with the possibility of contracting sexually transmitted diseases and/or becoming pregnant.
4. Report the crime to the police. Rape is a crime, and survivors should be encouraged to treat it as such. Most states require hospitals to report rapes to the police, and most police forces have trained female officers to handle the gathering of evidence. Rape crisis counselors often remain with survivors during the police questioning. Because police will often keep clothing as evidence, counselors may need to assist survivors in obtaining additional clothing.
5. Notify significant others. Encouraging survivors to notify family and friends who can provide immediate and on-going support is important. Because the experience of rape can be emotionally paralyzing, many survivors often enlist the help of counselors in initially contacting these people.
6. Encourage a follow-up counseling session. Counselors should schedule a time to meet face-to-face with survivors within a few days following the rape to discuss the physical and psychological responses to rape and the dynamics of the recovery process. However, many survivors want to forget about what has happened and will resist scheduling a counseling appointment right away. Counselors may then ask permission to call survivors in a few days or weeks to discuss the possibility of a meeting. If survivors continue to resist, counselors must, of course, respect their decision and wait for it to change.

Survivors who commit to long-term counseling care may then be exposed to any one or a combination of the following treatment strategies.

Stress Inoculation Training

The first comprehensive treatment model developed exclusively for counseling rape survivors was stress inoculation training (SIT) (Veronen & Kilpatrick, 1983). The goal of this treatment approach is for the client to gain a sense of mastery over her fears and anxieties by implementing a variety of coping skills. Applicable to both individual and group settings, SIT is divided into 2 phases. In phase 1, the counselor spends some time educating the client concerning the treatment philosophy of learning coping skills to alleviate intense fears and anxieties. The counselor also validates the client's fears and anxieties by informing her of the normality of such reactions to the traumatic event of rape. The counselor also explains that these reactions occur along three channels: physical, behavioral/motor, and cognitive.

In phase 2 of SIT the client is taught to utilize several coping skills aimed at reducing the fear and anxiety experienced in each of the three channels. In teaching a new coping skill, the counselor must first define it, explain what it can do, and then demonstrate how it is used by applying it to a problem unrelated to the rape. Once this exercise is processed and the client understands how it works, it is then applied to the rape-related problem. When addressing the fear and anxiety experienced in the physical channel, muscle relaxation and breathing control are most often used.

Muscle Relaxation

The Jacobsonian (**Jacobson,** 1938) tension-relaxation contrast training method is most commonly used to teach muscle relaxation. In the training sessions, the client focuses on relaxing all of her major muscle groups. The counselor then provides the client with a tape of the relaxation exercises that can be practiced at home.

Breathing Control

Breathing control exercises emphasize deep diaphragmatic breathing as a means to physical relaxation. The client is encouraged to practice this skill in each counseling session and at home.

To address the fear and anxiety that occurs in the behavioral channel, covert modeling and role playing are the coping skills typically taught by counselors.

Covert Modeling

In this exercise the counselor asks the client to imagine a frightening or anxiety-provoking situation. Once the client has a scenario in mind, the counselor then instructs her to visualize herself successfully confronting the problematic scene. Practiced often, the positive imagery gained as a result of this exercise can help her alleviate any fear or anxiety-provoking situations in the future.

Role Playing

In role playing the client and counselor act out new ways of reacting to old, problematic situations, thus teaching the client new ways of coping. The counselor and client take turns portraying the different characters in a feared or anxiety-provoking situation. Practicing the new behaviors gives the client a sense of confidence that helps reduce her fears and anxieties. This technique can also be utilized in a group setting in which group members act out several roles at once.

The coping skills of thought stopping and guided self-dialogue are best suited to calming the fears and anxieties experienced by the cognitive channel.

Thought Stopping

This coping strategy is designed to address the obsessive thinking patterns that develop in many survivors of rape and sexual assault. First, the client is asked to purposefully dwell on a troublesome thought for 30-45 seconds. Next, the counselor shouts in a loud voice "Stop!" Once this is repeated several times, the client is instructed to return to the thought and shout "Stop!" when ready. This process is repeated several times, then the client is asked to begin to silently verbalize the word "Stop!" whenever a troublesome thought begins to enter her awareness.

Guided Self-Dialogue

Using this approach, the counselor teaches the client to identify any irrational, maladaptive, or faulty self-statements taking place in her internal self-dialogue. She is then encouraged to replace these negative statements with more rational and adaptive self-verbalizations. For example, a client who experienced date-rape may irrationally conclude that she must somehow be partly responsible for what happened to her. This negative internal self-dialogue must be replaced with a more rational statement that acknowledges she is in no way responsible for the violent act that was committed against her.

The coping skills utilized by SIT are first practiced by the client on everyday, non-threatening stressors having no direct relationship to the sexual trauma (i.e., the pressures of a full-time job and single parenting). Once the client has gained a sense of mastery over the skills at this level, she is then encouraged to confront the trauma-related issues. Koss and Harvey (1991) modified their clinical approach to SIT by emphasizing the importance of establishing a trusting relationship with the client before proceeding with any type of treatment. Due to a lack of trust in others that has evolved since the crime, the client may be reluctant or unable to communicate with the counselor. Therefore, time must be taken to develop that sense of warmth, empathy and trust that is required for all working relationships.

Prolonged Exposure

A unique cognitive-behavioral approach, prolonged exposure (PE), was developed to specifically address the rape-related symptoms of PTSD (Foa, Rothbaum, Riggs, & Murdock, 1991). Prolonged exposure theorizes that rape-related PTSD results from the inadequate processing of rape stimuli, responses, and the meaning surrounding it. Therefore, PE requires the client to actively recall the rape memory until she is relieved of the painful intensity that the memory invokes.

Prolonged exposure is designed to be conducted in nine biweekly 90-minute sessions, with the first two sessions involving information gathering, treatment planning, and an explanation of the treatment rationale. The remaining sessions focus on having the client relive the rape experience in her mind and describe it vocally in the present tense. Initially, the client may be reluctant to remember or share the trauma in much detail. However, as counseling progresses, she should be encouraged to recall as complete a description of the event as possible, including what she was thinking and feeling. The counselor is to support her in this process and tape-record each session. For homework, the client is instructed to listen to the tape and process internally her thoughts and emotions. Because this is a highly-charged, emotionally stirring intervention, the counselor must be sure that the client is relaxed and calm before ending each counseling session.

Cognitive Processing Therapy

Resick and Schnicke (1992) developed a model for counseling rape survivors suffering from the symptoms of PTSD that goes beyond the memory processing approach of PE. Cognitive processing therapy (CPT) is designed to have the client vividly recall the rape and then directly confront any conflicts or maladaptive beliefs that might have developed as a result of the rape. In the first 2 sessions of the 12-session model, the client is asked to write a complete description of the event, including the important sensory information of thoughts and feelings. The client is then instructed to read the account aloud at home and in the counseling sessions with all the emotional intensity that can be recalled. The remaining sessions follow the cognitive restructuring method of providing corrective information regarding conflicts, faulty attributions or expectations, thus allowing the client to successfully process the trauma. For example, a client who was raped on her college campus may no longer feel safe attending classes and avoid returning to school to complete her degree. Therefore, CPT would first utilize its exposure component by encouraging her to recall the rape in written and verbal detail, and then move to dispel the faulty cognition that school is never a safe environment. A successful resolution would be to end her avoidance behavior, a classic symptom of PTSD, and return to school without fear and anxiety. In a controlled study, Resick and Schnicke found that CPT participants improved significantly on both PTSD and depression measures over a comparison sample waiting for group counseling.

Treatment planning typically involves the counselor putting together an intervention approach that most closely reflects his or her theoretical beliefs about what constitutes appropriate and effective techniques for the resolution of ASD and rape-related PTSD. **Foa and Rothbaum** (1990) suggested using exposure treatments, such as PE or CPT, if the client exhibits dissociative symptoms, such as numbing or cognitive avoidance; SIT is recommended for the client who is primarily experiencing chronic arousal and anxiety symptoms. And, for the client who appears to be manifesting the full spectrum of rape-related PTSD symptoms, it is suggested that the counselor incorporate both exposure therapy and SIT, beginning with SIT, in the treatment strategy.

Most treatment strategies can be used in a group or individual settings; the little research that has been conducted comparing the two settings is inconclusive. Self-help support groups that are offered by most rape crisis centers and mental health agencies are regarded as a helpful adjunct to individual counseling (Koss & Harvey, 1991). Among the advantages of group counseling are (a) reduction in feelings of isolation, (b) increased social support, (c) validation and normalization of feelings, (d) confirmation of the reality of the rape, (e) sharing of coping skills, (f) counter-action of self-blame, (g) increased self-esteem, and (h) decreased dependency (Koss & Harvey).

Group counseling can also be harmful in that it exposes the client very quickly to a wide range of intense emotions, both in herself and the other group members. The group experience may create over exposure for some clients, which may be burdensome and frightening. Therefore, the counselor must take special care to screen each client thoroughly to determine her readiness for such an experience. Clients who typically do not benefit from the group experience include those who have (a) substance abuse problems, (b) suicidal ideations, (c) self-mutilating problems with a diagnosis of borderline personality disorder, and (d) never disclosed the trauma to anyone or are having trouble remembering it (Koss & Harvey, 1991).

Selecting a particular treatment strategy can be difficult. The counselor must first understand the individual symptoms and circumstances of each client before proceeding in counseling. Many rape survivors wait years before seeking counseling, often presenting with the entire clinical picture of PTSD; others seek counseling immediately following the rape and are still in a state of shock and disbelief. Regardless of the time that has elapsed or the symptoms that are present, the counselor must proceed with the understanding that the client has experienced a traumatic event that has changed her life forever, and must now learn to live, not as a victim, but as a recovered survivor. Harvey (as cited in Koss & Harvey, 1991) describes the attributes of a client who has recovered from the trauma of sexual assault: (a) she has control over her memory, versus her memory having control over her; (b) her memory and feelings are integrated, one does not overwhelm the other; (c) her affect no longer overwhelms her; (d) she has control over feelings of anxiety, depression, and sexual dysfunction; (e) she is reconnected with others, and (f) she has assigned some tolerable meaning to the rape and to the self as a rape survivor. The counselor must work to build a trusting relationship with the client and provide a safe environment where she can begin this process of recovery.

CASE STUDY

The Rape

It is a stormy Friday afternoon, but Susan is happy to be leaving work until Monday morning. The single, white, 26 year old, energetic female has taken a position as a receptionist with an accounting firm, while she goes to college at night to finish her degree. Because she spends most of her time working and going to school, she is particularly excited about the date she has tonight. She met Jack a few weeks ago at school and has since enjoyed his company on a couple of other occasions. Her only concern is that he drinks a little too much, but decides not to worry in light of the fact that "no one is perfect."

Jack arrives 30 minutes early to find Susan just getting out of the shower. Dressed in her bathrobe, she invites him to fix a drink and watch TV or listen to some music while she finishes getting dressed. As she retreats to her bedroom, she wonders if he has not already been drinking, as evidenced by his bloodshot eyes and less-than-clear speech. But, she decides not to worry about it because, after all, "it is Friday night!"

As Susan stands before her bathroom mirror putting on her make-up, she senses a presence behind her. When she turns around, there stands Jack, totally naked. Startled and frightened, she demands to know what he is doing. He tells her that he thought it would be more fun to stay home tonight and "create our own excitement." Susan, nervous and panicked, tells him to put his clothes on and leave. To her horror, he just laughs, grabs her robe, forces her to her bed, and rapes her. Her screaming, crying, and pleading do nothing to discourage him. In fact, he threatens to kill her if she does not hush. Afterwards, he warns her not to say anything to anyone and jokes that it would simply be her word against his, with no one believing her. He also threatens to return if she talks. Fearing for her life, she remains silent. In the days and weeks following the attack, Susan drops out of school and moves back to her parents' home.

The Reaction

That was 11 years ago. Susan comes to counseling today still single, working as a receptionist, and living with her parents. She has tried, unsuccessfully, to date and return to school. However, both events remind her of Jack and the rape, creating extreme fear and anxiety. She has no friends outside of work, and never leaves the house alone. She tells you that "not a day goes by" that she does not think about what happened and complains of terrifying nightmares. She says she "snaps" at others for no reason, especially her parents. Once an energetic person, she says she barely has the strength to get out of bed each morning. She jokes that maybe she will stop going to bed, since she rarely sleeps anyway. Isolated, lonely and angry, Susan seeks counseling to help her overcome her fear of others. She says she has got to find a way to "get on" with her life.

Susan clearly meets the criteria for a DSM-IV (1994) diagnosis of Chronic PTSD. The life-threatening attack has left her emotionally paralyzed. She has experienced recurrent and intrusive distressing recollections of the rape for the past 11 years, including nightmares. And, whenever she tries to return to school where she met Jack or date other men, she becomes extremely distressed and gives up on doing either. Susan has refused to talk about the rape with anyone until now, indicating that she has tried to avoid the thoughts and feelings surrounding the attack. She is socially isolated, unable to develop friendships outside of work. She also has trouble sleeping and experiences irritability and outbursts of anger.

The Intervention

In treating Susan, the counselor first validates Susan's reactions to the rape as normal. Spending time with her and empathically listening to her concerns helps establish a safe and trusting relationship for the work that is to follow. Because Susan is having difficulty functioning on a daily basis, the counselor elects to first utilize SIT to teach Susan some badly needed coping strategies. Beginning with non-threatening events, the counselor teaches Susan to physically relax using controlled breathing and muscle relaxation. Next, the counselor teaches Susan how to react to troubling situations in ways that are calming through covert modeling and role playing. Finally, Susan is taught how to change her thinking about a fear or anxiety-provoking situation by practicing thought stopping and guided self-dialogue. Once Susan has mastered each of these coping skills, the counselor then moves to having her apply each one to the rape experience.

Because 11 years have passed, and Susan has never talked openly about the rape, the counselor concludes that her rape-related PTSD symptoms are caused from her inadequate processing of the traumatic event. Therefore, the counselor elects to utilize the cognitive-behavioral principals of PE and CPT as a strategies for helping Susan relive the night of the attack. First, the counselor educates Susan concerning this treatment philosophy and the need for her to vividly recall, both verbally and in writing, the rape, including the re-experiencing of all those terrifying thoughts and emotions. Susan is at first reluctant, but agrees to try. Remembering the details of the rape is no problem for Susan; putting them in writing and talking about them aloud prove to be very difficult, however. As Susan begins to recall the event, the counselor follows the CPT guidelines and has her confront many of her maladaptive beliefs. For example, because she answers the door in her bathrobe that night and did not lock her bedroom door, Susan feels that she is partly responsible for what happened to her. Also, since she had known Jack for only a few weeks, perhaps she should not have allowed him into her apartment, but should have met him out somewhere instead This, she reasons, would have "kept this from ever happening." In essence, she is imposing self-blame for what happened to her. As Susan processes these faulty beliefs, she begins to see the impact they have had on her life and how they have contributed to her feelings of shame and guilt. Once these beliefs are reconciled, Susan can clearly see that she is in no way responsible for what happened to her. And, she begins to feel better about herself, as her self-confidence and self-esteem increases.

Susan is also forced to realize the maladaptive beliefs she has developed concerning men. There is no mistaking the fact that Jack is a deplorable man. However, this does not mean that all men are evil, untrustworthy, and waiting to harm her. Gradually, through the use of her coping skills, Susan begins to gain control over these feelings and is able to date again. Using the same set of coping skills, Susan is also able to return to school. Her maladaptive belief that school is not safe because Jack had gone to school must be addressed in order for her to complete her degree and fulfill her life-long ambition of becoming a teacher. Although anxiety-provoking in the beginning, Susan stays with the treatment strategy and conquers her fears of attending college.

The Outcome

Susan spends 15 weeks in counseling, 3 weeks for the SIT component and 12 weeks for the cognitive-behavioral components (PE and CPT). Because Susan has not shared her date rape experience with anyone prior to now, the counselor decides against placing her in the group setting. In addition to the work she does with the counselor, Susan is required to complete weekly homework assignments. As recommended by the PE approach, Susan is instructed to go home and play the tape-recording of the session in which she is verbally re-experiencing the rape. As the tape is playing, Susan is asked to process internally any thoughts and emotions that are presenting themselves. Susan is also asked to take her written account of the rape home and read it daily, as CPT recommends, thinking through any thoughts and emotions that are troubling.

Susan is a success story. After 11 years she decides to seek counseling. She is also willing to do the hard work of recalling in vivid detail a crime that has been producing nightmares for many years. Susan is at first resistant to counseling. The counselor helps her to understand that avoidance is a coping skill she has developed over the past 11 years, but that it no longer serves her. Susan clearly wants help, but she does not want to confront the painful memories of the past, a common trait in someone with PTSD (Calhoun & Resick, 1993). In the end, Susan is able to think and talk about the rape without becoming overwhelmed with feelings of fear and anxiety. She no longer avoids talking about her experience, and, in fact, finds the courage to share it with others. Armed with her newly acquired coping skills, Susan eventually moves into her own apartment and starts a support group for survivors of rape.

SUMMARY

The threat of rape or sexual assault is a reality that women in the United States are confronted with daily. No matter what steps are taken to prevent such a horrible crime, she can never insulate herself from the possibility of it happening to her. As Koss (1993) stated, "Women truly have no safe haven from victimization because they are vulnerable both within and outside their homes" (p. 1062). Women not only fear the strangers on the street, but, with date, acquaintance, and marital rape, may also be afraid of those they know. Once a woman is raped, her life is never the same (Katz, 1993), and the healing process can take years. The trauma will be experienced through a host of physical, emotional and behavioral reactions. Some women report the crime and seek counseling immediately, and some wait many years, while others choose to live with their secret in silence. The counselor must understand where a woman is in her recovery journey to provide the most helpful assistance. For example, group counseling works well with women who can emotionally process what has happened to them. However, a group can be frightening and discouraging for a new client who has never talked about what happened to her (Koss & Harvey, 1991).

The treatments discussed in this chapter, SIT, PE, CPT, have limited support in the research literature. However, the empirical database remains insufficient regarding treatment strategies that are best suited for individual clients experiencing the wide range of ASD and PTSD symptoms. Clearly, more research needs to be done to assess intervention effectiveness in working with clients at different stages of recovery. The research concerning group counseling is also sparse and needs to be expanded. Finally, more research needs to be conducted on counseling special populations. Glaringly absent in the literature is data suggesting the best treatment approaches for women with different cultural and ethnic backgrounds.

Public awareness concerning the problem of rape and sexual assault in the United States has increased over the years due to the diligent efforts of victims' rights groups and rape crisis programs. Rape crisis centers can now be found in every state, offering immediate and long-term assistance for women. With increased public awareness and the strong support of community groups, the laws, policies, attitudes and beliefs about sexual violence are slowly changing. Eliminating sexual violence is the ultimate goal of all those who work with survivors. However, through program support and educational efforts, the immediate task of eliminating the myths surrounding rape and sexual assault is well underway.

REFERENCES

American Psychiatric Association. (1994). *Diagnostic and statistical manual of mental disorders* (4th ed.). Washington, DC: Author.

Barker-Collo, S. L., Melnyk, W. T., & McDonald-Miszczak, L. (2000). A cognitive-behavioral model of post-traumatic stress for sexually abused females. *Journal of Interpersonal Violence, 15*(4), 375-392.

Barlow, D. H. (1993). *Clinical handbook of psychological disorders* (2nd ed.). New York: Guilford Press.

Bownes, I., O'Gorman, E., & Sayers, A. (1991). Rape: A comparison of stranger and acquaintance assaults. *Medicine, Science and the Law, 31*, 102-109.

Breslau, N., Davis, G., Andeski, P., & Peterson, E. (1991). Traumatic events and posttraumatic stress disorder in an urban population of young adults. *Archives of General Psychiatry, 48*, 216-222.

Burgess, A., & Holmstrom, L. (1974). Rape trauma syndrome. *American Journal of Psychiatry, 132*, 981-986.

Calhoun, K. S., & Resick, P. A. (1993). Post-traumatic stress disorder. In D. Barlow (Ed.), *Clinical Handbook of Psychological Disorders* (2nd ed., pp. 48-98). New York: Guilford Press.

Cohen, L., & Roth, S. (1987). The psychological aftermath of rape: Long-term effects and individual differences in recovery. *Journal of Social and Clinical Psychology, 5*(4), 525-534.

Davis, G., & Breslau, N. (1994). Post-traumatic stress disorder in victims of civilian trauma and criminal violence. *Psychiatric Clinics of North America, 17*(2), 289-299.

Feagan, C. F. (1992). Rape trauma syndrome testimony as scientific evidence: Evolving beyond. *University of Missouri-Kansas City Law Review, 61*(1), 145-163.

Foa, E., & Rothbaum, B. (1990). Rape: Can victims be helped by cognitive behaviour therapy? In K. Hawton, & P. Cowen (Eds.), *Dilemmas and difficulties in the management of psychiatric patients* (pp. 197-204). New York: Oxford University Press.

Foa, E., & Rothbaum, B. (1998). *Treating the trauma of rape: Cognitive-behavioral therapy for PTSD*. New York: Guilford Press.

Foa, E. B., Rothbaum, B. O., Riggs, D. S., & Murdock, T. B. (1991). Treatment of posttraumatic stress disorder in rape victims: A comparison between cognitive-behavioral procedures and counseling. *Journal of Consulting and Clinical Psychology, 59*, 715-723.

Gidycz, C., & Koss, M. (1990). A comparison of group and individual sexual assault victims. *Psychology of Women Quarterly, 14*, 325-342.

Hackman, J. (*1995*). Henson v. State: Rape trauma syndrome used by the defendant as well as the victim. *The American Journal of Trial Advocacy, 19*(2),453-469.

Harney, P., & Muehlenhard, C. (1991). Rape. In E. Grauerholz, & M. Koralewski (Eds.), *Sexual coercion* (pp. 3-15). Lexington, MA: Lexington Books.

Hassel, R. A. (1981). The impact of stranger vs. non-stranger rape: A longitudinal study. Paper presented at the annual conference of the Association for Women in Psychology, Boston, MA.

Holzman, C. G. (1994). Multicultural perspectives on counseling survivors of rape. *Journal of Social Distress and the Homeless, 3*(1), 81-97.

Isley, P. J. (1991). Adult male sexual assault in the community: A literature review and group treatment model. In A. Burgess (Ed.), *Rape and sexual assault, III* (pp. 161-178). New York: Garland Publishing, Inc.

Jacobson, E. (1938). *Progressive relaxation.* Chicago: University of Chicago Press.

Jones, J., & Barlow, D. (1992). A new model of posttraumatic stress disorder: Implications for the future. In P. A. Saigh (Ed.), *Posttraumatic stress disorder* (pp. 147-165). New York: Macmillan.

Katz, J. H. (1993). *No fairy godmothers, no magic wands: The healing process after rape.* Saratoga, CA: R&E Publishers.

Kilpatrick, D., Edmunds, C., & Seymour, A. (1992). *Rape in America: A report to the nation.* Arlington, VA: National Victim Center.

Kilpatrick, D., Saunders, B., Veronen, L., Best, C., & Von, J. (1987). Criminal victimization: Lifetime prevalence, reporting to police, and psychological impact. *Crime and Delinquency, 33*, 479-489.

Kilpatrick, D. G., Veronen, L. J., Saunders, B. E., Best, C. L., Amick-McMullen, A. E., & Paduhovich, J. (1987). *The psychological impact of crime: A study of randomly surveyed crime victims* (Final report, grant No. 84-IF-CX-0030). Washington, DC: National Institute of Justice.

Koopman, C., Classen, C., & Spiegel, D. (1994). Predictors of posttraumatic stress symptoms among survuvors of the Oakland/Berkley, CA, firestorm. *American Journal of Psychiatry, 151*(16), 888-894.

Koss, M. P., (1993). Rape: Scope, impact, interventions, and public policy responses. *American Psychologist, 48*(10), 1062-1069.

Koss, M. P., Dinero, T. E., Seibel, C., & Cox, S. (1988). Stranger, acquaintance, and date rape: Is there a difference in the victim's experience? *Psychology of Women Quarterly, 12,* 1-24.

Koss, M. P., Gidycz, C. A., & Wisniewski, N. (1987). The scope of rape: Incidence and prevalence of sexual aggression and victimization in a national sample of higher education students. *Journal of Consulting and Clinical Psychology, 55,* 162-170.

Koss, M. P., & Harvey, M. R. (1991). *The rape victim: Clinical and community interventions* (2nd ed.). Newbury Park: Sage.

Koss, M. P., Koss, M. P., & Woodruff, W. J. (1990). Relations of criminal victimization to health perceptions among women medical patients. *Journal of Consulting and Clinical Psychology, 58,* 147-152.

Largen, M. (1988). Rape-law reform: An analysis. In A. Burgess (Ed.), *Rape and Sexual Assault* (Vol. 2, pp. 105-132). New York: Garland.

Louisiana Foundation Against Sexual Assault. (2000). *Acquaintance, date, and marital rape* [Brochure]. Independence, LA: Author.

Matheny, J., & Michels, P. (1989). Office counseling of rape victims. *The Journal of Family Practice, 28*(6), 657-660.

McCann, I. L., & Pearlman, L. A. (1990). *Psychological trauma and the adult survivor: Theory, therapy, and transformation.* New York: Brunner/Mazel.

Petrak, J. A., & Campbell, E. A. (1999). Post-traumatic stress disorder in female survivors of rape attending a genitourinary medicine clinic: A pilot study. *International Journal of STD and AIDS, 10*(8), 531-535.

Raitt, F., & Zeedyk, M. (1997). Rape trauma syndrome: Its corroborative and educational roles. *Journal of Law and Society. 24*(4), 552-568.

Resick, P. A., & Calhoun, K. S. (1996). Post-traumatic stress disorder. In C. G. Lindemann (Ed.), *Handbook of the treatment of the anxiety disorders* (2nd ed) (pp. 191-216). Northvale, NJ: Jason Aronson, Inc.

Resick, P. A., & Markaway, B. E., (1991). Clinical treatment of adult female victims of sexual assault. In C. R. Hollin & K. Howells (Eds.), *Clinical approaches to sex offenders and their victims* (pp. 261-284). New York: Wiley.

Resick, P. A., & Schnicke, M. K. (1992). Cognitive processing therapy for sexual assault victims. *Journal of Consulting and Clinical Psychology, 60*(5), 748-756.

Resnick, H., Kilpatrick, D., Dansky, B., Saunders, B., & Best, C. (1993). Prevalence of civilian trauma and posttraumatic stress disorder in a representative national sample of women. *Journal of Consulting and Clinical Psychology, 61*(6), 984-991.

Riggs, D., Rothbaum, B., & Foa, E. (1995). A prospective examination of symptoms of post-traumatic stress disorder in victims of nonsexual assault. *Journal of Interpersonal Violence, 10*, 210-214.

Rothbaum, B. O., & Foa, E. B. (1992). Exposure therapy for rape victims with post-traumatic stress disorder. *The Behavior Therapist, 15*, 219-222.

Rothbaum, B. O., Foa, E. B., Riggs, D. S., Murdock, T., & Walsh, W. (1992). A prospective examination of post-traumatic stress disorder in rape victims. *Journal of Traumatic Stress, 5*(3), 455-475.

Russell, D. E. H. (1984). *Sexual exploitation*. Beverly Hills, CA: Sage.

Sales, E., Baum, M., & Shore, B. (1984). Victim readjustment following assault. *Journal of Social Issues, 37*, 5-27.

Stewart, B., Hughes, C., Frank, E., Anderson, B., Kendall, K., & West, D. (1987). The aftermath of rape: Profiles of immediate and delayed treatment seekers. *Journal of Nervous and Mental Disease, 175*, 90-94.

Thornhill, R., & Palmer, C. (2000). *A natural history of rape: Biological bases of sexual coercion*. Cambridge, MA: MIT Press.

Veronen, L., & Kilpatrick, D. G. (1983). Stress management for rape victims. In D. Meichenbaum, & M. Jaremko (Eds.), *Stress management and prevention: A cognitive behavioral approach* (pp. 341-374). New York: Plenum.

Wyatt, G. E. (1992). The sociocultural context of African American and white American women's rape. *Journal of Social Issues, 48*, 77-91.

Young, K. (1993). The imperishable virginity of Saint Maria Goretti. In P. B. Bart & E. G. Moran (Eds.), *Violence against women* (pp. 105-113). Newbury Park, CA: Sage.

Zoellner, L., Foa, E., & Brigidi, B. (1999). Interpersonal friction and PTSD in female victims of sexual and nonsexual assault. *Journal of Traumatic Stress, 12*(4), 689-700.

Chapter 16

COUNSELING SEXUALLY HARASSED EMPLOYEES

Judith Morrison
Vice-President, ACT II Management

BACKGROUND

Introduction and Overview

Sexual harassment is not a new phenomenon, nor are the legal remedies against it. The Equal Employment Opportunity Commission (EEOC) established its present guidelines in 1980.What is new is the recognition of the need for training for mental health professionals to deal effectively with the psychological consequences of sexual harassment (Campbell, Raja, & Grining, 1999). Sexual harassment is an insidious concern in many areas of our lives, specifically in areas in which one person has power and authority over another person (Collins & Blodgett, 1981). Historically, the workplace was considered the main arena in which sexual harassment took place, but that is not the reality of the problem. Sexual harassment occurs in many other arenas that have power structures built into the roles of the organization or societal system; these arenas include the relationships with doctors, therapists, ministers, and teachers (Russell, 1984).

It appears that there are few environments that are safe from episodes of sexual harassment in our society today. This leads us to the question, "To Whom do people who are harassed most often turn to for help?" The research (Campbell et al., 1999) indicates that victims of sexual harassment often turn to mental health counselors for help. This response raises great concern because the literature also documents that mental heath counselors, as a group of professionals, are not well trained in the identification of episodes of sexual harassment, the legal process of filing complaints of sexual harassment, the criminal and employment consequences of the complaint process, the psychological consequences of harassment on victims, and most critically the therapy strategies that are necessary for working with the victims of sexual harassment (Campbell et al., 1999).

There is now increasing pressure for not only U. S. employers to adopt strategies to deal with sexual harassment but also for the mental health field to better train their counselors to deal with all aspects of the issue of sexual harassment (Fenley, 1988). The impetus for change comes from employment, legal, and societal sources. There is concern about economic efficiency, social equality, legal ramification, and international image of the U.S. as a world leader. In addition, the U.S. Supreme Court and EEOC have issued decisions, as well as federal guidelines, that impose an obligation to look at the issue of sexual harassment with renewed concern. There is an awareness that there is a need to develop the following: comprehensive educational programs on sexual harassment, methods of communicating about the prevention of sexual harassments, procedures for reporting incidents of sexual harassment as well as filing grievances, publication of clear consequences with discipline procedures for the sexual harassers, and effective methods for counseling the victims of sexual harassment.

Definition

The practice of sexual harassment (against men and women) is very prevalent in our society and the number of complaints filed with the U.S. Equal Employment Opportunity Commission (EEOC) and State Fair Employment Practice Agencies grew from 10,532 filed in FY 1992 to 15,628 filed in FY 1998 ("Sexual Harassment in the Workplace," 1999). Despite the increase in complaints, there continues to be confusion on a clear definition of sexual harassment and the behaviors that constitute harassment. In fact, sexual harassment is now being addressed as a form of workplace violence (U. S. Department of the Army, 2001).

The term sexual harassment was used for the first time in an article published in *The New York Times* on August 19, 1975 ("Sexual Harassment in the Workplace," 1999). The term sexual harassment has no clear, definite definition. Sexual harassment is generally defined as unwelcome physical or verbal conduct of a sexual nature in the workplace or academia. The most familiar context for sexual harassment is the workplace, however, this is not the only environment for sexual harassment. In employment, sexual harassment is defined as unwelcome sexual advances, requests for sexual favors, and other verbal or physical conduct that enters into employment decisions and/or conduct that unreasonably interferes with an individual's work performance or creates an intimidating, hostile, or offensive work environment (Havris, 1993). Sexual harassment is a form of discrimination, is illegal, and is damaging to the victim, the work environment, and the social community (Hotelling, 1991). In a more general context, "sexual harassment is most recently identified as a spectrum of exploitative behaviors in which power is misused and abused to victimize others" (Shrier, 1996, p. 25).

While these definitions reflect two of the most commonly accepted definitions of sexual harassment, it is important to emphasize once again that there is no precise definition of sexual harassment. With sexual harassment, as is true of other types of discriminatory behavior, it is not possible to list all the potentially inappropriate behaviors or actions that could be included in a general definition. This concept of an ambiguous definition allows sexual harassment to be defined by the situation in which it occurs. This openness of the definition was outlined by the Supreme Court's 1993 decision in Harris vs. Forklift Systems, Inc. "This is not, and by nature cannot be, a mathematically precise test" (U.S. Supreme Court, 1993).

Legal Overview

The Civil Rights Act of 1964 (the Act) makes it illegal to discriminate on the basis of race, color, religion, age, national origin, and sex. Title VII of the Act prohibits employers from, among other things, discriminating on the basis of sex with respect to compensation, terms, conditions, or privileges of employment. By definition, sexual harassment is another form of sex discrimination (Rubin, 1995). Sexual harassment was further extended from the work place to academic settings when a federal court decided in the case of Alexander v. Yale (1980) that "sexual harassment was a type of discrimination prohibited by Title IX of the Education Amendments of 1972" (Hotelling, 1991).

In actuality, under Title VII, there are two types of sexual harassment: quid pro quo (Latin for "this for that" or "something for something") and sexually hostile work environment. The hallmark of both types of sexual harassment is that the sexual behavior is unwelcome. "Unwelcome" means that the person did not invite or solicit advances; and this is determined by an objective standard and not the individual's personal feelings (Rubin, 1995).

Quid pro quo harassment refers specifically to work conditions that are contingent upon, or that involve the exchange of a job, job advancement, or tangible benefit for, express or implied sexual favors (Wagner, 1992). This type of harassment generally occurs when an individual is required to choose between submitting to sexual advances or losing a tangible benefit. An essential aspect of quid pro harassment is the harasser's power to control the employee's (the student's, the patient's or the client's) benefits. This type of harassment generally occurs in situation where one person has explicit power over another person. In order to meet a claim of quid pro quo harassment the following criteria must be met:

- The harassment was based on sex.
- The claimant was subjected to unwelcome sexual advances.
- A tangible economic benefit of the job (educational benefit or medical benefit) was conditional on the claimant's submission to the unwelcome sexual advances.
- It should be clearly understood that the acquiescence to sexual activity does not mean that the advances were not unwelcome.

In hostile work environment sexual harassment, continuous, frequent, repetitive offensive patterns, such as jokes, pictures, innuendoes, sex-role stereotyping, body part labeling by co-workers or clients, affect the conditions of the employment setting. The unwelcome conduct is so severe or pervasive that it changes the conditions of the person's employment and creates an intimidating, hostile, or offensive work environment (Rubin 1995), as well as a form of workplace violence. The work environment becomes so offensive that it adversely impacts an employee's job performance (Shrier, 1996) and/or affects the individual's reasonable comfort. In the case of Meritor Savings Bank v. Vinson, (U.S. Supreme Court, 1986), the U. S. Supreme Court found that a hostile work environment is unlawful sex discrimination even in the absence of the loss of tangible job benefit; this established the concept of the "chilling effect" (the fear of saying no because the harasser is the supervisor/the boss). This landmark court decision changed the arena for filing complaints of sexual harassment. In hostile work environment, the severity and pervasiveness of the actions are critical to the complaint process.

There are three criteria that must be met in a claim of harassment under hostile work environment:

1. The conduct was unwelcome.
2. The conduct was severe, pervasive, and regarded by the claimant as so hostile or offensive as to alter his/her conditions of employment.
3. The conduct was such that a reasonable person would find it hostile or offensive. The reasonable standard means that a reasonable person's work environment would be affected by the conduct. This statement of reasonable was later changed to state a reasonable woman standard. *(U.S. Circuit Court, 1991)*

Quid Pro Quo Harassment vs. Hostile Work Environment Harassment

What would be considered the differences between quid pro quo harassment and. hostile work environment harassment? There are criteria that set hostile work environment harassment apart form quid pro quo harassment. The hostile work environment must involve the following:

- Does not require an impact on an economic benefit.
- Can involve coworkers or third parties, not just supervisors,
- Is not limited to sexual advances; it can include hostile or offensive behavior based on the person's sex.
- Can occur even when the conduct is not directed specifically at the claimant but still impacts on his or her ability to perform the job,
- Typically involves a series of incidents rather than one incident (although a single offensive incident may constitute this type of harassment) (Shrier, 1996).

Behaviors That Constitute Sexual Harassment

According to the U.S. Merit Systems Protection Board (U.S. MSPB, 1994) report, the following behaviors constitute sexual harassment:

- Uninvited letters, telephone calls, or materials of a sexual nature
- Uninvited and deliberate touching, leaning over, or pinching
- Uninvited sexually suggestive looks, leering or gestures
- Uninvited pressure for sexual favors
- Uninvited pressure for dates
- Uninvited sexual teasing, jokes, remarks or questions.

The most significant aspects of these behaviors in the MSPB report is the dramatic percentage of men who felt and expressed their concern that these behaviors when uninvited were forms of sexual harassment. There is a new awareness that harassment is not perpetrated solely against women, but against men, children, students, patients, and clients. Additionally, it has become clear and has been adjudicated by the Supreme Court (Oncale v. Sundowner

Offshore Services, 1998) that sexual harassment can occur between members of the same-sex, and that this same-sex harassment is also illegal.

The Prevention of Sexual Harassment Policy

An appropriate policy that takes a proactive stand on preventing sexual harassment would include the following elements:

1. A clear statement that sexual harassment is illegal and will not be tolerated.
2. A clear definition of sexual harassment, including examples of quid pro quo and hostile work environment harassment.
3. A description of the behaviors that constitute sexual harassment.
4. The procedures for filing a complaint, including a statement that the incidents of harassment should be reported immediately.
5. A statement that complaints will be taken seriously and investigated immediately.
6. The procedures that should be followed in the investigation of a complaint.
7. A clear statement regarding the policy that retaliation for filing a complaint will not be tolerated.
8. A statement of the penalty for violating the policy.
9. A specific statement that reinforces that anyone found guilty of harassment will be disciplined appropriately. (Jones, 1996)

CULTURAL/GENDER CONSIDERATIONS

Victims of Sexual Harassment

Historically, the primary victims of sexual harassment were women. However the statistics are beginning to change. It is now estimated that up to 80% of working women will experience sexual harassment during their employment history and up to 15% of men will experience this type of harassment (Lumina Productions, 1999). Presently, men file 1 in 8 sexual harassment claims (Employers Publications, 1999).

These overall categories need to be broken down by gender into more specific groups that are harassed. Sexual harassment is now extending to child and adolescent sexual harassment, harassment in all levels of academia, and in the medical arena. This last category is extremely important because of the incidents of sexual harassment in the counseling relationship, even with the specific code of ethics established by the American Counseling Association.

Child and Adolescent Harassment

The Wall Street Journal (1999) reported that a survey conducted by *Teen People Magazine* revealed that 47% of their 1,000 teenage girl sample stated that they have been touched against their will at work. This number is frightening not only because of the rampart nature of existence of incidents of sexual harassment, but also because of the long term impacts of this harassment experience.

Lamb (1986) explained that teenage girls are still completing the following psychological tasks: separation, the development of a sense of separateness from parent; individualization, becoming her own distinct person separate from the family members; identity formation, finding a sense of the person she is and the person she would like to be; achieving intimacy, a process that allows her to develop closeness and exchanges confidences with selected peers and adults; developing a sense of mastery and confidence; and developing an understanding with control of her impulses. As Shrier (1996) wrote "The existence of chronic sexual harassment has the potential to have serious implication for adolescent girls' ability to negotiate this difficult period [and complex tasks], thus causing them to make limited choices and closes off their opportunities " (p.189). Additionally, sexual harassment also infringes on the full cultural development of adolescent girls. When sexual harassment is not curtailed and eliminated, the tolerance of the harassment perpetuates a social norm that women (girls) are second-class citizens (Shrier, 1996).

Sexual Harassment in Academia

Title IX of the Civil Rights Act of 1964 clearly prohibits sexual discrimination in education. As previously discussed, sexual harassment is a form of sexual discrimination. Further restrictions to the practice of sexual harassment in educational settings were strengthened with the 1972 Education Amendment which forbids discrimination by education programs receiving federal funds. The U.S. Court of Appeals in 1980 went further in explicitly adopting the EEOC guidelines for sexual harassment and extending them to the academic community (Jones, 1996). As presented by Shrier (1996) "The National Advisory Council on Women's Educational Programs defines sexual harassment as 'the use of authority to emphasize the sexuality or sexual identity of the student in a manner which prevents or impairs that student's full enjoyment of educational benefits, climate or opportunities'" (p. 204).

Shrier (1996) presented the following recent Harris Survey results. Approximately 80% of public school students in grades 8-11 experience some form of sexual harassment. These figures reflect 85% of girls and 75% of boys experience harassment (American Association of University Women, 1993). The literature (e.g., Charney & Russell, 1994; Dziech & Weiner, 1988; Roscoe, Goodwin, Repp, 1987) suggests that at the college level, 20-30% of the females 12% of the men experienced some form of sexual harassment. Stein (1986, 1991) wrote that sexual harassment behaviors, such as teasing about their developing bodies (especially about early development), name-calling, and gestures referring to weight and breast development, are extremely common in schools. These behaviors are most often targeted at girls, and generally go unrecognized by parents and school administrators. Sexual harassment has very specific impacts on the psychological development of adolescent girls (Shrier, 1996).

Sexual harassment in academia is not limited to the relationship between the academic staff and their students. Sexual harassment exists in all the relationships and organizational structures in which a power hierarchy comes into play. There are instances of harassment of junior faculty by senior faculty and harassment of faculty by students. Harassment of faculty by students generally occurs between female faculty and male students. This phenomenon is a by-product of our society's traditional socialization process. Shrier (1996) explained that the women in our culture who do possess power and hold positions of power are viewed as women first and powerful second, which results in the existence of lessened power. Bensen and Thomson (1982) named this type of sexual harassment, where a person in a lower position (a student) harasses a person of higher power (a professor) in the academic arena as contra-power sexual harassment.

Sexual Harassment in Medical Arena

Sexual harassment occurs in the medical environment on many different levels. Harassment occurs at all stages in the education, training, and workplaces of the medical field (Shrier, 1996). Harassment also occurs between patients and physicians when patients cannot receive treatment in a gender-safe environment.

In 1989, the American Medical Association adopted the EEOC guidelines to inform students, residents, faculty, and all employees in the medical workplace about their legal rights. In 1991, the American Psychiatric Association (APA) issued the following statement:

> The APA opposes and condemns all forms of harassment in the workplace, and further votes to advocate and lobby for legislative and judicial action to recognize,and facilitate any necessary treatment for victims of workplace harassment (APA, 1991).

Although many medical students experience harassment during their education, to date, the greatest number of reported complaints relate to women patients who experienced harassment from residents, attending physicians, and practicing physicians. While the behaviors that constitute sexual harassment according to EEOC guidelines, which apply to the medical arena, have already been identified, it is important to also look at the behaviors that could constitute sexual harassment in the process of providing medical services. These behaviors may be somewhat different due to the context in which medical services occur:

- Looking at a patient's anatomical parts during conversation instead of developing and making eye contact.
- Physicians who, uninvited, touch a pin on a person's jacket, perhaps the necklace on a patient, the patient's hair, earring; or pat the person on the thigh or another body parts.
- The use of sexist and sexually suggestive, often obscene language, slides, jokes, comments, riddles, limericks at work, in the teaching room, or the medical rounds or in clinics, in the explanation of medical conditions and possible treatments.
- Faculty, attending physicians, community physicians, and pre-clinical faculty who, uninvited and against another person's wishes, touch, fondle, and assault on the operating tables, in the laboratories during procedures, in lounges while providing medical information, and in call rooms while assigning rotations schedules to other medical personnel or scheduling medical procedures for patients. (Schrier, 1996)

Counselors may not be aware of all the behaviors in the medical arena that are considered sexual harassment according to EEOC guidelines. Counselors must gain a full understanding of these behaviors in order to help clients recognize and acknowledge harassment, as well as facilitate the process of clients learning to live with the experience of sexual harassment.

Sexual Harassment in the Courts

Schafran (1989, 1990, 1995) reported that female members of the legal system are accorded less credibility than men in the courtroom and, in addition, women attorneys, litigators, and witnesses are often the victims of unwanted and unprofessional behavior by judges, court personnel, and male counsel. This disrespect and inappropriate behavior takes a variety of forms such as sexual jokes and innuendoes or failing to call professional women by their professional titles instead of their surnames. These incidents of sexual harassment not only create emotional, psychological, and financial harm but also affect the judicial decision-making process and jury verdicts.

An individual who files a complaint of sexual harassment and enters the legal process is often re-victimized by judicial process. When counselors serve as witnesses in sexual harassment cases, they must be vigilant in ensuring that they do not become a player in this type of harassment.

Same Sex Harassment

A question that has been raised in the past is: Can there be sexual harassment between the people of the same sex? No matter what someone personally thinks or what the organization thinks, this year the U.S. Supreme Court answered this question and in doing so resolved a conflict among several federal appellate courts. In Oncale vs. Sundowner Offshore, Inc. (118 S. Ct. 998), the court ruled that the employers may be held liable for same-sex harassment under Title VII of the Civil Rights Act of 1964 (Marin, 1998).

Minorities Who Experience Sexual Harassment

Members of many minorities group are at an increased risk of experiencing sexual harassment (De Four, 1990; Schrier, 1996). There are very specific issues that arise for the minority victims of sexual harassment. As Shrier (1996) explained when the victim and the harasser are both members of the same racial, ethnic, or sexual orientation group difficulties arise. Victims may feel a group pressure to keep silent, and handle the matter within their own group, as opposed to filing a formal complaint thus exposing the group to public scrutiny and perhaps even reinforcement of negative stereotyping. For many victims, there is also a reluctance to expose a member of their own group to racism, ethnic slurs, and homophobic attitudes in the legal system. In addition, some minority women, due to their socialization process, are unsure whether to call the inappropriate behavior sexual harassment or racial discrimination (Shrier, 1996).

In some cultures, such as the Hispanic culture, which still adheres to traditional, rigid and perhaps polarized sex roles, a female victim of sexual harassment may be reluctant to report the incident. The exposure of the "sexual" incident may cause the girl to be viewed as dishonored, impure, and an embarrassment to her family. In fact, the actual revealing of the incident(s) of sexual harassment may cause the victim to be re-victimized by her own culture.

Fear prevents some minorities from reporting incidents of sexual harassment. Illegal aliens do not report incidents of sexual harassment for fear that the complaint processes will reveal their illegal employment status. Homosexual men and women may not report incidents of sexual harassment for fear of having their specific sexual orientation revealed.

DIAGNOSTIC FACTORS/MENTAL HEALTH ISSUES

Generally, sexual harassment is not a one-time incident, therefore, how the counselor approaches the therapeutic process may be influenced by recognizing and understanding the response stages that a victim experiences following an incident of harassment. Schrier (1996) delineated four stages of response to sexual harassment:

Stage 1: Confusion/self-blame/denial.
>With each incident, the victim hopes that the harassment will stop. When the harassment continues, it often leaves the victim feeling out of control and helpless.

Stage 2: Fear/anxiety.
>As the duration of the harassment continues, the victim feels trapped and becomes "paranoid." The victim begins to lose concentration, motivation, has lowering of work performance, misses work and has a general decline in self-esteem.

Stage 3: Depression/anger.
>Once the reality of the harassment settles in for the victim, the victim's general sense of anxiety changes to depression and anger. This anger triggers the beginning of the victim's taking back control of his/her life, but it is also accompanied by the victim leaving the work site, filing a formal protest and having increased feelings of self-doubt, and lowered self- esteem.

Stage 4: Disillusionment.
>The victim often finds that the organization does not respond with compassion and understanding to the disclosure of sexual harassment. The victim experiences sadness about his/her expectations of fairness, loyalty and justice. It is this realization that justice may not prevail, that may begin the development of effective and ineffective coping mechanisms for the victim.

Hotelling (1991) further suggested that there are three types of responses to sexual harassment: emotional responses, physical responses, and behavioral responses.

Emotional Responses

Some victims initially react to incidents of sexual harassment with denial of its occurrence. This reaction is part of the process of loss and change that a victim must process in order to survive the incident. The losses are internal and external losses (Shrier & Hamilton, 1996). The internal losses are losses of: self-esteem, self-confidence, trust in people (specifically men), and perhaps even a sense of loss of safety at the workplace. The external losses include loss of job, income, economic security, job opportunities, mentoring relationships, interpersonal relationships, and opportunities for special training and education.

Other victims react with disbelief, shock, and self blame (Dziech & Weiner, 1988). Additionally, victims can exhibit emotional responses of sadness, negative outlook, irritability, mood swings, impulsivity, hurt, depression, feeling of being trapped, emotional flooding, anxiety, fear of loss of control, excessive guilt, shame, obsessive thoughts, feelings of helplessness, and humiliation. The emotional responses are consistent with the emotions exhibited in situations of posttraumatic stress syndrome. (Schrier, 1996).

In addition, there can even be victims who are ambivalent about the incident or feel sympathy for the harasser (Dziech & Weiner, 1988). Jensen and Gutek (1982) found that women with traditional sex-role beliefs were most likely to blame themselves and other women. This was consistent with the information previously discussed on minorities as victims of sexual harassment.

Shrier (1996) reported a wide range of psychiatric disorders associated with sexual harassment experiences. The disorders include: DSM-IV (American Psychiatric Association, 1994), Code V diagnoses associated with marital, occupational, interpersonal, or bereavement issues. The disorders are commonly anxiety disorders (generalized anxiety disorder and post traumatic stress disorder), sleep disorders, depression disorders, and adjustment disorders.

Physical Responses

There are many physical responses and problems related to sexual harassment. Hotelling (1991) explained how the basis of these physical problems might be the emotions and feelings related to the incident of sexual harassment that have gone unexpressed. The physical symptoms that have been diagnosed as potentially resulting from sexual harassment are: insomnia, headaches, gastrointestinal problems, jaw tightening, neck and back aches, teeth grinding, dizziness, nausea, diarrhea, muscle spasms, pulse changes, weight loss, tiredness, increased perspiring, loss of appetite, binge eating, decreased sex drive, delayed recovery from illnesses and surgery, sleep disruption, increased respiratory and urinary tract infections, eczema, and recurrence of chronic illness (Alagna, King, & Lloyd, 1987; Himelein, Vogel, & Wachowiak, 1994; Hotelling, 1991; MacKinnon, 1979; Schrier, 1996).

Behavioral Responses

Fear, shame, guilt, and a lack of knowledge prevent some victims from reporting incidents of sexual harassment. These victim often develop behavioral coping mechanism that make them feel safer (Dziech & Wiener, 1984; Hotelling, 1991; Lenhart, 1991, 1996; Schrier, 1996). These behaviors often involve making themselves less attractive and appearing asexual by dressing down; avoidance of situations in which they could be alone, isolating themselves, keeping doors open; displacing anger at supportive people by yelling or even initiating impulsive accusations and litigation; and sudden and impulsive behavior such as precipitously leaving work or the academic setting in which the harassment occurred.; or the other extreme chronic ambivalence that can lead to self-doubt and the inability to make a decision.

Themes to be Addressed in the Counseling Process

There is no absolute answer to what is the best approach to use when counseling victims of sexual harassment. There is, however, some consensus on common themes that must be addressed in the counseling process (McCourt, Peel, & O'Carrol, 1998). McCourt et al. discussed the following themes that need to be addressed in sexual harassment counseling as they relate not only directly to the victim/survivor of sexual harassment, but also to the secondary victims of secondary harassment. The secondary victims of sexual harassment are the families, significant others, trusted persons, and co-workers.

There are four major themes that have to be addressed (McCourt et al., 1998) in counseling victims of sexual harassment. The first theme relates to trust issues, including the betrayal of trust that leads to self doubt. The second theme is the telling of the story over and over again until the victim has the story revealed enough times both in content and feeling to diffuse the emotions contained in the incident and move on. The third theme is the questioning of self with perhaps a sense of guilt. Guilt generally accompanies the loss and bereavement that is experienced in incidents of sexual harassment. Additionally, in working with feelings of guilt there is also a need for reality testing. The fourth theme is anger. Anger needs to be identified and appropriately focused, as it is often intense, unfocused, and inappropriately placed during the recovery after incidents of sexual harassment.

There are other common themes that must also be addressed during the counseling process (Alagna et al., 1987; Schier, 1998). These themes include powerlessness and isolation, depression, assertiveness and being in control, health issues, financial implications, work and career goals, sexual activity, and family support. These themes are complex issues impacted by additional variables such as gender of victim (Alagna et al., 1987; Collins & Blodgett, 1981; Ketring & Feinauer, 1999); history of the victim (Alagna et al., 1987); economic levels of the victim (Ingram, Corning, & Schmidt, 1996); and personality factors (Crow, Hartmen, Hammond, & Fok, 1995).

In order to better understand the themes, some are developed in more detail below.

- *Powerless and Isolation.* Victims feel that they are alone; "This has never happened to anyone else, no one will every understand, and there is something wrong with me." (Byerly, 1992).
- *Depression.* It is a normal reaction to feel depression as a part of grief (McCourt et al., 1998). Counselors must be alert, however, to signs of severe clinical depression. If the victim has no family or support system or if the victim is a member of a minority group, then the sense of hopelessness can be enhanced.
- *Assertiveness and Being in Control.* Counselors must facilitate the re-constructing of a victims self esteem and view of his/herself. This re-constructing is the initial stages of the transition from victim to survivor.

- *Health.* Stress creates health issues. The stress of sexual harassment can be reflected in new and chronic health symptoms. Counselors have to recognize the relationship between physical symptoms such as shingles, headaches, and incidents of sexual harassment.
- *Financial.* Sexual harassment has financial implications for the individual who has experienced the harassment, the harasser, and the organization. The crisis intervention role of the counselor often focuses on helping the victim to make effective decisions regarding the "handling" of the incident. The decision could have financial impacts, such as loss of income due to decision to leave the job to be away from the harasser or the overuse of sick leave due to the stress resulting from the reporting of the incident of sexual harassment.
- *Work and Career.* Sexual harassment cuts short an individual's opportunities for work and career advancement. Counselors must be aware that sexual harassment closes doors of employment through fear and retaliation.
- *Sexual Activity.* It is common for victims of sexual harassment to have difficulty with sexual relations. The misuse of power and lack of control are issues that often generalize from the incident of sexual harassment to an individual's sexual activity. Counselors may need to engage in counseling strategies that focus on creating a power balance in physical relationships.
- *Family Support.* According to McCourt et al. (1998), families tend to play three different roles in the recovery process for victims of sexual harassment. Some families are very supportive after incidents of sexual harassment, and other families are not supportive and can actually be critical, and some families actually place blame on the victim with beliefs like, "You must have known" (McCourt et al., p. 291). The counselor must be ready to provide nonjudgmental listening.

COUNSELING AND TREATMENT STRATEGIES

Changing Roles

The counselor has to play multiple roles at different stages of the therapeutic relationship and process. These phases and roles range from crisis intervention to problem solving techniques to being legal witnesses in the courtroom. All of the roles are relevant to the effective and successful therapeutic process. What is of significant importance is the change in the roles that counselors must play in the area of sexual harassment. The counseling relationship is no longer based solely on two-way communication and the building of a helping relationship process. Due to imposed legal constraints and long term psychological consequences for the victims of sexual harassment, the need has emerged for specific functions and tasks for the counselor to perform in the "world of sexual harassment." The counseling process is not left entirely to the discretion of the counselor; there is a two-part dimension to the relationship. There is the subjective part of the process, which is the traditional open and reflective relationship built on the needs and concerns of the client and the relationship building/story telling process with the counselor. And, there is the objective part of the counseling process, which is the product (outcome) dimension of the counseling process. The objective part of the counseling process must be addressed due to legal constraints, court mandated client referrals, and legal processes. The objective tasks include testing and assessment, expert witness, and litigation consulting (Friedland & Friedland, 1994).

Crisis Intervention

The first role that the counselor plays in the counseling process for victims of sexual harassment is crisis intervention. The counselor provides a safe environment and an opportunity for the victim to talk about "what has happened." An active, crisis intervention approach assists both the victim and the practitioner in assessing the nature of the crisis and the victim's response, in identifying and initiating effective coping mechanisms, and in exploring as well as anticipating stressors (past and future). This initial crisis intervention can also lead to identification and implementation of internal and external sources of support (Shrier, 1996).

One of the initial challenges for the counselor will be the recognition of sexual harassment (Himelein et al., 1994) due to the "apparent invisibility" (Kluft, 1989) of sexual harassment. The counselor helps the client identify and explore the incidence of harassment, and gain the strength to stop the harassment. The telling of the story often releases the burden of holding the secret. The counselor can serve as a role model and knowledge source to practice the communication skills and behaviors that are necessary to stop the harassment. Stopping the harassment can ultimately empower the victim to become a survivor and address the harasser. In this crisis role, the counselor assumes the stance that the harassment did occur, and therefore, is an ally to the victim (Shrier, 1996).

A second function of the crisis intervention role for the counselor is the initial diagnosing of the physical, psychological problems, symptoms, feelings, and behaviors of the victim. Responses of victims to sexual harassment are varied (Alagna et al., 1987; Bernstein. & Lenhart, 1993; Charney & Russsell, 1994; Hotelling, 1991; McCourt et al., 1998; Shrier; 1996).

Problem-Solving Role

Some of the therapeutic approaches to counseling the victims of sexual harassment involve the counselor playing a problem-solving role in the counseling. The counselor uses investigative methods to gain base line information to initiate a problem identification and solving orientation for the client (Spratlen, 1988). The investigative methods includes the use of the assessment process, the gathering of information through asking questions, and the telling of the story to gain the necessary information to facilitate the victim moving into an active role in his or her recovery. This active role in the problem-solving approach builds competencies in the victim and acts as a buffer against the victim's feelings of self-blame, loss of self-esteem, and depression.

In the problem-solving role, the practitioner has to be knowledgeable on multiple therapeutic interventions to counseling. The appropriate approach must be used with the victim of sexual harassment or the victim could be re-victimized. The questioning and assessment process in counseling itself can be perceived as intimidating and frightening. In this problem-solving role, the counselor helps the victim set goals concerning health issues, employment issues, and legal issues.

Educator Role

The counselor serves as a source of legal and technical information about sexual harassment to the victim, the family of the victim, and any other significant person in the person's live. The counselor explains the legal foundation, Title VII, for sexual harassment, as a form of sex discrimination, and explains how the law applies to all potential victims of sexual harassment. The counselor also must be able to identify and understand the behaviors that constitute sexual harassment in all work, educational, medical and court environments. Often the counselor is the first person to whom the victim turns after the incident or inappropriate behavior that he/she may have experienced. In fact, the victim may not even know what he/she just experienced, may not know how to label it, or may even be afraid to "make public" what has happened. The counselor has to be prepared to facilitate the identification of behaviors of sexual harassment, know how to label the incident that the person has just experienced , be able to begin the counseling process with the victim, and be able to refer the person to the appropriate sources to initiate the complaint process.

Referral Source

The counselor may need to refer the victim to several sources for help. The first referral may be to the equal employment opportunity (EEO) counselor at the work site. This EEO counselor begins the exploration of filing a formal complaint of sexual harassment with an employer. The counselor may see the need to refer the victim to a private lawyer to ensure that the person's rights are being protected in a formal complaint of sexual harassment.

As the individual mental health process progresses, the counselor may refer the client to a psychiatrist or medical doctor for medication to help with symptoms resulting from the harassment. The counselor, through the initial assessment and evaluation, may have assessed that psychopharmacological treatment might be indicated, but leaves the final determination of such to a medically trained professional.

In addition, as the victim moves through the phases and tasks of the counseling process, the client may need to work with other people who have been victims of sexual harassment. Many times a victim needs to feel like he/she is not alone in the process of healing from the effects of sexual harassment. Group counseling can facilitate the helping process and the transition from the victim of sexual harassment to the survivor of sexual harassment. Therefore, the counselor should have access to on-going groups for victims of sexual harassment and should know how to refer the victim to the appropriate group (Shrier, 1996).

Finally, the counselor has to be knowledgeable in religious/spiritual and self-help resources for the victims. Some individuals prefer to use self-help books, self-help tools (poetry writing/ personal journaling), and videos to work through the recovery process (McCourt et al., 1998). Other victims turn to religious convictions to find a meaning for the experience.

Expert Witness

During the litigation of a case of sexual harassment, the counselor may be called into court to provide expert testimony on many aspects of sexual harassment. The counselor's testimony in a deposition or a courtroom is generally based on a court ordered evaluation called a forensic evaluation. The forensic clinical evaluation has a different purpose than the standard clinical evaluation. The forensic evaluation is focused on asking questions that address the pertinent legal issues in the case. To conduct this type of evaluation, the counselor has to have a working knowledge of the legal standards embodied in the stature or case law in his or her particular jurisdiction. The expert recommendations must show relevance to identified legal issues of the case. The process of becoming an expert witness begins as soon as the counselor accepts a telephonic call from the attorney or from the court and agrees to become involved in the investigative part of the legal process. The role of the counselor then continues through the forensic evaluation, consultations with attorneys, report writing, and ends with providing testimony in the form of a deposition or direct testimony in the court.

Controversy exists about the possible impact of the court-mandated evaluations and where they should be part of the formal court testimony (Feldman-Schorrig & McDonald, 1992; Jensvold, 1993; Schier, 1996). Jensvold wrote that evaluations for sexual harassment in the workplace could be a misuse of the counseling process. Feldman-Schorrig and McDonald take the opposing position and they wrote, "Conducting forensic examinations properly can provide valuable material to bring into question the causation of a plaintiff's alleged emotional injuries"(p. 7). Schrier stated "that providing mental health input and psychiatric expertise to the bench and bar can represent another form of clinical effectiveness" (p.122).

No matter which side of the argument a counselor takes, it is paramount that the counselor be vigilant of not becoming part of the legal system to the detriment of the client. Counselors must remember that they play multiple roles in the area of sexual harassment. They provide court mandated forensic evaluations and serve as expert witnesses. At times, the roles may appear contradictory in purpose, but the overall objective of counseling victims of sexual harassment is to help the victims of harassment achieve a better understanding of their experience, develop effective coping mechanisms, move through the grief and loss process, become empowered as a problem solvers in the healing process, and "move on" with their lives. The expert witness should never negate the positive aspects of the counseling relationship.

Interventions Methodologies for Mental Health Counselors

Traditionally, sexual harassment training has centered on the work environment and how the environment could be changed. This orientation impacted on how the counselor could help the client. The counselor focused on crisis intervention   recognizing and stopping the harassment – while helping the client to continue to earn a living. Even though the workplace and employment concerns are still extremely relevant and crucial to the counseling process, the broader impact of sexual harassment is beginning to be addressed.

Only a few approaches to the therapeutic counseling process have addressed sexual harassment directly. Generally, all aspects of the sexual harassment, the prevention, the counseling, and the repercussions have been handled in the employment environment.

Therefore, the field of training counselors to deal with victims of sexual harassment in the mental health arena is relatively new (Campbell et al., 1999).

Counseling victims of sexual harassment begins with adherence to a fundamental model of mental health counseling with a specific approach to the counseling process. The model and approach are then integrated with the specific questions and steps that are necessary to complete all the roles required of the counselor in helping a victim of sexual harassment, as well as adhering to the legal responsibilities in such a case. The goals of effective treatment for victims of sexual harassment are similar to the goals associated with helping victims of all other gender-related sexual traumas. The goals and challenges to the counselor include helping the person to alter incorrect cognitions and re-construct effective thoughts and self talk; establishing appropriate affects and responses to past and present events; developing strategies to re-structure the power balance in the traumatic experience; and helping to cope with feelings of helplessness, shame, and vulnerability. An additional critical challenge is the confronting of maladaptive coping mechanisms that may lead to inappropriate behaviors, such as compulsive working; excessive use of alcohol; use of illicit drugs and misuse of prescription medications; and engaging in thrill-seeking behavior (Marmar, 1991; Marmar et al., 1993).

One effective approach to counseling victims of sexual harassment is the integration of the Capuzzi and Gross (1999) four-stage developmental model for the helping relationship. These four stages are: 1) relationship development, 2) extended exploration, 3) problem resolution, and 4) termination /follow-up. These stages, with specific models for behavior/stress/trauma experiences, set the foundation for the counseling process, but ultimately must be expanded and tailored to fit the needs of the victim of sexual harassment. Although the counselor may be working in a new arena of counseling, the effective use of these stages needs to be combined with Carkhoff's (1983) characteristics of an effective counselor. The counselor must exhibit a warm, approachable stance, be consistent, genuine, empathetic, and be an active listener.

McCourt et al. (1998) provided clear guidelines for the helping behavior of counselors. These behaviors were based on research conducted with secondary victims of sexual harassment. The behaviors include, active listening without judgment, availability of an accepting listener that reflects not formal training but the attitude of the trainer (being present and attending), modeling of composure and realistic decision making, informed referrals to appropriate support groups, providing of information when necessary and suggestions for self help like religious groups, keeping personal journals, and writing poetry.

The establishment of a caring, safe environment and relationship must begin at the very first session, the relationship development stage, because many victims of sexual harassment have had their basic trust in others severely damaged. In fact, it may be necessary for the counselor to actually discuss clear boundaries and prohibitions for a counselor in regard to physical or sexual contact with the client. These boundaries are ethical and moral boundaries, boundaries set by the American Counseling Association and other professional associations, and boundaries negotiated with the client to safeguard the counseling relationship and environment. This open discussion and commitment of adherence to these boundaries by the counselor acknowledge the client's sense of mistrust and fear regarding unwanted physical contact resulting from an incident of sexual harassment. Such a discussion may also encourage the revealing of the story of the incident of harassment. This up-front discussion is necessary to begin the process of creating a safe environment for two-way communication in the counseling relationship. Koss (1990) wrote, "[Practitioners], regardless of therapy format, can best serve their patients who have been sexually harassed by providing emotional support, a safe forum for expressing feelings, monitoring physical symptoms and coping behaviors, and engaging in specific problem solving" (p. 86).

The second phase, extended exploration, is the telling of the story to help release the feelings and thoughts related to the incident of sexual harassment. The telling of the story is handled with respect, care, and the ability of the counselor to suspend his/her own feelings, history, and perceptions about sexual harassment The counselor is attentive to the expressed and implied words, body, language, and demeanor of the client. The client may express many different feelings about what he/she thinks and feels about the incident of sexual harassment. Salisbury, Ginorio, and Remick (1986), and Shrier (1996) described the different emotional responses that victims of sexual harassment experience in regard to themselves, co-workers, managers, and the workplace. These emotions include confusion, self-blame, denial, fear, anxiety (feelings of being trapped and paranoid), depressed and angry, and disillusioned. These emotions must be expressed to start the healing process; the counseling session can provide a safe environment for expression. The expression of anger in the appropriate setting helps to prevent the expression of inappropriate anger targeted at the wrong person. During these first two stages, the counselor also establishes a preliminary treatment plan with the victim. The plan addresses confidentiality, length of counseling process, approach to treatment, and plans for possible litigation

The third phase, problem resolution, marks the transition for the client from a passive victim to an active person taking "back" control of her/his life. The counselor facilitates empowerment by exploring with the client the alternatives and options available, evaluating the risks and consequences of the option, and then determining an action plan with a time-frame for implementation. As previously discussed, the counselor must understand workplace policies on sexual harassment, the laws on sexual harassment, the process for filing a grievance or a complaint, as well as the potential consequences for "speaking out" about sexual harassment. The counselor should also be prepared to provide information about common emotional and interpersonal effects of sexual harassment.

The last phase, termination (follow-up), is the ending or the letting go of the counseling process. For victims of sexual harassment this phase is the point at which the victim has acquired the tools to move on with her/his life. It is the formal farewell portion of the counseling process. At the termination phase, the incident of sexual harassment should no longer be the defining junction in the individual's life. During the counseling process, the victim has acquired the self power to be a survivor and perhaps even enough inner strength to move into litigation against the harassers.

Specific Approaches for Counseling Victims of Sexual Harassment

There are some very specific models that have been developed for use in counseling victims of sexual harassment. Bernstein and Lenhart (1993) presented a six-step model for counseling victims of sexual harassment. These six steps could readily be incorporated as the tasks to be completed during the first three steps of the Capuzzi and Gross four-step model of counseling. The six steps are:

Step 1: Assessing the severity of the immediate crisis and validating the seriousness of the experience

Step 2: Evaluating the degree of depressive, psychosomatic, anxiety, and posttraumatic stress symptoms, both at the time of the patient's initial presentation and over the course of the treatment.

Step 3: Exploring and ventilating feelings of confusion/self-blame/denial, fear and anxiety, depression and anger, and disillusionment.

Step 4: Supporting Existing Adaptive Coping Strategies, Facilitating development of additional coping skills, and formulating a plan of action to reestablish a sense of control

Step 5: Assessing and protecting against potential losses or adverse consequences

Step 6: Dealing with losses.

The first two steps would be accomplished during the first stage of the Capuzzi and Gross model - relationship development. The third step would be included in the second phase of the Capuzzi and Gross model – extended exploration. And, the remaining three steps would be conducted during the third stage, problem resolution, of the Capuzzi and Gross model of effective counseling.

The final step of the Capuzzi and Gross model, termination, would be accomplished when the client is capable of deciding how to manage and bring closure to the crisis impact of the incident. Even when the counselor has helped the victim to prepare for closure of the counseling process, and the victim acknowledges that he/she is ready to move on, a reoccurrence of the effects of incident(s) of sexual harassment can still occur throughout the victim's life. Effective termination prepares the client for the cyclic nature of the recovery process and equips the client with the personal tools, internal and external support resources, and perhaps even organizational mechanisms to cope with the effects of sexual harassment.

Another counseling model that has been developed and used more specifically in the work place environment is the Morrison & Griggs (1996) Ten-Step Counseling Model for Work Behavior and Employment Counseling. This model reflects the specific components of the counseling process both on an individual session basis and in a larger organizational, employment context. These 10-steps can be seen as following the Capuzzi and Gross four stage model of relationship development, extended exploration, problem resolution, and termination/follow-up. However, while all the steps may be included in the Capuzzi and Gross model, they may be accomplished in a different sequential order. This difference in sequence is due to the context in which the model was designed and intended to be used (i.e., the work setting).

Step 1: Make a plan What has occurred?
Identification of problem with documentation of the issue.
Capuzzi and Gross- relationship development.

Step 2: Set a positive climate
Establishment of the relationship
Capuzzi and Gross- relationship development

Step 3: Elicit the client's story

Extended exploration of facts, feelings, thoughts, work context, and work consequences

Capuzzi and Gross- extended exploration

Step 4: Listen

The appropriate initial therapeutic and data gathering stance is to agree (and to convey the belief) that the harassment occurred essentially as described by the client

Capuzzi and Gross- relationship development

Step 5: Discuss and build on strengths

Capuzzi and Gross- extended exploration and problem identification

Step 6: Discuss problems and weakness

Capuzzi and Gross- extended exploration and problem identification

Step 7: Clarify what the clients tells and says are consequences

Capuzzi and Gross - extended exploration

Step 8: Agree on the problem and explore possible solutions

This marks the transition into problem solving and the client taking an active role in the recovery process

Capuzzi and Gross - problem solving

Step 9: Summarize the session, feedback and set goals

Capuzzi and Gross - beginning of termination phase

Step 10: Follow-up and evaluation

The "letting-go" by the counselor and the independence of the client

Capuzzi and Gross- termination phase

The Morrison and Griggs model adheres to the principles of the Capuzzi and Gross model. The incorporation of the principles of counseling with the procedures, regulations, and personnel/legal requirements of a work setting is important. The counselor has to be knowledgeable in these two areas and also be able to integrate these two sets of procedures and principles together to help the victim.

CASE STUDY

Ms. V., a 44 year old, intensive care nurse, was referred to therapy by her attorney for symptoms of anxiety and depression. Her symptoms were becoming worse as the court proceedings in regard to charges of sexual harassment that she had brought against the head physician in a major hospital were progressing. Ms. V. was recruited from a private home care nursing agency to head up the outpatient home care unit of the hospital. The recruiting physician was very helpful in the initial stages of the transition to hospital operated home care nursing.

About a month after Ms. V. began working, Dr. F., the administrative head of the department, began asking Ms. V. to have a working lunch with him alone in his office. Ms. V refused to meet him alone in his office, but offered instead to meet with him in the staff lounge or cafeteria. Dr. F. continued to press Ms. V. to have a private lunch with him. Finally, after Ms. V. persistently declined the lunch invitations, Dr. F. stopped talking to Ms. V. About six months later, it was time for Ms. V.'s performance review, and Dr. F., her reviewing supervisor, wrote a very critical performance evaluation with comments about her uncooperative approach to team work. Dr. F. had never counseled Ms. V. about any complaints or problems with her work. Ms. V. complained about her performance review, but Dr. F. informed her that she just was not a team player like some of the other nurses.

Another six months went by and there was an opening for a supervisory position. Ms. V. applied for the position, but was not selected by the selecting official, Dr. F. When Ms. V. asked for an explanation, she was told that if she would be more cooperative with the private working lunches that she would have a better chance of receiving a promotion.

After this incident of alleged sexual harassment, Ms. V. went to the Equal Employment Opportunity Office of her hospital and filed a formal complaint of sexual harassment. Ms. V. sought medical advice for her lack of sleep and took extended sick leave from her job on the advice of her medical physician.

As the complaint process was progressing, Ms. V. developed the symptoms of anxiety and depression. How would you approach counseling Ms. V. who was referred to you by her attorney?

Counseling and Treatment Strategies for Ms. V.

The initial step is to complete an assessment of the severity of the crisis situation for Ms. V. It is important to determine if the client's depression is so severe that she could be at risk of suicide. If she is at risk, suicide prevention techniques would immediately be put into place. Otherwise, once the initial assessment is made, although assessment continues throughout the counseling process, the practitioner works at building a trust relationship since the victim has experienced a breakdown in trust in other relationships in her work life and maybe even her personal life. A climate of trust allows the client to tell her entire story, with all details and description of the incidents of sexual harassment. The practitioner provides implicit permission that she/he believes Ms. V.'s story about the incident(s) of sexual harassment and is willing to listen to the story as often and in as much detail as she needs. The telling of the story is one of the steps in the transition of a victim to a survivor. This initial assessment and listening to the telling of the story are critical to the development of the counseling relationship.

Once the "facts" are disclosed, the client is often relieved of some of the burden of holding a "secret." The counselor creates a safe environment for exploring Ms. V.'s feelings with regard to the incidents of sexual harassment. Ms. V. might feel guilt and self-blame which can paralyze her. During the process, the counselor, who has fostered a relationship of trust, must help Ms. V. explore these feeling and any other feelings that emerge in association with the experiencing and disclosing of the incident of sexual harassment. These might include feelings of anger, isolation, depression, and a sense of powerlessness. The counselor might ask Ms. V. questions such as: Can you describe how you feel towards Dr. F? How do you feel now that you have told me the entire story of the incidents of sexual harassment? The counselor is also an educator of reality for Ms. V. and presents ideas such as: "You did nothing wrong, you were strong in your refusal to go to private lunches. You are a strong person to reveal the inappropriate and illegal behavior of the head physician. You are no longer alone in working through the effects of the sexual harassment."

At this point, the counselor can help Ms. V. develop both coping skills and empowerment skills so that she can begin to think about returning to work. Returning to work helps to minimize future economic losses and starts the client back on the road to being an empowered employee. The coping skills that could help Ms. V. are: an assertive style of communication, problem-solving techniques to explore how to proceed with the complaint process, and empowerment skills to request a transfer within the same hospital to a similar work setting with a different supervisor. These skills can also help to protect against further incidents of harassment and retaliation. The counselor might also find out the policy of Ms. V.'s workplace regarding the use and length of extended sick leave. One of the critical steps in the crisis intervention component of counseling the victims of sexual harassment is to help the client return to a safe work environment and not be in risk of future harassment and termination of her job – the source of livelihood and income. In helping with the transition to problem-solving behavior, and discovering what options are open for handling the complaint of sexual harassment, the counselor provides Ms. V. with information that is supportive of her during the work complaint process at the workplace.

Ms. V., who may be experiencing feelings of anger and revenge, should be discouraged from verbalizing uncontrolled feelings of anger as she begins her reentry into the workplace. She can be encouraged to develop assertive communication patterns that can increase her sense of control and self-respect and not display erratic behavior. Inappropriate conduct by Ms. V. at the workplace could have long-term detrimental impacts during the complaint process. The appropriate assertive communication patterns would involve the ability to say, "No" to anyone who wanted to openly discuss the incidents of harassment without Ms. V.'s initiative or permission, as well as "no" to inappropriate behavior.

In addition, it might help Ms. V. to practice the cognitive skill and ability to stay focused on the here-and-now and not revisit, in her mind, the incidents of harassment. Her ability to stay focused on the tasks of her job and not exhibit fearful, exaggerated behaviors and patterns at the workplace is important in protecting against future losses or adverse consequences at the workplace. A clear plan of how Ms. V. will reenter the work setting should be rehearsed in the safety of the counseling setting. The rehearsal of the return helps establish a sense of personal control.

A general sense of loss with any experience of sexual harassment will occur, and the counselor should help Ms. V. work through the loss and grief process. Patience and effective listening skills are essential. It is also important that Ms. V. learn coping skills that will help to provide some containment to the extent of the loss in the employment arena. Uncontrolled emotional outbursts and unpredictable behavior are not conducive to an effective workforce.

The final step that the counselor facilitates is the movement of Ms. V. from a victim to a survivor. This movement begins the termination phase of the counseling process. The task is to help Ms. V. decide how to manage and bring some closure to the crisis impact and long-term impacts of the sexual harassment experience. The incident of sexual harassment should no longer be the defining event of Ms. V.'s life.

SUMMARY

Sexual harassment is a widespread problem in our society. It is an illegal form of behavior, and it is also considered a form of workplace violence. Sexual harassment can result in great legal, financial, and social liabilities to an individual and an organization. But even more significant, sexual harassment creates emotional reactions and consequences that permeate an individual's entire life, as well as the entire workforce of an organization.

Sexual harassment occurs in almost every arena in which people interact with other people – the workplace, school environments, the medical arena, among others. However, until recently, the main focus of sexual harassment has been the prevention of sexual harassment only in the workplace. There is now a pressing need to address the consequences of sexual harassment at the organizational level, as well as the personal level. It is critical to train mental health providers with the skills and tools to help the "victim of sexual harassment" become a "survivor of sexual harassment."

REFERENCES

Algna, S.W., King, L.S., & Lloyd, C. (1987). The emotional consequences of gender-based abuse in the workplace: New counseling programs for sex discrimination. *Institute for Research on Women's Health, 6*, Washington, D.C., 155-182.

American Association of University Women. (1993). *Hostile hallways: The American association of women survey on sexual harassment in American schools.* Annapolis Junction, MD: Author.

American Psychiatric Association (1991). *Statement of Sexual Harassment.* Washington, D.C.: American Psychiatric Association Office of Government Relations.

American Psychiatric Association (1994). *Diagnostic and statistical manual of mental disorders* (4th ed.) Washington, D.C.: American Psychiatric Association.

Bensen, D. J., & Thomson, G. E. (1982). Sexual harassment on a university campus: The confluence of authority relations, sexual interest, and gender stratification. *Social Problems, 29*, 236-251.

Bernstein, A.E., & Lenhart S.A (1993). *Abuse of women, The psychological treatment of women.* Washington, D.C.: American Psychiatric Press.

Byerly, C. (1992). *The mother's book: How to survive the molestation of your child.* London: Allen & Unwin.

Campbell, R., Raja, S. & Grining, P. (1999). Training mental health professionals on violence against women. *Journal of Interpersonal Violence (14)*, 1003-1013.

Carhuff, R. R. (1983). *The art of helping* (5th ed.). Amherst, MA: Human Resource Development Press, Inc.

Capuzzi, D., & Gross, D. R. (1999). *Counseling and psychotherapy* (2nd ed.). Upper Saddle River, N.J.: Merrill.

Charney D. A., & Russell, R.C. (1994). An overview of sexual harassment. *American Journal of Psychiatry, 151*, 10-17.

Collins, E. G. C., & Blodgett, T. B. (1981). Sexual Harassment ... Some see it ...Some won't. *Harvard Business Review, 59* (No. 81203), 77-95.

Crow, S. M., Hartmen, S. J. Hammond, D., & Fok, L. Y. (1995). The impact of personality factors on sexual and non-sexual harassment sensitivity. *Women in Management Review, 10* (6). 9-20.

DeFour, D.C. (1990). The interface of racism and sexism on college campuses. In M.A. Paludi (Ed.) *Ivory power: Sexual harassment on campus* (pp. 45-52). Albany, N.Y.: State University of New York Press.

Dziech, D., & Wiener, L. (1988). *The lecherous professor: Sexual harassment on Campus.* Boston, MA: Beacon Press.

Ellison v. Brady, 924 F.2d. 872, 54 FEP Cases 1346, republished as amended, 55 FEP Cases 111 (9th Cir. 1991).

Employers Publications, (1999). Retrieved from: http://www.sexualharassmentpolicy. com/htm/new_problems.htm.

Feldman-Shorrig, S. P., & Mc Donald, J. J., Jr. (1992). The role of forensic psychiatry in the defense of sexual harassment cases. *Journal of Psychiatry and Law , 20,* 2-33.

Fenley, T. (1988). Dealing with sexual harassment: An American experience. *Equal Opportunities International 7,* 3-7.

Friedland, L., & Friedland, D. (1994)., Workplace harassment: What mental health practitioners need to know. In L. VandeCreek & S. Knapp (Eds.), *Innovations in clinical practice: A source book,* V. 13 (pp. 237-253). Sarasota, FL: Professional Resource Press/Professional Resource Exchange, Inc.

Hamilton, J. A., (1989). Emotional consequences of victimization and discrimination in "special populations" of women. *Psychiatric Clinic, 12,* 35-51.

Hamilton, J. A., Alagna, S.W., King, L.S. (1987). The emotional consequences of gender-based abuse in the workplace: New counseling programs for sex discrimination. In M. Braude (Ed.), *Women, power and therapy* (pp. 155-181). New York: Haworth.

Havris, K. (1999). Review of sexual harassment. *School Library Journal, 39,* 198-208.

Himelein, M., Vogel, R. E., & Wachowiak, D.G. (1994). Nonconsensual sexual experiences in precollege women: Prevalence and risk factors. *Journal of Counseling and Development, 72* (4), 411-422.

Hotelling, K. (1991). Sexual Harassment: A problem shielded by silence. *Journal of Counseling & Development* (69), 497-501.

Harvard Communication Letter (v. 2, 8), 1999. *Sexual Harassment in the workplace.*

Ingram, K. M., Corning, A., & Schmidt, F. D. (1996). The relationship of victimization experiences to psychological well-being among homeless women and low-income housed vs homeless females. *Journal of Counseling Psychology, 43* (2), 218-227.

Jensen, I. W., & Gutek, B.A. (1982). Attributions and assignments of responsibility in sexual harassment. *Journal of Social Issues, 38* (4), 121-136.

Jensvold, M. F. (1993). Workplace sexual harassment: The uses, misuse and abuse of psychiatry. *Psychiatric Annals, 23,* 43-445.

Jones, C. (1996). *Sexual harassment.* New York: Facts on File, Inc.

Ketring, S.A, & Feinauer, L.L., (1999). Perpetrator-victim relationship: Long-term effects of sexual abuse for men and women. *The American Journal of Family Therapy, 27*, 109-12.

Koss, M. P. (1990). Changed lives: The psychological impact of sexual harassment in ivory power. In M.A. Paludi (Ed.), *Ivory power: Sexual harassment on campus* (pp.73-92). Albany, NY: State University of New York Press.

Kluft, R. P. (1989). Treatment of victims of sexual abuse. *Psychiatric Clinic of North America, 12*, 385-408.

Lamb, D. (1986). *Psychotherapy with adolescent girls.* New York: Plenum.

Lenhart, S.A. (1991). Gender discrimination: A health and career development problem for women physicians. *Journal of American Medical Women Association, 46*, 77-82.

Lenhart. S. A. (1996). *The psychological impact of sexual harassment and gender discrimination in the workplace.* New York: Guilford.

Lumina Productions, Inc. (1999). *Sexual harassment in the workplace.* [Video]. Philadelphia, PA: Author. (Available from Author.)

MacKinnon, C. (1979). *Sexual harassment of working women.* New Haven, CT: Yale University Press.

Marin, K. M. (1998). New Rules for Sexual Harassment. *HR Magazine*, 1-7.

Marmar, C. R. (1991). Brief dynamic psychotherapy of posttraumatic stress disorder. Psychiatric Annals, 21, 405-419.

Marmar, C.R., Foy, D., Kagan, B., et al. (1993). An integrated approach for treating posttraumatic stress, in American Psychiatric Press Review of Psychiatry, 12, eds. Oldham, J.M., Riba, M.B., Tasman, A, Washington, D.C.: American Psychiatric Press, 239-272.

McCourt, J., Peel, J. C., & O'Carrol, P. (1998). The effects of child sexual abuse on the protecting parent(s): Identifying a counselling response for secondary victims. *Counseling Psychology Quarterly, 11*, (3). 283-299.

Morrison, J. P., & Griggs, E.G. (1996). *Ten-step counseling model for work behavior and employment counseling process ten-step, instructional methods training manual.* Washington, D.C.: U.S. Government Printing Office.

Roscoe, B., Goodwin, M. P., & Repp, S. E. (1987). Sexual harassment of university students and student –employees: findings and implications. *College Student Journal 21*, 254-273.

Rubin, P. N. (1995). *Civil rights and criminal justice: Primer on Sexual harassment.* NIJ Research in Action. Washington, D.C.: Government Printing Office.

Russell, D. E. (1984). *Sexual exploitation: Rape, child sexual, and workplace harassment.* Beverly Hills, CA: Sage.

Salisbury, J., Ginorio, A. B., & Remick, H. (1986). Counseling victims of sexual harrasment, *Psychotherapy, 23*, 316-324.

Schafran, L. H. (1989). Gender bias in the courts: An emerging focus for judicial reform. *Arizona State Law Journal 2*, 237.

Schafran, L. H. (1990). Overwhelming evidence: reports on gender bias in the courts. Trial 26:28-35.

Schafran, L. H. (1995). Credibility in the courts: Why is there a gender gap? *The Judges' Journal (Winter):5-6, 8-9,* 40-45.

Sexual harassment & Recent events. (1999, April 21). Wall Street Journal. P.47.

Shrier, D. K. (1996). *Sexual harassment in the workplace and academia.* Washington, D.C.: American Psychiatric Press, Inc.

Shrier, A. & Hamilton A. (1996). *Sexual harassment in the workplace and academia.* Washington, D.C.: American Psychiatric Press, Inc.

Spratlen, L. P. (1988). Sexual harassment counseling. *Journal of Psychosocial Nursing & Mental Health Services, 26* (2), 28-33.

Stein, N. (Ed.). (1986). *Who's hurt and who's liable: Sexual harassment in Massachusetts Schools.* Quincy, MA: Massachusetts Department of Education.

Stein, N. (Ed.). (1991). It happened here too: Sexual harassment in the schools (commentary). *Education Week, 25,* 32.

The Office of Civil Rights. (1997). Sexual Harassment: It's not academic. Website: hhtp://www.ed.gov./offices/OCR/ocrshpam.html.

U.S. Court of Appeal, 9th Circuit Court, Ellison v Brad, 1991.

U.S. Department of the Army, Headquarters, 25th Infantry Division (Light) & United States Army. (2001). *Green Tab Memorandum Safety-5. Violence in the workplace.* Schofield Barracks, HI: Author.

U.S. Merit System Protection Board. (1994). *Sexual harassment in the federal government: An update.* WDC: GAO.

U.S. Supreme Court, 477 U.S. 57, 40 FEP Case 1822, 1986.

U.S. Supreme Court, Harris v. Forklift System, Inc., 114S, Ct. 367, 1993.

VandeCreek, L, Knapp, S., & Freidland, D. (Eds.). (1994). Workplace harassment: What mental health practitioners need to know. *Innovations in clinical practice: A source book* (pp. 237-253). Sarasota, FL.

Wagner, E. J. (1992). *Sexual harassment in the workplace: How to prevent, investigate, and resolve problems in your organization.* New York: American Management Association.

Chapter 17

COUNSELING WOMEN CONSIDERING ABORTION

Valerie L. Schwiebert
Western Carolina University

Since the Supreme Court re-established legal **abortion** in the United States in the 1973 **Roe v. Wade** decision, abortion has been the topic of ongoing heated debate. Today, policies regarding legal abortion in the United States are debated in Congress, in local politics, and on the street corners of our smallest towns. Everyone seems to have an opinion, yet many myths and misconceptions continue to confuse the issue. In fact, 70% of Americans believe abortion should be legal in some form, however, wide disagreement exists as to under which circumstances it should be permitted (Rubin, 1994). This chapter begins with a brief **history** of abortion in America. This discussion is followed by an overview of the **demographics** of abortion, **abortion providers and services**, and **types** of abortion. This is followed by a discussion of **cultural and gender issues, and developmental issues** related to abortion. The chapter concludes with a discussion of **counseling issues** surrounding abortion and two case studies.

HISTORY OF ABORTION IN AMERICA

Contrary to popular opinion, the Roe v. Wade decision did not make abortion legal for the first time in the United States. In fact, abortion has been performed for thousands of years in every society that has been studied. It was legal in America until the mid to late 1800s when some states began passing laws making abortion illegal. It is interesting to note that the **American Medical Association** began the campaign against legal abortion, calling it immoral and dangerous. As a result, by 1910, all but one state had made abortion illegal except where necessary, in the doctor's judgment, to save a woman's life (National Abortion Federation, 2000).

The 1973 Roe v. Wade case was a challenge to the Texas law making abortions illegal except in cases where the woman's life was in danger. The ruling that resulted stated that the law was unconstitutional. The court found the right to privacy extends to the decision of a woman in consultation with her physician to terminate her pregnancy. Further, during the first trimester of pregnancy this decision may be made free of state interference except for the requirement that the abortion be performed by a licensed physician. After the first trimester, the state has a compelling interest in protecting the woman's health and may regulate abortion to promote that interest. At the point of **fetal viability** (the capacity for sustained survival outside the uterus), the state has a compelling interest in protecting potential life and may proscribe abortion, except when necessary to preserve the woman's life or health (Roe v. Wade, 1973).

In 1976, in the case **Planned Parenthood of Central Missouri v. Danforth**, a challenge was made to the Missouri law requiring parental consent to a minor's abortion, husband's consent to abortion, a woman's written informed consent, no second trimester abortions allowed by saline amniocentesis, and record keeping and reporting procedures. The court found that parental and spousal consent requirements were unconstitutional because they delegated to a third party an absolute veto power that the state did not itself possess. However, they also found that the requirement that a woman certify her consent is informed and given freely was constitutional as were the record keeping and reporting procedures. The ban on saline amniocentesis was also struck down because it was shown to be less dangerous to the woman's health than other available methods (Planned Parenthood of Central Missouri v. Danforth, 1976).

In 1979, in **Colautti v. Franklin**, a challenge was made to a Pennsylvania law requiring physicians intending to perform an abortion to determine that the fetus is not viable. The court ruled that the provisions were unconstitutional because they impose criminal liability on physicians regardless of their intent to violate the law and that the decision on viability must be left to the good faith judgment of the physician (Colautti v. Franklin, 1979).

In 1989, in **Webster v. Reproductive Health Services**, a challenge was made to Missouri's 1986 Act that declared that life begins at conception, forbid use of public funds for the purpose of counseling a woman to have an abortion not necessary to save her life, forbid the use of public facilities for abortions not necessary to save a woman's life, and required physicians to perform tests to determine viability of fetuses after 20 weeks gestational age. The court allowed the declaration that life begins at conception because there was no clear evidence that it would be used to restrict protected activities in the future. Should this occur at a later date, the affected parties could challenge the restrictions at that time. The court declined to address the constitutionality of the public funds provision. The court upheld the provision that barred the use of public facilities. The court upheld the provision requiring tests by interpreting it not to require tests that would be imprudent or careless to perform (Webster v. Reproductive Health Service). This decision is important because it opened the door for state regulation of abortion.

In 1992, **Planned Parenthood of Southeastern Pennsylvania v. Casey**, a challenge was made to Pennsylvania's 1989 Abortion Control Act. Specifically, the 1989 statute required that a woman wait 24 hours between consenting to and receiving an abortion, the woman be given state-mandated information about abortion and fetal development, a married woman inform her husband of her intent to have an abortion, minors' abortions be conditioned upon consent, and physicians performing abortions must provide annual statistical reports to the state. The court upheld all of the requirements except the husband-notification requirement. This ruling was important because the court upheld a woman's right to abortion under Roe v. Wade but revoked its long-standing definition of that right as "fundamental."

Currently, twenty states have passed requirements that a women receive information biased against abortion and, in all but one state, delay a set number of hours or days before having the abortion. Of these 20 state laws, 13 are currently in effect. In addition, 42 states have adopted laws mandating that a young woman obtain consent of or notify one or both parents prior to her abortion. Most of these laws contain a provision for judicial bypass if a young woman cannot involve her parents (Planned Parenthood, 1999).

DEMOGRAPHICS OF ABORTION

Statistics related to abortion must be interpreted with caution. Since social stigma surrounding the procedure still exists, some women may elect not to report having undergone the procedure. According to the Alan Guttmacher Institute (2000), each year more than 50% of pregnancies among American women are unintended. Of these, about half or 1.5 million each year are ended by abortion. In 1996, 1.37 million abortions took place, down from an estimated 1.61 million in 1990. From 1973 through 1996, more than 34 million legal abortions occurred. Each year, 2 out of every 100 women aged 15-44 have an abortion, 47% of them have had at least one previous abortion and 55% have had a previous birth. If current rates continue, it is estimated that nearly half of all women of reproductive age in the United States today will have had an abortion by the time they reach the age of 45 (Alan Guttmacher Institute, 2000).

Worldwide, each year an estimated 50 million abortions occur. Of these, 20 million procedures are obtained illegally.

Young women in the age group 25 and younger account for about 52% of all abortions in the United States. Women between the ages of 20 and 24 account for 32% of abortions performed in the United States, and about 20% of abortions are obtained by teenagers. Most of these abortions (91%) are obtained within the first trimester of pregnancy. In fact, over half of all abortions performed in the United States are obtained within the first 8 weeks of pregnancy. Only about 9% of abortions are performed during the second trimester and only about 100 are performed in the third trimester (approximately .01 percent). Fewer than 1% of all abortions in the United States occur after 21 weeks (Alan Guttmacher Institute, 2000).

Of the women obtaining abortions in the United States, 81% are unmarried, 63% have never been married, and 18% are separated, divorced, or widowed. Married women are about one sixth as likely as unmarried women to resolve unintended pregnancies through abortion. White women obtain 60% of all abortions although their abortion rate is well below that of minority women. Black women are more than 3 times as likely as white women to have an abortion, and Hispanic women are 2 times as likely to have an abortion. Catholic women are 29% more likely than Protestants to have an abortion (Alan Guttmacher Institute, 2000).

Abortion rates appear to be declining in recent years. In 1992, 1,529,000 abortions were performed. This was the first time since 1979 that less than 1,550,000 abortions were reported annually (Alan Guttmacher Institute, 1993). Though abortion rates are continuing to decline in the United States, these numbers are higher than those in any Western European country with accurate statistics, and lower than those of most Eastern European countries and developing nations (Henshaw, 1990).

The largest numbers of abortions are performed in the most populated states. For example, California reported 304,000 abortions in 1992 compared to 195,000 in New York and 97,000 in Texas. These states, plus Florida and Illinois, account for almost half of all abortions performed nationally. Abortion rates vary widely with New York and Hawaii having the highest rates at 46 abortions per 1,000 female residents aged 15-44 (Alan Guttmacher Institute, 1993). Factors affecting the abortion rates include the proportion of the population that is non-white and unmarried, degree of urbanization, extent of subsidies for abortion services for low-income women, and the availability of abortion services (Henshaw, 1998).

On average, women in the United States give at least 3 reasons for choosing abortions. Approximately 3/4ths say that having a baby would interfere with work, school, or other responsibilities. Approximately 2/3rds say they cannot afford a child, and one half say they do not want to be a single parent or are having problems with their husband or partner. About 14,000 women have abortions each year following a rape or incest (Alan Guttmacher Institute, 2000).

Women who undergo abortions after the first trimester do so for social, medical, and personal reasons. Problems with access to abortion services are a major factor in obtaining abortion after the first trimester. Six percent of women obtain abortions outside their home states and about 27% outside their home counties. Women living in rural areas may experience an even greater delay in locating abortion services. A second problem cited by women who obtain abortions after the first trimester is difficulty in obtaining financing. Lack of money delays abortions particularly for younger women and poor women. This has become a more significant problem since the implementation of the Hyde Amendment that blocks federal funding for abortion. Finally, legal restrictions, particularly for minors, may cause a delay in obtaining an abortion until after the first trimester (Planned Parenthood, 1999).

Medical reasons for delayed abortion after the first trimester include diagnosis of cancer, particularly hormone dependent cancer, severe cardiac conditions, pulmonary hypertension, uncontrolled diabetes, suicidal tendencies, substance abuse, and AIDS. Physician error in diagnosing pregnancy, and exposure to x-rays or prescription drugs that may cause malformation of the fetus may also cause a delayed abortion in the second or third trimesters. Finally, severe anomalies or chromosomal abnormalities may not be apparent until amniocentesis is performed between 16 and 20 weeks of pregnancy (Planned Parenthood, 1999).

Personal reasons for delaying abortion until after the first trimester include ignorance or unwillingness to acknowledge the pregnancy. This is especially prevalent among adolescents. In addition, women who have been raped or victims of incest may be unwilling to acknowledge the resulting pregnancy. Other personal reasons given for abortion after the first trimester include irregular menses or menopause resulting in the woman not recognizing she may be pregnant. Changes in relationships such as partner who dies or a woman who is abandoned by her partner may also result in the woman choosing to undergo abortion after the first trimester (Planned Parenthood, 1999).

ABORTION PROVIDERS AND SERVICES

Access to **abortion providers** and **services** has declined in recent years. Of the abortions performed in the United States, 93% are performed in clinics or doctors' offices. The number of abortion providers has declined by 14% between 1992 and 1996. In 1996, 86% of all U.S. counties lacked an abortion provider. These counties were home to 32% of all 15-44 year old women (those women most likely to seek abortion services). It is important to note that 43% of all abortion facilities in the United States only provide services through the 12th week of pregnancy (Alan Guttmacher Institute, 2000).

In 1997, the **average cost** of a nonhospital abortion with local anesthesia at 10 weeks gestation was $316 and ranged from $150 to $1,535. In nonhospital facilities offering both surgical and medical abortions in 1997, the cost of a medical abortion ranged from $100 to $1,250 with an average of $401. Only about 12% of all nonhospital providers offered their patients a medical abortion in 1997. Finally, 9 in 10 managed care plans routinely cover abortion or provide limited coverage (Alan Guttmacher Institute, 2000).

TYPES OF ABORTION

There are two general categories of abortion procedures, **surgical** and **medical**. Currently, over 95% of abortions performed in the United States use the **vacuum aspiration** method of surgical abortion. This method involves the insertion of a tube through the cervix into the uterus that then sucks out the products of the conception. This procedure is considered very safe and takes about 5 minutes to complete (Planned Parenthood, 1999). However, several side effects may occur. These include infection and possible perforation of the uterine wall. In addition, many women elect to have these procedures performed under general anesthesia, although it may be safely performed under local anesthesia, adding the complications associated with undergoing general anesthesia (Costa, 1996).

Another surgical technique is **dilatation and evacuation**. This method is used for abortions performed between 13 and 20 weeks of pregnancy. In most cases this is a two stage procedure. First the cervix must be dilated. Once the cervix is dilated, the physician removes the fetus and placenta using a combination of vacuum suction, forceps, and sharp curettage. This procedure may be done under general anesthesia, spinal or epidural anesthesia, or paracervical block. Possible complications include perforation of the uterus, cervical laceration, hemorrhage, an incomplete abortion, and infection. This procedure is considered safer and more effective than the instillation methods though it may be more emotionally traumatic for the healthcare staff in later pregnancies where the fetus must be dismembered to be removed (Costa, 1996).

Until recently, **intraamniotic instillations** were the most common method for abortions performed at 16 weeks or later. This procedure has been largely replaced by dilatation and evacuation for pregnancies before 20 weeks. In this procedure, under local anesthetic, a large needle is inserted into the uterus and used to withdraw amniotic fluid. A similar amount of saline solution is then infused into the uterine cavity. In most cases, the fetal heartbeat stops within 90 minutes and the woman goes into labor and delivers a dead fetus within 24 to 72 hours. This procedure carries a high risk of physical and psychological complications. These include birth of a live fetus, injection of saline into a vein, blood coagulation disorders, hemorrhage, and incomplete abortion. In addition, the psychological trauma for the woman who must endure long hours of pain and labor only to deliver a dead fetus is great (Costa, 1996).

Major surgery techniques include the **hysterotomy** and **hysterectomy**. A hysterotomy is similar to a cesarean section. An incision is made in the abdomen and the uterus. The fetus is then removed through the incision and the incision stitched closed. If done early enough in the second trimester, a hysterotomy may be done vaginally, eliminating the need for an abdominal incision. This procedure is used very rarely because it carries significant complications associated with major surgery. It is usually only performed in cases where other techniques have failed, numerous abortions have been previously performed, or the woman's medical condition makes other procedures unusable. Hysterectomy is performed even more rarely than hysterotomy. This involves the removal of the uterus and possibly ovaries. This is usually done only in cases where the procedure is needed for other reasons than abortion, such as in the case of a cancerous tumor. Both the hysterectomy and hysterotomy are performed under general anesthesia and carry with them the associated increased risks (Costa, 1996).

Although relatively safe, **abortion complications** of surgical abortion do exist. Most women experience some cramping and/or soreness following surgical abortion. These effects are transient and usually last only a day or two. In addition, some women may experience an incomplete abortion, infection, bleeding, damage to the uterus, complications from anesthesia, and death. For suction curettage abortions, the risk of death is less than 1 in 100,000. Overall, compared to other surgical procedures, legal abortion has a very low death-to-case rate, carrying approximately half the risk of death of a routine tonsillectomy. Of course, the risks associated with abortion increase with the length of pregnancy.

A relatively new method of abortion is **medical abortion** induced by a drug or a combination of drugs that usually can be administered orally. These drugs act to cause the uterus to expel the products of conception from the uterus. Examples of such drugs include Mifepristone or **RU-486** and Methotrexate (Costa, 1996). These procedures carry a much lower risk of complications than surgical abortions. No anesthesia is required, and because no instrument is inserted, there is no risk of cervical injury or uterine perforation. It is important however that these medications be taken only under the supervision of a physician. Side effects include uterine bleeding, nausea, diarrhea, weakness, fatigue, cramps, and abdominal pain. In rare cases, abortion is unsuccessful or the woman may require a blood transfusion due to loss of blood.

In addition to the medical and surgical procedures for abortion, it is important that counselors are aware that many **folk remedies** exist for abortion. These range from the infamous "coat hanger" inserted through the vagina into the uterus, to drinking poisons, consuming large amounts of aspirin, intense abdominal massage, and kicking or jumping on the woman's abdomen. These techniques are dangerous to the woman's health at best and may cause death in many cases. In addition, most have been proven ineffective in completing the abortion.

Surgical, medical, and folk methods of abortion carry some long term physical and psychological risks. According to the American College of Obstetricians and Gynecologists (1994), it is difficult to determine the effects of abortion on subsequent pregnancies. For individuals who have undergone one abortion by suction curettage, the risks for affecting subsequent pregnancy appear to be minimal. Studies to confirm this finding are difficult due to several issues. These include abortion techniques are now much safer than those used previously, many of the procedures used in early years are no longer performed, many studies do not indicate gestational age at which the abortions were performed making inferences difficult, and many women are reluctant to admit to prior abortions.

However, the American College of Obstetricians and Gynecologists (1994) acknowledges that though little is known about the risks for women having more than one abortion, some doctors believe that more than one abortion may have increased risks. These include increased risks of delivering a subsequent child with low birth weight or preterm, or difficulty conceiving. In addition, a study published by Daling (as cited in Costa, 1996) in 1994 found that women who had undergone an induced abortion had a 50 percent greater risk of developing breast cancer before age 45. This increase represents a change of one case per 100 to two cases per 100, a relatively small increase. This increase may be related to hormonal changes which occur in the breasts as a result of pregnancy and may be minimized by having an abortion as early as possible in the pregnancy, before the hormonal changes occur.

Long term psychological effects of abortion have also been reported in the literature, although there is much controversy surrounding the issue. Advocates of legal abortion claim that the negative effects of abortion, if any, are minimal and transient. They further claim that these effects are far outweighed by the relief that most women, if not all, experience following abortion. Abortion opponents, however, claim that most women suffer from some form of post-abortion syndrome. Symptoms of post-abortion syndrome, according to abortion opponents, include feelings of guilt and depression which may lead to difficulties such as substance abuse and suicidal tendencies.

A study by Adler (1992) concluded that the study of the psychological impact of abortion is complicated by a number of factors. These include methodological concerns such as sample representativeness, lack of baseline data, lack of long term studies, and the lack of studies that separate the experience of abortion from the characteristics of women seeking abortions and from the context of resolving an unwanted pregnancy.

Regardless of the overall conclusions of studies that attempt to document long term psychological consequences of abortion, similarities are consistently found among those women who report negative psychological effects following abortion. Adler (1992) found that women who were terminating wanted, personally meaningful pregnancies were more likely to experience emotional stress following abortion. In addition, women who lacked support from their parents or partners experienced higher levels of emotional stress following abortion. Finally, women who have abortions in the second or third trimesters or who feel uncertainty about the abortion decision report experiencing more emotional distress following abortion.

Sachdev (1993) found that for women who had undergone legal abortions in major hospitals adverse psychological reactions were influenced by the following several factors. These included emotional conflicts resulting from a woman's commitment to the pregnancy and her attitude toward abortion; the ease with which she was able to negotiate the medical system to obtain the abortion; the attitudes of the service providers; the woman's relationship with her partner involved in the pregnancy; and the woman's overall attitude toward sex.

In summary, Russo and Dabul (1997) found that "despite a concerted effort to convince the public of the existence of a widespread and severe post-abortion trauma, there is no scientific evidence for the existence of such trauma, even though abortion occurs in the highly stressful context of unwanted pregnancy." Russo and Dabul further discussed a growing concern related to the effect on women of the increasingly negative social and political climate surrounding abortion. While women in their study were interviewed from 1979 to 1987 when anti-abortion efforts to stigmatize abortion were not as prominent as today, women today may face extremely negative social and political pressures surrounding their decision to abort. Examples of these pressures include anti-choice groups who harass clinic staff, intimidate patients, and even result to murder of abortion clinic employees. In addition, they use graphic language and literature to punish women who elect abortion (e.g. "Women are baby-killers" and "Abortion is murder"). Further, anti-choice groups are more frequently using a new strategy to limit choice, advertising "counseling services" to women that are highly biased against abortion. Their anti-abortion stance is not reflected in their advertising and, therefore, many women may contact these associations to obtain information and counseling assuming the information provided will be non-biased. Many times, these "counseling" centers provide biased misinformation to women related to the psychological trauma of abortion in an attempt to sway the woman's decision.

CULTURAL AND GENDER CONSIDERATIONS

As evidenced in the demographic statistics discussed earlier in this chapter, differences in pregnancy rates, abortion, and other factors exist across cultural groups. In addition, though the focus of this chapter is on women considering abortion, it is important to consider men's roles in the pregnancy and pregnancy resolution. Counselors working with women considering abortion must be sensitive to the cultural and gender implications of the decision to terminate or carry a pregnancy to term.

According to the Centers for Disease Control and Prevention (1994), Black women have higher rates of unintentional pregnancy and three times the rate of abortion as White women do. However, research studies consistently document that Blacks tend to be less supportive of legalized abortion than Whites. In order to understand a Black woman's relationship to abortion, it is necessary to consider the effects of race, class and gender and how these are related to issues of power. Research indicates that for Whites, abortion is often understood and interpreted as more symbolic of a larger feminist or antifeminist orientation. For Black women, abortion is more of a practical consideration grounded in the realization of the consequences of unwanted pregnancies than it is a symbol of feminist or antifeminist orientation (Dugger, 1991). Dugger (1998) further stated that for Black women, the most important attitudinal determinant of their abortion attitudes is whether they believed women suffer from discrimination. In addition, education and the extent to which women were invested in the labor market more strongly predicted Black women's attitudes toward abortion than those of White women.

The degree of religiosity of Black women has also been found to be negatively related to opposition to abortion but positively associated with support for feminism, in direct contrast to findings in the White population. Wilcox and Thomas (1992) explained this difference by emphasizing the role the Black church plays in advocating racial equality and collective action, and these messages then spill over into the realm of gender politics, leading to increased support for feminism by Black women. Other issues related to abortion among Black women include a greater acceptance of nonnuclear family forms, out-of-wedlock births, perceptions of abortion as placing self-aggrandizement above concerns for preserving the Black family and community, and the sentiment that abortion is a form of Black genocide (Lynxwiler & Gay, 1994).

Contrary to popular opinion, statistics also suggest that Latina women have a higher abortion rate than White women. This finding seems counter-intuitive because Latina women are primarily Catholic and culturally highly invested in maternal roles (Koonin, Smith, & Ramick, 1995). Overall, Latino attitudes toward abortion tend to be more similar to that of the larger American population than to those of the Catholic church. That is, based upon the limited information available on Latino attitudes toward abortion, the majority of Latino individuals are not opposed to abortion under all circumstances, the official position of the Catholic church, but generally approve of abortion in the case of maternal or fetal health and rape. Additionally, although there is less acceptance of abortion for socioeconomic reasons, Latina women most frequently report this as their reason for undergoing abortion (Erickson & Kaplan, 1998). It is important to emphasize that there is a paucity of research on the reproductive patterns of Latinas in the United States. Further research, particularly emphasizing the differences among subgroups of Latinas (e.g., Mexican Americans, Puerto Rican Americans, Cuban Americans) is imperative if we are to understand the reproductive health behavior of this population.

Asian Pacific Islander American women also face unique challenges in reproductive health in the United States. These women may struggle to incorporate their own cultural roots and values with American values, norms, and beliefs while trying to negotiate the complex healthcare delivery system in the United States (Asian and Pacific Islanders for Reproductive Health, 1995). As with Latina women, there exists a paucity of information related to reproductive healthcare attitudes and practices of Asian Pacific Islanders in the United States and the diversity among this group of individuals (e.g., Chinese Americans, Filipino Americans, Vietnamese Americans) must also be appreciated.

For Asian Pacific Islander American (APIA) women, immigration history, acculturation, and settlement patterns must be considered, because APIA's are relatively recent immigrants to the United states, the majority of whom arrived in this country within the past 15 years (Lin-Fu, 1993). In addition, APIA immigration in this country has been marked by centuries of discrimination and exclusionary acts banning entry from many countries in Asia (Tanjasiri & Aibe, 1998). Because of the foreign born status and recency of immigration for the majority of this population, their abortion attitudes and practices in the United States may be significantly shaped by the knowledge, attitudes, and behaviors adopted from their countries of birth. According to Sachdev (1988), although Asian countries vary in their acceptance of abortion, in general, it has not been nearly as controversial an issue as it has become in the United States. In fact, all counties from which APIA immigrate either have laws which legalize abortion or have lenient enforcement of bans that allow abortions to be performed seemingly uninhibited except in the Phillipines. Though little information exists on the reproductive health of these women, it is clear that APIA women do utilize abortion in the United States and, in order to better understand these practices, more research is needed.

In summary, cultural factors and influences are important in counseling women considering abortion. While it is essential to remember that gross generalizations regarding attitudes and practices of any culture are unwarranted, some trends among women of diverse backgrounds have been found in the literature. Counselors must attempt to determine level of acculturation of the client if they are to assist the client in making culturally and personally appropriate decisions.

Another factor, often overlooked in discussions of abortion counseling, that must be considered is the role of men in pregnancy and the abortion decision. In order to understand the male role in pregnancy resolution, it is essential to consider the historical context of the male experience related to reproductive rights. In the 1973 Roe v. Wade decision, the court spoke directly to the woman's right to make a unilateral decision regarding whether to abort or bring a pregnancy to term. The court remained silent on the issue of father's rights. In 1976, the Planned Parenthood of Central Missouri v. Danforth decision, effectively denied men the right to have a legal voice in whether a pregnancy was to be brought to term ruling that the woman's interest in the pregnancy termination was paramount because it was she who was most directly physically effected by the decision. In contrast, federal child support enforcement legislation has made men legally and financially accountable for their partner's unilateral decisions (Marsiglio & Diekow, 1998).

Counselors working with women considering abortion must understand the context in which decisions between partners are made. In the United States, this social context occurs in a climate where partners' attitudes about the options for resolving a pregnancy and their strategies for arriving at a decision are in a structure that restricts men's ability to negotiate postconception decisions about their potential offspring (Marsiglio & Diekow, 1998). Counselors may work with the woman considering abortion, her partner, or a man whose partner has elected to undergo abortion either with or without his consent. In addition, there is research to suggest that understanding men's roles in the abortion decision is important because some findings suggest that male partners' coping expectations affect women's adjustment to the abortion process (Major, Cozzarelli, & Testa, 1992).

Research on the psychological and interpersonal experiences of men whose partners elected to have an abortion is very limited. In general, factors that effect how men experience and feel about resolving a pregnancy include their views about the morality of abortion, their feelings toward their partner, and their attitudes about becoming a father at this point in their life. Men differ widely in their perceptions of abortion. Some recognize the women's right to choose and others struggle with moral issues. Men with pro-choice views are unlikely to experience a great deal of emotional trauma if they feel as though having a child right now would disrupt their life plans dramatically. Those who have a pro-life stance may experience greater emotional distress. Overall, it appears that men respond to the abortion experience by being silent about their own pain and confusion (Marsiglio & Diekow, 1998). Although many men are upset about their partner's decision to abort, at least for a brief time, many others are indifferent to the decision, and some are simply relieved.

DEVELOPMENTAL FACTORS

The discussion to this point has emphasized the need for counselors working with women considering abortion to possess knowledge of the demographics of abortion, types of abortion and complications, access to abortion, and cultural and gender differences in perceptions of the abortion decision. In this section, the developmental issues that may impact the abortion decision are discussed. Since counselors approach working with clients from a developmental perspective, this section is particularly relevant to the discussion of working with clients dealing with abortion decisions.

A number of developmental issues must be considered when working with clients dealing with abortion decisions. These range from teenage pregnancy to unexpected pregnancy in later life. Teenage pregnancy is a significant issue in the United States. Each year, approximately 1 million adolescents become pregnant; of these, about 20% experience a spontaneous abortion and about an equal number terminate their pregnancy or carry to term. It should be noted, however, that teenage abortions constitute less than 25% of the abortions performed in the United States (Alan Guttmacher Institute, 1996). The majority of adolescents who undergo abortions are unmarried and terminating their first pregnancy (Russo, Horn, & Schwartz, 1992). When asked the reason for terminating their pregnancy, most teenagers say it is because they are not ready to raise a child.

Counselors working with pregnant teenagers considering abortion need to assess the developmental maturity of the client. In addition, there are developmental concerns associated with the physical effects of carrying a pregnancy to term while the teenage woman is herself still growing and developing. Counselors must be familiar with state and federal laws governing an adolescent's right to terminate her pregnancy and laws that govern parental consent. Finally, when considering teenage pregnancy, it is important to emphasize that decisions regarding abortion are only necessary when there is an unwanted pregnancy. Therefore, counselors need to consider proactive approaches when possible to prevent a pregnancy or future pregnancies among teenage clients (Adler, Smith, & Tschann, 1998).

Other developmental issues include women who are choosing to delay childbirth until later in life. Women who become pregnant before completing their postsecondary education or becoming established in their careers may wish to consider abortion. Women in the United States are increasingly choosing not only to delay pregnancy but alternative lifestyles. These new lifestyles, such as a woman choosing to bear children yet never marry or have a partner, may have implications for when the woman may choose to carry a pregnancy full term. If she has not yet established a career and is not yet able to care for the child, she may wish to consider abortion.

Finally, developmental issues are related to off-time life events for some women considering abortion. For example, a woman who has begun to experience symptoms of menopause may become pregnant. She may have considered herself unable to become pregnant because of the developmental changes associated with menopause, therefore, may be faced with an unwanted pregnancy. Other life events such as divorce, death, and illness may also affect a woman's decision to consider abortion.

DIAGNOSTIC ISSUES

Although the discussion so far has focused on abortion, one essential diagnostic feature has been overlooked. Counselors must be aware of the methods for diagnosing pregnancy. In order for the client to be faced with the abortion decision, she must be pregnant. While this may seem like an obvious statement, many women may believe they are pregnant or that they have engaged in acts that may result in pregnancy, when in fact, they are not pregnant or have misinformation regarding how one becomes pregnant. Since abortion options and the complications associated with abortion are affected by stage of pregnancy, it is essential that the counselor assist the client in ascertaining if she is pregnant and the length of the pregnancy as soon as possible.

There are several methods available for diagnosing pregnancy. Pregnancy test kits may be purchased at local pharmacies. These kits range in price from $12 to $30 depending on the brand of test and number of tests per kit. These tests use urine from the woman to detect a hormone produced by the pregnancy 17 to 20 days after fertilization (Planned Parenthood, 1999). The tests are relatively easy to use and have increased in accuracy in recent years. However, they are not 100% accurate and require that the individual follow the directions carefully and completely. They also require an ability to read and interpret the information correctly. The tests may report that the individual is not pregnant if taken too early and may also be inaccurate. These urine tests cannot be used to determine length of pregnancy.

Urine tests may also be performed by local free clinics and health departments. These tests are more accurate because they are performed and interpreted by trained clinicians. In addition, the woman is not alone and may access counseling services if necessary.

The most accurate test is a blood test, usually ordered and interpreted by a physician, and can detect a pregnancy as early as 7 days after fertilization (Planned Parenthood, 1999). These tests may be ordered through local clinics, college health centers, medical centers, or personal physicians. Though these tests are more invasive and costly, they are extremely accurate and may be used to determine the length of pregnancy. It should be remembered however that these tests may also give a false negative reading if administered too soon after conception.

Finally, pregnancy may be determined or confirmed through the use of ultrasound technology. In this procedure ultrasound technology is used to look into the uterus at the developing embryo. It may be used early in a pregnancy to see the rudiments of the fetal heart. It may also be used to determine length of pregnancy, number of fetuses and fetal status. This is an expensive procedure and requires a physician's order and interpretation.

COUNSELING ISSUES AND STRATEGIES

The first task for the counselor working with a client considering abortion is to clarify his or her own values and beliefs surrounding the abortion issue. This is particularly important because the topic of abortion tends to elicit strong emotional reactions either prochoice or prolife and is closely linked with an individual's religious and moral values (Armsworth, 1991). The counselor may wish to ask himself or herself questions such as: "Do I believe abortion is an option?" "Is abortion moral?" "Under what circumstances do I believe in abortion?" "Can I put aside my personal views on abortion and assist a woman in making a decision that is best for her even if it conflicts with my own views?" "If my position is so strong I cannot set it aside, should I tell the client so that he or she may make an informed choice regarding counselor selection?" "If I cannot work with a woman considering abortion, do I know the appropriate referral sources?" "Does the organization I work for have an official stance on abortion and how does that affect the services I may provide to my clients?"

This self reflection can help a counselor clarify his or her own perspectives on the abortion issue. Recognition of one's values and beliefs surrounding an emotionally charged issue is the first step in insuring that those beliefs do not unduly influence the client and her decision. It may be in the client's best interest if the counselor is able to share his or her own position on abortion so that the client may determine if counseling that matches or is contrary to the client's own beliefs and values is most useful to her (Armsworth, 1991). Once the client makes a commitment to counseling with the counselor based upon informed consent, the counselor may then focus on the client's concerns regarding her pregnancy.

The first client consideration when counseling a woman who suspects she may be pregnant is the confirmation of pregnancy, as well as testing for sexually transmitted diseases. As discussed above, the counselor must understand how the client determined she was pregnant. It may be that she missed her period and is assuming she is pregnant when, in fact, she is not pregnant. Counselors may take this opportunity to provide education related to pregnancy and sexuality. In addition, counselors must be familiar with local referral agencies that can either confirm or disconfirm a suspected pregnancy. In order to provide resources and counseling that is consistent with a client's religious, spiritual, and cultural beliefs, the counselor must openly address these areas with the client. Counselors should take care to provide referrals to agencies that provide unbiased services unless the client specifically requests a particular type of agency, either prochoice or prolife. At times, it may be appropriate for the counselor to accompany the client to obtain a pregnancy test. In other situations, a friend or significant other may wish to accompany the client or the client may choose to go alone.

Once it is accurately determined that the client is pregnant and the length of pregnancy is determined, the counselor may then begin to discuss options with the client. As previously discussed, many factors must be considered such as client developmental stage, cultural and religious background, age, planned pregnancy versus unplanned pregnancy, views on abortion, and level of partner support.

In particular, interventions that help the woman clarify the meaning of the pregnancy to herself and to own her decision may be critical in working with this population. This is based upon the finding that decision-making under stress seems to be a key factor in determining long-term adjustment and outcome related to abortion (Adler et al., 1990). The counselor must create an environment in which the client considers all factors related to her own situation without the counselor imposing judgement or values. Open discussion is essential and may be difficult to achieve because of the strong emotional views associated with abortion. In addition, clients may avoid seeking support because of real or imagined attitudinal barriers that exist in her mind or the minds of others (Armsworth, 1991).

As the counselor helps the client explore her situation and choices, it is important to offer education related to pregnancy and sexuality. If the client is to avoid unwanted pregnancy in the future, she must fully understand how one becomes pregnant and what one may do to prevent pregnancy. In addition, any misconceptions the client holds regarding being sexually active must be addressed. Again, the key to successfully working with clients in this population is creating an atmosphere where open discussion may take place. Issues surrounding sexuality and intercourse may be difficult for the client to discuss, although the discussion must occur so that the counselor can assess the accuracy of the client's information. A discussion of information related to future contraception is also of critical importance. The assessment of client knowledge may be particularly important when working with pregnant adolescents.

The counselor must eventually assist the client in coming to a decision regarding her pregnancy. All available options should be explored including keeping the baby, adoption, and abortion. As the counselor talks with the client about each option, it may help the client to envision herself choosing each option. What would she feel like? What might be the ramifications of such a decision? What would she do? How would others react? What are her fears about each option? What are the positive outcomes associated with each option? What choices does the client feel she can live with? Which choices are impossible for the client? What is going on in the client's life and what are her future plans? How would her decision affect her life? What are the client's spiritual and moral beliefs? What does the client believe is in her best interest in the long run? What can she afford?

This type of an approach assists the client in learning effective decision-making skills. In addition, it assists the counselor and client in identification of feelings, emotions and consequences that may result from the ultimate decision. The counselor and client may then work on strategies to minimize the negative effects of these feelings, emotions, and consequences on the client's overall wellness.

If the woman decides on an abortion, the counselor may help the client reframe negative feelings by pointing out that the woman is acting in the best interest of her potential child. Counselors can also emphasize that there is no one right decision that is right for everyone and that the client must make a decision for her. Potential reactions following an abortion, such as feelings of guilt, grief, and relief can also be discussed with the client in an attempt to normalize and minimize their impact.

A final consideration in the decision-making is who should the client involve in the process? The counselor must assist the woman in exploring her desire to involve her partner, friends, clergy, or family members. Who should be involved, if anyone, is an important consideration for the woman, and the counselor's own views regarding whether or not the woman should have a unilateral right to make the decision should not influence the client's decision to involve others. In the case of adolescents, the counselor needs to be knowledgeable of any court mandated consent and that the counselor explain the ramifications of these laws to the client.

Once the client has made the decision to abort, the counselor can help the client negotiate the medical system to undergo the abortion. This may involve providing referrals, information regarding consent, discussion of finances, and ongoing emotional and psychological support. Once the abortion has occurred, the counselor helps the client cope with any emotional and/or psychological responses to the abortion, such as feelings of grief, guilt, unhappiness, regret, relief, and anxiety. Many women develop an attachment to their fetuses, and abortion is experienced as the death of one's child, which may result in feelings of grief and guilt. The counselor must assess the degree of attachment the client feels toward her fetus to help the client as effectively as possible in the post-abortion phase.

Women who have undergone abortion prior to consulting a counselor, or women who have been seen by the counselor prior to the abortion who experience grief and guilt issues may benefit from participating in a ritual to bring closure to the abortion. Some women choose to revisit the abortion site and leave a rose or other rememberance. Other women choose to write letters to their unborn fetuses. For still others, the resolution of grief may come through practicing his or her faith, for example lighting a candle in church for her unborn child. Whatever the client's individual choice, counselors should support the woman in her attempts to bring closure to the abortion event and to come to terms with her grief. It is essential that the counselor support the woman in making the choice that the woman feels is best in her particualr circumstance. The following cases and discussions illustrate the application of the counseling issues and strategies discussed in this section.

CASE ONE

Trinity is a 23 year old, white, graduate student. She comes to the university counseling center and asks to see a counselor. The counselor notes that Trinity is obviously very distressed and begins to cry as they close the door to begin the counseling session. Trinity tells the counselor that she thinks she is pregnant. She missed her period and she is very regular, every 28 days. She states she should have begun her period three weeks ago. She says she is sexually active but is not currently in a monogamous relationship. She states that she did have a steady boyfriend until recently. She suspects he is the father. They broke up when he decided he wanted to see other women. She states that she uses birth control "most of the time." She states she has a diaphragm but does not use it because it is too uncomfortable. She states she "usually" asks her partner to wear a condom. She admits to unprotected intercourse on several occasions when her boyfriend "forgot" his condom, and she adds that he really did not like wearing a condom because it didn't "feel as good." She tells the counselor she has not had a physical examination by a medical doctor in the last 2 years and has not undergone any tests for sexually transmitted diseases. She continues, telling the counselor that many times she didn't actually plan to have intercourse with her boyfriend; it just "happens" after a night of drinking and "partying." She is currently in her second year of graduate school working toward her master's degree in business administration. She reports she is a "B" student with a current GPA of 3.4. She has not taken a pregnancy test to confirm whether she is or is not pregnant.

Discussion of Case One

One of the first considerations in working with Trinity is to determine if she is indeed pregnant and if so, the length of her pregnancy. The counselor offers to make an appointment for Trinity at the college infirmary for a physical examination, pregnancy testing, and screening for sexually transmitted diseases. Trinity agrees and an appointment is arranged for the next day. Trinity agrees to return to the counseling center the next week and a follow-up counseling appointment is made.

The results of the examination confirm that Trinity is pregnant with an estimated gestational age of 6 weeks since conception. The counselor has obtained a release of information consent form from Trinity and has also received the results from the physician's examination. The tests for sexually transmitted diseases were negative and Trinity was found to be otherwise in good health.

On the next visit, Trinity appears very distraught and emotional. She states she feels "terrible" and is nauseous all the time. She feels anxious and is unable to sleep or eat. She denies suicidal thoughts. She states she wants to terminate her pregnancy. The counselor validates her feelings and encourages her to begin discussing her decision and the implications of the decision. The counselor also asks Trinity about substance use. Trinity denies the use of any substances and states that she was drinking and partying with her boyfriend but since they broke up, she has not had anything to drink nor did she ever use drugs.

As the discussion continues, the counselor asks Trinity to consider all options including having the baby, adoption, and abortion. She also facilitates the client's exploration of her own values and beliefs related to each option and the consequences of each option. In addition, the counselor provides Trinity with information related to each of the three choices. At the end of the session, Trinity continues to feel she wants to terminate the pregnancy but is not certain. The counselor arranges for a follow-up appointment in three days and provides Trinity with information on a local Planned Parenthood chapter. Trinity agrees not to make any decisions until the next appointment and, if she feels overwhelmed or in danger of hurting herself, she agrees to contact the crisis line and/or the counselor.

When Trinity returns for her third appointment, she states she visited Planned Parenthood, talked with a counselor and obtained more information on her options. She states she is afraid that the abortion may be painful but feels it is the best option. She does not wish to interrupt her education and is financially and emotionally unable to care for a child. She states she does not wish to consult her family because she doesn't feel they would be supportive. In addition, she does not wish to consult the potential father because they are no longer seeing each other. She expresses no religious or moral convictions that would prevent her from obtaining the abortion. The counselor spends the session helping Trinity clarify her feelings and beliefs and exploring her decision to obtain an abortion.

At the end of the session, Trinity states that she intends to make an appointment with Planned Parenthood to obtain her abortion next week. The counselor asks her to call when she has made the appointment so that a follow-up counseling session may be scheduled. She also discusses what support Trinity may need from friends and the counselor, and possible feelings that may follow the procedure. Trinity states she has told her roomate and that she will accompany her to the clinic. Trinity feels she is supportive and will honor her confidence. The counselor notes that Trinity seems to feel comfortable with her decision though she is apprehensive.

Trinity calls the counseling center the next day and after arranging her appointment for the abortion. She states her roomate will accompany her and a follow-up counseling appointment is scheduled for the next week.

When Trinity arrives for her fourth appointment, she appears to be quiet and sad. She states she feels relieved and has been able to sleep and eat much better. She felt the abortion was "not as painful as I thought," but feels guilty and finds herself wondering what the baby would have been like. The counselor assures her that the grief process is normal and spends the remainder of the session providing support and exploring the client's feelings related to the pregnancy termination.

Future sessions will focus on helping Trinity accept her decision and resolve her feelings of guilt. In addition, although she appears to have accurate knowledge of pregnancy, contraception, and sexuality, her choices of not using a diaphragm and allowing her boyfriend to not use a condom because he didn't like the feeling indicate a lack of acceptance of responsibility for contraception on her part. She may not feel empowered enough to insist on the use of contraception or she may not really have believed she could become pregnant. In addition, she mentions that many times she did not intend to have intercourse but that sexual activity happened after drinking and "partying." These issues definitely warrant further exploration by the counselor since they have a direct influence on whether she may again experience unwanted pregnancy in the future. The counselor may wish to explore methods of contraception with the client and assist her in choosing a method that she will be able to use consistently. The counselor may also want to work on assertive communication skills with Trinity so that she may better communicate with future partners regarding sexual activity and contraception. The counselor should also undertake a thorough assessment of Trinity's substance use and possible abuse. This issue may become an additional focus of treatment in the counseling process.

CASE TWO

Shelly is a 36 year old, Hispanic woman. She reports being married for the past 6 years to her partner. They are both Catholic. They both have successful careers and work outside the home. Shelly is a biologist and her husband is an engineer. She comes to the community counseling center because she has been unable to get pregnant and this is causing a great deal of stress in her marriage. Shelly states that she and her husband have been trying to "get pregnant" for the past 5 years. They have undergone many physical tests and are currently working with a specialist in reproductive health. All of the physical tests indicated that neither she nor her husband have any physical reason for their current infertility. They both really want children and their respective families are pressuring them to begin a family. As the interview progresses, the counselor senses that Shelly needs to talk about something but does not feel quite comfortable discussing it. Finally, toward the end of the session and after asking the counselor again about the limits of confidentiality, Shelly tells the counselor that when she was in college, she had three abortions. Her husband and physicians know nothing of the abortions and her husband does not know she was sexually active before their relationship. She tells the counselor that after the third abortion, the doctor told her she would probably never be able to have children because of the possibility of extensive scarring to her uterus. She tells the counselor she believes this is why she has been unable to get pregnant. She asks the counselor what she should do.

Discussion of Case Two

Shelly expresses an overwhelming sense of guilt and grief. She feels isolated and alone. She does not feel she can tell her husband or he would leave her. She also does not feel she can tell her physician because she is afraid he will tell her husband. She has come to counseling to find a safe place to talk about her feelings. During the first session, she tearfully states repeatedly that she desparately wants children and wishes she had never had those abortions. She says she was emotionally immature and a "different person" back then. At the end of the first session, Shelly states she feels better because she was able to finally tell someone. She makes a follow-up appointment for the next week.

At the next appointment, Shelly states she still does not want to tell her husband. He is a strict Catholic and would never understand. She continues to express guilt and overwhelming sadness related to not being able to conceive. She states that if she were to get pregnant everything in her life would be perfect. She states that currently everything in her life is fine except the stress of "keeping the secrets" and not being able to get pregnant. The counselor continues to explore Shelly's feelings related to her previous abortions and learns that Shelly felt very positively about her decisions until she was unable to get pregnant. She states, "God is punishing me for those abortions." The counselor begins to explore ways Shelly may be able to forgive herself or seek forgiveness.

In the next several sessions, the counselor continues to work with Shelly toward decreasing her isolation. Together they brainstorm several options. Shelly states she has considered telling her priest because she knows he could not tell anyone. In addition, she asks the counselor about the limits of confidentiality with her physician. After thoroughly discussing all of her options, Shelly decides to make an appointment with her physician without her husband. She wants to tell the doctor of her previous medical history with the understanding that he will not share the information with anyone, including her husband. In addition, she decides to go to confession to "ask forgiveness for her sins" and "ask God to stop punishing her" and "help her get pregnant."

Shelly continues to meet with the counselor after her consultation with the physician and the priest. She met with the physician, and he told her he had suspected her previous history of abortion, but did not feel there was significant scarring that would lead to infertility. He attempted to assure her that this was not the direct cause of her infertility and that he would not share the information with her husband. She further states her experience in confession was very positive and that she felt things were "right" between her and God. She expresses a great deal of relief, although she continues to feel as though her inability to become pregnant is related to her previous abortions. The counselor continues to meet with Shelly with the goal of helping her work through her guilt and grief, and to provide support as she continues to undergo infertility treatment.

CONCLUSION

In summary, counselors working with women considering abortion must first explore their own beliefs and values surrounding this emotionally charged issue. The counselor must possess the knowledge and skills necessary to assist women in deciding whether to terminate or carry a pregnancy to term. Counselors must consider a variety of issues including developmental level of the client, availability of resources and social support, cultural and religious values and so on. In addition, counselors must be familiar with community resources and state and federal laws affecting the client's choices regarding abortion. In the counseling process, the counselor must first assist the client in confirming pregnancy, then assist the client in the decision-making process, and finally provide follow-up care and support.

REFERENCES

Adler, N. (1992). Psychological factors in abortion: A review. *American Psychologist, 47,* 1194.

Adler, N., David, H., Major, B., Roth, S., Russo, N., & Wyatt, G. (1990). *Psychological responses after abortion.* Washington, DC: American Psychological Association.

Adler, N., Smith, L., & Tschann, J. (1998). Abortion among adolescents. In L. Beckman, & S. Harvey (Eds.), *The new civil war: The psychology, culture and politics of abortion* (pp. 285-298). Washington, DC: American Psychological Association.

Alan Guttmacher Institute. (1993). *Facts in brief: Abortion in the United States.* New York: Author.

Alan Guttmacher Institute. (1996). *Facts in brief: Abortion in the United States.* New York: Author.

Alan Guttmacher Institute. (2000). *Facts in brief: Abortion in the United States.* New York: Author.

American College of Obstetricians and Gynecologists. (1994). *Induced abortion: Important medical facts* (brochure). Washington, DC: Author.

Armsworth, M. (1991). Psychological response to abortion. *Journal of Counseling and Development, 69,* 377-379.

Asians and Pacific Islanders for Reproductive Health. (1995). *The health and well being of Asian and Pacific Islander American women.* Oakland: Author.

Centers for Disease Control and Prevention. (1994). Abortion surveillance: Preliminary data - United States, 1992. *Morbidity and Mortality Weekly Report, 43,* 930-939.

Colauti v. Franklin. (1979). 439 U.S. 379.

Costa, M. (1996). *Abortion.* Santa Barbara, CA: ABC-CLIO.

Dugger, K. (1998). Black women and the question of abortion. In L. Beckman, & S. Harvey (Eds.), *The new civil war: The psychology, culture and politics of abortion* (pp. 107-131). Washington, DC: American Psychological Association.

Dugger, K. (1991). Race differences in the determinants of support for legalized abortion. *Social Science Quarterly, 72,* 570-587.

Erickson, P., & Kaplan, C. (1998). Latinas and abortion. In L. Beckman, & S. Harvey (Eds.), *The new civil war: The psychology, culture and politics of abortion* (pp. 133-155). Washington, DC: American Psychological Association.

Henshaw, S. (1990). Induced abortion: A world review. *Family Planning Perspectives, 22,* 76-89.

Henshaw, S. (1998). Barriers to access to abortion services. In L. Beckman, & S. Harvey (Eds.), *The new civil war: The psychology, culture and politics of abortion* (pp. 61-80). Washington, DC: American Psychological Association.

Koonin, L., Smith, J., & Ramick, M. (1995). Abortion surveillance in the United States, 1991. *Morbidity and Mortality Weekly Report, 44,* 23-53.

Lin-Fu, J.S. (1993). Asians and Pacific Islander Americans: An overview of demographic characteristics and health care issues. *Asian American and Pacific Islander Journal of Health, 1,* 20-36.

Lynxwiler, J., & Gay, D. (1994). Reconsidering race differences in abortion attitudes. *Social Science Quarterly, 75,* 67-84.

Major, B., Cozzarelli, C., & Testa, M. (1992). Male partners' appraisals of undesired pregnancy and abortion: Implications for women's adjustment to abortion. *Journal of Applied Social Psychology, 22,* 599-614.

Marsiglio, W., & Diekow, D. (1998). Men and abortion: The gender politics of pregnancy resolution. In L. Beckman, & S. Harvey (Eds.), *The new civil war: The psychology, culture and politics of abortion* (pp. 269-284). Washington, DC: American Psychological Association.

National Abortion Federation. (2000). *Abortion fact sheets.* Washington, DC: Author.

Planned Parenthood. (1999). *Facts Sheets.* New York, New York: Author.

Planned Parenthood of Central Missouri v. Danforth. (1976). 428 U.S. 52.

Planned Parenthood of Southeastern Pennsylvania v. Casey. (1992). 112 S. Ct. 2791.

Roe v. Wade. (1973). 410 US 113.

Rubin, E. (1994). *The abortion controversy: A documentary history*. Westport, CT: Greenwood Press.

Russo, N., & Dabul, A. (1997). The relationship of abortion to well being: Do race and religion make a difference? *Professional Psychology: Research and Practice, 28*, 269-280.

Russo, N., Horn, J., & Schwartz, R. (1992). U.S. abortion in context: Selected characteristics and motivations of women seeking abortions. *Journal of Social Issues, 48*, 183-202.

Sachdev, P. (1988). Abortion trends: An international review. In P. Sachdev (Ed.), *International handbook on abortion* (pp. 1-21). New York: Greenwood Press.

Sachdev, P. (1993). *Sex, abortion, and unmarried women*. Westport, CT: Greenwood Press.

Tanjasiri, S., & Aibe, S. (1998). Abortion and Asian Pacific Islander Americans. In L. Beckman, & S. Harvey (Eds.), *The new civil war: The psychology, culture and politics of abortion* (pp. 157-185). Washington, DC: American Psychological Association.

Webster v. Reproductive Health Services. (1989). 492 U.S. 490.

Wilcox, C., & Thomas, S. (1992). Religion and feminist attitudes among African American women: A view from the nation's capital. *Women & Politics, 12*, 19-40.

Chapter 18

COUNSELING AND SEXUALLY TRANSMITTED DISEASES

Timothy F. Dwyer and Susan H. Niemann
Our Lady of Holy Cross College, New Orleans

BACKGROUND

Sexually transmitted diseases (STDs) have continued to increase in the United States since the 1950s. Strong, DeVault, and Sayad (1996) cited a number of **social trends** and **cultural factors** considered to have contributed to this increase:

- Changes in sexual mores have led to widespread acceptance of sexual activity for both men and women outside of marriage.
- Since the 1960s and the advent of the birth control pill, condom use declined. Other methods of birth control do not possess the same prophylactic, or protection, from disease. Only with threat of AIDS and HIV did condom use begin to increase again.
- Educational efforts regarding STDs (and sexuality in general) are often constrained by conservative social factions pressing to limit frank discussion for fear that knowledge about sex causes people to engage in it.
- The often entangled moral and medical issues hamper funding for research and treatment of STDs. For example, funding for AIDS research did not expand until it was clear that heterosexuals as well as gay men were threatened (Shilts, 1987).
- The health care system cannot adequately met the societal demand for treatment. STDs are rampant in low-income, urban areas where healthcare service is limited.
- Moreover, racism and insensitivity to diversity and ethnic issues may also constrain adequate public health education and treatment programs.

- Funding for public health programs and health care agencies who are charged with providing education, diagnosis, treatment, partner tracing, and follow-up is often intensely competitive.
- Alcohol and drug abuse contribute indirectly to the spread of STDs by impairing people's ability judgement and decision making about sexual choices and conduct.

Moreover, Strong et al. (1996) noted certain **biological factors** that also contribute to the transmission of STDs:

- Many STDs are **asymptomatic.** That is, they produce no symptoms, especially in the early stages of the disease.
- Antibiotics that worked in the past are often no longer as effective in treating bacteria, because of the development of resistant strains of the pathogens. Infected people may continue to spread disease because they think they are cured or because they were asymptomatic. Follow-up examinations are needed to ensure that the initial treatment has worked, or else to try alternative treatment.
- Some STDs cannot be cured. A person who carries these viruses is always able to transmit them to others

The role of the counselor working with clients who have STDs, while important and necessary, has not been strongly emphasized in texts on sexuality counseling. Moreover, general STDs are scarcely discussed in the current counseling research literature. There have been few controlled studies examining whether or not clinician counseling in primary care settings is effective in reducing the incidence of STDs, (Aral & Peterman, 1993; Kamb et al., 1998;). However, recent systematic reviews highlight evidence that counseling interventions by health care professionals in a variety of settings can reduce specific STD risk behaviors (Kelly & Kalichman, 1995). Curiously, there are no recent studies which examine the specific role and interventions of counselors working with clients who have STDs, with the exception of persons living with HIV/AIDS.

Indeed, the predominant STD currently discussed in the professional counselor literature relates to clients with HIV and AIDS status in terms of prevention (Kelly & St.Lawrence, 1988), confidentiality (Harding, Gray, & Neal, 1993), duty to warn (Pais, Piercy, & Miller, 1998) disclosure of status (Serovich, 2000), sexual difficulties (Rosser, Metz, Bockting, & Buroker, 1997), and spirituality (Holt, Houg, & Romano, 1999), as well as issues related to counselor training in crisis management, support, and care for persons living with HIV and AIDS. Because these issues are discussed in a previous chapter (see Chapter 11), they are not substantively reviewed in this chapter.

Knowledge of the different disease types and treatments is essential for counselors today. Assessment of the health status and health care practices of clients should be a standard item when conducting an initial intake, along with complete and thorough sexual histories (Kelly & Kalichman, 1995) Completing a sexual history is especially important when working with young adults and clients exhibiting other potential risk behaviors. The aims of this chapter are: 1) to provide counselors with a solid knowledge base of the variety of STDs, their attendant characteristics, and a brief review of the standard medical treatments; 2) to provide counselors with relevant contextual, cultural and gender considerations; 3) to highlight important developmental and diagnostic factors; 4) to highlight specific strategies for assessment and treatment with clients presenting with STDs, and to suggest interventions for behavior that put clients and their partners at increased risk for disease transmission, and 5) to illustrate by clinical case example selected techniques and strategies for assisting clients with STDs.

An overarching aim of this chapter is to increase counselor awareness of the prevalence and health consequences of STDs. A thorough review of the incidence and transmission rates of STDs, as well as their specific disease types, is discussed in the following section.

Overview

Sexually transmitted diseases are infections and illnesses that are transmitted almost solely through sexual contact, such as sexual intercourse or oral or anal sex. A notable exception to this is HIV and AIDS which may be spread by contaminated intravenous drug needles or by blood transfusion. In the United States, the precise incidence of STDs is not clearly known. However, estimates of new cases of STDs range from 12 million (American Social Health Association, 1998) to 15.3 million each year (CDC, 1998). Approximately one-quarter of these new occurrences - over 3 million - are among teenagers, and nearly two-thirds of all newly reported cases are found in persons under the age of 25. In 1996, the National Institute of Health reported that of the top 10 reportable diseases in the Unites States, four are STDs: chlamydia, gonorrhea, AIDS, and syphilis (CDC, 1997).

The most prevalent STDs in the Unites States are chlamydial infection, gonorrhea, genital warts (Human papilloma virus), genital herpes, syphilis, hepatitis B, and HIV / AIDS. Other prevalent STDs include pelvic inflammatory disease, trichomoniasis, and chancroid. Each of these STDs will be discussed in terms of their prevalence, progression and symptomatology, and current medical treatment. For the professional counselors, accurate knowledge of the various STDs and their attendant risk factors is a primary information need.

SPECIFIC STDS

Chlamydia

Chlamydial infection - or **chlamydia** - is the most frequently reported infectious disease in the United States. It is caused by the bacterium *Chlamydia trachomatis*. Because approximately 75-80% of women and 50% of men have no symptoms, most people infected with chlamydia are not aware of their infections and, therefore, do not seek medical care or treatment. The time of exposure to occurrence is usually between 7-21 days. Severe underreporting of the incidence of this STD is suspected because of asymptomatic persons with infections who are not yet identified due to a lack of widely available screening. Thus, while over a half-million cases were reported in 1997, it is estimated that 4 million cases of chlamydia occur annually. There has been a 400 percent increase in the reported cases of chlamydia since 1987. However, the increase is not likely a true increase in the disease, but rather it reflects improved screening of asymptomatic persons and improved reporting.

When promptly diagnosed, chlamydia can be treated and easily cured. When symptoms do appear in women, they may present as vaginal discharge or pain with urination, and are similar to those of gonorrhea. In men, those presenting with symptoms may have discharge from the penis, burning urination, pain and swelling in testicles, or persistent low fever. Untreated chlamydia is especially dangerous and can cause severe, costly, reproductive and other health problems, including pelvic inflammatory disease (PID) in women. Forty-percent of women with untreated chlamydia will develop PID, which is thought to be a critical link to infertility and sometimes fatal tubal pregnancies. Untreated chlamydia in young men, which is common due to poor screening resources, typically causes urethral infection. Necessary medical treatment generally calls for antibiotics, such as doxycycline, tetracycline, or erythromycin.

Gonorrhea

An estimated 650,000 cases of **gonorrhea**, caused by *Neisseria gonorrhoeae*, occur annually in the U.S. It is estimated that 50-80% of women are asymptomatic, while others have symptoms similar to chlamydia. The time of exposure to occurrence with gonorrhea is 2 to 21 days. In slang terminology gonorrhea has been referred to as "the clap" or "the drip." In men, symptoms can include itching and burning or pain with urination and penile discharge. Most men seek treatment when symptoms reach this stage. If untreated the symptoms generally become more pronounced, though occasionally they diminish. However, even if the symptoms diminish, without treatment the bacteria are still present. Common medical treatment for gonorrhea is penicillin or other antibiotics.

Those who do not get treatment can infect their partners. Moreover, more serious complications can arise. In men, they can develop abscesses of the prostate gland. As with chlamydia, without adequate treatment 10 to 40% of infected women develop PID and suffer subsequent infertility problems. Gonorrhea may be also passed to an infant during childbirth, which can cause eye infection and blindness if not treated. Often times, a variety of antibiotics must be tried to rid the infection because the bacteria can evolve into resistant strains.

Genital Warts

Human Papilloma Virus (HPV) is the cause of the STD known as "**genital warts**" or *condyloma*. The virus is transmitted through direct contact with the warts, which are highly contagious. Many cases can be passed along by people who are asymptomatic or haven't noticed the warts. It appears as a variety of bumps (smooth, flat, round, or bumpy; clustered like miniature cauliflowers, or like tiny fingers; they may be colored gray, white, brown, pink, etc). In men, warts develop on the shaft or glans of the penis or around the anus. In women, they are found on the cervix, vaginal wall, vulva, or anus. The virus can be transmitted to a baby during childbirth if an infected mother has warts on her cervix or in her vagina. Moreover, genital warts seem to proliferate during pregnancy and regress after delivery.

Medical treatment is done by surgical removal, either by freezing (cryosurgery) laser therapy, cutting, or with a chemical solution. Removal of the warts is done for cosmetic reasons or for comfort. The virus remains in the body even after the warts are removed. The extent to which a person can transmit HPV after the warts have been removed is not known. However, in 80% of the cases the warts do eventually reappear.

An estimated 24 million people in the U.S. are infected, with as many as 1 million new cases each year. The time from exposure to occurrence is between 1 and 6 months, but usually within 3 months. Cervical infection with certain types of HPV are associated with more than 80% of the cases of invasive cervical cancer. It is especially important that any woman with a history of genital warts should have an annual Pap smear (note: it is generally recommended that all women should have Pap smear at least annually). In the U.S. an estimated 14,000 cases of invasive cervical cancer were diagnosed in 1998 (American Cancer Society, 1997). It is the second most common cancer among women worldwide. HPV has also been found in cancer of other organs, including the penis and anus.

Genital Herpes

Genital herpes is incurable. It is caused by the Herpes Simplex Virus (HSV) and is carried by 1 in 5 persons over the age of 12, or approximately 45 million individuals in the U.S. Indeed, those numbers are increasing by nearly a half-million per year (CDC, 1998). HSV occurs in two strains: Type 1 is responsible for cold sores and fever blisters around the mouth; Type 2 is usually associated with genital lesions around the penis, anus, perineum, vulva, and within the vagina. Serious complications from HSV are not all that common in adults. However, complications can result if the individual is in poor general health or has a compromised immune system. Newborns may contract HSV if they come into contact with active lesions during birth. This may result in infections of the eyes, skin, or mucous membranes, infections of the central nervous system or even death.

The first outbreak of genital herpes lasts an average of 12 days and the initial infection is the most severe. Within 3-20 days after exposure small bumps called vesicles or papules appear in areas around the genitals. They may itch at first, then form blisters which can rupture and form small painful ulcers. The period just prior to the outbreak of lesions is known as the prodrome. During this time, and while there are visible lesions, the virus is active. Generally, the affected areas shed live viruses which are spread upon contact. It should be noted, however, that some people with HSV may shed the virus without experiencing the symptoms. Many people have no symptoms after the first outbreak. Persons who experience recurrent herpes outbreak note they are often preceded by environmental factors such as stress, fatigue, exposure to extreme cold or sun, and certain foods.

Managing HSV with antiviral medication is often helpful in reducing or suppressing symptoms. Medication can be administered orally or topically. Other methods found to be useful in preventing, shortening, or lessening the severity of recurrent HSV outbreaks include: plenty of rest which enables the immune system to work most effectively and a balanced diet. Also, infected persons should observe foods that may trigger outbreaks. A warm, moist environment is an ideal host for HSV, therefore, infected persons should avoid tight clothes, nylon underwear and pantyhose and opt for loose-fitting, cotton clothing instead. Additionally, to keep the area cool and dry when lesions do begin to appear, it may be helpful to use an ice pack on lesions and baby powder or corn starch to absorb moisture.

It is important to recognize that HSV can be spread by hand, not only to another person but also to other parts of one's own body. Persons experiencing an outbreak should wash their hands frequently, and be careful not to touch one's eyes if one has had contact with an active lesion. Pregnant women and their partners who have HSV should discuss other reasonable precautions with their medical practitioners.

Hepatitis B

Hepatitis is a viral disease affecting the liver. Several types of the virus can be transmitted through sexual contact. The most common types are hepatitis A and B, and a third type, hepatitis C is more commonly passed via the bloodstream, but still may be passed through sexual contact There are an estimated 77,000 new cases of sexually transmitted hepatitis B infection occurring annually in the U. S. (American Social Health Association, 1998). Nearly a million people are currently living with sexually acquired hepatitis B, and although unaware, an estimated 1.5 million people in the U. S. are chronic carriers of the virus. While hepatitis A can also be transmitted through sexual contact, it is more often contracted through unsanitary conditions (i.e., contaminated food or water). It is believed to be transmitted sexually through infected fecal matter, for example, during oral-anal sex, or anal intercourse. The symptoms of hepatitis A are similar to hepatitis B, although the disease is not considered as dangerous. Individuals with hepatitis A generally recover within 6 weeks and develop immunity which protects them against reinfection. Hepatitis B is commonly spread through sexual contact, via blood, saliva, vaginal secretions, and urine. The incidence of hepatitis B is declining among gay men (possibly due to an increase in safer sex practices) and increasing among heterosexuals.

Hepatitis symptoms include fatigue, diarrhea, nausea, abdominal pain, jaundice, or yellowing of the whites of the eyes or skin (caused by accumulating blood pigments not destroyed by the liver), darkened urine, enlarged liver. There is currently no medical treatment available for hepatitis. Rest and fluids are recommended until the disease runs its course. Occasionally serious liver damage or death may result. The time of exposure to occurrence of symptoms is 1 to 4 months. Hepatitis B can be prevented by a widely available vaccine, though relatively few people take advantage of this. Health authorities, including counselors, can recommend routine vaccinations for persons at greater risk: people with more than one sexual partner, teenagers, gay men, IV drug users, and health care workers who come into contact with blood.

Syphilis

Syphilis is caused by the bacterium *T. pallidum,* a spiral shaped bacterium (or spirochete) that needs a warm moist environment, like the genitals or the mucous membranes inside the mouth, to survive. Since the 1980s the number of cases of syphilis has been dramatically increasing and in 1990, the rate was the highest it had been since the 1950s. It has continued to climb to over an estimated 100,000 cases annually (CDC, 1998). Globally, an estimated 12 million new cases of syphilis occurred in 1996 (World Health Organization, 1997). The rates reported among African Americans was nearly 50 times greater than that among whites (CDC, 1997).

Syphilis is generally spread though vaginal, anal, and oral sexual contact. However, an infected mother can pass the disease to her fetus through the placenta. Approximately 3,400 newborns acquire the infection from their mothers either before or during birth (Institute of Medicine, 1997). Because neonatal syphilis can lead to brain damage and death, women are often routinely screened for it within the first trimester.

Syphilis generally progresses thorough 4 discrete phases (primary, secondary, and two stages of tertiary - or early latency and latency), and is most often treated during the first two. Primary syphilis is when the first symptoms begin to appear or about 1-12 weeks after contact with an infected partner. A small, red, pea-sized bump develops into a round sore called a **chancre** (pronounced *shank-er*). It is usually painless and appears at the site where the bacteria initially entered the body: within the vagina or on the cervix for women, or on the glans or the shaft of the penis for men. The chancre can appear on the testicles, rectum, within the mouth or the lips as well. Unless it is in a visible area it can go undetected. Without treatment, it will disappear in 1-5 weeks, though the bacteria remain and the person is highly contagious.

After about 6 weeks after the chancre has disappeared, the primary syphilis develops into the secondary phase. The principal symptom at this stage is a skin rash that usually neither itches nor hurts. The rash can appear on the palms of the hand or soles of the feet, as well as other areas of the body. The person may also encounter flu-like symptoms. If the skin rash is swarming with spirochetes the person is highly contagious. Again, however, if the disease is not treated at this stage (and sometimes the symptoms may be so mild they may go unnoticed), the symptoms disappear within another 2-6 weeks. This begins the latent stage, and the person may never encounter another symptom for years, if ever again. A person may need a blood test to screen for the *T. pallidum*. After about a year, the bacteria can no longer be spread to sexual partners, although a pregnant woman can transmit the disease to her fetus.

Rarely in the U. S. do cases advance to this tertiary stage because treatment usually stops its progression. Symptoms at this stage can involve every organ of the body because the bacterium are circulating through the bloodstream. Large ulcers can develop within the muscles, liver, lungs, eyes, or endocrine system; heart disease may ensue; and "neurosyphilis" involving the brain, spinal cord can lead to muscular paralysis, psychosis, and eventually death. Penicillin (or other antibiotics) is still the treatment of choice for primary, secondary, and early latent phases of syphilis. Later stages would require additional treatments and injections.

Trichomoniasis

Among the variety of vaginal infections, the most common is **Trichomoniasis** or "trich" (pronounced "trick"), caused by *Trichomonas vaginalis*, a single cell protozoan. Globally, about 170 million people acquired this parasite in 1996 (World Health Organization, 1996). It is considered a hardy parasite that can survive many hospitable environments (e.g., on wet towels and toilet seats) but is principally transmitted by sexual intercourse. Even though they are asymptomatic, men may be carriers. If men do present with symptoms, they tend to be associated with urethritis, noted by painful and/or frequent urination. In women, symptoms are often extremely unpleasant and include intense itching of the vagina and vulva, unusual and malodorous discharge. It is estimated that 5 million cases of trichomoniasis occur annually in the U.S. (American Social Health Association, 1998). Suggested treatment is generally an antibiotic, but laboratory tests must be run to determine which is the appropriate one to be prescribed.

Other vaginal infections, or **vaginitis**, affect 3 out of 4 women at least once in their lives. While these other vaginal infections are not always sexually transmitted quite often they can be. Three most common types of vaginitis are bacterial vaginosis, candidiasis, and already discussed trichomonal infections. Moreover, public lice, or "crabs," and scabies are other parasites that are easily transmitted through sexual contact. However, they may likely be transmitted on towels, bedclothes, or underwear also.

Other STDs

There are a number of other sexually transmitted diseases bear mentioning. Though they are not as frequently occurring in the United States as they may be in some other developing countries, it is important that counselors be familiar with them. **Chancroid** is caused by a bacterium and creates a painful sore or group of sores on the penis. Women can carry the bacteria but remain asymptomatic. **Cytomegalovirus (CMV)** is among the herpes virus group and can affect people with immune deficiency problems. **Lymphogranuloma inguinale** appears on the genitals as single or multiple nodules. While not generally painful, these nodules become lumpy and bleed on contact. **Lymphomgranuloma venereum (LGV)** is also known as lymphogranuloma inguinale, tropical bubo, Nicholas-Favre disease, and sixth venereal disease, this is an infection of the chlamydia variety. It is still quite rare in the U.S. with estimates of infection that average between 250 to 400 people annually. It begins as a small but usually painless lesion at the site of infection and develops into painful swelling abscess in the groin. **Enteric infections** are infections caused by bacteria, viruses, and other organisms that are normally carried in the intestinal tract. They often result from anal sex, or oral-anal contact.

In summary, it is critically important that counselors remain informed of the variety and incidence of STDs, as well as their attendant health consequences and risks. Clearly, there are a number of considerations which may place some clients at great risk. In the next section cultural considerations related to STDs will be discussed.

GENDER AND CULTURAL CONSIDERATIONS

Arguably, the diagnosis and treatment of all medical conditions is strongly related to the **gender and cultural characteristics** of the individuals and/or groups affected. This is particularly so regarding STDs, a diverse collection of disorders whose only common characteristic is that their primary or sole method of transmission is through sexual contact. Attitudes towards sexuality, which vary across culture, greatly impact awareness, education, prevention, and treatment. Women are at significantly greater risk for sustaining long term damage from STDs, since their bodies are particularly hospitable to sexually transmitted organisms and may exhibit few initial symptoms. Additionally, women are often reluctant to seek treatment due to fear and stigma. STDs are associated with high-risk sexual behaviors; culturally, groups with less access to education about disease prevention, opportunities for responsible choices, or medical intervention are more likely to acquire STDs, and less likely to seek treatment promptly.

Counselors are challenged to conceptualize the problem of STDs from a cultural perspective, understanding the impact of gender, age, ethnicity, class, sexual orientation, and other contextual factors regarding prevention, diagnosis, and psychosocial aspects of treatment. Community counseling emphasizes prevention, empowerment, and advocacy, particularly for historically marginalized groups, which are often at greater risk for health problems in general and for sexually transmitted diseases in particular.

Attitudes towards Sexuality

In the United States, attitudes about sexuality are often paradoxical. On one hand, Americans consider themselves sexually liberated; television, movies, and popular music promote sexuality in an open, positive light, and media messages abound regarding the importance of being sexually attractive and open to sexual intimacies. While fear of HIV/AIDS has altered societal perceptions of unprotected sex as harmless, consensual sexual activity is still generally depicted as exciting, romantic and without lasting physical or emotional consequences. In popular media portrayals, it is rare to see discussions of contraception, much less concern regarding STDs. On the other hand, Americans are generally conservative regarding education about sexuality. Increasingly, sex education programs in public schools lean towards promoting abstinence from sexual activity as the only reasonable choice in preventing pregnancy, HIV/AIDS, and the spread of STDs. While popular teen movies, television and music present teen sexual activity as normal and expected, schools and other official lines of communication instruct adolescents to refrain from sexual activity in order to prevent STDs and other unwanted consequences of sexual activity. As a result, sexually active adolescents may be less likely to discuss their concerns about STDs with parents, teachers, or counselors.

While the gap between wishful thinking and actual behavior is clearly demonstrated by the widespread occurrence of STDs in teens and adults (Brandt, 1987; Nilsson Schonnesson, 1990), ambivalence and anxiety about sex prevents many from dealing with STDs rationally and directly. Singer (1994) noted that although many parents worry that sex education and condom availability encourage teenage sex, studies demonstrate that adolescents are already having unprotected sex at younger ages.

Moralistic views regarding high-risk behaviors that increase the likelihood of contracting STDs hinder effective prevention and treatment, and contribute to the emotional trauma experienced by individuals following diagnosis. Persons feeling shame regarding sexual behavior are less likely to seek medical attention or discuss their diagnosis with others, including future sexual partners. Furthermore, avoidance of sexual issues increases the stigma associated with STDs. Increasingly, counselors must examine their own attitudes towards and comfort level with sexuality and related issues in order to model open discussion and informed decision-making about sexual practices.

Women and STDs

Overall, the consequences for women who contract STDs appear to be more serious than those for men. Generally speaking, heterosexual women contract STDs more readily than men and risk greater damage to their health and reproductive functioning (Jacobson, 1992; Strong et al., 1996). The term "**biological sexism**" has been used to describe the biological and psychosocial disadvantages faced by women with STDs (Strong et al., 1996). Due to the fluid dynamics of intercourse, women are more likely than men to acquire a sexually transmitted infection from any single sexual encounter. For example, the risk of acquiring gonorrhea from a single coital event when one partner is infectious is 25% for men and 50% for women (Hatcher et al.,1990). Women's bodies are more susceptible to STDs, in part because the warm, moist interiors of the vagina and uterus are ideal environments for many organisms, and the thin, sensitive skin inside the labia, as well as the mucous membranes lining the vagina, are particularly permeable to infectious organisms (Strong et al.).

Women are less likely to seek treatment for STDs for a variety of reasons. One of the difficulties associated with seeking treatment is that initially, symptoms may be nonexistent or mild, especially in women (Amaral, 1998; Kelly, 1995). Two-thirds of clients at federally-funded STD clinics are males, largely because they recognize symptoms more readily. However, women tend to suffer more serious, often chronic physical consequences from STDs. Gonorrhea, syphilis, and chlamydia are particularly known for the inconspicuousness of their symptoms in the early stages. These STDs may progress into full-blown infections with potentially serious results when diagnosis and treatment is delayed. One example is pelvic inflammatory disease (PID), the leading cause of infertility in women, which is generally associated with untreated STDs. It has been estimated that between 100,000 and 150,000 women in the United States become infertile each year as a result of STDs (Barringer, 1993).

While the biological disadvantages of women regarding STDs are clear, less obvious are the psychosocial disadvantages. Many women diagnosed with chronic STDs view themselves as "damaged goods" (Nack, 2000). Low income women diagnosed with genital herpes identify various aspects of fear, including fear of rejection, of spreading the disease, and of the physical consequences, as the core psychosocial problem they face in making sense of their diagnosis (Gordon, 1999). Overall, women are more sensitive to the stigma associated with STDs, perhaps reflecting cultural stereotypes about sexually active women. While men who engage in sexual behavior with multiple partners are at increased risk for contracting STDs, they are less likely to be labeled as deviant or undesirable as are women who engage in these behaviors.

While men are at a biological advantage regarding the diagnosis and treatment of sexually transmitted diseases, they also face high risk and potential consequences. A survey conducted by a polling research agency found that based on questions asked of 1000 adult Americans, 62 percent of the men compared to 50 percent of the women were at moderate risk of conducting an STD. Among those who had protected sex, 69 percent of the women indicated that they were the ones who insisted on using a condom, compared to 12 percent of the men who did so. In addition, college-aged men have been found to be generally less knowledgeable about STDs regarding symptomology and methods of transmission (Frazer & Klein, 1985).

Cultural and Contextual Considerations

Regarding HIV/STD prevention, Pequegnat and Stover (1999) discussed several issues that have emerged as themes in research, theory, and practice regarding the prevention of sexually transmitted infections in women in general and in women of color in particular. First, unfavorable gender stereotypes, our cultural expectations of women, and prevalent social, political, and economic conditions significantly impact women's reproductive decision-making, self-protective behaviors, and their vulnerability to STDs. Second, a link between the high-risk behaviors associated with STD infection and prior sexual and physical abuse has been suggested; women who have been victims of trauma seem to be more likely to make unwise choices for themselves, or engage in self-defeating, re-victimizing behaviors, including engaging in unprotected sexual activity with multiple partners. Third, women are often called upon to fill multiple roles and act as designated caregivers in a family, often at the expense of their own caretaking needs. Women in caregiving roles may not take steps to protect themselves from possible infection from a partner, or even consider themselves at risk. Finally, Pequegnat and Stover noted that STD prevention should increasingly focus on development and refinement of female-controlled barrier methods of disease prevention, and in educating and empowering women to use these methods, since women are often at risk because of the behaviors of their partners rather than their own behaviors.

While STD infection cuts across ethnic and cultural lines, the high-risk behaviors associated STDs may be prevalent for some traditionally marginalized groups. Various ethnic minorities have been associated with higher numbers of reported STDs; for example, the Latino population has rates of primary and secondary syphilis that are five times greater and rates of gonorrhea that are three times greater than those of their European-American cohorts (CDC, 1994).

Acculturation in ethnic minorities has been associated with greater high-risk behaviors in Hispanic women (Newcomb et al., 1998). For Latinas, acculturation, including higher income and U.S. citizenship, is a potent predictor of sexual risk taking. Even though more acculturated Latinas have reported greater knowledge about STDs and greater access to health care services, they are more likely to take greater risks in their sexual relationships, such as failing to use condoms. Therefore, as Latina women acquire greater personal freedom from culturally constrained gender roles, they face the negative outcomes of unprotected sex, including STDs. The disparity between knowledge and behavior change may be due to the acculturation stress-related dilemma of feeling free to engage in more sexual behaviors, but not feeling entitled, from a gender role perspective, to make decisions about their partner's use of a condom.

There has been widespread perception that Asian Americans are at lower risk for HIV and other sexually transmitted diseases than the population as a whole. It has been suggested that due to cultural limitations regarding openly discussing sexuality, Asian-Americans are less knowledgeable about sexually transmitted diseases and less apt to discuss prevention than other ethnic groups. However, at least one study suggests that first-generation Asian-American adolescents are more aware of STDs, more willing to discuss the topic, and more willing to translate their knowledge into protective behaviors (Chan, 1997). While studies suggest that Asian American teens, like many adolescents, are prone to engaging in unprotected sex, frequency of high risk behavior and, therefore, rates of reported STDs are significantly lower.

Overall, STDs are more frequently identified in lower-income urban areas where health services are limited and health-care workers are often perceived as unresponsive to the community's needs. Racism, or at least an insensitivity to ethnic issues, may play a role in inadequate funding for public health programs that encompass education, diagnosis, treatment, partner tracing, and follow-up (Strong et al., 1996).

DEVELOPMENTAL AND DIAGNOSTIC FACTORS

Children and Adolescents

Children are rarely considered at high risk for STDs; yet, children who are victims of sexual abuse may acquire such infections (Hammerschlag, 1998). Sometimes, the discovery of an STD serves as a major component of the physical evidence of sexual violation of a child. Children who contract STDs through sexual trauma are particularly vulnerable to long-term emotional and physical consequences, since they are less likely to communicate about their symptoms and because they may build strong associations between the STD and the sexual abuse. It may not be until the symptoms of an STD become unbearable to the child or clearly noticeable to adults that medical treatment is sought.

About one-quarter of the 3 million new cases of STDs each year occur in teenagers (Francis, 1998). Adolescents are at particularly high risk for a variety of reasons, such as developmental characteristics that include challenging authority and building strong peer affiliations. Many teens experiment with sexual behaviors without seriously considering the full range of potential consequences. Furthermore, while teens often identify problematic social situations related to sex such as pregnancy, violence, alcohol use, and rape, few express concerns about sexually transmitted diseases (Noell, 1993). With teens, high-risk sexual behavior is related to a range of other behaviors, including antisocial behavior and drug and alcohol use. Substance abuse may promote other behaviors, such as running away from home and other forms of homelessness, which in turn increase exposure to STDs (Forst, 1994; McCarthy, Brack, Laygo, Brack, & Orr, 1997).

COUNSELING AND TREATMENT STRATEGIES

Psychoeducation for the Prevention of Sexually Transmitted Diseases

Increasingly, the counselor's role in promoting wellness involves working for systemic change. Counselors in a variety of settings, including agencies, schools, colleges, and private practice, are challenged to focus on prevention of sexually transmitted diseases through psychoeductional interventions with individuals and groups.

Promoting Safer Sexual Practices

While the most effective method of prevention for STDs is abstinence or complete and mutual monogamy between uninfected partners, these options are not realistic for many individuals and couples. Counselors need to help clients identify and target their high risk behaviors, and employ safer sexual practices. The simplest and most readily available method of STD risk reduction involves the consistent use of latex condoms. In the wake of the

HIV/AIDS epidemic, condom use has increased dramatically in gay and bisexual men, but less dramatically in women and heterosexual men. Several studies have shown that adolescents have reasonably high levels of knowledge about HIV/AIDS transmission and prevention, yet they still engage in risky sexual activities, including unprotected sex with multiple partners (Gillmore, 1992).

In spite of the growing rates of sexually transmitted infections, heterosexuals in the general population use condoms consistently only about 5% to 10% of the time with primary partners and about 15% of the time with secondary partners (Dolcini, Coates, Catania, Kegeles, & Hauck, 1995). Many reasons have been offered for not using condoms, including personal dislike, diminished sexual pleasure, lack of availability, and a partner's dislike or resistance (Corby, Wolitski, Thornton-Johnson, & Tanner, 1991). One study reported that male nonusers of condoms perceive less risk for STDs, hold negative views on their ability to discuss using condoms with a partner without reducing the sensation of the sexual encounter, and doubt their ability to effectively discuss condom use with any potential partners (Reis & Stephens, 1998). Women, in particular, cite their lack of self-efficacy in discussing or negotiating condom use, as well as their feelings of embarrassment in purchasing condoms (Helwig-Larsen & Collins, 1994). Promoting consistent condom use among female adolescents involves understanding and addressing complex sociocultural factors, including deep ambivalence regarding sexuality in general, women's sexuality in particular, and the sexuality challenges of adolescent girls. Regarding ethnicity, young Hispanic and African American women utilizing the services at an inner-city health clinic reported less use of condoms when they reported using other forms of birth control. However, these women were more likely to use condoms when they discussed the risks of STDs and condom use with friends, demonstrating the value of peer identification and validation (Roye, 1997). It seems that these women were more likely to take action to prevent pregnancy than disease, perhaps because pregnancy presents a more obvious and tangible threat, and because the women can control pregnancy through their own actions. Understanding the reasons men and women give for not using condoms is important in providing effective psychoeducation, since studies suggest that many who engage in high-risk behaviors are aware of the consequences but still do not use condoms regularly.

Factors associated with consistent condom use include favorable partner attitude, personally knowing someone with HIV/AIDS, social norms favoring condom use, and higher levels of social support and self-efficacy (Stark et al., 1998). Research by Stark et al. indicated that women who practice or intend to practice consistent condom use are more likely to talk with others about condoms, acknowledge the advantages of condoms, have higher self-efficacy for condom use, and indicate that people important to them favored condom use.

Helping to empower women and men to use condoms includes promoting opportunities for healthy decision-making. Since individuals who carry condoms are more likely to use them, counselors can encourage clients to address their reluctance in purchasing condoms through role-play or structured homework assignments. An important factor in promoting condom use appears to be helping individuals overcome reluctance to bring up the need for safer sex practices with their potential sexual partners. In helping clients approach sexual decision-making with intentionality, counselors may help clients gain greater control of sexual behaviors and risk management.

Ideally, condom use as a method of STD risk reduction is an issue for couples. An examination of college students in sexually active dating relationships found that while half of the respondents reported consistent condom use during the first month of the relationship, only 34% reported consistent use during the time of the study. Overall, couples subjectively reasoned that their partners were disease-free and unlikely to give them an STD, and that since they were using other birth control methods, such as birth control pills, it was no longer important to use condoms. Implications of these findings include the need to help couples in sexual relationships objectively assess for STD risk, and encourage condom use as a method of risk reduction (Civic, 2000). If successful interpersonal communication skills can be cultivated, then these skills can be applied to the negotiation of safer sexual practices between partners. Counselors can help clients develop strategies for using condoms in all of their sexual encounters, even when a partner is resistant, defensive, or manipulative (Williams, 1990). However, cultural ambivalence about sex roles come into play in dating relationships where differences in the allocation of power and responsibility often make it difficult for women to affect important sexual decisions such as condom use (Rostosky, Galliher, Vickerman, & Welsh, 1998). It would seem that couples who are more egalitarian in their attitudes and behaviors and who share power equally would be more likely to share in responsible decision-making regarding condom use.

Targeting High-risk Behaviors

In addition to encouraging condom use, counselors are challenged to help clients identify other high-risk behaviors associated with STDs. Individuals who engage in sexual activities with multiple partners are at greater risk for acquiring STDs, and for other often related conditions with long-term health implications. A link between frequent, emotionally unsatisfying sexual behavior and a history of unresolved sexual or physical trauma in women has been suggested (Pequegnat & Stover, 1999), raising concerns about the unintended consequences of self-defeating behaviors. Counselors working with women whose maladaptive patterns include sexual acting-out behaviors need to include STD and related reproductive health issues as a component of helping these clients gain a greater sense of self-worth and personal power in their relationships.

Both individual and group psychoeductional counseling interventions have been used to promote STD prevention by targeting high-risk behaviors. Brief counseling, based upon skills-development, has been effective in increasing condom use in women, suggesting that such interventions are feasible and effective within a community setting (Belcher et al., 1998). A culturally appropriate, theoretically based videotape developed in collaboration with local African American producers to promote condom use among 15-to-19 year old black males in an urban setting was found to be effective in increasing condom use, though patterns of high-risk behaviors and low perceived risk for STDs continued (DeLamater, Wagstaff, & Havens, 1998).

Assessing for STD Risk

In working with individuals, couples, and families, counselors may overlook the possibility of sexually transmitted diseases as a topic of clinical concern. Counselors need to address the issue of sexual behaviors and sexual health directly and openly with clients, including assessment of high-risk behaviors, and whether the client has been tested for STDs, or has any known sexual infections. Counselors can model responsible sexual behavior with clients in promoting informed choices about contraception and STD prevention. Common risk factors counselors should be routinely assessing include whether and how often clients have:

- unprotected sex (vaginal, anal, oral)
- had more than one sexual partner
- had sex with others in the past
- had a partner who had sex with other people in the past
- sex without knowing their partners medical history
- a history of mixing alcohol and drugs with sex which can impair judgement and/or ability to use condoms effectively
- feelings that often lead to taking risks with sex (e.g., insecurity, need to be loved, desire to be swept away, low self-esteem, etc.).

Counseling Biopsychosocial Issues for Clients with STDs

Individuals who are diagnosed with a sexually transmitted disease will face physical, emotional, and social challenges. While some STDs are curable, others are chronic, causing long-term consequences and the need for life-long management of physical, sexual, and reproductive behaviors. Individuals vary in their responses to acquiring STDs, but some common themes include managing physical and reproductive health issues, dealing with stigma, issues of esteem and loss, psychosexual considerations, and existential or spiritual dimensions.

Clients Diagnosed with STDs

For most, being diagnosed with an STD is an extremely unsettling and disorienting experience. Most STDs are associated with physical discomfort, including burning, itching, and unpleasant genital discharges, all of which worsen when prompt treatment is not sought. Women with chlamydia may suffer abdominal pain, and men and women with Herpes may experience recurring painful open lesions as well as flu-like symptoms. While many STDs, including chlamydia, gonorrhea, and syphilis can be cured with various antibiotics, untreated, these may lead to future medical problems. Chlamydia and gonorrhea are both strongly associated with pelvic inflammatory disease and infertility in women, and untreated syphilis can cause various diseases of the internal organs and neurological disorders. Other STDs, including herpes and venereal warts, are chronic conditions, often requiring ongoing medical management (Strong et al., 1996).

Initial reactions to the diagnosis of an STD may include shock and disbelief, fear and anxiety about treatment options and prognosis, anger and feelings of betrayal or loss of trust in partner, shame and embarrassment, and dismay or regret over unsafe sexual practices.

Dealing with Stigma

Individuals who contract STDs differ from those who acquire other infectious illness in the stigma associated with sexually transmitted infections. With most illnesses, individuals would have access to family and other support systems while pursuing treatment and managing symptoms. The embarrassment and shame often associated with acquiring an STD make it unlikely that a client will feel comfortable discussing the situation with many intimate associates.

Herpes, in particular, has been associated with symbolic stigma. An analysis of popular press accounts of herpes found herpes associated with discredited identity, including stigmatizing of individuals with herpes from administrative, moral, and scientific perspectives (Roberts, 1997). A qualitative study of 28 women diagnosed with herpes or HPV described a three-stage process of managing the stigma of chronic STDs. First, the majority of the women hid their infection from intimate others, through omission or by lying. Second, almost all used stigma transference to deflect the blame onto real or imaginary others. Finally, all of these women preventatively or therapeutically disclosed to intimate others. For these women, managing stigma was an ongoing process (Nack, 2000). Fear, often associated with disclosure, has been cited as persistent component of the daily lives of low income women with herpes (Gordon, 1999).

Loss of Esteem Issues

Related to stigma is the issue of loss of esteem. Upon being diagnosed with an STD, individuals may feel less personal worth due to their condition. Feeling "dirty" or "tainted" by infection can persist beyond treatment, even with curable STDs. Men and women diagnosed with genital warts, as well as with other STDs, have described fears of being rejected by future partners, even when their STDs were curable. This suggests a loss of esteem associated with contracting an STD, and that "curability" may not be a factor affecting the psychological symptomology of individuals with STDs (Edelman, 1995). As previously mentioned, women with chronic STDs have described their sexual selves as "damaged goods" (Nack, 2000). When they were able to forgive the partner perceived as responsible, and managed their chronic STDs through selective disclosure, distancing, and selectively choosing information, low income women regained more control over the fear in their lives (Gordon, 1999).

Psychosexual Considerations

The contagion factor necessitates changes in sexual practices of individuals with STDs. Clearly, those with chronic or as yet untreated STDs will need to manage sexual behaviors carefully to prevent the spread of disease to partners. Some psychosexual consequences of STDs include a loss of sexual self-esteem; some individuals diagnosed with HPV have reported that they have stopped being sexually active as a result of their diagnosis (Edelman,1995). In assessing for psychosexual concerns in clients with STDs, it is important to consider the complexity of client feelings regarding sexual identity and self-concept. While physically clients may be able to resume normal sexual activities using reasonable precautions, some may feel reluctant or uncomfortable with their sexuality. Clients may perceive themselves as less sexually desirable, or experience unreasonable fears about contracting STDs with future partners. These issues may impact their ability to trust or build intimacy in present or future relationships.

Existential/Spiritual Dimensions

Individuals will differ in how they make meaning of contracting an STD. Some may feel their STD is a punishment for immoral behavior, and feel somehow contaminated or unclean. For clients whose religious views include specific restrictions regarding sexual activity outside of marriage, STDs may seem like retribution for morally unacceptable acts. Shame at having contracted the disease may persist, especially if the condition is chronic, or if an untreated condition has lead to permanent reproductive problems.

For most, having an STD will be associated with loss, including the loss of a healthy or uninfected self for those who have contracted a chronic STD such as herpes. Others may feel loss associated with security or trust within a relationship. Many experience existential angst or feelings of "why me" in trying to make sense of their condition. In many cases, couples will have to wrestle with issues associated with the diagnosis of an STD, particularly when the one partner is perceived as to blame for infecting the other.

CASE STUDY

Melissa, a twenty-four year old graduate student, initiated counseling at her college counseling center a few weeks after discovering she had contacted herpes from her boyfriend of seven months. For several weeks, Melissa had been having symptoms including fever and achiness she had attributed to the flu; she was diagnosed during a visit to the campus health clinic. Melissa's boyfriend, who was asymptomatic but subsequently tested positive as well, was surprised but more outwardly accepting of the diagnosis.

Once Melissa's physical symptoms abated, she remained devastated about contracting an incurable STD. "I can't stop crying," she explained, "and I will never forgive Mark, as long as I live." She expressed anger and dismay that her boyfriend seemed to be taking the herpes in stride, figuring he was most likely responsible, since he had been with far more partners that she had in the past. Melissa expressed remorse over not using condoms and, of not knowing, somehow, that Mark was "infected." She expressed the fear that now that she has herpes, no one else will ever want to be with her, that she is somehow "damaged goods," and that she will never be the same.

Counseling Approach

Claire, Melissa's counselor, recognized that her counseling intervention would need to address several issues. Initially, Claire assessed Melissa as experiencing a crisis over her diagnosis, and helped Melissa regain her equilibrium. While Melissa exhibited a number of depressive symptoms, including periods of crying, inability to concentrate, and trouble sleeping, Claire concluded that these symptoms were situational and likely to abate in time, since Melissa described no significant history of depression in herself or family members. Claire focused on normalizing Melissa's feelings of shock, fear, and anger over her diagnosis.

Claire also assessed Melissa's support system and found that while she had generally positive relationships with her parents and an older sister, her family system did not allow for the open discussion of sexual topics. Melissa's strict Irish Catholic parents where opposed to extramarital sex, and she felt they would be very disappointed in her if they knew about the herpes. In addition, Melissa was far from her family home and had no family doctor she felt she could trust. Overall, her experience with the medical intervention of the herpes had been upsetting and confusing.

Claire worked with Melissa in helping the young woman feel more in control of her condition. She referred Melissa to campus health services, where she met with a health care professional who was able to address her medical and sexual concerns directly and sensitively. Claire offered additional referral sources, including support groups in the community that might help Melissa feel less isolated and uncertain, and therefore less afraid. The knowledge she gained about herpes, including ways she could moderate her symptoms through her lifestyle, gave Melissa a sense of control over her body and her future. Claire used a cognitive-behavioral approach in helping Melissa grieve the loss of her "uninfected" self while recognizing that she was still the same attractive, intelligent, and desirable young woman.

Over the following weeks, Melissa's feelings stabilized and she began to address some of the deeper concerns triggered by her diagnosis. Unsure of her feelings towards Mark, Melissa asked him to attend counseling with her; his refusal helped her conclude that the relationship was not healthy for her, and they parted amicably. Melissa worked through her anger at Mark, recognizing her need to blame him was not helpful to her own growth. She also forgave herself for not consistently using condoms, resolving to do so with future partners. Claire helped Melissa develop strategies for countering potential obstacles to consistent safer sex practices.

Finally, Claire guided Melissa in exploring her ambivalence about her sexuality in the context of her family of origin and her culture. In initially viewing herself as "damaged goods," Melissa identified feelings of shame related to sex and her worth as a woman. Melissa realized that she had at times been sexually active with men she hadn't deeply cared about, and that as a practicing Catholic, she had felt incongruent about this. Melissa realized that she had been passive consenting to sex and about using condoms, feeling a lack of entitlement in asserting herself with men. Claire helped Melissa face and dismiss her shame, and instead develop a resolve to be more intentional about her romantic and sexual relationships. In this way, Melissa was able to attach meaning to her diagnosis, framing herpes as a difficult blow that had nonetheless helped her develop intentionality about her sexual self and her goals for future relationship behavior.

SUMMARY

The aim of this chapter was to provide counselors and counseling students with the necessary knowledge of STDs and their medical features, treatments, and attendant health risks. Moreover, the purpose of this chapter was to provide a framework for conceptualizing the challenge of STDs through the lenses of gender, culture, and relevant developmental issues. The highlighted counseling issues are viewed as inextricably linked to the quality of the counseling relationship. Counselors' keen awareness and appreciation of these issues provide a richer contextual understanding of clients' biopsychosocial and spiritual concerns when diagnosed with an STD. The presented case study illustrates a poignant example of those issues and demonstrates the counseling role in supporting and intervening with the client.

Psychoeducational efforts toward prevention, early detection and treatment can depend in large part upon the counselor's role in conducting a thorough assessment of sexual history and also inquiring about current health and sexual practices. Additionally, counselors may enhance their efficacy for both prevention and intervention of STDs by remaining attentive to the identified psychosocial risk factors. Counselors should become aware of the local public health resources in their communities, and recognize that those agencies could become possible reciprocal referral sites.

The current research on STDs and counseling is predominantly focused on HIV and AIDS, and this remains a critically important issue. However, other STDs have seemingly fallen out of the research light in the recent counseling literature. Recognition of the roughly 15 million new cases of STDs annually in the U.S. is a startling fact. Counselors and counseling researchers need to join investigative teams with both medical and public health researchers to determine more effective STD intervention models and prevention methods. Both cross-disciplinary work and theory driven research investigations are critically lacking. The integration work of Stark et al. (1998) in utilizing a stages of change model in the prevention of STDs stands as a solid example of linking theory and practice and addressing multicultural issues. Finally, there is a need for further controlled clinical outcome studies to determine with greater specificity the effectiveness of counseling and prevention efforts.

REFERENCES

American Cancer Society. (1997). *Cancer Facts and Figures.* (Report 97-300M, No. 5008-97). Atlanta, GA: Author.

American Social Health Association. (1998). *Sexually transmitted diseases in America: How many cases and at what costs?* Menlo Park, CA: Kaiser Family Foundation.

Aral, S. O., & Peterman, T. A. (1993). Defining behavioral methods to prevent sexually transmitted diseases through intervention research. *Infectious Diseases Clinics of North America, 7*, 861-873.

Amaral, E. (1998). Current approach to STD management in women. *International Journal of Gynaecology and Obstetrics, 63*, 183-189.

Barringer, F. (1993, April 1). 1 in 5 in U.S. have sexually caused viral disease. *New York Times*, pp. A1, B9.

Belcher, L., Kalichman, S., Topping, M., Smith, S., Emshoff, J., Norris, F., Nurss, J. (1998). A randomized trial of a brief HIV risk reduction counseling intervention for women. *Journal of Consulting and Clinical Psychology, 66*, 856-861.

Brandt, A. M. (1987). *No magic bullet: A social history of venereal disease in the United States since 1880.* New York: Oxford University Press.

Centers for Disease Control. (1994). Trends in sexual risk behavior among high school students: United States, 1990, 1991, and 1993. *Morbidity and Mortality Weekly Report, 44*, 124-125; 131-132.

Centers for Disease Control. (1997). Summary of notifiable diseases in the United States, 1996. *Morbidity and Mortality Weekly Report, 45*, 1-103.

Centers for Disease Control. (1998). National Center for HIV, STD, and TB Prevention. *Sexually transmitted disease surveillance, 1997.* Atlanta, GA: Author.

Chan, C. S. (1997). *Attitudes towards sexuality and sexual behaviors of Asian-American adolescents. Implications for risk of HIV infection.* Boston, MA: University of Massachusetts, Institute for Asian American Studies.

Civic, D. (2000). College students; reasons for nonuse of condoms within dating relationships. *Journal of Sex and Marital Therapy, 26*, 95-105.

Corby, N. H., Wolitski, R. J., Thornton-Johnson, S., & Tanner, W. M. (1991). AIDS knowledge, perception of risk, and behaviors among female sex partners of injection drug users. *AIDS Education & Prevention, 3*, 353-366.

DeLamater, J., Wagstaff, D. A., & Havens, K. K. (1998). The impact of a culturally appropriate, STD/AIDS education and intervention on Black male adolescents' sexual and condom use behavior. (ERIC Document Reproduction Service No. ED 424328)

Dolcini, M. M., Coates, T. J., Catania, J. A., Kegeles, S. M., & Hauck, W. W. (1995). Multiple sexual partners and their psychosocial correlates: The populaton-based AIDS in multiethnic neighborhoods (AMEN) study. *Health Psychology, 13*, 395-407.

Edelman, D. (1995). The psychosocial impact of being diagnosed with genital human papillomarvirus. *Dissertation Abstracts International, 55* (8-A), 2286

Francis, S. (1998). The silent epidemic: Teens and sexually transmitted diseases. *Our Children, 23* (5), 32-33.

Forst, M. L. (1994). Sexual risk profiles of delinquent and homeless youths. *Journal of Community Health, 19*, 101-114.

Frazer, G., & Klein, D. (1985). A study of the awareness of selected college students concerning sexually transmitted diseases. (ERIC Document Reproduction Service No. ED 262298).

Gillmore, M. (1992). The process and pitfalls of developing a culturally relevant curriculum to reduce AIDS among sexually active teenagers. (ERIC Document Reproduction Service No. ED 424328)

Gordon, S. H. (1999). Low income women with genital herpes: Recognizing and managing their fear trajectory. *Dissertation Abstracts International, 60* (2-B), 577.

Hammerschlag, M. R. (1998). The transmissibility of sexually transmitted diseases in sexually abused children. *Child Abuse and Neglect, 22* (6), 23-35.

Harding, A. K., Gray, L. A., & Neal, M. (1993). Confidentiality limits with clients who have HIV: A review of ethical and legal guidelines and professional policies. *Journal of Counseling and Development, 71*, 297-305.

Hatcher, R, Stewart, F., Trussel, J., Kowal, D., Guest, F., Stewart, G., & Cates, W. (1990). *Contraceptive Technology: 1990-1991*. New York: Irving.

Helwig-Larsen, M., & Collins, B. E., (1994). The UCLA Multidimentional Condom Attitudes Scale: Documenting the complex determinants of condom use in college students. *Health Psychology, 13*, 224-237.

Holt, J. L., Houg, B. L., & Romano, J. L. (1999). Spiritual wellness for clients with HIV/AIDS: Review of counseling issucs. *Journal of Counseling and Development, 77*, 160-170.

Institute of Medicine. Committee on prevention and control of sexually transmitted diseases.(1997). In T.R. Eng, & W.T. Butler (Eds.), *The hidden epidemic: Confronting sexually transmitted diseases*. Washington, D.C.: National Academy Press.

Jacobson, J. L. (1992, May/June). The other epidemic. *World Watch*, pp. 10-17.

Kamb, M. L., Fishbein, M., Douglas, J.M., Rhodes, F., Rogers, J., Bolan, G., Zenilman, Hoxworth, T., Malotte, C. K., Iatesta, M., Kent, C., Lentz, A., Graziano, S., Byers, R. H., & Peterman, T. A., (1998). Efficacy of risk-reduction counseling to prevent human immunodeficiency virus and sexually transmitted diseases: A randomized controlled trial. Project RESPECT Study Group. *Journal of American Medical Association, 280*, 1161-1167.

Kelly, G. F. (1995). *Sexuality today: The human perspective.* Madison, WI: Brown & Benchmark.

Kelly, J. A. & Kalichman, S. C. (1995). Increased attention to human sexuality can improve HIV-AIDS prevention efforts: Key research issues and directions. *Journal of Consulting and Clinical Psychology, 63*, 907-918.

Kelly, J. A., & St. Lawrence, J. S. (1988). AIDS prevention and treatment: Psychology's role in the health crisis. *Clinical Psychology Review, 8*, 255-284.

McCarthy, C. J., Brack, C. J., Laygo, C. M., Brack, G., & Orr, D. P. (1997). A theory based investigation of adolescent risk behaviors and concern about AIDS. *The School Counselor, 44*, 185-197.

Nack, A. (2000). Damaged goods: Women managing the stigma of STDs. *Deviant Behavior, 21*, 95-121.

Newcomb, M. D., Wyatt, G. E., Romero, G. J., Tucker, M. B., Wayment, H. A., Caromona, J. V., Solis, B., & Mitchell-Kernan, C. (1998). Acculturation, sexual risk taking, and HIV health promotion among Latinas. *Journal of Counseling Psychology, 45*, 454-467.

Nilsson Schonnesson, L. (1990). Educational requirements of human sexuality in the counseling for and prevention of sexually transmitted diseases. *Seminars in Dermatology, 9*, 185-189.

Noell, J. (1993). Problematic sexual situations for adolescents: Alcohol and unsafe sex. *Health Values: The Journal of Health Behavior, Education, & Promotion, 17(6)*, 40-49.

Pais, S., Piercy, F., & Miller, J. (1998). Factors related to family therapists' breaking confidence when clients disclose high-risks-to-HIV/AIDS sexual behaviors. *Journal of Marital and Family Therapy, 24*, 457-472.

Pequegnat, W., & Stover, E. (1999). Considering women's contextual and cultural issues in HIV/STD prevention research. *Cultural Diversity and Ethnic Minority Psychology, 5*, 287-291.

Reis, J., & Stephens, Y. D. (1998). A discriminant analysis of young adults' knowledge of the human papillomavirus and self-efficacy of condom use. *Journal of Psychology and Human Sexuality, 10(2)*, 71-91.

Roberts, R. E. (1997). Power/knowledge and discredited identities: Media representations of herpes. *The Sociological Quarterly Review, 38*, 265-284.

Rosser, B. R., Metz, M. E., Bockting, W. O., & Buroker, T. (1997). Sexual difficulties, concerns, and satisfactions in homosexual men: An empirical study with implications for HIV prevention. *Journal of Sex and Marital Therapy, 23*, 61-73.

Rotosky, S. S., Galliher, R. V., Welsh, D. P. (1998). *Gender-roles, power, and condom use in adolescent dating relationships.* (ERIC Document Reproduction Service No. ED 424328)

Roye, C. F. (1997). Condom use by Hispanic and African American teens and young adults who use hormonal contraception: Implications for HIV prevention. *Journal of Health Education, 28(6)*, 61-66.

Serovich, J. M. (2000). Helping HIV-positive persons to negotiate the disclosure process to partners, family members, and friends. *Journal of Marital and Family Therapy, 26*, 365-372.

Shilts, R. (1987). *And the band played on: People, politics, and the AIDS epidemic.* New York: St. Martin's Press.

Singer, A. (1994). Why schools should make condoms available to teenagers. *Educational Leadership, 52(2)*, 78-79.

Stark, M. J., Tesselaar, H. M., O'Connell, A. A., Person, B., Galavotti, C., Cohen, A., & Walls, C. (1998). Psychosocial factors associated with the stages of change for condom use among women at risk for HIV and STDs: Implications for intervention development. *Journal of Consulting and Clinical Psychology, 66*, 967-978.

Strong, B., DeVault, C., & Sayad, B. W. (1996). *Core concepts in human sexuality.* Mountain View, CA: Mayfield Publishing Company.

Williams, K. N. (1990). *Interpersonal communication between partners: Addressing the issues of safe sex practices.* (ERIC Document Reproduction Service No. ED 321305)

World Health Organization. (1997). *World health report.* Geneva: Author.

World Health Organization. (1996). *Global prevalence and incidence of selected curable sexually transmitted diseases: Overview and estimates.* Geneva: Author.

BIOGRAPHICAL SKETCHES

EDITORS

Larry D. Burlew, EdD, LPC, is a professor in the Division of Counseling & HR at the University of Bridgeport in CT. He is a past president of the Association for Adult Development and Aging (AADA), a former governing council representative of the American Counseling Association (ACA), and a former editor of the *ADULTSPAN Journal: Development through Young, Middle, and Older Adulthood*. He currently does clinical work at Leeway, Inc., an HIV/AIDS inpatient facility in New Haven, CT. His counseling experience is with the following types of clients: college students; rape victims; domestic violence; EAP; gay men; HIV/AIDS victims; career development; addictions; and community mental health. He has published extensively with interest in topics like anti-gay hate crimes, career counseling, adult development, and clinical supervision. He has presented at local, state, and national conferences and has addressed topics including: multicultural issues; clinical supervision; older adults; euthanasia; counseling strategies/techniques; adult and career development; and violence. His interest in sexuality counseling stems from his work with adults and college students struggling with normative sexual development, sexual orientation, and sexual trauma. He can be reached at lburlew@bridgeport.edu.

David Capuzzi, PhD, LPC, is a past president of the American Counseling Association. He is a professor and coordinator of Counselor Education in the Graduate School of Education at Portland State University in Portland, OR. Dr. Capuzzi's publications have appeared in journals such as *Counselor Education and Supervision, Counseling and Values, Humanistic Education and Development, Generations*, and the *Journal for Specialists in Group Work*. From 1980-1984, he served as editor of the *School Counselor* for the American School Counselor Association. Dr. Capuzzi co-edited and authored *Youth at Risk* (2000), *Introduction to the Counseling Profession* (1997, 2001), *Introduction to Group Counseling* (1998, 2002), and *Counseling and Psychotherapy: Theories and Interventions* (1999) with Dr. Douglas R. Gross, professor emeritus, of Arizona State University. He is the author of *Suicide Prevention in the Schools* (1994) for the American Counseling Association. Dr. Capuzzi has won a number of awards for his contributions of service and expertise to professional groups. Among these are the Kitty Cole Human Rights Award of the American Counseling Association, the Leona Tyler Award of the Oregon Counseling Association, the Outstanding Service Award of the Western Region of the American Counseling Association and the Silver Award for Editorial Excellence of the Society of National Association Publications. A frequent keynoter and speaker for professional conferences and institutes, Dr. Capuzzi also has consulted with a variety of school districts and community agencies interested in initiating prevention and intervention strategies for youth at risk and adolescents at risk for suicide. He can be reached at capuzzida@pdx.edu.

CONTRIBUTORS

Tom Arbaugh, Jr., PhD, LPC, is an assistant professor at the Gulf Coast campus of the University of Southern Mississippi. He has been a school counselor, as well as a mental health counselor both in an agency and in private practice. Dr. Arbaugh has traveled extensively and has maintained an interest in multicultural issues. He is also active in state and national counseling organizations as seen by being the president of the Mississippi Association for Counselor Education and Supervision. He can be reached at tarbaugh@usm.edu.

Mary Ballard, PhD, earned her doctorate in Counselor Education from the University of New Orleans. She has worked as a school counselor and principal, and as an employee assistance counselor for the United States Postal Service. Currently, Dr. Ballard is an assistant professor of counseling at Southeastern Louisiana University and, as a Licensed Professional Counselor (LPC), maintains a private practice. Dr. Ballard is a member of the American Counseling Association (ACA), the Association for Counselor Education and Supervision (ACES), and the International Association for Addictions and Offender Counseling (IAAOC). She also serves on the executive board of the Louisiana Counseling Association (LCA), where she is editor of the *Louisiana Journal of Counseling* (LJC) and President of the Louisiana Association for Counselor Education and Supervision (LACES). Dr. Ballard has published numerous articles and conducted many presentations at the state, national and international levels. She can be contacted at mballard2@selu.edu.

Bob Barrett, PhD, LPC, is professor of counseling and coordinator of the doctoral program at the University of North Carolina at Charlotte and a psychologist in private practice. He is the co-author of *Gay Fathers* (Jossey Bass) and *Counseling Gay Men and Lesbians* (Brooks/Cole), and the author of many articles. His current interests are gay men and masculinity and spiritual experiences of gay men. He can be reached at bbarret@carolina.rr.com.

Jan R. Bartlett, PhD, is an assistant professor at Iowa State University. Dr. Bartlett has experience as both a K-12 school counselor and as a middle school and secondary teacher. Her research interests include the role of intergenerational connections in children and adolescent development, body image issues, and the role of school counselors in educational reform and as student advocates. She can be reached at jbartlet@iastate.edu.

Al Barton, MS, received his master's in counseling from the University of Arkansas. He is a Licensed Professional Counselor (LPC) and currently works with Piney Ridge Center, a residential setting for adolescent sexual offenders and their families.

Thomas W. Blume, PhD, LPC, LMFT, is an associate professor in the Department of Counseling, Oakland University, where he teaches in the Advanced Specialization in Couple and Family Counseling. Having entered the counseling field as an addiction counselor in Vietnam, he credits his ongoing experience with addicts and their families with having presented a significant challenge to the prevailing models of family therapy. During his doctoral studies in Marital and Family Therapy at Texas Tech University he began to develop a family counseling approach focused on couple and family members' efforts to integrate and reconcile their individual and group identities. Dr. Blume is currently conducting research on couples' experiences of major life disruptions and supervising a study of family counselors' attitudes and experiences regarding sexual issues with couples. He has a private family counseling and mediation practice in Bloomfield Hills, Michigan. He can be reached at blume@oakland.edu.

Hunter Downing-Alessi, PhD, is an associate professor of Counselor Education at Southeastern Louisiana University in Hammond, LA. She received her doctorate from the University of New Orleans in 1991. She has taught courses in Educational Psychology and Counselor Education since 1987, working with both undergraduate and graduate students. She has been active in the Louisiana Counseling Association, and the American Counseling Association, and has served as President of the Louisiana Association of Counselors and Supervisors. She is presently the Chair of the Department of Counseling, Family Studies, and Educational Leadership at SLU. She has worked with battered women, abused children, and adolescents both in private practice, and as a supervisor of counselors-in-training. Her research interests include cognition, cognitive development, and abuse-related memory issues. She can be reached at hdowning@selu.edu.

Timothy F. Dwyer, PhD, LPC, is an assistant professor of Marriage and Family Counseling and the Director of the Rev. Thomas E. Chambers Counseling and Training Center at Our Lady of Holy Cross College in New Orleans. Dr. Dwyer is also an adjunct professor of clinical psychiatry at Louisiana State University School of Medicine, and an Approved Supervisor and Clinical Member of AAMFT. After receiving his PhD in marriage and family therapy from Purdue University, Dr. Dwyer moved to New Orleans to teach and practice. He has published in the area of clinical supervision and counselor training, medical family therapy, and has presented at many national conferences. He can be reached at Tdwyer@olhcc.edu

Janet H. Fontaine, PhD, is an associate professor in the Department of Counseling at Indiana University of Pennsylvania where she teaches diversity courses and supervises advanced counseling practica and interns in the graduate counseling program. She has been researching and writing in the area of sexual minority youth for over ten years and has had numerous articles on the topic of sexual diversity published in national journals. In conjunction with Dr. Kathy Wilson, Outreach Coordinator for the Denver Gender Identity Center, she has made several national presentations on the topic of transgender issues for counselors at the American Counseling Association's national conferences in WDC and San Antonio, TX. Dr. Fontaine has become an activist to bring transgender issues into the mainstream of the counseling profession. She can be reached at fontaine@grove.iup.edu

Arpana G. Inman, PhD, is an assistant professor in the Counseling Psychology progeram at Lehigh University in Bethlehem, PA. Her scholastic and research interests are in the area of multicultural issues and span several topics including acculturation, biculturalism, ethnic/racial identities and the psychology of women. She has presented nationally and internationally and published in these areas. She can be reached at 610-758-3227

Colleen R. Logan, PhD, is a Licensed Professional Counselor (LPC) in both Texas and Virginia, and maintains a private practice in the Montrose area of Houston. She is an assistant professor at the University of Houston-Victoria where she teaches graduate counseling courses. She has authored a number of articles concerning the complex issues facing sexual minorities. Dr. Logan is a sought-after speaker and trainer, conducting numerous presentations at the local, state and national levels regarding the myriad issues facing gay, lesbian, bisexual and transgendered individuals. She is a past president of the Association of Gay, Lesbian and Bisexual Issues in Counseling (AGLBIC), a division of the American Counseling Association. She is also co-author of an upcoming book with Dr. Robert Barret titled, *Counseling Gays and Lesbians: A Practice Primer*. She can be reached at clogan6987@aol.com.

Mary L. Loos, JD, shares her life and recovery with her soul-mate, Dr. Michael D. Loos, in Laramie, WY, where they enjoy such activities as snowshoeing in winter and golf in summer. She is currently employed as an Assistant Attorney General at the Office of the Attorney General for the State of Wyoming, Cheyenne, WY. Educational and career-related achievements to date include: B.S. (psychology, 1992), Arkansas State University, Jonesboro, AR; J.D. (1995), University of Arkansas School of Law, Fayetteville, AR; admitted to practice law in Arkansas (1995) and Wyoming (1999); Certified Mediator since 2001. She would like to recognize and thank Beveraly Dubose Cochran for sharing the principles of recovery since August 11, 1986.

Michael D. Loos, PhD, received his doctorate in Counselor Education in 1998 from the University of Arkansas. He is a National Certified Counselor, Licensed Professional Counselor, and Licensed Addictions Therapist. His interests in addictions brought him to the University of Wyoming. Dr. Loos has been engaged in alcohol, drug abuse, and mental health counseling as a clinical practitioner and supervisor since 1969, working in diverse settings including mental health centers, prisons, public sector addictions treatment programs, acute care hospitals, private psychiatric hospitals, and private practice. Since joining the faculty at UW, Dr. Loos has re-worked the addiction curricula and is providing technical assistance supporting outcome research at the community level for the improvement of addiction related treatment services as evidenced in community-based indicators. His current research interests include topics associated with addiction treatment and prevention, provision of research-based counseling services, addiction and the elderly, and the enhancement of counselor preparation. Dr. Loos is the principal investigator on a subcontract with the Mountain West Addiction Technology Transfer Center to develop and enhance evidenced-based addiction education and training for practitioners throughout Wyoming. He can be reached at MDLoos@uwyo.edu.

E. Christine Moll, PhD, is a counselor educator at Canisius College in Buffalo, New York. Additional professional experience includes serving as the Director of Counseling Services at Canisius College and working for Catholic Charities in Western New York as an outreach therapist for individuals over 60 who were too frail to seek counseling outside their homes. She is a past president of the New York Counseling Association and is currently the president of the Association for Adult Development and Aging, a division of ACA. She also serves on the Editorial Review Board of the *Journal of Counseling and Development*. She can be reached at moll@canisius.edu.

Judith Morrison, PhD, is the vice-president of ACT II Management Company, a consulting firm providing management training to the private sector and the Federal government. She got her doctorate in Leadership and Counseling from Barry University in Miami Shores, FL. She has been an adjunct professor at The Johns Hopkins University and Barry University. Her research interests include death and dying, career development, and management training. She can be reached at juddell@aol.com.

Susan H. Niemann, PhD, LPC, is an assistant professor of counseling at Our Lady of Holy Cross College in New Orleans. Dr. Niemann was a middle school and high school educator before earning her doctorate in counseling at the University of New Orleans. Along with teaching, she maintains a clinical practice in the New Orleans area. An advocate for persons with disabilities and their families, Dr. Neimann writes and conducts research in the area of disability and family and is an active presenter at local, regional, and national levels.

Larry Phillips, EdD, LPC, is an associate professor of counseling at the University of Bridgeport, teaching in the naturopathic medicine, mental health counseling, and human services programs. He is a licensed psychologist and mental health counselor and has formerly worked as director of the counseling center at Franklin Pierce College. He can be reached at larry.phillips12@verizon.net.

Mark Pope, EdD, is an associate professor of Counseling and Family Therapy at the University of Missouri – St. Louis. He has had a major impact on the field of counseling through his pioneering, sustained, and wide-reaching work on lesbian, gay, and bisexual (LGB) issues that includes: pioneering counseling services, pioneering advocacy efforts, pioneering efforts to start LGB divisions in professional organizations, pioneering efforts to break the lavender ceiling in professional organizations' high level leadership, and pioneering scholarship efforts on LGB issues in career development, assessment with LGB populations, multicultural-LGB intersections, LGB gerontology, and gay sexuality. He is the American Counseling Association's president for 2003-2004 and a former president of both the National Career Development Association and the Association for Gay, Lesbian, and Bisexual Issues in Counseling. He can be reached at pope@jinx.umsl.edu.

Tarrell Awe Agahe Portman, PhD, LMHC, NCC, is an assistant professor at the University of Iowa. Dr. Portman has 15 years experience in public schools as an educator and a school counselor. As a counselor educator she teaches school counseling courses at the master's level and counselor education courses at the doctoral level. Her research interests are in the areas of school counselor identity development, supervision, technology, and multicultural counseling. She can be reached at tportman@blue.weeg.uiowa.edu.

Catherine Buffalino Roland, EdD, LPC, has been on the faculty of the Counselor Education program at the University of Arkansas since 1993. She has also worked as a Dean of Student Affairs, Director of a Counseling Center, and a clinician. Special populations she has worked with include families in conflict, midlife to older women in transition, and survivors of sexual abuse/trauma. Originally from New York, Dr. Roland has published regularly and has presented at local, state, and national conferences. She is a past president of the Association for Adult Development and Aging (AADA), and is the current editor of *ADULTSPAN: Development Through Young, Middle, and Older Adulthood.* It is Dr. Roland's hope that clinical issues of adult survivors will be illuminated for counselors, and that we will continue the quest for effective treatment strategies for this population. She can be reached at croland@mail.uark.edu.

Daya Singh Sandhu, EdD, NCC, NCSC, CPC, is Chair of the Department of Educational and Counseling Psychology at the University of Louisville. Dr. Sandhu has a special interest in school counseling, multicultural counseling, neurolinguistic programming, and the role of spirituality in counseling and psychotherapy. He has published more than 50 articles in state, national, and international journals, as well as authoring or editing more than 6 texts. He has made more than 100 presentations at the international, state, and local levels. His presentations focused on a wide variety of subjects that can be broadly classified under school counseling and multicultural counseling.

Valerie L. Schwiebert, PhD, is an associate professor of counseling in the Department of Human Services at Western Carolina University. She received her master's degree in rehabilitation counseling, specialist degree in counseling, and her doctorate in Counselor Education with a graduate certificate in gerontology from the University of Florida. Additionally, she has a small private practice where she works primarily with women and older persons. Dr. Schwiebert is a National Certified Counselor, National Certified Gerontological Counselor, Licensed Professional Counselor, and Certified Rehabilitation Counselor. She is the recipient of awards for her research and has authored 3 books and numerous journal articles. She can be reached at vschwieb@WCUVAX1.WCU.EDU.

Jennifer A. Walker, PhD, LPC, is an assistant professor in the Department of Counseling and Family Therapy at Saint Louis University. Jennifer has worked as a counselor educator for the past 6 years, and has a background in agency counseling. Jennifer's research interests include multicultural training in counseling programs, HIV/AIDS, and theoretical formulation in counseling students. She can be reached at walkerj@SLU.EDU

INDEX

T

U

V